Lecture Notes in Computer Science 5931

Commenced Publication in 1973
Founding and Former Series Editors:
Gerhard Goos, Juris Hartmanis, and Jan van Leeuwen

Martin Gilje Jaatun Gansen Zhao
Chunming Rong (Eds.)

Cloud Computing

First International Conference, CloudCom 2009
Beijing, China, December 1- 4, 2009
Proceedings

 Springer

Volume Editors

Martin Gilje Jaatun
SINTEF IKT
NO-7465, Trondheim, Norway
E-mail: martin.g.jaatun@sintef.no

Gansen Zhao
South China Normal University
School of Computer Science
Guangzhou, China
E-mail: zhaogansen@gmail.com

Chunming Rong
University of Stavanger
Faculty of Science and Technology
Department of Electrical and Computer Engineering
NO- 4036, Stavanger, Norway
E-mail: chunming.rong@uis.no

Library of Congress Control Number: 2009939453

CR Subject Classification (1998): C.2.1, C.1.4, C.2.4, D.4.2, D.4.3, D.4.7, E.1

LNCS Sublibrary: SL 5 – Computer Communication Networks and Telecommunications

ISSN   0302-9743
ISBN   3-642-10664-1 Springer Berlin Heidelberg New York
ISBN   978-3-642-10664-4 Springer Berlin Heidelberg New York

Typesetting: Camera-ready by author, data conversion by Scientific Publishing Services, Chennai, India
Printed on acid-free paper   SPIN: 12810659   06/3180   5 4 3 2 1 0

Preface

This volume contains the proceedings of CloudCom 2009, the First International Conference on Cloud Computing. The conference was held in Beijing, China, during December 1–4, 2009, and was the first in a series initiated by the Cloud Computing Association (www.cloudcom.org). The Cloud Computing Association was founded in 2009 by Chunming Rong, Martin Gilje Jaatun, and Frode Eika Sandnes. This first conference was organized by the Beijing Jiaotong University, Chinese Institute of Electronics, and Wuhan University, and co-organized by Huazhong University of Science and Technology, South China Normal University, and Sun Yat-sen University.

Ever since the inception of the Internet, a "Cloud" has been used as a metaphor for a network-accessible infrastructure (e.g., data storage, computing hardware, or entire networks) which is hidden from users. To some, the concept of cloud computing may seem like a throwback to the days of big mainframe computers, but we believe that cloud computing makes data truly mobile, allowing a user to access services anywhere, anytime, with any Internet browser. In cloud computing, IT-related capabilities are provided as services, accessible without requiring control of, or even knowledge of, the underlying technology. Cloud computing provides dynamic scalability of services and computing power, and although many mature technologies are used as components in cloud computing, there are still many unresolved and open problems.

The CloudCom 2009 conference provided a dynamic forum for engineers and scientists in academia, industry, and government to exchange ideas and experiences in developing: cloud/grid architectures; load balancing schemes; Optimal deployment configurations; consistency models; virtualization technologies; middleware frameworks; software as a service (SaaS); hardware as a service (HaaS); data grid & Semantic Web; Web services; security and risk; fault tolerance and reliability; auditing, monitoring and scheduling; utility computing; high-performance computing; and peer-to-peer computing, all within the concept of cloud computing.

Almost 200 papers were submitted, from all around the world. The Program Chairs rejected 20 clearly out-of-scope papers without review, and these are not included in the acceptance ratio calculation. All relevant submissions were reviewed by at least three Technical Program Committee members or external reviewers. In order to ensure a high quality, out of 167 papers in the submission and review system only 44 regular full-length papers were accepted for oral presentation and inclusion in the proceedings, reflecting a 27% acceptance rate. Since cloud computing is a relatively new field, we also included some contributions in the short paper sessions representing ongoing research and interesting ideas. All of these papers and topics provided novel ideas, new results, work in progress, and state-of-the-art techniques in this field. We thus made every effort to stimulate the future research activities in the area of cloud computing, to encourage the dissemination of various research results and ideas, and to make CloudCom2009 a real forum for cloud computing research and technology. The program also included four invited talks from James Yeh, Geoffrey Fox, Chunming Rong, and Rajkumar Buyya.

Organization of conferences with a large number of submissions requires a lot of hard work and dedication from many people. We would like to take this opportunity to thank numerous individuals whose work made this conference possible and ensured its high quality. First and foremost, we thank the authors of submitted papers for contributing to the conference technical program. We are also grateful to the Program (Vice) Chairs, for their hard work and commitment to quality when helping with the paper selection. We would also like to thank all Program Committee members and external reviewers for their excellent job in the paper review process. We are indebted to the Publicity Chairs for advertising the conference, to the Local Organizing Committee for managing registration and other conference organization-related tasks, and to Beijing Jiatong University, Chinese Institute of Electronics, and Wuhan University for hosting the conference. We are also grateful to Liang Yan and Jie Lian for their intrepid efforts managing the two mirrors of the conference website, and to EasyChair for providing the conference management system.

Special thanks to Hamid R. Arabnia, University of Georgia, Han-Chieh Chao, National Ilan University, Frode Eika Sandnes, Oslo University College, Chunming Rong, University of Stavanger, and Hai Jin, Huangzhong University of Science and Technology, for organising special issues in the *Journal of Supercomputing*, the *Journal of Internet Technology*, and the *Journal of Computer Science and Technology*.

October 2009   Martin Gilje Jaatun
                                                                             Gansen Zhao
                                                                             Chunming Rong

Conference Organization

Honarary General Chair

Jichuan Wu   Chinese Institute of Electronics, China

General Chairs (Academic)

Deyi Li   Chinese Academy of Engineering, China
Hai Jin   Huazhong University of Science & Technology,
                              China

General Chair (Organizing)

Yun Liu   Beijing Jiaotong University, China

Program Chairs

Martin Gilje Jaatun   SINTEF ICT, Norway
Gansen Zhao   South China Normal University/Sun Yat-sen
                              University, China

Program Vice Chairs

Geoffrey Fox   Indiana University, USA
Ho-fung Leung   Chinese University of Hong Kong, China
Omer F. Rana   Cardiff University, UK
Waleed Smari   University of Dayton, USA
Luca Spalazzi   Universitá Politecnica delle Marche, Italy
Yun Yang   Swinburne University of Technology, Australia
Shi Ying   Wuhan University, China

Award Chair

David Bader   Georgia Institute of Technology, USA

Panel Chairs

Rajkumar Buyya	University of Melbourne and Manjrasoft, Australia
Hai Jin	Huazhong University of Science and Technology, China

Steering Committee

Chunming Rong	University of Stavanger, Norway (Chair)
Hai Jin	Huazhong University of Science and Technology, China
Martin Gilje Jaatun	SINTEF, Norway
Rulin Liu	Chinese Institute of Electronics, China

Advisory Committee

Hamid R. Arabnia	University of Georgia, USA
Han-Chieh Chao	National Ilan University, Taiwan, China
Geoffrey Fox	Indiana University, USA
Benxiong Huang	Huazhong University of Science and Technology, China
Chung-Ming Huang	National Chung Kung University, Taiwan, China
Victor Leung	University of British Columbia, Canada
Jianhua Ma	Hosei University, Japan
Mark Musen	Stanford University, USA
Jong Hyuk Park	Kyungnam University, Korea
Frode Eika Sandnes	Oslo University College, Norway
Cho-Li Wang	University of Hong Kong, China
Zhiwei Xu	Chinese Academy of Science, China
Laurence T. Yang	St. Francis Xavier University, Canada

Finance Committee

Runhua Lin	Chinese Institute of Electronics, China (Chair)
Zhenjiang Zhang	Beijing Jiaotong University, China (Co-chair)
Gansen Zhao	South China Normal University/Sun Yat-sen University, China (Co-chair)

Organizing Committee

Yong Li	Beijing Jiaotong University, China (Chair)
Kaihong Dong	Chinese Institute of Electronics, China (Co-chair)

Bing Li   Wuhan University, China (Co-chair)
Yanning Zhang   Beijing Jiaotong University, China (Co-chair)
Dan Tao   Beijing Jiaotong University, China
Liang Yan   University of Stavanger, Norway
Jin Liu   Wuhan University, China
Yimin Zhang   Chinese Institute of Electronics, China

Web Administration Chairs

Jie Lian   Beijing Jiaotong University, China
Qing Liu   Beijing Jiaotong University, China

Publicity Chair

Paul Van Binst   Université Libre de Bruxelles, Belgium

Publication Chair

Wei Sun   Sun Yat-sen University, China

European Liaison Chair

Erik Hjelmås   Gjøvik University College, Norway

American Liaison Chair

Naixue Xiong   Georgia State University, USA

Asia Liaison Chair

Robert Hsu   Chung Hua University, Taiwan

Oceania Liaison Chair

Oliver Sinnen   University of Auckland, New Zealand

Program Committee

Gagan Agrawal   Ohio State University, USA
Ahmed Al-Dubai   Napier University, UK
Bernady Apduhan   Kyushu Sangyo University, Japan
Atta Badii   University of Reading, UK

Mark Baker	University of Reading, UK
Kyrre Begnum	Oslo University College, Norway
George Bosilca	University of Tennessee, USA
Sergey Bratus	Dartmouth College, USA
Lawrie Brown	ADFA, Australia
Rajkumar Buyya	University of Melbourne and Manjrasoft, Australia
Jian Cao	ShangHai Jiao Tong University, China
David Chadwick	University of Kent, UK
Ruey-Maw Chen	National Chin-Yi University of Technology, Taiwan, China
Dickson Chiu	Dickson Computer Systems, Hong Kong, China
Kenneth Chiu	Binghamton University, USA
Fabio M. Costa	Universidade Federal de Goiás, Brazil
Yuanshun Dai	University of Electronic Science and Technology of China, China
Reggie Davidrajuh	University of Stavanger, Norway
Robert Deng	Singapore Management University, Singapore
Frederic Desprez	INRIA, France
Wanchun Dou	Nanjing University, China
Chenggong Fan	EMC China Research Center, China
Dan Feng	Huazhong University of Science and Technology, China
Jürgen Fuss	University of Applied Sciences - Hageberg, Austria
Stefanos Gritzalis	University of the Aegean, Greece
Daniel Grosu	Wayne State University, USA
Nils Gruschka	NEC Laboratories Europe, Germany
Peiyuan Guo	Beijing Technology and Business University, China
Thomas Hacker	Purdue University, USA
Yanbo Han	Chinese Academy of Sciences, China
Zhen Han	Beijing Jiaotong University, China
Qing He	Chinese Academy of Sciences, China
Neil Chue Hong	OMII, UK
Hui-Huang Hsu	Tamkang University, Taiwan, China
Yongfeng Huang	Tsinghua University, China
Yo-Ping Huang	National Taipei University of Technology, Taiwan, China
Ray Y.M. Huang	National Cheng Kung University, Taiwan, China
Marty Humphrey	University of Virginia, USA
Michel Hurfin	Irisa, INRIA, France
Ren-Hung Hwang	National Chung Cheng University, Taiwan, China

Jörg Hähner	Leibniz University of Hannover, Germany
Luigi Lo Iacono	NEC Laboratories Europe, Germany
Alexandru Iosup	TU Delft, The Netherlands
Mike (Hua) Ji	Juniper Networks, USA
Thilo Kielmann	Vrije Universiteit, The Netherlands
Hiroaki Kikuchi	Tokai University, Japan
Romain Laborde	University Paul Sabatier, France
Bing Li	Wuhan University, China
Juanzi Li	Tsinghua University, China
Wenjun Li	Sun Yat-sen University, China
Xuhui Li	Wuhan University, China
Yan Li	Intel, China
Yong Li	Beijing Jiaotong University, China
Zhi Li	800APP, China
Peter Linington	University of Kent, UK
Jiming Liu	Hong Kong Baptist University, Hong Kong, China
Yun Liu	Beijing Jiaotong University, China
Peng Liu	PLA University of Science and Technology, China
Seng Wai Loke	La Trobe University, Australia
Shizhu Long	BORQS, China
Jinhu Lv	Chinese Academy of Science, China
Huadong Ma	Beijing University of Posts and Telecommunications, China
Antonio Maña Gomez	University of Malaga, Spain
Ian Marshall	Lancaster University, UK
Hong Mei	Peking University, China
Hein Meling	University of Stavanger, Norway
Kai Xiang Miao	Intel China Research Center, China
José A. Montenegro	Universidad de Málaga, Spain
David Moreland	CSIRO, Australia
Gero Mühl	Technical University of Berlin, Germany
Tadahiko Murata	Kansai University, Japan
Simin Nadjm-Tehrani	Linköping University, Sweden
Dimitris Nikolopoulos	Virginia Tech, USA
Josef Noll	UniK, Norway
Oleksandr Otenko	Oracle, UK
Maria S. Perez-Hernandez	Universidad Politécnica de Madrid, Spain
Radu Prodan	University of Innsbruck, Austria
Depei Qian	BeiHang University, China
Huaifeng Qin	Platform Computing, China
Julian L. Rrushi	Oak Ridge National Laboratory, USA
Ali Shahrabi	Glasgow Caledonian University, UK
Kuei-Ping Shih	Tamkang University, Taiwan, China

Timothy K. Shih	NTUE, Taiwan, China
Qinbao Song	Xian Jiao Tong University, China
Willy Susilo	University of Wollongong, Australia
Jie Tang	Tsinghua University, China
Yong Tang	South China Normal University, China
Feiyue Wang	Chinese Academy of Sciences, China
Guojun Wang	Central South University, China
Junfeng Wang	Sichuan University, China
Peng Wang	Chengdu University of Information Technology, China
Qing Wang	Chinese Academy of Sciences, China
Yi Wang	Google China Research Lab, China
Von Welch	University of Illinois, USA
Gilbert Wondracek	TU Vienna, Austria
Song Wu	Huazhong University of Science and Technology, China
Xinran Wu	Intel Research China, China
Jinhua Xiong	Institute of Computing Technology, CAS, China
Dongyan Xu	Purdue University, USA
Zhiyong Xu	Suffolk University, USA
Lu Yan	University of Hertfordshire, UK
Shoubao Yang	USTC, China
Geng Yang	Nanjing University of Post & Telecommunications, China
Chao-Tung Yang	Tunghai University, Taiwan, China
Hongyu Yao	Yoyo System, China
Jon (Jong-Hoon) Youn	University of Nebraska at Omaha, USA
Feng Yu	Southeast University, China
Huashan Yu	Peking University, China
Nenghai Yu	University of Science and Technology of China, China
Zhiwen Yu	Northwestern Polytechnical University, China
Sherali Zeadally	University of the District of Columbia, USA
Cheng Zeng	Wuhan University, China
Li Zha	Institute of Computing Technology, CAS, China
Feng Zhang	Sun Yat-sen University, China
Li Zhang	BeiHang University, China
Tingting Zhang	Mid Sweden University, Sweden
Zonghua Zhang	NICT, Japan
Wenyin Zhao	KingQue Cor., China
Weimin Zheng	Tsinghua University, China
Zhibin Zheng	HUAWEI, China

Sheng Zhong	SUNY Buffalo, USA
Wenhui Zhou	China Mobile Research Institute, China
Jinzy Zhu	IBM Software Group Services, China
Peidong Zhu	National University of Defense Technology, China
Deqing Zou	Huazhong University of Science and Technology, China
Knut Øvsthus	Bergen University College, Norway

External Reviewers

Azab, Abdulrahman	Slagell, Adam
Cao, Zhidong	Sonmez, Ozan
Chang, Lei	Sun, Xiaoping
Chen, Jidong	Sun, Yibo
Chen, Xi	Tang, Lei
Chen, Xu	Ting, Chuan-Kang
Chen, Yu	Voorsluys, William
Deng, Fang	Wang, Chi
Ding, Zhijun	Wang, Lei
Garg, Nandan	Wang, Rui
Hao, Lu	Wang, Xingang
He, Chengwan	Wang, Zhu
He, Keqing	Wu, Ling
Huang, Bo	Wu, Qian
Huang, Jiung-yao	Xiao, Chunxian
Huang, Xiaomeng	Xiao, Junchao
Ibrahim, Shadi	Xiaolong, Zheng
Jeng, Yu-Lin	Yang, Bo
Liu, Haiwen	Yang, Qiusong
Liu, Jeff	Yang, Ziye
Liu, Jin	Yigitbasi, Nezih
Long, Qin	Zaman, Sharrukh
Luo, Xiangfeng	Zhai, Haoliang
Muñoz, Antonio	Zhang, Chi
Nyre, Åsmund Ahlmann	Zhang, Junsheng
Ostermann, Simon	Zhao, Zhuofeng
Peng, Rong	Zheng, Zibin
Rekleitis, Evangelos	Zhou, Aoying
Schneider, Joerg	Zhou, Guofu
Schoenherr, Jan H.	Zhou, Shuigeng
Shi, Feng	Zhydkov, Dmytro
Shi, Xuanhua	

Table of Contents

1. Invited Papers

2. Full Papers

3. Short Papers

The Many Colors and Shapes of Cloud

James T. Yeh

IBM Corporation

Abstract. While many enterprises and business entities are deploying and exploiting Cloud Computing, the academic institutes and researchers are also busy trying to wrestle this beast and put a leash on this possible paradigm changing computing model. Many have argued that Cloud Computing is nothing more than a name change of Utility Computing. Others have argued that Cloud Computing is a revolutionary change of the computing architecture. So it has been difficult to put a boundary of what is in Cloud Computing, and what is not. I assert that it is equally difficult to find a group of people who would agree on even the definition of Cloud Computing. In actuality, may be all that arguments are not necessary, as Clouds have many shapes and colors. In this presentation, the speaker will attempt to illustrate that the shape and the color of the cloud depend very much on the business goals one intends to achieve. It will be a very rich territory for both the businesses to take the advantage of the benefits of Cloud Computing and the academia to integrate the technology research and business research.

M.G. Jaatun, G. Zhao, and C. Rong (Eds.): CloudCom 2009, LNCS 5931, p. 1, 2009.

Biomedical Case Studies in Data Intensive Computing

Geoffrey Fox[1,2], Xiaohong Qiu[1], Scott Beason[1], Jong Choi[1,2], Jaliya Ekanayake[1,2], Thilina Gunarathne[1,2], Mina Rho[2], Haixu Tang[2], Neil Devadasan[3], and Gilbert Liu[4]

[1] Pervasive Technology Institute
[2] School of Informatics and Computing
[3] The Polis Center
[4] School of Medicine Indiana University
{gcf,xqiu,smbeason,jychoi,jekanaya,tgunarat,mrho,
hatang}@indiana.edu,
{ndevadas,gcliu}@iupui.edu

Abstract. Many areas of science are seeing a data deluge coming from new instruments, myriads of sensors and exponential growth in electronic records. We take two examples – one the analysis of gene sequence data (35339 Alu sequences) and other a study of medical information (over 100,000 patient records) in Indianapolis and their relationship to Geographic and Information System and Census data available for 635 Census Blocks in Indianapolis. We look at initial processing (such as Smith Waterman dissimilarities), clustering (using robust deterministic annealing) and Multi Dimensional Scaling to map high dimension data to 3D for convenient visualization. We show how scaling pipelines can be produced that can be implemented using either cloud technologies or MPI which are compared. This study illustrates challenges in integrating data exploration tools with a variety of different architectural requirements and natural programming models. We present preliminary results for end to end study of two complete applications.

Keywords: MapReduce, Clouds, MPI, Clustering, Sequencing, Dryad. Hadoop.

1 Introduction

Data Intensive Computing is very popular at this time. Partly this is due to the well understood data deluge with all activities including science, government and modern Internet (Web 2.0) systems all generating exponentially increasing data. One special driver is that Web Search and related data mining can use an especially simple programming model MapReduce of which there are now several implementations. It is attractive to understand how generally applicable MapReduce is to other data intensive problems as one can expect excellent commercial support for software in this area. We have looked at the impact of clouds and compared Yahoo (Hadoop) and Microsoft (Dryad) implementations of the MapReduce step presenting Dryad results here. We choose two biomedical applications. The first addresses the structure of Gene families and the processing steps involve sequence alignment, clustering and visualization after projecting sequences to 3 dimensions using Multidimensional

M.G. Jaatun, G. Zhao, and C. Rong (Eds.): CloudCom 2009, LNCS 5931, pp. 2–18, 2009.

scaling MDS. The second application involves correlating electronic patient records with environmental information (from Geographical Information Systems) associated with the patient location. Here the end to end study involves substantial data validation, processing with many standard tools such as those in R but also many possible other applications such as Multidimensional Scaling dimension reductions and Genetic algorithm based optimizations.

We present performance results from Tempest – An Infiniband connected 32 node system running Windows HPCS with each node having 24 cores spread over 4 Intel chips. Such a modest cluster can fully process all stages of the 35,000 element Alu study in less than a day and is suitable for up to 200,000 sequences even though all steps in analysis are of $O(N^2)$ time complexity. We estimate that a 1024 node Tempest architecture cluster would tackle well our million sequence goal. We find systems easy to use and program as well as giving good wall clock execution time. Some of our studies used a slightly older cluster Madrid with 8 nodes each with four AMD Opteron chips with 4 cores each. Section 2 presents some overall architecture comments while sections 3 and 4 describe the two main applications. Section 5 has conclusions and future work.

2 Data Intensive Computing Architecture

The computer architecture needed to support data intensive computing is obviously complex and varied. Here we do not discuss virtualization or issues of distributed systems which although important are not the topic of this paper. We abstract many approaches as a mixture of pipelined and parallel (good MPI performance) systems, linked by a pervasive storage system. Here we have many interesting possibilities including Amazon and Azure "Blob" storage, traditional supercomputer environment like Lustre plus importantly the file systems (such as Cosmos from Microsoft or HDFS from Hadoop) supporting the new MapReduce systems. These cloud/Web 2.0 technologies support a computing style where data is read from one file system, analyzed by one or more tools and written back to a database or file system. An important feature of the newer approaches is explicit support for file-based data parallelism which is needed in our applications. In figure 1, we abstract this disk/database-compute model and assume it will underlie many applications even when some of resources will be local and others in the cloud or part of a large grid. In figures 2 and 3 we give in more detail the data pipelines used in the applications of sections 3 and 4 respectively.

We record in table 1, the major facilities used in this study. Note they run Windows (HPC Edition) and stress both multicore and traditional parallelism. The largest Tempest cluster has 768 Intel Cores spread over 32 nodes while the smaller one Madrid has 128 Opteron cores spread over 8 nodes. Our work [5, 19, 21] stresses both Windows and Linux so we can explore Hadoop, Dryad and the emerging cloud approaches. This paper focuses on results from the Windows clusters.

Table 1. Hardware and software configurations of the clusters used in this paper. In addition a traditional 8-node Linux Cluster "Gridfarm" was used to run statistics package R in section 4.

System/ Size	CPU	Memory	Operating System	Network
Tempest 32 Cluster + 1 Head	4 Intel Six CoreXenon E7450 2.4 GHz	Cluster:48 GB Head: 24 GB 12 MB Cache	Windows Server 2008 HPC Ed. (SP1)	1 Gbps Ethernet
Madrid 8 Cluster + 1 Head	4 AMD Quad Core. Opteron 8356 2.3GHz	Cluster:16 GB Head: 8 GB 2 MB Cache	Windows Server HPC Ed. (SP1)	20Gbps Infiniband

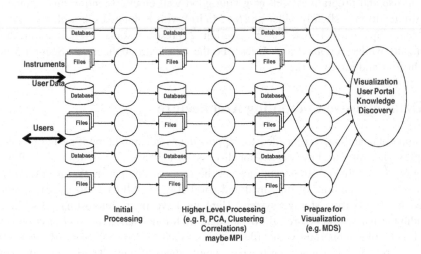

Fig. 1. A Data intensive computing architecture

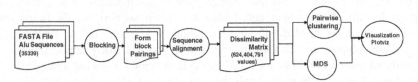

Fig. 2. Stages of Gene sequencing application processing pipeline

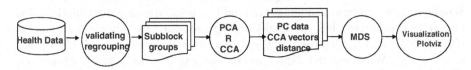

Fig. 3. Stages of health application processing pipeline

3   Gene Sequencing Applications

3.1   Alu Sequencing Studies

The Alu clustering problem [13] is one of the most challenging problem for sequencing clustering because Alus represent the largest repeat families in human genome. There are about 1 million copies of Alu sequences in human genome, in which most insertions can be found in other primates and only a small fraction (~ 7000) are human-specific insertions. This indicates that the classification of Alu repeats can be deduced solely from the 1 million human Alu elements. Notable, Alu clustering can be viewed as a classical case study for the capacity of computational infrastructures because it is not only of great biological interests, but also a problem of a scale that will remain as the upper limit of many other clustering problem in bioinformatics for the next few years, e.g. the automated protein family classification for a few millions of proteins predicted from large metagenomics projects.

3.2   Smith Waterman Dissimilarities

The first step is to identify human Alu gene sequences which were obtained by using Repeatmasker [14] with Repbase Update [15]. We have been gradually increasing the size of our projects with the sample in this paper having 35339 sequences (while we are preparing to analyze 300,000) and requires a modest cluster such as Tempest (768 cores). Note from the discussion in section 3.1, we are aiming at supporting problems with a million sequences -- quite practical today on TeraGrid and equivalent facilities given basic analysis steps scale like $O(N^2)$.

We used open source version [16] of the Smith Waterman – Gotoh algorithm SW-G [17, 18] modified to ensure low start up effects by each thread/processing large numbers (above a few hundred) at a time. Memory bandwidth needed was reduced by storing data items in as few bytes as possible.

3.2.1   Performance of Smith Waterman Gotoh SW-G Algorithm with MPI

The calculation of the 624 million independent dissimilarities is of course architecturally simple as each computation is independent. Nevertheless it shows striking structure shown in figure 4. As in previous papers [5, 21], we look at different patterns denoted as (Thread per process) x (MPI process per 24 core node) x (Number of Nodes) or in short the pattern *txmxn*. We have for Tempest defined in table 1, *n* <=32 and *txm* <= 24. We present results in terms of parallel overhead f(P) defined for Parallelism P by

$$f(P) = [PT(P) - P(Ref)T(Ref)] / (P(Ref)T(Ref)) \qquad (1)$$

Where we set usually Ref =1 but later we use Ref as the smallest number of processes that can run job efficiently.

The striking result for this step is that MPI easily outperforms the equivalent threaded version of this embarrassingly parallel step. In figure 4, all the peaks in the overhead correspond to patterns with large values of thread count *t*. On figure 4, we note that MPI intranode 1x24x32 pattern completes the full 624 billion alignments in

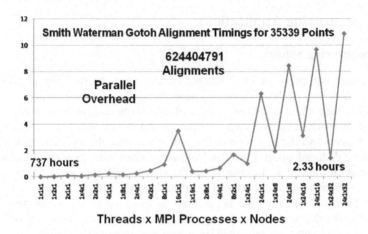

Fig. 4. Performance of Alu Gene Alignments for different parallel patterns

2.33 hours – 4.9 times faster than threaded implementation 24x1x32. This 768 core MPI run has a parallel overhead of 1.43 corresponding to a speed up of 316.

The SW-G alignment performance is probably dominated by memory bandwidth issues but we are still pursuing several points that could affect this but not at our highest priority as SW-G is not a dominant step. We have tried to identify the reason for the comparative slowness of threading. Using Windows monitoring tools, we found that the threaded version has about a factor of 100 more context switches than in case where in MPI we have one thread per process. This could lead to a slow down of threaded approach and correspond to Windows handing of paging of threads with large memory footprints [30]. We have seen this effect in many related circumstances. There is also an important data transfer effect that we discuss in the following subsection.

3.2.2 The O(N²) Factor of 2 and Data Transfer

There is a well known factor of 2 in many $O(N^2)$ parallel algorithms such as those in direct simulations of astrophysical stems. We initially calculate in parallel the Distance or Dissimilarity $D(i,j)$ between points (sequences) i and j and as discussed above this is done in parallel over all processor nodes selecting criteria $i < j$ to avoid calculating both $D(i,j)$ and the identical $D(j,i)$. This can require substantial file transfer as it is unlikely that nodes requiring $D(i,j)$ in a later step, will find that it was calculated on nodes where it is needed.

For example the MDS and PW(PairWise) Clustering algorithms described in next 2 sections, require a parallel decomposition where each of N processes (MPI processes, threads) has 1/N of sequences and for this subset {i} of sequences stores in memory $D(\{i\},j)$ for all sequences j and the subset {i} of sequences for which this node is responsible. This implies that we need D (i,j) and D (j,i) (which are equal) stored in different processors/disks). This is a well known collective operation in MPI called either gather or scatter. Note that we did NOT get good performance for data transfer of $D(i,j)$ to its needed final processor from either MPI (it should be a seconds on Petabit/sec Infiniband switch) or Dryad. We intend to make the needed collective (reduction) primitives more precise and expect substantial performance improvement. However, for the results presented here the timings include the I/O necessary to write results from each process to local disk. An additional step was necessary in our processing workflow to combine the results into a single file used in downstream processing such as clustering and MDS.

3.2.3   Use of Dryad in Smith-Waterman Computation

We performed a detailed study [19, 29] of DryadLINQ – Microsoft's implementation of MapReduce [31, 32] for the computation described in previous subsection for MPI. It is nontrivial to produce final output – the $D(i,j)$ in a form suitable for use in next stage of pipeline – this is currently a single final file holding all the independent dissimilarities.

We adopted a coarse grain task decomposition approach [29] which requires minimum inter-process communicational requirements to ameliorate the higher communication and synchronization costs of the DryadLINQ parallel runtime compared to MPI. To explain our algorithm, let's consider an example where N gene sequences produces as discussed above, a pairwise distance matrix of size NxN. We decompose the computation task by considering the resultant matrix and group the overall computation into a blocks by dividing original matrix into BxB subblocks where B is a multiple (>2) of the available computation nodes. As discussed above, due to the symmetry of the distances $D(i,j)$ and $D(j,i)$ we only calculate the distances in the blocks of the upper triangle of the blocked matrix. Diagonal blocks are especially handled and calculated as full sub blocks. As the number of diagonal blocks is B and total number $B(B+1)/2$, there is no significant compute overhead added by ignoring symmetry in diagonal blocks. The blocks in the upper triangle are partitioned (assigned) to the available compute nodes and an DryadLINQ "Apply" operation is used to execute a function to calculate (N/B)x(N/B) distances in each block. After computing the distances in each block, the function calculates the transpose matrix of the result matrix which corresponds to a block in the lower triangle, and writes both these matrices into two output files in the local file system. The names of these files and their block numbers are communicated back to the main program. The main program sorts the files based on their block number s and perform another DryadLINQ "Apply" operation to combine the files corresponding to a row of blocks in a single large row block.

Figures 5, 6 and 7 present our initial results. Fig. 5 compares the DryadLINQ performance with that of MPI showing the DryadLINQ performance lies between two different versions of the MPI code [29]. In figure 6, we take a fixed Alu dataset of 10,000 sequences and compare its performance as a function of the number of nodes. Note in all these figures we scale results so perfect scaling would correspond to a flat curve independent of the value of the abscissa. Figure 6 only shows some 20% increase in execution time as the core count increases. One problem with current MapReduce implementations is that they are not set up to do dynamic scheduling that help efficiency of a pleasing parallel job mix of inhomogeneous tasks. We examine this in fig. 7 where we artificially increase the scatter in the sequence lengths of the input data. The "real" data shown in figures 5 and 6 has a standard deviation of the

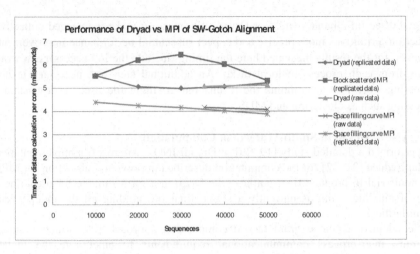

Fig. 5. Comparison of Dryad MapReduce framework with MPI on Smith Waterman Gotoh distance calculations on first step of Alu sequence study pipeline as a function of number of sequences from 10,000 to 50,000. Those "marked replicated" are generated artificially to have uniform inhomogeneity. The raw data for 35339 and 50,000 sequences are also shown.

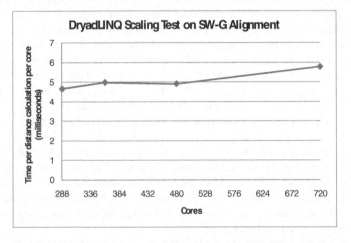

Fig. 6. Scaling test of Dryad MapReduce framework on Smith Waterman Gotoh distance calculations on first step of Alu sequence study pipeline as a function of number of cores

length that is 10% of the mean length. However in figure 7 we increase the standard deviation up to 75% of the mean. By randomizing the sequences in each block we are still able to maintain good performance as seen in fig. 7.

Note that fig. 7 shows both the actual computation and total time including data reorganization for the MPI step. Currently we are extending these results to quantify the comparison between Hadoop [33] and DryadLINQ. In previous work, we have found similar performance between these two MapReduce implementations with Dryad showing somewhat better results [34, 35] in some cases.

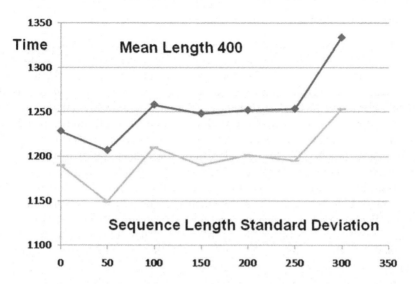

Fig. 7. Study of DryadLINQ processing time on Tempest with statistically load balanced inhomogeneous data with a fixed mean length of 400 characters. The top curve shows the total processing time while the bottom has the final data distribution stage excluded.

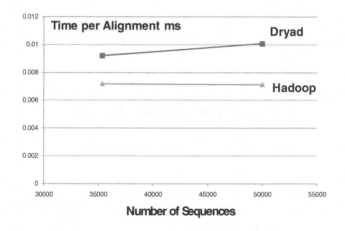

Fig. 8. Study of DryadLINQ (on Windows HPCS) v Hadoop (on RedHat Enterprise Linux) processing Smith Waterman pairwise computations on an IBM IDataplex for samples of 35,339 and 50,000 sequences. The results are presented as time per pair.

We performed initial experiments on an IBM IDataplex with 32 nodes each with 32GB memory and two Intel Xeon L5420   CPU's with 4 cores at 2.50GHz. Surprising the Java alignment code used in Hadoop ran faster (20%) per distance calculation than the C# version and the results in fig. 8 have been corrected for this. Even with this, the Dryad run is somewhat slower than Hadoop in fig. 8.

3.3 Pairwise Clustering

As data sets increase in size, we expect some applications to require particularly robust algorithms that are as insensitive as possible to well known difficulties such as "trapping in local minima". This increases computing challenge which grows to accommodate data set size and the needed increased robustness of results. For example, clustering methods like Kmeans are very sensitive to false minima but some 20 years ago a more robust EM (Expectation Maximization) method using annealing (deterministic not Monte Carlo) was developed by Ken Rose (UCSB) [1], Fox and others [4]. In this algorithm, the annealing is in distance (as represented by D(i,j)) resolution. One slowly lowers a Temperature T that implements an algorithm sensitive to distance scales of order $T^{0.5}$. This method has the interesting feature that it automatically splits clusters when instabilities detected. Further it has a highly efficient parallel algorithm which we have studied in detail in earlier papers on smaller problems [5]. These clustering approaches are fuzzy methods where points are assigned probabilities for belonging to a particular cluster.

There are striking differences between the parallel pattern dependence of figures 4 and 9 which shows the performance of Pairwise Clustering. In all cases MPI is used as communication mechanism between nodes but we can use any mix of threading and MPI on a single node. For figure 4 intranode MPI always gave best performance but in figure 9, intranode threading is the best at high levels of parallelism but worst at low parallelism. We have analyzed this in detail elsewhere and found it is a consequence of MPI communication overheads that increase as data parallel unit (of

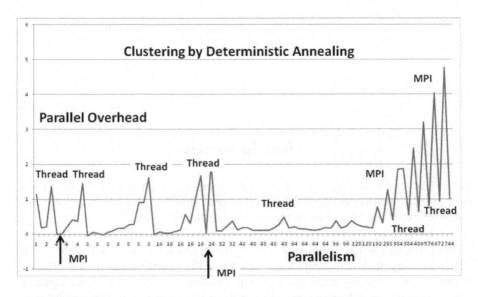

Fig. 9. Paralled Overhead (equation 1) normalized to 4 way parallel MPI job. It is plotted upto 744 way parallel case.

size 35339/(m n)) decreases. For large data parallel units MPI is fastest but for smaller ones used here in production, threading. The poor threaded performance for low levels of parallelism is due to context switches for large memory jobs discussed in section 3.2.1.

The original clustering work was based in a vector space (like Kmeans) where a cluster is defined by a vector as its center. However in a major advance 10 years ago [2, 3], it was shown that one could use a vector free approach and operate with just the dissimilarities D(i,j). This unfortunately does increase the computational complexity from O(N) to O(N^2) for N sequences. It appears however more natural and even essential for studies of gene sequences which do not have Euclidean vectors easily associated with them. We completed these pairwise vector free algorithms and implemented them in parallel. We have discussed elsewhere [5] detailed algorithm and performance issues. Here we report the clustering as part of a large end to end component of our "Million Sequence Analysis as a Service project". All capabilities discussed in this paper will be made available as cloud or TeraGrid services over the next year.

3.4 Multidimensional Scaling MDS

Given dissimilarities D(i,j), MDS finds the best set of vectors $\underline{\mathbf{x}}_i$ in any chosen dimension d (d=3 in our case) minimizing:

$$\Sigma_{i,j} \, \text{weight}(i,j) \, (D(i,j)^m - |\underline{\mathbf{x}}_i - \mathbf{x}_j|^n)^2 \qquad (2)$$

The form of the weight(i,j) is chosen to reflect importance of a point or perhaps a desire (Sammon's method with weight(i,j)=1/ D(i,j)) to fit smaller distance more precisely than larger ones. The index n is typically 1 (Euclidean distance) but 2 also useful. m is 1 in this paper but m=0.5 is interesting.

We have previously reported results using Expectation Maximization and we are exploring adding to this deterministic annealing to improve robustness. Here we use a different technique exploiting that (2) is "just" χ^2 and one can use very reliable nonlinear optimizers to solve it [20]. We have implemented and got good results with the Levenberg–Marquardt approach (adding suitable multiple of unit matrix to nonlinear second derivative matrix) to χ^2 solution.

This "MDS as χ^2" approach allows us to incorporate some powerful features including very general choices for the weight(i,j) and n. Our MDS service is fully parallel over unknowns $\underline{\mathbf{x}}_i$. Further it allows "incremental use"; fixing an MDS solution from a subset of data and adding new points at a later time. One can also optimally align different versions of MDS (e.g. different choices of weight(i,j) to allow precise comparisons. All our MDS services feed their results directly to powerful Point Visualizer. Figure 10 shows the end to end Alu study after SW-G alignments, pairwise clustering and MDS projection. One sees three small clusters red (2794 points), yellow (3666) and green (1838 sequences) isolated from larger (27041) collection of blue sequences that are presumably older. Note that total time for all 3 steps on the full Tempest system is about 6 hours and clearly getting to a million sequences is not unrealistic and would take around a week on a 1024 node cluster.

Fig. 10. Pairwise Clustering of 35339 Alu Sequences visualized with MDS

4   Linking Environment and Health Data

4.1   Introduction

Another area where our tools are naturally used comes in Geographical information systems where we have already presented results [21]. Here we link environmental and patient (health) data. This is challenging as a community's vulnerability and impact may depend on special concerns like environmentally sensitive areas or historical structures, socioeconomic conditions, and various social concerns such as the degree of public trust, education levels, literacy, and collective action and solidarity. The event impact must account for a blend of physical and social measures.

One example is the SAVI Community Information System (www.savi.org)1 is one of the nation's largest community information systems [22]. SAVI, designed to improve decision-making in Central Indiana communities, includes over a ~22 million individual data values, and provides over 161,322 event datasets, 3,099 basic indicators on the socio-economic conditions, health, economy, housing, and many other aspects of the community. Further it makes them available for 11 types of geographic areas, such as census tracts, neighborhoods, and school corporations. The SAVI system is now being used by a variety of other sectors for community development, public health research, education, program planning, disaster mitigation planning and more.   Only recently has the field of social epidemiology begun to develop the theoretical tools that make possible the identification of explanatory pathways from the physical and social infrastructure to health-related behaviors, which then lead to adverse health outcomes [23-25]. We see geographic clustering [21, 36] in many health outcomes because social environment has an effect on health and/or health behaviors [26-28].

4.2   Correlating Environment and Patient Data

We used an ongoing childhood obesity study as our first application to test the relevance of our tools in the area of linking environment and social/health data. [6-7] Obesity is presently one of the most pervasive, serious, and challenging health problems facing the world. Over the past 30 years, the obesity rate has nearly tripled for children ages 2 to 5 years (from 5 to 14 percent) and tripled for youth ages 12 to 19 years (from 5 percent to 17 percent). The obesity rate for children 6 to 11 years of age has quadrupled from 4 to 19 percent. What is causing the dramatic and threatening rise in obesity? Bray concisely captured the etiology of obesity in metaphor: "Genes load the gun, the environment pulls the trigger." 23 Genetic factors are thought to account for 25-40% of the variance in BMI (Body Mass Index) by determining differences in such things as resting metabolic rate and weight gain in response to overfeeding. However, it is highly improbable that changes in genetic factors explain the rapid increases in obesity prevalence over the past two decades. [26] Rather the obesity epidemic is almost certainly rooted in environmental factors that promote excessive caloric intake and sedentary lifestyle [8].

In addition to physical environmental factors, social environmental factors also have bearing on obesity by facilitating or constraining behavior. Specific social environmental factors that have been examined include crime, safety, social support, social networks, and neighborhood socioeconomic status. Perceived (or actual) lack of a safe environment is a significant barrier to physical activity. According to a study conducted by the Centers for Disease Control in 2004, persons who perceived their neighborhoods as less than extremely safe were more than twice as likely to have no leisure-time physical activity, and those who perceived their neighborhoods as not at all safe were nearly three times as likely to have no leisure-time physical activity. Research also indicates that parental concerns about traffic and crime have a strong influence on children's physical activity levels and that child and parent perceptions of the environment are as important as the actual environment.

This motivates studies that study linkage between patient health and environment factors. We can examine urban planning data that provides information on characteristics of the built environment, such as street features, land use mix, and neighborhood greenness. We examine insurance information from patient medical records as an indicator of family-level social environment. We examine U.S. Census and Uniform Crime Report information for areas surrounding patients' residential addresses as indicators of neighborhood social environment. Here we are setting up the infrastructure linking the tool R with our other tools described in section 3 and only have preliminary results on this use case for our new generation of large scale data analysis tools. As there are some 30 patient attributes and over one hundred environmental attributes, tools like MDS that reduce dimensionality were a focus.

4.3 Canonical Correlation Analysis and Multidimensional Scaling

The canonical correlation analysis (CCA) is a tool of multivariate statistical analysis for finding correlations between two sets of variables [9, 10]. Here we are applying CCA to correlate patient health and environmental factors. Our full data set we used for this research consists of over 314,000 real-life patient records collected over 15 years and measured on about 180 variables, mostly related with biological and environmental factors. We stored our full data set (with size 832 MB) in a database system for easy exploration and fast extraction. Among the full data set, we only used the cleanest data for our initial studies. For performing CCA over the patient data set and conducting various kinds of statistical analysis, we used R, one of the most well-known statistical computing environments. R expedites complicated statistical data

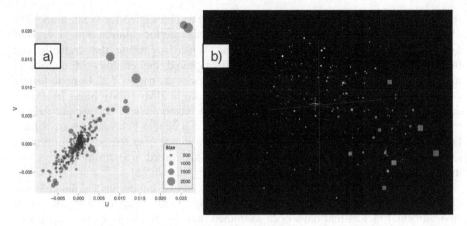

Fig. 11. a) The plot of the first pair of canonical variables for 635 Census Blocks and b) the color coded correlation between MDS and first eigenvector of PCA decomposition

manipulations with ease by utilizing highly optimized and multi-threaded numeric packages, such as BLAS, Goto-BLAS [11], and ATLAS [12]. Another advantage in using R is that we can use various open-source add-on packages for additional functionalities. For example, with the help of packages for databases, such as PostgreSQL and MySQL, we can directly access the data stored in the database system.

The core idea in CCA is to find an optimal linear projection of two sets of data in a sense that the correlation of them in the projected space, also called "canonical space", is maximized. More specifically, for the given two sets of data matrix X and Y, the CCA seeks two optimal projection vectors $\underline{a}$ and $\underline{b}$, which make the following correlation maximum:

$$\rho = \mathrm{corr}(\underline{U},\underline{V}),$$

where $\underline{U} = \underline{a}^T X$ and $\underline{V} = \underline{b}^T Y$ are vectors in the canonical space. One can see that the vector $\underline{U}$ and $\underline{V}$, known as *canonical correlation variables*, are the new representation of the data matrix X and Y in the canonical space, transformed by the projection vector $\underline{a}$ and $\underline{b}$ respectively..

In our project, the CCA is a good match as we have two sets of data – patient and environmental data – and want to find out which variables of environmental data have some connections to patient's obesity or more generally their health. For this purpose, we can use X as an environmental data and Y as a patient data with the CCA formalism to find the best optimal canonical variables $\underline{U}$ and $\underline{V}$, which maximize the correlation between the patient and the environmental data. As an alternative to CCA, which maximizes vector in both data sets, one can find the vectors $\underline{a}$ and $\underline{b}$ by fixing the vector in one sector. For example with our health data set, we can find new projection vector $\underline{a}$ by fixing $\underline{b}$ in terms of Principle Components (PC) of the patient data matrix Y.

Since the well known CCA algorithm itself is not our focus in this paper, we will not present more details in As an example of CCA results to the patient data set, we found the optimal correlation in the canonical space (Figure 11a)). Those results can feed in to the MDS to find more robust structures in 3-dimension (Figure 11b). More details can be found in [9, 10, 30]. Each point corresponds to one of 635 Census blocks. We color projections on a green (lowest) to red/mauve (highest) scale and see clear clustering of the different colors in different regions of MDS. The low (green) values occur together and are well separated from the high weighted red and mauve points. In these plots the MDS was weighted (using weight(i,j) in equation (2)) proportional to the number of patients in block. Figures 11b) show correlations for a pure principal component analysis PCA and similar results are seen for the optimal CCA vector $\underline{U}$. The correlation between PCA eigenvector and MDS decomposition was 0.86 (using CCA applied to MDS and environmental data) where as correlation is 0.67 between MNDS and the optimal vector $\underline{U}$ from patient analysis.

In processing CCA in our project, we have used R as statistical computing environments to utilize various matrix manipulation and linear algebra packages with efficiency. Also, by building R with multi-threaded enabled BLAS libraries, we got parallel speed up in our 8 core Linux cluster nodes "Gridfarm". We are continuing these studies on Tempest using a Genetic algorithm to find the optimal set of environment features and this type of loosely coupled problem is suitable for clouds and we will look at an Hadoop/Dryad implementation. We believe linking of R and MapReduce will be very powerful as is the current MPI link.

5 Conclusions

This paper examines the technology to support rapid analysis of genome sequencing and patient record problems that typify today's high end biomedical computational challenges. As well as our local sample problems, we would like to refine and test the technology on a broader range of problems. To encourage this, we will make key capabilities available as services that we eventually be implemented on virtual clusters (clouds) to address very large problems. Relevant services we will make available include the basic Pairwise dissimilarity calculations, R (done already by us and others), MDS in EM and χ^2 forms; the vector and pairwise deterministic annealing clustering including support of fingerprints and other "unusual" vectors. Our point viewer (Plotviz) will be made available either as download (to Windows!) or as a Web service. We note all our current code is written in C# (high performance managed code) and runs on Microsoft HPCS 2008 (with Dryad extensions).

Cloud technologies such as Hadoop and Dryad are very attractive as robust commercially supported software environments. Further many services will run on virtual machine based clouds such as Azure and EC2. In our two problems, we have found steps that currently need MPI. These run well but do not have the intrinsic flexibility and robustness of MapReduce. We note that our MPI applications are not like traditional particle dynamics or differential equation solvers with many small messages. Rather they can be implemented efficiently with only MPI Barrier, Broadcast and Reduction operations which are typical of linear algebra. We are exploring [34, 35] extensions of MapReduce – we call them MapReduce++ -- that support the iterative structure of parallel linear algebra. We expect these to be an attractive implementation paradigm for biomedical applications and allow easy porting of our current MPI codes.

In summary, we've shown two examples of data intensive science applications in area of biology and health using several modern technologies. We suggest that these ideas will support new generations of large scale data analysis systems for patient records, demographic data and next generation gene sequencers.

References

1. Rose, K.: Deterministic Annealing for Clustering, Compression, Classification, Regression, and Related Optimization Problems. Proceedings of the IEEE 80, 2210–2239 (1998)
2. Hofmann, T., Buhmann, J.M.: Pairwise data clustering by deterministic annealing. IEEE Transactions on Pattern Analysis and Machine Intelligence 19, 1–13 (1997)
3. Klock, H., Buhmann, J.M.: Data visualization by multidimensional scaling: a deterministic annealing approach. Pattern Recognition 33(4), 651–669 (2000)
4. Granat, R.A.: Regularized Deterministic Annealing EM for Hidden Markov Models, Ph.D. Thesis, UCLA (2004)
5. Fox, G., Bae, S.-H., Ekanayake, J., Qiu, X., Yuan, H.: Parallel Data Mining from Multicore to Cloudy Grids. In: Proceedings of HPC 2008, High Performance Computing and Grids Workshop, Cetraro Italy, July 3 (2008)
6. Liu, G., Wilson, J., Rong, Q., Ying, J.: Green neighborhoods, food retail, and childhood overweight: differences by population density. American Journal of Health Promotion 21(I4 suppl.), 317–325 (2007)
7. Liu, G., et al.: Examining Urban Environment Correlates of Childhood Physical Activity and Walkability Perception with GIS and Remote Sensing. In: Geo-spatial Technologies in Urban Environments Policy, Practice, and Pixels, 2nd edn., pp. 121–140. Springer, Berlin (2007)
8. Sandy, R., Liu, G., et al.: Studying the child obesity epidemic with natural experiments, NBER Working Paper in (May 2009), http://www.nber.org/papers/w14989
9. Hardoon, D., et al.: Canonical correlation analysis: an overview with application to learning methods. Neural Computation 16(12), 2639–2664 (2004)
10. Härdle, W., Simar, L.: Applied multivariate statistical analysis, pp. 361–372. Springer, Heidelberg (2007)
11. Goto, K., Van De Geijn, R.: High-performance implementation of the level-3 blas. ACM Trans. Math. Softw. 35(1), 1–14 (2008)
12. Whaley, R., Dongarra, J.: Automatically tuned linear algebra software. In: Proceedings of the 1998 ACM/IEEE conf. on Supercomputing (CDROM), pp. 1–27 (1998)
13. Batzer, M.A., Deininger, P.L.: Alu repeats and human genomic diversity. Nat. Rev. Genet. 3(5), 370–379 (2002)
14. Smit, A.F.A., Hubley, R., Green, P.: Repeatmasker (2004), http://www.repeatmasker.org
15. Jurka, J.: Repbase Update: a database and electronic journal of repetitive elements. Trends Genet. 9, 418–420 (2000)
16. Waterman, S.: Software with Gotoh enhancement, http://jaligner.sourceforge.net/naligner/
17. Smith, T.F., Waterman, M.S.: Identification of common molecular subsequences. Journal of Molecular Biology 147, 195–197 (1981)

18. Gotoh, O.: An improved algorithm for matching biological sequences. J. of Molecular Biology 162, 705–708 (1982)
19. Ekanayake, J., Balkir, A.S., Gunarathne, T., Fox, G., Poulain, C., Araujo, N., Barga, R.: DryadLINQ for Scientific Analyses. In: Proceedings of eScience conference (2009), http://grids.ucs.indiana.edu/ptliupages/publications/DryadLINQ_for_Scientific_Analyses.pdf
20. Kearsley, A.J., Tapia, R.A., Trosset, M.W.: The Solution of the Metric STRESS and SSTRESS Problems in Multidimensional Scaling Using Newton's Method, technical report (1995)
21. Qiu, X., Fox, G.C., Yuan, H., Bae, S.-H., Chrysanthakopoulos, G., Nielsen, H.F.: Parallel Clustering and Dimensional Scaling on Multicore System. In: Bubak, M., van Albada, G.D., Dongarra, J., Sloot, P.M.A. (eds.) ICCS 2008, Part I. LNCS, vol. 5101, pp. 407–416. Springer, Heidelberg (2008)
22. Frederickson, K.E.: Enhanced Local Coordination and Collaboration through the Social Assets and Vulnerabilities Indicators (SAVI) Project. In: Proceedings of the American Public Health Association Annual Conference, Washington, D.C (1998)
23. American Public Health Association, National Public Health Week, Eliminating Health Disparities: Communities Moving from Statistics to Solutions, Toolkit (2004)
24. Berkman, L.F., Glass, T.: Social integration, social networks, social support, and health. In: Berkman, L.F., Kawachi, I. (eds.) Social Epidemiology, pp. 137–173. Oxford University Press, New York (2000)
25. Shaw, M., Dorling, D., Smith, G.D.: Poverty, social exclusion, and minorities. In: Marmot, M., Wilkinson, R.G. (eds.) Social Determinants of Health, 2nd edn., pp. 196–223. Oxford University Press, New York (2006)
26. Berkman, L.F., Kawachi, I.: A historical framework for social epidemiology. In: Berkman, L.F., Kawachi, I. (eds.) Social Epidemiology, pp. 3–12. Oxford Univ. Press, New York (2000)
27. Kawachi, I., Berkman, L.F. (eds.): Neighborhoods and Health. Oxford University Press, New York (2003)
28. Robert, S.: Community-level socioeconomic status effects on adult health. Journal of Health and Social Behavior 39, 18–37 (1998)
29. Qiu, X., Ekanayake, J., Beason, S., Gunarathne, T., Fox, G., Barga, R., Gannon, D.: Cloud Technologies for Bioinformatics Applications. In: 2nd ACM Workshop on Many-Task Computing on Grids and Supercomputers (SuperComputing 2009), Portland, Oregon, November 16 (2009), http://grids.ucs.indiana.edu/ptliupages/publications/MTAGS09-23.pdf
30. Fox, G., Qiu, X., Beason, S., Choi, J.Y., Rho, M., Tang, H., Devadasan, N., Liu, G.: Case Studies in Data Intensive Computing: Large Scale DNA Sequence Analysis as the Million Sequence Challenge and Biomedical Computing Technical Report, August 9 (2009), http://grids.ucs.indiana.edu/ptliupages/publications/UsesCasesforDIC-Aug%209-09.pdf
31. Isard, M., Budiu, M., Yu, Y., Birrell, A., Fetterly, D.: Dryad: Distributed data-parallel programs from sequential building blocks. In: European Conference on Computer Systems (March 2007)
32. Yu, Y., Isard, M., Fetterly, D., Budiu, M., Erlingsson, Ú., Gunda, P., Currey, J.: DryadLINQ: A System for General-Purpose Distributed Data-Parallel Computing Using a High-Level Language. In: Symposium on Operating System Design and Implementation (OSDI), CA, December 8-10 (2008)
33. Apache Hadoop, http://hadoop.apache.org/core/

34. Ekanayake, J., Qiu, X., Gunarathne, T., Beason, S., Fox, G.: High Performance Parallel Computing with Clouds and Cloud Technologies (August 25, 2009) (to be published as book chapter),
http://grids.ucs.indiana.edu/ptliupages/publications/
cloud_handbook_final-with-diagrams.pdf
35. Ekanayake, J., Fox, G.: High Performance Parallel Computing with Clouds and Cloud Technologies. In: Jaatun, M.G., Zhao, G., Rong, C. (eds.) CloudCom 2009. LNCS, vol. 5931, Springer, Heidelberg (2009),
http://grids.ucs.indiana.edu/ptliupages/publications/
cloudcomp_camera_ready.pdf
36. Qiu, X., Fox, G.C., Yuan, H., Bae, S.-H., Chrysanthakopoulos, G., Nielsen, H.F.: Parallel Clustering And Dimensional Scaling on Multicore Systems. In: Bubak, M., van Albada, G.D., Dongarra, J., Sloot, P.M.A. (eds.) ICCS 2008, Part I. LNCS, vol. 5101, pp. 407–416. Springer, Heidelberg (2008),
http://grids.ucs.indiana.edu/ptliupages/publications/
hpcsApril12-08.pdf

An Industrial Cloud: Integrated Operations in Oil and Gas in the Norwegian Continental Shelf

Chunming Rong

Department of Electrical Engineering and Computer Science
University of Stavanger, N-4036 Stavanger, Norway
chunming.rong@uis.no

Abstract. Cloud computing may provide the long waiting technologies and methodologies for large scale industrial collaboration across disciplines and enterprise boundaries. Industrial cloud is introduced as a new inter-enterprise integration concept in cloud computing. Motivations and advantages are given by a practical exploration of the concept from the perspective of the on-going effort by the Norwegian oil and gas industry to build industry wide information integration and collaboration. ISO15926 is recognized as a standard enabling cross boundaries data integration and processing.

Keywords: cloud computing, integrated operations.

1 Introduction

In a large scale industrial operation, making the right decisions depends on the accurate overview of the current operation status built upon the received operational data flow. The challenge is to deal with the information flow in an *integrated, cost efficient?, secure* and *reliable* way, while confronting the following: the data flow increases in both quantity and complexity; the received information may often cross disciplines and even company or enterprise boundaries; new information may also be data-mined or extracted from existing information. Furthermore, consistent views of the situations among different involved members should be maintained to avoid conflicts and errors. For real time operational control, the accurate overview must be constantly maintained during the operation. In addition, before being used in a decision making process, information quality should be ensured for both retrieved and extracted data, by consulting related information, e.g. historic events, or current statuses of the other connected components. To exchange, process and analyze the increasing digital data flows from industrial operations, an integrated information platform should be established in an industry wide effort.

Cloud computing technology has the potential to meet the above mentioned challenges. The general goal of cloud computing is to obtain better resource utilization and availability among connected entities. Existing cloud computing models have been focused on providing cost effective services for enterprise, or small and medium businesses. Within an enterprise, information may be interpreted and classified according to the organizational authority of the enterprise. On the other

M.G. Jaatun, G. Zhao, and C. Rong (Eds.): CloudCom 2009, LNCS 5931, pp. 19–23, 2009.

hand, due to political and social differences, information integration efforts in the public domain have often met with difficulties in reaching consensus for large scale data interpretations. For an industry wide collaboration, the involvement of an industry wide authority or association is essential for leadership and consensus on information classification, standardization and interpretation. An industrial wide collaboration has its unique characters and challenges. Applying cloud computing across enterprises has many implied obstacles, but the benefits and potentials encourage us to explore applications of the concept. Existing general solutions such as the information grid [1] are not adequate to deal with the complexity involved. To facilitate the information convergence across enterprises, an industrial cloud is introduced in our paper [2] as a new inter-enterprise integration concept in cloud computing, providing a convenient, integrated and cost efficient? solution in large scale industrial collaborations.

2   Integrated Operations in the Norwegian Continental Shelf

The global energy situation has been dependent on oil and gas products for the last decades. The recent energy crisis occurs in a combination of increasing demand and reduction of production reserves. The Norwegian Continental Shelf (NCS) is a case in point. Many of the oil and gas fields on the NCS had their peak production periods in the 1990s. The situation reflects on both less volume and higher unit costs in their oil and gas production. Consequently, the rise of consumer energy prices was inevitable in order to keep up with demand, while production from such fields on the NCS was approaching the limit for what was profitable. To prevent many of the fields from planned shutdown, the oil and gas industry in Norway recognizes the needs to apply new technologies and methodologies to improve the production process with a cheaper, faster, automated and collaborative solution. Better access to relevant data and tighter collaboration between geographically distributed personnel should lead to faster and better decisions.

Furthermore, the reduction in oil reserves has pushed the exploration of new oil and gas fields further north and even into the arctic region, e.g. the recent Snow-White field is currently the north-most field in operation on the NCS. In addition to the remoteness of the area, rough weather and oceanic conditions are obviously associated with such operations in the high north. Hence, asset and resource management through remote and distributed control is preferred. However, it leads to heavy demands on the communication links and information flow. Additional complexity comes from the connecting and integrating business processes and information sources across organizational boundaries. Furthermore, the environmental vulnerability of the high north areas requires special attention in such operations, and the tolerance for environmental hazards should be approaching zero as a commitment for such exploration licenses. Therefore, the capability of real time monitoring and control is essential for a successful remote operation, between fields and operation centers located elsewhere. Heavily instrumented facilities must be installed for remote data retrieval and control. Key work processes must also be renewed with automated real time data handling embedded.

To meet all the requirements and at the same time maintain profitable operations, the Norwegian Oil Industry Association (OLF) and its associated members have joined forces on a vision of large scale industrial collaboration on the NCS, called Integrated Operations (IO) [3], defined as "collaboration across disciplines, companies, organizational and geographical boundaries, made possible by real-time data and new work processes, in order to reach safer and better decisions – faster". The key element in IO is the integrated digital information platform to provide industrial services and solutions for those interconnected entities. The goal is to increase the amount of oil extracted from the reservoir while reducing the cost, and to be able to operate safely and sustainably in remote, vulnerable and hazardous areas. According an OLF study [4], the effort of IO is predicted to add value of USD 50 billion to the NCS operations, based on the reduced costs and increased production. Integrated operations are recognized as a key element in the future of the oil and gas industry, e.g. the on-going IO in the High North (IOHN) project [5] consists of key members from both IT, defense, and oil and gas operator and service companies in NCS.

The development of IO can be characterized as an industrial effort on cloud computing. A prerequisite for the development of next generation of IO is a robust digital infrastructure and a platform for effective and efficient information exchange. For the oil and gas industry on the NCS, all production platforms and most of other installations are connected with communication fibers and some with redundant communication links through e.g. radio or satellite. The available communication infrastructure is modern and unique. Above physical level, there is the so called SOIL Network (Secure Oil Information Link) to provide the inter-enterprise information exchange network. The infrastructure makes possible further development of a robust industry-wide digital platform using the cloud computing concept, providing not only effective and efficient information exchange but also enabling service delivery.

Information integration is essential to allow the data exchange and sharing across boundaries, and to support data interpretation, information validation and related web services for data mining. Many sub-domain standards exists side by side, e.g. within the sub-domain of drilling and completion alone, there are more than five different communication standards to relate to, e.g., WITSML [6] or OPC-UA [7]. The development of the ISO 15926 [8] based oil and gas ontology has provided opportunities to unify and integrate different data standards and to apply information validation and reasoning methodology. Together with the POSC Caesar organization [9], the work of realizing IO has encouraged the implementation of many enabling technologies and standards such as semantic web and ISO15926 by the members of OLF.

Many fields on the NCS have been modernized with heavily instrumented facilities. The advance in sensor and actuator technologies allows increasing amount of data to be retrieved and delivered in real time over the information infrastructure. Different kinds of data are retrieved from the instrumented installations and stored in distributed databases. Both current and historic data are available from these databases for decision making. The databases may also be available cross enterprise boundaries. This huge amount of data may now be made accessible in real-time for personnel located far away from the offshore platform. However, humans have a limited ability to deal with large amounts of data, especially when it arrives constantly and simultaneously. Hence, it is important to automate the data processing, and filter out unnecessary information and present what is relevant for the tasks at hand. Among the related efforts in IO, the TAIL IO project [10] is most noticeable.

Real time operational control is a significant part of the proposed IO architecture. Recent developments in information and communication technologies enable a more cost efficient utilization of real-time data from the offshore installations, allowing a tighter integration of offshore and onshore personnel, operator companies and service companies.

By integrating and presenting relevant data, new work benches and visualization solutions have been developed to provide an overview of the current state of various systems at the remote installation. Personnel collaborate across a distance sharing this common view of the data. This may result in improvements within fields such as production optimization, process optimization, better work planning, better risk and personnel safety management.

3 Conclusion

Collaboration between different companies in an industry is important to meet the challenges of the future. The effort of realizing the vision of IO in NCS has explored many enabling technologies and methodologies such as cloud computing and semantic web with implementation and field tests. However, there remain many challenges, e.g. unified industry wide data standards (of which ISO15926 is recognized as a strong candidate), work flow and work processes renewal, security, reliability and availability. To establish an industrial cloud, the involvement of industry wide authorities or associations, like OLF and POSC Caesar is essential for leadership and consensus reaching. Implementation of IO on the NCS shall enable real time data decision-making worldwide and provide new collaboration models that link offshore installations, onshore headquarters and service companies. The related innovations in technologies, methodologies and work processes have great potential to create new value and opportunities and to lead us to safer, faster and better decisions.

References

1. Alonso, O., Banerjee, S., Drake, M.: The Information Grid: A Practical Approach to the Semantic Web,
   http://www.oracle.com/technology/tech/semantic_technologies/
   pdf/informationgrid_oracle.pdf
2. Wlodarczyk, T., Rong, C., Thorsen, K.A.: Industrial Cloud: Toward Inter-Enterprise Integration. In: Jaatun, M.G., Zhao, G., Rong, C. (eds.) CloudCom 2009. LNCS, vol. 5931, pp. 460–471. Springer, Heidelberg (2009)
3. OLF, Website on Integrated Operations, http://www.olf.no/io
4. OLF, Potential value of Integrated Operations on the Norwegian Shelf, OLF report (2006),
   http://www.olf.no/getfile.php/zKonvertert/www.olf.no/
   Aktuelt/Dokumenter/Potential%20value%20of%20Integrated%
   20Operations%20on%20the%20Norwegian%20Shelf.pdf

5. Integrated Operations in the High North (IOHN),
   http://www.posccaesar.org/wiki/IOHN
6. Energistics, http://www.witsml.org
7. POSC Caesar Association, http://www.posccaesar.org
8. ISO, ISO 15926: Industrial automation systems and integration – Integration of life-cycle
   data for process plants including oil and gas production facilities,
   http://www.iso.org
9. OPC Foundation, http://www.opcfoundation.org
10. StatoilHydro and consortium consisting of ABB, IBM, Aker Solutions and SKF, TAIL IO,
    http://www-05.ibm.com/no/solutions/chemicalspetroleum/
    tail.html

Cloudbus Toolkit for Market-Oriented Cloud Computing

Rajkumar Buyya[1,2], Suraj Pandey[1], and Christian Vecchiola[1]

[1] Cloud Computing and Distributed Systems (CLOUDS) Laboratory,
Department of Computer Science and Software Engineering,
The University of Melbourne, Australia
{raj,spandey,csve}@csse.unimelb.edu.au
[2] Manjrasoft Pty Ltd, Melbourne, Australia

Abstract. This keynote paper: (1) presents the 21st century vision of computing and identifies various IT paradigms promising to deliver computing as a utility; (2) defines the architecture for creating market-oriented Clouds and computing atmosphere by leveraging technologies such as virtual machines; (3) provides thoughts on market-based resource management strategies that encompass both customer-driven service management and computational risk management to sustain SLA-oriented resource allocation; (4) presents the work carried out as part of our new Cloud Computing initiative, called Cloudbus: (i) Aneka, a Platform as a Service software system containing SDK (Software Development Kit) for construction of Cloud applications and deployment on private or public Clouds, in addition to supporting market-oriented resource management; (ii) internetworking of Clouds for dynamic creation of federated computing environments for scaling of elastic applications; (iii) creation of 3rd party Cloud brokering services for building content delivery networks and e-Science applications and their deployment on capabilities of IaaS providers such as Amazon along with Grid mashups; (iv) CloudSim supporting modelling and simulation of Clouds for performance studies; (v) Energy Efficient Resource Allocation Mechanisms and Techniques for creation and management of Green Clouds; and (vi) pathways for future research.

Keywords: Cloud Computing, Cloudbus, Virtualization, Utility Computing.

1 Introduction - Technology Trends

In 1969, Leonard Kleinrock, one of the chief scientists of the original Advanced Research Projects Agency Network (ARPANET) project which seeded the Internet, said [1]: *"As of now, computer networks are still in their infancy, but as they grow up and become sophisticated, we will probably see the spread of 'computer utilities' which, like present electric and telephone utilities, will service individual homes and offices across the country."* This vision of computing utilities, based on a service provisioning model, anticipated the massive transformation of the entire computing industry in the 21st century whereby computing services will be readily available on demand, like water, electricity, gas, and telephony services available in today's society. Similarly, computing service users (consumers) need to pay providers only when they access computing

M.G. Jaatun, G. Zhao, and C. Rong (Eds.): CloudCom 2009, LNCS 5931, pp. 24–44, 2009.

services, without the need to invest heavily or encounter difficulties in building and maintaining complex IT infrastructure by themselves. They access the services based on their requirements without regard to where the services are hosted. This model has been referred to as *utility computing*, or recently as *Cloud computing* [2].

Cloud computing delivers infrastructure, platform, and software (application) as services, which are made available as subscription-based services in a pay-as-you-go model to consumers. These services in industry are referred to as Infrastructure as a Service (IaaS), Platform as a Service (PaaS), and Software as a Service (SaaS), respectively. Berkeley Report [3] released in Feb 2009 notes - "Cloud computing, the long-held dream of computing as a utility, has the potential to transform a large part of the IT industry, making software even more attractive as a service".

Clouds aim to power the next generation data centers by architecting them as a network of virtual services (hardware, database, user-interface, application logic) so that users are able to access and deploy applications from anywhere in the world on demand at competitive costs depending on users Quality of Service (QoS) requirements [4]. It offers significant benefit to IT companies by freeing them from the low level tasks of setting up basic hardware (servers) and software infrastructures and thus enabling them to focus on innovation and creating business value for their services.

The business potential of Cloud computing is recognised by several market research firms including IDC (International Data Corporation), which reports that worldwide spending on Cloud services will grow from $16 billion by 2008 to $42 billion in 2012. Furthermore, many applications making use of Clouds emerge simply as catalysts or market makers that bring buyers and sellers together. This creates several trillion dollars of business opportunity to the utility/pervasive computing industry, as noted by Bill Joy, co-founder of Sun Microsystems [5].

Cloud computing has high potential to provide infrastructure, services and capabilities required for harnessing this business potential. In fact, it has been identified as one of the emerging technologies in IT as noted in "Gartner's IT Hype Cycle" (see Figure 1). A "Hype Cycle" is a way to represent the emergence, adoption, maturity and impact on applications of specific technologies.

Cloud computing is definitely at the top of the technology trend, reaching its peak of expectations in just 3-5 years. This trend is enforced by providers such as Amazon[1], Google, SalesForce[2], IBM, Microsoft, and Sun Microsystems who have begun to establish new data centers for hosting Cloud computing applications such as social networking (e.g. Facebook[3] and MySpace[4]), gaming portals (e.g. BigPoint[5]), business applications (e.g., SalesForce.com), media content delivery, and scientific workflows. It is predicted that within the next 2-5 years, Cloud computing will become a part of mainstream computing; that is, it enters into the plateau of productivity phase.

---

[1] http://www.amazon.com/
[2] http://www.salesforce.com/
[3] http://www.facebook.com/
[4] http://www.myspace.com/
[5] http://www.bigpoint.net/

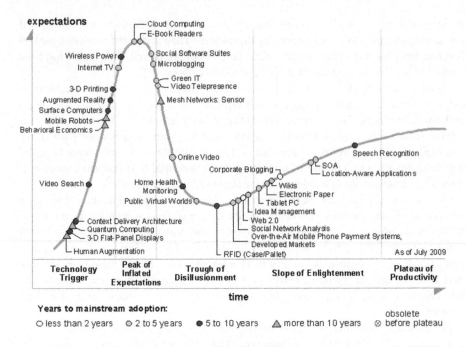

Fig. 1. Hype Cycle of Emerging Technologies, 2009 - Source: Gartner (August 2009)

The rest of the paper is organized as follows: Section 2 presents a high-level definition of Cloud computing followed by open challenges and a reference model; Section 3 presents Cloudbus vision and architecture in conformance with the high-level definition; Section 4 lists specific technologies of the Cloudbus toolkit that have made the vision a reality; Section 5 talks about integration of the Cloudbus toolkit with other Cloud management Technologies; and finally, Section 6 concludes the paper providing insights into future trends in Cloud computing.

2 Cloud Computing

Cloud computing [3] is an emerging paradigm that aims at delivering hardware infrastructure and software applications as services, which users can consume on a pay-per-use-basis. As depicted in Fig. 1, Cloud computing is now at the peak of its hype cycle and there are a lot of expectations from this technology. In order to fully understand its potential, we first provide a more precise definition of the term, then introduce a reference model for Cloud computing, and briefly sketch the challenges that lies ahead.

2.1 Cloud Definition

The cloud symbol traditionally represents the Internet. Hence, Cloud computing refers to the practice of moving computing to the Internet. Armbrust et al. [3] observe that *"Cloud computing refers to both the applications delivered as services over the*

Internet and the hardware and system software in the data centers that provide those services". This definition captures the real essence of this new trend, where both software applications and hardware infrastructures are moved from private environment to third parties data centers and made accessible through the Internet. Buyya et al. [2] define Cloud as *"a type of parallel and distributed system consisting of a collection of interconnected and virtualized computers that are dynamically provisioned and presented as one or more unified computing resources based on service-level agreements"*. This definition puts Cloud computing into a market oriented perspective and stresses the economic nature of this phenomenon.

The key feature, emerging from above two characterizations is the ability to deliver both infrastructure and software as services that are consumed on a pay-per-use-basis. Previous trends were limited to a specific class of users, or specific kinds of IT resources; the approach of Cloud computing is global and encompasses the entire computing stack. It provides services to the mass, ranging from the end-users hosting their personal documents on the Internet to enterprises outsourcing their entire IT infrastructure to external data centers. Service Level Agreements (SLAs), which include QoS requirements, are set up between customers and Cloud providers. An SLA specifies the details of the service to be provided in terms of metrics agreed upon by all parties, and penalties for violating the expectations. SLAs act as a warranty for users, who can more comfortably move their business to the Cloud. As a result, enterprises can cut down maintenance and administrative costs by renting their IT infrastructure from Cloud vendors. Similarly, end-users leverage the Cloud not only for accessing their personal data from everywhere, but also for carrying out activities without buying expensive software and hardware.

Figure 2 shows the high level components of the service-oriented architectural framework consisting of client's brokering and coordinator services that support utility-driven management of Clouds: application scheduling, resource allocation and migration of workloads. The architecture cohesively couples the administratively and topologically distributed storage and compute capabilities of Clouds as parts of a single resource leasing abstraction [4]. The system will ease the cross-domain integration of capabilities for on-demand, flexible, energy-efficient, and reliable access to the infrastructure based on emerging virtualization technologies [6,7].

The Cloud Exchange (CEx) acts as a market maker for bringing together service producers and consumers. It aggregates the infrastructure demands from the application brokers and evaluates them against the available supply currently published by the Cloud Coordinators. It aims to support trading of Cloud services based on competitive economic models such as commodity markets and auctions. CEx allows the participants (Cloud Coordinators and Cloud Brokers) to locate providers and consumers with fitting offers. Such markets enable services to be commoditized and thus, can pave the way for the creation of dynamic market infrastructure for trading based on SLAs. The availability of a banking system within the market ensures that financial transactions pertaining to SLAs between participants are carried out in a secure and dependable environment. Every client in the Cloud platform will need to instantiate a Cloud brokering service that can dynamically establish service contracts with Cloud Coordinators via the trading functions exposed by the Cloud Exchange.

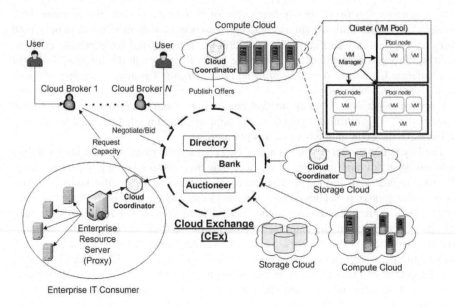

Fig. 2. Utility-oriented Clouds and their federated network mediated by Cloud exchange

2.2 Open Challenges

Cloud computing introduces many challenges for system and application developers, engineers, system administrators, and service providers. Fig. 3 identifies some of them. Virtualization enables consolidation of servers for hosting one or more services on independent virtual machines in a multi-tenancy manner. When a large number of VMs are created they need to be effectively managed to ensure that services are able to deliver quality expectations of users. That means, VMs need to be migrated to suitable servers when QoS demand on services is high and later get consolidated dynamically to a fewer number of physical servers.

One of the major concerns when moving to Clouds is related to security, privacy, and trust. Security in particular, affects the entire cloud computing stack. The Cloud computing model promotes massive use of third party services and infrastructures to host important data or to perform critical operations. In this scenario, the trust towards providers is fundamental to ensure the desired level of privacy for applications hosted in the Cloud. At present, traditional tools and models used to enforce a secure and reliable environment from a security point of view are the only ones available.

Besides security, there are legal and regulatory issues that need to be taken care of. When moving applications and data to the Cloud, the providers may choose to locate them anywhere on the planet. The physical location of data centers and clusters determines the set of laws that can be applied to the management of data. For example, specific cryptography techniques could not be used because they are not allowed in some countries. Simply, specific classes of users, such as banks, would not be comfortable to put their sensitive data into the Cloud, in order to protect their customers

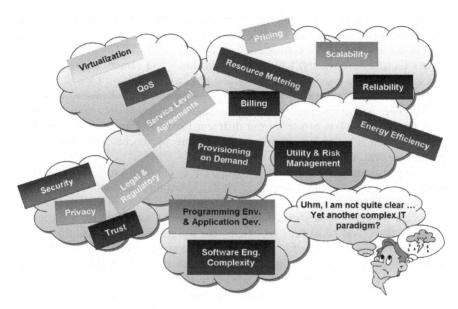

Fig. 3. Cloud computing challenges

and their business. At present, a conservative approach is taken for what concerns hosting sensitive data. An interesting initiative is the concept of availability zones[6] promoted by Amazon EC2. Availability zones identify a set of resources that have a specific geographic location. Currently there are two regions grouping the availability zones: US and Europe. Although this initiative is mostly concerned with providing of better services in terms of isolation from failures, network latency, and service downtime, it could be an interesting example for exploring legal and regulatory issues.

In most cases, the desired level of security is established within a Service Level Agreement (SLA). SLAs also establish the price of services, and specific activities such as resource metering, billing, and pricing have to be implemented in order to charge users. At present, the adopted solutions fall into the "pay-as-you-go" model, where users are charged according to the use they make of the service. More sophisticated and flexible pricing policies have to be developed and put in place in order to devise an efficient pricing model for the Cloud computing scenario.

As services are offered on a subscription basis, they need to be priced based on users' QoS expectations that vary from time to time. It is also important to ensure that whenever service providers are unable to meet all SLAs, their violation needs to be managed to reduce penalties.

Data centers are expensive to operate as they consume huge amount of electricity. For instance, the combined energy consumption of all data centers worldwide is equivalent to the power consumption of Czech Republic. As a result, their carbon footprint on the environment is rapidly increasing. In order to address these issues, energy efficient resource allocation and algorithms need to be developed.

---

[6] http://aws.amazon.com/ec2/

In addition, practical and engineering problems are yet to be solved. Cloud computing infrastructures need to be scalable and reliable. In order to support this, a large number of application service consumers from around the world, Cloud infrastructure providers (i.e., IaaS providers) have been establishing data centers in multiple geographical locations to provide redundancy and ensure reliability in case of site failures. Cloud environments need to provide seamless/automatic mechanisms for scaling their hosted services across multiple, geographically distributed data centers in order to meet QoS expectations of users from different locations. The scaling of applications across multiple-vendor infrastructures requires protocols and mechanisms needed for the creation of InterCloud environments.

From applications' perspective, the development of platform and services that take full advantage of the Cloud Computing model, constitute an interesting software engineering problem.

These are some of the key challenges that need to be addressed for a successful adoption of the Cloud computing paradigm into the mainstream IT industry. R&D initiatives in both academia and industry are playing an important role in addressing these challenges. In particular, the outcome of such research in terms of models, software frameworks, and applications constitute the first tools that can be used to experience Cloud computing. The Cloudbus Toolkit is a step towards this goal.

2.3 Cloud Computing Reference Model

Fig. 4 provides a broad overview of the scenario envisioned by Cloud computing. This scenario identifies a reference model into which all the key components are organized and classified. As previously introduced, the novelty of this approach intercepts the entire computing stack: from the system level, where IT infrastructure is delivered on demand, to the user level, where applications transparently hosted in the Cloud are accessible from anywhere. This is the revolutionary aspect of Cloud computing that makes service providers, enterprises, and users completely rethink their experience with IT.

The lowest level of the stack is characterized by the physical resources, which constitute the foundations of the Cloud. These resources can be of different nature: clusters, data centers, and desktop computers. On top of these, the IT infrastructure is deployed and managed. Commercial Cloud deployments are more likely to be constituted by data centers hosting hundreds or thousands of machines, while private Clouds can provide a more heterogeneous environment, in which even the idle CPU cycles of desktop computers are used to leverage the compute workload. This level provides the "horse power" of the Cloud.

The physical infrastructure is managed by the core middleware whose objectives are to provide an appropriate runtime environment for applications and to utilize the physical resources at best. Virtualization technologies provide features such as application isolation, quality of service, and sandboxing. Among the different solutions for virtualization, hardware level virtualization and programming language level virtualization are the most popular. Hardware level virtualization guarantees complete isolation of applications and a fine partitioning of the physical resources, such as memory and CPU, by means of virtual machines. Programming level virtualization provides sandboxing and managed executions for applications developed with a specific

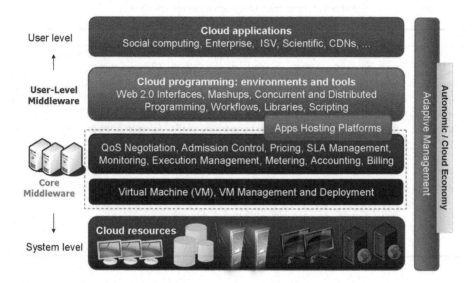

Fig. 4. Cloud computing reference model

technology or programming language (i.e. Java, .NET, and Python). Virtualization technologies help in creating an environment in which professional and commercial services are integrated. These include: negotiation of the quality of service, admission control, execution management and monitoring, accounting, and billing.

Physical infrastructure and core middleware represent the platform where applications are deployed. This platform is made available through a user level middleware, which provides environments and tools simplifying the development and the deployment of applications in the Cloud. They are: web 2.0 interfaces, command line tools, libraries, and programming languages. The user-level middleware constitutes the access point of applications to the Cloud.

At the top level, different types of applications take advantage of the offerings provided by the Cloud computing reference model. Independent software vendors (ISV) can rely on the Cloud to manage new applications and services. Enterprises can leverage the Cloud for providing services to their customers. Other opportunities can be found in the education sector, social computing, scientific computing, and Content Delivery Networks (CDNs).

It is quite uncommon for a single value offering to encompass all the services described in the reference model. More likely, different vendors specialize their business towards providing a specific subclass of services that address the needs of a market sector. It is possible to characterize the different solutions into three main classes: Software as a Service (SaaS), Platform as a Service (PaaS), and Infrastructure / Hardware as a Service (IaaS/HaaS). Table 1 summarizes the nature of these categories and lists some major players in the field.

Table 1. Cloud computing services classification

Category	Characteristics	Product Type	Vendors & Products
SaaS	Customers are provided with applications that are accessible anytime and from anywhere.	Web applications and services (Web 2.0)	SalesForce.com (CRM) Clarizen.com (Project Management) Google Documents, Google Mail (Automation)
PaaS	Customers are provided with a platform for developing applications hosted in the Cloud.	Programming APIs and frameworks; Deployment system.	Google AppEngine Microsoft Azure Manjrasoft Aneka
IaaS/HaaS	Customers are provided with virtualized hardware and storage on top of which they can build their infrastructure.	Virtual machines management infrastructure, Storage management	Amazon EC2 and S3; GoGrid; Nirvanix

Infrastructure as a Service (IaaS) or Hardware as a Service (HaaS) solutions deliver IT infrastructure based on virtual or physical resources as a commodity to customers. These resources meet the end user requirements in terms of memory, CPU type and power, storage, and, in most of the cases, operating system as well. Users are billed on a pay-per-use basis. They have to set up their applications on top of these resources that are hosted and managed in data centers owned by the vendor. Amazon is one of the major players in providing IaaS solutions. Amazon Elastic Compute Cloud (EC2) provides a large computing infrastructure and a service based on hardware virtualization. By using Amazon Web Services, users can create Amazon Machine Images (AMIs) and save them as templates from which multiple instances can be run. It is possible to run either Windows or Linux virtual machines, for which the user is charged per hour for each of the instances running. Amazon also provides storage services with the Amazon Simple Storage Service (S3)[7], users can use Amazon S3 to host large amount of data accessible from anywhere.

Platform as a Service solutions provide an application or development platform in which users can create their own application that will run on the Cloud. More precisely, they provide an application framework and a set of API that can be used by developers to program or compose applications for the Cloud. PaaS solutions often integrate an IT infrastructure on top of which applications will be executed. This is the case of Google AppEngine and Microsoft Azure, while other solutions, such as Manjrasoft Aneka, are purely PaaS implementations.

Google AppEngine[8] is a platform for developing scalable web applications that run on top of data centers maintained by Google. It defines an application model and provides a set of APIs that allow developers to take advantage of additional services such as Mail, Datastore, Memcache, and others. AppEngine manages the execution of applications and automatically scales them up/down as required. Google provides a

---

[7] http://aws.amazon.com/s3/
[8] http://code.google.com/appengine/

free but limited service, while utilizes daily and per minute quotas to meter and price applications requiring a professional service. Azure[9] is a cloud service operating system that serves as the development, run-time, and control environment for the Azure Services Platform. By using the Microsoft Azure SDK, developers can create services that leverage the .NET Framework. These services have to be uploaded through the Microsoft Azure portal in order to be executed on top of Windows Azure. Additional services, such as workflow execution and management, web services orchestration, and access to SQL data stores, are provided to build enterprise applications. Aneka [20], commercialized by Manjrasoft, is a pure PaaS implementation and provides end users and developers with a platform for developing distributed applications for the Cloud by using .NET technology. The core value of Aneka is a service oriented runtime environment that is deployed on both physical and virtual infrastructures and allows the execution of applications developed by means of various programming models. Aneka provides a Software Development Kit (SDK) helping developers to create applications and a set of tools for setting up and deploying clouds on Windows and Linux based systems. Aneka does not provide an IT hardware infrastructure to build computing Clouds, but system administrators can easily set up Aneka Clouds by deploying Aneka containers on clusters, data centers, desktop PCs, or even bundled within Amazon Machine Images.

Software as a Service solutions are at the top end of the Cloud computing stack and they provide end users with an integrated service comprising hardware, development platforms, and applications. Users are not allowed to customize the service but get access to a specific application hosted in the Cloud. Examples of SaaS implementations are the services provided by Google for office automation, such as Google Mail, Google Documents, and Google Calendar, which are delivered for free to the Internet users and charged for professional quality services. Examples of commercial solutions are SalesForce.com and Clarizen.com, which provide online CRM (Customer Relationship Management) and project management services, respectively.

3 Cloudbus Vision and Architecture

Fig.5 provides a glimpse in the future of Cloud computing. A Cloud marketplace, composed of different types of Clouds such as computing, storage, and content delivery Clouds, will be available to end-users and enterprises.

Users can interact with the Cloud market either transparently, by using applications that leverage the Cloud, or explicitly, by making resource requests according to application needs. At present, it is the responsibility of the users to directly interact with the Cloud provider. In the context of a real Cloud marketplace, users will indirectly interact with Cloud providers but they will rely on a *market maker* or *meta-broker* component, which is in charge of providing the best service according to the budget and the constraints of users. A Cloud broker client, directly embedded within applications, or available as a separate tool, will interact with the market maker by specifying the desired Quality of Service parameters through a Service Level Agreement. As a

---

[9] http://www.microsoft.com/azure/

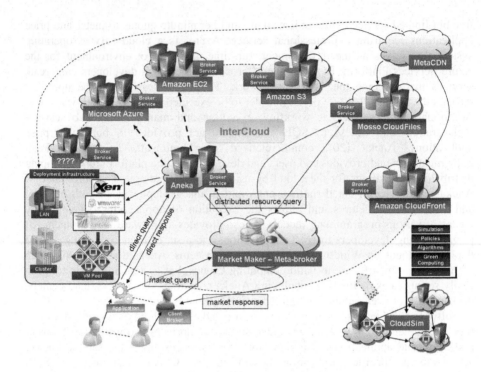

Fig. 5. Cloud computing marketplace

result of the query, the meta-broker will select the best option available among all the Cloud providers belonging to the Cloud marketplace. Such interaction will take place through native interfaces exposed by the provider or via standardized brokering services.

In order to increase their chances of providing a better service to customers, different Cloud providers could establish peering arrangements among themselves in order to offload to (or serve from) other providers' service requests. Such peering arrangements will define a Cloud federation and foster the introduction of standard interface and policies for the interconnection of heterogeneous Clouds. The integration of different technologies and solutions into a single value offering will be the key to the success of the Cloud marketplace. PaaS solutions, such as Aneka [20], could rely on different providers for leveraging the workload and balance the use of private resources by provisioning virtual resources from public Clouds. This approach not only applies for compute intensive services, but also for storage and content delivery. MetaCDN [8], which is a Content Delivery Cloud, aims to provide a unified access to different storage Clouds in order to deliver a better service to end-users and maximize its utility.

The scenario projected by using the Cloud marketplace has its own challenges. Some of them have been already discussed in Section 2.2. In order to make this vision a reality, considerable amount of research has to be carried out through vigorous experiments. Simulation environments will definitely help researcher in conducting

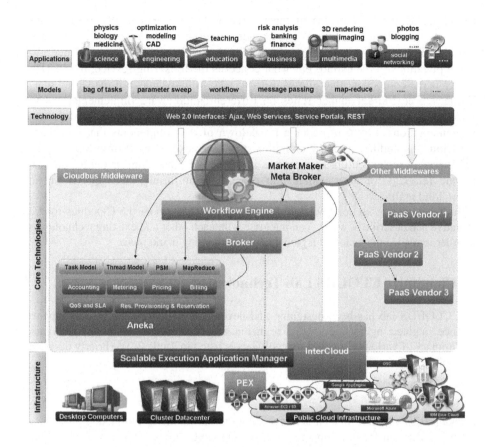

Fig. 6. The Cloudbus Toolkit. The picture represents a layered view of the collection of technologies and components for market oriented Cloud computing available within the Cloudbus Toolkit.

repeatable and controllable experiments, while devising new policies and algorithms for resource provisioning or new strategies for an effective and energy efficient use of physical resources. Simulation toolkits, should be able to model any possible scenario and any layer of the Cloud computing reference model: from the fundamental components of the infrastructure, such as physical nodes, data centers, and virtual machines, to the high level services offered to end users. This will help researchers to finely reproduce their problem frame they want to solve and to obtain reliable results.

The Cloudbus Toolkit is a collection of technologies and components that comprehensively try to address the challenges involved in making this vision a concrete reality. Fig. 6 provides a layered view of the entire toolkit and puts it into the context of a real Cloud marketplace. At the top of the stack, real life applications belonging to different scenarios (finance, science, education, engineering, multimedia, and others) leverage the Cloud horse power. Resources available in the

Cloud are acquired by means of third party brokering services that mediate the access to the real infrastructure. The Cloudbus toolkit mostly operates at this level by providing a service brokering infrastructure and a core middleware for deploying applications in the Cloud. For what concerns the brokering service, the Market maker is the component that allows users to take full advantage of the Cloud marketplace. The Market maker relies on different middleware implementations to fulfill the requests of users: these can be Cloudbus technologies or third parties implementations. Fig. 6 provides a breakdown of the components that constitute the Cloudbus middleware. Technologies such as Aneka or Workflow Engine provide services for executing applications in the Cloud. These can be public Clouds, private intranets, or data centers that can all be uniformly managed within an InterCloud realm.

In the following sections, we will present more details about the Cloudbus toolkit initiative and describe how they can integrate with each other and existing technologies in order to realize the vision of a global Cloud computing marketplace.

4   Cloudbus / CLOUDS Lab Technologies

The CLOUDS lab has been designing and developing Cloud middleware to support science, engineering, business, creative media, and consumer applications on Clouds. A summary of various Cloudbus technologies is listed in Table 2. We briefly describe each of these technologies in the following sub-sections.

4.1   Aneka

Aneka [20] is a "Platform as a Service" solution for Cloud computing and provides a software platform for developing and deploying applications in the Cloud. The core features of Aneka are: a) a configurable software container constituting the building blocks of the Cloud; b) an open ended set of programming models available to developers to express distributed applications; c) a collection of tools for rapidly prototyping and porting applications to the Cloud; d) a set of advanced services that put the horse power of Aneka in a market oriented perspective.

One of the elements that make Aneka unique is its flexible design and high level of customization allowing it to target different application scenarios: education, engineering, scientific computing, and financial applications. The Aneka container, which is the core of the component of any Aneka based Cloud, can be deployed into any computing resource connected to the Internet whether it be physical or virtual. This makes the integration with public and private Clouds transparent; and specific services for dynamic provisioning of resources are built into the framework in order to exploit the horse power of the Cloud.

A collection of standardized interfaces, such as Web Services, make Aneka completely integrate with client applications and third party brokering services that can negotiate the desired Quality of Service and submit applications to Aneka Clouds.

Table 2. Components of Cloudbus Toolkit

Technology	Description
Aneka	A software platform for developing and deploying Cloud computing applications.
Broker	A middleware for scheduling distributed applications across Windows and Unix-variant distributed resources.
Workflow Management System	A middleware that handles dependent tasks, implements scheduling algorithms and manages the execution of applications on distributed resources.
Market Maker/ Meta-Broker	A matchmaker that matches user's requirements with service providers' capabilities at a common marketplace.
InterGrid	A model that links islands of Grids through peering arrangements to enable inter-Grid resource sharing.
MetaCDN	A system that intelligently places users' content onto "Storage Cloud" resources based on their QoS and budget preferences.
Energy Efficient Computing	A research on developing techniques and technologies for addressing scalability and energy efficiency.
CloudSim	A simulation toolkit that helps users model: compute, storage, network and other related components of Cloud data centers.

4.2 Broker

The Grid Service Broker [9] mediates access to distributed physical and virtual resources by (a) discovering suitable data sources for a given analysis scenario, (b) selecting suitable computational resources, (c) optimally mapping analysis jobs to compute resources, (d) deploying and monitoring job execution on selected resources, (e) accessing data from local or remote data source during job execution and (f) collating and presenting results. It provides a platform on which enhanced resource brokering strategies can be developed and deployed.

The broker supports various application models such as parameter sweep, workflow, parallel and bag of tasks. It has plug-in support for integration with other middleware technologies such a Globus [21], Aneka [20], Unicore [22] and ssh plug-in for accessing Condor [23], Unix based platforms via fork, PBS [24] and SGE [25]. The broker can provision compute and storage services in Cloud resources via SSH. It also provides QoS parameters in its service description for applications requiring a mix of public and private Cloud resources. For e.g. part of an application workload can be offloaded to Amazon EC2 and rest to local resources dynamically.

4.3 Workflow Engine

The Workflow Management System (WMS) [10] aids users by enabling their applications to be represented as a workflow and then execute on the Cloud from a higher level of abstraction. The WMS provides an easy-to-use workflow editor for application composition, an XML-based workflow language for structured representation, and a user-friendly portal with discovery, monitoring, and scheduling components. It can be used with either Aneka [20] and/or Broker [9] to manage applications running on distributed resources. These tools put together enables users to select distributed resources on Clouds and/or Grids, upload/download huge amount of data to/from selected resources, execute applications on distributed resources using various scheduling algorithms and monitor applications' progress in real-time.

The WMS has been used for several real-world applications such as: fMRI brain imaging analysis [11,10], evolutionary multi-objective optimizations using distributed resources [11] and intrusion detection systems with various models [12].

4.4 Market Maker/Meta-broker

Market Maker/Meta-broker [13,14] is a part of Cloud infrastructure that works on behalf of both Cloud users and Cloud service providers. It mediates access to distributed resources by discovering suitable Cloud providers for a given user application and attempts to optimally map users' jobs and requirements to published services. It is a part of a global marketplace where service providers and consumers join to find suitable match for each other. It provides various services to its customers such as resource discovery, meta-scheduler, reservation service, queuing service, accounting and pricing services.

4.5 From InterGrid to InterCloud

In the coming years, users will be able to see a plethora of Cloud several providers around the world desperate to provide resources such as computers, data, and instruments to scale science, engineering, and business applications. In the long run, these Clouds may require sharing its load with other Cloud service providers as users may select various Cloud services to work on their applications, collectively. Therefore, dispersed Cloud initiatives may lead to the creation of disparate Clouds with little or no interaction between them. The InterCloud model will: (a) promote interlinking of islands of Clouds through peering arrangements to enable inter-Cloud resource sharing; (b) provide a scalable structure for Clouds that allow them to interconnect with one another and grow in a sustainable way; (c) create a global Cyberinfrastructure to support e-Science and e-Business applications.

At present, the InterGrid project [15] is a first step towards realizing the InterCloud vision. It has been implemented using the existing Grid infrastructure. The system uses virtual machines as building blocks to construct execution environments that span multiple computing sites. The computing sites could be a combination of physical machines hosted on Grid sites or virtual machines running on cloud infrastructures, such as Amazon EC2.

4.6 MetaCDN

MetaCDN [8] is a system that exploits "Storage Cloud" resources offered by multiple IaaS vendors, thus creating an integrated overlay network that provides a low cost, high performance CDN for content creators. It removes the complexity of dealing with multiple storage providers, by intelligently matching and placing users' content onto one or many storage providers based on their quality of service, coverage and budget preferences. By using a single unified namespace, it helps users to harness the performance and coverage of numerous "Storage Clouds".

4.7 Energy Efficient Computing

In order to support elastic applications, Cloud infrastructure providers are establishing Data Centers in multiple geographic locations. These Data Centers are expensive to operate since they consume significant amount of electric power. For instance, the energy consumption of Google Data Center is equivalent to the power consumption of cities such as San Francisco. This is not only increasing the power bills, but also contributing to global warming due to its high carbon footprint. Indeed, the ICT sector is currently responsible for about 2 percent of global greenhouse gas emissions.

In our current research, we are investigating and developing novel techniques and technologies for addressing challenges of: application scalability and energy efficiency with the aim of making a significant impact on industry producing service-oriented Green ICT technologies. As part of this, we explored power-aware scheduling [16], which is one of the ways to reduce energy consumption when using large data-centers. Our scheduling algorithms select appropriate supply voltages of processing elements to minimize energy consumption. As energy consumption is optimized, operational cost decreases and the reliability of the system increases.

4.8 CloudSim

The CloudSim toolkit [17] enables users to model and simulate extensible Clouds as well as execute applications on top of Clouds. As a completely customizable tool, it allows extension and definition of policies in all the components of the software stack. This makes it suitable as a research tool as it can relieve users from handling the complexities arising from provisioning, deploying, configuring real resources in physical environments.

CloudSim offers the following novel features: (i) support for modeling and simulation of large scale Cloud computing infrastructure, including data centers on a single physical computing node; and (ii) a self-contained platform for modeling data centers, service brokers, scheduling, and allocations policies. For enabling the simulation of data centers, CloudSim provides: (i) virtualization engine, which aids in creation and management of multiple, independent, and co-hosted virtualized services on a data center node; and (ii) flexibility to switch between space-shared and time-shared allocation of processing cores to virtualized services. These features of CloudSim would speed up the development of new resource allocation policies and scheduling algorithms for Cloud computing.

CloudSim evolved from GridSim [18], a Grid simulation toolkit for resource modeling and application scheduling for parallel and distributed computing. GridSim provides a comprehensive facility for creating different classes of heterogeneous resources that can be aggregated using resource brokers for solving compute and data intensive applications. It provides a framework for incorporating failures, advance reservations, allocation policies, data models, network model extensions, background traffic and load, and so forth, which are also present in the CloudSim toolkit.

5 Related Technologies, Integration, and Deployment

The Cloudbus toolkit provides a set of technologies completely integrated with each other. More importantly, they also support the integration with third party technologies and solutions. Integration is a fundamental element in the Cloud computing model, where enterprises and end-users offload their computation to third party infrastructures and access their data anytime from anywhere in a ubiquitous manner.

Many vendors provide different solutions for deploying public, private, and hybrid Clouds. At the lowest level of the Cloud computing reference model, virtual server containers provide a management layer for the commodity hardware infrastructure: VMWare[10], Xen [7], and KVM[11] (Kernel-based Virtual Machine) are some of the most popular hypervisors available today. On top of these, "Infrastructure as a Service" solutions such as Amazon EC2, Eucalyptus [28], and OpenNebula [29] provide a high level service to end-users. Advanced resource managers such as OpenPEX [27] complete the picture by providing an advance reservation based approach for provisioning virtual resources on such platforms. Technologies such as Aneka and the Workflow Engine can readily be integrated with these solutions in order to utilize their capabilities and scale on demand. This applies not only for compute type workloads, but also for storage Clouds and CDNs, as demonstrated by the MetaCDN project. At a higher level, the Market maker and the Grid Service Broker are able to provision compute resources with or without a SLA by relying on different middleware implementations and provide the best suitable service to end-users.

The Cloudbus toolkit is a work in progress, but several Cloudbus technologies have been already put into action in real scenarios. A private Aneka Cloud has been deployed at GoFront[12] in order to increase the overall productivity of product design and the return of investment of existing resources. The Workflow Engine has been used to execute complex scientific applications such as functional Magnetic Resonance Imaging (fMRI) workflows on top of hybrid Clouds composed of EC2 virtual resources and several clusters in the world [10, 11]. Various external organizations, such as HP Labs are using CloudSim for industrial Cloud computing research.

Furthermore, Aneka has been extended to support dynamic pooling of resources from public Clouds. This capability of Aneka enables creation of hybrid Clouds by leasing additional resources from external/public Clouds such as Amazon EC2 whenever the demand on private Cloud exceeds its available capacity. In addition, Aneka supports federation of other private Clouds within an enterprise, which are managed through Aneka or other vendor technologies such as XenServer and VMWare.

---

[10] http://www.vmware.com
[11] http://www.linux-kvm.org
[12] http://www.gofront.com

Moreover, some of our Cloudbus technologies have been utilized by commercial enterprises and they are demonstrated at public international events such as the 4th IEEE International Conference on e-Science held in Indianapolis, USA; and the 2nd IEEE International Scalable Computing Challenge hosted at the 9th International Conference on Cluster Computing and Grid (CCGrid 2009) held in Shanghai, China. These demonstrations included fMRI brain imaging application workflows [11, 19], and gene expression data classification [26] on Clouds and distributed resources.

6 Future Trends

In the next two decades, service-oriented distributed computing will emerge as a dominant factor in shaping the industry, changing the way business is conducted and how services are delivered and managed. This paradigm is expected to have a major impact on service economy, which contributes significantly towards GDP of many countries, including Australia. The service sector includes health services (e-health), financial services and government services. With the increased demand for delivering services to a larger number of users, providers are looking for novel ways of hosting their application services in Clouds at lower cost while meeting the users' quality of service expectations. With increased dependencies on ICT technologies in their realization, major advances are required in Cloud Computing to support elastic applications offering services to millions of users, simultaneously.

Software licensing will be a major hurdle for vendors of Cloud services when proprietary software technologies (e.g. Microsoft Windows OS) have to be made available to millions of users via public virtual appliances (e.g. customized images of OS and applications). Overwhelming use of such customized software would lead to seamless integration of enterprise Clouds with public Clouds for service scalability and greater outreach to customers. More and more enterprises would be interested in moving to Clouds for cooperative sharing. In such scenarios, security and privacy of corporate data could be of paramount concern to these huge conglomerates. One of the solutions would be to establish a globally accredited Cloud service regulatory body that would act under a common statute for certifying Cloud service providers, standardizing data formats, enforcing service level agreements, handling trust certificates and so forth.

On one hand, there are technological challenges; on the other, there are issues with balancing usage cost and services delivered. Cloud service providers are already tussling by advertising attractive pricing policies for luring users of all kinds to use their services (e.g. Amazon, SalesForce, Google, etc.). As the market condition is determined through cutthroat competition between many vendors, dynamic negotiations and SLA management will play a major role in determining the amount of revenue to be generated for service providers. Similarly, users will be able to choose better services that fit their requirements and budget. They will be evaluating services based on their level of QoS satisfaction, so that they get the right value for the price paid.

As the price for commodity hardware and network equipments for a data center is already getting cheaper, significant part of the total cost of operating Cloud services in industrial scale is determined by the amount of energy consumed by the data center. To conserve energy and save cooling costs, data centers could adopt energy efficient resource allocation policies. Moreover, they could use renewable sources of energy to power up their centers and leave the least carbon footprint, in the long run.

A daunting task for any vendor is to keep its Cloud services alive and running for as long as it takes. As users gradually become dependent on Cloud services, a sudden disruption of any of the services will send a ripple effect around the world that could: destabilizing markets (e.g. financial institutions such as banks depending on Clouds), paralyzing IT services (e.g. gmail services) and so forth. For preventing these effects arising from vendor "lock-in", interoperability issues between Cloud service providers should be adequately addressed.

Nevertheless, Cloud Computing is the technology for realizing a long awaited dream of using distributed compute, storage resources and application software services as commodities (computing utilities).

As the technology is gradually changing from Cluster and Grid computing to Cloud computing, the Cloudbus toolkit is also evolving towards being more robust and scalable to support the hype. We are continuously consolidating our efforts to enhance the toolkit such that it is able to support more and more users.

Acknowledgments. All members of our CLOUDS Lab have been actively contributing towards various developments reported in this paper. In particular, we would like to thank Srikumar Venugopal, Xingchen Chu, Rajiv Ranjan, Chao Jin, Michael Mattess, William Voorsluys, Dileban Karunamoorthy, Saurabh Garg, Marcos Dias de Assunção, Alexandre di Costanzo, Mohsen Amini, James Broberg, Mukaddim Pathan, Chee Shin Yeo, Anton Beloglazov, Rodrigo Neves Calheiros, and Marco Netto.

References

[1] Kleinrock, L.: A Vision for the Internet. ST Journal of Research 2(1), 4–5 (2005)

[2] Buyya, R., Yeo, C.S., Venugopal, S.: Market-Oriented Cloud Computing: Vision, Hype, and Reality for Delivering IT Services as Computing Utilities, Keynote Paper. In: Proceedings of the 10th IEEE International Conference on High Performance Computing and Communications, Dalian, China, September 25-27 (2008)

[3] Armbrust, M., Fox, A., et al.: Above the Clouds: A Berkeley View of Cloud Computing. Technical Report No. UCB/EECS-2009-28, University of California at Berkley, USA (February 10, 2009)

[4] Buyya, R., Yeo, C.S., Venugopal, S., Broberg, J., Brandic, I.: Cloud Computing and Emerging IT Platforms: Vision, Hype, and Reality for Delivering Computing as the 5th Utility. Future Generation Computer Systems 25(6), 599–616 (2009)

[5] London, S.: Inside Track: The high-tech rebels. Financial Times, September 6 (2002)

[6] VMware: Migrate Virtual Machines with Zero Downtime,
http://www.vmware.com/

[7] Barham, P., Dragovic, B., Fraser, K., Hand, S., Harris, T., Ho, A., Neugebauer, R., Pratt, I., Warfield, A.: Xen and the Art of Virtualization. In: Proceedings of the 19th ACM Symposium on Operating Systems Principles. ACM Press, New York (2003)

[8] Broberg, J., Buyya, R., Tari, Z.: MetaCDN: Harnessing 'Storage Clouds' for High Performance Content Delivery. Journal of Network and Computer Applications 32(5), 1012–1022 (2009)

[9] Venugopal, S., Nadiminti, K., Gibbins, H., Buyya, R.: Designing a Resource Broker for Heterogeneous Grids. Software: Practice and Experience 38(8), 793–825 (2008)

[10] Pandey, S., Voorsluys, W., Rahman, M., Buyya, R., Dobson, J., Chiu, K.: A Grid Workflow Environment for Brain Imaging Analysis on Distributed Systems. In: Concurrency and Computation: Practice and Experience. Wiley Press, New York (2009)

[11] Pandey, S., Dobson, J.E., Voorsluys, W., Vecchiola, C., Karunamoorthy, D., Chu, X., Buyya, R.: Workflow Engine: fMRI Brain Image Analysis on Amazon EC2 and S3 Clouds. In: The Second IEEE International Scalable Computing Challenge (SCALE 2009) in conjunction with CCGrid 2009, Shanghai, China (2009)

[12] Pandey, S., Gupta, K.K., Barker, A., Buyya, R.: Minimizing Cost when Using Globally Distributed Cloud Services: A Case Study in Analysis of Intrusion Detection Workflow Application, Technical Report, CLOUDS-TR-2009-6, Cloud Computing and Distributed Systems Laboratory, The University of Melbourne, Australia, August 7 (2009)

[13] Garg, S.K., Venugopal, S., Buyya, R.: A Meta-scheduler with Auction Based Resource Allocation for Global Grids. In: Proceedings of the 14th IEEE International Conference on Parallel and Distributed Systems. IEEE CS Press, Los Alamitos (2008)

[14] Garg, S.K., Buyya, R., Siegel, H.J.: Time and Cost Trade-off Management for Scheduling Parallel Applications on Utility Grids. Future Generation Computer Systems (July 25, 2009) (in press), doi:10.1016/j.future.2009.07.003

[15] de Assunção, D., Buyya, M., Venugopal, S.: InterGrid: A Case for Internetworking Islands of Grids. Concurrency and Computation: Practice and Experience 20(8), 997–1024 (2008)

[16] Kim, K.H., Buyya, R., Kim, J.: Power Aware Scheduling of Bag-of-Tasks Applications with Deadline Constraints on DVS-enabled Clusters. In: Proceedings of the 7th IEEE International Symposium on Cluster Computing and the Grid (CCGrid). IEEE CS Press, Los Alamitos (2007)

[17] Buyya, R., Ranjan, R., Calheiros, R.N.: Modeling and Simulation of Scalable Cloud Computing Environments and the CloudSim Toolkit: Challenges and Opportunities, Keynote Paper. In: Proceedings of the 7th High Performance Computing and Simulation (HPCS 2009) Conference, Leipzig, Germany (2009)

[18] Buyya, R., Murshed, M.: GridSim: A Toolkit for the Modeling and Simulation of Distributed Resource Management and Scheduling for Grid Computing. Concurrency and Computation: Practice and Experience (CCPE) 14(13-15), 1175–1220 (2002)

[19] Pandey, S., Jin, C., Voorsluys, W., Rahman, M., Buyya, R.: Gridbus Workflow Management System on Clouds and Global Grids. In: Proceedings of the 4th International Conference on eScience, pp. 323–324 (2008)

[20] Vecchiola, C., Chu, X., Buyya, R.: Aneka: A Software Platform for.NET-based Cloud Computing. In: Gentzsch, W., Grandinetti, L., Joubert, G. (eds.) High Performance & Large Scale Computing, Advances in Parallel Computing. IOS Press, Amsterdam (2009)

[21] Foster, I., Kesselman, C.: Globus: A Metacomputing Infrastructure Toolkit. International Journal of Supercomputer Applications 11(2), 115–128 (1997)

[22] Erwin, D.W., Snelling, D.F.: UNICORE: A grid computing environment. In: Sakellariou, R., Keane, J.A., Gurd, J.R., Freeman, L. (eds.) Euro-Par 2001. LNCS, vol. 2150, p. 825. Springer, Heidelberg (2001)

[23] Thain, D., Tannenbaum, T., Livny, M.: Distributed Computing in Practice: The Condor Experience. Concurrency and Computation: Practice and Experience (CCPE) 17, 323–356 (2005)

[24] Bayucan, A., Henderson, R., Lesiak, C., Mann, B., Proett, T., Tweten, T.: Portable Batch System: External Reference Specification, Technical report, MRJ Technology Solutions (1999)

[25] Gentzsch, W.: Sun Grid Engine: Towards Creating a Compute Power Grid. In: Proceedings of the 1st International Symposium on Cluster Computing and the Grid (CCGRID 2001), Brisbane, Australia. IEEE CS Press, Los Alamitos (2001)

[26] Chu, X., Vecchiola, C., Abedini, M., Buyya, R.: Microarray Gene Expression Data Analysis for Cancer Diagnosis on Enterprise Clouds. In: The Second IEEE International Scalable Computing Challenge (SCALE 2009), CCGrid 2009, Shanghai, China (2009)

[27] Venugopal, S., Broberg, J., Buyya, R.: OpenPEX: An Open Provisioning and EXecution System for Virtual Machines, Technical Report, CLOUDS-TR-2009-8, CLOUDS Laboratory, The University of Melbourne, Australia, August 25 (2009)

[28] Nurmi, D., Wolski, R., Grzegorczyk, C., Obertelli, G., Soman, S., Youseff, L., Zagorodnov, D.: The Eucalyptus Open-source Cloud Computing System. In: Proceedings of the 9th IEEE/ACM International Symposium on Cluster Computing and the Grid (CCGrid 2009), Shanghai, China, pp. 124–131 (2009)

[29] Sotomayor, B., Montero, R.S., Llorente, I.M., Foster, I.: Capacity Leasing in Cloud Systems using the OpenNebula Engine. In: Workshop on Cloud Computing and its Applications 2008 (CCA 2008), Chicago, Illinois, USA (October 2008)

Self-healing and Hybrid Diagnosis in Cloud Computing[*]

Yuanshun Dai[1,2], Yanping Xiang[1], and Gewei Zhang[2]

[1] Collaborative Autonomic Computing Laboratory, School of Computer Science,
University of Electronic Science and Technology of China
[2] Department of Electrical Engineering and Computer Science, University of Tennessee, USA
ydai1@ece.utk.edu, yanping_xiang@yahoo.com.cn,
sundaywork@gmail.com

Abstract. Cloud computing requires a robust, scalable, and high-performance infrastructure. To provide a reliable and dependable cloud computing platform, it is necessary to build a self-diagnosis and self-healing system against various failures or downgrades. This paper is the first to study the self-healing function, a challenging topic in today's clouding computing systems, from the consequence-oriented point of view. To fulfill the self-diagnosis and self-healing requirements of efficiency, accuracy, and learning ability, a hybrid tool that takes advantages from Multivariate Decision Diagram and Naïve Bayes Classifier is proposed. An example is used to demonstrate that this proposed approach is effective.

Keywords: Self-healing, Autonomic computing, Multivariate Decision diagram, Naïve Bayes.

1 Introduction

An evolutionary trend in computing has started to take place called cloud computing, which aims to realize Massive-Scale Service Sharing over the Internet. Cloud computing is a general term for anything that involves delivering hosted services over the Internet. These services are broadly divided into four categories: Infrastructure-as-a-Service (IaaS), Platform-as-a-Service (PaaS), Software-as-a-Service (SaaS), and Data-as-a-Service (DaaS). Since cloud computing can offer ready access to entirely new business capabilities, less expensive IT resources, and unrivaled flexibility for businesses of every size, it appears to offer significant economic benefits if the risks can be offset , thus becoming a hot topic for major vendors, including top firms such as Amazon, Google, and Microsoft. Cloud computing service providers will need a robust, scalable, and high-performance infrastructure to compete in this emerging market; therefore, the many challenges involved in adopting cloud computing must be thoroughly investigated.

A cloud can be defined as a pool of computer resources that can host a variety of different workloads, including batch-style back-end jobs and interactive user

---

[*] Partially supported by National Science Foundation, USA (No. 0831609 and 0831634).
Partially supported by National Natural Science Foundation of China (No. 60974089).

M.G. Jaatun, G. Zhao, and C. Rong (Eds.): CloudCom 2009, LNCS 5931, pp. 45–56, 2009.
© Springer-Verlag Berlin Heidelberg 2009

applications [1]. Clouds are used by a huge number of people. The resource sharing at various levels results in various clouds. In sum, they represent a very complex system. As computer systems become increasingly large and complex, their dependability and autonomy play a critical role in supporting next-generation science, engineering, and commercial applications [2-3]. Clouds offer the automatic resizing of virtualized resources. Cloud scalability is mainly enabled by increasing the number of working nodes and requires dynamic self-configuration in accordance with high-level policies (representing business-level objectives). Cloud computing provides computing services to large pools of users and applications, and, thus, Clouds are exposed to a number of dangers such as accidental/deliberate faults, virus infections, system failures etc. [4]. As a result, clouds often fail, become compromised, or perform poorly, therefore becoming unreliable. Consequently, in cloud computing, the challenge to design, analyze, evaluate, and improve dependability remains. Clouds are generally massive and complex. In order to cope with their existing complexity and reduce the continued development of their complexity, the difficult but obviously interesting option of endowing clouds with the abilities of self-diagnosis and self-healing presents itself. A possible solution may reside in autonomic computing that enables systems to manage themselves without direct human intervention.

Autonomic computing is about shifting the burden of managing systems from people to technologies. The aim of autonomic computing is to develop the systems' capabilities of self-managing the distributed computing resources, to adapt to unpredictable changes while hiding the system's intrinsic complexity to users. The idea of Autonomic computing is to mimic the autonomic nervous systems found in biology, as first presented by IBM researchers [5] and extensively studied in follow-up research [6-8]. This autonomic nervous system controls important bodily functions (e.g. respiration, heart rate, and blood pressure) in an unconscious manner. Today's computing systems are like humans that lack autonomic nervous systems, consequently resulting in unreliability and vulnerability. Autonomic computing systems have four fundamental features: be self-configuring, self-healing, self-optimizing, and self-protecting [5]. To provide a reliable and dependable cloud computing platform, it is necessary to build a self-diagnosis and self-healing system against various failures or downgrades.

Self-healing is the capability to discover, diagnose, and react to system disruptions. The main objective of adding self-healing features to any system is to maximize the availability, survivability, maintainability, and reliability of the system [5]. Systems designed to be self-healing are able to heal themselves at runtime in response to changing environmental or operational circumstances. Clouds are a large pool of easily usable, accessible, and volatile virtualized resources. They need to be self-healing because they are so complex, continuously adapting to additions, removals, and failures of nodes/resources. The enormity of how to self-configure according to a dynamically changing environment is out of the scope of this paper. This paper instead proposes a novel solution in self-healing that is based on consequence-oriented diagnosis and healing..

Instead of detecting the causes that lead to the symptoms, consequence-oriented diagnosis offers predictions of the consequences resulting from the symptoms. In the consequence-oriented concept, the efficiency, accuracy, and learning ability of the diagnosis tool are important. Thus, a new hybrid diagnosis tool that combines the

Multivariate Decision Diagram (MDD) and Naïve Bayes Classifier is developed. Whereas the MDD can quickly categorize the degree of the severity of consequences according to the symptoms, the Naïve Bayes classification provides a more precise prediction on different candidate consequences associated with the corresponding probabilities. Naïve Bayes learning is used to integrate the machining learning ability into this system. In addition, these two methodologies operate in a holistic manner.

The rest of the paper is organized as follows: Section 2 presents self-diagnosis and self-healing. Section 3 focuses on the hybrid diagnosis tool, the kernel of the self-healing system. Section 4 gives an example to show the effectiveness of the self-healing function. In Section 5, the conclusion is provided.

2   Self-diagnosis and Self-healing

Self-healing, automatically detecting errors and recovering from failures, is a challenging topic in cloud computing. Current self-healing is far from perfect. Most self-healing systems diagnose and heal the failure after failure occurs rather than anticipating failures. Accurate self-healing instead needs to involve more complicated computation, analysis, and decision processes, analyzing system-level models and making decisions in a holistic manner. Suspect events including abnormal cases that are detected should lead to the analysis to anticipate/forestall failure.

Traditional mechanisms for diagnosis and healing test and locate bugs that should be removed from software codes. However, such procedures have to stop the program and recompile it, which is not suitable for the self-healing function in cloud computing because the hosts in clouds are massive and are not expected to reboot or stop programs for recompilation. Moreover, the bugs and locations of the problems can vary, so it is impractical to ask the host itself to precisely locate errors and to intelligently remove them from the codes as if a professional programmer.

To make self-healing more tractable, we hereby present consequence-oriented diagnosis and recovery. Even though there are numerous and various bugs, the consequence on the host's performance may be similar. For example, a memory leak may be caused by forgetting to release memory occupied by some objects when deleted. As a result, after running a long time, the host fails to properly work due to the exhaustion of its memory. Such a bug may exist at an arbitrary module/class/function/line in different programs. However, wherever the error exists or whatever types of programs they are, the consequence on the host is similar, i.e., memory consumption. Therefore, consequence-oriented healing is designed to help the hosts recover by reclaiming the leaked memory without stopping the current processes or rebooting the computer.

A software system may contain various faults/errors/bugs that reside in different modules, classes, or lines and lead to some symptoms. These symptoms can be monitored in the real-time system, see e.g. [9-10]. The influences of the bugs, the symptoms in the system, are accumulated so as to cause a certain consequence that affects the overall performance and quality of the service or task. Thus, an innovative direction for the ultimate objective of self-healing is presented here. Gleaning the symptoms through monitoring, the host predicts or diagnoses the possible consequences from the symptoms.

The consequence oriented concept is predictive and preventative by diagnosing the symptoms detected in the real-time, before the catastrophic failures really occur. This new concept can prevent serious consequences derived from the monitored symptoms in advance. Based on the concept of consequence-oriented self-healing, the two important functions of self-diagnosis and self-healing will be discussed as follows:

2.1   Consequence-Oriented Self-diagnosis

Unlike traditional fault detection and isolation (FDI) methods, consequence oriented diagnosis diagnoses not only the content of the consequences but also the severity levels, according to the symptoms. Because self-healing is real-time, the timing for diagnosis and healing is important. Some diagnosis and prescriptions are time consuming and can only be applied in situations with minor symptoms that are not very serious; they cannot be applied to serious problems which may quickly bring the system down. At this point, some quick diagnoses and prescriptions (though not so precise) should be applied in order to prevent complete failure as obtaining a precise diagnosis after the system has gone down or the mission has failed is worthless.

Therefore, the severity levels of the consequences should be diagnosed first. There are several requirements for the diagnosis of consequence severity. First, it should be quick and straightforward because the severity level will determine the next step of consequence diagnosis and start the different categories of the healing method. Second, the definition of the severity levels should be related to the degree the system can afford the detected symptoms because the timing for healing is critical. Third, the severity levels should also reflect how far the current state is away from a serious consequence, which tells an approximate duration for the next diagnosis and healing to prevent the occurrence of system failures. Thus, the definitions of the severity levels should be carefully analyzed and preset according to these requirements. The MDD (Multivariate Decision Diagram), introduced later in Section 3.1, is very effective and efficient in satisfying the above requirements for the severity diagnosis.

After determining the severity levels, the consequence diagnosis enters the next phase. This phase first determines the category of consequences corresponding to the severity levels. Then, which diagnosis system to be used is decided based on the category because each category of consequence has its own diagnosis system trained particularly for a set of consequences. Here, we use the Naïve Bayes classifier system, further elaborated in Section 3.2. Following that, the corresponding prescription needs to be opened and executed for healing. Finally, the healing result feeds back to adjust the Naïve Bayes network in the diagnosis system through certain machine learning mechanisms.

In accordance with these requirements, the consequence-oriented diagnosis integrates different tools as needed in a holistic system. We name this approach as the hybrid diagnosis which integrates the Multivariate Decision Diagram and the Naïve Bayes Classifier.

2.2   Consequence Oriented Self Healing

Accompanying the consequence oriented concept, self-healing needs to be implemented via three necessary components: Prescriptions, Healing Categories, and Recursive Healing Method.

As an important component in consequence-oriented healing, we hereby propose the idea of Prescriptions. The prescription ought to recover the patient host and processes from or prevent serious consequences or failures. However, different prescriptions are aimed at fulfilling different requirements, so it is possible for a certain prescription to satisfy some requirements but sacrifice others, especially when some requirements are in conflict or present tradeoffs.

The host will choose corresponding categories of self-healing approaches according to determined severity levels. Four typical healing categories are described here.

Minor severity level: The patient process is allowed to continue running. In the meantime, follow-up diagnosis steps are executed to find the possible consequences and then decide the corresponding prescriptions to heal it.

Major severity level: The patient process is suspended immediately and then the follow-up diagnosis starts to detect the consequences and recover from/prevent the consequence.

Serious level: If the patient process has the potential to cause the destruction of the entire system, then the fastest and simplest way is to kill this dangerous process. However, before the process becomes serious (such as during the earlier minor or major phases), the host should have initiated another backup process to run for the same function, though ineffectively.

Catastrophic level: If the host is detected with catastrophic failure (unable to run), then reboot the system. After rebooting, the previously monitored and stored states of all processes can help restart the system from the latest checkpoint.

Even though we introduced four different categories for healing according to four severity levels, it does not affect the generality of this framework. More categories can be added as needed in reality.

After identifying the possible consequences (named as diseases hereafter), the healing process starts to recover from them. The recursive healing method is presented as follows:

After the diagnosis, the host determines a prescription for healing the identified disease. The host runs the prescription. The results after the healing are fed back. However, if the problem still persists, the second option for prescription output by the hybrid diagnosis can be tried, or further diagnosis is completed and another prescription is tried. This step can be recursively attempted for several rounds until one prescription works to alleviate the consequence. In the case all attempts are useless; the host can restart the corresponding processes or reboot the operation system. Before the restart process, some important variables or states can be recorded in order to allow the system to recover back to the latest healthy check-point. The healing results will also be reported to the diagnosis modules for learning. As it is possible that the patient host lacks sufficient resources to support the healing, in such cases, the system can assign another host to heal the patient host.

The above recursive healing method not only tries multiple prescriptions according to the possibilities assigned by the hybrid diagnosis but also utilizes other hosts to realize peer healing if the current host itself has inadequate resources to execute the prescriptions.

3   Hybrid Diagnosis Approach

The hybrid diagnosis approach is a general concept that represents a combination of the analytical tools cooperating together to realize the diagnosis purpose as shown in Fig. 1.

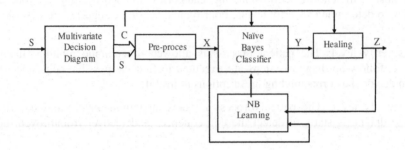

Fig. 1. Hybrid diagnosis integrating the MDD and the Naïve Bayes Classifier

There are several important modules for the hybrid diagnosis. The first module is to quickly get the overall severity levels in order to decide which type of healing method or prescription to apply. Depending on the severity, the corresponding diagnosis and healing category can be selected, e.g. some severe problems need quick solutions whereas some minor problems need intelligent solutions. Determining a wrong category may lead to missing the best recovery time. Thus, we implement the MDD (Multivariate Decision Diagram) [11], to determine severity levels, which is very efficient as the first module in Fig. 1.

Then, the Naïve Bayes Classifier is applied to infer the possible consequences. First, the severity level C output from the MDD module feeds forward to the Healing module for selecting the corresponding healing categories. The severity level C also feeds forward to diagnosis module to determine which model to apply. The symptoms S are pre-processed to X and then feed into the Naïve Bayes Classifier to derive the possibilities associated with corresponding consequences. Finally, the results are the consequences (Y) out of the diagnosis for self-healing. Then, the healing module selects and runs the corresponding prescription with the result Z. After that, the Naïve Bayes learning is applied to train the Naïve Bayes network and then to adjust the parameters.

The MDD and Naïve Bayes network integrate together to realize the hybrid diagnosis function. The following subsections respectively show how to deploy them into this hybrid diagnosis.

3.1   Multiple-valued Decision Diagrams (MDD)

The Multiple-valued decision diagram (MDD) [12] is a natural extension of Binary Decision Diagram (BDD)[13-14] to the multiple-valued case. A MDD is a directed acyclic graph (DAG) with up to n sink nodes, each labeled by a distinct logic value 0, 1, ..., n-1. Each non-sink node is labeled by an n-valued variable and has n outgoing edges, one corresponding to each logic value. MDDs have been used in multiple-valued logic design in the circuit area. They have recently been adapted to the reliability analysis of fault tolerant systems in Xing & Dai [11].

The MDD-based approach is very efficient in determining the severity level of the system, because the MDD is ready and the criteria for severity levels of context indices are also set by models in advance. The resulting almost one-step inference, important in deciding the right healing category, serves as the basis for timely diagnosis and healing.

3.2 The Naïve Bayes Classifier

A Naïve Bayes classifier is a simple probabilistic classifier based on applying Bayes' theorem. The Naïve Bayes model is a specific form of Bayesian network which is widely used for classification. Fig.2 shows graphically the structure of the Naïve Bayes. It contains two kinds of nodes: a class node and attribute nodes. In the Naïve Bayes, though each attribute node has one class node as its parent, there are no direct links among attributes.

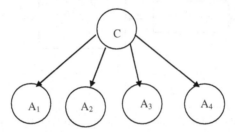

Fig. 2. An example of the Naïve Bayes

Classification is one of the most remarkable problems in machine learning and data mining. Consider the classification problem: Let C be the random variable denoting the class of an instance. Let $(A_1, A_2, A_3,..., A_n)$ represent the observed attributes with discrete values. The goal is to estimate the maximum posterior probability for an instance. The Bayes theorem can be used to calculate the probability of class value c given an instance X with a set of attribute values $\{a_1, a_2, ..., a_n\}$:

$$P(C = c \mid A_1 = a_1,..., A_n = a_n) = \frac{P(C = c)P(A_1 = a_1,..., A_n = a_n \mid C = c)}{P(A_1 = a_1,..., A_n = a_n)} \tag{1}$$

P $(A_1=a_1,...,A_n=a_n)$ is a constant if the values of the attribute variables are known; $P(C=c)$ is the prior probability which can be obtained from statistics. So $P(A_1=a_1,...,A_n=a_n|C=c)$ is the bottleneck for the calculation. Naïve Bayes models assume that all attributes are conditionally independent given the class, called the conditional independent assumption. Then:

$$P(A_1 = a_1,..., A_n = a_n \mid C = c) = \prod_{i=1}^{n} P(A_i = a_i \mid C = c) \tag{2}$$

The Naïve Bayes classifier combines the Naïve Bayes probability model with a decision rule. One common rule is to select the class that is most probable. The Naïve Bayes Classifier assigns the most probable category according to the following formula:

$$C_{nb} = \arg\max_{c \in C} P(C = c) \prod_{i=1}^{n} P(A_i = a_i \mid C = c) \qquad (3)$$

The Naïve Bayes classifier is applied to our consequence oriented diagnosis. In Fig. 3, the input set S is a cluster of symptoms and some other related context measures gleaned by monitoring the patient process. Then, the pre-process converts the symptom set S into a set of qualitative attributes for the Naïve Bayes as a sequence of intervals. It maps every symptom value into a qualitative value according to its corresponding interval. Different measures have their own mapping rules which depend on their characteristics.

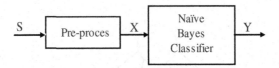

Fig. 3. The Naïve Bayes Classifier in the hybrid diagnosis

Then, the output of pre-process X= {a_1, a_2, ..., a_n} feeds forward into the module Naïve Bayes classifier for classification. The normal output of a Naïve Bayes Classifier is the most probable category. In our system, the output of the module Naïve Bayes Classifier Y = {p_1, p_2, ..., p_n} is a set in which each element is the probability of each category which corresponds to the predicted consequence. Y is the result of the diagnosis according to the input, which feeds into the healing module to find the corresponding prescriptions and recover from/prevent the predicted consequence(s). The predicted consequence with the largest probability is the most possible one. The number of iterations for the recursive healing method depends on the configuration and severity changing. The healing module selects and runs the corresponding prescription with the result Z. Z is a set of results in which each element is the result whether the problem is alleviated or not through the cure, according to the corresponding predicted consequence.

The Naïve Bayes learning is applied to train the Naïve Bayes network and then to adjust the parameters. Z and X become the input of the NB (NB refers to the Naïve Bayes) learning module as shown in Fig. 1. The NB learning module adds sample data to the whole dataset, and then a new learning process is executed which can update the condition probability table (CPT). This is very important in the real-time environment. The newest result can be applied to self-diagnosis immediately. However, the drawback is also obvious, i.e. computing cost using this method is very expensive. Another method is to use a suitable-size subset of data for incremental Naïve Bayes learning, which starts a new learning process when the amounts of sample data reach a threshold. Obviously, in this case, the Naïve Bayes network cannot be updated in time when new sample data come.

The Naïve Bayes is one of the most efficient and effective inductive learning algorithms for machine learning and data mining. The condition independent assumption is clearly violated in real-world problems. However Naïve Bayes classifiers often work better in many complex real-world situations [15]. A lot of research [16] has been done to relax the independence assumption of the Naïve Bayes approach. In this diagnosis system, dependencies among attributes should be taken into account in the future research.

4 Example

An example is used here to illustrate the process of self-diagnosis and self-healing. We applied the above self-diagnosis and self-healing system onto three often occurring malfunctions in computing systems: CPU Overload, Memory Leak, and High Average Disk Queue Length.

As mentioned in Section 2, self-diagnosis is used here to predict the possible consequences from the symptoms. First, the MDD is applied to quickly assess the overall severity levels to determine which category of healing method or prescription to apply. In the first step, the three symptoms are represented by a set with three elements $S = \{s_1, s_2, s_3\}$: where s_1 is the degree of severity of CPU overload, s_2 is the severity of memory leak, and s_3 is the severity of hard-disc I/O. We define three levels of severity according to specific criteria for each element, including Good Status, Minor Problem, and Serious Problem as denoted by 0, 1 and 2, respectively. Given the combination of the symptoms of the three components (CPU, Memory, and Hard-disk), we also define the severity levels of system in three levels as well: Good Status (0), Minor Problem (1), and Serious Problem (2). Then, we built the MDD as depicted in Fig. 4. Input the series of detected symptoms into the MDD to find the path that reaches a certain system severity level (the bottom line in Fig. 4). For example, if all components (CPU, Memory and Hard-disc I/O) are in good status staying at 0, the severity level of the system is good; if any one component stays at status 2 (serious problem), the severity level of the system goes to status 2. Thus, the first module in the hybrid diagnosis approach (Fig. 4.) can be used to quickly determine the severity level of the system given a set of detected symptoms.

If the MDD outputs a good status, then there is no need to go through the following much more complicated diagnosis processes. If the MDD outputs a minor problem, then the following procedures are triggered without stopping any program. Otherwise, if the MDD outputs a serious situation, some suspect programs (those that consume the most resources, such as Memory) are suspended and then the following diagnosis starts. After the problems are solved by our self-healing mechanism, the suspended programs resume and continue running.

After that, as Fig. 3 shows, the Naïve Bayes Classifier module is applied to the diagnosis. The pre-process maps the symptom set S into a set of qualitative attributes for the Naïve Bayes. Then, the output of pre-process X goes through the module Naïve Bayes Classifier. Fig.5 represents our structure of the Naïve Bayes Classifier for classification. Attribute nodes are CPU, Memory and Hard-disc I/O. Each attribute

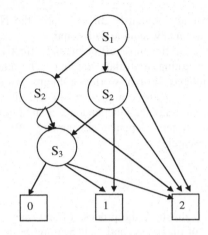

Fig. 4. The MDD for severity analysis

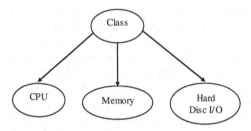

Fig. 5. The Naïve Bayes model for classification

node has the class node as its parent. The class node has three states corresponding to the predicted consequences (i.e. Too much CPU consumption; Not enough memory; Slow Hard-Disk I/O).

In this Hybrid diagnosis, $X = \{a_1, a_2, a_3\}$ is inputted into the Naïve Bayes Classifier module, where each attribute value belongs to a sequence of intervals. For example, the value of the attribute CPU $a_1 \in \{$ 0-20% CT, 20%CT-40%CT, 40%CT-60%CT, 60%CTe-80%CT, 80%CT-100%CT$\}$, where CT denotes CPU Time. After the classification, we obtain the diagnosis result $Y = \{p_1, p_2, p_3\}$ is a set in which p_1 is the probability of "Too much CPU consumption", p_2 is the probability of "Not enough memory", and p_3 is the probability of "Slow Hard-Disk I/O". We need to process the self-healing according to the sequence of the probability corresponding to respective consequences. The most possible consequence is healed by a given prescription first and then by the second until the problems are really solved. The healing module we implemented here is consequence-oriented healing, the same as proposed in the above Section 2. In this case, we studied three consequences and designed three corresponding prescriptions to heal them.

After the healing, we scan to determine actual problems, denoted by Z. In this case $Z = \{z_1, z_2, z_3\}$, where z_i takes binary values $\{0, 1\}$. '1' denotes the corresponding consequence is actually confirmed, and '0' denotes that the corresponding consequence does not exist. For example, $Z = \{1, 0, 0\}$ represents the case that the system records the consequences related to CPU speed.

X and Z act as the input of the NB learning module for training the CPT directly. The updated Naïve Bayes can be applied to the self-diagnosis immediately.

5 Conclusion

To provide a reliable and dependable cloud computing platform, it is difficult but obviously interesting to build a self-diagnosis and self-healing system to prevent/forestall various failures or downgrades. Self-healing is a challenging topic in today's cloud computing systems. This paper proposes a novel solution in self-healing that is based on the consequence-oriented diagnosis and healing. Consequence-oriented diagnosis offers the prediction of the consequence from the symptoms instead of detecting the causes that lead to the symptoms. To fulfill the self-diagnosis and self-healing requirements of efficiency, accuracy, and learning ability, a hybrid tool that combines the MDD and Naïve Bayes Classifier was proposed. An example is employed to show the effectiveness of our approach. However, much more research and experimentation should be conducted to pioneer future work in this area.

References

1. Erdogmus, H.: Cloud Computing. IEEE Software 26(2), 4–6 (2009)
2. Dai, Y.S., Xie, M., Poh, K.L.: Markov Renewal Models for Correlated Software Failures of Multiple Types. IEEE Trans. Relia. 54, 100–106 (2005)
3. Dai, Y.S., Marshall, T., Guan, X.H.: Autonomic and Dependable Computing: Moving Towards a Model-Driven Approach. J. Comput. Sci. 2(6), 496–504 (2006)
4. Xie, M., Dai, Y.S., Poh, K.L.: Computing Systems Reliability: Models and Analysis. Kluwer Academic Publishers, New York (2004)
5. Kephart, J.O., Chess, D.M.: The Vision of Autonomic Computing. IEEE Computer 36(1), 41–50 (2003)
6. Motuzenko, P.: Adaptive Domain Model: Dealing with Multiple Attributes of Self-managing Distributed Object Systems. In: 1st International Symposium on Information and Communication Technologies, pp. 549–554 (2003)
7. Paulson, L.: Computer System, Heal Thyself. Computer 35(8), 20–22 (2002)
8. Patterson, D., Brown, A., Broadwell, P., et al.: Recovery Oriented Computing roc): Motivation, Definition, Techniques, and Case Studies. Technical Report CSD-02-1175, Univ. of California-Berkeley (2002)
9. Hinchey, M., Dai, Y.S., Rash, J.L., Truszkowski, W., Madhusoodan, M.: Bionic Autonomic Nervous System and Self-healing for NASA ANTS Missions. In: 22nd Annual ACM Symposium on Applied Computing, pp. 90–96 (2007)
10. Dai, Y.S., Hinchey, M., Madhusoodan, M., Rash, J.L., Zou, X.: A Prototype Model for Self-Healing and Self-reproduction in Swarm Robotics System. In: 2nd IEEE Symposium on Dependable, Autonomic and Secure Computing, pp. 3–11 (2006)
11. Xing, L., Dai, Y.S.: Reliability Evaluation using Various Decision Diagrams. In: 10th Annual International Conference on Industrial Engineering Theory, Applications and Practice, pp. 448–454 (2005)

12. Miller, D.M., Drechsler, R.: Implementing a Multiple-Valued Decision Diagram Package. In: 28th International Symposium on Multiple-Valued Logic, pp. 27–29 (1998)
13. Lee, C.Y.: Representation of Switching Circuits by Binary-Decision Programs. Bell Systems Technical J. 38, 985–999 (1959)
14. Akers, S.B.: Binary Decision Diagrams. IEEE Trans. Computers 27(6), 509–516 (1978)
15. Domingos, P., Pazzani, M.: On the Optimality of the Simple Bayesian Classifier under Zero-one Loss. Machine Learning 29, 103–137 (1997)
16. Friedman, N., Geiger, D., Goldszmidt, M.: Bayesian Network Classifiers. Machine Learning 29(2-3), 131–163 (1997)

Snow Leopard Cloud: A Multi-national Education Training and Experimentation Cloud and Its Security Challenges

Erdal Cayirci[1], Chunming Rong[1], Wim Huiskamp[2], and Cor Verkoelen[2]

[1] Electrical Engineering & Computer Science Department,
NATO Joint Warfare Center / University of Stavanger,
Stavanger, Norway
{erdal.cayirci,chunming.rong}@uis.no
[2] TNO Defence, Safety and Security,
The Hague, The Netherlands
{wim.huiskamp,cor.verkoelen}@tno.nl

Abstract. Military/civilian education training and experimentation networks (ETEN) are an important application area for the cloud computing concept. However, major security challenges have to be overcome to realize an ETEN. These challenges can be categorized as security challenges typical to any cloud and multi-level security challenges specific to an ETEN environment. The cloud approach for ETEN is introduced and its security challenges are explained in this paper.

Keywords: Snow Leopard, military simulation, training, shared scenarios, LVC, multi-resolution simulation, exercise, experiment.

1 Introduction

In recent years, modern armed forces have been developing their persistent networks for training, education and experimentation. The US Joint National Training Capability (JNTC) [1], which provides a persistent network for joint (i.e., multi-service, army, navy, air force and marines together) training services, is an example. The North Atlantic Treaty Organization (NATO) is also developing a persistent training capability for NATO, its nations and partners. This initiative is lead by NATO ACT (Allied Command Transformation) and is known as Program Snow Leopard. The enabling network for Snow Leopard is called NATO Education and Training Network (NETN) [2, 3]. The NATO Modeling and Simulation Task Group MSG-068 has been tasked to develop NETN standards and recommendations and to demonstrate their practicality.

Snow Leopard will use the MSG-068 NETN recommendations for delivering to the Alliance and its Partners a persistent, distributed education and training capability that supports training spanning from strategic down to tactical level across the full spectrum of operations, leveraging national expertise and capabilities. Snow Leopard has four pillars organized as separate projects: advanced distributed learning (ADL),

M.G. Jaatun, G. Zhao, and C. Rong (Eds.): CloudCom 2009, LNCS 5931, pp. 57–68, 2009.

Fig. 1. The Structure of Snow Leopard

shared scenarios, NATO Training Federation (NTF) and NATO Live, Virtual, Constructive (NLVC) federation. These pillars will be available as services to NATO Headquarters, Nations and Partners over a persistent network.

Snow Leopard connectivity should be flexible in the sense that nations and organizations that have access to the Snow Leopard infrastructure will be able to perform exercises or experiments in different configurations. In some cases all nations may want to join a specific event, in other cases, a (small) number of nations may use Snow Leopard for a particular training exercise or mission preparation event. The preparation time to set up a particular event should be minimized as a result of the permanent character of Snow Leopard.

The following applications are foreseen in Snow Leopard:

- Simulation systems (including simulated radio and data links), possibly with hardware in the loop for training purposes.
- Command and control (C2) systems, mainly identical to the applications that are used operationally.
- Video teleconferencing (VTC) for exercise mission briefings, mission planning and after action review. VTC is also used for technical briefings, technical planning and technical after action review.
- VoIP for technical management and control (before, during and after the exercise).
- Network remote management, control and monitoring.
- Network time synchronization (using Network Time Protocol NTP).

Classified data storage and data exchange for planning, training, results, documentation and shared scenarios should also be accessible from all sites [13]. This includes:

- E-mail
- Webservers and collaborative workspaces
- FTP servers (e.g. to distribute scenario data)

A subset of these services and data can be classified as NATO Secret, and may be accessible only for a subset of users. Nations or organizations that are not involved in a particular event taking place on the Snow Leopard infrastructure should not have access to the data related to that event. Therefore, security services are also required for the realization of the concept.

Two NATO training centers have an important role in the implementation of Snow Leopard: Joint Forces Training Center (JFTC) in Bydgoszcz, Poland and Joint Warfare Center (JWC) in Stavanger, Norway, which are responsible for tactical and operational/higher level training respectively. JFTC will be the hub for tactical level live, virtual and constructive simulations called NATO Live Virtual Constructive (NLVC) federation. On the other hand JWC is the hub for another simulation federation called NATO Training Federation (NTF). JFTC and JWC will start providing services from new facilities in 2010 and 2011 respectively. In new facilities both para-virtualization and clustering techniques will be used extensively for operating system, platform, network and application virtualizations.

The MSG-068 TG has already made some key decisions for the simulation infrastructure to fulfill the Snow Leopard requirements: Interoperability between live, virtual and constructive simulations will be based on the High Level Architecture (HLA, IEEE 1516 [7-11]), as agreed by NATO STANAG 4603 [14] and NATO M&S Master Plan [13]. A modular federation object model (FOM) [1, 10] approach will be applied to extend the well-known HLA real-time platform reference FOM (RPR FOM V2). The Combined Federated Battle Laboratories Network (CFBLNet) will provide the secure network link among JWC, JFTC, NATO, Partner and Contact Nations. NETN will allow the centers, headquarters and units in these nations to dynamically access the training, education and experimentation resources, i.e., software, platforms, architectures and data available in JWC and JFTC, as well as in the nations.

Snow Leopard can be a good candidate to create a multi-national joint education, training and experimentation cloud (ETEC). NETN can be perceived as a very large cloud public to accredited sites in nations, and also connects other national private clouds like JNTC. It can provide:

- Shared resources applications like joint exercise management module (JEMM) and joint exercise scenario tool (JEST), simulation systems like joint theater level simulation (JTLS), joint conflict and tactical simulation (JCATS) and virtual battlespace simulation (VBS2)[4] in the form of software as a service (SaaS)
- Central Runtime Infrastructure (RTI) component of HLA, HLA federation execution control tools, exercise logging services, database management systems, Wiki and other web services in the form of platform as a service (PaaS)
- CFBLNet, video teleconference (VTC), voice over IP (VoIP), network control and monitoring, network time protocol servers and other infrastructure elements in the form of infrastructure as a service (IaaS).

An ETEC can also be very useful for civilian purposes like training and education for large scale complex crises response operations because:

- A common architecture and collaboration environment is needed also for civilian purposes, such as, complex national or multinational crises management.
- For local crises management training, small organizations often cannot afford maintaining an organization and architecture for exercising and training.

60   E. Cayirci et al.

ETEC can provide not only IaaS, PaaS and SaaS but also other services like exercise/training planning and management. Therefore, ETEC is a very attractive concept for Snow Leopard. However security is a major challenge for the realization of ETEC concept. In this paper we introduce ETEC for Snow Leopard and its security challenges. In Section 2 the conventional approach proposed by MSG-068 and our ETEC approach are introduced and compared. Then we examine the security challenges typical for any cloud in Section 3. Multi level security (MLS) is not a necessity but may increase ETEC capabilities and efficiency considerably. In Section 4 various forms and challenges of MLS are introduced. We conclude our paper in Section 5.

2 ETEC Architecture for Snow Leopard and Its Advantages

In the first quarter of 2009, MSG-068 completed the technical recommendations for Snow Leopard, and the Taskgroup tested the practicality of the recommendations in experiments throughout 2009. The current design of Snow Leopard, i.e., new facilities and MSG-068 recommendations, is depicted in Figure 2.

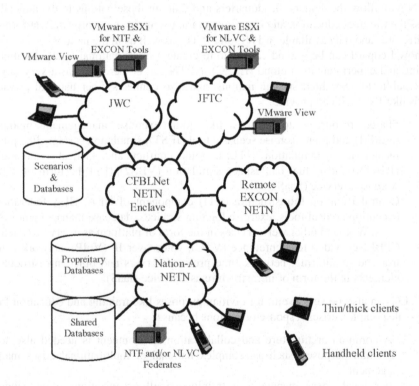

Fig. 2. NETN as it is designed

MSG-068 recommends CFBLNet as the networking infrastructure for Snow Leopard. CFBLNet is a network built and maintained by its members. The network consists of sites, national *Point of Presence* (PoPs), infrastructure, services and knowledge management. The national/organizational PoP is the connection from the national/organizational *Wide Area network* (WAN) to the international part of the CFBLNet WAN. The CFBLNet *BlackBone* (i.e., Black backbone) provides a common, closed, unclassified IP routed network layer implementation using a mixture of both ATM and IP bearer networks. Its primary purpose is to transport encrypted traffic throughout the network. *Enclaves* are the cryptographic protected networks on top of the CFBLNet BlackBone. Each enclave has a *classification* and a *marking* indicating security level and the countries allowed connecting. CFBLNet enclaves can be accredited upto NATO Secret level events. The classification, i.e., NATO Secret, NATO Restricted, NATO Unclassified and Unlimited, of an enclave can change from one event to another. However, an enclave can only have a single classification level at a time. It is possible to connect an enclave to other NATO networks. In this case guards (data-diodes) and firewalls are used to apply strict flow control mechanisms.

MSG-068 also recommends an RPR2 based FOM and HLA 1516-2009 for federating live virtual constructive simulations. The reference Federation Agreement and FOM Document (FAFD) for NETN was completed in May 2009. Since this topic is outside the scope of this paper, we do not give the details about FAFD. Interested reader can find more detailed information about FAFD in [1, 11, 12].

Two important parts of NETN will be JFTC and JWC local area networks (LAN) which consist of completely virtualized services. These networks and all the virtualized functional area services (FAS) running on them will be carefully designed and accredited for each event, i.e., an exercise or experimentation, through a process, which typically lasts 12 months.

Most challenging FAS in this environment are related to computer assisted exercise (CAX) support. There are four classes of CAX services: CAX planning and management, complex military simulation systems, interfaces between simulation and C2 systems and experimentation services. Especially the simulation tools are different from typical services. They are a very complex set of processes that work together and interact with each other. Therefore, JWC is rigorously testing virtualization environments (VMware ESXi and VMware View) for the simulation tools. Most of the results from the preliminary tests run in a small testbed in Stavanger, Norway were positive. Some minor problems were corrected by configuration changes, i.e., higher RAM available, etc. In October 2009, the fully virtualized architecture for computer assisted exercises will be tested for the first time during a major exercise.

In the following years, a new set of services will be introduced with Snow Leopard. The services that include also the new tools can be categorized as follows:

- Advanced distributed learning tools and databases
- Shared scenario and database resources
- NATO training federation (NTF), i.e., an HLA federation made up of constructive, virtual and live simulation systems (Note that NTF was already successfully used in a major exercise).

-   NATO live virtual constructive (NLVC) federation for low level tactical training
-   Exercise/experiment planning and management tools, such as joint exercise management module (JEMM) and joint exercise scenario tool (JEST)
-   All kinds of functional area services (FAS), such as command and control (C2) systems, logistics systems and operational planning tools.

The infrastructure for Snow Leopard, i.e., NETN, is already partly available in JWC and JFTC. NETN will extend it mainly with distributed exercise control (EXCON) capabilities and an architecture that allows national simulation and C2 systems to join NTF or NLVC.

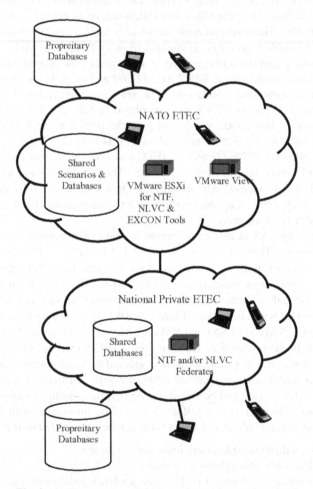

Fig. 3. NATO education training and experimentation cloud

Figure 3 shows the proposed ETEC approach for NETN, which can further increase the efficiency and flexibility of NETN. JWC and JFTC facilities and infrastructure allow quick adaptation of the ETEC approach. National private ETECs can also join the NATO ETEC to create more flexibility and extensive usage. Therefore, we can perceive the overall architecture as a hybrid cloud that has both public and private components. Propriety databases can also be used with this cloud. They may remain outside of the ETEC, but can become available through a controlled access from inside the ETEC. A NATO ETEC can reduce the cost of NATO exercises and experiments considerably because:

- Handheld devices and terminals cheaper than typical client workstations, can use all the services in ETEC without any configuration requirement as long as they can gain access to the ETEC.
- Hardware for servers are procured for only one site.
- Software licenses are obtained for only one site. Licenses may be shared between users that don't require permanent use. For example, VBS2.
- Software and hardware configurations and upgrades are carried out at only one site. Therefore operations and maintenance costs are reduced.

Nations and Partners can use this architecture not only for NATO exercises but also to train their tactical forces for coalition operations more efficiently and less costly. For example several nations can train their tactical forces for a coalition operation without involving any NATO Headquarters by using NATO ETEC. Moreover, such an ETEC can be opened for UN and other international governmental and non-governmental organizations, which cannot afford to procure and maintain such a complex training and experimentation cloud.

However the ETEC approach for NETN also has many challenges and most of these challenges are related to security, especially to multi-level security. In the following sections we explain the security challenges of ETEC.

3 Security Challenges for Cloud Computing

Major security challenges for ETEC, which are also typical for any cloud, can be listed as follows:

Privacy: Users must rely on the ETEC administration for the protection of their privacy and security of their proprietary data because the first and most important difference of ETEC from the conventional approach is that the users do not own the hardware and software. Instead they receive the services available in ETEC based on a per use service model. For a NATO ETEC, there are two sides of this issue: nations and national data, NATO and NATO data. This issue can be even more challenging if Partner and Contact nations are allowed to use NATO ETEC resources. It may be needed to keep some data always invisible to some ETEC users. Alternatively, some data provided by a NATO organization or a nation for use during an event may not be releasable to the participants although they are using it during the event. For example, the JWC exercise flow (JEMM) database for an exercise is not releasable to any nation or NATO organization after that exercise ends. This policy is implemented because some parts of the exercise data can be used in the next exercise. When these data are prematurely available to the training audience of the next exercise it may hinder achieving the exercise objectives. It may be desirable to use own data that is secured locally while receiving IaaS, PaaS and SaaS from ETEC, and sharing these data only with the users approved by the owner of the data. Data segregation, which ensures that reliable encryption is always available, is also an issue related to privacy. Of course encryption brings up the requirement for a secure, efficient and practical key distribution scheme. It is not easy to design a secure key distribution scheme for such a dynamic and flexible environment.

Anonymity and Traffic Analysis: Not only the private data owned by a particular user, but also the anonymity of the users may need to be protected. In addition, ETEC should prevent users from unauthorized analysis of the network traffic to derive some information about the operational postures of the units. For example certain patterns of network traffic among certain headquarters before an air-to-ground attack package starts flying in a simulation during an exercise may be very important intelligence for a user that represents the opposing forces. Therefore, ETEC should protect anonymity and prevent (undesired) traffic analysis. Keeping the data and service locations anonymous and using techniques like load balancing both for servers and networking resources can help dealing with this issue.

Single Point to Attack and Single Point of Failure: Although centralization of services increases the security of a system by reducing the size of infrastructure to protect, that also creates points of gravitation for attacks. Services in a cloud can be a very attractive target for hackers. Moreover, when a system is hacked and/or fails, the impact is much bigger comparing to distributed computation approaches. Therefore, ETEC requires comprehensive intrusion prevention, detection and response techniques and fault tolerance measures. Actually we can state that both clustering and para-virtualization techniques that will be used in JWC and JFTC are naturally fault tolerant. Still there are key services, and when one of them are compromised, all elements in the cloud can be affected.

Large Databases and High Number of Clients: The centralization of services also reduces the probability of configuration errors since there is no need for local system administrators. Therefore, at the first glance it looks like the points that can be exploited by the hackers are less comparing to the conventional approach. However, a cloud typically has huge number of users, much bigger databases and a much higher number of processes. This creates new opportunities for denial of service attacks. For example a single malicious user that uses multiple identities, i.e., sybil attack, can attempt to consume as much system resources as possible. The cloud can be accessible from many different points by many users using generic and simple client devices, it is therefore not an easy task to detect an intruder. Huge databases, high number of users and services also make the detection of bugs, covert channels and bypasses a very difficult task. Therefore each module, component and their contents should be carefully verified and accredited before putting into service. This may increase the time required to modify a cloud or adding a new piece of data or software into it.

Denial of Service (DoS) Attacks in Medium Access Control (MAC) and Higher Layers of Networking Protocols: Malicious intermediate nodes in the routes between the users/clients and centralized services can degrade the service quality. Although this kind of attacks is not specific to cloud computing, users of clouds are more sensitive to it because they are highly dependent on the centralized resources. Resource centralization also makes the organization of such attacks easier. Some examples for this kind of attacks are as follows:

- A malicious node may **selectively forward** the packets coming from the cloud or the users. Although the attack is organized in network layer, it has also effects in transport layer. In transport layer protocols like TCP, a missing packet indicates congestion, which means reducing the transmission speed by starting slow start process from the beginning. Since the malicious node drops only some random packets, it is not easy to discover it.
- A malicious node may not forward any packet to or from a cloud. This attack has a bigger impact comparing to selective forwarding. However, it is also easier to detect and recover from.
- A malicious node can do **acknowledgement spoofing**. There are various impacts of this. By acknowledgement spoofing congestion can be created. Alternatively, acknowledgements can be replayed, which indicates negative acknowledgement in various TCP derivatives like TCP-Reno.
- If wireless links are involved in any part of the communications, the security risks are even higher. For example, clear to send (CTS) signals can be jammed to organize very cost effective and practical jamming attacks in MAC layer for IEEE 802.11. Similarly, request to send signals broadcasted periodically can jam a wireless IEEE 802.11 channel very effectively.

Self-configuring, Self-optimizing, Self-monitoring and Self-healing Procedures: Cloud computing requires algorithms for self configuration, self optimization, self monitoring and self healing. These processes may create opportunities to exploit for security attacks because of two reasons: First their implementation may have some bugs, and a hacker can use those bugs to gain access to a service. Second, a hacker may make these processes misbehave to degrade the services or to gain access to a service. For example a malicious user may change some system variables to show a system resource busy, and make a load balancing algorithm assign no task to the system resource, which is available in reality.

4 Multi-Level Security for ETEC

All the security challenges explained in Section 3 are also valid for an ETEC. In addition to those, an ETEC, especially a NATO ETEC, has another major challenge, which is multi-level security (MLS). Within current collective mission simulation environments all security domains are required to agree on a common security classification. Information kept within each security domain must then be altered to comply with the agreed common security classification. This requires a costly and time consuming effort per collective mission simulation (re)configuration. There is an increasing need for a security solution that enables the sharing of simulation information across these security domains to establish collective simulations without a potential information leakage and confidentiality breach. This problem of information flow has been identified in the NATO M&S Master Plan [13] (Section 3.9).

In the current NETN design, an enclave in CFBLNet can have a single security classification. This means that only users that have a security clearance equal to or higher than the security classification of the enclave can access the enclave, and data that has higher classification level cannot be processed in the enclave. CFBLNet procedures allow changing the security level of an enclave from time to time. However, an enclave can have only a single security classification level at a time. There can be multiple enclaves for NETN with different security classification. Each of these enclaves means separate clouds that require separate servers, i.e., both hardware and software. This can be called multiple single level security (MSL), and seems the only practical option in the beginning. It is also possible to connect enclaves with different security classification through mail guards and firewalls that apply strict flow control mechanisms (e.g. data diodes).

Benefits of a NATO ETEC can be fully achieved when true multi level security (MLS) is realized. That means all users with different clearances can access a cloud, and an automated security mechanism can guarantee the following:

- A user cannot access a service that has higher security classification than his/her clearance. Please note that a service can be software, platform, infrastructure or data in ETEC.
- A process can read and write an object if it has a classification level equal to the classification of the object.
- A process can read an object with a classification label of a lower level than its own clearance.
- A process cannot write to an object with a lower classification level to prevent leakage.
- A process cannot read or write to an object that has higher classification level, which is also related to the first item in this list.

A reliable *flow control* mechanism is required in order to meet these requirements. That can be achieved by labeling each data item, service and user with its security classification and clearance, and by implementing procedures for the automated security mechanism based on these labels. Of course, *service labeling* is a major challenge when it is an ETEC because an ETEC is characterized by huge number of users and very large databases. Moreover, *clearance management* for the users in such a dynamic environment with so many users is not an easy task. We expect that service labeling and clearance management for an ETEC will be much more complex than key management in mobile ad hoc networks.

Efficient *sanitization* techniques allow a reader to see parts of a document, which has security classification lower or equal to his/her clearance, although the classification of the overall document is higher. Sanitization is almost a "mission impossible". First, sanitization requires an intelligence to decide which parts of a service cannot be seen by a particular user and should be removed before serving the user. Second, it also requires an effective and scalable implementation for high number of users and large databases. Please note that some of the services in ETEC, such as live and virtual simulations are real time services and have very stringent latency constraints. Moreover, utilities in some applications make this task harder. For example, some documents may keep editing information to be capable for undoing changes later. Therefore, the parts deleted during sanitization can be undone if the mechanism misses those utilities.

Information kept within a simulator includes for instance models, attributes and values. In relation to simulation new factors complicate the problem of sanitization:

- The value as such of a particular object may be unclassified (e.g. a geographical position as shown on a C2 system), but derived values may be classified under certain conditions. For example, velocity of the object can be derived from its position updates. The average velocity may be unclassified, however, the breaking capabilities or turn rates (when avoiding threats) may be classified.
- Combinations of unclassified values may disclose classified data. For example, position information of a strike package provides details about the doctrines that are used for specific operations.
- Data rates as such may provide classified information.

The ongoing MLS research activity investigates, through use-cases, how information classification and release within the simulation context should be handled. The techniques developed for flow control and sanitization of simulation data should be carefully designed such that adversaries cannot find and exploit covert channels or bypass the security mechanisms.

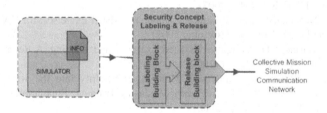

Fig. 4. Labeling and release mechanism for simulations

Finaly HLA components and procedures like object models, RTI and FEDEP may have a role in enhancing security in an ETEC. The information elements of the simulation are described within the Federation Object Model. The FOM is used to determine and define classified information elements. The actual prevention of releasing classified information is initially based on the individual classified information elements using some kind of release mechanism that is integrated into the HLA middleware (RTI).

The proposed security mechanisms/processes to prevent information leakage should become an integral part of the simulator development process, such as the HLA FEDEP (or its successor DSEEP) process.

5 Conclusion

The ACT Program Snow Leopard is aiming to deliver a persistent network that consists of ADL, shared scenarios and live, virtual, constructive simulation capabilities. MSG-068 NETN TG is developing standards and recommendations to be used by Snow Leopard. Technical recommendations are almost completed and testing of these recommendations has started. Virtualization related testing were conducted during a large military exercise in late October 2009. The experimentation and demonstration for overall NETN recommendations will be conducted during a large standalone experiment event in the second half of 2010. These efforts can lead to a multi national education training and experimentation cloud. However, the cloud approach has some major security challenges to tackle with first. Some of these challenges are typical to any cloud. There are also multi level security requirements for fully utilizing ETEC concept. Concepts for addressing MLS in distributed simulation environments have been identified and will be developed and tested in the following years. Once developed and validated, these measures will greatly enhance the advantages and flexibility of ETEC for distributed training in a multi-national context.

References

1. Lofstrand, B., Khayari, R., Keller, K., Greiwe, K., Hulten, T., Bowers, A., Faye, J.-P.: Logistic FOM Module in Snow Leopard: Recommendations by MSG-068 NATO Education and Training Network Task Group. In: Fall Simulation Interoperability Workshop (SIW) (September 2009)
2. Cayirci, E.: Exercise Structure for Distributed Multi-resolution NATO Computer Assisted Exercises. In: ITEC 2007 (May 2007)
3. Cayirci, E.: Distributed Multi-resolution Computer Assisted Exercises. In: NATO Modelling and Simulation Conference (October 2007)
4. Cayirci, E., Marincic, D.: Computer Assisted Exercises and Training: A Reference Guide. John Wiley and Sons, Chichester (2009)
5. McGowan, G., Raney, C.: Integrating Multi-Level Security into the Joint Warfighter Training Environment. In: The Interservice/Industry Training, Simulation & Education Conference (I/ITSEC), Orlando (2008)
6. Knapp, G.F.: The Joint National Training Capability, The cornerstone of Training Transformation. In: NATO Modelling and Simulation Conference, Koblenz (2004)
7. IEEE Std 1516 ™ -2000: IEEE Standard for Modeling and Simulation (M&S) High Level Architecture (HLA) - Framework and Rules
8. IEEE 1516.1™ -2000: IEEE Standard for Modeling and Simulation (M&S)
9. High Level Architecture (HLA) - Federate Interface Specification
10. IEEE 1516.2™ -2000: IEEE Standard for Modeling and Simulation (M&S) High Level Architecture (HLA) - Object Model Template (OMT) Specification
11. IEEE Standard1516.3-2000, IEEE Recommended Practice for High Level Architecture (HLA) Federation and Development and Execution Process FEDEP
12. MSG-068 NETN TG Technical Report Draft 1.3, NATO Modeling and Simulation Group, NATO Research and Technology Organization, Paris (2009)
13. NATO M&S Masterplan (AC/323 (SGMS) D/2 Version 1.0 (1998)
14. NATO STANAG 4603 Modelling and Simulation Architecture Standards for technical interoperability: High Level Architecture (HLA)

Trust Model to Enhance Security and Interoperability of Cloud Environment[*]

Wenjuan Li[1,2] and Lingdi Ping[1]

[1] College of Computer Science and Technology, Zhejiang University,
Hangzhou, Zhejiang 310058, China
[2] Hangzhou Normal University, Hangzhou, Zhejiang 310012, China
liellie@163.com, Ldping@cs.zju.edu.cn

Abstract. Trust is one of the most important means to improve security and enable interoperability of current heterogeneous independent cloud platforms. This paper first analyzed several trust models used in large and distributed environment and then introduced a novel cloud trust model to solve security issues in cross-clouds environment in which cloud customer can choose different providers' services and resources in heterogeneous domains can cooperate. The model is domain-based. It divides one cloud provider's resource nodes into the same domain and sets trust agent. It distinguishes two different roles cloud customer and cloud server and designs different strategies for them. In our model, trust recommendation is treated as one type of cloud services just like computation or storage. The model achieves both identity authentication and behavior authentication. The results of emulation experiments show that the proposed model can efficiently and safely construct trust relationship in cross-clouds environment.

Keywords: cloud computing, trust model, heterogeneous domain, role, trust recommendation.

1 Introduction

Cloud computing based on many other existing technologies is a new method for sharing infrastructure which provides customers with extremely strong computation capability and huge memory space while with low cost. But now cloud computing is faced with many problems to be resolved especially security. Till now most IT enterprises' cloud platforms are heterogeneous, independent and not interoperable. For the benefit of human society and the development of cloud computing, one uniform and interoperable cross-clouds platform will surely be born in the near future. And in cross-clouds environment, security is the most important issue. Compared to traditional technologies, cloud has many specific features, such as it is ultra-large-scale and resources belong to each cloud providers are completely distributed, heterogeneous and totally virtualized. Traditional security mechanisms such as identity validation,

---

[*] This project is supported by Chinese National Advanced Science and Technology 863(2008BA21B03 and 2008AA01A323).

M.G. Jaatun, G. Zhao, and C. Rong (Eds.): CloudCom 2009, LNCS 5931, pp. 69–79, 2009.

authentication and authorization were no longer suitable for cloud. Trust which is originally society notion in constructing human beings' relationship is now an essential substitute for former security mechanism in distributed environments. Some experts said the biggest issue of cloud computing 2009 is trust [6].

While in fact trust is the most complex relationship between entities because it is extremely abstract, unstable and difficult to be measured and managed. Today there is no special trust model for cloud computing environment. But as we know cloud has inextricably linked to distributed systems, so we try to establish our cloud trust model on the basis of in-deep research of previous studies.

This paper proposed a novel trust model which ensured the security of cloud entities both customers and providers in cross-clouds applications. It divided cloud nodes into two categories: customers and servers and designed different trust strategies for them. Trust domains were established based on independent single-cloud platform. Trust choice and update strategies took into account both the independence of nodes and manageable of domains. What's more, trust recommendation in this model was treated and managed as one type of cloud services.

This paper was constructed as follows: part 2 describes the main concept of trust and part 3 analyzes and compares several existing trust models. Part 4 introduces the new cross-clouds trust model. Part 5 shows results of our emulation experiments and the last part is conclusion and future work.

2 Definitions

2.1 Trust Relationship

The following are some correlative definitions:

* Definition1: *Trust* is referred to the recognition of entity's identity and the confidence on its behaviors. Trust is subjective behavior since entity's judgement is usually based on its own experiences. Trust is described by trust value.
* Definition2: *Trust value* or *trust degree* is used to measure the degree of trust. Trust value often depends on special time and special context.
* Definition3: *Direct trust* means trust that is obtained by entities' direct interaction.
* Definition4: *Indirect trust* or *recommended trust* means trust that is obtained from credible third party who has direct contact with the designated one. Recommended trust is one important way to obtain trust degree of unknown entities.

2.2 Classification of Trust

Trust can be classified into different categories according to different standards.

* According to attributes: identity trust and behavior trust
* According to obtaining way: direct trust and recommended trust
* According to role: code trust, third party trust and execution trust, etc.
* According to based theory: subjective trust and objective trust.

2.3 Features of Trust

In our opinion trust has the following main features:

* *Subjective, uncertainty and fuzzy.*
* *Asymmetry.* If A and B have to set up trust relationship, A's evaluated trust for B can be different from B for A
* *Inconstancy and context-sensitive.* Trust is changing along with special time and special context..
* *Condition based transitivity.* A's trust value for B is always unequal to the recommended trust that is received from C. There always exists a recommendation factor.

3 Trust Models in Distributed Environment [7-11]

With the widespread application of large scale and distributed systems such as Grid computing, Ubiquitous computing, P2P computing and Ad hoc networks, trust models fit for them have been in-depth researches. In this part we discuss the previous trust models designed for distributed systems.

3.1 PKI Based Trust Model

This trust model depends on a few leader nodes to secure the whole system. The leaders' validity certifications are signed by CA. GSI Security Infrastructure of Globus the most famous Grid toolkit is also based on PKI technology. GSI introduces the concept of user agent. PKI model may cause uneven load or a single point of failure since it rely on leader nodes too much.

3.2 Network Topology Based Trust Model

This trust model is constructed on the basis of network topology. Each entity's trust is evaluated according to its location in system topology and it usually uses tree or graph traversal algorithm. Trust management mechanism in this model is relatively simple. But due to the extremely complexity of network environment, trust values are often inaccurate which may cause system security risks.

3.3 Basic Behavior Based Trust Model

This model uses history trade records to compute trust. One entity's trust is gained by considering both former trade experiences and other nodes' recommendation. Trust value is relatively complete and reliable in this model while at the same time with large-scale computation and other burden.

3.4 Domain Based Trust Model

This trust model is mostly used in Grid computing. It divides Grid environment into several trust domains and distinguishes two kinds of trust. One is in-domain trust relationship and the other is inter-domain trust relationship. It establishes different strategies for them. The mechanism of this model is reasonable in that since nodes in the same domain usually are much more familiar, they generally have higher trust degree for each other. This algorithm is low computational complexity because in-domain trust's computation only depends on the number of nodes in a domain and inter-domain trust only depends on the number of domains. Domain based model can be seen as a compromise between PKI and network topology. But just like PKI, it may cause network bottleneck and a single point of failure and it ignores the trust decision independence of entities.

3.5 Subjective Trust Model

Distributed applications are often faced with two major security scenarios. First, user programs may contain malicious codes that may endanger or weaken resources. Second, resources once infected by network attacks may damage user applications. So Subject logic based trust model divides trust into several subclass: execution trust, code trust, authority trust, direct trust and recommendation trust and so on. Also it designs different strategies for each kind of trust. Subjective trust is a subjective decision about specific level of entity's particular characters or behaviors. Entity A trusts entity B means A believes that B will perform certain action in some specific situation. Probability theory for example D-S theory or fuzzy mathematics is the basic tool to define trust. But generally speaking subjective trust cannot reflect fuzziness and is only reasoning on probability models which were over formalized and far away from real essence of trust management. Literature [9] proposed a new subjective trust model based on cloud model which can better describe the fuzziness and randomicity. There are other defects such as it cannot realize the integration of identity and behavior certification and the mechanism is so complex that it is difficult to realize the system based on it.

3.6 Dynamic Trust Model

Dynamic trust mechanism is a new and hot topic of security research for distributed applications. Construction of dynamic trust relationship needs to solve the following mathematics issues.

* To decide trust degree space. Always it is defined by fuzzy logics.
* To design mechanism of acquirement of trust value. There are two kinds of methods: direct or indirect.
* To design mechanism of trust value evaluation or evolution.

The research of dynamic trust model is still at the initial stage with a lot of problems to be resolved.

* Definition confusion of dynamic trust relationship. Since trust is a subjective concept there is no universal definition that can be widely accepted.
* Diversity of trust model. Dynamic trust models are based on special application environment and lack universality.
* Difficulties in the evaluation of trust model performance.
* Lack of the realization or application of model.

4 Proposed Trust Model

We proposed a novel trust model that can be used in large-scale and completely distributed cross-clouds environment based on the previous research. The following is the detail of our model.

The model differentiates two kinds of cloud roles: client and server or customer and provider. Clients are enterprises or individuals who choose to use cloud services, while service nodes are resources of cloud providers. Resources that belong to the same providers will attend the same trust domain and each domain set trust agent.

4.1 Trust Relationship Table

Each client stores and maintains a customer trust table.

Table 1. Customer trust table

Domain name	Service type	Trust value/trust degree	Generation time

The key of the table showed above contains the first and second attributes. Domain name is one cloud provider's unique identity in uniform cloud platform. Service type can be computation, storage and so on. In our model, the most specific service type is trust recommendation. When customer uses certain provider's service for the first time, it will use recommended trust provided by the other familiar providers to compute original trust. After the trade, it updates the corresponding trust according to trade result, and also it updates the recommendation factor of corresponding providers. Recommendation factor here is the trust value of recommendation service. Trust value or trust degree is used for trade judgement. The last column "generation time" is used to update trust.

Providers rely on their domain trust agent to manage trust. Agent stores and maintains domain trust table which records other domains' trust. Domain trust is used when one provider cooperates with some others, turns over customer's services, recommends trust, etc. Each time when two providers cooperate for the first time, they can also request for trust recommendation from their familiar domains. In this case recommendation is also one cooperation type. Table2 below is domain trust table.

Table 2. Domain trust table

Domain name	Cooperation type	Trust value/trust degree	Generation time

4.2 Realization Mechanism

Figure 1 shows the basic realization framework of the new model.

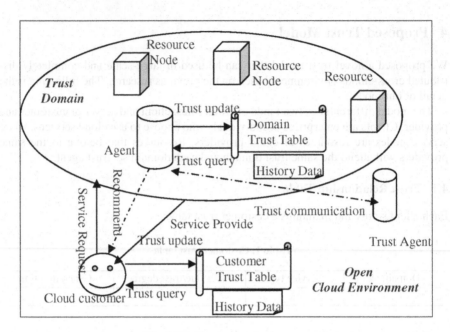

Fig. 1. Realization mechanism

4.2.1 Trust Decision

Safe transactions in cross-clouds environment are ensured by trust mechanism of which the key is trust decision. When customers want to use cloud services, they have to make trust decision. Also when service providers want to cooperate, they have to make trust decision. Explicit trust decision needs a *threshold*. Unless trust value is bigger than or trust degree is higher than the threshold, entities will not continue their transaction. In our model, threshold is customizable and cloud entity or trust domain can independently set its threshold according to its current level of security.

The general process of trust decision in our model is as follows: first of all, to search corresponding value of special trading partner in local trust table (for customer is customer trust table and for provider is domain trust table). If there exists the value and it exceeds the threshold, entity will agree to continue the transaction else transaction will be suspended. If no corresponding record is found, entity will broadcast trust request within familiar domains. And original trust for counterparty will be calculated using the received recommendation trust and corresponding recommendation factor.

Algorithm to Obtain Direct Trust for the familiar nodes.

```
DirectSearch(nodeB,serviceType){/*example      of      nodeA
searches nodeB's trust in local trust table*/

        Boolean found=false;

        TargetNode *isTargetNode=nodeA.dir;

        While(!found||isTargetNode!=null) {
```

```
if(isTargetNode->id==nodeB) {
                  found=true;
   for(;isTargetNode->context==serviceType||isTargetNode!=
nodeB;isTargetNode =isTargetNode->next)
   { if(isTargetNode->context==serviceType)
   {return isTargetNode->trustValue;}
   }
   } else { isTargetNode=isTargetNode->next;}
           }
         if(!found) {return -1;}
   }
```

Algorithm to Compute Recommendation Trust.

```
   RecommendSearch(nodeB,serviceType){/*example   of   nodeA
calculates nodeB's recommendation trust */
     Boolean found=false;
     float trustValue;
     RecomNode *isRecomNode=nodeA.dir;
     While(!found||isRecomNode!=null){
       if(isRecomNode->context==recommendation){
         trustValue=requestforRecom(isRecomNode,nodeB,
           serviceType);/*Agent   will   reply   recommendation
         trust for nodeB of the special trade type*/
         }
       if(trustValue>=0){
         found=true;
         return trustValue*isRecomNode->trustValue;
         }
       isRecomNode=isRecomNode->next;
       }
     if(!found) return -1;
   }
```

We suppose that rows in each trust table are already sorted by trust value in descending order. And for simplicity in recommendation circumstances, entity just chooses to use the recommendation trust of the node with highest recommendation factor. Besides since trust is always context dependent, our algorithms take into account service types.

4.2.2 Trust Update

Two factors cause the update of trust: one is time and the other is re-evaluation of trust after each transaction. Time influence is continuous while transactions' are leaping. So the model adopts different strategies to evaluate them. It tends to use appropriate attenuation function to measure time influence. And in contrast it counts much on the evaluation of last time transaction rather than history cooperation data. Below is the different update policy for different cloud role.

* For customers:

    * To set a time-stamp and periodically delete expired records.

Example of Time Update.

```
ETimeUpdate(){
  DirNode *isDirNode=nodeA.dir;
  DirNode *p=nodeA.dir;
  IsDirNode= IsDirNode->next;
  While(p!=null) {
if(isDirNode->time>=MAXTIME) {
  p->next=IsDirNode->next;
    Delete IsDirNode;
    p=p->next;
    IsDirNode=p->next;
  } else {
    p=p->next;
    IsDirNode=p->next;}
  }
}
```

* To re-evaluate trust after each transaction. If it is the first time, customer will increase one record in customer trust table to store the new provider's trust and at the same time update the recommendation service trust of providers who offered recommended trust. Else it just replaces the old trust with the new one.
* For agents:

    * To refresh trust using proper time attenuation function.
    * To update domain trust value after each cooperation with other domains.

5   Emulation Experiment and Results

We designed simulation experiments realizing the emulation of cross domain transactions based on proposed model and traditional domain-based model. The experiments set up two evaluation factors: trust accuracy and transaction success rate. *Trust accuracy* means the ratio of obtaining correct trust value through trust mechanism to the total number of evaluations. *Transaction success rate* means the ratio of success transactions to the ideal number of transactions.

Simulation experiments simulated cloud platform that contained 2000 nodes and 10 trust domains. In initial time, node randomly became a customer node or joined a domain and became a resource node. Each node should complete 100 times transactions. For each customer node each time, it randomly chose a certain domain to provide download service. For each resource node each time, the specific domain it belonged to randomly chose another domain to cooperate. So the total number of transactions was 200,000. Since each time before nodes began transaction they made trust decisions, the total number of trust evaluations was also 200,000. Malicious node or bad nodes in the experiments were referred to those who refused to provide services or deliberately cheat in trust recommendation. The following two figures show the results.

The results show the proposed model can ensure higher transaction success rate on the basis of relative higher trust accuracy compared to simple domain-based model in cross-domain environment with transaction fraud and malicious recommendation.

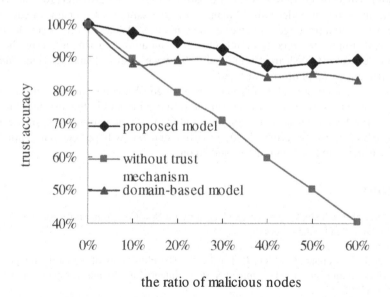

the ratio of malicious nodes

Fig. 2. Result of Trust Accuracy. X-axis represents the ratio of malicious nodes and Y-axis represents trust accuracy.

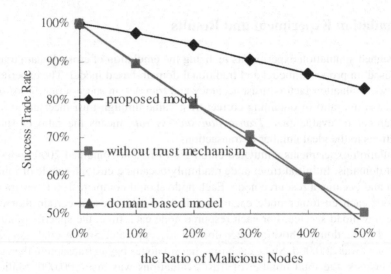

the Ratio of Malicious Nodes

Fig. 3. Result of Success Transaction Rate. X-axis represents the ratio of malicious nodes and Y-axis represents success trade rate.

6 Conclusion and Future Work

This paper introduces a novel trust model that can be used in cross-clouds environment. We distinguished two different roles in cloud: customer and provider. Resources that belong to the same provider will be managed in the same trust domain. In each trust domain we set up a trust agent to charge domain's trust. What's more the model treats recommendation as one type of cloud service. Simulation experiments show the proposed model can establish trust relationship between customer and provider and between different cloud platforms fast and safe.

In future, there are still a lot of issues to be studied. We will establish a cross-clouds security prototype system and implement the proposed model in the test-bed. Since in reality entities behaviors are more complex and there are many other potential security risks in ultra-large-scale cross-clouds environment, we will perfect our model and improve its performance when in use and so on.

References

1. Foster, I., Kesselman, C.: The Grid: Blueprint for a New Computing Infrastructure. Morgan Kaufmann, San Francisco (1999)
2. Chinacloud.cn, http://www.chinacloud.cn
3. Foster, I., Kesselman, C., Nick, J., Tuecke, S.: The Physiology of the Grid: an Open Grid Services Architecture for Distributed Systems Integration. Technical report, Global Grid Forum (2002)
4. Xu, Z., Feng, B., Li, W.: Cloud Computing Technology. Publishing House of Electronics Industry, Beijing (2004)
5. Gartner.: Security Issue of Cloud Computing,
   http://cio.ctocio.com.cn/12/8723012.shtml

6. Urquhart, J.: The Biggest Cloud-Computing Issue of 2009 is Trust (2009),
   http://news.cnet.com/8301-19413_3-10133487-240.html
7. Li, W., Wang, X., Fu, Y., Fu, Z.: Study on Several Trust Models in Grid Environment. Journal of Fuzhou University Natural Science Edition 34(2), 189–193 (2006)
8. Blaze, M., Ioannidis, J., Keromytis, A.D.: Experience with the KeyNote Trust Management System. Applications and Future Directions. In: iTrust 2008, pp. 284–300 (2003)
9. Meng, X., Zhang, G., Kang, J., Li, H., Li, D.: A New Subjective Trust Model Based on Cloud Model. In: ICNSC 2008, 5th IEEE International Conference on Networking, Sensing and Control Sanya China, April 6-8, pp. 1125–1130 (2008)
10. Xiao-Yong, L.I., Xiao-Lin, G.U.I.: Research on Dynamic Trust Model for Large Scale Distributed Environment. Journal of Software 18(6), 1510–1521 (2007)
11. Song, S., Hwang, K., Macwan, M.: Fuzzy Trust Integration for Security Enforcement in Grid Computing. In: Jin, H., Gao, G.R., Xu, Z., Chen, H. (eds.) NPC 2004. LNCS, vol. 3222, pp. 9–21. Springer, Heidelberg (2004)
12. Altman, J.: PKI Security for JXTA Overlay Network, Technical Report,TR-I2-03-06, Palo Alto; Sun Microsystem (2003)
13. Perlman, R.: An Overview of PKI Trust Models. IEEE Network 13, 38–43 (1999)
14. Dou, W., Wang, H., Jia, Y., Zou, P.: A Recommendation-Based Peer-to-Peer Trust Model. Software Journal 15(4), 571–583 (2004)
15. Gan, Z., Zeng, G.: A Trust Evaluation Model Based on Behavior in Grid Environment. Computer Application and Software 22(2), 63–64 (2005)
16. Zhu, J., Yang, S., Fan, J., Chen, M.: A Grid&P2P Trust Model Based on Recommendation Evidence Reasoning. Journal of Computer Research and Development 42(5), 797–803 (2005)
17. Li, X., Michael, R., Liu, J.: A Trust Model Based Routing Protocol for Secure Ad Hoc Network. In: Proceedings of the 2004 IEEE Aerospace Conference, vol. 2, pp. 1286–1295 (2004)
18. Lin, C., Varadharajan, V., Wang, Y.: Enhancing Grid Security with Trust Management. In: Proceedings of the 2004 IEEE International Conference on Service Computing, pp. 303–310 (2004)
19. Azzendin, F., Maheswaran, M.: Evolving and Managing Trust in Grid Computing Systems. In: Proceedings of the 2002 IEEE Canadian Conference on Electrical & Computer Engineering, vol. 3, pp. 1424–1429 (2002)
20. Abdul-Rahman, A., Hailes, S.: Supporting Trust in Virtual Communities. In: Proceedings of the 33rd Hawaii International Conference on System Sciences, Hawaii, vol. 1 (2000)
21. Wang, L., Yang, S.: A Trust Model in Grid Environment. Journal of Computer Engineering and Application 40(23), 50–53 (2004)
22. Foster, I., Kesselman, C., Tsudik, G., Tuecke, S.: A Security Architecture for Computational Grids. In: The 5th ACM Conference on Computer and Communication Security, pp. 83–92 (1998)
23. Foster, I., Zhao, Y., Raicu, I., Lu, S.: Cloud Computing and Grid Computing 360-Degree Compared. In: Grid Computing Environments Workshop, GCE 2008. IEEE, Los Alamitos (2008)

Dynamic Malicious Code Detection
Based on Binary Translator

Zhe Fang, Minglu Li, Chuliang Weng, and Yuan Luo

Department of Computer Science,
Shanghai Jiaotong University
pighogswine@sjtu.edu.cn,
{li-ml,weng-cl,luoyuan}@cs.sjtu.edu.cn

Abstract. The binary translator is a software component of a computer system. It converts binary code of one ISA into binary code of another ISA. Recent trends show that binary translators have been used to save CPU power consumption and CPU die size, which makes binary translators a possible indispensable component of future computer systems. And such situation would give new opportunities to the security of these computer systems. One of the opportunities is that we can perform malicious code checking dynamically in the layer of binary translators. This approach has many advantages, both in terms of capability of detection and checking overhead. In this paper, we proposed a working dynamic malicious code checking module integrated to an existent open-source binary translator, QEMU, and explained that our module's capability of detection is superior to other malicious code checking methods while acceptable performance is still maintained.

Keywords: binary translator, malicious code, dynamic detection.

1 Introduction

The Binary translator is a software component of a computer system. It converts binary code of one instruction set architecture (ISA) into binary code of another ISA. After the conversion, the binary translator executes the converted binary code and manages the runtime environment. A binary translator might interpret and execute one instruction at a time in some cases (e.g. in BIOS code). But in most cases, it translates code at basic block or greater granularity which involves intermediate language (IL) generation, optimization and assembling.

Binary translators have long been the solution to emulate or virtualize one ISA as another ISA, so as to resolve ISA compatibility issues between the software and the CPU. Sun's binary translator UQDBT [1] could virtualize SPARC as x86, or vice versa. Intel's binary translator IA32-EL [2] could virtualize Itanium as x86. In such a sense, binary translators enable the underlying CPUs to execute a greater variety of software already existent, stable, powerful and popular, and thus have great significance in extending the underlying CPU's market share.

M.G. Jaatun, G. Zhao, and C. Rong (Eds.): CloudCom 2009, LNCS 5931, pp. 80–89, 2009.
© Springer-Verlag Berlin Heidelberg 2009

Moreover, recent trends have put binary translators into new use. Instead of tackling ISA compatibility issues, binary translators have been used to save CPU power consumption and CPU die size. Transmeta's binary translator CMS [3] virtualizes its own VLIW [4] CPU Astro into x86 and saved power greatly while sacrificing limited performance. Binary translators could also save CPU die size. For example, modern out-of-order super-scalars' [5] dynamic instruction scheduling mechanism, such as implementation of Tomasulo [6], consumes a lot of circuit, if this scheduler could be replaced by binary translator's scheduling function, the die size and IC complexity could decrease considerably.

With future CPU design and manufacturing requiring more and more on minimizing power consumption and minimizing die size, binary translations have good reason to be an indispensable software component on a computer system. And this gives new opportunities to the security of computer systems.

One of the opportunities is that malicious code checking can be performed dynamically in the layer of binary translators. This approach has several advantages:

- Binary translators have full control of which binary code are translated and executed, which promises that no malicious code could bypass the binary translator without being translated, since the underlying CPU simply could not execute untranslated binary code of another ISA.
- Binary translators are usually much more complicated than a simple instruction-by-instruction interpreter such as Bochs [7]. They usually aggressively optimize the binary code, and cache the translated binary code for later effective reuse. This means that for some already-checked secure code in cache, the checking time overhead is almost zero when being executed again.
- Most binary translators translate binary code dynamically. This provides dynamic malicious code checking with more runtime information. For example, an indirect branch instruction's target address is stored in a register and can only be determined at run time. For traditional static malicious code checking methods [8], indirect branch's target address cannot be determined because there is only a scan and match of patterns in the binary file thus providing no runtime register values. In contrast, for dynamic malicious code checking in a binary translator, the mentioned target address in the register is available at run time, in that this dynamic information is required by the binary translator to detect whether the next basic block at the target address is not yet executed or already executed and thus stored in cache of translated code.
- Since binary translators collect considerable information, such as instruction decoding information, to understand the binary code in order to translate it, we can use this information to perform dynamic code checking with limited time overhead. For example, binary translators decode each instruction to intermediate language before optimization, and the decoded information can be used for dynamic malicious code checking as well, and there is no further decoding time overhead. In comparison, other virtual machine-based code checking methods such as a sandbox [9], requires to do all the work by itself for the sole intention of malicious code detection, which imposes painful time overhead during execution.

In this paper, we will introduce first our dynamic malicious code checking module as a whole and then each component respectively in detail. During the explanation of each component, their advantages are also pointed out, and the reason should also be clear after the explanation of each component's mechanism. Finally, there is a performance evaluation of our dynamic malicious code checking module and a conclusion.

2 Related Work

The idea of our work is different from sandbox [9], in that sandbox requires extra CPU and memory resources of the computer system for virtual machines, while our solution observes that binary translator might become indispensable for computer systems as described in the previous section and we can take advantage of it for security purposes. The security mechanism for JVM goes beyond sandbox [11], and is more close to the idea of our work. However, only a limited variety of software runs on JVM, such a security solution has limited monitoring scope, while on a computer system with binary translator, all software runs on the binary translator, sometimes including the operating system [3, 10].

There is also a great amount of clever work based on static malicious code detection [8, 12]. But our work also takes advantage of runtime dynamic information as described in the previous section. Note that dynamic detection also means there should be restrictions on runtime overhead, which is not as sensitive an issue for static solutions.

3 DMCC Module Overview

The dynamic malicious code checker (DMCC) module is a security extension to the binary translator. DMCC module is responsible for dynamically checking the code being translated and taking initiatives if malicious code is detected. Fig. 1 illustrates the architectural overview of DMCC module and the binary translator. In our prototype, the open-source binary translator QEMU [10] is used as base code, but we only rely on QEMU's features that are general to most binary translators, which makes DMCC module a more general security solution.

In Fig. 1, all the arrows represent data flow. Binary code image for translation is first retrieved by the decoder. The decoder converts each instruction into its corresponding intermediate language representation. Then, the optimizer collects these ILs and does all kinds of optimization on them. Finally, the code generator generates binary code of the underlying CPU's ISA with the optimized ILs and stores these codes in the binary translator's cache for execution. The cache will not be invalidated unless the original code image is modified due to SMC or the binary translator decides to retranslate it more aggressively seeking better performance for frequently used code. DMCC rules are malicious code rules specified by the user. The DMCC parser takes them as input and yields functions used by the DMCC engine.

As shown in Fig. 1, the DMCC module is composed of the DMCC rules, the DMCC parser and the DMCC engine. The extended binary translator is composed of the DMCC engine, the decoder, the optimizer, the code generator, and the cache. As shown in Fig. 1, the DMCC rules and the DMCC parser are offline parts of the

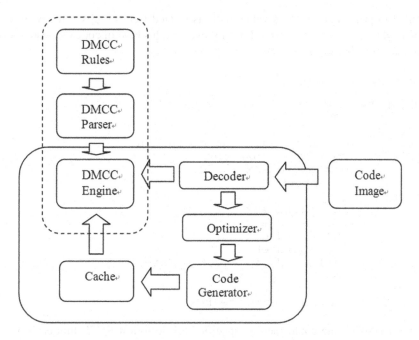

Fig. 1. The DMCC Module and Binary Translator Overview

extended binary translator. Code image is standalone because it is merely binary code on the media or loaded to memory, which is to be translated. Note that the cache is also an integrated part of the binary translator because it also includes the functionality that manages the cache, such as cache lookup.

4 DMCC Module Components

The DMCC rules, the DMCC parser and the DMCC engine of the DMCC module is elaborated on respectively in this section.

4.1 DMCC Rule

The DMCC rules are specified in a text file by the user. The user could be anti-virus experts, system administrators or so. The rules can be replaced or extended according to new security requirements and situations.

The user specifies the rule according to a simple rule grammar. The following is an example. In our example, an x86 self-modifying code snippet is used as imaginary malicious code, our goal is to specify the corresponding rule as general as possible for the DMCC module to detect it and its variants.

In this snippet, the second and the third "inc ebx" instruction will be overwritten by two "nop" instructions when executing "rep stosb" instruction. So when "write_hex" is called to print register ebx's value, 0x02 is printed (register ebx actually only incremented twice), instead of 0x04. It is possible that this kind of code can lead to even more malicious behaviors.

A self-modifying code snippet

```
no_operation:
            nop
start:
            mov byte  al, [no_operation]
            xor dword ebx, ebx
            mov dword ecx, 0x02
            rep stosb
mark:
            inc dword ebx
            inc dword ebx
            inc dword ebx
            inc dword ebx
            call dword [function_pointer]
            ret
end:
function_pointer: dd write_hex
```

And a DMCC rule could then be specified as the following. Within each pair of braces is one DMCC rule. In a rule file, multiple DMCC rules can be provided. On each line is a rule statement. There are two kinds of statements, instruction type and constraint. In order to accurately specify a constraint, some instruction types or their operand types are numbered for reference, such as "inst0" and "reg3".

On Line2, "inst0" says it could be any instruction type.

On Line3, "mov reg0, mem0" says it is a "mov" instruction type, with a register operand as target and a memory operand as source.

On Line4, it constrains that the "reg0" operand on Line4 must be register al, which is required by "rep stosb" on Line8.

On Line5, it constrains that the "mem0" operand on Line4 must point to the "inst0" instruction on Line1.

On Line6, "mov reg3, imm0" says it is a "mov" instruction type, with a register operand as target and an immediate operand as source.

On Line7, it constrains that the "reg3" operand on Line6 must be register ecx, which is required by "rep stosb" on Line8.

On Line 8, "rep stosb" says it is a "rep stosb" instruction type. Note that this instruction takes register al and ecx as implicit operands.

On Line9 ~ Line14, the statements make sure that the instructions replaced by "inst0" are precisely on the instruction boundary. "%" is modulo operation.

Comparing the code snippet and the DMCC rule, we can see that the DMCC rule is more general and can be even more powerful if there is a wise user to specify the rules. In addition, the DMCC rule is also designed for dynamic checking, which will be elaborated on in detail with the DMCC parser.

A DMCC rule correspondent to the previous self-modifying code snippet

```
1          {
2          inst0;
3          mov reg0, mem0;
4          reg0 == al;
5          mem0 == CURRENT - (SIZEOF(inst0));
6          mov reg3, imm0;
7          reg3 == ecx;
8          rep stosb;
9          inst1;
10         inst2;
11         inst3;
12         inst4;
13         SIZEOF(inst1) == SIZEOF(inst2) ==
SIZEOF(inst3) == SIZEOF(inst4);
14         SIZEOF(inst0) * imm0 % SIZEOF(inst1) == 0;
15         ret
16         }
17
18         {
19         /* other rules */
20         }
```

4.2 DMCC Parser

The DMCC parser parses the DMCC rules. It takes the DMCC rule file as input and outputs a source file, which contains several functions for the DMCC engine to call. These functions take an execution trace, which is a list of instructions as input, and outputs whether malicious code is detected. One thing to emphasize is that the input execution trace is a sequence of instructions in their execution order, rather than a sequence of instructions in their code image layout order. Thus in the input execution trace, branch instructions are also eliminated, because all the instructions are already in their execution order and any branch instruction information is unnecessary in this case. For example, code image like the following:

```
            xor ebx, ebx;
            je taken;
fall_through:
            inc ebx;
            /* ... */
taken:
            dec ebx;
```

would yield according to dynamic information an input execution trace as:

```
            xor ebx, ebx;
            inc ebx;
```

or an input execution trace as:

```
            xor ebx, ebx;
            dec ebx;
```

The input execution trace is dynamically collected and provided by the DMCC engine which is a module inside the binary translator. The input execution trace provided in execution order benefits malicious code checking considerably, in that it provides which instructions sequence is actually to be processed by the CPU in order. In contrast, a list of instructions in code image layout order lacks dynamic information, such as the target of an indirect branch, or the result of self-modifying code. Even if the input CPU state and memory state is provided, it is hard to figure out the actual execution order, because other inputs such interrupts are almost impossible to predict or provide in a reasonable way. So doing dynamic malicious code checking in binary translator is a corollary choice.

By calling the functions generated by the DMCC parser, whether the input execution trace is malicious code is checked against the DMCC rules implemented by the functions. In fact, more complicated checking method can be implemented based on the dynamic information provided by the DMCC engine as needed, but since it's not designed so, extending the DMCC parser might not be as easy a task as extending the DMCC rule for non-developer users.

4.3 DMCC Engine

The DMCC engine is an integrated component added to the binary translator. It has three main functionalities: collect and provide input execution trace for the DMCC parser generated functions, perform checking by calling these functions, and take initiatives if malicious code is detected.

The DMCC engine collects information in two ways, by monitoring the binary translator's decoding process and by looking into binary translator's cache. For code that has never been executed, the DMCC engine monitors the decoder to collect the input execution trace. Since code image that has never executed must not have been translated, it must not have been decoded. So the decoding order is the same as the execution order. Thus, the DMCC engine could collect a list of instructions in execution order. For code that has already been executed and cached, the DMCC engine looks into the cached decoding information and forms a list of instructions as input execution trace accordingly.

One issue should be noted that many binary translators such as QEMU do a kind of optimization called "chaining". "Chaining" requires more consideration when collecting an input execution trace in the binary translator's cache. Here is an example to explain the issue. In Fig. 2, BB1' is translated code cache for the basic block BB1, while BB2' is translated code cache for the basic block BB2. At the end of execution of BB1' a branch instruction targeted to BB2 is to be executed. According to the definition of a basic block, the last instruction is always a branch instruction or the like, such as a call instruction. When encountering such a branch, the control is transferred to the binary translator. The binary translator looks up for the translated code cache of BB2. If BB2' is found, the binary translator transfers control to BB2'; if not, translate BB2 first and then transfer to BB2'. Transferring control back and forth is time consuming, because the execution context is switched back and forth and a lot of load and store instructions take place. This is where "chaining" comes to place. It modifies the branch target of BB1' from the binary translator to BB2' if it exists, and thus saves context switches dramatically. But the issue from the DMCC engine point

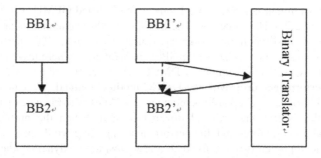

Fig. 2. An example of "Chaining" optimization

of view is that, after executing BB1', the control will not be transferred to the binary translator, so the DMCC engine could not monitor and collect cached decoding information of BB2' once BB1' starts to execute. So the DMCC engine has to be considerate enough to check if BB1' is "chained" to BB2'. If so, the cached decoding information of BB2' should be collected before BB1' starts to execute.

5 Performance Evaluation

The DMCC will harm the performance of the system as a trade-off for security. We estimated the performance drop with different numbers of DMCC rules specified with SPECINT 2000. Note that due to the difficulty to find such great numbers of DMCC rules, we make the DMCC module to treat duplicate rules as entirely independent ones.

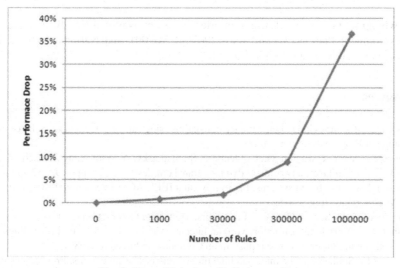

Fig. 3. Binary Translator Performance Drop

The test environment is a RHEL5.2 Linux with modified QEMU 0.10 working on an AMD Athlon 2.71GHz processor. The SPECINT 2000 benchmarks are built with the default configuration in the same environment by GCC. The performance is measured by means of the product of the SPEC benchmarks, where less means better.

In Fig. 3, the x axis is the number of DMCC rules specified; the y axis is the SPE-CINT 2000 performance drop with the DMCC module enabled. We can see that our DMCC module imposes acceptable percentage ($< 3\%$) of performance drop when the number of rules is less than several dozen thousand. When the number of rules reaches several hundred thousand, the performance is getting wildly poor.

The possible approach is that only keep a few most active dynamic checking rules in the DMCC module, and for those checking that could be done outside of binary translator, such as those can be checked statically, move them outside.

6 Conclusion

As a conclusion, the DMCC module can work quite well to dynamically detect malicious code that can be specified with our DMCC rule grammar. The significance is that the DMCC module has advantage over both static malicious code checking and virtual sandbox checking. The former lack dynamic runtime information while the latter causes too much overhead.

The DMCC module also has acceptable performance at its current complexity when the number of DMCC rules is limited to several dozen thousand.

In future work, we will enhance the DMCC parser, in order to make the DMCC rule grammar more expressive and so more powerful. Also, we will enhance the binary translator's chaining mechanism so that it supports the DMCC module better. And hopefully, we will provide more mechanism that takes more advantage of dynamic information in the binary translator.

Acknowledgments. This work was supported in part by National Key Basic Research and Development Plan (973 Plan) (No. 2007CB310900), and National Natural Science Foundation of China (No. 90612018).

References

1. Ung, D., Cifuentes, C.: Dynamic binary translation using run-time feedbacks. Science of Computer Programming 60(2) (2006)
2. Baraz, L., Devor, T., Etzion, O., Goldenberg, S., Skaletsky, A., Yun Wang Zemach, Y.: IA-32 execution layer: a two-phase dynamic translator designed to support IA-32 applications on Itanium®-based systems. In: 36th Annual IEEE/ACM International Symposium on Micro-architecture (2003)
3. The Technology Behind Crusoe™ Processors, Transmeta Corporation (2000)
4. Fisher, J.A.: Very long instruction word architectures and the ELI-512. In: Proceedings of the 10th annual international symposium on Computer architecture (1983)
5. Smith, J.E., Sohi, G.S.: The micro-architecture of superscalar processors. Proceedings of the IEEE (1995)

6. Tomasulo, R.M.: An efficient algorithm for exploiting multiple arithmetic units. IBM Journal of research and Development (1967)
7. Lawton, K.P.: Bochs: A Portable PC Emulator for Unix/X. Linux Journal (1996)
8. Mihahai, C.: Static analysis of executables to detect malicious patterns. In: Proceedings of the 12th conference on USENIX Security Symposium (2006)
9. Natvig, K.: Sandbox Technology inside AV Scanners. In: Virus Bulletin Coference (2001)
10. Bellard, F.: QEMU, a Fast and Portable Dynamic Translator, USENIX (2005)
11. Gong, L.: Going beyond the sandbox: An overview of the new security architecture in the Java development kit 1.2. In: Proceedings of the USENIX Symposium on Internet Technologies and Systems (1997)
12. Sung, A.H.: Static analyzer of vicious executables (SAVE). In: 20th Annual Computer Security Applications Conference (2004)

A Privacy Manager for Cloud Computing

Siani Pearson, Yun Shen, and Miranda Mowbray

HP Labs, Long Down Avenue, Stoke Gifford, Bristol BS34 8QZ, UK
{siani.pearson,yun.shen,miranda.mowbray}@hp.com

Abstract. We describe a privacy manager for cloud computing, which reduces
the risk to the cloud computing user of their private data being stolen or misused, and also assists the cloud computing provider to conform to privacy law.
We describe different possible architectures for privacy management in cloud
computing; give an algebraic description of obfuscation, one of the features of
the privacy manager; and describe how the privacy manager might be used to
protect private metadata of online photos.

Keywords: Cloud computing, privacy.

1 Introduction

In this paper we describe a privacy manager for cloud computing, which reduces the
risk to the cloud computing user of their private data being stolen or misused, and also
assists the cloud computing provider to conform to privacy law.

Cloud computing, in which services are carried out on behalf of customers on
hardware that the customers do not own or manage, is an increasingly fashionable
business model. The input data for cloud services is uploaded by the user to the cloud,
which means that they typically result in users' data being present in unencrypted
form on a machine that the user does not own or control. This poses some inherent
privacy challenges.

There is a risk of data theft from machines in the cloud, by rogue employees of
cloud service providers or by data thieves breaking into service providers' machines,
or even by other customers of the same service if there is inadequate separation of
different customers' data in a machine that they share in the cloud. Governments in
the countries where the data is processed or stored may have legal rights to view the
data under some circumstances [1,2]. There is also a risk that the data may be put to
unauthorized uses. It is part of the standard business model of cloud computing that
the service provider may gain revenue from authorized secondary uses of the user's
data, most commonly the targeting of advertisements. However, some secondary data
uses would be very unwelcome to the data owner (such as, for example, the resale of
detailed sales data to their competitors). At present there are no technological barriers
to such secondary uses.

There are, however, some legal constraints on the treatment of users' private
data by cloud computing providers. Privacy laws vary according to jurisdiction, but
EU countries generally only allow personally-identifiable information to be processed
if the data subject is aware of the processing and its purpose, and place special

M.G. Jaatun, G. Zhao, and C. Rong (Eds.): CloudCom 2009, LNCS 5931, pp. 90–106, 2009.
© Springer-Verlag Berlin Heidelberg 2009

restrictions on the processing of sensitive data (for example, health or financial data), the explicit consent of the data owner being part of a sufficient justification for such processing [3]. They generally adhere to the concept of *data minimization*, that is, they require that personally identifiable information is not collected or processed unless that information is necessary to meet the stated purposes. In Europe, data subjects can refuse to allow their personally identifiable data to be used for marketing purposes [4]. Moreover, there may be requirements on the security and geographical location of the machines on which personally identifiable data is stored. A UK business processing data about individual customers with some cloud computing services could find itself in breach of UK data processing law, if these services do not give assurances that the machines they use are adequately secure [5]. European law limiting cross-border data transfers also might prohibit the use of the cloud computing services to process this data if they stored data in countries with weak privacy protection laws [6].

The structure of the paper is as follows. In section 2 we present our solution, which is in the form of a privacy manager for cloud computing. In section 3 we discuss different architectures for privacy management in cloud computing, giving an overview of how the privacy manager may be used. We also describe how Trusted Computing mechanisms [7] can optionally be used to enhance privacy management. In Section 4 we describe obfuscation in mathematical terms. We give an algebraic formulation of the task of obfuscation, and algebraic specifications of different obfuscation methods suitable for particular examples. In Section 5 we discuss an application scenario, the management of online photos, and present the user interface for the privacy manager for this application. In Section 6 we review previous approaches to privacy management for data repositories. The paper concludes with a general analysis and discussion of next steps.

2   Our Solution: Privacy Manager

Our contribution to addressing these problems is a Privacy Manager, which helps the user manage the privacy of their data in the cloud. As a first line of defence, the privacy manager uses a feature called *obfuscation*, where this is possible. The idea is that instead of being present unencrypted in the cloud, the user's private data is sent to the cloud in an encrypted form, and the processing is done on the encrypted data. The output of the processing is de-obfuscated by the privacy manager to reveal the correct result. (We call it obfuscation rather than encryption because some of the information present in the original data is in general still present in the obfuscated data.) The obfuscation method uses a key which is chosen by the user and known by the privacy manager, but which is not communicated to the service provider. Thus the service provider is not able to de-obfuscate the user's data, and the un-obfuscated data is never present on the service provider's machines. This reduces (or even eliminates) the risks of theft of this data from the cloud and unauthorized uses of this data. Moreover, the obfuscated data is not personally identifiable information, and so the service provider is not subject to the legal restrictions that apply to the processing of the unobfuscated data. Where obfuscation is practical, the principle of data minimization gives a legal impetus to use it.

However, it is not practical for all cloud applications to work with obfuscated data. For applications for which users have to upload some private data to the cloud, the privacy manager contains two additional features, called *preferences* and *personae*, which help the users to communicate to service providers their wishes for the use of this personal data. These two features do not guarantee that a user's wishes will be observed if the service provider is not trustworthy. However they assist trustworthy service providers to respect privacy laws that require the user's consent.

The preferences feature allows users to set their preferences about the handling of personal data that is stored in an unobfuscated form in the cloud. A similar approach has been taken within P3P [8] and PRIME [9]. It communicates these preferences to a corresponding policy enforcement mechanism within the cloud service. The preferences can be associated with data sent to the cloud, and preferably cryptographically bound to it (by encrypting both the policy and data under a key shared by the sender and receiver). For stickiness of the privacy policy to the data, public key enveloping techniques can be used. Alternatively, it is possible to use policy-based encryption of credential blobs (a form of Identity-Based Encryption (IBE) technology) [10]: the policies could be used directly as IBE encryption keys to encrypt the transferred material [11]. Part of the preference specification could involve the purpose for which the personal data might be used within the cloud, and this could be checked within the cloud before access control were granted, using mechanisms specified via [12].

The persona feature allows the user to choose between multiple personae when interacting with cloud services. In some contexts a user might want to be anonymous, and in others he might wish for partial or full disclosure of his identity. The user's choice of persona provides a simple interface to a possibly complex set of data use preferences communicated to the service provider via the preference feature, and may also determine which data items are to be obfuscated.

This paper extends the basic idea of a client-based Privacy Manager introduced in [13]. We describe several different possible architectures for usage of a Privacy Manager in cloud computing, not just one in which the privacy manager is within the user's client; we show how trusted computing can be used to enhance this approach; we give a general mathematical description of the obfuscation mechanisms used within the Privacy Manager; and we describe an application to a particular scenario – photo management in the cloud – and a demonstration of the Privacy Manager that allows investigation of how the Privacy Manager can operate in practice to help users protect their private information in the cloud.

3 Architectural Options

In this section we describe different possible architectures for privacy management within cloud computing, and demonstrate how trusted computing can be used to strengthen this approach. The most appropriate architecture to be used depends upon the cloud infrastructure deployed for a particular environment, and the trust relationships between the parties involved.

3.1 Privacy Manager in the Client

The overall architecture of our solution is illustrated in Figure 1. Privacy Manager software on the client helps users to protect their privacy when accessing cloud services. A central feature of the Privacy Manager is that it can provide an obfuscation and de-obfuscation service, to reduce the amount of sensitive information held within the cloud. For further detail, see Section 4. In addition, the Privacy Manager allows the user to express privacy preferences about the treatment of their personal information, including the degree and type of obfuscation used. Personae – in the form of icons that correspond to sets of privacy preferences – can be used to simplify this process and make it more intuitive to the user. So for example, there could be an icon with a mask over a face that corresponds to maximal privacy settings, and other icons that relate to a lower level of protection of certain types of personal data in a given context. The user's personae will be defined by the cloud service interaction context. Personae may be defined by the user, although a range of default options would be available.

Trusted computing solutions, like those being developed by the Trusted Computing Group (TCG) [14], can address the lower-level protection of data, and this can be exploited in our solution. The TCG is an organization set up to design and develop specifications for computing platforms that create a foundation of trust for software processes, based on a small amount of extra hardware called a Trusted Platform Module (TPM) [14]. This tamper-resistant hardware component within a machine acts as a root of trust. In the longer term, as specified by TCG, trusted computing will provide cryptographic functionality, hardware-based protected storage of secrets, platform attestation and mechanisms for secure boot and integrity checking [7]. Allied protected computing environments under development by certain manufacturers and open source operating systems such as Linux can support TCG facilities further. For details about how trusted computing might be used to enhance privacy, see [15].

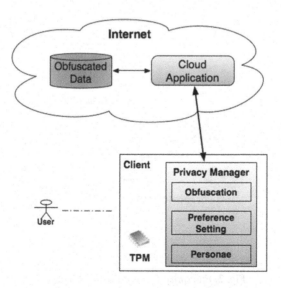

Fig. 1. Client-Based Privacy Manager

As an enhancement to our solution, a TPM on the client machine can be used to protect the obfuscation keys and provide further benefits. The privacy manager software and the methods linking sensitive data to pseudonyms can be protected by a TPM (see Figure 1). The TPM can provide encryption services and also allow integrity checking of the Privacy Manager software. In general, the main benefits that trusted computing could provide for client-based privacy management are hardware-based cryptographic functionality, confidentiality and integrity. In terms of confidentiality, it decreases the risk of unsecured access to secret material, by means of tamper-resistant hardware-based protection of keys. Moreover, protected data on the platform is not usable by other platforms. Trusted computing could yield greater trust in integrity of the privacy management software, integrity of the involved platforms, and platform identities.

3.2 Privacy Manager in a Hybrid Cloud

As an alternative, as illustrated in Figure 2, the Privacy Manager may be deployed in a local network, or a private cloud, to protect information relating to multiple parties. This would be suitable in environments, such as enterprise environments, where local protection of information is controlled in an adequate manner and its principal use would be to control personal information passing to a public cloud. The Privacy Manager can itself be virtualized within the internal cloud. Note that the TPM could also be virtualized, within the private cloud.

Advantages to this approach include that the benefits of the cloud can be reaped within the private cloud, including the most efficient provision of the Privacy Manager functionality. It can provide enterprise control over dissemination of

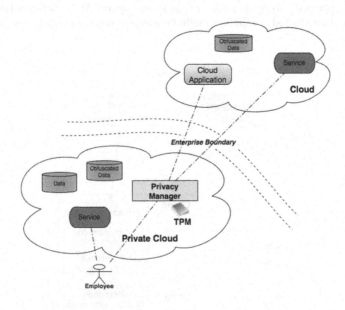

Fig. 2. Enterprise-focused Privacy Manager

sensitive information, and local compliance. A significant issue however is scalability, in the sense that the Privacy Manager might slow down traffic, provide a bottleneck and may not be able to adequately manage information exposed between composed services.

There are various different options with respect to this type of architecture. For example, the proxy capability could be combined, even in a distributed way, with other functionalities, including identity management. Another example is that trusted virtual machines [16] could be used within the privacy cloud to support strong enforcement of integrity and security policy controls over a virtual entity (a guest operating system or virtual appliance running on a virtualized platform). It would be possible to define within the Privacy Manager different personae corresponding to different groups of cloud services, using different virtualized environments on each end user device. In this way, virtualization is used to push control from the cloud back to the client platform. As with the previous architecture, there could be mutual attestation of the platforms, including integrity checking.

3.3 Privacy Infomediary within the Cloud

Figure 3 shows how the Privacy Manager may be deployed as (part of) a privacy infomediary [17], mediating data transfer between different trust domains. The Privacy Manager would act on behalf of the user and decide the degree of data transfer allowed, based upon transferred user policies and the service context, and preferably also an assessment of the trustworthiness of the service provision environment. Notification and feedback by the Privacy Manager to the user would also be preferable here, in order to increase transparency and accountability.

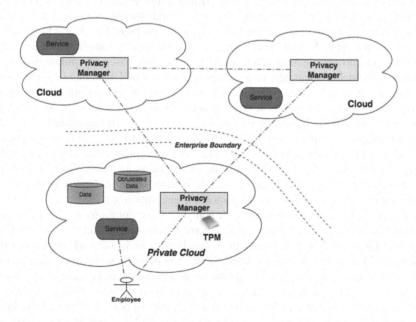

Fig. 3. Privacy Manager within the Cloud

The infomediary could be a consumer organization or other entity that is trusted by the users. It might alternatively be an entity that already exists within the cloud in order to provide an alternative function, such as an identity provider or auditor, and the functionality could be an extension of that. For example, the open source project Otemba [18] implements key management and user management, separating crypto-graphic keys from the cloud infrastructure. A key management role might be extended to a general infomediary role.

The infomediary may also play a role in checking that the user preferences are sat-isfied before providing a decryption key for decrypting any data that needs to be de-crypted in order for the cloud service to be provided (for example, it could be a Trust Authority in order to provide IBE decryption keys [10,11]). Again, trusted infrastruc-ture [7] could be useful in ensuring that the infrastructural building blocks of the cloud are secure, trustworthy and compliant with security best practice.

The following section provides more detail about the obfuscation mechanism used by the Privacy Manager, in these different cases.

4   Obfuscation

The aim of obfuscation is to solve the following general problem. A user has private data x. He wishes to carry out some communication protocol with a service provider, which will enable him to learn the result of some function f on x, without revealing x to the service provider. (The function f may itself depend on some data known to the service provider but not to the user, and on some data supplied by the user which is not private).

If the user and service provider are both willing to use whatever protocol will solve the problem, and have sufficient computing power and storage to do so, Yao's proto-col for secure two-party computation [19] solves this problem for any f which can be expressed as a circuit. In fact, Yao's protocol can be used to ensure that the service provider learns no information at all about x. So in this case, any polynomial-time application could be calculated in a completely obfuscated fashion. In fact, Yao's protocol can be used to ensure that the service provider learns no information at all about x. Yao's protocol requires several rounds of interactions between the user and service provider, which depend on the choice of f. Gentry [20] has recently removed this requirement for interaction by constructing a remarkable encryption scheme which allows the service provider to calculate the encrypted value of $f(x)$ given the encrypted value of x, for *any* f which can be expressed as a circuit, while also ensur-ing that the service provider learns no information about x. Gentry's encryption scheme improves on prior work on homomorphic encryption, eg. [21].

However, there are two problems with applying these solutions in cloud comput-ing. The first is efficiency. Gentry's full scheme is impractical due to its rather high computational complexity. Although there has been a body of work improving the efficiency of Yao's protocol and related secure computation techniques such as pri-vacy-preserving data mining [21,22], when the input data x is large these methods can still require a large amount of storage or computation on the part of the user. One of the attractions of cloud computing is that it can enable users to process or store large amounts of data at times of peak demand without having large amounts of computing resources in-house. The other problem is that cloud computing providers may not be willing to rewrite their applications. If this is the case, the user has to calculate $f(\underline{x})$ using only the functions provided by the service, which in this section are denoted $f_1, \ldots, f_n$. The set of functions f for which it is possible to do this without revealing $\underline{x}$ to the service provider depends on $f_1, \ldots, f_n$ and on the extent of the user's computing resources. For some specialized cloud computing services, only one function is provided, which will typically be a MapReduce-style function [23] if the input data is a large data set; some more generic services offer full SQL SELECT functionality [24].

The requirement that we make of obfuscation in this paper is only that it is difficult for the service provider to determine $\underline{x}$ given the obfuscated data. It may be that the service provider can easily obtain some information about $\underline{x}$, but not enough to determine $\underline{x}$. As a different example of obfuscation methods that allow some but not all information about the input data to be learned from the obfuscated data, Narayanan and Shmatikov [25] describe an obfuscation method which allows individual records to be retrieved from an obfuscated database by anyone who can specify them precisely, while making "mass harvesting" queries matching a large number of records computationally infeasible. As remarked in [25], there is a tension between the strict security definitions and loose notions of efficiency used by the cryptography community, and the strict efficiency requirements but loose security requirements of the database community. Like the database community we prioritize efficiency over strength of the security definition, as it is essential for us that the privacy manager be practical and scalable to implement.

4.1 The Algebra of Obfuscation

The general algebraic description of obfuscation is as follows. Suppose you wish to use an application to calculate the result of a function f on an input $\underline{x}$, without revealing $\underline{x}$ to the application. The application can calculate functions $f_1, \ldots, f_n$. (Typically, but not necessarily, one of these will be equal to the function f). You can use the application to compute function f in an obfuscated fashion if for some positive integer m there are encryption functions $o_1, \ldots, o_m$ such that it is difficult to determine $\underline{x}$ from the tuple $o_1(k,\underline{x}), \ldots, o_m(k,\underline{x})$ without knowing the key k, and a decryption function d such that for all inputs $\underline{x}$ and keys k,

$$d(k, \ f_1(o_1(k,\underline{x})), \ldots, f_m(o_m(k,\underline{x}))) = f(\underline{x}) \tag{1}$$

To perform the obfuscated calculation, first encrypt $\underline{x}$ with each of the encryption functions to form the tuple $(o_1(k,\underline{x}), \ldots, o_m(k,\underline{x}))$, using a key k known to you but not to the application. Send the values in the tuple to the application, to compute the values $f_1(o_1(k,\underline{x})), \ldots, f_m(o_m(k,\underline{x}))$. Finally, apply the decryption function to obtain $f(\underline{x})$ from the key k and the values output from the application. Since the only information the application receives is the tuple $(o_1(k,\underline{x}), \ldots, o_m(k,\underline{x}))$, it is difficult for the application to determine $\underline{x}$.

We now give some examples of calculating functions an obfuscated fashion. Since we are interested in using cloud applications, in the examples the functions $f_1, \ldots, f_n$ are typically SQL SELECT commands or MapReduce-style functions of a list (possibly a very long list) of values, indexed by a finite index set I.

Example 1: Using Privacy Homomorphisms

Privacy homomorphisms were first introduced by Rivest, Adelman and Dertouzos [26], who give several examples. A privacy homomorphism is a family of functions (e_k, d_k, f, g) where e_k is an encryption function depending on key k, such that for each key k and messages $a_1, \ldots, a_r$,

$$d_k(g(e_k(a_1), \ldots, e_k(a_r))) = f(a1, \ldots, ar) \tag{2}$$

If you wish to calculate function f and know a privacy homormorphism (e_k, d_k, f, g), you can use it to calculate f in an obfuscated fashion via an application that can calculate the function g. Set $m=1$ and $f_1=g$, and for each $\underline{x} = (x_i : i \text{ in } I)$, i in I and key k, set $o_i(k, \underline{x}) = e_k(x_i)$. Set d to be the function sending (k, y) to $d_k(y)$ for all y. Then by equation (2), equation (1) holds.

Example 2: TC3 Health

TC3 Health [27] is a cloud-based company which checks health insurance claims on behalf of insurance companies. The functions that they calculate have the property that if a patient identifier (a name, say, or a hospital ID) is replaced everywhere in the input by a pseudonym, the resulting output is the same as that obtained by replacing the patient identifier by the pseudonym everywhere in the original output. They are therefore able to offer a service which checks the claims without requiring patient identifiers to be released to the cloud: the insurance companies replace the patient identifiers with (unique) pseudonyms, send the result as input to TC3 Health, and translate back the pseudonyms in the output. In terms of equation (1) above, $m=1$, the key k is the insurance company's map from patient identifiers to pseudonyms, o_1 is the application of this map and d is the application of the inverse map.

Example 3: Share Investment Web Site

In this example the function calculated is the current value of a portfolio of shares $\underline{x} = (x_i : i \text{ in } I)$ where I is a set of companies and x_i is the number of shares of company i in the portfolio. The application offers the same function, which calculates the sum over i in I of $x_i . v_i$, where v_i is the current value of a share in company i: the value v_i is known to the application, but the share owner does not know the value without help from the application. A straightforward way of performing this calculation in an obfuscated fashion is choose k to be a positive integer and set

$$m=1, \quad o_1(k, \underline{x}) = k.\underline{x}, \quad d(k, \underline{y}) = k^{-1}.\underline{y} \text{ for all } k, \underline{x}, \underline{y} \tag{3}$$

In fact, some people use just this obfuscation method when they calculate the value of their portfolios online. However, $o_1(\underline{x})$ reveals the set of companies whose shares are contained in the portfolio (and also their relative frequency). This information might be enough to identify an individual investor. Moreover, the key k must be a divisor of the highest common factor of the entries of $o_1(\underline{x})$, and so may be easy to guess given $o_1(\underline{x})$ and some likely bounds on the total value of the portfolio. An obfuscation method that does not give away as much information is to construct several different portfolios, such that $\underline{x}$ is a linear combination of these portfolios, and derive the value of $\underline{x}$ from the values of these portfolios.

For example, choose a key k consisting of a map $k_0: I \rightarrow \{1,2\}$, two portfolios $\underline{k_1}$, $\underline{k_2}$, and two integers k_3, k_4 greater than 1. For any portfolio $\underline{x}$ write $\underline{x}^{(k,1)}$, $\underline{x}^{(k,2)}$ for the portfolios $(x_i: i$ in I, $k_0(x_i)=1)$ and $(x_i: i$ in I, $k_0(x_i)=2)$ respectively. Set $m=3$ and define the obfuscation functions by

$$o_1(k,\underline{x}) = \underline{x}^{(k,1)} + \underline{k}_1, \; o_2(k,\underline{x}) = \underline{x}^{(k,2)} + \underline{k}_2,$$

$$o_3(k,\underline{x}) = k_3 . \underline{k}_1 + k_4 . \underline{k}_2 + (k_3 - \min\{k_3,k_4\}).\underline{x}^{(k,1)} + (k_4 - \min\{k_3,k_4\}).\underline{x}^{(k,2)}$$

(4)

If you know the triple $(o_1(k,\underline{x}), o_2(k,\underline{x}), o_3(k,\underline{x}))$ but not k, it is difficult to guess $\underline{x}$, and also difficult to guess the set of companies i such that $x_i > 0$ or the relative values of these x_i. Define the deobfuscation function d by

$$d(k,v_1,v_2,v_3) = (\min\{k_3, k_4\})^{-1}. (k_3.v_1 + k_4.v_2 - v_3) \text{ for all } v_1,v_2,v_3$$

(5)

It is straightforward to check that equation (1) holds for these obfuscation functions and deobfuscation function, when both f and f_1 are the function that returns the value of the portfolio. So this allows the value of portfolio $\underline{x}$ to be calculated in an obfuscated fashion.

Example 4: Simple Obfuscation of SQL Queries
Suppose that $\underline{x} = (x_i: i$ in $I)$ describes the content of a SQL database: each x_i is a database row, containing entries $x_i(1), \ldots, x_i(c)$ in columns 1 to c. For $j=1,2,..c$ let nj be the name of column j, and let Vj be the set of values that are permitted in column j. The application can perform SQL queries, and we would like to compute an SQL query of the form

```
SELECT <ex 1> WHERE <ex 2> GROUP BY <ex 3> ORDER BY
<ex 4> LIMIT n
```

in an obfuscated fashion, where

- <ex 1> is a nonempty list of terms of the form MAX(ni), SUM(ni), COUNT(*) or ni for some $1 \leq i \leq c$,
- <ex 2> is obtained by combining terms of the form ni = nj, ni = v, or ni > v (for some $1 \leq i, j \leq c$ and v in V_i) using the logical operators AND, OR and NOT,
- <ex 3> is a possibly nonempty list of column names,
- <ex 4> is an element of <ex 1> or its negative, or is empty
- n is either a positive integer or infinity; if it is infinity then the "LIMIT n" clause is omitted from the query.

If any of <ex 2>, <ex 3>, <ex 4> are empty then the relevant subclause is omitted from the query. Examples of such queries include, for instance,

```
SELECT MAX(n3) WHERE ((n7 != v7 OR n3 <= v3) AND n1 = n2 )

SELECT n1, SUM(n5), COUNT(*) GROUP BY n1 ORDER BY -
SUM(n5) LIMIT 10
```

The key k used for the obfuscation of such a query consists of $c+1$ functions

$$\pi: \{1,2,\ldots,c\} \rightarrow \{1,2,\ldots,c\}, \; k_i: V_i \rightarrow V_{\pi(i)} \quad (1 \leq i \leq c)$$

(6)

chosen such that k_i is sum-preserving if SUM(ni) is in <ex 1>, and is order-preserving if either MAX(ni) is in <ex 1>, ni > v appears in <ex 2>, or ni appears in <ex 4>. The obfuscation function o_1 is given by

$$o_1: (k, \underline{x}) \rightarrow (y_i: 1 \leq i \leq c) \text{ such that for all } i, \ y_{\pi(i)} = k_i(x_i) \quad (7)$$

To calculate the query in an obfuscated form, an obfuscated query is performed on $o_1(k, \underline{x})$, where the obfuscated query f_1 (which depends on the original query and on k) is obtained by substituting each column name ni in the original query by nj where $j = \pi(i)$, and substituting each value v in the original query occurring in a substring of form ni = v or ni > v by the value $k_i(v)$. The answer $(ans_1, ..., ans_a)$ is then decrypted using function d, (which again depends on the original query and k), where

- $d(ans_1, ..., ans_a) = (d'(ans_1), ..., d'(ans_a))$,
- $d'(ans_j) = k_i^{-1}(ans_j)$ if the jth element of <ex 1> in the original query is ni, MAX(ni) or SUM(ni),
- $d'(ans_j) =$ is ans_j if the jth element of <ex 1> in the original query is COUNT(*).

It is straightforward to check that the result of this calculation is the same as the result of performing the original query on $\underline{x}$, so equation (1) holds.

Example 5: More Complicated SQL Query Obfuscation
In the previous example, the value of an entry in the obfuscated input database depended only on the value of one entry in the original database. It is possible to calculate selected SQL queries in an obfuscated fashion in such a way that the entries in some columns of the obfuscated database depend on multiple entries in the original database. As an example, consider the two queries

```
SELECT SUM(n2) WHERE n1 = v

SELECT n1 GROUP BY n1
```

and suppose that the values in column 1 of the original database are particularly sensitive, so for extra protection we want to avoid having any entry in the obfuscated database depend solely on an element in column 1 of the original database. Pick a key k consisting of $c+3$ one-to-one functions

$$\pi: \{1, ..c\} \rightarrow \{1, ...c\}, \ q: V_{\pi(1)} \rightarrow \{0,1\}, \ k_0: V_1 \rightarrow V_{\pi(1)},$$
$$k_i: V_i \rightarrow V_{\pi(i)}, \ 1 \leq i \leq c \quad (8)$$

where k_2 is chosen to be sum-preserving, and q can be expressed in the SQL query language. Set $m=1$ and define the obfuscation function o_1 by

$$o_1: (k, \underline{x}) \rightarrow (y_i: 1 \leq i \leq c) \text{ such that } y_{\pi(i)} = k_i(x_i) \text{ for all } i > 1,$$
$$y_{\pi(1)} = k_j(x_1) \text{ where } j = q(y_{\pi(2)}) \quad (9)$$

The same obfuscation function can be used for both queries. Write m1, m2 for the names of columns $\pi(1)$, $\pi(2)$, and w0, w1 for the values $k_0(v)$, $k_1(v)$. In the case of the first query, set f_1 to be the function calculating the query

```
SELECT SUM(m2) WHERE ((m1=w0 AND q(m2)=0) OR (m1=w1 AND
q(m2)=1))
```

and set d to be the function sending (k,y) to $k_2^{-1}(y)$. In the case of the second query, set f_1 to be the function calculating the query

```
SELECT m1, q(m2) GROUP BY m1, q(m2)
```

and set d to be the function which, given key k and a list of pairs $(y1,y2)$ with $y2$ in $\{0,1\}$, calculates $k_{y2}^{-1}(y1)$ for each pair in the list and returns a list of the unique results obtained. As for the other examples, it is straightforward to check that for both of the queries equation (1) holds (with $m=1$), so that the query is calculated in an obfuscated fashion.

In this section we have described various different obfuscation mechanisms that can be used by the Privacy Manager. Different functions, with varying degrees of obfuscation, can be specified within preferences available to the user via the Privacy Manager. This process can be made more intuitive via the use of personae, as described in Section 2. The following section provides an illustration of this approach which is fully implemented.

5 Online Photo Scenario

This section looks at a particular scenario, and describes how the privacy manager could operate in this scenario. In particular, we discuss the user interface for the privacy manager for this application.

5.1 Scenario: Cloud Photo Application

Vincent, a professional photographer and freelance writer for a geographic magazine, loves taking photographs, travelling, and writing articles. He is also a social man and likes to share his photos with family members and members of the photographic forums that he subscribes to.

Vincent recently bought a new professional digital camera with a built-in Global Positioning System (GPS) module, which provides a NMEA data stream from which the camera can extract the positional information (longitude and latitude) and record in the image metadata the location that the picture was taken. This feature helps him track and organize pictures geographically.

Vincent uses a commercial digital imaging web site to share his pictures online and order various products displaying his photos, such as postcards, T-shirts, and calendars. He likes the web site's simple and straightforward user interface. However, he soon realizes that the positional information contained in the pictures shot by his new camera may reveal the location of his house and his travel patterns, as such GPS information can be easily and accurately visualized in Google Earth.

With an increasing number of people using GPS-enabled cameras, the company owning the web site rolls out a new privacy manager assisting people to obfuscate certain metadata attributes which may reveal their private information – for example location information. By using this privacy manager, only the owner of the pictures can have access to the obfuscated attributes. The quality of the pictures is not affected. To demonstrate the scalability of our proposed obfuscation methods, we implemented two functions k_i for use in simple SQL query obfuscation (see example 4

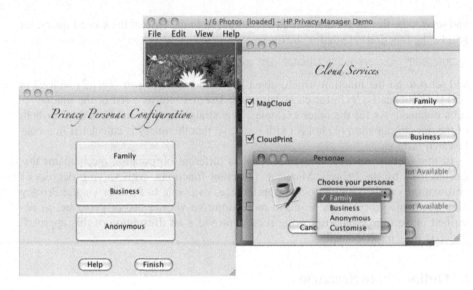

Fig. 4. Privacy Manager User Interface

of Section 4): *add*, which adds a secret number to an unencrypted numerical value, and *Caesar*, which does Caesar's Alphabet encryption using a secret alphabet order and shift value. Our implementation was not optimized for speed, but carried out 100,000 *add* calculations in 0.6s, and 100,000 *Caesar* calculations in 1.03s.

5.2 Privacy Manager User Interface

We have built a demonstrator of the use of the privacy manager within this scenario. The user interface for the privacy manager is shown in Figure 4. The end user selects the pictures that will be shared through certain cloud services. Specific personae, e.g. family, business, or anonymous, can be applied to obfuscate certain attributes associated with the pictures. The user can also customize the personae (i.e. choosing which attributes are to be obfuscated, and by which obfuscation methods) by changing the default settings via the privacy personae configuration window. By using the Privacy Manager, only the owner has control over the attributes, and the underlying obfuscation methods (as stated in Section 4) are transparent to the end users. Nevertheless, this method will not affect photo quality and still allows the photos to be further encrypted.

6 Previous Approaches to Privacy Management for Data Repositories

Since in this paper we are interested in managing the privacy of data which is sent to a database in the cloud, in this section we place this work in a wider context by reviewing previous general approaches to privacy management for data repositories, for which various techniques have been developed to ensure that stored data is accessed in a privacy compliant way.

Some mechanisms and solutions have been built to encrypt confidential data when it is stored in data repositories, for example solutions using Translucent Databases [28]. Most of these solutions focus on confidentiality and access control aspects, and have little flexibility in providing policy-driven mechanisms encompassing aspects beyond authentication and authorization. [29,30] describe access control policy-based encryption mechanisms for XML documents. [29] describes mechanisms for fine-grained encryption of parts of XML documents, in which decryption keys can either be granted to data receivers or collected from LDAP servers, based on data receivers' credentials. [30] focuses on related cryptographic mechanisms.

Hippocratic Databases [31] include mechanisms for preserving the privacy of the data they manage. Their proposed architecture is based on the concept of associating privacy metadata (i.e. privacy policies) to data stored in data repositories, along with mechanisms to enforce privacy. The drawback of this approach is that it might require substantial changes to current data repository architectures, and therefore might take a long time and require substantial investment (by all the involved parties) to succeed. In addition, this approach does not take into account that the management of privacy spans across the database boundaries: such management has to be carried out within a broader context within cloud computing.

Although now withdrawn from production, IBM Tivoli Privacy Manager [32] provided mechanisms for defining fine-grained privacy policies and associating them with data. The privacy policies contain authorization constraints along with constraints on contextual information and intent. This approach addressed the privacy management problem purely from an access control perspective within a single enterprise. It did not include additional aspects relevant for privacy management within cloud computing such as trust management and dealing with ongoing privacy obligations dictated by legislation and enterprises' guidelines.

An alternative approach is based on an adaptive privacy management system where data are retrieved from standard data repositories, and parts of these data are encrypted and associated with privacy policies [33]. This aims to make use of current data repository technologies and reduce to the minimum the impact on them, in terms of required changes: interactions with data repositories can still happen but in a way that confidential data is protected and contextually released, in a fine-grained way, based on the fulfilment of associated privacy policies.

7 Analysis and Next Steps

The current state of this work is that we have a working implementation of the obfuscation feature of the privacy manager, both for the online photo application described in this paper and for another scenario that we have implemented [13] which is based on SalesForce.com's sales force automation suite [34]. The techniques described in examples 5 and 6 of Section 4 are implemented within our code, and it would be relatively simple to extend this to implement the other examples. Our next steps are to extend this implementation to a greater range of cloud scenarios, including more complex ones.

Ideally, the privacy manager might be extended to allow consideration of trust assessment of third parties (risk management [35], reputation management [36], etc.), policy enforcement on service side (cf. sticky policies, involvement of Trust Authorities [11]), feedback and notification, subject data access requests, etc. We plan to consider these aspects in the EnCoRe project [37].

Our solution is not suitable for all cloud applications. Theoretically, as discussed in Section 4, *any* application which calculates a function of the input that can be expressed as a circuit could be calculated in a fully obfuscated fashion, if the service provider were willing to implement the application using Yao's protocol [19] or Gentry's encryption scheme [20]: however, the implementation of these for a large data set x may be impractical when resources are limited. For users with access to limited computing resources there is a tradeoff between the extent to which data is obfuscated and the set of applications that can effectively be used, even when the service provider gives full cooperation. Nevertheless, if the service provider cooperates then the other features of our solutions can still be used.

The picture is different if the service provider does not provide full cooperation. Some cloud service providers that base their business models on the sale of user data to advertisers (or other third parties) may not be willing to allow the user to use their applications in a way that preserves his privacy. Other providers may be willing to respect users' privacy wishes, but not to implement the service-side code that is necessary for some of the privacy manager's features. Yet other service providers may claim to cooperate, but not be trustworthy. In these cases, the features of our solution other than obfuscation will not be effective, since they require the honest cooperation of the service provider.

There is still a possibility that in these cases a user may be able to use obfuscation to protect the privacy of his data. However, the ability to use obfuscation without any cooperation from the service provider depends not only on the user having access to sufficient computing resources to carry out the obfuscation and de-obfuscation, but also on the application having been implemented in such a way that it will work with obfuscation. For example, a service that is customized with a map showing the area around a US user's zip code might theoretically be implemented in a way that would allow a user to obtain the correct customized result without revealing his zip code to the service provider. But a common method of implementing this type of service is to pass the input zip code directly to a map server, and mash up the map with the result from the rest of the service. With such an implementation it is difficult for the user to obtain the correct result without revealing the correct zip code to the application. As a more general example, for some applications it may be difficult to discover the set of input values that are treated as valid by the application. Without some knowledge of the set of valid inputs, it is not possible to design an obfuscation function such that the obfuscated input data is still valid input.

Despite this, we believe that many existing cloud services could be used in an obfuscated fashion without any cooperation from the service provider.

8 Conclusion and Acknowledgements

In conclusion, we have described a Privacy Manager and shown that this is a practical approach. We have also explored how the architecture would vary for different scenarios.

An earlier draft of this paper benefitted from helpful feedback from John Erickson and Guillaume Belrose.

References

1. Regulation of Investigatory Powers Act, Part II, s 28, UK (2000)
2. Uniting and Strengthening America by Providing Appropriate Tools Required to Intercept and Obstruct Terrorism (USA PATRIOT ACT) Act, Title V, s 505 (2001)
3. Organization for Economic Co-operation and Development (OECD): Guidelines Governing the Protection of Privacy and Transborder Flow of Personal Data. OECD, Geneva (1980)
4. EU Data Protection Directive (95/46/EC) (1995)
5. Salmon, J.: Clouded in uncertainty – the legal pitfalls of cloud computing. Computing magazine, September 24 (2008), http://www.computing.co.uk/computing/features/2226701/clouded-uncertainty-4229153
6. Mowbray, M.: The Fog over the Grimpen Mire: Cloud Computing and the Law. Scripted Journal of Law, Technology and Society 6(1) (April 2009)
7. Pearson, S. (ed.): Trusted Computing Platforms. Prentice-Hall, Englewood Cliffs (2002)
8. World Wide Web Consortium (W3C): Platform for Privacy Preferences (P3P) Project, http://www.w3.org/P3P
9. PRIME, Privacy and Identity Management for Europe, https://www.prime-project.eu/
10. Boneh, D., Franklin, M.: Identity-Based Encryption from the Weil Pairing. In: Goos, G., Hartmanis, J., van Leeuwen, J. (eds.) CRYPTO 2001. LNCS, vol. 2139, pp. 213–229. Springer, Heidelberg (2001)
11. Casassa Mont, M., Pearson, S., Bramhall, P.: Towards Accountable Management of Identity and Privacy: Sticky Policies and Enforceable Tracing Services. In: IEEE Workshop on Data and Expert Systems Applications, pp. 377–382. IEEE Computer Society Press, Washington (2003)
12. Casassa Mont, M., Thyne, R.: A systemic approach to automate privacy policy enforcement in enterprises. In: Danezis, G., Golle, P. (eds.) PET 2006. LNCS, vol. 4258, pp. 118–134. Springer, Heidelberg (2006)
13. Mowbray, M., Pearson, S.: A client-based privacy manager for cloud computing. In: COMSWARE 2009. ACM, New York (2009)
14. Trusted Computing Group: Trusted Platform Module (TPM) Specifications (2009), https://www.trustedcomputinggroup.org/specs/TPM/
15. Pearson, S.: Trusted Computing: Strengths, Weaknesses and Further Opportunities for Enhancing Privacy. In: Herrmann, P., Issarny, V., Shiu, S.C.K. (eds.) iTrust 2005. LNCS, vol. 3477, pp. 305–320. Springer, Heidelberg (2005)
16. Dalton, C., Plaquin, D., Weidner, W., Kuhlmann, D., Balacheff, B., Brown, R.: Trusted virtual platforms: a key enabler for converged client devices. In: ACM SIGOPS Operating Systems Review, vol. 43(1), pp. 36–43. ACM, New York (2009)

17. Gritzalis, D., Moulinos, K., Kostis, K.: A privacy-enhancing e-business model based on in-fomediaries. In: Gorodetski, V.I., Skormin, V.A., Popyack, L.J. (eds.) MMM-ACNS 2001. LNCS, vol. 2052, pp. 72–83. Springer, Heidelberg (2001)
18. Otemba project: The Reasons for Otemba's Existence, http://sourceforge.net/apps/trac/otemba/wiki/Reasons%20for%20existence
19. Yao, A.C.: How to Generate and Exchange Secrets. In: 27th Symposium of Foundations of Computer Science (FoCS), pp. 162–167. IEEE Press, New York (1986)
20. Gentry, C.: Fully Homomorphic Encryption Using Ideal Lattices. In: 41st ACM Symposium on Theory of Computing, Bethesda, Maryland, USA, May 31-June 2 (2009), pp. 169–178 (2009)
21. Boneh, D., Goh, E.-J., Nissim, K.: Evaluating 2-DNF formulas on ciphertexts. In: Kilian, J. (ed.) TCC 2005. LNCS, vol. 3378, pp. 325–341. Springer, Heidelberg (2005)
22. Lindell, Y., Pinkas, B.: Privacy Preserving Data Mining. J. Cryptology 15(3), 151–222 (2002)
23. Liu, K.: Privacy Preserving Data Mining Bibliography, http://www.cs.umbc.edu/~kunliu1/research/privacy_review.html
24. Dean, J., Ghemawat, S.: Map Reduce: Simplified data processing on large clusters. Communications of the ACM 51(1) (2008)
25. Date, C.J.: A guide to the SQL standard. Addison-Wesley Longman Publishing Co., Boston (1986)
26. Narayanan, A., Shmatikov, V.: Obfuscated Databases and Group Privacy. In: Proceedings of the 12th ACM conference on Computer and Communications Security, pp. 102–111
27. Rivest, R., Adelman, L., Dertouzos, M.L.: On data banks and privacy homomorphisms. In: DeMillo, R.A., et al. (eds.) Foundations of Secure Computation, pp. 168–179. Academic Press, New York (1978)
28. Amazon Web Services LLC: Case Studies: TC3 Health, http://aws.amazon.com/solutions/case-studies/tc3-health/
29. Wayner, P.: Translucent Databases, Flyzone Press (2002)
30. Bertino, E., Ferrari, E.: Secure and Selective Dissemination of XML Documents. In: Proc. TISSEC, pp. 290–331. ACM, New York (2002)
31. Miklau, G., Suciu, D.: Controlling Access to Published Data Using Cryptography. In: VLDB, VLDB Endowment (2003)
32. Agrawal, R., Kiernan, J., Srikant, R., Xu, Y.: Hippocratic databases. In: Proc. VLDB, VLDB Endowment, pp. 143-154 (2002)
33. IBM: IBM Tivoli Privacy Manager for e-Business (2009), http://www-01.ibm.com/software/tivoli/products/privacy-mgr-e-bus/
34. Casassa Mont, M., Pearson, S.: An Adaptive Privacy Management System for Data Repositories. In: Katsikas, S.K., López, J., Pernul, G. (eds.) TrustBus 2005. LMXS, vol. 3592, pp. 236–245. Springer, Heidelberg (2005)
35. Salesforce.com, Inc.: Sales Force Automation, http://www.salesforce.com/products/sales-force-automation/
36. Haimes, Y.Y.: Risk Modeling, Assessment, and Management. Systems, Man, and Cybernetics, Part C: Applications and Reviews 29(2), 315 (1999)
37. Despotovic, Z., Aberer, K.: P2P reputation management: Probabilistic estimation vs. social networks. Management in Peer-to-Peer Systems, Computer Networks 50(4), 485–500 (2006)
38. EnCoRe: EnCoRe: Ensuring Consent and Revocation, http://www.encore-project.info

Privacy in a Semantic Cloud: What's Trust Got to Do with It?

Åsmund Ahlmann Nyre and Martin Gilje Jaatun

SINTEF ICT, NO-7465 Trondheim, Norway
{Asmund.A.Nyre,Martin.G.Jaatun}@sintef.no
http://www.sintef.no/ses

Abstract. The semantic web can benefit from cloud computing as a platform, but for semantic technologies to gain wide adoption, a solution to the privacy challenges of the cloud is necessary. In this paper we present a brief survey on recent work on privacy and trust for the semantic web, and sketch a middleware solution for privacy protection that leverages probabilistic methods for automated trust and privacy management for the semantic web.

1 Introduction

Cloud Computing will be an enabler for the Semantic Web, e.g. by distributing analysis, transformation and querying of data [1]. The Semantic Web as envisioned by Berners-Lee et al. [2] represents a shift from machine readable data towards machine understandable data, allowing machines (e.g. agents) to make intelligent decisions based on the meaning of data on the web.

Similarly, securing the Semantic Web constitutes a shift from current security solutions relying on humans to perform intelligent decisions and assessments, to a semantic security solution where this can be done by automatic and autonomous agents. Providing a basis for such intelligence is assumed to be a highly difficult and complex task [3], but is nevertheless a prerequisite for the anticipated wider adoption of the Semantic Web and semantic technologies.

According to a recent survey on European citizens' perceptions on privacy [4], two-thirds of participants said to be concerned that organisations holding personal information would not handle them appropriately, which is the at the same level as the previous [5]. The survey also showed that four out of five EU citizens feel uneasy about transmitting personal data on the internet due to lack of security, while only one out of five said they used tools for technologies to increase the level of security. This indicates that there is a strong need for better and more reliant privacy control to combat the current threat, and an even stronger one for the future threats.

However, any such privacy enhancing technology is not anticipated to be implemented and deployed in operational environments without providing significant evidence of its correctness and fitness for use. This paper will sketch the first step in creating a privacy middleware for the Semantic Web to be adopted and deployed by the industry.

M.G. Jaatun, G. Zhao, and C. Rong (Eds.): CloudCom 2009, LNCS 5931, pp. 107–118, 2009.

The remainder of the paper is organised as follows. In section 2 we give a brief overview of existing approaches and solutions to privacy and trust and investigate the current challenges. Next, in section 3 we outline our approach to privacy enforcement through integrated trust and privacy management. Our solution is then discussed in Section 4, before we give our concluding remarks and outline further research in Section 5.

2   Foundations

Although practical security solutions for the semantic web remain elusive, there is an ample body of relevant security knowledge to draw upon. In the following we provide a brief survey on the state of the art of privacy and trust on the semantic web.

2.1   Privacy

The semantic web opens a whole new world of automated data collection and aggregation, surpassing current web searches by far in terms of precision. It is evident that privacy protection will be an absolute necessity for it to be accepted and fully utilised by end users.

Privacy Preferences and Policies. All major web sites with user interaction currently provide privacy policies describing how personal information will be handled. The fact that such policies are not understood (or even read) by users, served as one of the main motivations for the early Privacy Enhancing Technologies (PETs) [6,7,8]. The W3C recommendation Platform for Privacy Preferences (P3P) specification [8] utilises a mark-up language to allow websites to declare their privacy policy in a standardised fashion, which again allow user agents to display the policy in a way users can easily understand. P3P does not provide privacy on its own, but merely helps users make informed decisions about interacting with specific websites. Much of the criticism towards this specification [9] stems from the failure to adhere to privacy standards and regulations.

With semantically annotated policies, privacy negotiations may be conducted autonomously by agents. Several policy languages have been proposed for both security and privacy policy specification (e.g. [10,11,12]). By matching users' policies (or preferences) with web services' policies, privacy can be maintained automatically without the need for manual investigation. A review and comparison of current policy languages [13] suggest that policy languages in general are quite expressive, but further work is required especially for improved usage control and minimal information disclosure. Another point being made is the need for user-friendly interfaces and the ability to adapt to changing preferences and requirements.

Privacy through Anonymity. A way to protect one's privacy is to remain anonymous, e.g. by providing only non-identifiable information. This is common in the health sector, where e.g. medical status needs to be published in a way so that the patient's identity is not revealed. K-anonymity [14] is one approach to restrict semi-identifiable information such that at least K subjects share any combination. Other approaches include general anonymity, pseudo anonymity and trap-door anonymity. Pseudo anonymity refers to situations where the identity of users are not their real identity (e.g. usernames, subscriber ID, etc) and thereby provide protection from entities that do not know the link between the pseudonym and the real identity. To be anonymous, a user must not identify herself with anything that can link information from different sources.

However, for some types of services, e.g. online social networks (Facebook, LinkedIn, etc.), the benefit is greatly reduced if identity information is not provided. Anonymity is therefore not the answer to all privacy problems.

Privacy Regulations. Unlike other security mechanisms, privacy is also protected by law. Hence, any privacy policy (and preference) should be according to the privacy legislation of the given country. EU directives on privacy protection [15,16] place requirements on member states' legislation as to how personal information is stored, handled and shared. The P3P specification has been criticised for its lack of support for such legislation. The architecture proposed in [17] uses the principles from the EU directives as a foundation for its legislation compliance. The architecture is capable of mediating between users, websites and legislation, to ensure that all parties' requirements are satisfied. While most privacy enhancing technologies are focused solely on protecting personal information explicitly given by users, this architecture is determined to protect both active data (controlled by user, e.g. credentials), semi-active data (partly controlled by user, e.g. sensor data) and passive data (uncontrolled by user, e.g. surveillance cameras).

Privacy through Usage Control. Park and Sandhu [18] proposed the generic UCON usage control model aimed at being generic enough to encompass both traditional access control, Digital Rights Management (DRM) and trust management. As noted by the authors, privacy management (i.e. controlling personal information) may be seen as the reversed version of DRM; where users are placing restrictions on service providers' use of information. The basic model is built up of subjects, objects, rights, authorisations, obligations and conditions. Subjects and objects are similar to that of other access control mechanisms, with the distinction that their attributes may be mutable, i.e. they may change due to access requests. Rights are not considered static and the existence of a certain right or privilege is determined by a usage decision function upon requesting to invoke it. Authorisations determine whether the subject is allowed to perform the requested operation on the object. Obligations refer to the mandatory requirements a subject must fulfil before or during usage while conditions describe how environmental or system status may influence usage decisions.

Privacy Policy Enforcement. The current web provides no means of controlling information after it has been published. Anything on the web is visible by all, and is generally hard (or even impossible) to remove. Thus, the best privacy policy would be never to make personal information available to anyone. However, that would also greatly reduce the usefulness of the web, especially the interactive, user-driven services.

Policy enforcement has traditionally (e.g. for access control) been done by a central entity, typically the provider. However, with distributed information and ubiquitous environments, the information provider might be required to enforce restrictions on remote devices. Realising this, Sandhu et al. [19] propose a client-side enforcement strategy based on trusted computing and Privacy Enforcement Implementation (PEI) models.

The approach taken by Lioudakis et al. [17] is to establish a privacy infrastructure similar to that of public keys (PKI). Service providers implement a Discrete Box functioning as a privacy proxy for end-users. Whether to grant requests for personal information is handled by the containing Policy Decision Point and Policy Enforcement Point (PDP/PEP) of the Discrete Box. Policies considered for such a decision include both statutory, service provider and user policies. The idea is that the service provider's privacy proxy guarantees that all applicable policies (regardless of origin) are met whenever access to personal information is granted. To prevent misbehaving privacy proxies, the infrastructure is equipped with a set of Privacy Authorities to supervise service providers' adherence to general legislation, user policies and their own specific policies. There are apparent similarities with the Certificate Authority required for the X.509 Certificate infrastructure [20]. Additionally, when applied to the semantic web, each user agent must have its own privacy proxy (Discrete Box), which is a major challenge in terms of scalability.

As stated earlier, the P3P specification [8] offers no enforcement guarantees, and hence the user must determine on its own whether to trust the service provider to adhere to its own policy.

Commercially available privacy management systems (e.g. IBM's Enterprise Privacy Architecture) assume centralised data storage, which leaves them unable to cope with distributed data on the semantic web. The system proposed by Song et al. [21], utilises social networks as a model to control private data flow within enterprises, not across organisational boundaries.

2.2   Trust Management

Trust, and more specifically trust management, has received considerable attention from security researchers over the past years [22], apparently without being able to make a definite impact on services that are actually deployed on the internet.

The problem with *trust* is that it takes various meanings in various contexts. In a PKI, a certificate is said to be trusted if the link between the owner entity (e.g. user) and the public key is either known in advance, or is confirmed by a trusted entity. On the current web, the content of a web page is assumed to be trusted if it is provided by a trusted source (as seen by the user). What constitutes a trusted source, is not trivially explained.

Definitions. Trust is not easily defined and many definitions exist both within computer science and social sciences [23,24,25]. Mayer et al. [24] state that organisational studies dealing with trust has been hampered by lack of consensus on contributing factors, trust itself and outcomes of trust. This is supported by a survey of organisational trust [25] and a computer science counterpart [23] where several definitions of trust are listed based on different factors and viewpoints. The common factors of these definitions are vulnerability and risk, implying that the trustor must be vulnerable to the actions of the trustee and that the inherent risk is recognised and accepted in order to call it trust. Mayer et al. argue that it is the recognition of risk that separates trust from confidence, where the latter does not consciously consider the risk involved. Cooperation is another factor that may be both a contributing factor and an outcome of trust. Trust may result in cooperation and cooperation may result in trust, but they are not dependent on one another. Entities may be forced to cooperate without any trust relation. Similarly, predictability of entities may be a contributing factor of trust, however only if performance is satisfactory. If always performing badly, predictability may lead to decreased trust [24].

We choose to use the definition from [24] where trust is defined as *the willingness of a party to be vulnerable to the actions of another party based on the expectation that the other will perform a particular action important to the trustor, irrespective of the ability to monitor and control that other party.*

Trust Models. As with trust definitions; several different trust models have been proposed over the years, covering different aspects and views of trust. Many of the models that have been proposed have been targeting a very specific use (e.g. e-commerce) and therefore have sacrificed completeness for simplicity, while others have attempted to specify general and somewhat complex trust models.

Mayer et al. [24] focused on a general model. They viewed a trust relation as dependent on the trustor's willingness to trust and the trustworthiness of the trustee (as seen by the trustor). The main factors of trustworthiness were identified as ability, benevolence and integrity. On the trustor's part, disposition to trust and perceived risk were identified as the most influential factors with regards to trust. Furthermore, the outcome of a trust relation (experience) is assumed to influence one or more of the trustworthiness factors and hence the trustworthiness of the trustee.

The work by Marsh [26] was an early attempt to establish a formalism for trust in computer science in general, and artificial intelligence in particular. The formalism allows agents to compute a trust value based on a set of factors in order to arrive at a trust decision automatically. The complexity of the model makes it difficult to use in practise, however as inspiration the model has contributed greatly to advances in research on trust.

Acknowledging that the complexity of several proposed models does not necessarily give better trust assessments, Conrad et al. [27] proposed a lightweight model for trust propagation. The parameters self confidence, experience, hearsay and prejudice are used to model and assess trust. This computational model also allows agents to compute a trust value to automatically perform trust decisions.

The degree of self confidence determines how much influence own experience and hearsay would have on the computed trust value. The prejudice determines the initial value of experience and hearsay, before experience is accumulated.

In the model proposed by Gil and Artz [28] the idea is to arrive at content trust, where the information itself is used for trust calculation. This allows for a whole new range of parameters (such as bias, criticality, appearance, etc.) to be used when assessing trust in resources. The problem of such parameters is that they require user input, which conflicts with the assumption of agents conducting the assessment autonomously.

Trust Propagation. Golbeck and Hendler [29] describe an algorithm for inferring trust and reputation in social networks when entities are not connected directly by a trust relationship. This is done by computing the weighted distance from the source to the sink. Any distrusted entity is not included in the computation since the trust assessments done by such entities are worthless. Guha et al. [30] introduce the notion of distrust to address the problem of expressing explicit distrust as a contrast to the absence of trust. Absence of trust may come from lack of information to conduct a proper trust assessment, while distrust expresses that a proper assessment have been conducted and that the entity should not be trusted. Furthermore, they argue that distrust could also be propagated and proposes several propagation models in addition to trust transitivity, including co-citation, which is extensively used for web searches.

Huang and Fox [31] claim that not all kinds of trust can be assumed to be transitive. They note that trust based on performance, i.e. an entity performing as expected repeatedly, is not necessarily transitive, while trust based on a belief that the entity will perform as expected often is.

3   Probabilistic Privacy Policy Enforcement

From the discussions above we know that some of the proposed PETs assume that entities will always adhere to and enforce their own policies, either because they are trusted or because there is an infrastructure in place that would not allow them to misbehave. As a consequence, enforcement is seen as binary, either it is done or it is not.

While assuming that all entities will enforce relevant policies is clearly not a good idea, there are quite some difficulties involved in relying on trusted computing for guarantees.

1. Trusted computing requires an infrastructure (hardware and software) for it to work. Hence, any entity that does not comply with this not allowed to take part.
2. Trusted third parties are needed and are not easily established. Although some have been successfully established for the X.509 Public Key Infrastructure, it is not generally viewed as an unconditional success [32].
3. There may be situations where users do want to communicate with entities not part of the privacy infrastructure, even though this would generally

conflict with their privacy requirements. Users would therefore be forced to disable any PET functionality in order to do this.

4. With any such system, there is a critical mass of users/providers that must be attained before users will view investments in such tools beneficial.

Example 1. Consider three websites; one evil, one benign and one somewhere in between (probably owned by Google). All provide a privacy policy, possibly very different from one another. Using mere policies, no distinction is made as to the level of trust to be placed in the websites' adherence to their policies, i.e. there is no enforcement. Using trusted computing, only the benign website will be included in the infrastructure, and hence communication with possibly misbehaving websites are impossible (using privacy management).

A user may want to interact with such shady websites despite warnings of misbehaviour and would therefore greatly benefit from a privacy technology that would:

1. Alert the user of the trustworthiness of the website.
2. Record the user's willingness to interact and the willingness to (potentially) be vulnerable to exploit.
3. Provide means to mitigate the risk and calculate criticality and consequence of interaction (e.g. distribution of personal data).
4. Provide anonymity where where appropriate.

We therefore propose a probabilistic approach to policy enforcement, where users are given a probability that their requirements will be respected and polices enforced. Thus when interacting with websites who are known to be less trustworthy, policy adherence is given by a probability metric that the website will actually enforce its own policies. Our enforcement model does not include a privacy or trust model, i.e. it is only occupied with how to handle uncertainty in enforcement and provide a tool for interacting with non-conforming entities while minimising the risks involved.

3.1   Personal Data Recorder

The semantic web offers great opportunities for information aggregation, which is generally difficult to protect oneself from.

Example 2. Consider the situation where a user wanting to stay unidentified has provided his postal code and anonymous e-mail address to a website. Later he also provides age and given name (not the full name) and the anonymous e-mail address. Now, the website is able to combine the data (postal code, age and given name) to identify the anonymous user.

Protecting users from this kind of aggregation requires complete control of what information has been distributed and to whom. In our scheme, this is done by the Personal Data Recorder (PDR), which basically records what data is transmitted to which receivers. Thus in the above example, the second interaction with the website should have been blocked, since it enables the website to reveal the user's identity. The PDR allows the user to view himself through the eyes of the receiving party, and thereby perform aggregation to see whether too much information is provided.

3.2   Personal Data Monitor

The personal data monitor (PDM) is responsible for computing and assessing policies and behaviour, and to update the personal data recorder with inferred knowledge. A problem with the PDR is that it is not capable of handling re-distribution of data (receiver forwards the data to other recipients). However, all personal data are assumed accompanied by a privacy policy and obligations. Using the probabilistic privacy enforcement described earlier, the PDM is able to compute the probability that the receiving entity is redistributing information. That is, the PDM will determine the likelihood that the personal information distributed to the receiver will also reach other. This need not be criminal or shady activity either, it is actually quite common in business life. For instance, sending an e-mail with a business proposition to a specific employee of a company, it is likely that other employees in that company also will receive the e-mail (e.g. his superior). The PDM is in such a case responsible for inferring other recipients and to include such information in the Personal Information Base.

Information that is made publicly available on the Internet, would generally be considered to be available to all. Hence, any interaction later on should consider this information when assessing the kind of information to reveal.

3.3   Trust Assessment Engine

The Trust Assessment Engine (TAE) is responsible for calculating trust values of different entities in order to determine their trustworthiness. The TAE is thus focused solely on assessing communicating parties and does not take into account risk willingness, vulnerability and criticality.

3.4   Trust Monitor

The trust monitor (TM) is responsible for detecting events that might affect the perceived trustworthiness and the willingness to take risks. The trust monitor is thus responsible for calculating and deciding on what is an acceptable trust level, given the circumstances. Any computed trust value and feedback received from cooperating entities is stored in the trust assessment repository.

3.5   Policy Decision Point

The Policy Decision Point (PDP) is responsible for the final decision on whether to engage in information exchange and if so; under what conditions. The PDP collects the views of both the TM and the PDM and compares their calculations to the policies and requirements found in the policy repository. The decision is reported back to the TM and PDM to allow recalculation in case the decision alters the calculated trust values or distribution of personal information.

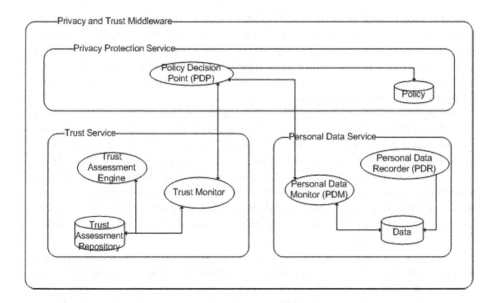

Fig. 1. Middleware architecture for probabilistic privacy management

4 Discussion

The practical application of Privacy Enhancing Technologies is limited by the human cognitive capacity – or rather, the lack thereof. However, even on the semantic web, information is ultimately communicated from one human to another, and thus if we want to apply trust to this equation, we have to base ourselves on human notions of trust, which are neither binary nor straight-forward.

In fact, the word "trust" is used to mean many things even in a human context, and is often misunderstood when applied to end-user applications. One example is the Pretty Good Privacy (PGP) program, which allows users to collect public keys of friends and associates, and subsequently assign a "trust level" to these keys. A common misconception is that this trust level reflects on the degree of certainty that the given key is the correct key for that particular associate; while in reality it reflects to which degree the user is willing to trust *other* keys signed by that particular associate. These concepts are quite different: While I am confident that I have the right key for my friend Bob on my computer, I also know that Bob is a fool who at regular intervals is sending money to Nigerian princesses, and also freely signs any key that comes his way.

Our proposed middleware relies heavily on the Personal Data Recorder, but it is clear that this element will not be able to cope with passive data collection; in a real-life example, this would require you to e.g. carry a device that could detect all surveillance cameras and record what they capture of your movements. However, since the possibilities for aggregation are so abundant on the semantic web, it is vital that any new PET takes steps to limit unnecessary information spread.

In one way, it may seem that a PET application that introduces anonymous or pseudonymous data would be anathema to the semantic web, since nobody wants inaccurate or false data in their system. However, we do not advocate that information that a person *wants* to be disseminated should be anonymised, but rather that the user should be in control of her own information (as in the spirit of European privacy legislation).

One might argue that it would be better if the option to remain anonymous were offered by the various providers, but currently it seems that the providers have no incentive for offering such an option – to the contrary, providers seem to want to go to great lengths to collect as much information as possible. If we want to be able to communicate with whomever we want, but still want to have protection against aggregation, it seems the only solution is to lie. Since most humans are bad liars, our privacy middleware will help users to "lie" consistently, allowing them to reap the benefits of the semantic web and cloud computing without sacrificing their privacy.

However, as already mentioned, there are circumstances when use of a service precludes anonymity – e.g. when ordering a book from Amazon.com, you *have* to provide a valid postal address, or you will never receive your purchase. Thus the trust aspect of the middleware is used to automatically determine which information is necessary to divulge, and performing a risk calculation. Combined with the personal data recorder, there are multiple opportunities for automatic extensions, e.g. calculating the impact of mergers (when your local Mom & Pop bookstore is acquired by Waldenbooks) or changes in privacy policies.

5   Conclusion and Further Work

In this paper we have outlined existing approaches to privacy and trust management and the fundamental challenges of the emerging semantic web. We have proposed a new way of handling policy enforcement remotely, based on computing the probability that the recipient will adhere to the established policies. The probability is computed on the basis of trust assertions, user's willingness to trust, and the personal information involved. We believe that such an approach would facilitate a gradual deployment of software since it may prove beneficial to users, regardless of whether other users have adopted it.

We acknowledge that these are early thoughts and that proper justification and simulations should be provided before the benefits of our proposed approach can be rightfully claimed. In particular, a more detailed description of how the Personal Data Recorder and Personal Data Monitor should be designed to meet the goals stated is an important subject for further research. Also, the interface between a trust management system and the personal data service needs to be properly specified to clearly separate the responsibilities of the two, so as to allow for different trust management systems to be utilised. Verification of the approach through simulation or user-testing forms a natural next step.

References

1. Mika, P., Tummarello, G.: Web semantics in the clouds. IEEE Intelligent Systems 23, 82–87 (2008)
2. Berners-Lee, T., Hendler, J., Lassila, O.: The semantic web. Scientific America, 34–43 (2001)
3. Bussler, C.: Is semantic web technology taking the wrong turn? Internet Computing, IEEE 12, 75–79 (2008)
4. Data protection in the european union - citizens' perceptions. Flash Eurobarometer 225, The Gallup Organization (2008)
5. Data protection. Special Eurobarometer 192, European Opinion Research Group EEIG (2003)
6. Burkert, H.: Privacy-enhancing technologies: typology, critique, vision. In: Agre, P., Rotenberg, M. (eds.) Technology and Privacy: The New Landscape, pp. 125–142. MIT Press, Cambridge (1997)
7. Goldberg, I., Wagner, D., Brewer, E.: Privacy-enhancing technologies for the internet. In: Proc. of 42nd IEEE Spring COMPCON. IEEE Computer Society Press, Los Alamitos (1997)
8. Cranor, L., Langheinrich, M., Marchiori, M., Reagle, J.: The platform for privacy preferences 1.0 (p3p1.0) specification. W3C Recommendation (2002)
9. EPIC: Pretty poor privacy: An assessment of p3p and internet privacy. Technical report, Electronic Privacy Information Center (2000)
10. Kagal, L., Finin, T., Joshi, A.: A policy based approach to security for the semantic web. In: Fensel, D., Sycara, K., Mylopoulos, J. (eds.) ISWC 2003. LNCS, vol. 2870, pp. 402–418. Springer, Heidelberg (2003)
11. Bonatti, P., Olmedilla, D.: Driving and monitoring provisional trust negotiation with metapolicies. In: Sixth IEEE International Workshop on Policies for Distributed Systems and Networks, pp. 14–23 (2005)
12. Damianou, N., Dulay, N., Lupu, E., Sloman, M.: The ponder policy specification language. In: Sloman, M., Lobo, J., Lupu, E.C. (eds.) POLICY 2001. LNCS, vol. 1995, pp. 18–38. Springer, Heidelberg (2001)
13. Duma, C., Herzog, A., Shahmehri, N.: Privacy in the semantic web: What policy languages have to offer. In: Eighth IEEE International Workshop on Policies for Distributed Systems and Networks, POLICY 2007, pp. 109–118 (2007)
14. Sweeney, L.: K-Anonymity: a model for protecting privacy. International Journal on Uncertainty, Fuzziness and Knowledge-based Systems 10, 557–570 (2002)
15. EU: Directive 2002/58/ec of the european parliament and of the council concerning the processing of personal data and the protection of privacy in the electronic communications sector. Official Journal of the European Communities (2002)
16. EU: Directive 95/46/ec of the european parliament and of the council of 24 october 1995 on the protection of individuals with regard to the processing of personal data and on the free movement of such data. Official Journal of the European Communities (1995)
17. Lioudakis, G.V., Koutsoloukas, E.A., Dellas, N.L., Tselikas, N., Kapellaki, S., Prezerakos, G.N., Kaklamani, D.I., Venieris, I.S.: A middleware architecture for privacy protection. Computer Networks 51, 4679–4696 (2007)
18. Park, J., Sandhu, R.: The UCON$_{ABC}$ usage control model. ACM Transactions on Information Systems Secuity 7, 128–174 (2004)
19. Sandhu, R., Zhang, X., Ranganathan, K., Covington, M.J.: Client-side access control enforcement using trusted computing and PEI models. Journal of High Speed Networks 15, 229–245 (2006)

20. Housley, R., Polk, W., Ford, W., Solo, D.: RFC 3280: Internet X.509 Public Key Infrastructure Certificate and Certificate Revocation List (CRL) Profile. RFC Editor (2002)
21. Song, R., Korba, L., Yee, G.: Privacy management system using social networking. In: Korba, L. (ed.) IEEE International Conference on Systems, Man and Cybernetics, ISIC, pp. 3327–3332 (2007)
22. Varadharajan, V.: A note on Trust-Enhanced security. Security & Privacy, IEEE 7, 57–59 (2009)
23. Artz, D., Gil, Y.: A survey of trust in computer science and the semantic web. Web Semantics: Science, Services and Agents on the World Wide Web 5, 58–71 (2007)
24. Mayer, R., Davis, J., Schoorman, F.: An integrative model of organizational trust. Academy of Management Review 2, 709–734 (1995)
25. Bigley, G., Pearce, J.: Straining for shared meaning in organization science: Problems of trust and distrust. Academy of Management Review 23, 405–421 (1998)
26. Marsh, S.P.: Formalizing Trust as a Computational Concept. PhD thesis, Department of Comuting Science and Mathematics, University of Sterling (1994)
27. Conrad, M., French, T., Huang, W., Maple, C.: A lightweight model of trust propagation in a multi-client network environment: to what extent does experience matter? In: The First International Conference on Availability, Reliability and Security, ARES 2006, 6 p. (2006)
28. Gil, Y., Artz, D.: Towards content trust of web resources. In: WWW 2006: Proceedings of the 15th international conference on World Wide Web, pp. 565–574. ACM, New York (2006)
29. Golbeck, J., Hendler, J.: Accuracy of metrics for inferring trust and reputation in semantic web-based social networks. In: Motta, E., Shadbolt, N.R., Stutt, A., Gibbins, N. (eds.) EKAW 2004. LNCS (LNAI), vol. 3257, pp. 116–131. Springer, Heidelberg (2004)
30. Guha, R., Kumar, R., Raghavan, P., Tomkins, A.: Propagation of trust and distrust. In: WWW 2004: Proceedings of the 13th international conference on World Wide Web, pp. 403–412. ACM, New York (2004)
31. Huang, J., Fox, M.S.: An ontology of trust: formal semantics and transitivity. ACM, New York (2006)
32. Lopez, J., Oppliger, R., Pernul, G.: Why have public key infrastructures failed so far? Internet Research 15, 544–556 (2005)

Data Protection-Aware Design for Cloud Services

Sadie Creese[1], Paul Hopkins[1], Siani Pearson[2], and Yun Shen[2]

[1] International Digital Laboratory, University of Warwick, Coventry, UK.
[2] HP Labs, Long Down Avenue, Bristol, UK. BS34 8QZ
{Sadie.Creese,P.D.Hopkins}@warwick.ac.uk,
{Siani.Pearson,Yun.Shen}@hp.com

Abstract. The Cloud is a relatively new concept and so it is unsurprising that the information assurance, data protection, network security and privacy concerns have yet to be fully addressed. This paper seeks to begin the process of designing data protection controls into clouds from the outset so as to avoid the costs associated with bolting on security as an afterthought. Our approach is firstly to consider cloud maturity from an enterprise level perspective, describing a novel capability maturity model. We use this model to explore privacy controls within an enterprise cloud deployment, and explore where there may be opportunities to design in data protection controls as exploitation of the Cloud matures. We demonstrate how we might enable such controls via the use of design patterns. Finally, we consider how Service Level Agreements (SLAs) might be used to ensure that third party suppliers act in support of such controls.

Keywords: Data protection, information security, privacy, cloud computing, design pattern, capability maturity model.

1 Introduction

Cloud computing offers a utility model for IT, enabling users to access applications, middleware and hardware via the Internet as opposed to owning it themselves. The vision for the Cloud is one where applications, platforms and infrastructure can all be consumed as and when required. The ability to rapidly scale-up and scale-down is perceived by many to directly lead to cost savings. Other benefits include fast access to new applications, easier ability to try things out before large-scale investment and staying on the leading edge. 'Cloud nirvana' is a future where cloud service providers (SPs) utilise the cloud to deliver dynamic capability enhancements, resources are switched on and off like taps, and users can switch suppliers quickly in order to access the best solution on the market. Current expectations of the market potential remain high, with Gartner predicting a services market value of $150bn by 2013 [1].

The adoption of cloud services will vary across enterprises and users. Early take-up appears to be within the technology sector with other potential users voicing concerns surrounding security and privacy of data. Undoubtedly, any model which involves data assets residing on equipment not within users' immediate control needs to address security and privacy. In 'cloud nirvana' environments this will only become more

M.G. Jaatun, G. Zhao, and C. Rong (Eds.): CloudCom 2009, LNCS 5931, pp. 119–130, 2009.

acute, and potentially more challenging. Current recommendations and approaches to information security in the cloud are essentially based on today's best practice surrounding traditional outsourcing. Certainly, this is an obvious and valid starting point, and one which is recognised by those operating in the data-centre and secure-hosted service space, since they already possess the relationships, infrastructure, and business models which could easily be extended into a cloud service domain.

However, the cloud vision does offer some particularly challenging privacy problems that are unlikely to be sufficiently addressed by today's best practice [2]. Privacy can be thought of as a human right that is rather complex to analyse [3]. We focus in this paper on the issue of privacy in the sense of data protection (processing of data on identifiable living people), as defined by Directive 95/46/EC [4]. There are differing interpretations of what this may mean in a practical sense, since users of cloud services are likely to have varying expectations of confidentiality, control, and service responsiveness in response to their changing privacy requirements. The protection of these expectations will be met to equally varying degrees by the legal and regulatory structures in operation, which in themselves could vary as a cloud service could transcend national boundaries.

We seek here to begin addressing whether there are opportunities to *design-in* data protection during this cloud start-up phase, so avoiding costly future bolt-ons and suboptimal protection resulting from design decisions in conflict with data protection needs. We cannot provide a complete treatment in a paper of this size; instead we focus on three aspects of the cloud deployment lifecycle: Firstly, we consider cloud adoption at the enterprise level and the likely maturity characteristics, developing a novel capability maturity model for enterprises exploiting cloud services. We use this maturity model as a basis for identifying opportunities for designing in privacy, and capture this analysis in a privacy maturity model. Secondly, we consider the design stage for a cloud service and how we might use design patterns to enable enterprises to adopt data protection design principles. Finally, we consider how the use of third party suppliers of cloud services might impact upon privacy, and how the associated risks might be mitigated via the use of Service Level Agreements (SLAs).

2 Related Work

Whilst there is no existing published work directly considering how to develop mechanisms for designing in data protection controls in the cloud, there are a range of work areas upon which our research is based. We discuss these here.

The point of a *capability maturity model* (CMM) is generally to understand the maturity of organisations through various characteristics: see [5] for detailed definition and history. Such maturity models can help facilitate process development and enterprise evolution by identifying maturity milestones and benchmarks for comparison. Thus, it is possible to plan, prioritise and invest in order to progress along the maturity model until the most effective and beneficial state is achieved for the enterprise. It should be noted that it is unlikely always to be the case that a higher maturity leads to greater profit in a commercial organisation, or that cloud deployment makes sense for every application (see [6]). By considering a maturity model for cloud exploitation we hope to identify the key developmental stages for a number of enterprise characteristics, which in turn will have implications for information security and data protection strategies. Hence it may be possible to anticipate future needs and begin delivering techniques for architecting data-protection aware clouds. A number of Cloud maturity models have been proposed, for example see [7,8,9]. In [7] a cloud maturity model is presented that is specifically aimed at data centres. Whilst it offers inspiration when considering a model for exploitation of cloud by an enterprise, it cannot be directly applied. Wardley [9] implies that to achieve cloud maturity the following are likely to exist (accumulatively as maturity grows): resilient architecture, SLAs, an option to run the service in-house, evidential portability between SPs, third party assurance and monitoring of services, a marketplace of providers with easy switching, third party management of cloud market exploitation. However, as for [7], the detail is missing.

Dr. Dobb's Jake Sorofman [8] proposes a slightly different model where: the lowest level of cloud maturity involves adoption of virtualisation for seamless portability of applications and a shared server infrastructure; level two is cloud experimentation where a cloud is deployed (internally or externally) based on controlled and bounded deployments; level three is cloud foundations where governance, controls, procedures, policies and best practice begin to form initially focused on internal and non-mission critical applications; level four cloud advancement sees the scaling up of the volume of cloud applications and broad-based deployments; and level five is cloud actualisation where dynamic workload balancing occurs across multiple utility clouds and applications are distributed based on cloud capacity, cost and proximity to users. This does not break down maturity across enterprise characteristics, but is the closest to what we require and, in combination with a detailed capability model for service-oriented architectures (SOAs) designed by IBM (see [10]) forms the foundation upon which we design our new capability maturity model for cloud.

Privacy design techniques are not a new concept: various companies, notably Microsoft [11], have produced detailed privacy design guidelines. Cannon has described processes and methodologies about how to integrate privacy considerations and engineering into the development process [12]. Privacy design guidelines in specific areas are given in [13,14], and [2] considers the case of cloud computing. In November 2007 the UK Information Commissioners Office (ICO) [15] (an organisation responsible for regulating and enforcing access to and use of personal information), launched a Privacy Impact Assessment (PIA) [15] process (incorporating privacy by design) to help organizations assess the impact of their operations on personal privacy. This process assesses the privacy requirements of new and existing systems; it is primarily intended for use in public sector risk management, but is increasingly seen to be of value to private sector businesses that process personal data. Similar methodologies exist and can have legal status in Australia, Canada and the USA [16]. This methodology aims to combat the slow take-up to design in privacy protections from first principles at the enterprise level, see [17] for further discussion, [18] for further background, and [19] for a useful classification system for online privacy.

However, whilst there is a body of privacy design guidelines, there exist no practical techniques for designing specifically for cloud environments. To do this we choose to focus on the utility of *design patterns* [20]. We believe that in some circumstances they could be useful since the use-cases that drive cloud computing are familiar ones and so design patterns to fit these can be produced [21]. Some previous work has been carried out in the privacy design pattern area, but not for cloud computing:

[22] describes four design patterns that can aide the decision making process for the designers of privacy protecting systems. These design patterns are applicable to the design of anonymity systems for various types of online communication, online data sharing, location monitoring, voting and electronic cash management and do not address use within an enterprise.

3   Cloud Capability Maturity Model

We begin by considering capability maturity for enterprises exploiting clouds, considering a number of key characteristics: business strategy, governance, procurement methods, applications, information and information security.

Table 1. Capability Maturity Model for Cloud Computing

	Level 1 Initial Services	Level 2 Architected Services	Level 3 Aligned and responsive	Level 4 Measurable	Level 5 Optimised and Dynamically Reconfigurable
Business Perspective	Componentised business units	Strategy and vision for broad adoption across business	Cloud services integrated across business	Impact of cloud on business lines measured	Multiple cloud suppliers used, seamless transition
Cloud Governance	Due diligence of external suppliers	Based on best practice	Cloud and enterprise practice / processes aligned	Compliance metrics established and applied	Dynamically monitored and enforced
Procurement Methods	Standard contractual arrangements utilised	Best practice in cloud procurement adopted, SLAs emerging	Support team established, common service environment, automated SLAs	Cloud procurement cycles measured for deployment efficiency and consumption	Dynamic and changing SLAs and optimisation
Cloud Applications	Additional functionality and siloed applications	Applications enable new enterprise activities	Process integration across enterprise, enhanced productivity	Cloud applications measured for impact	Bespoke and dynamically changing service offerings
Information Perspective	Cloud services offer information based applications to silos	Enterprise service meta-data available	Single enterprise ontology, shared with partners to enhance delivery	Cloud based information services measured for quality	Information services evolving in response to changing enterprise strategy
Infosec	Monitoring and control at gateway and enterprise network boundary	SLAs include infosec, idm across the enterprise and in cloud	Monitoring and auditability integrated across enterprise	Cloud infosec measured for impact on risks	Auto enforcement of changing cloud infosec strategies, multi-level security in place
	quick-win	*business-wide benefits*	*clear alignment between enterprise and suppliers*	*mature deployment and significant gains*	*leader in cloud capabilities*

We present our capability maturity model for enterprises exploiting cloud services in Table 1 above. Level 1 represents today's environment where users of cloud services are adopting offerings to enable additional functionality, and controlling the risks via standard outsourcing risk management processes. The cloud service is consumed within a business unit and is typically siloed off from the rest of the enterprise. Information security is focused at the perimeter. At Level 2 best practice begins to emerge surrounding the adoption of cloud services within an enterprise, and the enterprise begins to roll out a broader adoption strategy. This in turn generates enterprise level metadata which underpins new information based services. At Level 3 cloud and other business processes become aligned, enabling a more integrated management activity. This in turn delivers enhanced productivity. It also facilitates a single enterprise cloud ontology, which when shared with partners and suppliers can directly enhance delivery. The importance of cloud to the enterprise results in a dedicated support function being maintained within the enterprise. The information security function delivers monitoring and audibility across the enterprise. At Level 4 the impact of cloud on the enterprise becomes measurable, compliance metrics are established and services and applications are measured for quality. Information security functions for cloud are also measured for impact on the overall risk mitigation strategy. At Level 5 cloud services become dynamically reconfigurable in response to the increased awareness delivered by the various metrics and changing operating requirements. Governance mechanisms can be dynamically monitored and enforced. Procurement methods become dynamic, with SLAs requiring an agile and perhaps automated solution, in order to provide the agility required by the enterprise. Information security mechanisms also require additional automation and multi-level security solutions will need to be present and effective.

From an enterprise perspective it is at the points of crossing maturity levels that change is likely, for all characteristics. With change comes the potential for introduction of information security vulnerabilities, and alongside opportunities for designing in privacy. Consider the governance perspective: in the lower maturity levels best practice will be based upon existing outsourcing practice. However, as cloud exploitation matures this is unlikely to be sufficient since the dynamic business models and agility of service deployment will move at a faster pace. New best practice in risk management will certainly be required, and this will impact governance.

We can use this cloud exploitation capability maturity model to motivate a privacy maturity model for clouds which elucidates the enterprise architecture characteristics which will offer opportunities to deliver privacy preserving functionality, and will necessarily vary as cloud adoption matures.

4   Examples of Privacy Controls in Cloud Computing

It is possible to represent a privacy maturity model by capturing key privacy controls that have been identified in Table 1 above. These controls are shown in Table 2, and are loosely based upon the simpler model for privacy risks (in general) described in [24]. The controls are focused at an appropriate level to allay potential concerns relating to why personal information is collected, and how it will be used in the cloud or passed on to affiliated clouds at different maturity levels. However, the relative control level is selected according to the cloud maturity level. As an example, obligation management can evolve with increasing privacy risks, such that at preliminary stage contracts are used for legal compliance for data treatment, this would correspond to the initial services maturity level defined in Table 1. Before any transition to the use of 'architected services', obligations must be defined within the organisation and for third parties with whom information is shared, which may assure the user in a more mature or advanced level. However, obligations should be automated to facilitate management processes and therefore enable the transition for cloud service providers to a level at which they can be dynamically composed and measured (e.g. level 4 and above). Finally, at the highest level the obligation management procedure is continually refined and improved with respect to the enterprise's continuous exploitation of cloud services while responsibly protecting the individuals' private information [25]. Hence, in order to transition across the relative maturity levels; the privacy controls are also required to transition; however, given the relationship is business- and regulatory- context dependant, the mapping cannot be guaranteed to be linear with businesses given freedom on their adoption of controls relative to their maturity in the use of cloud services. We hope to develop this mapping as part of future work.

In the next section, we demonstrate how guidance about designing such privacy controls into cloud services may be achieved by means of design patterns, and discuss a *sticky privacy policies* pattern in detail.

Table 2. Examples of Privacy Controls in Cloud Computing

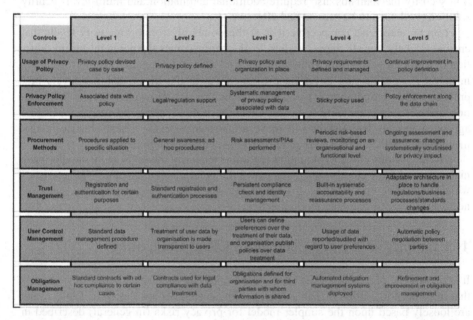

Controls	Level 1	Level 2	Level 3	Level 4	Level 5
Usage of Privacy Policy	Privacy policy devised case by case	Privacy policy defined	Privacy policy and organization in place	Privacy requirements defined and managed	Continual improvement in policy definition
Privacy Policy Enforcement	Associated data with policy	Legal/regulation support	Systematic management of privacy policy associated with data	Sticky policy used	Policy enforcement along the data chain
Procurement Methods	Procedures applied to specific situation	General awareness, ad hoc procedures	Risk assessments/PIAs performed	Periodic risk-based reviews, monitoring on an organisational and functional level	Ongoing assessment and assurance: changes systematically scrutinised for privacy impact
Trust Management	Registration and authentication for certain purposes	Standard registration and authentication processes	Persistent compliance check and identity management	Built-in systematic accountability and reassurance processes	Adaptable architecture in place to handle regulations/business processes/standards changes
User Control Management	Standard data management procedure defined	Treatment of user data by organisation is made transparent to users	Users can define preferences over the treatment of their data, and organisation publish policies over data treatment	Usage of data reported/audited with regard to user preferences	Automatic policy negotiation between parties
Obligation Management	Standard contracts with ad hoc compliance to certain cases	Contracts used for legal compliance with data treatment	Obligations defined for organisation and for third parties with whom information is shared	Automated obligation management systems deployed	Refinement and improvement in obligation management

5 Designing Privacy into the Cloud via Design Patterns

The examples of privacy controls in cloud computing given above show that there will be multiple opportunities to *design in* data protection. In order to exploit these opportunities we require methods that can support an enterprise through its evolution towards maturity, which can incorporate anecdotal advice as well as more formal prescriptive solutions. Such methods also need to be flexible enough to incorporate solutions of varying types, including: processes; techniques; methods; training; software configurations; applications; communications protocols. We have selected *design patterns* [20] since they meet all of these requirements.

Key aspects of design patterns have already been introduced in Section 2. There are multiple approaches one might take to how solutions for different maturity levels of Table 1 are reflected into the corresponding design patterns. Our approach is to have the patterns correspond to giving further details of techniques in each 'cell' of Table 2, so that for each maturity level there would be a set of patterns. Where closely related techniques could be used across more than one level of Table 1, a single pattern may be used and the distinction between maturity levels made within the *context* and *solution* descriptions (see example below); in such a case a subjective judgement is needed, in the sense that if the variation is great then a new pattern would be created.

We describe below a draft design pattern for building a data protection mechanism into a cloud, specifically *Sticky Privacy Policies*. This pattern provides a method for addressing maturity within the enterprise use of privacy policy (identified by our capability maturity analysis outlined above); it corresponds to the control for Privacy Policy Enforcement used at level 4 in Table 2. Due to space limitations we concentrate on this example. We have also defined a number of others in a similar manner, including: obligation management, data fragmentation, user interface design techniques, risk assessment, reputation management, and user anonymisation.

Sticky Privacy Policy Example

Name: Sticky Privacy Policies   **Classification:** Privacy Policy Enforcement

Intent: to bind a privacy policy to the data to which it refers

Motivation: The sticky privacy policy would ensure that policies relating to data are propagated and enforced along all supply chains in the cloud ecosystem and all mechanisms through which the data is stored, processed and shared.

Context: You are designing a cloud service solution and want to make sure that multiple parties are aware of and act in accordance with your policies as personal and sensitive data is passed along the chain of parties storing, using and sharing that data.

Problem: Data could be treated by receivers in ways that the data subject or initiator would not like. The policy could be ignored or separated from the data.

Forces: Factors related to Privacy Policy specification and maintenance and user control (in Table 2) are relevant, as well as contextual factors, notably user trust. For example, in situations where the user has low trust in the service providers, or they have unknown length and composition, the level of user control required increases, gradually implementing the solution set from this pattern.

Solution: Enforceable 'sticky' electronic privacy policies: personal information is associated with machine-readable policies, which are preferences or conditions about how that information should be treated (for example, that it is only to be used for particular purposes, by certain people or that the user must be contacted before it is used) in such a way that this cannot be compromised. When information is processed, this is done in such a way as to adhere to these constraints. These policies are associated with data using cryptographic mechanisms. At level 5, Identifier-Based Encryption (IBE) [26] is particularly appropriate as it means that a third party needs to check certain properties at the time of decryption, before a decryption key is released.

Design Issues
- To what level of granularity of data should the policy be attached? It could be anything from a personal data element (e.g. name, etc.) to a whole database
- It might be better to have a reference to a policy bound to the data rather than the actual policy bound to the data, for practicality reasons
- Need to be compatible with current/legacy systems
- Need to provide mechanism to enforce and audit between parties
- Need to provide mechanism for the parties to assess their enforcement abilities
- Need to provide economically feasible mechanism to enforce the policy.

Consequences: *Benefits:* Policies can be propagated throughout the cloud, strong enforcement of these policies, strong binding of data to policies, traceability (for the IBE approach [26]). Multiple copies of data each have the policy attached.

Liabilities: Scalability and practicality: if data is bonded with the policy, this makes data heavier and potentially not compatible to current information systems. It may be difficult to update the policy once the data is sent to the cloud, as there can be multiple copies of data and it might not be known where these are. Once the data is decrypted and in clear, the enforcement mechanism becomes weak, i.e. it is hard to enforce that the data cannot be shared further in clear, but must instead be passed on in the sticky policy form; therefore, audit must be used to check that this does not happen.

Known Uses: Policy specification, modelling and verification tools include EPAL [27], OASIS XACML [28], W3C P3P [29] and Ponder [30]. Various different solutions to sticky policies are compared in [31]. Notably, a technical solution for sticky policies and tracing services is introduced in [26] that leverages Identifier-Based Encryption (IBE) and trusted technologies. This solution requires enforcement for third party tracing and auditing parties. An alternative solution that relies on a Merkle hash tree has been proposed by Pöhls in [32]. A unified policy model is discussed in [33], which discusses steps towards privacy management for an organisation or across organisations within a federated identity management environment.

Related Patterns: obligations (obligations can be stuck to data), identity management (e.g. polices bound to data managed in identity management system), audit, Digital Rights Management (DRM).

Our conclusion is that a pattern approach is viable and scalable. However, patterns can only be as good as experience and analysis allow and so they will need to be evolved and refined. But they could offer a practical approach to enabling the adoption of best practice in discrete steps as an enterprise builds towards their optimum level of cloud exploitation maturity.

6 Maintaining Data Protection in the Cloud via SLAs

Whilst patterns provide an intuitive way to engage with system architects and policy developers during cloud service design, they may not be ideal for enabling contractual risk management maturity in deployed cloud services. Service level agreements (SLAs) are an industry standard approach for controlling risk, and so are a more natural starting point. For many outsourced services the SLA is a key document as it attempts to define the relationship between the customer and provider of a service, the service itself and the parameters which can be used to define performance of the service supplier [34]. In practice the SLA can have many more functions, dependant upon the service type and level (of Table 1) to which it is targeted. An enterprise may have a number of SLA agreements which can either be standalone or with multiple dependencies. For example, the hosting of a single server on which Human Resources (HR) data is stored may have a separate SLA from that of the database that it hosts and from that of the provision of the supported HR service.

In general, SLAs can be split into three functional areas [35], which may be simplified as: service description (including roles and responsibilities); SLA governance (identifying metrics and the process for dispute resolution); SLA change management (managing uncertainty and renegotiating services in the agreement). In order to be effective SLAs are broken down into specific service objectives with key performance indicators (KPIs) specifying the service delivered by the outsourced service. One of the key difficulties [36] is mapping the service KPI to a meaningful metric and ensuring that there is a shared understanding of that metric with the provider and the customer.

While recent work [37] has attempted to define KPIs for information security, to the best of our knowledge KPIs for information privacy have yet to be adequately tackled. The reason for this is probably twofold: firstly, as considered in Section 3, privacy is a broader topic and there are many different interpretations based upon societal, cultural and contextual factors; secondly, the privacy of an individual is interpreted through a number of data protection laws, which can potentially be contradictory, sector specific and vary between countries even when they interpret the same principles or directive (as is the case in the EEA).

At the lowest level (Level 1) of maturity cloud services (cf Table 1) are not too dissimilar to the current services we use today; standard contractual methods are used and SLAs will typically be natural language documents; thus high-level requirements will be directly translated into the SLA, where possible. For example, the UK Data Protection eighth principle states that personal data "should not be transferred outside the EEA unless an adequate level of data protection is ensured" and this can be directly expressed as a condition against which certain actions could constitute a serious breach of SLA.

The SP has the responsibility of designing and operating a system such that this breach is not the case and yet currently no standards or mechanisms exist for assessing the effectiveness or suitability of the design. By contrast as the cloud matures (cf Table 1) so a broader number of suppliers become interdependent and are used in a more dynamic manner. Increasing dynamics for quality of service and choice has already been recognised within other projects examining Grid [38] and SOA [39]. These projects have highlighted the need to be able to handle: SLAs that are composed of a hierarchy of technologies to comprise an overall service level objective within an agreement; service provision that may need to change between providers either for functional, price or quality reasons; the SLA subsequently being negotiated, planned and deployed. A requirement of the SLA is that they are expressed in parameters that are tangible and can be processed by machines rather than requiring interpretation at human quarterly review meetings.

We believe that by exposing and interpreting these clauses as service level objectives within an SLA, we will provide engineering requirements against which we can map design solutions. For example, the 'sticky policy' design pattern can be used to ensure that the user can be assured that the data processor has correct instructions for each individual data item as to where it may be transferred and processed (e.g. outside of the EEA/Safe Harbour etc) and gain assurance in so doing. However, challenges still remain in strongly defining both the design pattern properties (such as the ability to strongly identify processing parties, via IBE) and the detail required by the service level objective to satisfy the service user (such as identifying all data processors). Clearly, both objective and data protection properties must be expressed in a solution neutral format as well as having a common ontology that can be encoded within a machine readable format around which communication can take place. Due to space limitations we are unable to present any further examples. It may be possible to define a pattern which communicates how an enterprise should seek to utilise SLAs as it matures; however, at this time the technical capability does not exist to actually support the higher levels of maturity envisaged.

7 Conclusion and Acknowledgements

We have demonstrated that through the creation of novel capability maturity models for cloud exploitation and associated privacy requirements in an enterprise we can begin to identify opportunities to produce methods for designing data protection into clouds. Design patterns provide a good mechanism for expressing such techniques in a manner which could be useful at all levels of maturity. We believe that such patterns could also be applicable for architecting SLAs. Our future work will include a more complete analysis of where the maturity models indicate opportunities for designing in privacy, including an assessment of those which should be considered high priority. It is clear that privacy controls (cf. Table 2) could be highly context-dependent. To avoid overlooking the subtleties of individual privacy concerns, which may vary with context, we must be careful not to use too general a template. Further research is required to elucidate the user related contextual factors affecting the degree of privacy protection that is necessary for a given context. Such factors include: sensitivity of data, location of data, sector, contractual restrictions, cultural expectations, user trust (in organisations, etc.), trustworthiness of partners, security deployed in the infrastructure, etc. We will explore the use of recommendations which could be deduced via a decision based support system that assesses context, and then outputs a list of recommendations and controls, as has been done with [23]. Further analysis is also required to study the utility of the design pattern approach by application to a case study, and the issues surrounding legal protections and their inclusion in SLA design patterns.

This research is being conducted as part of the EnCoRe project [40], focused on delivering usable consent and revocation controls for managing personal data and considering amongst others cloud service operating environments.

References

1. Gartner: Forecast: Sizing the Cloud; Understanding the Opportunities in Cloud Services (March 2009)
2. Pearson, S.: Taking Account of Privacy when Designing Cloud Computing Services. In: ICSE-Cloud 2009, Vancouver. IEEE, Los Alamitos (2009); HP Labs Technical Report, HPL-2009-54 (2009), http://www.hpl.hp.com/techreports/2009/HPL-2009-54.html
3. Solove, D.J.: A Taxonomy of Privacy. University of Pennyslavania Law Review 154(3), 477 (2006), http://papers.ssrn.com/sol3/papers.cfm?abstract_id=667622
4. Council Directive 95/46/EC. On the protection of individuals with regard to the processing of personal data and on the free movement of such data. OJ, L281, pp. 31-50 (1995)
5. Wikipedia (2009), http://en.wikipedia.org/wiki/Capability_Maturity_Model
6. Smith, R.: Cloud Maturity Models Don't Make Sense (2008), http://www.informationweek.com/blog/main/archives/2008/12/cloud_maturity.html;jsessionid=OL1NSZLUOGDMCQSNDLPCKHSCJUNN2JVN
7. Urquhart, J.: A maturity model for cloud computing (2009), http://news.cnet.com/8301-19413_3-10122295-240.html
8. Sorofman, J.: The cloud computing adoption model (2009), http://www.ddj.com/architect/211201818
9. Wardley, S.: Maturity models for the cloud (2009), http://blog.gardeviance.org/2008/12/maturity-models-for-cloud.html
10. OpenGroup: A Maturity Model for SOA (2009), http://www.opengroup.org/projects/soa-book/page.tpl?CALLER=faq.tpl&ggid=1319
11. Microsoft Corporation: Privacy Guidelines for Developing Software Products and Services, Version 2.1a (2007), http://www.microsoft.com/Downloads/details.aspx?FamilyID=c48cf80f-6e87-48f5-83ec-a18d1ad2fc1f&displaylang=en
12. Cannon, J.C.: Privacy: What Developers and IT Professionals Should Know. Addison-Wesley, Reading (2004)
13. Patrick, A., Kenny, S.: From Privacy Legislation to Interface Design: Implementing Information Privacy in Human-Computer Interactions. In: Dingledine, R. (ed.) PET 2003. LNCS, vol. 2760, pp. 107–124. Springer, Heidelberg (2003)
14. Belloti, V., Sellen, A.: Design for Privacy in Ubiquitous Computing Environments. In: Proc. 3rd conference on European Conference on Computer-Supported Cooperative Work, pp. 77–92 (1993)
15. Information Commissioner's Office: PIA handbook (2007), http://www.ico.gov.uk/
16. Office of the Privacy Commissioner of Canada: Fact sheet: Privacy impact assessments (2007), http://www.privcom.gc.ca/
17. Information Commissioners Office: Privacy by Design. Report (2008), http://www.ico.gov.uk
18. Jutla, D.N., Bodorik, P.: Sociotechnical architecture for online privacy. IEEE Security and Privacy 3(2), 29–39 (2005)
19. Spiekermann, S., Cranor, L.F.: Engineering privacy. IEEE Transactions on Software Engineering, 1–42 (2008)
20. Alexander, C., Ishikawa, S., Silverstein, M., Jacobson, M., Fiksdahl-King, I., Angel, S.: A Pattern Language: Towns, Buildings, Construction. Oxford University Press, Oxford (1977)

21. Arista, Cloud Networking: Design Patterns for 'Cloud Centric' Application Environments (2009),
    http://www.aristanetworks.com/en/
    CloudCentricDesignPatterns.pdf
22. Hafiz, M.: A collection of privacy design patterns. Pattern Languages of Programs, 1–13 (2006)
23. Pearson, S., Sander, T., Sharma, R.: A Privacy Management Tool for Global Outsourcing. In: DPM 2009. LNCS, vol. 5939. Springer, Heidelberg (2009)
24. The Institute of Internal Auditors: Managing and Auditing Privacy Risks,
    http://www.theiia.org/download.cfm?file=33917
25. Casassa Mont, M.: Dealing with privacy obligations: Important aspects and technical approaches. In: Katsikas, S.K., López, J., Pernul, G. (eds.) TrustBus 2004. LNCS, vol. 3184, pp. 120–131. Springer, Heidelberg (2004)
26. Casassa Mont, M., Pearson, S., Bramhall, P.: Towards Accountable Management of Identity and Privacy: Sticky Policies and Enforceable Tracing Services. In: Mařík, V., Štěpánková, O., Retschitzegger, W. (eds.) DEXA 2003. LNCS, vol. 2736, pp. 377–382. Springer, Heidelberg (2003)
27. IBM, The Enterprise Privacy Authorization Language (EPAL), EPAL specification, v1.2 (2004),
    http://www.zurich.ibm.com/security/enterprise-privacy/epal/
28. OASIS, eXtensible Access Control Markup Language (XACML),
    http://www.oasis-open.org/committees/
    tc_home.php?wg_abbrev=xacml
29. Cranor, L.: Web Privacy with P3P. O'Reilly & Associates, Sebastopol (2002)
30. Damianou, N., Dulay, N., Lupu, E., Sloman, M.: The Ponder Policy Specification Language (2001),
    http://wwwdse.doc.ic.ac.uk/research/policies/index.shtml
31. Tang, Q.: On Using Encryption Techniques to Enhance Sticky Policies Enforcement, Technical Report TR-CTIT-08-64, Centre for Telematics and Information Technology, University of Twente, Enschede (2008)
32. Pöhls, H.C.: Verifiable and Revocable Expression of Consent to Processing of Aggregated Personal Data. In: Chen, L., Ryan, M.D., Wang, G. (eds.) ICICS 2008. LNCS, vol. 5308, pp. 279–293. Springer, Heidelberg (2008)
33. Schunter, M., Waidner, M.: Simplified privacy controls for aggregated services - suspend and resume of personal data. In: Borisov, N., Golle, P. (eds.) PET 2007. LNCS, vol. 4776, pp. 218–232. Springer, Heidelberg (2007)
34. Clarke, I., Miller, S.G.: Protecting Free Expression Online with Freenet. IEEE Computing (2002)
35. Rhea, S., Eaton, P., Geels, D., Weatherspoon, H., Zhao, B., Kubiatowicz. J.: Pond: the OceanStore Prototype. In: FAST 2003 (2003)
36. Huang, C.D., Goo, J.: Rescuing IT Outsourcing- Strategic Use of Service Level Agreements, IT Pro. (2009)
37. Yearworth, M., Monahan, B., Pym, D.: Predictive Modelling for Security Operations Economics, HPL-2006-125 (2006)
38. EU FP7 Network of Excellence(2009), http://www.coregrid.net/
39. EU FP7 Project SLA Aware Infrastructure (2009), http://sla-at-soi.eu/
40. EnCoRe: Ensuring Consent and Revocation project (2008),
    http://www.encore-project.info

Accountability as a Way Forward for Privacy Protection in the Cloud

Siani Pearson[1] and Andrew Charlesworth[2]

[1] HP Labs, Long Down Avenue, Stoke Gifford, Bristol, UK BS34 8QZ
[2] Centre for IT and Law, University of Bristol, Queens Road, Bristol, UK BS8 1RJ
Siani.Pearson@hp.com, a.j.charlesworth@bris.ac.uk

Abstract. The issue of how to provide appropriate privacy protection for cloud computing is important, and as yet unresolved. In this paper we propose an approach in which procedural and technical solutions are co-designed to demonstrate accountability as a path forward to resolving jurisdictional privacy and security risks within the cloud.

Keywords: Accountability, cloud computing, privacy.

1 Introduction

Cloud computing is a means by which highly scalable, technology-enabled services can be easily consumed over the Internet on an as-needed basis [1]. The convenience and efficiency of this approach, however, comes with privacy and security risks [2]. A significant barrier to the adoption of cloud services is thus user fear of confidential data leakage and loss of privacy in the cloud. Furthermore, the cross-jurisdictional nature of clouds presents a new challenge in maintaining the data protection required by current legislation including restrictions on cross-border data transfer.

At the broadest level, privacy is a fundamental human right that encompasses the right to be left alone, although an analysis of the term is complex [3]. In the commercial, consumer context, privacy entails the protection and appropriate use of the personal information of customers, and the meeting of expectations of customers about its use. For organisations, privacy entails the application of laws, policies, standards and processes by which Personally Identifiable Information (PII) of individuals is managed.

We focus in this paper on: privacy in the sense of data protection, as defined by Directive 95/46/EC [4] (rather than the narrower US sense of data security); data that is PII (information that can be traced to a particular individual, such as a phone number or social security number); the corporate entity seeking to contract for services in the cloud, either for its own use, or to offer to its customers, as this entity is most likely to have resources to use our proposed path of technical and procedural solutions. However, our solution is not EU-specific, and is compatible with privacy principles underlying American and Asia-Pacific regulation and legislation, as well as a self-regulatory approach.

M.G. Jaatun, G. Zhao, and C. Rong (Eds.): CloudCom 2009, LNCS 5931, pp. 131–144, 2009.
© Springer-Verlag Berlin Heidelberg 2009

This paper proposes the incorporation of complementary regulatory, procedural and technical provisions that demonstrate accountability into a flexible operational framework to address privacy issues in this cloud computing scenario. The structure of the paper is as follows: consideration of open issues that relate to cloud computing and privacy; an explanation of accountability and how this might apply in cloud computing; proposal of legal mechanisms, procedures and technical measures that tie in with this approach; an assessment of this approach and conclusions.

2 Privacy Issues for Cloud Computing

Privacy is a key business risk and compliance issue, as it sits at the intersection of social norms, human rights and legal mandates [5]. Conforming to legal privacy requirements, and meeting client privacy expectations with regard to PII, require corporations to demonstrate a context-appropriate level of control over such data at all stages of its processing, from collection to destruction. The advantages of cloud computing – its ability to scale rapidly (through subcontractors), store data remotely (in unknown places), and share services in a dynamic environment – can thus become disadvantages in maintaining a level of privacy assurance sufficient to sustain confidence in potential customers. For example:

- **Outsourcing.** Outsourcing of data processing invariably raises governance and accountability questions. Which party is responsible (statutorily or contractually) for ensuring legal requirements for PII are observed, or appropriate data handling standards are set and followed [6]? Can they effectively audit third-party compliance with such laws and standards? To what extent can processing be further sub-contracted, and how are the identities, and *bona fides*, of sub-contractors to be confirmed? What rights in the data will be acquired by data processors and their sub-contractors, and are these transferable to other third parties upon bankruptcy, takeover, or merger [7]? 'On-demand' and 'pay-as-you-go' models may be based on weak trust relationships, involve third parties with lax data security practices, expose data widely, and make deletion hard to verify.
- **Offshoring.** Offshoring of data processing increases risk factors and legal complexity [8]. Issues of jurisdiction (whose courts can/will hear a case?), choice of law (whose law applies?) and enforcement (can a legal remedy be effectively applied?) need to be considered [9]. A cloud computing service which combines outsourcing and offshoring may raise very complex issues [10].
- **Virtualization.** There are security risks in sharing machines, e.g. loss of control over data location, and who has access to it. Transactional data is a byproduct with unclear ownership, and it can be hard to anticipate which data to protect. Even innocuous-seeming data can turn out to be commercially sensitive [11].
- **Autonomic technology.** If technological processes are granted a degree of autonomy in decision making, e.g. automatically adapting services to meet changing needs of customers and service providers, this challenges enterprises' abilities to maintain consistent security standards, and to provide appropriate business continuity and back-up, not least as it may not be possible to determine with any specificity where data processing will take place within the cloud [12].

As cloud computing exhibits all the aspects above, privacy solutions need to address a combination of issues, and this may require new and even unique mechanisms rather than just a combination of known techniques for addressing selected aspects. For example, privacy problems when transferring PII across borders within a group of companies can be addressed via Binding Corporate Rules, and yet this approach would not be available to a corporation seeking to adopt a cloud computing solution where PII will be handled by third party cloud service providers.

Overall, the speed and flexibility of adjustment to vendor offerings, which benefits business and motivates cloud computing uptake, brings a higher risk to data privacy and security. This is a key user concern, particularly for financial and health data.

2.1 Mapping Legal and Regulatory Approaches

Effective corporate governance is vital to compliance with the type of regional block regulatory governance models which underpin Binding Corporate Rules in Europe and Cross Border Privacy Rules in Asia-Pacific Economic Cooperation (APEC) countries. Organizations that process PII must safeguard it (including limiting its use and disclosure) or face legal, financial and reputational penalties. Where there are inadequate information governance capabilities in the cloud, this will severely restrict the outsourcing of key business processes using cloud-based service marketplaces.

Companies and governmental organisations are increasingly aware of the need to integrate privacy into the technology design process [13, 14]. However, tools and technical controls alone cannot fully address privacy issues in cloud computing, due to diverse privacy obligations upon, and privacy practices within, organisations [15]. Cloud service providers (SPs) and marketplace providers need to design their processes to ensure those obligations and practices can be mapped against a combination of technical and procedural measures, which together provide broad assurance that appropriate contextual safeguards apply to PII processing in the cloud. Context is key to requirements. Identical information collected in different contexts by different entities might involve totally divergent data protection criteria [16, 17].

Such a mapping exercise requires an understanding of the rationales for, and the objectives of, the protection of PII, and how these translate to the cloud computing environment. If cloud computing is to reach its full potential, where customers are willing to entrust PII to such a service marketplace, these criteria need to be met:

1. a determination of risks and requirements involved in a given interaction situation e.g. consideration of the underlying legal, policy and social context.
2. a determination of what protective measures (procedural and/or technological) are appropriate, based on this information.
3. effective ways of providing assurance and auditing that potential partners protect PII, in accordance with contextually appropriate protective measures.
4. a degree of transparency, in the sense of visibility into the data protection obligations and processes of potential suppliers.

Requirements arising from applying privacy legislation to the cloud are considered in [2]. A key issue is the need to respect cross-border transfer obligations. As this is particularly difficult to ensure within cloud computing, it is suggested that legislation will need to evolve to allow compliance in dynamic, global environments. The notion of accountability is likely to provide a way forward, as discussed in this paper.

3 Accountability: A Way Forward

In this section we examine what accountability is and how we believe accountability and corporate responsibility with regard to the use of PII might be applicable in cloud computing. In doing so, we present how accountability can help fill the gaps identified above. Finally, we explain what procedural measures are needed, and the basis of a technological approach to provide accountability.

3.1 What Is Accountability?

It is important to clearly define what is meant by 'accountability' as the term is susceptible to a variety of different meanings within and across disciplines. For example, the term has been used for a number of years in computer science to refer to an imprecise requirement that is met by reporting and auditing mechanisms (see for example, [18]). In this paper the context of its use is corporate data governance (the management of the availability, usability, integrity and security of the data used, stored, or processed within an organization), and it refers to the process by which a particular goal – the prevention of disproportionate (in the circumstances) harm to the subjects of PII – can be obtained via a combination of public law (legislation, regulation), private law (contract), self-regulation and the use of privacy technologies (system architectures, access controls, machine readable policies).

To date, national and international privacy protection approaches have been heavily influenced by public law, and premised upon 'command and control' regulatory strategies. However, such legislative and regulatory mechanisms have declined in effectiveness as technological developments render the underlying regulatory techniques obsolete. Effective privacy protection for PII in some business environments is thus heavily compromised, and the ability of organizations to meaningfully quantify, control, and offset, their business risk is significantly impeded.

> It enjoins upon 'data controllers' a set of largely procedural requirements for their processing activities, and therefore conveys the impression that formal compliance will be enough to legitimise their activities. It encourages a box-ticking mentality, rather than a more systemic, and systematic, approach to fulfilling its values. [19]

The EU data protection regime, in particular, lacks effective regulatory responses for key developing technologies, such as mobile e-commerce and cloud computing [20]. Equally, self-regulation, in isolation, has failed to gain traction as a plausible alternative for effective privacy protection, with weak risk assessment and limited compliance checking [21].

Accountability in our sense will be achieved via a combination of *private* and *public* accountability. Public accountability is derived from an active interaction between: subjects of PII; regulatory bodies, such as Information Commissioners; data controllers. It is premised upon highly transparent processes. Private accountability, in contrast, is derived from the interaction between data controllers and data processors, and is premised on contract law, technological processes, and practical internal compliance requirements. The objective of such accountability is not to meet 'a set of largely procedural requirements for ... processing activities' but rather to reduce the risk of disproportionate (in context) harm to the subjects of PII, and thus reduce or permit the amelioration of negative consequences for the data controller. It reflects an acceptance that absolute reduction of harm to the subjects of PII is an impossible goal in a disaggregated environment, such as a cloud service, and that the ability to respond flexibly and efficiently (or systemically and systematically) to harms arising will provide a more efficient form of privacy protection than enforcing blunt and/or static 'tick-box' compliance criteria.

Weitzner *et al* have previously used the term "information accountability" to refer to checking 'whether the policies that govern data manipulations and inferences were in fact adhered to' [22]. Our usage of the term 'accountability' differs from this to the extent that adherence to policy becomes less critical than achieving a proportionate and responsive process for reacting to context-dependent privacy risks.

Crompton *et al* note that in contrast to the EU's 'adequacy' regime, 'accountability' is increasingly popular in jurisdictions such as Australia, Canada and the US [23]. As discussed below, accountability in this context means placing a legal responsibility upon an organization that uses PII to ensure that contracted partners to whom it supplies the PII are compliant, wherever in the world they may be. Our accountability model reflects the basic premise of this approach, but expands upon it in suggesting ways in which organizations might take the 'accountability' approach further in order to develop a reflexive privacy process.

3.2 How Accountability Might Provide a Way Forward for Privacy Protection within Cloud Computing

Solutions to privacy risks in the cloud involve reintroducing an element of control. For the corporate user, privacy risk in cloud computing can be reduced if organisations involved in cloud provision use a combination of privacy policies and contractual terms to create accountability in the form of transparent, enforceable commitments to responsible data handling [2, 19]. Specifically, accountable organisations will ensure that obligations to protect data (corresponding to user, legal and company policy requirements) are observed by all processors of the data, irrespective of where that processing occurs.

Through contractual agreements, all organizations involved in the cloud provision would be accountable. While the corporate user, as the first corporate entity in the cloud provision, would be held legally accountable, the corporate user would then hold the initial service provider (SP1) accountable through contractual agreements, requiring in turn that SP1 hold its SPs accountable contractually as well. This is analogous to some existing cases in outsourcing environments, where the transferor is held accountable by regulators even when it is the transferee that does not act in accordance with individuals' wishes [23].

The following elements are key to provision of accountability within the cloud:

-   **Transparency.** Individuals should be adequately informed about how their data is handled within the cloud and the responsibilities of people and organisations in relation to the processing of PII should be clearly identified. As with other disaggregated data environments, transparency in cloud computing is important not only for legal and regulatory reasons, but also to avoid violation of social norms [24]. In the context of this paper, transparency means a level of openness about an entity's handling of PII that permits meaningful accountability.

- **Assurance.** The corporate user provides assurance and transparency to the customer/client through its privacy policy, while requiring similar assurances from the SP through contractual measures and audits.
- **User trust.** Accountability helps foster user trust. When it is not clear to individuals why their personal information is requested, or how and by whom it will be processed, this lack of control will lead to suspicion and ultimately distrust [25]. There are also security-related concerns about whether data in the cloud will be adequately protected [6].
- **Responsibility.** Most data protection regimes require a clear allocation of responsibility for the processing of PII, as existing regulatory mechanisms rely heavily upon user and regulator intervention with responsible parties. Disaggregated data environments, e.g. mobile e-commerce and cloud computing, can hinder determination of that responsibility. Predetermining responsibility, via contract, as information is shared and processed within the cloud, pre-empts perceptions of regulatory failure, which may erode user trust. It also permits companies to assess their trading risks in terms of potential financial losses and data privacy breaches. This knowledge can be used to establish organisational and group privacy and security standards, and to implement due diligence/compliance measures which conform to regulatory parameters, but which are otherwise negotiable between contracting organisations, based on relevant operational criteria [20].
- **Policy compliance.** Accountability helps ensure that the cloud service complies with laws, and also the mechanisms proposed in this paper help compliance with cloud provider organisational policies and user preferences, and with auditing.

With a legal and regulatory approach, location is paramount to enforcement. With accountability, location either becomes less relevant to the customer/client because of assurances that data will be treated as described regardless of jurisdiction or becomes transparent through contracts specifying where data processing will take place. In the accountability model, the corporate user works with legal and regulatory bodies to move data between jurisdictions through mechanisms such as Binding Corporate Rules and intra-company agreements. For the corporate user, the flexibility to move customer/client data between jurisdictions has a big impact on cost.

With accountability, regulators enforce the law on the 'first in the chain' in regard to the misdeeds of anybody in the chain, including those further along. However, whether any regulatory framework will be effective depends upon a number of characteristics including the background of the regulator (country, resources available to prosecute, etc.). This approach is more effective if action can be taken against an organization that has a presence in the regulator's home jurisdiction.

Accountability is included in various privacy frameworks, including Canada and USA and the APEC privacy framework. In the EU it applies in the restricted sense that data controllers (DCs) are directly responsible for the actions of their data processors (DPs) (and thus for clouds of DPs and sub-DPs). The difference in approaches becomes more obvious where there are multiple DCs; if these are responsible separately (DCs in common, but not joint DCs) it is hard to police via the EU model, as the data subject (DS) may be unable to identify and enforce rights against a specific DC in a cloud computing environment with a mix of DCs and DPs.

The key issue in responsibility (and accountability) terms under EU law is who is making the decision about the particular processing purpose, and not who is carrying out the processing. A central problem in the mobile e-commerce and cloud computing environments is that it is unclear to the DS if, and if so, where, a breach is taking place, so that they can enforce rights against the relevant DC. The contractual approach provides a mechanism for avoiding that accountability-negating uncertainty, in a manner which permits the DC to demonstrate compliance with the substantive law (and boost user trust), without undue reliance upon the flawed mechanism in the legislation. The accountability process is expanded outwards by the initial DC to DPs and other DCs by contract, then information that the initial DC derives from the accountability processes can be passed upwards to the regulator and downwards to the DS, so that both can perform the functions envisaged by the legislation.

In conclusion, accountability can play a role in ensuring that laws that apply to cloud computing are enforced. There is a role for regulators in the form of criminal penalties for misuse. Also, there is a role for technology, as considered below.

3.3 Procedural Approach

Procedural is used here in the sense of governance, business practices (e.g. strong privacy policies) and contractual agreements. Privacy policies can be defined at a number of levels and be reflected within internal and external corporate policy statements, contracts, Service Level Agreements (SLAs), security policies, etc. Policies are passed on when sharing information with third parties and organisational policies are used to help ensure legal compliance. In general, they should be based upon established privacy principles, such as the OECD privacy principles [26] and regulatory requirements specific to the region(s) in which the company is operating.

For our approach, cloud computing providers should move away from terms and conditions of service towards contracts between the client and the initial service provider (SP), and between that SP and other cloud providers. This approach is consistent with industry self-regulation (for example, Truste certification [27]). At issue in cloud computing is that most policies have a clause that frees the company to change its policy at any time, often, but not always, with some form of notice. These clauses may need to be re-examined in the cloud environment, where data is perhaps not as easily destroyed or returned to its original owner.

The corporate user has options that the consumer does not in using contracts as a governance measure for control within the cloud environment. Contractual obligations are those imposed on an entity by incorporation in a contract of similar legally binding agreement between that entity and other party. The corporate user has experience in using contracts to control offshoring and outsourcing relationships. These experiences can be leveraged in the cloud.

SLAs for the cloud are still being developed and there are still a number of open issues [28]. SLAs can be informal or formal with the former being more in the nature of a promise than a contract and the latter being ancillary to a contract between parties, with breach of an SLA term not being in general as severe as a breach of contract. Moreover, third parties (i.e users) would not easily be able to rely on the terms of an SLA between a cloud computing company and a corporation selling such services onwards (i.e. the customer), as there are processes for varying the terms, without the need to renegotiate the whole SLA with customers.

Nevertheless, specific contractual agreements can be used between the cloud provider and the corporate user, just as contracts are used today with traditional SPs. SPs can pass on obligations to subcontractors via contracts – they would require written permission to subcontract with agreements that must be no less restrictive than the agreement the corporate user has with the SP, and reserve the right to enter at will into additional confidentiality agreements directly with the subcontractors. Such contracts have to be plausibly capable of supporting meaningful enforcement processes, and capable of at least some degree of meaningful oversight/audit. The contracts can be used to:

1. address the issue of location – by requiring prior written consent for transfers to any third country
2. restrict use of data
3. prevent copying or reproducing of data without express written permission, except as technically necessary to fulfil the agreement (e.g. backup protection)
4. restrict employee access to the associated data (e.g. on a need to know basis), require that the SP provide employee privacy training, and require employees to sign confidentiality agreements
5. specify security levels – at least the same level of care applied to the SP's own similar data, but not less than a reasonable level of care, implementation of any security measures required by applicable laws
6. require immediate notification by specified means (e.g., via telephone with written follow-up), for any suspected data breach, and cooperation in resolving
7. reserve the right to audit
8. require upon request or at termination, that PII be delivered back to the data controller or data subject, and all copies be destroyed.

3.4 Co-design Involving Technological Approach

We now explain our technological approach and how it ties in with the procedural approach.

The direction in which we are carrying out research is to underpin the procedural approach above with a technological approach that helps provide accountability. In this, natural language policies in the contract are associated with lower-level policies that are machine-readable and that can be acted upon automatically within the cloud without the need for human intervention. These policies define the usage contraints of the associated PII. In this approach, as with Weitzner's approach [22], the data is accessible, but its usage is constrained. The main problem in the cloud is how this can be enforced: one option is a Creative Commons-type approach [29], where holders are made aware of their obligations and their behaviour can be audited with regard to this. If more enforcement is required, obligation management and identity management [30] could be used to manipulate data and aid data minimisation, deletion and management of notifications to individuals, but it is difficult to envisage how such a technical solution could work within non-constrained cloud environments.

Although we do not in general hide the data within the cloud, there is still the possibility to obscure it in some contexts: for example, sensitive data can in some cases be obfuscated in the cloud [31] and multi-party security (zero knowledge) techniques can be used [32].

In our approach, the machine-readable policies would include preferences or conditions about how PII should be treated (for example, that it is only to be used for particular purposes, by certain people or that the user must be contacted before it is used). When PII is processed, this is done in such a way as to adhere to these constraints. Existing policy specification, modelling and verification tools that can be used as a basis for this representation include EPAL [33], OASIS XACML [34], W3C P3P [35] and Ponder [36]. Policies can be associated with data with various degrees of binding and enforcement. Trusted computing and cryptography can be used to stick policies to data and ensure that that receivers act according to associated policies and constraints, by interacting with trusted third parties [37, 38]. Strong enforcement mechanisms include Digital Rights Management (DRM) techniques [39] and enforceable 'sticky' electronic privacy policies [37, 40].

Accountability and good privacy design go together, in that privacy protecting controls should be build into different aspects of the business process. This should be a reflexive process in that it is underpinned by a non-static compliance mechanism that is an ongoing process of privacy review throughout the contractual chain. There will be developmental, contractual and technical processes in play that encourage an organisation's cloud contractors to review and improve their privacy standards on an ongoing basis – this discourages 'cheating' by contractors, rewards effective privacy protections, and prioritises the prevention of disproportionate (in context) privacy harms over inconsequential, (in context) privacy harms. This contrasts with the application of privacy protection in a 'box-ticking fashion', where checking 'our contractor is 'adequate' according to this set of static criteria' is likely to either waste resources on low risk privacy harms or fail to identify developing high risk privacy harms. Audit information can be produced, e.g. by logging, usage of third parties and tracking [41]. In particular, sticky policy techniques can be used to ensure an audit trail of notification and disclosure of data to third parties [37]. Third party certifiers or auditors can periodically verify data protection controls, and also underpin a range of new accountability-related services that offer a cloud computing infrastructure assurances as to the degree of privacy offered (e.g. analogous to privacy seal provision for web services [42] and mechanisms for privacy assurance on the service provider side [43]).

It is necessary to utilize security techniques within the cloud to protect PII from unauthorised access or modification, and to protect backup, protect and manage multiple data copies and delete PII. To limit who has access to personal information within an organisation, privacy-aware access control [44] deployed within that organization can make decisions and enforce access control policies, intercepting queries to data repositories and returning sanitized views (if any) on requested data.

Policy enforcement within the cloud is a difficult issue – and a combined technical and procedural approach to this is preferable. The strongest binding between these would be if the wording in the contracts can be translated into machine-readable policies that are bound to data, and then enforced within the cloud. However, this binding cannot be an exact one from laws to human-readable policies to machine-readable policies, due to interpretation of the law, and furthermore only a restricted part of this translation process can be easily automated. Translation of legislation/regulation to machine readable policies has proven very difficult, although there are several examples of how translations of principles into machine readable/actionable policies can be done, e.g. Privacy Incorporated Software Agent (PISA) project [45] (deriving and modelling privacy principles from [27]); Sparcle project [46], (transforming natural based policies into XML code that can be utilized by enforcement engines); REALM project [47] (translating high level policy and compliance constraints into machine readable formats); Breaux and Antón [48] (extracting privacy rules and regulations from natural language text); OASIS LegalXML [49] (creating and managing contract documents and terms).

Our approach is to add a technical descriptor at the bottom of a contract that describes what a cloud SP should do. For example, there could be a policy text in words that forms part of the contract, then a legal XML expression corresponding to this also within the contract [46]. Also, there could be a mapping from legal XML expression to a policy associated with data covered by the contract, and this policy might be expressed in a language like XACML [34]. However, there are currently gaps between these layers, so further work is needed to allow and provide an automatic translation. In addition, the mapping needs to be agreed, perhaps involving a third party to pre-define clauses and their meanings. A similar approach could be taken to that proposed for assurance control policies [43], to avoid having to use a fine-grained ontological approach. In general, there is a tension between flexibility of expression and ease of understanding of such policies. There is a role for standardization as these technical policies need to be understood by multiple parties so that they can be dealt with and enforced by policy decision points and policy enforcement points within the cloud infrastructure. Current technical policies of this type are access control policies, obligations and security policies. More work needs to be done in defining these, and we are working on this within the Encore project [50].

As an extension of this approach, there can be a role for infomediaries, e.g. as a Trust Authority [37], to check policies apply before allowing the decryption of data, and to play a role in auditing at this point. They could help check the situation before authorising access to personal information, e.g. via IBE [37], or else using secret sharing techniques where the decryption key is broken down and shared between multiple parties, a certain number of whom need to agree in order to be able to build up the decryption key, in a process that exploits Shamir's key sharing algorithm (analogous to the approach used in [51]). Potentially, privacy infomediaries [52] could be used in other ways that help provide accountability, e.g. by acting as insurance brokers and paying claims in case of privacy breaches. Who plays the role of privacy infomediary could vary according to the context; it could be a trusted identity provider for a federated set of services, a web proxy at an enterprise boundary, or a consumer organisation.

Mechanisms for checking compliance will be a mixture of procedural and technical, involving both auditing and regulatory aspects. There is also a role for risk and trust assessment (including reputation management) [53] before issuing contracts, to help satisfy regulators that best practice is being carried out, and in measuring metrics specified within SLAs. Decision support tools might be useful for lawyers representing the cloud providers, and to determine appropriate actions that should be allowed and to assess risk before PII is passed on (this could be part of a Privacy Impact Assessment [54]). In addition automated access control decision-making could incorporate privacy policy checking.

If trusted infrastructure [38,,55] were available within the cloud, it could help: ensure that the infrastructural building blocks of the cloud are secure, trustworthy and compliant with security best practice; determine and provide assurance regarding location [56]; provide a basis for enhanced auditing of platforms [38, 55]. Furthermore, trusted virtual machines [57] can support strong enforcement of integrity and security policy controls over a virtual entity; for different groups of cloud services, there could be different personae and virtualized environments on each end user device.

4 Analysis of Our Approach

We believe accountability is a useful basis for enhancing privacy in many cloud computing scenarios. Corporate management can quickly comprehend its links with the recognized concept of, and mechanisms for achieving, corporate responsibility. An effective approach will require a combination of procedural and technical measures to be used and co-designed. In essence, this would use measures to link organisational obligations to machine readable policies, and mechanisms to ensure that these policies are adhered to by the parties that use, store or share that data, irrespective of the jurisdiction in which the information is processed (ideally, with a technical basis for enforcement backing up contractual assurances that incorporate privacy). Companies providing cloud computing services would give a suitable level of contractual assurances, to the organisation that wishes to be accountable, that they are can meet the policies (i.e. obligations) that it has set, particularly PII protection requirements. Technology can provide a stronger level of evidence of compliance, and audit capabilities.

While our approach can provide a practical way forward, it has limitations. First, while contracts provide a solution for an initial SP to enforce its policies along the chain, risks that cannot be addressed contractually will remain. For example, data generally has to be unencrypted at the point of processing, creating a security risk and vulnerability due to the cloud's attractiveness to cybercriminals. Secondly, only large corporate users are likely to have the legal resources to replace generic SLAs with customized contracts. Finally, adding requirements to the vendor chain will increase the cost of the service. Use of contracts will be most effective for more sensitive or more highly regulated data that merits additional and more costly protection. We believe that this approach should be scalable.

Accountability is not a substitute for data protection laws, nor would our approach render other approaches for privacy enhancement unnecessary; rather, it is a practical mechanism for helping reduce end user privacy risk and enhance end user control.

5 Conclusions

The current regulatory structure places too much emphasis on recovering if things go wrong, and not enough on trying to get organizations to 'do the right thing' for privacy in the first place. Provision of a hybrid accountability mechanism via a combination of legal, regulatory and technical means leveraging both public and private forms of accountability could be a practical way of addressing this problem; it is a particularly appropriate mechanism for dealing with some of the privacy issues that arise and are combined within cloud computing. Specifically, we advocate a co-regulation strategy based on a corporate responsibility model that is underpinned primarily by contract, and which thus places the onus upon the data controller to take a more proactive approach to ensuring compliance, but at the same time works to encourage cloud service vendors and their subcontractors to compete in the service provision arena, at least in part, on the basis of at least maintaining good, and ideally evolving better, privacy enhancing mechanisms and processes. Further work needs to be done to effectively realize this approach, and we are continuing research in this area within the Encore project [50].

Acknowledgments. This work has greatly benefitted from input by Stacy Martin and MariJo Rogers, and broadly related discussions with colleagues from Encore project, Marty Abrams, Malcolm Crompton, Paul Henrion, Wayne Pauley and Scott Taylor.

References

1. HP cloud website, http://h71028.www7.hp.com/enterprise/us/en/technologies/cloud-computing.html?jumpid=ex_r2858_us/en/large/tsg/go_cloud
2. Pearson, S.: Taking Account of Privacy when Designing Cloud Computing Services. In: ICSE-Cloud 2009, Vancouver. IEEE, Los Alamitos (2009); HP Labs Technical Report, HPL-2009-54 (2009), http://www.hpl.hp.com/techreports/2009/HPL-2009-54.html
3. Solove, D.J.: A Taxonomy of Privacy. University of Pennsylvania Law Review 154(3), 477–564 (2006)
4. Council Directive 95/46/EC: On the protection of individuals with regard to the processing of personal data and on the free movement of such data. OJ, L281, pp. 31–50 (1995)
5. Ackerman, M., Darrell, T., Weitzner, D.: Privacy in Context. Human Computer Interaction 16(2), 167–176 (2001)
6. Cloud Security Alliance: Security Guidance for Critical Areas of Focus in Cloud Computing (2009), http://www.cloudsecurityalliance.org/guidance/csaguide.pdf
7. Gellman, R.: Privacy in the Clouds: Risks to Privacy and Confidentiality from Cloud Computing. World Privacy Forum (2009), http://www.worldprivacyforum.org/pdf/WPF_Cloud_Privacy_Report.pdf
8. Abrams, M.: A Perspective: Data Flow Governance in Asia Pacific & APEC Framework (2008), http://ec.europa.eu/justice_home/news/information_dossiers/personal_data_workshop/speeches_en.htm
9. Kohl, U.: Jurisdiction and the Internet. Cambridge University Press, Cambridge (2007)
10. Mowbray, M.: The Fog over the Grimpen Mire: Cloud Computing and the Law. Script-ed Journal of Law, Technology and Society 6(1) (April 2009)
11. Hall, J.A., Liedtka, S.L.: The Sarbanes-Oxley Act: implications for large-scale IT outsourcing. Communications of the ACM 50(3), 95–100 (2007)
12. McKinley, P.K., Samimi, F.A., Shapiro, J.K., Chiping, T.: Service Clouds: A Distributed Infrastructure for Constructing Autonomic Communication Services. In: Dependable, Autonomic and Secure Computing, pp. 341–348. IEEE, Los Alamitos (2006)
13. Microsoft Corporation: Privacy Guidelines for Developing Software Products and Services, v2.1a (2007), http://www.microsoft.com/Downloads/details.aspx?FamilyID=c48cf80f-6e87-48f5-83ec-a18d1ad2fc1f&displaylang=en
14. Information Commissioners Office: Privacy by Design, Report (2008), http://www.ico.gov.uk

15. Bamberger, K., Mulligan, D.: Privacy Decision-making in Administrative Agencies. University of Chicago Law Review 75(1) (2008)
16. Nissenbaum, H.: Privacy as Contextual Integrity. Washington Law Review 79(1), 119–158 (2004)
17. 6, P.: Who wants privacy protection, and what do they want? Journal of Consumer Behaviour 2(1), 80–100 (2002)
18. Cederquist, J.G., Conn, R., Dekker, M.A.C., Etalle, S., den Hartog, J.I.: An audit logic for accountability. In: Policies for Distributed Systems and Networks, pp. 34–43. IEEE, Los Alamitos (2005)
19. UK Information Commissioner's Office A Report on the Surveillance Society (2006)
20. Charlesworth, A.: The Future of UK Data Protection Regulation. Information Security Technical Report 11(1), 46–54 (2006)
21. Charlesworth, A.: Information Privacy Law in the European Union: E. Pluribus Unum. or Ex. Uno. Plures. Hastings Law Review 54, 931–969 (2003)
22. Weitzner, D., Abelson, H., Berners-Lee, T., Hanson, C., Hendler, J.A., Kagal, L., McGuinness, D.L., Sussman, G.J., Waterman, K.K.: Transparent Accountable Data Mining: New Strategies for Privacy Protection. In: Proceedings of AAAI Spring Symposium on The Semantic Web meets eGovernment. AAAI Press, Menlo Park (2006)
23. Crompton, M., Cowper, C., Jefferis, C.: The Australian Dodo Case: an insight for data protection regulation. World Data Protection Report 9(1) (2009)
24. Dolnicar, S., Jordaan, Y.: Protecting Consumer Privacy in the Company's Best Interest. Australasian Marketing Journal 14(1), 39–61 (2006)
25. Tweney, A., Crane, S.: Trustguide2: An exploration of privacy preferences in an online world. In: Cunningham, P., Cunningham, M. (eds.) Expanding the Knowledge Economy. IOS Press, Amsterdam (2007)
26. Organization for Economic Co-operation and Development: Guidelines Governing the Protection of Privacy and Transborder Flow of Personal Data. OECD, Geneva (1980)
27. Truste: Website (2009), http://www.truste.org/
28. SLA@SOI: Website (2009), http://sla-at-soi.eu/
29. Creative Commons: Creative Commons Home Page (2009), http://creativecommons.org
30. Casassa Mont, M.: Dealing with privacy obligations: Important aspects and technical approaches. In: Katsikas, S.K., López, J., Pernul, G. (eds.) TrustBus 2004. LNCS, vol. 3184, pp. 120–131. Springer, Heidelberg (2004)
31. Mowbray, M., Pearson, S.: A Client-Based Privacy Manager for Cloud Computing. In: Proc. COMSWARE 2009. ACM, New York (2009)
32. Yao, A.C.: How to Generate and Exchange Secrets. In: Proc. FoCS, pp. 162–167. IEEE, Los Alamitos (1986)
33. IBM: The Enterprise Privacy Authorization Language (EPAL), EPAL specification, v1.2 (2004), http://www.zurich.ibm.com/security/enterprise-privacy/epal/
34. OASIS: XACML, http://www.oasis-open.org/committees/tc_home.php?wg_abbrev=xacml
35. Cranor, L.: Web Privacy with P3P. O'Reilly & Associates, Sebastopol (2002)
36. Damianou, N., Dulay, N., Lupu, E., Sloman, M.: The Ponder Policy Specification Language (2001), http://wwwdse.doc.ic.ac.uk/research/policies/index.shtml
37. Casassa Mont, M., Pearson, S., Bramhall, P.: Towards Accountable Management of Identity and Privacy: Sticky Policies and Enforceable Tracing Services. In: Mařík, V., Štěpánková, O., Retschitzegger, W. (eds.) DEXA 2003. LNCS, vol. 2736, pp. 377–382. Springer, Heidelberg (2003)

38. Pearson, S.: Trusted computing: Strengths, weaknesses and further opportunities for en-hancing privacy. In: Herrmann, P., Issarny, V., Shiu, S.C.K. (eds.) iTrust 2005. LNCS, vol. 3477, pp. 305–320. Springer, Heidelberg (2005)
39. Kenny, S., Korba, L.: Applying Digital Rights Management Systems to Privacy Rights Management Computers & Security 21(7) (2002)
40. Tang, Q.: On Using Encryption Techniques to Enhance Sticky Policies Enforcement. TR-CTIT-08-64, Centre for Telematics and Information Technology, Uni. Twente (2008)
41. Golle, P., McSherry, F., Mironov, I.: Data Collection with self-enforcing privacy. In: CCS 2006, Alexandria, Virginia, USA. ACM, New York (2006)
42. Cavoukian, A., Crompton, M.: Web Seals: A review of Online Privacy Programs. In: Privacy and Data Protection (2000), http://www.privacy.gov.au/publications/seals.pdf
43. Elahi, T., Pearson, S.: Privacy Assurance: Bridging the Gap between Preference and Prac-tice. In: Lambrinoudakis, C., Pernul, G., Tjoa, A.M. (eds.) TrustBus. LNCS, vol. 4657, pp. 65–74. Springer, Heidelberg (2007)
44. Casassa Mont, M., Thyne, R.: A Systemic Approach to Automate Privacy Policy En-forcement in Enterprises. In: Danezis, G., Golle, P. (eds.) PET 2006. LNCS, vol. 4258, pp. 118–134. Springer, Heidelberg (2006)
45. Kenny, S., Borking, J.: The Value of Privacy Engineering. JILT, 1 (2002), http://elj.warwick.ac.uk/jilt/02-1/kenny.html
46. IBM: Sparcle project, http://domino.research.ibm.com/comm/research_projects.nsf/pages/sparcle.index.html
47. IBM: REALM project, http://www.zurich.ibm.com/security/publications/2006/REALM-at-IRIS2006-20060217.pdf
48. Travis, D., Breaux, T.D., Antón, A.I.: Analyzing Regulatory Rules for Privacy and Secu-rity Requirements. Transactions on Software Engineering 34(1), 5–20 (2008)
49. OASIS: eContracts Specification v1.0 (2007), http://www.oasis-open.org/apps/org/workgroup/legalxml-econtracts
50. EnCoRe: Ensuring Consent and Revocation project (2008), http://www.encore-project.info
51. Flegel, U.: Pseudonymising Unix Log Files. In: Davida, G.I., Frankel, Y., Rees, O. (eds.) InfraSec 2002. LNCS, vol. 2437, pp. 162–179. Springer, Heidelberg (2002)
52. Gritzalis, D., Moulinos, K., Kostis, K.: A Privacy-Enhancing e-Business Model Based on Infomediaries. In: Gorodetski, V.I., Skormin, V.A., Popyack, L.J. (eds.) MMM-ACNS 2001. LNCS, vol. 2052, pp. 72–83. Springer, Heidelberg (2001)
53. Pearson, S., Sander, T., Sharma, R.: A Privacy Management Tool for Global Outsourcing. In: DPM 2009 (2009)
54. Warren, A., Bayley, R., Charlesworth, A., Bennett, C., Clarke, R., Oppenheim, C.: Privacy Impact Assessments: international experience as a basis for UK guidance. Computer Law and Security Report 24(3), 233–242 (2008)
55. Trusted Computing Group (2009), https://www.trustedcomputinggroup.org
56. Pearson, S., Casassa Mont, M.: A System for Privacy-aware Resource Allocation and Data Processing in Dynamic Environments. In: I-NetSec 2006, vol. 201, pp. 471–482. Springer, Heidelberg (2006)
57. Dalton, C., Plaquin, D., Weidner, W., Kuhlmann, D., Balacheff, B., Brown, R.: Trusted virtual platforms: a key enabler for converged client devices. Operating Systems Re-view 43(1), 36–43 (2009)

Towards an Approach of Semantic Access Control for Cloud Computing

Luokai Hu[1,2], Shi Ying[1], Xiangyang Jia[1], and Kai Zhao[1,3]

[1] Wuhan University, State Key Lab of Software Engineering, 430072 Wuhan, China
[2] Hubei University of Education, Computer School, 430205 Wuhan, China
[3] Xinjiang University, Department of Computer, 830046 Urumchi, China
Luokaihu@gmail.com

Abstract. With the development of cloud computing, the mutual understandability among distributed Access Control Policies (ACPs) has become an important issue in the security field of cloud computing. Semantic Web technology provides the solution to semantic interoperability of heterogeneous applications. In this paper, we analysis existing access control methods and present a new Semantic Access Control Policy Language (SACPL) for describing ACPs in cloud computing environment. Access Control Oriented Ontology System (ACOOS) is designed as the semantic basis of SACPL. Ontology-based SACPL language can effectively solve the interoperability issue of distributed ACPs. This study enriches the research that the semantic web technology is applied in the field of security, and provides a new way of thinking of access control in cloud computing.

Keywords: Semantic Web, Access Control, SACPL, ACOOS, Cloud Computing.

1 Introduction

With the development of Internet and computer software technology, there is a long-term existence of a new trend expected to continue, which is the so-called Cloud Computing. Applications and storage of information will be significant changed in Cloud Computing environment. Applications and data are no longer running and kept in the personal desktop computer, but all are hosted to the "Cloud", which is a cloud-like collection formed by various personal computers and servers that can be visited via the Internet. Cloud computing will allow users from anywhere in the world to access applications and data and you will no longer be restricted on the desktop, which makes remote collaboration easier.

Cloud computing, with a great flexibility and ease of use, makes the safety of data and applications becoming one of the biggest problems. Because Web-based applications have potential security risks, many companies prefer to remain applications (services) and data under the control of their own. In fact, applications and information using of cloud hosting, in rare cases, has the risk of loss of data or illegal access. The data security and backup tool in a big cloud hosting company may be better than

M.G. Jaatun, G. Zhao, and C. Rong (Eds.): CloudCom 2009, LNCS 5931, pp. 145–156, 2009.
© Springer-Verlag Berlin Heidelberg 2009

in the average enterprise. Nevertheless, even if the security threats of the critical data and services hosted in different places are perceived, it may prevent some companies to do so. Therefore, the access to applications or data needs to have appropriate permissions. Traditional syntax-based access control methods can not provide the semantic interoperability for software network environment, such as cloud computing, because of the distributed ACPs among various PCs and servers in various places.

The semantic web is an extension of the current web in which information is given well-defined meaning, better enabling computers and people to work in cooperation [1]. This article proposes a semantic access control approach, which applies Semantic Web Technology to access control method. This study provided a new train of thought for access control in cloud computing environments.

2 Related Works

An access control system is typically described in three ways: access control policies, access control models and access control mechanisms [2]. Policy defines the high level rules according to which access control must be regulated. Model provides a formal representation of the ACPs. Mechanism defines the low level functions that implement the controls imposed by the policy and formally stated in the model.

Access Control Policies can be generally divided into three main policy categories: Discretionary Access Control (DAC), Mandatory Access Control (MAC), and Role-Based Access Control (RBAC). Early DAC models, such as the access control matrix model [3] and the HRU (Harrison–Ruzzo–Ullman) model [4], provide a basic framework for describing DAC policy. In these models, it is the users' discretion to pass their privileges on to other users, leaving DAC policies vulnerable to Trojan Horse attacks [2]. The lattice-based multilevel security policy [5], policies represented by the Bell–LaPadula model [6,7] and the Biba model [8] are typical MAC policies. RBAC policies employ roles to simplify authorization management for enforcing enterprise-specific security policies [9].

By combining a formal framework and a logic-based language, Jajodia et al. developed the authentication specification language (ASL) that can be used to identify different AC policies that can coexist within the same system and be enforced by the same security server [10].

Furthermore, Security Assertion Markup Language (SAML) [11] is an XML framework identified by organization for the advancement of structured information standards (OASIS) security services to exchange authorization information. For AC application across enterprises, Belokosztolszki and Moody proposed meta-policies [12]. Hada and Kudo presented XML access control language (XACL), an XML-based language for provisional authorization, articulating the security policies to be enforced for specific access to XML documents and provides a sophisticated AC mechanism, which enables an initiator to securely browse and update XML documents [13].

EXtensible Access Control Markup Language (XACML) [14], a standard AC policy description language used in e-business, was proposed by organization for the advancement of structured information standards committee, and defined as an XML schema for both AC policy language and a request/response language. XACML can be applied to represent the functionalities of most policy representation mechanisms and express AC statements (who can access what, where and when) [15].

Determined semantics information can ensure the existence of a common understanding for the unknown entities previously. Not only can the policy interaction among multiple systems but also the conflict detection and coordination be realized. Recent studies proposed the policy specification based on Semantic Web technology. KAoS uses DAML as the basis for representing and reasoning about policies within Web Services, Grid Computing, and multi-agent system platforms [16]. KAoS also exploits ontology for representing and reasoning about domains describing organizations of human, agent, and other computational actors.[17] Rei is a deontic logic-based policy language that is grounded in a semantic representation of policies in RDF-S [18]. However, developers of KAoS augured that the pure OWL based method has difficulty in definition of some types of policy [17]. On the basis of XACML and RBAC, access control oriented ontology is used as the semantic annotation of policy specification. Our approach has more powerful description capability than the pure OWL, which is more suitable to implement mutual understanding and semantic interoperability of distributed policy in cloud computing environments.

3 Access Control Oriented Ontology System

Access Control Oriented Ontology System (ACOOS) is designed to provide the common understandable semantic basis for access control in cloud computing environments. ACOOS can be divided into four parts, Subject Ontology, Object Ontology, Action Ontology and Attribute Ontology. In this paper, the Web Ontology Language (OWL) is selected as the modeling language of ACOOS. Specifically, its sub-languages OWL DL is used in order to ensure the completeness of reasoning and decidability.

Ontology is helpful to construct authorization policy within the scope of whole cloud computing environment based on policy definition elements with determined semantics. All authorization entities (subject, object or action) and their attributes should be understood as the unambiguous meaning in the cloud computing environment. The action should be determined in according with the policy to ensure that policy administrator of cloud computing environment can define the ACPs and entities which can be understood by other administrators in different applications.

(1) Subject Ontology
Subject is the entity that has a number of action permissions over object. In the cloud computing environment, a subject can be a user, a user group, an organization, a role, a process, a service and so on, which can also be called Cloud Droplet. There is no absolute boundary between subject and object. The object entity in some scene of applications may also appear as the subject in the scene of other applications, and vice versa. The attribute of a subject is described by the data property and object property of OWL with *hasSubjectDataAttribute* and *hasSubjectAttribute* respectively.

The role in subject ontology represents the capability of a subject to implement a task. Access permission of resources can be encapsulated in the role. If a subject is assigned to a role, it can access the resources indirectly.

In the ontology, the role assignment of subject can be generally grouped in two ways. The first one is explicit assignment, that is, directly use of object properties such as *playsRole* to assign a role for a subject. The second is implicit assignment, that is, through the describing subject attributes and attribute requirement of role respectively, the subject that meets the requirements of the role attribute can be assigned with the corresponding role. The second approach is recommended to achieve the dynamic role assignment more effectively.

The use of role is one of the methods to achieve fine-grained access control. The method described in this article supports the role-based access control. The role of access control can be used as the subject of ACPs.

(2) Object Ontology
Object is the entity as receptor of action and is need for protection. In the cloud computing environment, the typical object can be data, documents, services and other resources. The attribute of an object is described by the data property and object property of OWL with *hasObjectDataAttribute* and *hasObjectAttribute* respectively. Similar to the role of subject, object group can also be used to define the rule to organize objects. Each object group in fact establishes a new object concept, all object individuals of the object concept have object attribute values of the object group. The formal representation using description logic is as follows:

$$ObjectGroup_i \equiv \forall hasObjAtt_1.AttriValue_{i1} \sqcap \exists hasObjAtt_1.AttriValue_{i1} \sqcap ...$$

$$\sqcap \forall hasObjAtt_n.AttriValue_{in} \sqcap \exists hasObjAtt_n.AttriValue_{in}$$

$\forall i (i=1,2,...,m)(m<=n)$, $hasObjAtt_i$ is the sub property of object property *hasObjectAttribute* or data property *hasObjectDataAttribute*

(3) Action Ontology
As concerned with the cloud computing technology, usually a large number of subjects and objects but only a relatively small number of actions could be found, such as reading, writing and execution and so on. In addition, in the cloud computing environment, the procedure often requires the ability to work in parallel, therefore, some actions should be increased such as parallel read, parallel write, parallel execution, parallel reading and writing, parallel writing and reading and so on. However, in the business area of cloud computing, there are relatively more actions named business function process. Action also has properties, known as the *ActionAttribute*, which describes various information of action for authorization and management.

Similar to the role and object group, action group can be defined with helpful for the definition of rules. The definition of action group, nearly the same with the object group, will not repeat it again.

(4) Attribute Ontology
Attribute types are defined in the attribute ontology, can be used to define the attribute of almost all entities, including the subject, object and action.

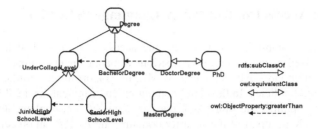

Fig. 1. An example of partial order in attribute ontology

In the ACP, the attribute value of entities is often needed to determine whether meet the Permit conditions or Deny ones. An important issue in attribute definition is the partial order between attribute values. For the attribute value of data property, its partial order can be defined according with the actual numerical value. For the non-data property of attribute values, the manual approach is recommended to explicitly define partial order between attribute values. The following approach of ontology representation for partial order is proposed in this paper.

1) The partial order definition of non-data property attributes value:

① If class A_i and A_j satisfy $A_i \sqsubseteq A_j$, A_j is greater than A_i in the partial order ;

② If class A_i and A_j satisfy $A_i \sqsubseteq \exists greaterThan.A_j$, A_i is greater than A_j in the partial order ;

③ Leaf class is the class that has no subclass. Only the attribute class at the leaf node can be the attribute of entities.

2) The approach of adding an attribute:

① If the adding attribute class A_x is the subclass of an existing attribute class A_E in ontology, the subclass relationship of A_x and A_E ($A_x \sqsubseteq A_E$) should be added by manual. Find the class A_E^k that is "only greater" than class A_x and the class A_E^j that is "only less" than A_x in the subclass chain of class A_E ($A_E^i \mid i = 1...n, A_E^i \sqsubseteq A_E$) and create the relation $A_x \sqsubseteq \exists greaterThan. A_E^j$ and $A_E^k \sqsubseteq \exists greaterThan.A_x$ respectively. The attribute class MasterDegree needs to be added into the attribute ontology in Fig. 1, the following relations needs to be created:

DoctorDegree $\sqsubseteq \exists greaterThan.MasterDegree$, MasterDegree $\sqsubseteq \exists greaterThan.BachelorDegree$.

② If the adding class A_x is the equivalent class of an existing class A_E in the ontology, the equivalent class relationship A_x and A_E ($A_x \equiv A_E$) is needed to add by manual, no other relation should be added.

③ Can not add new super class of an attribute class with existing super class, that is, the multiple inheritance is not allowed.

4   Semantic Access Control Policy Language (SACPL)

In the distributed computing environment, the access control method has changed
from the centralized management into a distributed management approach. There has
been policy markup language, such as XACML, to support description and management of distributed policies. In the cloud computing environment, as the development
of distributed computing, the same ACP may be deployed and implemented in many
points of the whole or a part of the security domain. The ACP of an object (resource)
may be completed by a number of departments even organizations, such as information systems department, human resources and financial department. The same ACP
may be applied to the internal network protection, e-mail system, remote access systems, or a cloud computing platform. As a result, in cloud computing environment,
the issue of interoperability among policies is more important than ever before.

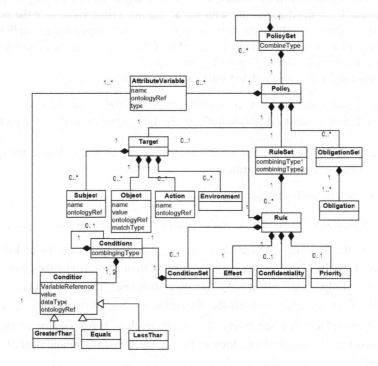

Fig. 2. Meta Model of the SACPL

4.1   Meta-model of SACPL

In this paper, through the semantic annotation of XACML, an ontology-based Semantic Access Control Policy Language (SACPL) is proposed. Specifically, subject, object, action and attribute variables as the basic semantic element are annotated by
ACOOS and some syntax elements such as priority and confidentiality is added. The
language can be applied to access control of cloud computing environments and the

semantic access control is realized. Figure 2 gives the Meta Model of the SACPL language.

4.1.1 Rule and Rule Set

The typical access control applications scenario might be as follows. When a subject requests to perform an action on an object, the corresponding rules are evaluated by the enforcement engine for the request. A typical access control rule is expressed as a 3-tuple subject, object, action, such that a subject can perform some action on an object [19]. The SACPL language extends the typical access control rule 3-tuple to include conditions, confidentiality and priority as we now discuss.

Each access control rule defines a specific combination of: zero or one target, a condition set, an effect, zero or one priority and confidentiality of a rule. The target of the rule includes action, subject that issues the action, object that accepts the action and the environment. Action defines what operations (query, update, execution, or even more detailed action, etc.) of the target are controlled by the rules for more fine-grained access control. If the action part is empty, then the rule is effective for all actions of the subject and object. The subject and the object here can be a single user, a role or user group of security domain for support of RBAC. If the target or part of the target is empty, then use the target defined in policy.

The confidentiality of a rule is used for feedback of the refused request and an example is given in section 4.3. The effect of a rule defines an authorization result predetermined by the rule-making of the action when the target and condition are matched. A rule can have various effects (e.g., allow/deny/oblige/refrain). Since allow and deny rules are the most common ones, this paper focuses on these two kinds of rules. Allow rules authorize a subject to access a particular object. Deny rules explicitly prohibit a subject from accessing a particular object.

The conditions of a rule define a logical expression for factors beyond the target that affect the applicability of the rules (such as state information of resource). The expression can be and/or relation of several conditions. If the conditions are empty, the rule applies in all circumstances. The conditions of the rules need to use the semantic variables defined in the policy, which is generally used to represent the attributes of subject, object and action. It can also be called semantic attribute variables, which can effectively avoid the problem of incomprehensibility of policy caused by the heterogeneous of variables in the syntax layer.

Rule set describes how to compose the various rules on generating the final authorization results of the policy. There are four combination algorithms, Deny-overrides, Permit-overrides, First-applicable, and Priority-overrides. The first three algorithms are recommended by XACML, will not repeat them here. They also can be applied to the policy combination. Rule-maker could specify the priority of rules in the priority-overrides algorithm subjectively, which is not recommended for policy combination. In addition, the Only-one-applicable algorithm is also suitable for the policy combination.

The pseudo-code of Priority-overrides algorithm is as follows.

```
Decision priorityOverrideRuleCombingAlgorithm(Rule
rules[], COMBTYPE comtype){
```

```
/* The priority is initialized as 0. The priority is
defined as five grades and expressed with an integer 1-
5, the greater the value, the higher the priority
level. 0 indicates that the priority of rule is not
set, that is the default value.*/
   int priority = 0 ;
/* Authorization result is initialized as Deny. Au-
thorization result is defined as four kinds of situa-
tion and expressed with enumeration type, namely: Deny,
Permit, Indeterminate and NotApplicable.*/
   Decision decision = NotApplicable ;
   Rule ruleSP = NULL ;
   int n = 0;
   for(i=0; i<lengthof(rules); i++){
     decisionTemp = evaluate(rules[i]) ;
     priorityTemp = checkPriority (rules[i]) ;
     if(priorityTemp > priority){
        if(decisionTemp == Deny||decisionTemp == Permit){
          decision = decisionTemp ;
          priority = priorityTemp ;
          n=ruleSP.flush() ;
        }
     }
     else if (priorityTemp == priority)
        n = ruleSP.addRule(i) ;
   }
   if(n>0){
     if(comtype == DenyOverrides)
      decision = denyOverridesRuleCombiningAlgorithm() ;
     else if(comtype == PermitOverrides)
      decision =permitOverridesRuleCombiningAlgorithm();
     else if(comtype == FisrtApplicableOverrides)
      decision = firstOverridesRuleCombiningAlgorithm();
     else
      return NotApplicable ;
   }
      return decision ;
}
```

4.1.2 Policy and Policy Set

Policy is the smallest component in SACPL. Each SACPL policy contains a group of access control rules based on the same target of the policy. Policy is logical form of structure and expression of access control rules in a security domain. The policy target and rule target have the same structure, it will not repeat them. The reason why a policy also has a target is as follows.

1. When the rules in a rule set have the same subject, object, action or environment, they are unnecessary specified in the rules repeatedly but inherit from the policy.
2. The target of policy can be used as an index. When an access request arrives, the corresponding policy could be found more quickly so that efficiency of the entire access control will be improved.

Attribute variables of policy give the definition of semantic variables that would be used in the conditions of the policy's rules. Attribute variables are usually the attributes of subjects, objects and actions.

Policy Set is the structure form of the distributed policies in cloud. URL reference is employed to organize the policy or policy set to form a new policy set, which can not be used in the rule set. Different from the policy set definition of XACML, the policy set of SACPL does not contain a target.

Finally, each SACPL policy description document should be attached on the digital signature of policy maker to ensure its authenticity and reliability.

4.2 Syntax Structure of SACPL

We propose XML-based syntax structure to support semantic policy description model based on SACPL meta-Model. SACPL syntax structure is shown in Fig. 3. Since the description of policy is more complex than policy set, this paper focuses on the specification of policy. It should generate semantic description document with the extension name of SACPL when SACPL language is used to describe semantic ACPs.

We next use an example to illustrate the basic element of SACPL. In plain language, a policy is:

- Any staff who has greater than or equal to master degree can read the company's technical documentation, but it can not be modified.

The following xml-based policy document illustrates the policy of the above company using SACPL.

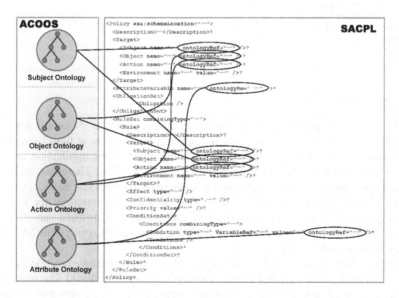

Fig. 3. Syntax Structure of SACPL and Relationship between ACOOS and SACPL

```
<Policy xsi:schemaLocation="http://www.sklse.org/ac/SACPL-1.0-schema.xsd">
 <Target>
  <Subject name="employee" ontologyRef="http://www.sklse.org/onto4AC#OfficerWorker" />
 </Target>
 <AttributeVariable name="degree" type="subject" ontologyRef="www.sklse.org/onto4AC#
EducationalLevel" />
 <RuleSet combining="priorityOverride">
  <Rule>
   <Target>
    <Object name="book"
ontologyRef="http://www.sklse.org/onto4AC#TechnicalDocumentation" />
     <Action name="read" ontologyRef="http://www.sklse.org/onto4AC#OnlineRead" />
   </Target>
   <Effect type="Permit" />
   <Confidentiality type=" Secret" />
   <Priority value="2" />
   <ConditionSet>
    <Conditions combiningType="OR">
     <Condition type="GreaterThan" VariableReference="degree" value="master"
dataType="http://www.w3c.org/2001/XMLSchema#String"
ontologyRef="http://www.sklse.org/onto4AC#MasterDegree" />
      <Condition type="Equals" VariableReference="degree" value="master"
dataType="http://www.w3c.org/2001/XMLSchema#String"
ontologyRef="http://www.sklse.org/onto4AC#MasterDegree" />
    </Conditions>
   </ConditionSet>
  </Rule>
  <Rule>
   <Target>
    <Object name="book"
ontologyRef="http://www.sklse.org/onto4AC#TechnicalDocumentation" />
     <Action name="modify" ontologyRef="http://www.sklse.org/onto4AC#OnlineModify" />
   </Target>
   <Effect type="Deny" />
   <Confidentiality type="Secret" />
   <Priority value="3" />
  </Rule>
 </RuleSet>
</Policy>
```

4.3 Context of SACPL

SACPL provides a semantic policy description language which is suitable for cloud computing environment. However, specific applications may have their own special way to describe the attributes of entities and the request of the application environments may be different from the request description of SACPL. Therefore, request of specific environment should be translated into the request which can be recognized by SACPL, named SACPL Context. SACPL Context still uses ontology for semantic annotating of four basic elements (subject, object, action and attribute variable). The semantic interoperability is achieved through the same ontology system (ACOOS) between SACPL and SACPL Context.

Take the policy of section 4.2 as an example. A company employee named Jack (ontology annotation), with bachelor degree (ontology annotation), would like to read the company's technical documentation (ontology annotation) "file://company/tc/SRS1.0". According to the partial order of degree defined in ACCOS, it can be reasoned that the authorization result of the access request is Deny. The corresponding Request and Response Context is as follows.

```
<Request>
  <Subject value="Jack" ontologyRef="http://www.sklse.org/onto4AC#OfficerWorker">
    <Attribute value="Bachelor" dataType="http://www.w3c.org/2001/XMLSchema#String"
ontologyRef="http://www.sklse.org/onto4AC#BachelorDegree "></Attribute>
  </Subject>
  <Object value="file://company/tc/SRS1.0"
dataType="http://www.w3c.org/2001/XMLSchema#anyURL"
ontologyRef="http://www.sklse.org/onto4AC#TechnicalDocumentation">
  </Object>
  <action value="read" ontologyRef="http://www.sklse.org/onto4AC#OnlineRead"></action>
<Request>
```

Because the confidentiality of rule is "secret", the reason for the Deny is empty (NULL) in the Response Context, that is, the details of violated rule can not be revealed.

```
<Response>
  <Decision>Deny</Decision>
  <Reason>NULL</Reason>
</Response>
```

5 Conclusion

Ontology is ideal for cloud computing environment with characteristics of decentralized and highly heterogeneous. The specification of security policy and security property of different resources (entities) will have clear semantics using ontology-based, the same set of lexical semantic descriptions. Considering the limitations of traditional access control method in the cloud computing, this paper introduces the Semantic Web technologies to the distributed role-based access control method and proposes an ontology-based Semantic Access Control Policy Language (SACPL). Some syntax elements of XACML, such as subject, object, action and attribute variables, are annotated with semantic information using the Access Control Oriented Ontology System (ACOOS) and some syntax elements are added such as priority and confidentiality. This approach can solve the problem of semantic interoperability and mutual understanding on the distributed access control policies of resources when we do the cross-organizational work together. This study provides a new method for ACP specification in cloud computing environment. However, there are several issues in our next study. The approach of automatic conflict resolution for rules or policies and semantics-based access control mechanism for variable granularity are the focus of our future work.

Acknowledgments. This work was supported by the National Natural Science Foundation of China under Grant (No. 60773006), the National Research Foundation for the Doctoral Program of Higher Education of China (No. 20060486045) and the youth project "A Semantic Security Policy Language and its Application" of Hubei University of Education Grant.

References

1. Berners-Lee, T., Hendler, J., Lassila, O.: The semantic web. Scientific American (2001)
2. Samarati, P., de di Vimercati, S.C.: Access control: Policies, models, and mechanisms. In: Focardi, R., Gorrieri, R. (eds.) FOSAD 2000. LNCS, vol. 2171, pp. 137–196. Springer, Heidelberg (2001)
3. Lampson, B.W.: Protection. In: Proceedings of the 5th Princeton Symposium on Information Science and Systems, pp. 437–443 (1971); ACM Operating Systems Review 8(1), 18–24 (1974)
4. Harrison, M.H., Ruzzo, W.L., Ullman, J.D.: Protection in operating systems. Communications of the ACM 19(8), 461–471 (1976)
5. Denning, D.E.: A lattice model of secure information flow. Communications of the ACM 19(5), 236–243 (1976)
6. Bell, D.E., LaPadula, L.J.: Secure Computer Systems: Mathematical Foundations, vol. 1, Technical Report MTR-2547, MITRE Corporation (1973)
7. Bell, D.E., LaPadula, L.J.: Secure Computer System: Unified Exposition and Multics Interpretation, Technical Report MTR-2997, Rev. 1, MITRE Corporation (1976)
8. Biba, K.J.: Integrity Considerations for Secure Computer Systems, Technical Report MTR-3153, Rev. 1, MITRE Corporation (1977)
9. Sandhu, R.S., Coyne, E.J., Feinstein, H.L., Youman, C.E.: Role-based access control models. IEEE Computer 29(2), 38–47 (1996)
10. Jajodia, S., Samarati, P., Sapino, M.L., Subrahmanian, V.S.: Flexible support for multiple access control policies. ACM Transactions on Database Systems 26(2), 214–260 (2001)
11. OASIS, Security Assertion Markup Language Version 1.1 (2003),
    `http://www.oasis-open.org/committees/download.php/3406/`
    `oasis-sstc-saml-core-1.1.pdf`
12. Belokosztolszki, A., Moody, K.: Meta-policies for distributed role-based access control systems. In: Proceedings of the Third International Workshop on Policies for Distributed Systems and Networks, pp. 106–115 (2002)
13. Hada, S., Kudo, M.: XML document security based on provisional authorization. In: Proceedings of the Seventh ACM Conference on Computer and Communications Security, pp. 87–96 (2000)
14. OASIS, Extensible Access Control Markup Language (XACML) Version 2.0 (2005),
    `http://docs.oasis-open.org/xacml/2.0/`
    `access_control-xacml-2.0-core-spec-os.pdf`
15. Lorch, M., Kafura, D., Shah, S.: An XACML-based policy management and authorization service for globus resources. Grid Computing, 208–210 (2003)
16. Johnson, M., et al.: KAoS semantic policy and domain services: An application of DAML to Web-Services-based grid architectures. In: Proceedings of the AAMAS 2003 Workshop on Web Services and Agent-Based Engineering, Melbourne, Australia (2003)
17. Tonti, G., et al.: Semantic web languages for policy representation and reasoning: A comparison of KAoS, Rei and Ponder. In: Proceedings of the 2nd International Semantic Web Conference, Florida, USA (2003)
18. Kagal, L.: Rei: A Policy Language for the Me-Centric Project. HP Labs Technical Report, HPL-2002-270 (2002)
19. Denning, D.E., Denning, P.J.: Cryptography and Data Security. Addison-Wesley, Reading (1982)

Identity-Based Authentication for Cloud Computing

Hongwei Li[1], Yuanshun Dai[1,2], Ling Tian[1], and Haomiao Yang[1]

[1] Collaborative Autonomic Computing Lab, School of Computer Science and Engineering,
University of Electronic Science and Technology of China
hongwei-li@tom.com, ruan052@126.com, yanghaomiao@sohu.com
[2] Innovative Computing Lab, Department of Electronic Engineering & Computer Science,
University of Tennessee, Knoxville, USA
ydai1@eecs.utk.edu

Abstract. Cloud computing is a recently developed new technology for complex systems with massive-scale services sharing among numerous users. Therefore, authentication of both users and services is a significant issue for the trust and security of the cloud computing. SSL Authentication Protocol (SAP), once applied in cloud computing, will become so complicated that users will undergo a heavily loaded point both in computation and communication. This paper, based on the identity-based hierarchical model for cloud computing (IBHMCC) and its corresponding encryption and signature schemes, presented a new identity-based authentication protocol for cloud computing and services. Through simulation testing, it is shown that the authentication protocol is more lightweight and efficient than SAP, specially the more lightweight user side. Such merit of our model with great scalability is very suited to the massive-scale cloud.

Keywords: cloud computing, identity-based cryptography, authentication.

1 Introduction

Cloud computing is a style of computing in which dynamically scalable and often virtualized resources are provided as a service over the Internet. Users need not have knowledge of, expertise in, or control over the technology infrastructure 'in the cloud' that supports them [1,2]. Authentication, thus, becomes pretty important for cloud security. Applied to cloud computing and based on standard X.509 certificate-based PKI authentication framework, SSL Authentication Protocol (SAP) [3] is low efficient. The authors of Grid Security Infrastructure (GSI) conceded that the current GSI technique has a poor scalability [4]. W.B. Mao analyzed that this scalability problem is an inherent one due to the use of SAP [5].

Grid computing and cloud computing are so similar that grid security technique can be applied to cloud computing. Dai et al. made great contribution to Grid security [6-9]. Recently, identity-based cryptography (IBC) is developing very quickly [10-12]. The idea of applying IBC to grid security was initially explored by Lim (2004) [13]. Mao et al. (2004) proposed an identity-based non-interactive authentication framework for grid [5]. The framework is certificate-free. But the unique Private Key

M.G. Jaatun, G. Zhao, and C. Rong (Eds.): CloudCom 2009, LNCS 5931, pp. 157–166, 2009.
© Springer-Verlag Berlin Heidelberg 2009

Generator (PKG) becomes the bottleneck of framework. Lim and Robshow (2005) proposed a hybrid approach combining IBC [14]. The approach solves escrow and distribution of private key. However, the non-interactive and certificate-free quality is lost. Chen (2005) revisited the GSI in the GT version2 and improved the GSI architecture and protocols [15]. It is significant to study IBC and cloud computing.

In this paper, based on identity-based hierarchical model for cloud computing (IBHMCC) and corresponding encryption and signature schemes, an identity-based authentication for cloud computing (IBACC) is proposed. IBACC is more efficient and lightweight than SAP, specially the more lightweight user side, which contributes good scalability to the much larger cloud systems.

The remaining of the paper is organized as the following. Section 2 introduces the identity-based hierarchical model for cloud computing (IBHMCC). In section 3, we propose identity-based encryption and signature technology for the IBHMCC. Section 4 proposes identity-based authentication mechanism for cloud computing. Section 5 makes the performance analysis for our new protocols and did simulated experiments to validate the techniques.

2 Identity-Based Hierarchical Model for Cloud Computing

As shown in Fig.1, IBHM for cloud computing (IBHMCC) is composed of three levels. The top level (level-0) is root PKG. The level-1 is sub-PKGs. Each node in level-1 corresponds to a data-center (such as a Cloud Storage Service Provider) in the cloud computing. The bottom level (level-2) are users in the cloud computing. In IBHMCC, each node has a unique name. The name is the node's registered distinguished name (DN) when the node joins the cloud storage service. For example, in the Fig.1, DN of the root node is DN_0 , DN of node M is DN_M and DN of node N is DN_N. We define the identity of node is the DN string from the root node to the current node itself. For example, the identity of entity N is $ID_N = DN_0 \parallel DN_M \parallel DN_N$. " $\parallel$ " denotes string concatenation. We further define $ID_N \mid_0 = DN_0$, $ID_N \mid_1 = DN_0 \parallel DN_M$, $ID_N \mid_2 = DN_0 \parallel DN_M \parallel DN_N$ .The rule is applicable to all nodes in the hierarchical model.

The deployment of IBHMCC needs two modules: Root PKG setup and Lower-level setup.

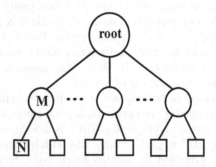

Fig. 1. IBHM for cloud computing

Root PKG setup: Root PKG acts as follows:

1. Generate group G_1, G_2 of some prime order q and an admissible pairing $\hat{e}: G_1 \times G_1 \rightarrow G_2$;
2. Choose an arbitrary generator $P \in G_1$;
3. Choose cryptography hash functions $H_1: \{0,1\}^* \rightarrow G_1, H_2: G_2 \rightarrow \{0,1\}^n$ for some n;
4. Pick a random $\alpha \in \mathbb{Z}_q^*$ and set $Q_0 = \alpha P$, $P_0 = H_1(DN_0), S_0 = \alpha P_0$. The root PKG's master key is S_0 and the system parameters are $< G_1, G_2, \hat{e}, Q_0, P, P_0, H_1, H_2 >$.

Lower-level setup

1. Assume there are m nodes in the level-1. For each node, the root PKG acts as follows (let X be an arbitrary node in the m nodes):
2. Compute the public key of node $X : P_X = H_1(ID_X)$, where $ID_X = DN_0 \parallel DN_X$;
3. Pick the secret point $\rho_X \in \mathbb{Z}_q^*$ for node $X . \rho_X$ is only known by node X and its parent node;
4. Set the secret key of node $X : S_X = S_0 + \rho_X P_X$;
5. Define the Q-value: $Q_{ID_X \parallel} = \rho_X P . Q_{ID_X \parallel}$ is public.

After the above five steps are finished, all nodes in the level-1 get and securely keep their secret keys and the secret points. On the other hand, the public key and the Q-value are publicized.

Then, Each node in the level-1 similarly repeats the above steps (2-5). Similarly, all nodes in level-2 keep the secret keys and the secret point while publicizing the public key and Q-value.

3 Identity-Based Encryption and Signature for IBHMCC

In the cloud computing, it is frequent for the entities to communicate mutually. To achieve the security in the communication, it is important to propose an encryption and signature schemes. Therefore, we propose an identity-based encryption (IBE) and identity-based signature (IBS) schemes for IBHMCC in the following.

3.1 Identity-Based Encryption

IBE is based on the above Root PKG setup and Lower-level setup algorithms. It is composed by two parts: Encryption and Decryption.

Encryption: Assume E_1 and E_2 are two entities in the cloud computing. The identity of entity E_2 is $ID_{E_2} = DN_0 \parallel DN_1 \parallel DN_2$. To encrypt message m with ID_{E_2}, E_1 acts as follows:

1. Compute

$$P_1 = H_1(DN_0 \parallel DN_1) \tag{1}$$

$$P_2 = H_1(DN_0 \| DN_1 \| DN_2) \tag{2}$$

2. Choose a random $r \in \mathbb{Z}_q^*$;

3. Output the ciphertext

$$C = < rP, rP_1, rP_2, H_2(g^r) \oplus m > \tag{3}$$

where $g = \hat{e}(Q_0, P_0)$ which can be pre-computed.

Decryption: After receiving the ciphertext $C = <U_0, U_1, U_2, V>$, entity E_2 can decrypt C using its secret key $S_{E_2} = S_0 + \rho_1 P_1 + \rho_2 P_2$, where ρ_1 is the secret point of node $DN_0 \| DN_1$, ρ_2 is the secret point of node $DN_0 \| DN_1 \| DN_2$:

1. Compute

$$d = \frac{\hat{e}(U_0, S_{E_2})}{\prod_{i=1}^{2} \hat{e}(Q_{ID_{E_2}|i}, U_i)} \tag{4}$$

where $Q_{ID_{E_2}|1} = \rho_1 P, Q_{ID_{E_2}|2} = \rho_2 P$;

2. Output the message $m = H_2(d) \oplus V$.

3.2 Identity-Based Signature

IBS is also based on Root PKG setup and Lower-level setup algorithms. It incorporates two algorithms: signature and verification.

Signature: To sign message m, entity E_2 acts as follows:

1. Compute $P_m = H_1(DN_0 \| DN_1 \| DN_2 \| m)$;
2. Compute $\delta = S_{E_2} + \rho_2 P_m$, where ρ_2 is the secret point of entity E_2;
3. Output the signature $< \delta, P_m, Q_{ID_{E_2}|1}, Q_{ID_{E_2}|2} >$.

Verification: Other Entities can verify the signature by acting as follows: Confirm

$$\hat{e}(P, \delta) = \hat{e}(P, \rho_2 P_m) \; \hat{e}(Q_0, P_0) \prod_{i=1}^{2} \hat{e}(Q_{ID_{E_2}|i}, P_i) \tag{5}$$

if the equation is true, the signature is validated.

4 Identity-Based Authentication for Cloud Computing

In this section, based on the former IBE and IBS schemes, an identity-based authentication for cloud computing (IBACC) is proposed.

(1) $C \rightarrow S$: **ClientHello** ($n_C, ID, specification_C$)
   ClientHelloDone
(2) $S \rightarrow C$: **ServerHello** ($n_S, ID, specification_S$)
   ServerKeyExchange ($E_{P_C}[F_{CS}]$)
   IdentityVerify ($Sig_{S_S}[M]$)
   ServerHelloDone
(3) $C \rightarrow S$: **ClientFinished**

Fig. 2. Identity-based Authentication Protocol

where

n_C, n_S : the fresh random number

ID : the session identifier

$specification_C$: the cipher specification of C

$specification_S$: the cipher specification of S

F_{CS} : a pre-master secret used to generate the shared key

$E_{P_C}[F_{CS}]$: encrypt F_{CS} with the public key P_C of entity C using the encryption algorithm of IBE

M : all handshake messages since the ClientHello message

$Sig_{S_S}[M]$: sign M with the private key S_S of entity S using the signature algorithm of IBS

In step (1), the client C sends the server S a ClientHello message. The message contains a fresh random number n_C , session identifier ID and $specification_C$. $Specification_C$ extends from TLS to handle the IBE and IBS schemes. For example, $Specification_C$ could be the form $TLS\_IBE\_IBS\_WITH\_SHA\_AES$. IBE and IBS are used as secure transporting and authentication. SHA is the hash function. AES is the symmetric encryption algorithm.

In step (2), the server S responds with a ServerHello message which contains a new fresh random number n_S , the session identifier ID and the cipher specification $specification_S$. The $specification_S$ is S 's supporting ciphersuite. Then C chooses a pre-master secret F_{CS} and encrypts it with the public key P_C of entity C using the encryption algorithm of IBE. The ciphertext is transmitted to C as ServerKeyExchange message. Then S generates a signature $Sig_{S_S}[M]$ as the IdentityVerify message to forward to C . Finally, The ServerHelloDone message means the step (2) is over.

In step (3), C firstly verifies the signature $Sig_{S_S}[M]$ with the help of ID_S . Pass of verification means S is the valid owner of ID_S . This completes authentication form

S to C .Then C decrypts the $E_{P_C}[F_{CS}]$ with its private key S_C . Because of the fresh F_{CS} , the correct decryption indicates C is the valid owner of ID_C . This step authenticates the validity of C . The ServerFinished message means the step (3) finishes.

Eventually, a shared secret key between C and S is calculated by $K_{CS} = PRF(F_{CS}, n_C, n_S)$, where PRF is pseudo-random function.

5 Performance Analysis and Simulation

In this section, performance comparisons between SAP and IBACC are firstly discussed. Then simulation experiment gives precise results.

5.1 Communication Cost

The comparison of communication cost between the two different protocols is shown in table 1. Note that only dominant communication is considered, i.e. certificate, signed or encrypted messages, which may have the greatest consumptions of the network bandwidth.

Table 1. Comparison of communication cost

SAP		IBACC	
Certificate	RSA Signature	IBS Signature	IBE Ciphertext
2	2	1	1

Reference [3] shows that communication cost of SAP is two public key certificates and two RSA signatures. However, in the IBACC, the communication cost is only one IBS signature and one IBE ciphertext.

5.2 Computation Cost

The comparison of computation cost between the two different protocols is shown in table 2. Note that only dominant computation is considered, i.e. encryption, decryption and authentication.

Table 2. Comparison of computation cost

	SAP	IBACC
Client	1 ENC_R , 1 SIG_R and Authenticating server	1 ENC_I and 1 SIG_I
Server	1 DEC_R , 1 SIG_R and Authenticating client	1 DEC_I and 1 VER_I

Where

ENC_R = RSA encryption

DEC_R = RSA decryption

ENC_I = IBE encryption

DEC_I = IBE decryption

SIG_R = RSA signature

SIG_I = IBS signature

VER_I = IBS signature verification

Authenticating server=Including building certification path of server and verifying signatures.

Authenticating client= Including building certification path of client and verifying signatures.

The paper [3] showed that in the SAP, the computation cost of client was one RSA encryption, one RSA signature and Authenticating server. The computation cost of server was one RSA decryption, one RSA signature and Authenticating client. However, in the IBACC, the computation cost of client is one IBE encryption and one IBS signature. The computation cost of server is one IBE decryption and one IBS signature verification.

5.3 Simulation and Experiment Results

Simulation Platform and Reference

The platform of simulation experiment is GridSim [16] which is a simulation platform based on Java. Special users and resources can be generated by rewriting these interfaces. This aligns well with various users and resources of cloud computing. Furthermore, GridSim is based on SimJava which is a discrete event simulation tool based on Java and simulates various entities by multiple thread. This aligns well with randomness of cloud computing entity action. Therefore, it is feasible to simulate our proposed authentication protocol of cloud computing by GridSim.

The simulation environment is composed of four computers which are all equipped with P4 3.0 CPU, 2G memory. Certification chain is important for SAP. The shorter, the better. The shortest certification chain includes all 4 certifications: CA_1, client and CA_2, server. There are a cross authentication for CA_1 and CA_2. It is in this scene that SAP and IBACC are compared. Based on openssl0.9.7, SAP is implemented. Pairing computing adapts the algorithms of reference [17]. To precisely simulate the network delay, there are 25~45ms waiting time before messages are sent.

Simulation Results and Analysis

Fig.3 illustrates the authentication time of IBACC is approximately 571 ms while that of SAP is 980 ms. That is to say, authentication time of IBACC is 58% of that of SAP. Fig.4 shows thecommunication cost of IBACC is approximately 1785 bytes while that of SAP is 5852 bytes. That is to say, communication cost of IBACC is 31% of that of SAP. The simulation results confirm that the communication cost of IBACC is less and the authentication time is shorter.

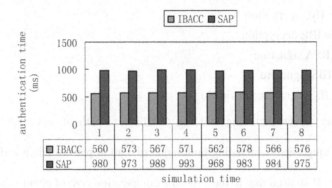

Fig. 3. Comparison of authentication time

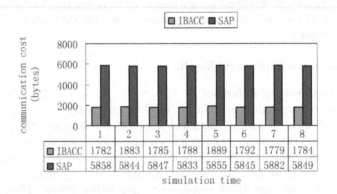

Fig. 4. Comparison of communication cost

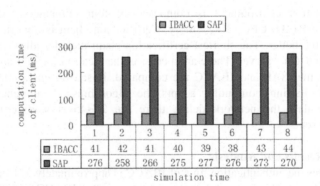

Fig. 5. Comparison of computation time of client

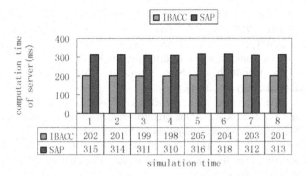

Fig. 6. Comparison of computation time of server

As shown in Fig.5, computation time of client for IBACC is approximately 41 ms while that for SAP is 272 ms. That is to say, computation time of client for IBACC is 15% of that for SAP. Fig.6 illustrates computation time of server for IBACC is approximately 202 ms while that for SAP is 313 ms. That is to say, computation time of server for IBACC is 65% of that for SAP. The simulation results confirm that both client and server of IBACC are more lightweight than those of SAP.

Furthermore, computation time of client is 20% of that of server in IBACC. This aligns well with the idea of cloud computing which allows the user with an average or low-end platform to outsource its computational tasks to more powerful servers. As a result, the more lightweight user side can connect more servers and contribute to the larger scalability.

6   Conclusion

Authentication is necessary in Cloud Computing. SSL Authentication Protocol is of low efficiency for Cloud services and users. In this paper, we presented an identity-based authentication for cloud computing, based on the identity-based hierarchical model for cloud computing (IBHMCC) and corresponding encryption and signature schemes. Being certificate-free, the authentication protocol aligned well with demands of cloud computing. Performance analysis indicated that the authentication protocol is more efficient and lightweight than SAP, especially the more lightweight user side. This aligned well with the idea of cloud computing to allow the users with an average or low-end platform to outsource their computational tasks to more powerful servers.

References

1. Erdogmus, H.: Cloud Computing: Does Nirvana Hide behind the Nebula? IEEE Software 26(2), 4–6 (2009)
2. Leavitt, N.: Is Cloud Computing Really Ready for Prime Time? Computer 42(1), 15–20 (2009)

3. Freier, A.O., Karlton, P., Kocher, P.C.: The SSL Protocol, Version 3.0.INTERNET-DRAFT (November 1996), http://draft-freier-ssl-version3-02.txt

4. Foster, I., Kesslman, C., Tsudik, G.: A Security Architecture for Computational Grids. In: ACM Conference on Computers and Security, pp. 83–90 (1998)

5. Mao, W.B.: An Identity-based Non- interactive Authentication Framework for Computational Grids, May 29 (2004),
http://www.hpl.hp.com/techreports/2004/HPL-2004-96.pdf

6. Dai, Y.S., Pan, Y., Zou, X.K.: A hierarchical modelling and analysis for grid service reliability. IEEE Transactions on Computers 56(5), 681–691 (2007)

7. Dai, Y.S., Levitin, G., Trivedi, K.S.: Performance and Reliability of Tree-Structured Grid Services Considering Data Dependence and Failure Correlation. IEEE Transactions on Computers 56(7), 925–936 (2007)

8. Dai, Y.S., Levitin, G.: Reliability and Performance of Tree-structured Grid Services. IEEE Transactions on Reliability 55(2), 337–349 (2006)

9. Dai, Y.S., Xie, M., Wang, X.L.: Heuristic Algorithm for Reliability Modeling and Analysis of Grid Systems. IEEE Transactions on Systems, Man, and Cybernetics, Part A 37(2), 189–200 (2007)

10. Boneh, D., Gentry, C., Hamburg, M.: Space Efficient Identity Based Encryption without Pairings. In: Proceedings of FOCS 2007, pp. 647–657 (2007)

11. Boneh, D.: Generalized Identity Based and Broadcast Encryption Schemes. In: Pieprzyk, J. (ed.) ASIACRYPT 2008. LNCS, vol. 5350, pp. 455–470. Springer, Heidelberg (2008)

12. Boyen, X.: General Ad Hoc Encryption from Exponent Inversion IBE. In: Naor, M. (ed.) EUROCRYPT 2007. LNCS, vol. 4515, pp. 394–411. Springer, Heidelberg (2007)

13. Lim, H.W., Robshaw, M.: On Identity- Based. Cryptography and Grid Computing. In: Bubak, M., van Albada, G.D., Sloot, P.M.A., Dongarra, J. (eds.) ICCS 2004. LNCS, vol. 3036, pp. 474–477. Springer, Heidelberg (2004)

14. Lim, H.W., Robshaw, M.: A dynamic key infrastructure for GRID. In: Sloot, P.M.A., Hoekstra, A.G., Priol, T., Reinefeld, A., Bubak, M. (eds.) EGC 2005. LNCS, vol. 3470, pp. 255–264. Springer, Heidelberg (2005)

15. Chen, L., Lim, H.W., Mao, W.B.: User-friendly grid security architecture and protocols. In: Proceedings of the 13th International Workshop on Security Protocols (2005)

16. Buyya, R., Murshed, M.: GridSim: a toolkit for the modeling and simulation of distributed resource management and scheduling for grid computing. Journal of concurrency and computation practice and experience 14(13-15), 1175–1220 (2002)

17. Barreto, P.S.L.M., Kim, H.Y., Lynn, B., Scott, M.: Efficient algorithms for pairing-based cryptosystems. In: Yung, M. (ed.) CRYPTO 2002. LNCS, vol. 2442, pp. 354–368. Springer, Heidelberg (2002)

Strengthen Cloud Computing Security with Federal Identity Management Using Hierarchical Identity-Based Cryptography

Liang Yan[1], Chunming Rong[1], and Gansen Zhao[2]

[1] University of Stavanger, Norway
{liang.yan,chunming.rong}@uis.no
[2] South China Normal University, China
zhaogansen@gmail.com

Abstract. More and more companies begin to provide different kinds of cloud computing services for Internet users at the same time these services also bring some security problems. Currently the majority of cloud computing systems provide digital identity for users to access their services, this will bring some inconvenience for a hybrid cloud that includes multiple private clouds and/or public clouds. Today most cloud computing system use asymmetric and traditional public key cryptography to provide data security and mutual authentication. Identity-based cryptography has some attraction characteristics that seem to fit well the requirements of cloud computing. In this paper, by adopting federated identity management together with hierarchical identity-based cryptography (HIBC), not only the key distribution but also the mutual authentication can be simplified in the cloud.

1 Introduction

Cloud Computing is a new computing model that distributes the computing missions on a resource pool that includes a large amount of computing resources. It is the result of development of infrastructure as a service (IAAS), platform as a service (PAAS), and software as a service (SAAS). With broadband Internet access, Internet users are able to acquire computing resource, storage space and other kinds of software services according to their needs. In cloud computing, with a large amount of various computing resources, users can easily solve their problems with the resources provided by a cloud. This brings great flexibility for the users. Using cloud computing service, users can store their critical data in servers and can access their data anywhere they can with the Internet and do not need to worry about system breakdown or disk faults, etc. Also, different users in one system can share their information and work, as well as play games together. Many important companies such as Amazon, Google, IBM, Microsoft, and Yahoo are the forerunners that provide cloud computing services. Recently more and more companies such as Salesforce, Facebook, Youtube, Myspace etc. also begin to provide all kinds of cloud computing services for Internet users.

M.G. Jaatun, G. Zhao, and C. Rong (Eds.): CloudCom 2009, LNCS 5931, pp. 167–177, 2009.

Currently, as shown in Figure 1, there are mainly three types of clouds: private clouds, public clouds and hybrid clouds [15]. Private clouds, also called internal clouds, are the private networks that offer cloud computing services for a very restrictive set of users within internal network. For example, some companies and universities can use their internal networks to provide cloud computing services for their own users. These kinds of networks can be thought as private clouds. Public clouds or external clouds refer to clouds in the traditional sense [13], such as enterprises that provide cloud computing services for the public users. Hybrid clouds are the clouds that include multiple private and/or public clouds [14]. Providing security in a private cloud and a public cloud is easier, comparing with a hybrid cloud since commonly a private cloud or a public cloud only has one service provider in the cloud. Providing security in a hybrid cloud that consisting multiple service providers is much more difficult especially for key distribution and mutual authentication. Also for users to access the services in a cloud, a user digital identity is needed for the servers of the cloud to manage the access control. While in the whole cloud, there are many different kinds of clouds and each of them has its own identity management system. Thus user who wants to access services from different clouds needs multiple digital identities from different clouds, which will bring inconvenience for users. Using federated identity management, each user will have his unique digital identity and with this identity, he can access different services from different clouds.

Identity-based cryptography [10] is a public key technology that allows the use of a public identifier of a user as the user's public key. Hierarchy identity-based cryptography is the development from it in order to solve the scalability problem. Recently identity-based cryptography and hierarchy identity-based cryptography have been proposed to provide security for some Internet applications. For example, applying identity-based cryptography in the grid computing and web service security have been explored in [11] [8] [12] and [5].

This paper proposes to use federated identity management in the cloud such that each user and each server will have its own unique identity, and the identity is allocated by the system hierarchically. With this unique identity and hierarchical identity-based cryptography (HIBC), the key distribution and mutual authentication can be greatly simplified.

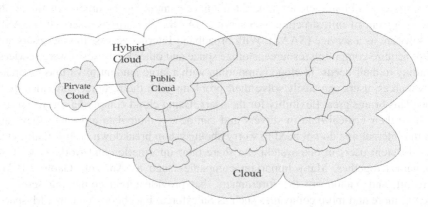

Fig. 1. Cloud type

The rest of this paper is organized as follows. In Section 2, we introduce security problems and related solutions in cloud computing. In Section 3, we describe the principle of identity-based cryptography and HIBC. In Section 4, we describe how to use federated identity management and HIBC in the cloud computing system to provide security. Section 5 concludes the paper.

2 Security in Cloud Computing

Cloud computing have many advantages in cost reduction, resource sharing, time saving for new service deployment. While in a cloud computing system, most data and software that users use reside on the Internet, which bring some new challenges for the system, especially security and privacy. Since each application may use resource from multiple servers. The servers are potentially based at multiple locations and the services provided by the cloud may use different infrastructures across organizations. All these characteristics of cloud computing make it complicated to provide security in cloud computing. To ensure adequate security in cloud computing, various security issues, such as authentication, data confidentiality and integrity, and non-repudiation, all need to be taken into account. Currently, WS-Security service is wildly used in the cloud to provide security for the system. In WS-Security, XML encryption and XML signature are used to provide data confidentiality and integrity. Mutual authentication can be supported by adding X.509 certificate and Kerberos tickets into SOAP message header.

As mentioned earlier, there are three types of clouds in general: private cloud, public cloud and hybrid cloud. In a public cloud, resources are dynamically provisioned on a fine-grained, self-service basis over the Internet. Services in the cloud are provided by an off-site third-party provider who shares resources and bills on a fine-grained utility computing basis. While in most private clouds, with limited computing resources, it is difficult for a private cloud to provide all services for their users, as some services may more resources than internal cloud can provide. Hybrid cloud is a potential solution for this issue since they can get the computing resources from external cloud computing providers. Private clouds have their advantages in corporation governance and offer reliable services, as well as they allow more control than public clouds do. For the security concerns, when a cloud environment is created inside a firewall, it can provide its users with less exposure to Internet security risks. Also in the private cloud, all the services can be accessed through internal connections rather than public Internet connections, which make it easier to use existing security measures and standards. This can make private clouds more appropriate for services with sensitive data that must be protected. While in a hybrid cloud, it includes more than one domain, which will increase the difficulty of security provision, especially key management and mutual authentication. The domains in a hybrid cloud can be heterogeneous networks, hence there may be gaps between these networks and between the different services providers. Even security can be well guaranteed in each of private/public cloud, while in a hybrid cloud with more than one kind of clouds that have different kinds of network conditions and different security policies, how to provide efficient security protection is much more difficult. For example, cross domain authentication can be a problem in a hybrid cloud with different domains. Although some authentication services such as Kerberos can provide multi-domain authentication, but one of the requirements for the multi-domain Kerberos authentication is that the Kerberos server in each domain needs to share a secret key with servers in other Kerberos domains and every two Kerberos servers need to be registered with each other. The problem here is if there are N Kerberos domains and each of them want to trust each other, then the number of key exchanges is N(N-1)/2. For a hybrid cloud with a large number of domains, this will bring a problem for scalability. If different networks in a hybrid cloud using different authentication protocols, this problem can be more complex.

In a cloud, the cloud computing system needs to provide a strong and user-friendly way for users to access all kinds of services in the system. When a user wants to run an application in the cloud, the user is required to provide a digital identity. Normally, this identity is a set of bytes that related to the user. Based on the digital identity, a cloud system can know what right this user has and what the user is allowed to do in the system. Most of cloud platforms include an identity service since identity information is required for most distributed applications [3]. These cloud computing systems will provide a digital identity for every user. For example, user with a Windows Live ID can use cloud computing services provided by Microsoft and user who wants to access cloud computing services from Amazon and Google also needs an Amazon-defined identity and Google account. Here, each of these companies is a public cloud. The problem here is this digital identity can only be used in one private cloud or one public cloud. Users want to access services in the cloud that provided by different clouds will need to have multiple identities, each for one of the cloud. This is obviously not user friendly.

To solve these problems in the cloud, we propose to use federated identity management in clouds with HIBC. The proposed scheme does not only allow users from a cloud to access services from other clouds with a single digital identity, it also simplifies the key distribution and mutual authentication in a hybrid cloud.

3 Identity-Based Cryptography and Signature

Identity-based cryptography and signature schemes were firstly proposed by Shamir [10] in 1984. But only in 2001, a efficient approach of identity-based encryption schemes was developed by Dan Boneh and Matthew K. Franklin [2] and Clifford Cocks [4]. These schemes are based on bilinear pairings on elliptic curves and have provable security. Recently hierarchical identity-based cryptography (HIBC) has been proposed in [6, 7] to improve the scalability of traditional identity-based cryptography scheme.

Identity-based cryptographic scheme is a kind of public-key based approach that can be used for two parties to exchange messages and effectively verify each other's signatures. Unlike in traditional public-key systems that using a random string as the public key, with identity-based cryptography user's identity that can uniquely identify that user is used as the public key for encryption and signature verification. Identity-based cryptography can ease the key management complexity as public keys are not required to be distributed securely to others. Another advantage of identity-based encryption is that encryption and decryption can be conducted offline without the key generation center.

In the identity-based cryptography approach, the PKG should creates a "master" public key and a corresponding "master" private key firstly, then it will make this "master" public key public for all the interested users. Any user can use this "master" public key and the identity of a user to create the public key of this user. Each user wants to get his private key needs to contact the PKG with his identity. PKG will use the identity and the "master" private key to generate the private key for this user. In Dan Boneh and Matthew K. Franklin's approach, they defined four algorithms for a complete identity-based cryptography system. It includes setup, extract, encryption and decryption.

1. **Setup:** PKG create a master key K_m and the system parameters P. K_m is kept secret and used to generate private key for users. System parameters P are made public for all the users and can be used to generate users' public key with their identities.

2. **Extract:** When a user requests his private key from the PKG, PKG will use the identity of this user, system parameters P and master key K_m to generate a private key for this user.

3. **Encryption:** When a user wants to encrypt a message and send to another user, he can use the system parameters P, receiver's identity and the message as input to generate the cipher text.

4. **Decryption:** Receiving a cipher text, receiver can use the system parameters P and his private key got from the PKG to decrypt the cipher text.

In a network using identity-based cryptography, the PKG needs not only to generate private keys for all the users, but also to verify the user identities and establish secure channels to transmit private keys. In a large network with only one PKG, the PKG will have a burdensome job. In this case, HIBC [6] can be a better choice. In a HIBC network, a root PKG will generate and distribute private keys for domain-level PKGs and the domain-level PKGs will generate and distribute private keys to the users in their own domain. HIBC is suitable for a large scale network since it can reduce the workload of root PKG by distribute the work of user authentication, private key generation and distribution to the different level of PKGs. It can also improve the security of the network because user authentication and private key distribution can be done locally. The HIBC encryption and signature algorithms include root setup, lower-level setup, extraction, encryption, and decryption.

1. **Root setup:** root PKG will generate the root PKG system parameters and a root secret. The root secret will be used for private key generation for the lower-level PKGs. The root system parameters are made publicly available and will be used to generate public keys for lower-level PKGs and users.

2. **Lower-level setup:** Each lower-level PKG will get the root system parameters and generate its own lower-level secret. This lower-level secret will be used to generate private keys for the users in its domain.

3. **Extract:** When a user or PKG at level t with its identity ($ID_1,..., ID_t$) requests his private key from its upper-level PKG, where ($ID_1,..., ID_i$) is the identity of its ancestor at level i ($1 \leq i \leq t$), the upper-level PKG will use this

identity, system parameters and its own private key to generate a private key for this user.

4. **Encryption:** User who wants to encrypt a message M can use the system parameters, receiver's identity and the message as input to generate the cipher text.

   C = Encryption (parameters, receiver ID, M).

5. **Decryption:** Receiving a cipher text, receiver can use system parameters and his private key got from the PKG to decrypt the cipher text.

   M = Decryption (parameters, k, C), k is the private key of the receiver

6. **Signing and verification:** A user can use parameters, its private key, and message M to generate a digital signature and sends to the receiver. Receiver and verify the signature using the parameters, message M, and the sender's ID.

   Signature = Signing (parameters, k, M), k is the sender's private key.

   Verification = (parameters, sender ID, M,Signature).

There are some inherent limitations with the identity-based cryptography [1]. One of the issues is the key escrow problem. Since users' private keys are generated by PKG, the PKG can decrypt a user's message and create any user's digital signature without authorization. This in fact means that PKGs must be highly trusted. So the identity-based scheme is more appropriate for a closed group of users such as a big company or a university. Since only under this situation, PKGs can be set up with users' trust.

In a system using HIBC, every PKG in the hierarchy knows the users' private keys in the domain under the PKG. Although key escrow problem can not be avoided, this can limit the scope of key escrow problem. Another drawback of the identity-based cryptography is the revocation problem. Because all the users in the system use some unique identifiers as their public keys, if one user's private key has been compromised, the user need to change its public key. For example, if the public key is the user's name, address, or email address, it is inconvenient for the user to change it. One solution for this problem is to add a time period to the identifier as the public key [2], but it can not solve this problem completely.

4   Using Federated Identity Management in Cloud

4.1   Federated Identity Management in the Cloud

Compared with centralized identity, which is used to deal with security problems within the same networks, federated identity is adopted to deal with the security problems that a user may want to access external networks or an external user may want to access internal networks. Federated identity is a standard-based mechanism for different organization to share identity between them and it can enable the portability of identity information to across different networks. One common use of federated identity is secure Internet single sign-on, where a user who logs in successfully at one organization can access all partner networks without having to log in again. Using identity federation can increase the security of network since it only requires a user to identify and authenticate him to the system for one time and this identity information can be used in different networks. Use of identity federation standards can not only help the user to across multiple networks include external networks with only one time log in, but also can help users from different networks to trust each other.

Using identity federation in the cloud means users from different clouds can use a federated identification to identify themselves, which naturally suit the requirement of identity based cryptography in cloud computing. In our approach, users and servers in the cloud have their own unique identities. These identities are hierarchical identities. To access services in the cloud, users are required to authenticate themselves for each service in their own clouds. In some cases, servers are also required to authenticate themselves to users. In a small and closed cloud, this requirement can be satisfied easily. While in a hybrid cloud, there are multiple private and/or public clouds and these clouds may rely on different authentication mechanisms. Providing effective authentications for users and servers from different cloud domains would be difficult. In this paper, we propose to use federated identity management and HIBC in the cloud. In the cloud trusted authority PKGs are used and these PKGs will not only act as PKGs in traditional identity-based cryptography system but also allocate hierarchical identities to users in their domains. There is a root PKG in overall domain of each cloud, and each sub-level domain (private or public cloud) within the cloud also has its own PKG. The root PKG will manage the whole cloud, each private cloud or public cloud is the first level and users and servers in these clouds are the second level. The root PKG of the cloud will allocate and authenticate identities for all the private and public clouds. For example, it can allocate identity UiS to a private cloud of University of Stavanger. Each private cloud and public cloud uses its own domain PKG to allocate and manage the identities of all the users and servers in its own cloud. Each user and server in this domain has its own identity and this identity is a hierarchical identity, which includes both the identity of the user or server and the identity of the domain. For example, the identity of user Alice in the private cloud of University of Stavanger can be UIS.Alice.

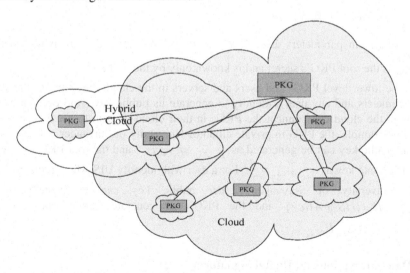

Fig. 2. Federated identity management in cloud

4.2 Key Generation and in the Cloud

Using HIBC in the cloud, an important part is key generation and distribution. As shown in [6], the security of HIBC scheme is based on the using of admissible pairing. Let G_1 and G_2 be two groups of some large prime order q and G_1 is an additive group and G_2 is a multiplicative group, we can call $\hat{e}$ an admissible pairing if $\hat{e}$: $G_1 \times G_2 \rightarrow G_2$ have the following properties.

1. **Billinear:** For all $P, Q \in G_1$ and $a, b \in Z_q^*$, $\hat{e}(aP, bQ) = \hat{e}(P, Q)^{ab}$.
2. **Non-degenerate:** There exits $P, Q \in G_1$, such that $\hat{e}(P, Q) \neq 1$.
3. **Computable:** For all $P, Q \in G_1$, there exits a efficient way to calculate $\hat{e}(P, Q)$.

An admissible pairing can be generated by suing a Weil pairing or a Tate pairing [2]. Here, in the cloud we use two levels PKG, the root PKG is $level_0$ PKG and the PKGs in the private or public clouds are $level_1$ PKGs. The root setup can be done as follow:

1. Root PKG generates G_1, G_2 and an admissible pairing $\hat{e}(aP, bQ) = \hat{e}(P, Q) \neq 1 (G_1, G_2, \hat{e}, P_0, Q_0, H_1, H_2)$ $\qquad \hat{e}$: $G_1 \times G_2 \rightarrow G_2$.
2. Root PKG chooses $P_0 \in G_1$ and $s_0 \in Z_q^*$ and set $Q_0 = s_0 P_0$.
3. Root PKG chooses hash function $H_1 : \{0,1\}^* \rightarrow G_1$ and $H_2 : G_2 \rightarrow \{0,1\}^n$.

Then the system parameters are $(G_1, G_2, \hat{e}, P_0, Q_0, H_1, H_2)$ and are public available, s_0 is the root PKG's secret and is known only by the root PKG.

For the lower level PKGs and users and servers in the cloud, they can use the system parameters and any user's identity to generate its public key. And every user or servers in the cloud can connect the PKGs in their cloud domain to get their private keys. For example, the PKG in private cloud of University of Stavanger with identity UIS, its public key can be generated as $p_{uis} = H_1(UIS)$ and the root PKG can generate its private key as $s_{uis} = s_0 P_{uis}$. For a user with identity UIS.Alice in the private cloud University of Stavanger, her public key can be generated as $P_{uisalice} = H_1(UIS \| Alice)$ and the PKG can generate her private key as $s_{uisalice} = s_{uis} + s_{uis} P_{uisalice}$.

4.3 Date Encryption and Digital Signature

In the cloud, one of the most important security problems are mutual authentication between users and servers, protection of data confidentiality and integrity during data transmission by encryption using secret keys. In a cloud using federated identity, any user and server has its unique identity and any user and server can get the identity of any other user/server by request with the PKGs. With HIBC, the public key distribution can be greatly simplified in the cloud. Users and servers do not need to ask a public key directory to get the public key of other users and servers as in traditional public key schemes. If any user or server wants to encrypt the data that transmitted in the cloud, the sender can acquire the identity of the receiver, then the sender can encrypt the data with receiver's identity.

Currently, WS-Security (Web service Security) protocol which can provide end-to-end message level security using SOAP messages is widely applied in cloud computing to protect the security of most cloud computing related web services. WS-Security uses SOAP header element to carry security-related information. Since SOAP message is a kind of XML message and ordinarily XML message representation is about 4 to 10 times large compared with their equivalent binary formats, adding security information into SOAP header will greatly increase the costs of data communication and data parsing. For example, if XML signature is used to protect data integrity or authentication, the SOAP header will include the signature information about the signature method, signature value, key info and some reference information like digest method, transforms, and digest value. And the key info element may include keys names certificates and some public key management information [16]. If RSA and X.509 are chosen as the public key cryptography and certificate format in XML signature, the key info element in the SOAP header usually includes a public key certificate or a reference pointing to a remote location. While using HIBC in a cloud, any user and server can get its own private key from its domain PKG and can calculate the public key of any other party in the cloud knowing its identity. Then it is easy for a sender to add a digital signature using its private key and for a receiver to verify a digital signature using the sender's public key. Then the key info may be not needed in the SOAP header, and this will greatly reduce the SOAP messages need to be transmitted in the cloud and thus save the cost.

4.4 Secret Session Key Exchange and Mutual Authentication

Identity-based cryptography is a public key cryptography scheme, it is much slower when it is compared with symmetric key cryptography. In practice, public key cryptography is not used for data encryption in most of the clouds. For example, in XML encryption, XML data is encrypted using symmetric cryptography such as AES and Triple-DES. This secret symmetric key is encrypted using the public key encryption and added in the SOAP message and then transmitted to the receiver. While in the cloud with HIBC, this secret symmetric key distribution can be avoided since identity-based cryptography can be used for secret session key exchange. According to [9], for every two parties in the system using identity-based cryptography, it is easy for each one of the two parties to calculate a secret session key between them using its own private key and public key of other party, this is call identity-based non-interactive key distribution. For example, two parties Alice and Bob in a cloud with their public keys and private keys P_{alice}, Q_{alice}, P_{bob} and Q_{bob} can calculate their shared secret session key by computing

$$K_s = \hat{e}(Q_{alice}, P_{bob}) = \hat{e}(Q_{bob}, P_{alice}) \tag{1}$$

This means in a cloud using HIBC, each user or server can calculate a secret session key between it and the other party it wants to communicate with without message exchange. This advantage of identity-based cryptography can not only reduce message transmission but also can avoid session key disclosure during transmission.

This secret session key can be used not only for data encryption, but also for mutual authentication [8]. We assume if a user with identity $Alice@UiS$ and a server with identity $Storage@google$ in the cloud want to authenticate each other. First, they can calculate a secret session key K_s between them. Then Alice can send a message to the server as:

$Alice \rightarrow Server : Alice @ UiS, M, f(K_s, Alice @ UiS, Storage @ google, M)$

Here M is a randomly selected message and f is a one way hash function. Here, to compute the correct hash value, a correct secret session key K_s is needed. Since K_s computation requires Alice's private key and this private key can only be allocated from the PKG in the private cloud of University of Stavanger, thus Alice can be verified that she is a legal user of this cloud. Also the server can authenticate itself to Alice the same way. We can notice that this mutual authentication does not include any certification form a third party.

4.5 Key Escrow

For a system using identity-based cryptography, key escrow problem is inherent and can not be avoided since PKG knows the private keys of all the users. While in the hierarchical identity-based cryptography system, only the PKG in the same domain as the users can knows their private keys. PKGs in other domains or at other levels can not know these private keys, such the key escrow problem can be restricted in a small range.

5 Conclusion

The quick development of cloud computing bring some security problems as well as many benefits to Internet users. Current solutions have some disadvantages in key management and authentication especially in a hybrid cloud with several public/private clouds. In this paper, we depicted the principles of identity-based cryptography and hierarchical identity-based cryptography and find the properties of HIBC fit well with the security demands of cloud. We proposed to use federated identity management and HIBC in the cloud and depicted how can the system generate and distribute the public and private keys to users and servers. Compared with the current Ws-Security approach, we can see our approach has its advantages in simplifying public key distribution and reducing SOAP header size. Also we showed how the users and servers in the cloud can generate secret session key without message exchange and authenticate each other with a simple way using identity-based cryptography. Also we can see the key escrow problem of identity-based cryptography can be restricted with HIBC approach.

References

1. Beak, J., Newmarch, J., Safavi-Naini, R., Susilo, W.: A Survey of Identity-Based Cryptography. In: Proc. of the 10th Annual Conference for Australian Unix User's Group (AUUG 2004), pp. 95–102 (2004)
2. Boneh, D., Franklin, M.: Identity-based Encryption from the Weil Pairing. In: Kilian, J. (ed.) CRYPTO 2001. LNCS, vol. 2139, pp. 433–439. Springer, Heidelberg (2001)
3. Chappell, D.: A Short Introduction to Cloud Platforms,
   http://www.davidchappell.com/CloudPlatforms-Chappell.pdf
4. Cocks, C.: An Identity-based Encryption Scheme Based on Quadratic Residues. In: Proceeding of 8th IMA International Conference on Cryptography and Coding (2001)
5. Crampton, J., Lim, H.W., Paterson, K.G.: What Can Identity-Based Cryptography Offer to Web Services? In: Proceedings of the 5th ACM Workshop on Secure Web Services (SWS 2007), Alexandria, Virginia, USA, pp. 26–36. ACM Press, New York (2007)
6. Gentry, C., Silverberg, A.: Hierarchical ID-Based cryptography. In: Zheng, Y. (ed.) ASIACRYPT 2002. LNCS, vol. 2501, pp. 548–566. Springer, Heidelberg (2002)
7. Horwitz, J., Lynn, B.: Toward Hierarchical Identity-Based Encryption. In: Knudsen, L.R. (ed.) EUROCRYPT 2002. LNCS, vol. 2332, pp. 466–481. Springer, Heidelberg (2002)
8. Mao, W.: An Identity-based Non-interactive Authentication Framework for Computational Grids. HP Lab, Technical Report HPL-2004-96 (June 2004)
9. Sakai, R., Ohgishi, K., Kasahara, M.: Cryptosystems based on pairing. In: Proceedings of the 2000 Symposium on Cryptography and Information Security, Okinawa, Japan (January 2000)
10. Shamir, A.: Identity-based cryptosystems and signature schemes. In: Blakely, G.R., Chaum, D. (eds.) CRYPTO 1984. LNCS, vol. 196, pp. 47–53. Springer, Heidelberg (1985)
11. Lim, H.W., Robshaw, M.J.B.: On identity-based cryptography and GRID computing. In: Bubak, M., van Albada, G.D., Sloot, P.M.A., Dongarra, J. (eds.) ICCS 2004. LNCS, vol. 3036, pp. 474–477. Springer, Heidelberg (2004)
12. Lim, H.W., Paterson, K.G.: Identity-Based Cryptography for Grid Security. In: Proceedings of the 1st IEEE International Conference on e-Science and Grid Computing (e-Science 2005). IEEE Computer Society Press, Los Alamitos (2005)
13. Defining Cloud Services and Cloud Computing,
    http://blogs.idc.com/ie/?p=190
14. IBM Embraces Juniper For Its Smart Hybrid Cloud, Disses Cisco (IBM),
    http://www.businessinsider.com/2009/2/
    ibm-embraces-juniper-for-its-smart-hybrid-cloud-disses-cisco-ibm
15. http://en.wikipedia.org/wiki/Cloud_computing#cite_note-61
16. XML Signature Syntax and Processing (Second Edition),
    http://www.w3.org/TR/xmldsig-core/#sec-KeyInfo

Availability Analysis of a Scalable Intrusion Tolerant Architecture with Two Detection Modes

Toshikazu Uemura[1], Tadashi Dohi[1], and Naoto Kaio[2]

[1] Department of Information Engineering, Graduate School of Engineering
Hiroshima University, 1–4–1 Kagamiyama, Higashi-Hiroshima, 739–8527 Japan
[2] Department of Economic Informatics, Faculty of Economic Sciences
Hiroshima Shudo University, 1–1–1 Ohzukahigashi, Asaminami-ku, Hiroshima, 739–3195,
Japan
dohi@rel.hiroshima-u.ac.jp, kaio@shudo-u.ac.jp

Abstract. In this paper we consider a discrete-time availability model of an intrusion tolerant system with two detection modes; automatic detection mode and manual detection mode. The stochastic behavior of the system is formulated by a discrete-time semi-Markov process and analyzed through an embedded Markov chain (EMC) approach. We derive the optimal switching time from an automatic detection mode to a manual detection mode, which maximizes the steady-state system availability. Numerical examples are presented for illustrating the optimal switching of detection mode and its availability performance. availability, detection mode, EMC approach, Cloud computing environment.

Keywords: SITAR, availability, intrusion tolerance, discrete-time modeling, detection mode, EMC approach, cloud computing circumstance.

1   Introduction

Cloud Computing is one of computing technologies in which dynamically scalable and often virtualized resources are provided as a service over the Internet. Since users need not have knowledge of expertise and the technology infrastructure in the network that supports them, recently this low-cost computing paradigm is becoming popular as an expected Internet-based computing in the next generation. Since the cloud computing is highly vulnerable to the Internet epidemics, many attacking events compromise a huge number of host computers rapidly and cause DoS around the Internet. Such epidemics result in extensive widespread damage costing billions of dollars, and countering the propagating worms in time becomes an increasingly emergency issue on the Internet security. Although traditional security approaches which may be categorized into *intrusion detection approaches* establish proactive barriers like a firewall, unfortunately, the efficiency of a single barrier is not still enough to prevent attack from sophisticated new skills by malicious attackers. As the result, the number of network attack incidents is tremendously increasing day by day. In contrast to pursue the nearly impossibility of a perfect barrier unit, the concept of *intrusion tolerance* is becoming much popular in recent years. An intrusion tolerant system can avoid severe security failures caused by intrusion and/or attack and can provide the intended services to users in a timely manner even under attack. This is inspired from traditional techniques commonly used for

M.G. Jaatun, G. Zhao, and C. Rong (Eds.): CloudCom 2009, LNCS 5931, pp. 178–189, 2009.
© Springer-Verlag Berlin Heidelberg 2009

tolerating accidental faults in hardware and/or software systems, and can provide the system dependability which is defined as a property of a computer-based system, such that reliance can justifiably be placed on the service it delivers [1]. So far, most efforts in security have been focused on specification, design and implementation issues. In fact, several implementation techniques of intrusion tolerance at the architecture level have been developed for real computer-based systems. For an excellent survey on this research topic, see Deswarte and Powell [2].

In other words, since these methods can be categorized by a design diversity technique in secure systems and need much cost for the development, the effect on implementation has to be evaluated carefully and quantitatively. To assess quantitatively security effects of computer-based systems, reliability/performance evaluation with stochastic modeling is quite effective. Littlewood *et al.* [4] applied fundamental techniques in reliability theory to assess the security of operational software systems and proposed some quantitative security measures. Jonsson and Olovsson [3] also developed a quantitative method to study attacker's behavior with the empirical data observed in experiments. Ortalo, Deswarte and Kaaniche [7] used both privilege graph and Markov chain to evaluate system vulnerability, and derived the mean effort to security failure. Uemura and Dohi [8] focused on the typical DoS attacks for a server system and formulated an optimal patch management problem via continuous-time semi-Markov models (CTSMM). Recently, the same authors [9] considered a secure design of an intrusion tolerant database system [12] with a control parameter to switch an automatic detection mode to a manual detection mode after receiving an attack, and described its stochastic behavior by a CTSMM. In this way considerable attentions have been paid to stochastic modeling in security evaluation of computer-based systems.

In this paper we consider an existing system architecture with intrusion tolerance, called SITAR (Scalable Intrusion Tolerant Architecture). SITAR was developed in MCNC Inc. and Duke University [11]. Madan *et al.* [5], [6] considered the security evaluation of SITAR and described its stochastic behavior by a CTSMM. More precisely, they investigated effects of the intrusion tolerant architecture under some attack patterns such as DoS attacks. In this paper we consider the similar but somewhat different models from Madan *et al.* [5], [6]. By introducing an additional control parameter [9], [12], called the switching time from an automatic detection mode to a manual detection mode, we consider a discrete-time semi-Markov model (DTSMM). The authors considered in their previous work [10] to control the patch release timing from a vulnerable state. In COTS (commercial-off-the-shelf) distributed servers like SITAR, on the other hand, the intrusion-detection function equipped for a proactive security management is not perfect and is often switched to a manual detection mode, in order to detect intrusions/vulnerable parts more speedy [9], [12]. Then the problem here is to find the optimal switching time which maximizes the steady-state system availability. We describe the stochastic behavior of the underlying SITAR with two detection modes and develop an availability model based on a DTSMM.

The paper is organized as follows: In Section 2 we explain SITAR and describe the stochastic behavior [5], [6]. Section 3 concerns the EMC approach and obtain the representation of an embedded DTMC in a DTSMM. We derive the steady-state probability in the DTSMM by using the mean sojourn time and the steady-state probability in the embedded DTMC. In Sections 4 and 5, we formulate the maximization problems of steady-state system availability in continuous-time and discrete-time cases, respectively. Actually, we showed in a different context that the control scheme which included auto patch would be useful to guarantee several security attributes [12], but at the same time that the design of the optimal PPMT was quite effective to optimize some quantitative measures [9]. We derive analytically the optimal PPMTs maximizing the system availability. It is worth mentioning in these optimization phases that the treatment of DTSMM is rather complex. Numerical examples are presented in Section 6 for illustrating the optimal preventive patch management policies and performing sensitivity analysis of model parameters. It is illustrated that the preventive patch management policies can improve effectively the system availability in some cases, and that the implementation of both preventive maintenance and intrusion tolerance may lead to keeping the whole Internet availability/survivability. Finally the paper is concluded with some remarks in Section 7.

2   SITAR

The SITAR is a COTS distributed server with an intrusion tolerant function [11] and consists of five major components; proxy server, acceptance monitor, ballot monitor, adaptive reconfiguration module, and audit control module. Since the usual COTS server is vulnerable for an intrusion from outside, an additional intrusion tolerant structure is introduced in SITAR. Madan *et al.* [5], [6] described the stochastic behavior of SITAR by means of CTSMM and gave its embedded DTMC representation. Figure 1 depicts the configuration of SITAR behavior under consideration. Let G be the normal state in which the COTS server can protect itself from adversaries. However, if a vulnerable part is detected by them, a state transition occurs from G to the vulnerable state V.

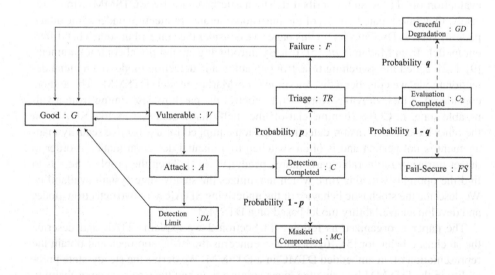

Fig. 1. Block diagram of SITAR behavior

Further if adversaries attack the vulnerable part, the state moves to A. On the other hand, if the vulnerable part is detected by vulnerability identifiers such as benign users, the vulnerable state V goes back to the normal state G again.

In the attack state A, two possible states can be taken. If the problem caused by the attack cannot be resolved and the containment of the damaged part fails, the corresponding event can be regarded as a security failure, and the initialization/reconfiguration of the system is performed as a corrective maintenance (repair) at DL. After completing it, the system state makes a transition to G again and becomes as good as new. While, if the intrusion/attack is detected, then the state goes to C. In the state C, one of two instantaneous transitions without time delay, which are denoted by dotted-lines in Fig. 1, can occur, $i.e.$, if the damaged part by attacking is not so significant and does not lead to a serious system failure directly, the system state makes a transition from C to MC with probability $1 - p$ $(0 \leq p \leq 1)$, and the damaged part can be contained by means of the fail safe function. After the containment, the system state moves back to G by masking the damaged part.

Otherwise, $i.e.$ if the containment of the damaged part with serious effects to the system fails, the state goes to TR with probability p. We call this probability the *triage probability* in this paper. In the state TR, several corrective inspections are tried in parallel with services. If the system is diagnosed as failure, the state moves to F, the service operation is stopped, and the recovery operation starts immediately. After completing the recovery from the system failure, the system becomes as good as new in G. Otherwise, it goes to the so-called non-failure state denoted by C_2. Here, two states can be taken; it may be switched to the gracefully service degradation in GD with probability q $(0 \leq q \leq 1)$, or the service operation is forced to stop and the corrective maintenance starts immediately.

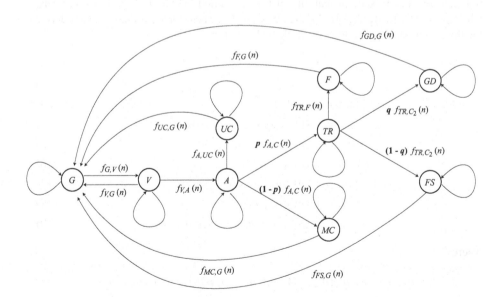

Fig. 2. Transition diagram of DTSMM

The main differences from Madan *et al.* [5], [6] are (i) an automatic intrusion-detection can be switched to a manual detection mode at any timing in A, although Madan *et al.* [5], [6] did not take account of switching of automatic detection mode, (ii) In two states C and C_2 instantaneous transitions are allowed in the present model, although Madan *et al.* [5], [6] assumed random transitions with time delay. We define the time interval from G to G as one cycle and suppose that the same cycle repeats again and again over an infinite time horizon. For respective states, let $F_{i,j}(n)$ $(i, j \in \{G, V, A, PM, UC, C, MC, TR, C_2, FS, GD, F\}$ denote the discrete transition probability distributions with p.m.f. $f_{i,j}(n)$ in the DTSMM, where $f_{i,j}(0) = 0$ and mean $\mu_{i,j}$ (> 0).

In Fig. 2, we give the trandition diagram of the DTSMM. It is assumed that the automatic detection function in SITAR is switched just after n_0 (≥ 0) time unit elapses in an active attack state A in the DTSMM. More specifically, let $F_{A,UC}(n)$ be the transition probability from A to UC which denotes the manual detection mode. When it is given by the step function, *i.e.*, $F_{A,UC}(n) = 1$ $(n \geq n_0)$ and $F_{A,UC}(n) = 0$ $(n < n_0)$, the switching time from an automatic detection mode to a manual detection model is given by the (integer-valued) constant time n_0. From the preliminary above, we formulate the steady-state system availability as a function of the switching time n_0.

3   Availability Analysis

3.1   EMC Approach

The embedded DTMC representation of the DTSMM is illustrated in Fig.3. Let p_k, h_k and π_k denote the steady-state probability of the DTSMM in Fig.2, the mean sojourn time and the steady-state probability of the embedded DTMC in Fig. 3, respectively, where $k \in \{G, V, A, DL, MC, TR, FS, GD, F\}$. From the definition, we can derive the the steady-state probability π_k of the DTSMM by

$$\pi_G = h_G/\phi, \tag{1}$$

$$\pi_V = h_V/\phi, \tag{2}$$

$$\pi_A = p_A h_A/\phi, \tag{3}$$

$$\pi_{DL} = p_A(1 - p_{MC} - p_{TR})h_{DL}/\phi, \tag{4}$$

$$\pi_{MC} = p_A p_{MC} h_{MC}/\phi, \tag{5}$$

$$\pi_{TR} = p_A p_{TR} h_{TR}/\phi, \tag{6}$$

$$\pi_{FS} = p_A p_{TR} p_{FS} h_{FS}/\phi, \tag{7}$$

$$\pi_{GD} = p_A p_{TR} p_{GD} h_{GD}/\phi, \tag{8}$$

$$\pi_F = p_A p_{TR}(1 - p_{FS} - p_{GD})h_F/\phi, \tag{9}$$

where

$$\phi = h_G + h_V + p_A\Big[h_A + (1 - p_{MC} - p_{TR})h_{DL} + p_{MC}h_{MC}$$
$$+ p_{TR}\big\{h_{TR} + p_{FS}h_{FS} + p_{GD}h_{GD} + (1 - p_{FS} - p_{GD})h_F\big\}\Big]. \tag{10}$$

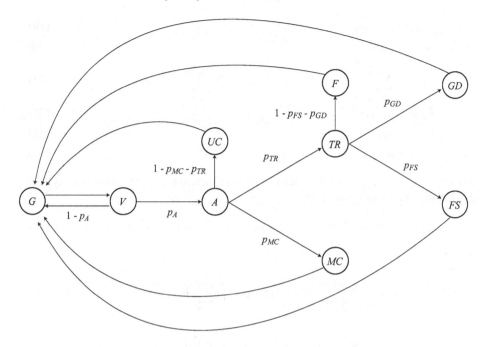

Fig. 3. EMC representation

3.2 Semi-markov Model

From the transition diagram of the DTSMM in Fig.3, we obtain

$$p_A = \sum_{x=0}^{\infty} \sum_{w=x}^{\infty} f_{V,G}(w) f_{V,A}(x), \tag{11}$$

$$p_{MC} = p_{MC}(n_0) = (1-p) F_{A,C}(n_0 - 1), \tag{12}$$

$$p_{TR} = p_{TR}(n_0) = p F_{A,C}(n_0 - 1), \tag{13}$$

$$p_{FS} = (1-q) \sum_{z=0}^{\infty} \sum_{y=z}^{\infty} f_{TR,F}(y) f_{TR,C_2}(z), \tag{14}$$

$$p_{GD} = q \sum_{z=0}^{\infty} \sum_{y=z}^{\infty} f_{TR,F}(y) f_{TR,C_2}(z) \tag{15}$$

and

$$h_G = \mu_{G,V}, \tag{16}$$

$$h_V = \sum_{x=0}^{\infty} \sum_{w=0}^{x-1} w f_{V,G}(w) f_{V,A}(x) + \sum_{x=0}^{\infty} \sum_{w=x}^{\infty} x f_{V,G}(w) f_{V,A}(x), \tag{17}$$

$$h_A = h_A(n_0) = \sum_{n=0}^{n_0-1} \overline{F}_{A,C}(n), \tag{18}$$

$$h_{DL} = \mu_{UC,G}, \tag{19}$$

$$h_{MC} = \mu_{MC,G}, \tag{20}$$

$$h_{TR} = \sum_{z=0}^{\infty}\sum_{y=0}^{z-1} y f_{TR,F}(y) f_{TR,C_2}(z) + \sum_{z=0}^{\infty}\sum_{y=z}^{\infty} z f_{TR,F}(y) f_{TR,C_2}(z), \tag{21}$$

$$h_{FS} = \mu_{FS,G}, \tag{22}$$

$$h_{GD} = \mu_{GD,G}, \tag{23}$$

$$h_F = \mu_{F,G}, \tag{24}$$

where $\overline{F}_{A,C}(n) = 1 - F_{A,C}(n)$. Then it is straightforward to get the steady-state system availability as a function of n_0 by

$$AV(n_0) = \pi_G + \pi_V + \pi_A + \pi_{MC} + \pi_{TR} + \pi_{GD} = U(n_0)/T(n_0), \tag{25}$$

where

$$U(n_0) = H_{G,V} + \sum_{x=0}^{\infty}\sum_{w=x}^{\infty} f_{V,G}(w) f_{V,A}(x)\left\{ \sum_{n=0}^{n_0-1} \overline{F}_{A,C}(n) + \alpha F_{A,C}(n_0 - 1)\right\}, \tag{26}$$

$$T(n_0) = H_{G,V} + \sum_{x=0}^{\infty}\sum_{w=x}^{\infty} f_{V,G}(w) f_{V,A}(x)\left\{ \sum_{n=0}^{n_0-1} \overline{F}_{A,C}(n)\right.$$
$$\left. + \mu_{DL,G}\overline{F}_{A,C}(n_0 - 1) + \beta F_{A,C}(n_0 - 1)\right\}, \tag{27}$$

$$\overline{F}_{A,C}(n) = 1 - F_{A,C}(n-1) = \sum_{k=n}^{\infty} f_{A,C}(k), \tag{28}$$

$$h_{G,V} = \mu_{G,V} + \sum_{n=0}^{\infty} n f_{V,A}(n)\overline{F}_{V,G}(n) + \sum_{n=0}^{\infty} n f_{V,G}(n)\overline{F}_{V,A}(n), \tag{29}$$

$$\alpha = (1-p)h_{MC} + p(h_{TR} + p_{GD}h_{GD}), \tag{30}$$

$$\beta = \alpha + p\left\{p_{FS}h_{FS} + (1 - p_{FS} - p_{GD})h_F\right\}. \tag{31}$$

In the above expressions, α and β mean that the mean up time and the total mean time length from state C to G, respectively.

3.3 Optimal Switching Time

Taking the difference of $AV(n_0)$ with respect to n_0, we define

$$q(n_0) = \left\{1 + (\alpha - 1)r_{A,C}(n_0)\right\}T(n_0)$$
$$- U(n_0)\left\{1 + (\beta - \mu_{DL,G} - 1)r_{A,C}(n_0)\right\}, \tag{32}$$

where $r_{A,C}(n_0) = f_{A,C}(n)/\overline{F}_{A,C}(n)$ is the discrete hazard rate. We make the following two parametric assumptions:

Table 1. Dependence of steady-state system availability on parameter r in discrete-time operation

		Case 1			Case 2	
r	n_0^*	$AV(n_0^*)$	Δ (%)	n_0^*	$AV(n_0^*)$	Δ (%)
1	∞	1	0	1	0.9322	0.0788
2	∞	1	0	8	0.9328	0.0162
3	∞	1	0	17	0.9338	0.0071
4	∞	1	0	25	0.9348	0.0043
5	∞	1	0	32	0.9358	0.0031

		Case 3			Case 4	
r	n_0^*	$AV(n_0^*)$	Δ (%)	n_0^*	$AV(n_0^*)$	Δ (%)
1	1	0.9322	10.5087	1	0.9322	3.5860
2	1	0.9322	10.1917	1	0.9322	3.4108
3	1	0.9322	9.8861	1	0.9322	3.2414
4	2	0.9324	9.6078	3	0.9326	3.1157
5	3	0.9327	9.3587	5	0.9330	3.0072

(A-1) $\alpha + \mu_{DL,G} < \beta$,

(A-2) $\alpha\mu_{DL,G} < h_{G,V}(\beta - \alpha - \mu_{DL,G})$.

From the definition it is evident that $\alpha < \beta$. The assumption **(A-1)** implies that the sum of mean up time after state C and the mean time overhead for switching to a manual detection mode is strictly smaller than the total mean time length. On the other hand, the assumption **(A-2)** seems to be somewhat technical but is needed to guarantee a unique optimal switching time. These both assumptions were numerically checked and could be validated in many parametric cases.

We characterize the optimal switching time from an automatic detection mode to a manual detection mode maximizing the steady-state system availability as follows:

Proposition: (1) Suppose that $F_{A,C}(n)$ is strictly IHR (Increasing Failure rate), *i.e.*, the hazard rate $r_{A,C}(n)$ is strictly increasing in n, under **(A-1)** and **(A-2)**. (i) If $q(0) > 0$ and $q(\infty) < 0$, then there exist (at least one, at most two) optimal switching time n_0^* $(0 < n_0^* < \infty)$ satisfying the simultaneous inequalities $q(n_0^* - 1) > 0$ and $q(n_0^*) \leq 0$. The corresponding steady-state system availability $AV(n_0^*)$ must satisfy

$$K(n_0^* + 1) \leq AV(n_0^*) < K(n_0^*), \qquad (33)$$

where

$$K(n) = \frac{1 + (\alpha - 1)r_{A,C}(n)}{1 + (\beta - \mu_{DL,G} - 1)r_{A,C}(n)}. \qquad (34)$$

(ii) If $q(0) \leq 0$, then the optimal switching time is $n_0^* = 0$, *i.e.*, it is always optimal to detect in only a manual mode, and the corresponding maximum steady-state system availability is given by

$$AV(0) = \frac{h_{G,V}}{H_{G,V} + \mu_{DL,G} \sum_{x=0}^{\infty} \sum_{w=x}^{\infty} f_{V,G}(w)f_{V,A}(x)}. \qquad (35)$$

Table 2. Dependence of steady-state system availability on parameter ξ in discrete-time operation

ξ	Case 1			Case 2		
	n_0^*	$AV(n_0^*)$	Δ (%)	n_0^*	$AV(n_0^*)$	Δ (%)
0.01	∞	1	0	∞	0.9692	0
0.05	∞	1	0	∞	0.9439	0
0.2	∞	1	0	17	0.9338	0.0071
0.5	∞	1	0	2	0.9323	0.1113

ξ	Case 3			Case 4		
	n_0^*	$AV(n_0^*)$	Δ (%)	n_0^*	$AV(n_0^*)$	Δ (%)
0.01	111	0.9470	2.1128	∞	0.9531	0
0.05	8	0.9335	7.2209	15	0.9346	1.9234
0.2	1	0.9322	9.8861	1	0.9322	3.2414
0.5	1	0.9322	10.5898	1	0.9322	3.6307

(iii) If $q(\infty) \geq 0$, then the optimal switching time is $n_0^* \rightarrow \infty$, i.e., it is always optimal to detect in only an automatic mode, and the corresponding maximum steady-state system availability is given by

$$AV(\infty) = \frac{h_{G,V} + (\mu_{A,C} + \alpha) \sum_{x=0}^{\infty} \sum_{w=x}^{\infty} f_{V,G}(w) f_{V,A}(x)}{H_{G,V} + (\mu_{A,C} + \beta) \sum_{x=0}^{\infty} \sum_{w=x}^{\infty} f_{V,G}(w) f_{V,A}(x)}. \qquad (36)$$

(2) Suppose that $F_{A,C}(n)$ is DHR (Decreasing hazard Rate), i.e., the hazard rate $r_{A,C}(n)$ is decreasing in n, under **(A-1)** and **(A-2)**. If $AV(0) > AV(\infty)$, then $n_0^* = 0$, otherwise, $n_0^* \rightarrow \infty$.

Proof: Taking the difference of Eq.(32), we obtain

$$q(n_0 + 1) - q(n_0) =$$
$$\sum_{x=0}^{\infty} \sum_{w=x}^{\infty} f_{V,G}(w) f_{V,A}(x) \Big[\{T(n_0 + 1) - T(n_0)\} - \{U(n_0 + 1) - U(n_0)\}$$
$$+ r_{A,C}(n_0 + 1) \Big\{ (\alpha - 1)T(n_0 + 1) - (\beta - \mu_{DL,G} - 1)U(n_0 + 1) \Big\}$$
$$+ r_{A,C}(n_0) \Big\{ (\alpha - 1)T(n_0) - (\beta - \mu_{DL,G} - 1)U(n_0) \Big\} \Big]. \qquad (37)$$

If $F_{A,C}(n)$ is strictly IHR, the r.h.s. of Eq.(37) is strictly negative under **(A-1)** and **(A-2)**, and the function $q(n_0)$ is strictly decreasing in n_0. Since the steady-state system availability $AV(n_0)$ is a strictly quasi-concave in n_0 in the sense of discrete, if $q(0) > 0$ and $q(\infty) < 0$, then there exists at least one at most two optimal switching time n_0^* ($0 < n_0^* < \infty$) so as to satisfy $q(n_0^* - 1) > 0$ and $q(n_0^*) \leq 0$ which lead to the inequalities in Eq.(33). If $q(0) \leq 0$ or $q(\infty) \geq 0$, then the function $AV(n_0)$ decreases or increases, and the resulting optimal switching time becomes $n_0^* = 0$ or $n_0^* \rightarrow \infty$. On the other hand, if $F_{A,C}(n)$ is DHR, the function $AV(n_0)$ is a quasi-convex function of n_0 in the sense of discrete, and the optimal switching time is given by $n_0^* = 0$ or $n_0^* \rightarrow \infty$.

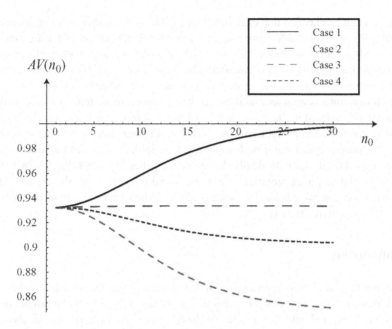

Fig. 4. Behavior of system availability $AV(n_0)$

4   Numerical Examples

In this section we derive the optimal switching time n_0^* numerically and quantify the steady-state system availability. Suppose the following parametric circumstance: $\mu_{G,V} = 72C\mu_{V,G} = 15C \ \mu_{V,A} = 24C\mu_{DL,G} = 15C\mu_{MC,G} = 12C\mu_{TR,F} = 6C\mu_{TR,C_2} = 8C\mu_{FS,G} = 30, \ \mu_{GD,G} = 40$ and $\mu_{F,G} = 48$. Especially we concern the following four cases:

(i) Case 1: $p = 0$, *i.e.*, the system state makes a transition from C to MC with probability one.

(ii) Case 2: $p = 0.5$ and $q = 0.5$.

(iii) Case 3: $p = 1$ and $q = 0$, *i.e.*, the service operation at C_2 is forced to stop with probability one.

(iv) Case 4: $p = 1$ and $q = 1$, *i.e.*, the graceful degradation can be observed with probability one.

Suppose that $f_{A,C}(n)$ is given by the negative binomial p.m.f.:

$$f_{A,C}(n) = \binom{n-1}{r-1} \xi^r (1-\xi)^{n-r}, \tag{38}$$

where $\xi \in (0,1)$ and $r = 1, 2, \cdots$ is the natural number. Figure 4 illustrates the behavior of the steady-state system availability with respect to the switching time n_0. From this figure, it can be checked that each behavior of $AV(n_0)$ is rather different from each other among four cases. Table 1 presents the dependence of optimal switching time and its associated system availability for varying the parameter r under four different scenarios, where the increment Δ is calculated by $\{AV(n_0^*) - AV(\infty)\} \times 100/AV(n_0^*)$. By switching from an automatic mode to a manual mode at the best timing, it is seen that the steady-state system availability can be improved more than the case without switching to the manual mode. Especially, in Case 3, it is worth noting that the system availability could be improved up to $\Delta = 10.5\%$. Further, we execute the sensitivity analysis of optimal switching time for varying ξ in Table 2. It could be observed that the system availability monotonically decreased as ξ increased and that the increment of system availability was remarkable in Case 3 and Case 4. From these quantitative results it can be concluded that the control of the switching time would be useful to improve the system availability.

5   Conclusion

In this paper we have considered an availability models of an intrusion tolerant system by introducing a control parameter called the switching time from an automatic detection mode to a manual detection mode. We have derived the optimal time analytically so as to maximize the steady-state system availability. We have also investigated quantitative effects of the optimal control of switching timing in numerical examples. The lesson learned from the numerical examples was that the optimal switching could improve the system availability effectively. Hence, it has been shown that the combination between an intrusion tolerance architecture and a control of detection mode was quite effective in some cases. In the future work, we will examine an effect of the optimal switching policy on the mean time to security failure which is an alternative dependability/security measure of intrusion tolerant systems.

Acknowledgments

This research was partially supported by the Ministry of Education, Science, Sports and Culture, Grant-in-Aid for Scientific Research (C), Grant No. 21510167 (2009–2011) and the Research Program 2008 under the Center for Academic Development and Cooperation of the Hiroshima Shudo University, Japan.

References

1. Avizienis, A., Laprie, J.C., Randell, B., Landwehr, C.: Basic concepts and taxonomy of dependable and secure computing. IEEE Transactions on Dependable and Secure Computing 1(1), 11–33 (2004)
2. Deswarte, Y., Powell, D.: Internet security: an intrusion-torelance approach. Proceedings of the IEEE 94(2), 432–441 (2006)
3. Jonsson, E., Olovsson, T.: A quantitative model of the security intrusion process based on attacker behavior. IEEE Transactions on Software Engineering 23(4), 235–245 (1997)

4. Littlewood, B., Brocklehurst, S., Fenton, N., Mellor, P., Page, S., Wright, D., Doboson, J., McDermid, J., Gollmann, D.: Towards operational measures of computer security. Journal of Computer Security 2(2/3), 211–229 (1993)
5. Madan, B.B., Goseva-Popstojanova, K., Vaidyanathan, K., Trivedi, K.S.: Modeling and quantification of security attributes of software systems. In: Proceedings of 32nd Annual IEEE/IFIP International Conference on Dependable Systems and Networks (DSN 2002), pp. 505–514. IEEE CS Press, Los Alamitos (2002)
6. Madan, B.B., Goseva-Popstojanova, K., Vaidyanathan, K., Trivedi, K.S.: A method for modeling and quantifying the security attributes of intrusion tolerant systems. Performance Evaluation 56(1/4), 167–186 (2004)
7. Ortalo, R., Deswarte, Y., Kaaniche, M.: Experimenting with quantitative evaluation tools for monitoring operational security. IEEE Transactions on Software Engineering 25(5), 633–650 (1999)
8. Uemura, T., Dohi, T.: Quantitative evaluation of intrusion tolerant systems subject to DoS attacks via semi-Markov cost models. In: Denko, M.K., Shih, C.-S., Li, K.-C., Tsao, S.-L., Zeng, Q.-A., Park, S.-H., Ko, Y.-B., Hung, S.-H., Park, J.-H. (eds.) EUC-WS 2007. LNCS, vol. 4809, pp. 31–42. Springer, Heidelberg (2007)
9. Uemura, T., Dohi, T.: Optimizing security measures in an intrusion tolerant database system. In: Nanya, T., Maruyama, F., Pataricza, A., Malek, M. (eds.) ISAS 2008. LNCS, vol. 5017, pp. 26–42. Springer, Heidelberg (2008)
10. Uemura, T., Dohi, T., Kaio, N.: Availability modeling of an intrusion tolerant system with preventive maintenance. In: Sheu, S.-H., Dohi, T. (eds.) Advanced Reliability Modeling III – Global Aspect of Reliability and Maintainability, pp. 655–662. McGraw Hill, New York (2008)
11. Wang, F., Gong, F., Sargor, C., Goseva-Popstojanova, K., Trivedi, K.S., Jou, F.: SITAR: A scalable intrusion-tolerant architecture for distributed services. In: Proceedings of 2nd Annual IEEE Systems, Man and Cybernetics, Information Assurance Workshop, West Point, NY (June 2001)
12. Wang, H., Liu, P.: Modeling and evaluating the survivability of an intrusion tolerant database system. In: Gollmann, D., Meier, J., Sabelfeld, A. (eds.) ESORICS 2006. LNCS, vol. 4189, pp. 207–224. Springer, Heidelberg (2006)

Data Center Consolidation: A Step towards Infrastructure Clouds

Markus Winter[1,2]

[1] Otto-von-Guericke-University Magdeburg,
Department of Technical and Business Information Systems,
VLBA Lab, P.O. Box 4120, 39016 Magdeburg, Germany
[2] Hosting Infrastructure Management, SAP AG,
Raiffeisenring 15, 68789 St. Leon-Rot, Germany
ma.winter@sap.com

Abstract. Application service providers face enormous challenges and rising costs in managing and operating a growing number of heterogeneous system and computing landscapes. Limitations of traditional computing environments force IT decision-makers to reorganize computing resources within the data center, as continuous growth leads to an inefficient utilization of the underlying hardware infrastructure. This paper discusses a way for infrastructure providers to improve data center operations based on the findings of a case study on resource utilization of very large business applications and presents an outlook beyond server consolidation endeavors, transforming corporate data centers into compute clouds.

Keywords: data center consolidation, virtualization, very large business applications, VLBA, virtual computing, adaptive computing, grid computing, IaaS, SaaS.

1 Introduction

Today, application service providers (ASP) face a challenging dilemma. Looking back at the old monolithic mainframe computing installations of the 1970s, one of the main drivers to switch to x86 personal computers and the client/server architecture were significant lower costs for hardware and operations. Now, more than 30 years later, the x86-architecture has been mostly established as the "traditional" computing platform in data centers around the world. However, the situation has changed over the years and we see a different picture today [1]. Looking at corporate data centers, we see large volumes of servers that were installed over the last years; their number still continues to grow. In most landscapes it is almost impossible to keep an overview on and track of the huge "server fleets". Due to the increasing amount of heterogeneous software installations and required computing units in corporate environments, the costs for management and operations of data center infrastructure has been growing ever since. Some data center operators wish the good old times of a few "giant computers" were coming back, even though the costs associated with mainframe computing have always been too high in the past. – Today, however, funding the operations of many small

M.G. Jaatun, G. Zhao, and C. Rong (Eds.): CloudCom 2009, LNCS 5931, pp. 190–199, 2009.
© Springer-Verlag Berlin Heidelberg 2009

servers with complex software installations is also a significant part of corporate spending. To make the situation even more difficult, limitations of the x86-architecture and the increase in processing power[1] lead to underutilized hardware usage. The introduction of new software at a company usually requires new server units in the data center – new applications result in more computing units ("server sprawl"). Sizing of new physical servers is done with regard to peak situations, thus intensifying efficiency problems in today's data centers. Servers consume electric energy, require cooling and occupy floor space – no matter whether they are highly utilized or underutilized. In times of global warming, climate discussions, "Green IT" initiatives and intensive efforts of the entire industry to lower costs, IT decision-makers face more and more pressure to increase the efficiency of their IT infrastructure and operations [2].

This paper discusses ways to overcome the exposed dilemma, how to consolidate corporate data center infrastructures and presents a transformation path towards cloud computing variants. The focus lies on large corporate environments or hosting providers which act as application service providers (ASP) for very large business applications (VLBA). Data center operations are defined as the professional mass business for IT infrastructure, characterized by high volume, specially designed building infrastructure for high energy consumption, sufficient heat dissipation, access security and redundancy of all critical components[2] [3].

Additionally, this paper provides an excerpt of a case study analyzing data center resource consumptions of VLBAs to identify potential room for consolidation.

2 New Computing for Data Centers

Given the challenging situation for IT infrastructure providers, new technologies and concepts are developed to overcome the limitations of traditional physical computing environments with regards to flexibility, resource management and data center operation costs. Virtualization is one of the key technologies to abstract computing resources and to separate actual physical resources from their presentation and from their way of consumption. In general, resources can refer to hardware, software or a logical component such as an IP or other access address. Virtualization technology applies to all levels of IT infrastructure, like the virtualization of networks (VLANs) or the virtualization of computing resources into virtual machines (Virtual Computing) [4]. It affects the entire data center.

Virtual Computing provides flexible computing resources and the possibility to consolidate operating system environments onto fewer physical computers. It enables data center operators to assign computing resources as needed to virtual machines and to react quickly on changing load situations. Adding new physical servers for each new operating system environment is no longer necessary, as remaining free capacities on existing servers can be used for hosting multiple operating system environments on a single computing unit. Hence, sizing of new environments no longer requires addressing the maximum peak of an entire application lifecycle but can be done dynamically and as needed for each virtual server [5]. With this technology, the traditional relationship between application and physical hardware is redefined to

---

[1] See Moore's law [6].
[2] Office equipment and small departmental server rooms do not fall under that definition.

the need of computing resources. Now, IT administrators have the possibility to view the entire data center as a virtual pool of aggregated resources instead of looking at physical resource silos.

This view on resources is also known in the area of Grid Computing. The principle of the interconnected use of computing resources grouped in logical resource clusters plays an important role supporting capacity management in data centers. In combination with the flexible assignment of resources through Virtual Computing, data center operators can deliver computing resources "on-demand" with the requested sizing [7].

Another concept to assign resources in the data center is known as Adaptive Computing. Adaptive Computing focuses on applications and services and enables the flexible assignment of IT infrastructure, consisting of network, computing nodes and central storage systems. It can be defined as virtualization of entire complex application landscapes – found, for example, in SAP® environments. There, a special management software called Adaptive Computing Controller (ACC) is available to manage entire landscapes and the central assignment of resources to SAP applications [8, 9]. The perspective of Adaptive Computing is from application down to infrastructure, limited to the size of a single computing node. Virtual Computing, on the other hand, looks bottom-up from IT infrastructure to applications, sizing and delivering the most adequate computing node.

3 The Transformation of Data Centers

Due to the described situation and challenges for data center service providers, DC infrastructure needs to change over the next years. Figure 1 highlights a possible transformation path from a "traditional" silo operation mode, via a consolidation phase with "hybrid" operations of internal "resource pool" infrastructures and external compute cloud consumption towards a utility computing model, where infrastructure and entire application software is delivered as a utility service.

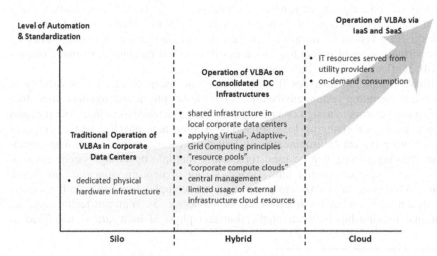

Fig. 1. The transformation path for corporate data centers

With the technology and principles of Virtual-, Adaptive- and Grid Computing, in combination with effective automation, IT decision-makers can find a way out of the infrastructure dilemma. They can transform their data center from a "traditional" silo operations mode into an internal "infrastructure cloud". For example, instead of managing 100 physical servers, each with 4 GB of main memory (RAM), as individual hardware units, data center operators can invest in a resource pool model: Based on larger computing nodes, they can run four servers, each with 128 GB of RAM, and use virtualization technology to create 100 virtual machines utilizing resources from this pool. This brings flexibility and allows them to adjust the resource situation for each virtual machine (VM) individually. Of course, there are more criteria for sizing than just RAM. In a real-life scenario, other parameters such as CPU utilization, data throughput and economic reasons play an important role as well.

However, simply implementing these principles and technologies is not the solution. There are technical challenges to be overcome along the way. First of all, business software in today's corporate data center environments usually runs on dedicated hardware. The resources required for a consolidated infrastructure need to be accurately determined to ensure proper sizing and stable operations of "traditional" VLBAs.

The second challenge is the proper management of the virtualized, consolidated IT infrastructures described above. Moving away from physical resource silos into shared resource pools ("internal clouds") requires a diligent management of available computing capacity. Where, in the traditional world, resources are basically sitting and waiting to be consumed whenever the peak situation might occur, in the world of a consolidated IT infrastructure, these unused resources may be consumed by or allocated to other systems. This leads to a situation where systems compete for available computing capacity; a set of rules needs to be created and implemented to operate this competition, the basic necessity being adequate planning.

Looking further down the road at current trends and developments, it is likely that computing resources will be consumed as a utility service – similar to electrical power. Several providers already offer "Software as a Service" (SaaS) or "Infrastructure as a Service" (IaaS), for example Amazon on the cutting edge, making Cloud Computing available to everyone in the first place. For data center decision-makers, this is a new dimension of looking at IT resources. The transformation from physical assets into virtualized corporate compute clouds is one step. However, dealing with resources that are no longer part of internal IT processes, is a second and more difficult one. The external cloud brings new challenges, starting with corporate policies, local as well as international legal matters and security concerns – let alone the technical difficulties. Therefore, this transition will likely be a phased approach, similar to the proposal in Figure 1. In the long run, it will go beyond mere data center consolidation – but rather go through a transformation from today's "silo operations" towards an IT resource consumption model. However, consolidation is an essential first step of this journey.

4 Consolidation Study

In order to explore the possibilities for consolidation in server environments for VLBAs, a case study was initiated to collect resource utilization data. The goal of this study is to support the theory of traditional IT environments being oversized thus offering significant room for consolidation. With the help of the data collected in this case study, it should be possible to review the actual physical resource consumption of VLBAs and to find possible sizing parameters for a consolidated IT infrastructure.

In this paper only an excerpt of the results of this study, including a limited view on CPU and RAM, is discussed. Information beyond this status report is available in other publications or will be made available once the project and ongoing analysis have been completed.

For this case study, a set of approximately 700 physical servers had been selected. The servers were a subset from a large data center provider containing multiple different customer environments of a global corporation, running mainly SAP database applications of production, quality assurance and development systems. The servers were monitored for several months and a three-month timeframe (full business quarter) was selected for detailed analysis.

4.1 Data Collection

To determine the required data for this analysis, first a level of abstraction needed to be defined. The actual physical capacity of IT resources could be calculated just by the technical specifications of each system. But in order to gain more actual insight into the amount of resources effectively consumed by the operated systems, periodic resource utilization data was collected. The physical server was defined as the reading point for data collection. This required an applicable choice of abstraction and measurement units.

With regard to the focus of this study, four measurable dimensions were selected to review server consolidation options: processor load (CPU), main memory consumption (RAM), hard disk throughput (disk input/output (I/O)) and network throughput (network I/O). All four make up characteristic criteria for the selection of servers and their connections in a consolidated landscape. – Data stored on hard disks was not considered, as data throughput is required to have sufficient bandwidth at each individual server. Thus, total storage capacity in the backend was not relevant for this analysis. The four specified dimensions were determined through available routines of available operating systems and servers monitored over a longer period. The quality and accuracy of the data was constantly supervised, the collection process monitored.

Nagios[3] standard software collected the performance data samples every 1 to 5 minutes for CPU utilization, main memory consumption, network I/O and disk I/O. To ensure high data quality, the collected raw data was transferred into a separate database to avoid compression in Nagios built-in round-robin database files. As preparation for data analysis, the required data was selected out of the available Nagios measurements. For CPU, this is a percentage value indicating processor utilization.[4] For the main memory consumption, the total amount of available RAM and used RAM was recorded in Gigabytes. Disk utilization was measured in Kilobytes of

---

[3] http://www.nagios.org

[4] Based on the hypothesis that there is a significant underutilization of resources, especially CPU, and the fact that a consolidation target landscape would be built with new and much more powerful hardware, the inaccuracy of looking at non-normalized CPU data was accepted for this analysis.

read and write operations. Network throughput was measured in Kilobytes of incoming and outgoing traffic. All data was collected in time intervals of 5 minutes. Data that for technical reasons had to be collected in tighter or wider intervals was aggregated into 5 minute average values to enable comparison.

4.2 Data Analysis

Timeframe for this analysis was the fourth quarter of 2008. Data is available for all 92 days in that period. Unfortunately, not all of the total 718 distinct servers were reporting correct data from day one and some of them did not report all four data dimensions properly for the entire timeframe. While this slightly influenced data quality, it did not significantly impact the analysis due to the high number of samples collected. For the first eleven days, only 75 servers reported data; starting with day 12, the total number of monitored servers was included into the collection. These initial difficulties explain the visible interference in Figure 3 that shows the total and consumed amount of main memory.

The collected data was partitioned into CPU utilization intervals to allow for a statement regarding CPU utilization in general. The utilization scale ranges from 0% to 100% CPU utilization, partitioned into 20 intervals of 5% increments. All collected samples were assigned into one of the intervals. This made it possible to gain an overview on the frequency in which the collected server data values appeared in which part of the CPU utilization scale. The resulting CPU data samples per CPU utilization interval are presented in Figure 2 and show the time servers spent per interval per month. The total amount of data points is considered 100%; Figure 2 displays the data points in each interval.

An average 68,27% of all collected samples are in the interval between zero and five percent CPU utilization. All monitored servers spend 93,35% of their online time with up to a maximum of 30% CPU utilization. Looking at the values above 50% CPU utilization, they still represent 360.224 data points or almost 67 hours of time within the three month period when summarized. Percentage-wise this might not

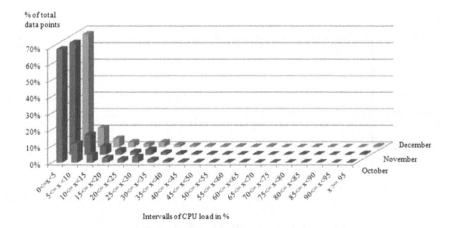

Fig. 2. CPU data samples per CPU utilization interval

seem too important, however, it is vital for VLBA landscapes as these 67 hours, when broken down into calendar days, represent almost 44 minutes per calendar day in which the system is under load. Looking at the servers causing the load, a more de-tailed analysis makes it evident that less than 1% of the total number of monitored servers cause the CPU values of above 50%. This is a first confirmation of the under-utilization hypothesis as it turns out that CPU utilization is not the bottleneck for the large majority of monitored systems. Of course, peak situations for servers occur, but for the summarized majority of system uptime CPU load is in fact rather low. This is somewhat a contradiction to findings in previous studies, where CPU was assumed as the bottleneck resource for applications and their consolidation onto fewer physical hardware [10].

The analysis of main memory utilization followed a slightly different approach. The available five-minute data points from all servers were summarized to obtain the total amount of available and consumed memory per time slot. For each calendar day, the maximum value was identified (peak of the day) and is shown in Figure 3 as the total amount of available RAM (dashed red line) and as the amount of RAM used per day (continuous blue line).

The total amount of memory results in a constant line with only slight fluctuations because of the fluctuating number of servers delivering data. This is no surprise, as physical servers in live production environments usually do not undergo change to prevent downtimes.

The amount of memory actually in use results in a more fluctuating line, yet the fluctuations are still within a very limited scope. This shows that main memory utili-zation of the analyzed VLBAs was relatively constant. The reasons for this are likely to be the same: configurations and settings of applications in production environments do not change frequently; system utilization in the monitored environment was rather constant.

Overall memory utilization turns out to be comparably low. On average, only 32,26% of the total amount of RAM is in use. This makes it clear that there is indeed

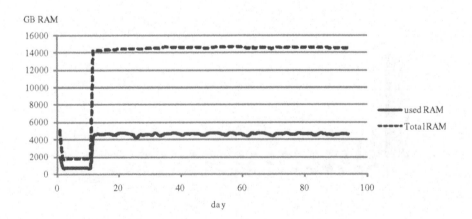

Fig. 3. Main memory (RAM) utilization per day

room for improvement and consolidation. Even though RAM is a significant cost driver when purchasing new servers, the results show that a large amount is never actually used. This makes it necessary to review initial sizing procedures of system environments for applications.

These results are a second confirmation of the hypothesis that environments are oversized and resources underutilized. The findings of this case study show that RAM utilization is rather static and suggest to look at RAM as an initial sizing parameter for consolidated VLBA environments.

5 Results and Outlook

In this time of global economic crisis, companies fight harder than ever for market share, and margin pressure increases. Innovations are vital to "achieve more with less", companies look at creating more output through less input to be spearheading the competition. This demand for an increase in efficiency is also seen in IT. IT decision-makers are asked to streamline their operations and optimize their infrastructures. Consolidation of applications and hardware in corporate data center environments has already started and represents a first step into a new era of corporate computing.

Looking only at the two utilization dimensions CPU load and RAM usage, this case study has shown that there is significant room for consolidation of physical server environments in corporate data centers, especially with regards to very large business applications. It can be stated that CPU load is not a limiting factor for consolidation. Assuming that the systems in this case were sized according to the SAP sizing guidelines[5] [11], the utilization is within expected range and within the vendor's recommendations. As virtual machines can be moved between physical hosts without downtime, CPU utilization can be load-balanced within an entire physical resource pool. This is in line with the results of other studies and virtual machine distribution models with regard to resource consumption [10]. For further sizing calculations, a virtualization overhead should be taken into account.

RAM utilization in this case turned out to be rather constant and as the reconfiguration of RAM usually requires (operating) system downtime. RAM load balancing is only possible via online migration of VMs between physical hosts, but does not change the actual consumption of RAM by the application. Due to the more static resource consumption, RAM utilization was hence recommended as the primary sizing parameter.

After reaching an (assumed) consolidation maximum in highly efficient corporate data centers, the next step is to ask the question whether computing infrastructure will after all need to remain in corporate data centers in the future.

The development of the electrical power grid about a hundred years ago comes to mind where electrical power was initially generated by each factory in their own power plant. After the power grid was in place, there was suddenly a way of consuming electrical energy from a service provider – and the rest is history [12]. The

---

[5] Sizing is recommended to target 30 - 50% CPU utilization in order to avoid negative impact on system response times for transactions.

ongoing growth of the Internet creates new services and the possibility to consume IT resources in a way similar to the power grid. Still, data centers are far from facing extinction. In a next round of consolidation, according to thought leaders in the industry, data centers will scale up to large service providers, and the industry is heading towards utility computing [13, 14].

Technical challenges aside, there is a need to rethink the operation of VLBAs and IT infrastructure in general. The transition from "self-produced" computing towards a consumer role will take some time and require hybrid model architectures to manage both worlds: local system operations in "home-grown" data center environments on the one hand and the consumption of computing resources out of a giant compute cloud on the other. For business applications, topics well-known and lessons learned during many years of internal operations such as system availability, reliability, service levels, interfaces and security need to be mapped onto external cloud providers. In internal data centers, local access control over hardware, building security and physical location of data convey a very tangible feeling of safety. This subjective feeling of having everything under control needs to be developed for IT provided through external computing resources as well. Where is my data located in the cloud? Who can potentially access it? From which countries in the world do cloud providers operate? Are there probably other legal terms of data security and governmental access? These and many more questions will have to be answered and legal aspects to be addressed. In the end, trust is something that requires time and can only partly be built through technology.

30 years ago, the mainframe faced dramatic change, driven by the motivation to increase efficiency and reduce costs. Today, it is still this same motivation that pushes the industry forward. Consolidation remains key. Time will tell if the cloud mantra will prove to be a sustainable model. For sure it offers tangible benefits today and the promise of even more efficient IT tomorrow.

References

1. Ceruzzi, P.E.: A History of Modern Computing, 2nd edn. MIT Press, Cambridge (2003)
2. Bittman, T.J., Dawson, P.: Virtualization Changes Virtually Everything. Gartner Research, ID G00156488 (03-28-2008)
3. Sartor, D., Stein, J., Tschudi, W., Xu, T.: High Performance Data Centers – a research roadmap. Lawrence Berkeley National Laboratory, LBNL-53483, Berkeley, California, USA (2004),
   http://hightech.lbl.gov/documents/
   DataCenters_Roadmap_Final.pdf (02-20-2009)
4. Nair, R., Smith, J.E.: Virtual Machines – Versatile Platforms for Systems and Processes. Morgan Kaufmann Publishers/ Elsevier, Amsterdam (2005)
5. Osterburg, S., Pinnow, A., Rautenstrauch, C., Winter, M.: Neue Computing-Grundlagen für das Rechenzentrum. In: Informatik Spektrum, vol. 32(2), pp. 118–126. Springer, Berlin (2009), http://www.springerlink.com/content/38131333342j5843 (12-16-2008)
6. Tanenbaum, A.S.: Structured Computer Organization, 4th edn. Simon & Schuster, Upper Saddle River (1999)

7. Foster, I., Kesselman, C.: The Grid: Blueprint for a New Computing Infrastructure, 2nd edn. Morgan Kaufmann Publishers, San Francisco (2004)
8. Schmalzhaf, G.: SAP Adaptive Computing – Implementation and Operation. Galileo Press, Bonn (2007)
9. Mißbach, M., Gibbels, P., Karnstädt, J., Stelzel, J., Wagenblast, T.: Adaptive Hardware Infrastructures for SAP. Galileo Press, Bonn (2005)
10. Bichler, M., Speitkamp, B.: Allocation Problems in Large-Scale Server Consolidation, TUM Working Paper, ISR-0001-1922.6 (2008)
11. Janssen, S., Marquard, U.: Sizing SAP Systems. Galileo Press, Bonn (2007)
12. Bryant, L., Hunter, L.C.: A History of Industrial Power in the United States. In: The Transmission of Power, vol. 3, pp. 1780–1930. MIT Press, Cambridge (1991)
13. Carr, N.: The big switch: rewiring the world, from Edison to Google, 1st edn. W.W. Norton & Company, New York (2008)
14. Foster, I.: There's Grid in them thar Clouds (2008),
    http://ianfoster.typepad.com/blog/2008/01/
    theres-grid-in.html (2008-03-18)

Decentralized Service Allocation in a Broker Overlay Based Grid

Abdulrahman Azab and Hein Meling

Dept. of Electrical Engineering and Computer Science, University of Stavanger,
4036 Stavanger, Norway
{abdulrahman.azab,hein.meling}@uis.no

Abstract. Grid computing is based on coordinated resource sharing in a dynamic environment of multi-institutional virtual organizations. Data exchanges, and service allocation, are challenging problems in the field of Grid computing. This is due to the decentralization of Grid systems. Building decentralized Grid systems with efficient resource management and software component mechanisms is a need for achieving the required efficiency and usability of Grid systems. In this work, a decentralized Grid system model is presented in which, the system is divided into virtual organizations each controlled by a broker. An overlay network of brokers is responsible for global resource management and managing allocation of services. Experimental results show that, the system achieves dependable performance with various loads of services, and broker failures.

Keywords: Grid computing, Peer-to-peer computing, Virtual organization management.

1 Introduction

Grid computing is the computing paradigm which is concerned with "coordinated resource sharing and problem solving in dynamic, multi-institutional virtual organizations" [1]. A virtual organization (VO) can be defined as a collection of computing nodes in which each participating node can acquire or provide services from/to other nodes inside/outside the organization [2]. The main aspect in cloud computing is transparency, while in Grid computing is coordinated resource sharing. The common aim of both paradigms is to achieve decrease in the need for additional expensive hardware and increase in computing power and storage capacities [3]. Building a decentralized computing infrastructure which fulfills the requirements of both Grid computing and Cloud computing, requires implementing a decentralized multi-VO Grid model in which the complexity of the entire system is transparent to regular participants. For a decentralized multi-VO Grid system, it is required to implement both, local Resource Management, RM, within each VO, and global RM among the grid. Two main issues are essential for both local and global RM: decentralized allocation of tasks to suitable nodes to achieve local and global load balancing, and handling of both regular node and broker [1] failures.

M.G. Jaatun, G. Zhao, and C. Rong (Eds.): CloudCom 2009, LNCS 5931, pp. 200–211, 2009.
© Springer-Verlag Berlin Heidelberg 2009

This paper presents a decentralized multi-VO RM model based on hybrid peer- to-peer communication [4]. The proposed model is implemented on HIMAN [5, 6] Grid middleware. The Grid system is divided into a set of virtual organizations. Each VO contains a set of regular nodes and one broker. Rules of resource sharing within a virtual organization are well known by each node and controlled and managed by brokers. A broker is responsible for receiving requests for resources, comparing the requirements in each request with the resource specifications of the available nodes, and direct requests to suitable nodes. Brokers from different VOs construct a cooperative collection called, *Broker Overlay*. The idea is to provide each participating node with the ability to offer and claim computational resources. In addition, the complexity of the system is transparent to regular nodes in the broker overlay, as each node interacts only with the attached broker. Both regular node and broker failures are handled.

Machine organization [7] in most existing Grid systems is either flat [8, 12, 23, and 22] or hierarchical [9, 10, 11, and 17], in a single VO. Multi-VO model is implemented in some Grid systems: EGEE [18] and D4Science [19] implements centralized task allocation using a central broker. Grid3 [20], which is based on VOMS [16], implements centralized RM through management servers. DEISA [21] uses a central batch scheduler for task allocation. In GHOSTS [24], each VO implements local RM model, and the framework implements centralized global RM. In NorduGrid [25], information about available resources is stored on dedicated database servers, and task allocation is carried out by local brokers on client nodes. None of these systems provides an efficient failure handling for both regular nodes and brokers.

The paper is organized as follows: Section 2 gives an overview for the system architecture. Section 3 describes the resource information exchange mechanism. Section 4 describes the service allocation model. Section 5 describes the failure handling mechanism. Section 6 describes the simulation model and presents the performed experiments and discussion of the results. Section 7 presents conclusions.

2 Architectural Overview

The proposed architecture is based on global resource sharing based on collaboration of virtual organizations. Each virtual organization is set up as a domain. Each domain consists of one domain controller (i.e. Broker), and a collection of regular nodes. Fig. 1 shows the architecture of the Grid as a collection of virtual organizations. Components of the grid system are:

A service, in this architecture refers to a computational task. It has five execution parameters: 1) Required CPU, the computational power required for running the service. 2) Required Memory, the memory size required for running the service. 3) Expiration Time, the amount of time to wait before the allocation. 4) Creation Time, the time at which the service is created for allocation. 5) Allocation attempts, the maximum number of attempts to deploy the service before it is expired.

A regular node, refers to each non-broker node in the Grid. Each regular node can be a member of one virtual organization, and can submit and/or run a service. A regular node is also responsible for periodically sending information about the current available resource state of the node to its broker. Each regular node has two resource

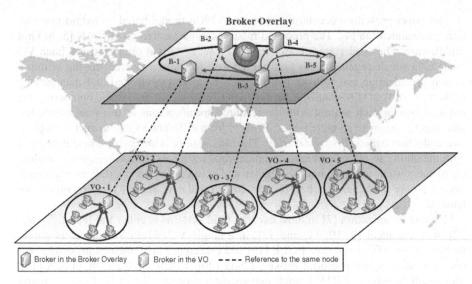

Fig. 1. Grid architecture

parameters: 1) Available CPU, which refers to the available computational power in the node, and 2) Available Memory space. Regular is equivalent to Peer in HIMAN, which contains two components: *Worker* (W), which is responsible for task execution, and *Client* (C), which is responsible for task submission[1] [6].

A broker, is a node which works as a virtual organization controller, can also work as a regular node in case of lack of available regular nodes. It is responsible for: 1) Allocating services to suitable nodes. A suitable node for a service is elected by performing a matchmaking process between the service requirements and the available resources of attached Grid nodes [13]. 2) Storing the current resource state for local nodes (i.e. in the same virtual organization) as well as global nodes (i.e. in other virtual organizations).

A virtual organization, is an overlay of nodes, which may be allocated in different regions and members of different organizations. Each VO is composed of one broker and regular nodes. Each VO is structured as a star logical topology, so that; communication is between the broker and regular nodes. There is no communication between regular nodes within the same virtual organization.

The broker overlay, is the overlay network between brokers through which communication and data exchange between different virtual organizations is performed. For the broker overlay, four different network topologies are assumed: Ring, hypercube, wire-*k*-out, and fully connected. Based on the communication topology, each broker will have a number of neighbor brokers, those brokers with which direct communication can be established.

---

[1] In HIMAN, the client component is responsible also for task allocation [6]. In this model, it is carried out by the broker.

3 Resource Information Exchange

Resource information for each participating node is stored in a three field Resource Information Data Block, RIDB. The three fields represent: 1) Available CPU, 2) Available Memory, and 3) Time of last read. The third field, time of last read, is included to indicate if this read is too old so that it may not be dependable for allocation actions.

Each broker maintains a set of RIDBs for all nodes in the system. Periodically, each regular node in a virtual organization reads the local current resource state (i.e. available CPU, and available Memory) in a data block and sends this block along with the reading time to its broker. Each time a broker receives a resource information block from a local node; it removes the previously stored reading, and replaces it with the current. Brokers also periodically exchange resource information through the broker overlay. Each broker performs one exchange operation with a single neighbor broker[2] each time unit. The exchange operation is done by updating each resource information data set in each of the two brokers with the newest data blocks.

4 Service Allocation

Allocation of services to nodes is done through brokers. Submitting new services to brokers for allocation can be implemented in two ways: centrally, through a service allocation server connected to all brokers, or through the brokers by including a service allocation portal in each broker. In this work, allocation through the brokers is implemented. A service allocator component is included in each regular node for forwarding services to the attached broker. The allocation model is depicted in Fig. 2.

Each broker has a service queue. When a service allocator sends a new service to a broker, it is automatically appended to the end of the service queue. Each time unit a broker picks the first service from the queue and starts a lookup process among the RIDBs, in order to find a suitable node with matching resource state to the resource requirements of the service. The Allocation algorithm is described in Fig. 3. The broker starts the lookup first among RIDBs of the local nodes. If no suitable resource found, the broker repeats the operation among RIDBs of global nodes. If a global node matches, the broker passes the service to that node's broker with high priority, so that it will be placed at the first position in the queue. The reason is to reduce the allocation time since there has been already previous allocation attempt(s). If there is no matching global node found, the service is passed to any neighbor broker, based on the topology. The allocation attempts parameter of a service is decremented each time the service is transferred to a new broker queue.

4.1 Service Validation Parameters

Each time unit, a broker checks the *expiration time* and *allocation attempts* values for each service in the local service queue. For a service S:

---

[2] Neighbor brokers for a broker are those which it has direct communication with, according to the topology of the broker overlay.

```
If (S.ExpirationTime < (CurrentTime - S.CreationTime) OR
S.AllocationAttempts ==0)
      // Service S is expired
      Remove(S); //from local service queue
```

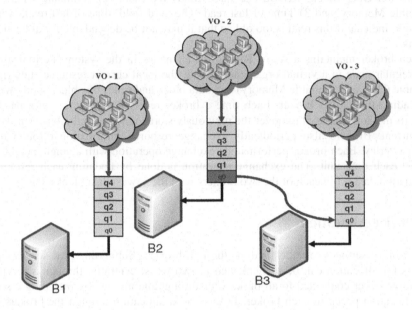

Fig. 2. Service Allocation model

5 Failure Handling

Two types of failure are considered: regular node failure and broker failure. Regular node failures are managed in the same failure handling mechanism in HIMAN [6, 15]. In this paper, focus is on broker failure. In a virtual organization, it is assumed that each regular node has direct communication only with its broker. In addition, each node in the Grid holds a list of information about all existing brokers in the broker overlay. This information is updated periodically in regular nodes through their local brokers.

When a broker failure occurs, a regular node will detect the broker failure when it attempts to send its resource information to the broker. In case of broker failure, all regular nodes in the local virtual organization of the failed broker will be detached from the Grid. Once a broker failure is detected, a regular node sends a membership request to the first broker in the list. If the request is granted, the node will set the new broker as the attached broker, and add it as a neighbor; otherwise the request is repeated to the next broker in the list. Fig. 4 describes the failure handling algorithm implemented in regular nodes. The algorithm is repeated each time unit.

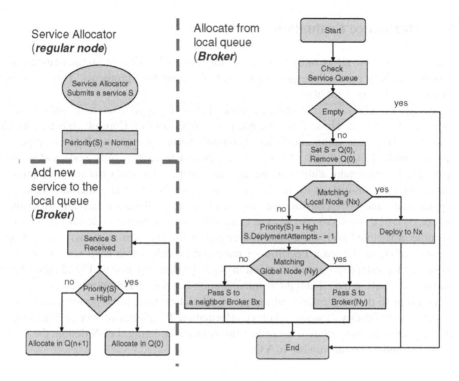

Fig. 3. Service Allocation algorithm

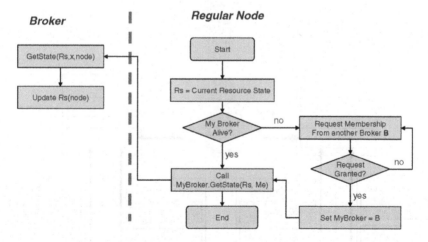

Fig. 4. Failure handling, and resource information sending algorithm

6 Performance Evaluation

The simulation model is built using PeerSim [14]; a Java-based simulation-engine designed to help protocol designers in simulating their P2P protocols. This work is based on cycle-based simulation.

GridNode class is a reference for node objects. GridAllocator and Grid-FailureControl classes are included as references for Control objects which simulate service allocation and failure handling. Three cycle-driven Protocol classes are also built: 1) Grid CD Protocol, included in each regular node and is responsible for communicating with the attached broker and sends the resource information in each simulation cycle. 2) Allocation Protocol, included in each regular node and is responsible for responding to the Allocation requests from the broker. 3) Grid Broker Protocol, included in each broker node for performing the tasks associated with the broker (described in the previous sections). The Idle Protocol is in the main PeerSim package and is included in each node to be responsible for establishing communication with neighboring nodes. Fig. 5 describes the Grid simulation model and the communication between different protocols.

To evaluate the performance of the proposed architecture, three performance metrics are used: Validity of stored resource information, Efficiency of service allocation, and Impact of broker failure on resource information updating. Let **N** denote the total Grid size, and **M** be the number of VOs.

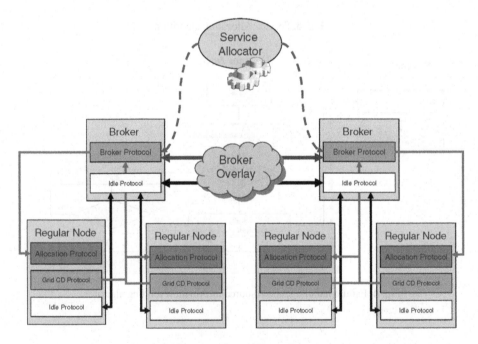

Fig. 5. Grid simulation model

6.1 Validity of Stored Resource Information

This metric is implemented through measuring the efficiency of the resource information exchange algorithm in keeping resource information up to date. The implemented methodology is to depict the deviation of the reading time values of RIDBs stored in the resource information data set, from the current cycle in a broker, with the simulation cycles. The results are read from one broker. For this performance metric, topologies for the broker overlay are ring and fully connected. A total of 120 simulation cycles are used. Two experiments are performed with the following configuration: 1) N = 100, K = 20. 2) N = 500, M = 100. The results are shown in fig 6.

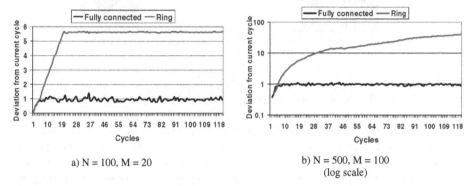

a) N = 100, M = 20   b) N = 500, M = 100
(log scale)

Fig. 6. Deviation of the resource information reading time from the current cycle among simulation cycles

As expected Fig. 6 shows that the deviation is much more less for the fully connected topology than for the ring topology. In addition, when the network size and the number of brokers were increased, in experiment 2, the deviation remained at the same level for fully connected topology, but increased for the ring topology. This can be attributed to the fact that, in a fully connected topology, all brokers are neighbors and can exchange resource information. This increases the probability of getting fresher data. In the ring topology a broker has only two neighbors. Increasing the number of brokers, the number of broker neighbors increases for the fully connected topology, but remains two for the ring topology. This reduces the chance of reaching data stored in far brokers (i.e. with large number of hops between) in ring topology, so, the deviation increases.

6.2 Efficiency of Service Allocation

In this metric we measure the efficiency of the allocation algorithm for distributing services among available suitable nodes, using different broker overlays. The network size is fixed to 500 nodes, and 100 virtual organizations. The implemented methodology is to depict the total number of waiting services, in broker queues, and the number of expired services with the simulation cycle. The results are collected from all brokers.

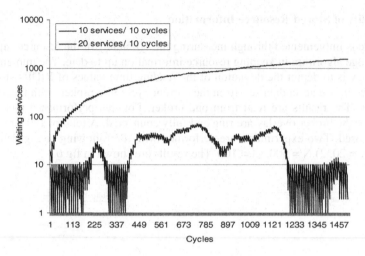

Fig. 7. Number of waiting services plotted against simulation cycles for periodic allocation using a fully connected broker overlay topology, for 10 and 20 services per 10 cycles

The main allocation method is: One broker periodical allocation. In this method, nodes of one VO deploy a number of services to the broker each specific number of cycles. The idea is to focus all the allocation traffic on one broker, as the worst case, to measure the efficiency of service exchange. Only the fully connected topology is tested with a total number of cycles of 1500. Two experiments are performed with the following configuration: 1) Total of 1500 services deployed as 10 services per 10 cycles. 2) Total of 3000 services deployed as 20 services per 10 cycles. The results are depicted for experiment 1 and experiment 2 in fig 7 using logarithmic scale.

In Fig. 7, it is clear that in case of allocating 10 services every 10th cycle; the system can produce a dependable performance. It is noticed that some bottlenecks can occur, but the system can recover. In case of allocating 20 services every 10th cycle, it is clear that the system becomes overloaded with service allocation requests. This occurs as a result of submitting all services to one broker. It can be concluded that, in periodical allocation, the allocation ratio of 10 services every 10th cycle (i.e. 1 Service/ cycle), is acceptable and can be handled in a Grid system of $N >= 500$, and 100 brokers with fully connected broker topology. If the ratio increased to 2 services/ cycle, the system, with the same network size will become overloaded.

6.3 Impact of Broker Failure on Resource Information Updating

The aim of the experiments in this section is to measure the impact of broker failures on the validity of stored resource information. Experiment 2 in Sec 7.1, is repeated with adding injected broker failures during the simulation. With the existence of broker failures, it is expected that the deviation of the reading time values of RIDBs from the current cycle will increase due to failure. The reason is that resource information of the regular nodes which have been attached to the failed broker, will remain old and not updated until they are attached to other brokers and start sending resource information blocks. In the following experiments, a new parameter is taken into account: *Data Age*, the maximum age, in cycles, of resource information in a broker resource data set. In each simulation cycle, the broker protocol checks the reading time of each block in the resource information data set. If the reading time of a block is < (Current time – Data Age), then, this block is removed from the data set. If a new block for the same node is received later, in an exchange operation, it is added to the data set. The following experiments are performed by varying the value of Data Age.

Four topologies are used: ring, fully connected, and Wire-k-Out ($k = 60$), and hyper-cube. The network size is fixed to $N = 500$, and $M = 100$. The number of simulation cycles is 300. Two experiments are performed with varying the total number of failures: 1) Data age of 10 cycles with 4 injected broker failures, and 2) Data age of 20 cycles with 8 injected broker failures. The results are depicted in fig 8.

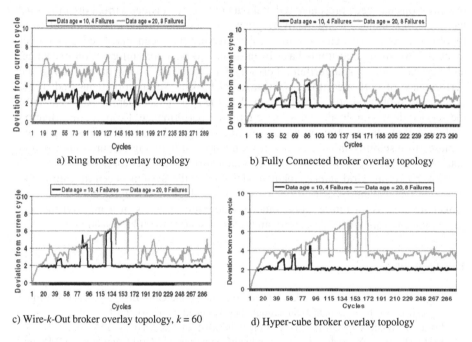

a) Ring broker overlay topology

b) Fully Connected broker overlay topology

c) Wire-k-Out broker overlay topology, $k = 60$

d) Hyper-cube broker overlay topology

Fig. 8. Impact of failures on the deviation of the resource information for: data age of 10 cycles with 4 injected broker failures, and data age of 20 cycles with 8 injected broker failures

In Fig. 8 it is clear that when the Data Age value decreases, the impact of failure decreases. This is because old data associated with unreachable nodes is periodically deleted from the resource information data sets. It is also clear that for fully connected, wire-k-out, and hyper-cube topologies, the system can recover from failures and return to stable state. In case of ring topology, the deviation has terrible variation and unstable. This can be described that, because of the lack of possible direct communications between brokers, it takes time for a broker to reach data stored in non-neighbor brokers. It can also be noticed that the magnitude of deviation caused by failure increases each time a new failure occurs, in fully connected, wire-k-out, and hyper-cube topologies. This increase is not noticed in ring topology. This increase can be described as follows: when a broker fails, all attached nodes attempt to join virtual organizations of other brokers. As the number of failures increases, the number of regular nodes attached to existing brokers also increases, So when a failure occurs then, the number of detached nodes will be larger than those in the previous failures, which causes increase in the number of old data blocks in brokers' data sets.

It can be concluded that the ring topology which is implemented in many hybrid peer-to-peer systems, is not applicable in case of assuming broker failures.

7 Conclusions

Grid simulation model which is built based on the concept of collaboration of virtual organizations has been presented. Global data exchange between virtual organizations has been implemented using the overlay network between brokers, based on different topologies. Four topologies for the broker overlay has been discussed and implemented. Two main algorithms have been described: resource information exchange, and service allocation algorithm. Performed experiments aimed at evaluating the performance of both algorithms with different broker overlay topologies and in the presence of broker failures. Results show that, the system can adapt to some extent to the service deploying load, and achieve required performance. Resource information exchange algorithm is efficient for the tested topologies, but in case of ring topology, it biases to instability in case of failures, and slow in updating resource information data due to the lack of possible direct communications between brokers.

Broker overlay Grid management model retains the system decentralization and increases the scalability. Ring broker overlay topology is not applicable in case of broker failures. As a future work, other collaboration aspects in a multi-virtual organization environment (e.g. security and rules of sharing) will be considered.

References

1. Foster, I., Kesselman, C., Tuecke, S.: The Anatomy of the Grid: Enabling Scalable Virtual Organizations. International J. Supercomputer Applications 15(3) (2001)
2. Foster, I.: What is the Grid? A Three Point Checklist. In: GRIDToday (July 20, 2002)
3. Foster, I., Zhao, Y., Raicu, I., Lu, S.: Cloud Computing and Grid Computing 360-Degree Compared. In: Grid Computing Environments Workshop, GCE 2008, pp. 1–10 (2008)
4. Androutsellis-Theotokis, S., Spinellis, D.: A survey of peer-to-peer content distribution technologies. ACM Computing Surveys 36(4), 335–371 (2004)
5. Kholidy, H.A., Azab, A.A., Deif, S.H.: Enhanced "ULTRA GRIDSEC": Enhancing High Performance Symmetric Key Cryptography Schema Using Pure Peer To Peer Computational Grid Middleware (HIMAN). In: ICPCA 2008, vol. 1, pp. 26–31 (2008)
6. El-Desoky, A.E., Ali, H.A., Azab, A.A.: A Pure Peer-To-Peer Desktop Grid framework with efficient fault tolerance. In: ICCES 2007, pp. 346–352 (2007)
7. Krauter, K., Buyya, R., Maheswaran, M.: A Taxonomy and Survey of Grid Resource Management Systems. Software—Practice And Experience 32, 135–164 (2002)
8. Condor project, http://www.cs.wisc.edu/condor/
9. The Globus toolkit, http://www.globus.org/toolkit/

10. Open-source software for volunteer computing and grid computing,
    http://boinc.berkeley.edu/
11. Kacsuk, P., Podhorszki, N., Kiss, T.: Scalable desktop Grid system. In: Daydé, M., Palma, J.M.L.M., Coutinho, Á.L.G.A., Pacitti, E., Lopes, J.C. (eds.) VECPAR 2006. LNCS, vol. 4395, pp. 27–38. Springer, Heidelberg (2007)
12. Luther, A., Buyya, R., Ranjan, R., Venugopal, S.: Peer-to-Peer Grid Computing and a. NET-based Alchemi Framework. Wiley Press, New Jersey (2005)
13. Azab, A.A., Kholidy, H.A.: An adaptive decentralized scheduling mechanism for peer-to-peer Desktop Grids. In: ICCES 2008, pp. 364–371 (2008)
14. Montresor, A., Jelasity, M.: PeerSim: A Scalable P2P Simulator,
    http://peersim.sourceforge.net/
15. El-Desoky, A.E., Ali, H.A., Azab, A.A.: Improving Fault Tolerance in Desktop Grids Based on Incremental Checkpointing. In: ICCES 2006 (November 2006)
16. EU DataGrid Java Security Working Group. VOMS Architecture v1.1,
    http://grid-auth.infn.it/docs/VOMS-v1_1.pdf
17. Asia-Pacific Grid, http://www.apgrid.org/
18. EGEE: Enabling Grids for E-Science in Europe, http://public.eu-egee.org/
19. D4Science: DIstributed colLaboratories Infrastructure on Grid ENabled Technology 4 Science. http://www.d4science.eu/
20. Gardner, R.: Grid3: An Application Grid Laboratory for Science. In: Computing in High Energy Physics and Nuclear Physics 2004, Interlaken, Switzerland, September 27-October 1, p. 18 (2004)
21. Lederer, H., Pringle, G.J., Girou, D., Hermanns, M.-A., Erbacci, G.: DEISA: Extreme Computing in an Advanced Supercomputing Environment. NIC Series, vol. 38, pp. 687–688 (2007)
22. Coulson, G., Clarke, M.: A Distributed Object Platform Infrastructure for Multimedia Applications. Computer Communications 21(9), 802–818 (1998)
23. Boloni, L., Jun, K., Palacz, K., Sion, R., Marinescu, D.C.: The Bond Agent System and Applications. In: Kotz, D., Mattern, F. (eds.) MA 2000, ASA/MA 2000, and ASA 2000. LNCS, vol. 1882, pp. 99–113. Springer, Heidelberg (2000)
24. Kooburat, T., Muangsin, V.: Centralized Grid Hosting System for Multiple Virtual Organizations, ANSCSE10 (March 22-24, 2006)
25. NorduGrid: Nordic Testbed for Wide Area Computing and Data Handling,
    http://www.nordugrid.org/

DisTec: Towards a Distributed System for Telecom Computing*

Shengqi Yang, Bai Wang, Haizhou Zhao, Yuan Gao, and Bin Wu

Beijing Key Laboratory of Intelligent Telecommunications Software and Multimedia,
Beijing University of Posts and Telecommunications,
Beijing, China
sheng_qi.yang@yahoo.com.cn

Abstract. The continued exponential growth in both the volume and
the complexity of information, compared with the computing capacity
of the silicon-based devices restricted by Moore's Law, is giving birth
to a new challenge to the specific requirements of analysts, researchers
and intelligence providers. With respect to this challenge, a new class of
techniques and computing platforms, such as Map-Reduce model, which
mainly focus on scalability and parallelism, has been emerging. In this
paper, to move the scientific prototype forward to practice, we elaborate
a prototype of our applied distributed system, *DisTec*, for knowledge
discovery from social network perspective in the field of telecommunications. The major infrastructure is constructed on Hadoop, an open-
source counterpart of Google's Map-Reduce. We carefully devised our
system to undertake the mining tasks in terabytes call records. To illustrate its functionality, DisTec is applied to real-world large-scale telecom
dataset. The experiments range from initial raw data preprocessing to
final knowledge extraction. We demonstrate that our system has a good
performance in such cloud-scale data computing.

1 Introduction

Large-scale data interpreting, computing and analyzing have stimulated great
interests in recent years, while the emergence of modern communication facilities has made these problems ubiquitous [1]. The resulted various applications
and methods have been widely implemented not only in research domains, such
as biology, climate modeling, energy systems, homeland security, and computational science [2, 3], but also in human daily lives, such as emails, calls and

* This work is supported by the National Natural Science Foundation of China under
  Grant No.60402011, the National Key Technology R&D Program of China under
  Grant No.2006BAH03B05. It is also supported by IBM China Research Laboratory,
  the Specialized Research Fund for the Joint laboratory between Beijing Univer-
  sity of Posts and Communications and IBM China Research Laboratory (Project
  No.JTP200806014-3).

M.G. Jaatun, G. Zhao, and C. Rong (Eds.): CloudCom 2009, LNCS 5931, pp. 212–223, 2009.

increasing mature WWW-based applications [4,5,6]. While especially for the new types of services enabled by *Cloud Computing* most recently, the sheer volume of data has led these applications to parallelism or distribution on commodity clusters [7,8].

In today's extremely challenging business environment, telecom operators are under intense pressure to manage customer relationships, process call logs and make business-oriented solutions. Generally, all of these operations are tightly relied on analysis of terabytes of Call Detail Records (CDRs). High-end data warehouses and powerful Business Intelligence (BI) solutions are thus becoming essential tools to help carriers meet profit goals [9, 10, 11]. Meanwhile, the Map-Reduce [4] computational model, first popularized by *Google* for handling extremely large-scale data, is widely applied both in specific research [12, 3, 8] and public utilities [13,14,15]. This up-to-date technique and its related projects [16,14] create particular opportunities for both telecom operators and high-level service providers.

In response to these challenges and opportunities, in this work, we introduce our on-going constructing system, **DisTec**, to provide access to huge telecom datasets and business solutions for telecom marketing. Basing on a distributed cluster infrastructure and *Hadoop* [5] platform built on it, a number of data mining algorithms were re-implemented parallely. More importantly, we elaborate several application scenarios as real-word requirements of telecom industry, with the aid of methods of social network analysis (SNA). As a system, we also resolve to provide an unified process of applications, ranging from data preprocessing to result reports generating. By employing a large volume of CDRs obtained from telecom operator, we validate our system from the view of scalability, effectiveness and efficiency. In summary, DisTec takes the following challenges as its destination as well as the contribution to this work:

- Towards a comprehensive architecture, DisTec integrates legacy systems and provides a layer of virtualization to overcome underlying variety and complexity.
- DisTec stores large scale CDRs in a distributed manner and provides the capability of data-intensive computing.
- DisTec provides timely and effective solutions for telecom operators regardless of the sheer volume of data.
- Based on call network, novel SNA methods are proposed to assist operator marketing and CRM operations.
- APIs and user-end tools have been published for accessing the services of DisTec conveniently and safely.

The rest of this paper is organized as follows: Section 2 presents a rough description of preliminary knowledge. Section 3 introduces an overview of our systems. Implementation and critical features are discussed in section 4. In Section 5, we are devoted to the exploration of a large volume of call records. Experimental results are soundly presented. Section 6 briefly discusses our experience in using Hadoop. Finally, we conclude our work in Section 7.

2 Preliminary

2.1 Map-Reduce Model and Hadoop Implementation

Inspired by the *map* and *reduce* primitives present in functional programming languages [4], Map-Reduce highly abstracts previous complex parallel computation into a fault-tolerant, data distribution and load balancing library. As a open-source implementation, Hadoop [5] closely resembles Google's [4] and receives numerous contributions from both enthusiastic developers and industrial giants, such as *Yahoo, Amazon, eBay*, etc. After initially launched, a job automatically partitions the input into a set of logical *splits*. Then *Mappers* will be invoked to handle the splits that have been assigned to them by the *Master*. These Mappers are geographically distributed in order to process the splits of data locally. The output is temporarily stored in a local *intermediate file*, which will be accessed further by the *Reducer*. Reducers will be invoked not until all map tasks have finished. They will iterate all values that share the same key and then output final results. Master plays the role of central commander, which coordinates Mappers and Reducers. This deliberate device efficiently simplifies the schedule task [17].

2.2 Social Network Analysis

A social network is generally represented as a graph-like structure made of nodes (individuals or organizations, such as persons or web sites) and links (a specific type of interdependency, such as kinship and friendship). Because network based complex social structure can well capture the intricate connection properties of individuals, social network analysis has gained a significance both in scientific works [18, 19, 10, 9] and in industrial applications [20, 21] during the past few years. For its inherent facility in revealing patterns of human communication, retrieved call network from CDRs can well provide major business insights for designing such strategies [9].

3 Constructing Methodology and Application Scenarios

We next briefly describe the overview architecture (also as a blueprint) of *DisTec*. As Fig. 1 presents, DisTec has a hierarchical architecture consisting four main layers: infrastructure, basic service, high layer service and public interface.

Infrastructure refers to the underlying architecture, including *cluster environment, layer of virtualization, distributed computing platform* [15, 5, 13] and *data management utilities* [22, 6, 23]. As one of enabling technologies, virtualization multiplex hardware and thus provides flexible and transparent perspective [12, 7]. Besides, the key benefits of Hadoop - simplicity, scalability and fault-tolerance [3] - also facilitate platform managers and upper layer service providers (SPs).

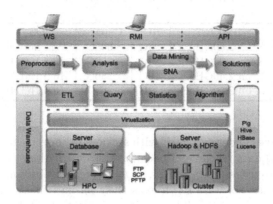

Fig. 1. DisTec overview

Fig. 2. Application scenarios in DisTec

Basic service is built on top of the virtualization layer, intending to provide both a general support of high layer applications and a channel for end-users to access underlying utilities and metadata. Traditional Algorithms here have been re-designed in a Map-Reduce form. *Statistic* and *query* are also implemented efficiently to face large-scale datasets.

High layer service mainly provides four kinds of services: *Preprocess, Analysis, Data Mining & SNA* and *Solutions*. These four parts can be served as undependent applications or be organized as a flow that can be executed one pass. Service in this layer, such as complex algorithms of data mining and SNA, involve several basic services and produce a number of intermediary results.

Table 1. Hardware Environment

Type	N_{node}	CPU	ROM	Capacity	OS	DBMS
HPC	1	Xeon 2.60GHz ×4	6G	600G	Win Server	Win SQL
HPC	1	Xeon 2.00GHz ×4	4G	250G	Red Hat 4	
HPC	1	Xeon 2.40GHz ×4	6G	250G	Red Hat 4	Oracle
Cluster	40^1	Xeon 3.20GHz ×2	2G	6T	Red Hat 4	$*^2$

Public Interface render end-users with services to conveniently access hardware, software, and data resource. To achieve this destination, we publish three kind of interfaces to users: *Web Service, Remote Method Call* and *API*.

Many activities use software services as their business basis [7]. Hence it is essential to make services accessible to various users through local or Internet-based interfaces. To provide flexible service as well as ensure the safety of our system, we predefine several user roles, including developer, researcher, data manager, domain expert, analyst and decision maker. Fig. 2 demonstrates the possible application scenarios of DisTec associated with its potential users.

4 Implementation

4.1 Hardware Construction

Table 1 summarizes the hardware environment of DisTec. It can be seen that different platforms have been incorporated in DisTec via virtualization technique. On top of cluster, HDFS (Hadoop Distributed File System) organizes huge dataset into even sized blocks and provides high throughput access to data blocks while hides its obscure construction from developers.

4.2 Data Model

Based on HDFS, a set of open-source data management software [22,23,24] have been employed to satisfy high layer OLAP-like operations. Fig. 3 demonstrates a row structure in the *table* that we store CDRs. Row key *"123"* is an identity number which represents a telecom service subscriber. The content of the row is grouped by two *column families*. The first family ("cust_info:") contains the basic registration information, such as customer identity, age, sex, city code, etc. The second family ("call_info:") contains the detailed call information associated to this subscriber. We organize *cell* values according to customer's call partners. Each cell contains all the call information between the customer ("123") and a specific partner (such as "456" or "789"). By using the timestamp mechanism of HBase, each slice in a cell represents a call event between the customer and his(her) call partner and the timestamp is set to be call's time. HBase physically

---

[1] Hadoop platform is deployed on cluster composed of 1 master and 32 slaves.

[2] Under constructed using [5,22,23,24].

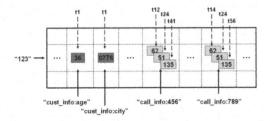

Fig. 3. An example of row that stores CDRs in DisTec

distributes large-scale CDRs and is particular well adapted to data-intensive operations [22].

4.3 Critical Requirements

There are still some vital requirements for constructing a comprehensive distributed system. Although some of them are beyond the scope of this work, we list them as our possible future works:

– **QoS:** The services provided by DisTec should guarantee QoS for users, such as CPU bandwidth and memory size.
– **Security:** As in [7], DisTec offers security services and credential delegation to access available resources in a virtual organization.
– **Service flow:** Complicated demands of users are usually composed by a number of inside services in DisTec. These basic services should be performed coordinately.
– **Control:** DisTec provides a centralized control via the master node, which schedule job tasks, report execution status and recover from mistakes.

5 Case Studies

We next validate DisTec by an analyzing procedure. The data employed here comes from CDRs of a telecom operator, describing call behaviors of people in a city in China. The raw data spans 5 months and is as large as 210 gigabytes (0.72 billion call records). Each call record contains 40 detailed attributes, including information of customers, calls and switches. Our experiments on this huge dataset are inspected from the scalability and the performance.

5.1 Preprocessing

Raw data directly extracted from switch log may be extremely large, mixed with abundant irrelevant attributes and missing values. Thus it is an important step to smooth out noise, select proper attributes and correct inconsistence in the raw data. Specifically, this step includes anonymous replacing, attribute selection and records selection.

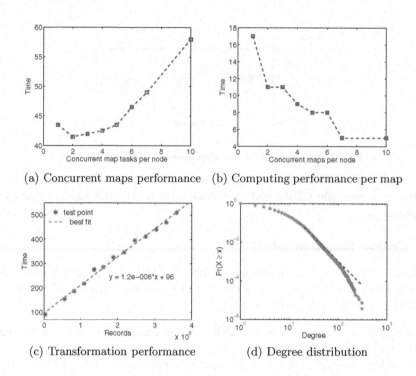

(a) Concurrent maps performance   (b) Computing performance per map

(c) Transformation performance   (d) Degree distribution

Fig. 4. Preprocess

For its extremely large scale, we can not have a complete performance experiments. Hence we just employ a small section of data (12G) to introduce our experience in using distributed computing platform. Fig. 4(a) shows that the peak performance appears when there are 2 concurrent maps on each node. When the concurrent map number is more than five per node, the performance would decay even below that of one per node. Moreover, we also investigate time consumed by one map. The result in Fig. 4(b) shows when map number increases, the average time consumed by each task decreases significantly. At the same time, I/O overhead begins to dominate CPU time and thus the integrated performance decays. Therefore it is an important task to make a balance between number of map tasks and the efficiency to arrive at an optimum result.

After preprocessing, raw data is reduced into 45 gigabytes (0.36 billion call records). Before come into analysis, another task is to transform call records into an appropriate format. Especially in SNA, data is generally constructed as a network, represented as adjacency list. Fig. 4(c) depicts the time consumed in this transformation with respect to different input records size. We find out that the time spent is linearly correlated with the input size. It takes less than 10 minutes to transform 0.36 billion records into a network containing 1.5 million customers and their detailed call info. The degree distribution is described in Fig. 4(d).

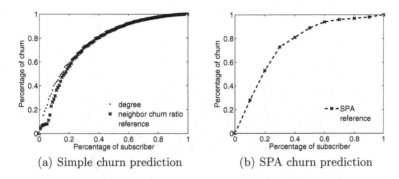

(a) Simple churn prediction   (b) SPA churn prediction

Fig. 5. Churn prediction

5.2 Customer Churn

The problem of churn prediction has been addressed by academicians as well as BI practitioners. In this subsection, we demonstrate an example of churn prediction using DisTec. Compared with traditional solutions, such as *Bayes classification* and *Decision Tree*, which mainly rely on customer attributes (profiles), however here we focus on the link properties of customers. In Fig. 5(a), the red line shows that the customer who has low degree in the call network would more likely churn. The green line shows that a user probably churns if his(her) friends has a high churn ratio. Accordingly, these two line both demonstrate the social ties effect on individual behaviors. Besides, we also implemented the *SPA* method in [9] and the result is depicted in Fig. 5(b). For its spreading process quite resembles *PageRank*, it is especially appropriate to implement this algorithm in Map-Reduce model.

5.3 Network Evolution

From dynamic view, analysis on evolving trend of call network is essential to help telecom operators make business strategies. Here, we propose an effective algorithm that can generate an evolving timeline throughout the lifecycle of the network. Our method is optimized for Map-Reduce model and thus guarantees its efficiency. We calculate the distance between each two successive snapshots of a network, $\delta(k, k + 1)$, as the accumulation of the distance between each corresponding nodes pair $\tilde{d}_{t,t+1}(v)$ in these two snapshots, which is defined as:

$$\tilde{d}_{t,t+1}(v) = \begin{cases} |\log \frac{d_t(v)+1}{1}| & v \in V_d \\ |\log \frac{1}{d_{t+1}(v)+1}| & v \in V_b \\ |\log \frac{d_t(v)}{d_{t+1}(v)}| + |\log \frac{adj_t(v) \bigcap adj_{t+1}(v)}{adj_t(v) \bigcup adj_{t+1}(v)}| & v \in V_s \end{cases} \quad (1)$$

According to Formula 1, the skeleton of the algorithm is presented as Algorithm 1 and 2. By applying this algorithm, we eventually generate the evolving timeline

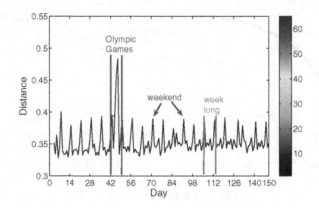

Fig. 6. Network Evolution Timeline

Algorithm 1. *TrackMapper*(k, v)

1: construct $adj_t(k)$
2: **for all** each change point t **do**
3:     calculate $\tilde{d}_{t,t+1}(k)$ according to Formula 3
4:     output $< t, \tilde{d}_{t,t+1}(k) >$
5: **end for**

---

spending 101 seconds (as a comparison, the stand-alone version costs more than 3 hours). In Fig. 6, we can easily find out the maximum point which appears at the Olympic Games period. Besides, we also locate the call pattern that shows periodicity.

5.4 Public Services

In DisTec, we provide a set of useful interfaces to users. Here we introduce a search service as an illustration.

Firstly, call network should be loaded into HBase as the table format discussed above. Fig. 7(a) shows the load performance on different records size. This operation is also a Map-Reduce process. We observe that the time spent is almost linear to the input size. It costs less than 40 minutes to load the complete 0.36 billion CDRs. After that, we also perform a search test on the distributed data table. With respect to the different size of table, the time spent on different number of search request are almost the same. It shows that the search performance have little relationship with the table size. Fig. 7(c) demonstrates an application that has subscribed our search service over Web Service. It costs only around several seconds to extract an egocentric network consisting of several hundreds nodes.

Algorithm 2. *TrackReducer*(k, iter)

1: $\delta(k, k+1) \Leftarrow 0$
2: $s \Leftarrow 0$
3: **for all** *value* $\in$ *iter* **do**
4:     $\delta(k, k+1) \Leftarrow \delta(k, k+1) + value$
5:     $s \Leftarrow s + 1$
6: **end for**
7: $\delta(k, k+1) \Leftarrow \delta(k, k+1)/s$
8: output $< k, \delta(k, k+1) >$

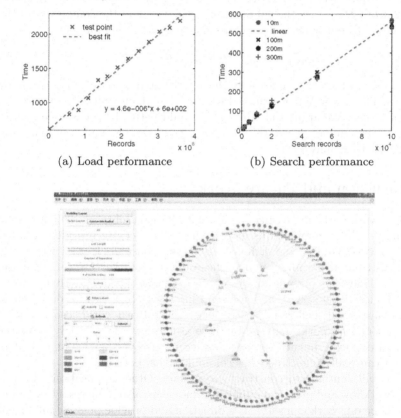

(a) Load performance   (b) Search performance

(c) Egocentric network

Fig. 7. Public service

6 Discussion

In this section, we would like to amplify some critical points and share our experience in using the Map-Reduce computing model. Hadoop platform is tightly related with the underlying hardware environment. Any deficiency of the cluster hardware, such as the frequency of CPU, I/O rate and network bandwidth, may influence the performance of high level applications. To achieve a desirable performance, some parameters, such as the block size, map number and reduce number, should be set appropriately. Increasing the number of tasks increases the framework overhead, but also increases load balancing and lowers the cost of failures. Block size generally defines the minimum number of maps (64MB as default). This number is practically determined by the number of cluster nodes, the number of CPU cores, the split size of input data and the complexity of the map function. To our experience, we propose to set the map number as:

$$N_{map} = N_{nodes} \times N_{core} \times \theta_{fun} \times \lambda \qquad (2)$$

Here, θ_{fun} stands for the complexity of the algorithm. In practice, θ_{fun} is usually less than 5. The factor λ is determined by block size, bandwidth of network and user's experience. We argue that this value would better be set between 0.5 to 1.5. Finally, the number of reduces is usually driven by the number of maps and seems to be 1 to 2 times of it.

7 Conclusion and Future Work

Motivated by recently increasing request for the capability of data intensive computing in telecommunications industy, in this paper, we introduce a novel system prototype, DisTec, and demonstrate how to construct it using the widely accepted distributed paradigm and service oriented architecture (SOA). From the industrial view, we present our system from the aspects of underlying infrastructure, middle level service and user-end interface. To illustrate our system, we employ large-scale call records and devise several real-world scenarios with the aid of social network analysis. In these studies, we do not only show the efficiency of our experiments but also resolve to discover particular insight in CDRs that can really reflect people's communication patterns.

Next we will continue to construct our system. Other applications, such as *MOLAP*, workflow and practical public interfaces, are also to be resolved. Essentially, we hope our work can serve as a direction and provide possible intelligent solutions for telecom operators.

References

1. Gorton, I.: Software architecture challenges for data intensive computing. Software Architecture, 4–6 (February 2008)
2. Kouzes, R.T., Anderson, G.A., Elbert, S.T., Gorton, I., Gracio, D.K.: The changing paradigm of data-intensive computing. Computer 42(1), 26–34 (2009)

3. Zaharia, M., Konwinski, A., Joseph, A.D., Katz, R.H., Stoica, I.: Improving mapreduce performance in heterogeneous environments (August 2008)
4. Dean, J., Ghemawat, S.: Mapreduce: Simplified data processing on large clusters. In: OSDI 2004, pp. 137–150 (2004)
5. Hadoop, `http://hadoop.apache.org/`
6. Hive, `http://hadoop.apache.org/hive/`
7. Vaquero, L.M., Merino, L.R., Caceres, J., Lindner, M.: A break in the clouds: Towards a cloud definition. SIGCOMM 39(1), 50–55 (2009)
8. Armbrust, M., Fox, A., Griffith, R., Joseph, A.D., Katz, R., Konwinski, A., Lee, G., Patterson, D., Rabkin, A., Stoica, I., Zaharia, M.: Above the clouds: A berkeley view of cloud computing (February 2009)
9. Dasgupta, K., Singh, R., Viswanathan, B., Chakraborty, D., Mukherjea, S., Nanavati, A.A., Joshi, A.: Social ties and their relevance to churn in mobile telecom networks. In: EDBT 2008, pp. 668–677 (2008)
10. Nanavati, A.A., Gurumurthy, S., Das, G., Chakraborty, D., Dasgupta, K., Mukherjea, S., Joshi, A.: On the structural properties of massive telecom call graphs: findings and implications. In: CIKM 2006, pp. 435–444 (2006)
11. Onnela, J.P., Saramaki, J., Hyvonen, J., Szabo, G., Lazer, D., Kaski, K., Kertesz, J., Barabasi, A.L.: Structure and tie strengths in mobile communication networks. PNAS 104, 7332–7336 (2007)
12. Wang, L., Tao, J., Kunze, M., Castellanos, A.C., Kramer, D., Karl, W.: Scientific cloud computing: Early definition and experience. In: HPCC 2008, pp. 825–830 (2008)
13. Amazon web services, `http://aws.amazon.com/`
14. Google appengine, `http://code.google.com/appengine/`
15. Microsoft azure, `http://www.microsoft.com/azure/default.mspx`
16. Chang, F., Dean, J., Ghemawat, S., Hsieh, W.C., Wallach, D.A., Burrows, M., Chandra, T., Fikes, A., Gruber, R.E.: Bigtable: A distributed storage system for structured data. In: OSDI 2006, pp. 205–218 (2006)
17. Papadimitriou, S., Sun, J.: Disco: Distributed co-clustering with map-reduce. In: ICDM 2008, December 2008, pp. 512–521 (2008)
18. Watts, D.J., Strogatz, S.H.: Collective dynamics of 'small-world' networks. Nature 393(6684), 440–442 (1998)
19. Barabasi, A.L., Albert, R.: Emergence of scaling in random networks. Science 286(5439), 509–512 (1999)
20. kxen, `http://www.kxen.com/index.php`
21. xtract, `http://www.xtract.com/`
22. Hbase, `http://hadoop.apache.org/hbase/`
23. Pig, `http://hadoop.apache.org/pig/`
24. Zookeeper, `http://hadoop.apache.org/zookeeper/`

Cloud Computing Boosts Business Intelligence of Telecommunication Industry

Meng Xu, Dan Gao, Chao Deng, Zhiguo Luo, and Shaoling Sun

China Mobile Communications Corporation, China
{xumeng,gaodan,dengchao,luozhiguo,
shunshaoling}@chinamobile.com

Abstract. Business Intelligence becomes an attracting topic in today's data intensive applications, especially in telecommunication industry. Meanwhile, Cloud Computing providing IT supporting Infrastructure with excellent scalability, large scale storage, and high performance becomes an effective way to implement parallel data processing and data mining algorithms. BC-PDM (Big Cloud based Parallel Data Miner) is a new MapReduce based parallel data mining platform developed by CMRI (China Mobile Research Institute) to fit the urgent requirements of business intelligence in telecommunication industry. In this paper, the architecture, functionality and performance of BC-PDM are presented, together with the experimental evaluation and case studies of its applications. The evaluation result demonstrates both the usability and the cost-effectiveness of Cloud Computing based Business Intelligence system in applications of telecommunication industry.

Keywords: Business Intelligence, Cloud Computing, BI application in telecommunication Industry.

1 Introduction

1.1 Business Intelligence

Business intelligence (BI) refers to the use of company data to facilitate decision-making by decision-makers, which means understanding current functioning and anticipating actions for well-informed steering of the enterprise. Intelligence tools are based on the use of an intelligence information system which is supplied with different data extracted from production data, information concerning the company or its environment and economic data. A tool called ETL (Extract, Transform and Load) is therefore responsible for extracting data from different sources, cleaning them up and loading them into a data warehouse. BI technologies provide historical, current, and predictive views of business operations. Common functions of business intelligence technologies are reporting, OLAP, analytics, data mining, business performance management, benchmarking, text mining, and predictive analytics.

Recently, BI applications at CMCC focus on the field of business analysis. While, as the growing of user scale and the rising of service requirement, more and more

M.G. Jaatun, G. Zhao, and C. Rong (Eds.): CloudCom 2009, LNCS 5931, pp. 224–231, 2009.

systems will need BI, such as Network Management Signaling Monitoring System and so on. Specifically, China Mobile can use BI in the following fields:

Business Analysis includes multi-dimensions data analysis, data exploration, statistic report form generation, data mining and so on, which are used to help decision-makers to make decisions of production management and marketing strategy.

Network Management includes network management signaling analysis, statistics and mining, which are used to support network optimization and failure analysis.

Mobile Internet includes the mobile internet accessing logs analysis, mining and so on, which are used to support personalized recommendation, advertisement marketing and so on.

1.2   New Challenges to the Business Intelligence System of CMCC

With the enlargement of user scale and the rising of complexity of business application, the business intelligence system of CMCC faces new challenges.

Firstly, there're mass data generated by large number of users' activity and variety of services waiting to be mined. The data scale of CMCC Service Support field reaches 6000 TB at the beginning of 2009. For example, a middle level branch of CMCC has more than 10 million users, and its CDR (calling detail records) will be 12-16TB in 12 months. For one simple application, the data after ETL process would be at 10 GB level.

Secondly, with the increasing requirements of business intelligence applications, the business intelligence system requires higher computing capability as well as larger storage capacity to IT platform. In most situations, the decision-makers hope to get result in short response time to lead them to make correct operational decision.

Traditional business intelligence platforms commonly provide data mining algorithm in a centralized environment with a few UNIX servers. However, the centralized configurations of these platforms result in low scalability and high cost which can further weaken an organization's competitiveness and limit the development of business intelligence systems. Using a mainstream commercial business intelligence platform, for example, an application based clustering algorithm can only support 1 million user's data for knowledge discovery processing, which keeps a gap with real demand.

1.3   The Emerging Cloud Computing

With the increasing of the requirements of large scale data storage and computation, cloud computing emerges at a historic moment. Cloud computing offers large scale data storage and computation services delivered through huge data centers.

Cloud computing data centers provide IT supporting Infrastructure of parallel computation through PC cluster servers. The combination of Google File System (GFS) [1] and MapReduce programming frame, as is typical in their deployment, represents the necessary confluence of data distribution and parallel computation. Hadoop [2] is an open source implementing of MapReduce and GFS, which gives an opportunity to everyone who are willing to adopt new technology. Data mining algorithms based MapReduce are increasing concerned by researcher and engineer.

Google built several data mining applications based on MapReduce [3][4]. Researchers of Stanford University developed some data mining algorithm based on MapReduce to evaluate MapReduce performance on multi-core and multiprocessor system [5][6], and some algorithms were open source to a project called Mahout [7]. But, data mining application based MapReduce is not widely adopted by industry except few Internet service providers, such as Google, Yahoo, etc. Therefore, further research and development of BI system in telecommunication Industry based on cloud computing platform is needed.

2 Cloud Computing Based Business Intelligence System

A new parallel data mining framework based on cloud computing, which is called BC-PDM, is developed to solve problems mentioned above.

2.1 BC-PDM Architecture

BC-PDM is developed based on Cloud Computing platform of CMRI. The architecture of BC-PDM is depicted in Figure 1 as follows:

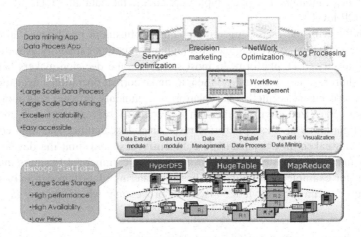

Fig. 1. BC-PDM Architecture

The feature of each layer is introduced as follows:

1) Business application layer implements business applications of telecommunication industry for marketing department making decisions of marketing strategy, such as service optimization, precision marketing, network optimization and log processing.
2) BC-PDM layer implements functions comprising: Data Extract and Load module supporting variety of data format, Data Management module for data management and remote access control, Parallel data processing module and Parallel

data mining module offering the ability of processing large scale datasets, Visualization module presenting BI results to users.

3)   Hadoop platform layer consists of DFS, MapReduce and HugeTable.

Google File System (GFS) typically underling the MapReduce system can provide an efficient and reliable distributed data storage as well as file control service needed by applications involving large databases.

MapReduce is an easy-using parallel programming paradigm suitable for large scale, data intensive parallel computing applications, which at the same time offering load balancing and fault tolerance.

HugeTable offers online *ad hoc* querying based on HBase with partial SQL support.

2.2   Features of BC-PDM

BC-PDM includes functions as following: remote data transmission, data extract, data load, parallel data process, parallel data mining, data management, visualization, workflow management and web workflow management, etc.

1) **Remote data transmission:** Allows user to upload and download data from remote external system securely and conveniently;

2) **Data extract:** Extract data from DFS to BC-PDM;

3) **Parallel data process:** Provides 14 different parallel data process operations of 6 categories based on MapReduce, such as Statistic, attribute processing, data sampling, join, redundancy data processing, etc.

4) **Parallel data mining:** Offers 9 algorithms of 3 categories based on MapReduce including Clustering, Classifier and Association Analysis;

5) **Data management:** Provides remote access control and data management which includes data and its meta data;

6) **Visualization:** Presents knowledge mined from huge amount of data to users;

7) **Workflow management:** Offers GUI for users to design BI application by drag and drop operations;

An example of GUI of BC-PDM is shown in Figure 2, which can help users in designing BI application with a graphical layout by allowing drag-and-drop of modules.

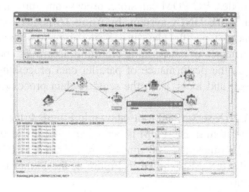

Fig. 2. GUI of BC-PDM

2.3 Experiment Evaluation

According to data scale, a BC-PDM configuration of 16 PC nodes is selected to compare with an UNIX server system. The experiment environments list as follows:

Table 1. Comparison of experiment environment between cloud computing platform and an existing commercial BI tool

	BC-PDM	an existing commercial BI tool
Hardware	16 PC nodes	UNIX server: P570_LP1
	Total CPU: 64 core,	P570_LP1:PowerPC_POWER5 2198 MHz
	Total Memory: 128GB, total Storage: 24T	CPU: 8 core, Memory: 32GB
Software	BI software: BC-PDM	BI software: SPSS Clementine v10.1
	operating system: Linux	operating system: Unix/Windows XP

Evaluation Method

The experiment evaluates BC-PDM at three aspects: correctness, performance and scalability. In detail, it comprises testing and proving whether the correctness satisfies industry standard; testing the performance of parallel data processing and parallel data mining models compared with existing serial tool; and testing the scalability of parallel functions with the number of nodes increased.

Evaluation Results of Correctness

The correctness of both parallel data processing and parallel data mining algorithms satisfies application requirements. The result of parallel data processing is consistent with serial data processing completely. Parallel data mining algorithm models are correct when using UCI data. Moreover, the correctness of parallel data mining algorithm satisfies industry standard when using real data. Classification accuracy achieves 70%, clustering gets high similarity, and strong association rules are consistency.

Evaluation Results of Performance

When there are 256 nodes, BC-PDM can store, process and mine the data at hundreds TB level. Compared to the UNIX system, by using 16 nodes configuration of BC-PDM, the performance of parallel data processing improves about 12 to 60 times; meanwhile, the performance of data mining algorithm improves about 10 to 50 times. As shown in Figure 3, the performance of parallel data processing of BC-PDM exceeds the UNIX server and tools, even the scale of data processed is 10 times than that of the latter.

Compared to the UNIX server and tools shown in Figure 4, the performance of the Paprior and PC45 algorithm in BC-PDM is better. Specifically, even the scale of data used in BC-PDM is 10 times and 100 times than that used in UNIX server, the response time is still shorter. Also shown in Figure 4, the Pkmeans algorithm in BC-PDM is same excellent.

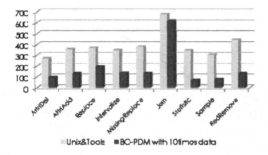

Fig. 3. Performance comparison of parallel data processing

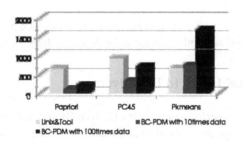

Fig. 4. Performance comparison of parallel data mining algorithm

Evaluation Results of Scalability

The number of nodes is increased from 32 to 64 and 128 to test the scalability of parallel data processing and parallel data mining modules. The experiment results indicate that the parallel data processing has excellent scalability; meanwhile, the parallel data mining algorithm has acceptable scalability. As shown in Figure 5, it can be seen that there are 11 parallel data process operations with good scalability, whose speedup ratio increases nearly linearly with the number of nodes.

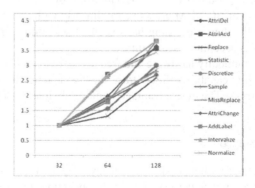

Fig. 5. Scalability of parallel data processing

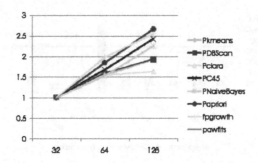

Fig. 6. Scalability of parallel data mining algorithm

Figure 6 indicates that some of the algorithms (i.e. FP-growth, PC45 and Pnaive-Bayes) achieved desired scalability; other algorithms also have suitable scalability.

3   Advantages and Issues to Be Solved

BC-PDM supports high-performance, cost-effective BI application in Telecommunication Industry with huge amounts of data for accurate business marketing. Although with some issues to be resolved, BC-PDM as a data mining framework has some features which still can not be realized by commercial software.

3.1   Advantages

BC-PDM can process and mine data at hundreds TB level with high performance, while commercial data mining software can not process such large scale data because data to be processed of these software must be load in memory in advance.

The performance of parallel data processing and mining of BC-PDM is 10 times better than that of current commercial systems for processing GB level data. For example, the response time to process 1.2 TB data using BC-PDM is about 40 minutes.

The speedup ratio of BC-PDM grows nearly linearly with the increase of data node numbers. The parallel data processing has excellent scalability, and the parallel data mining algorithm has acceptable scalability.

BC-PDM uses commodity hardware and free software to archive cost-effectiveness with higher processing capability. In contrast, the cost is much higher for UNIX servers and Storage Arrays. The cost advantage is more obvious with the growth of data scale.

3.2   Issues to Be Solved

It is important to choose a better parallel strategy of data processing and data mining algorithms to archive higher performance in the meantime to ensure the correctness satisfies industry standard.

User-access authority and data-access authority are needed due to information security. Moreover, data privacy processing and encryption must be considered in order to protect user privacy.

BC-PDM offers services through GUI and Web Service API, and HugeTable further provides querying by SQL. On the other hand, there are still works to be done, such as seamless transplant of current application system to BC-PDM.

4 Conclusions and Future Works

The BC-PDM framework which integrates data mining applications on MapReduce and HDFS platform is a preliminary implementation of cloud computing based BI. The above experiment results verified that data mining application on MapReduce could process large scale data and speed up the response time effectively. Moreover, BC-PDM has advantages which commercial BI software do not support, such as large scale data, high performance, massive scalability, cost-effectiveness and customization. Nonetheless, BC-PDM is an experimental framework at present. Further development and improvement is needed at aspects such as functionality, performance and reliability to meet requirements of CMCC's business applications. To provide standard BI service based on cloud computing, which encourages user participation, is our research direction in future.

Cloud computing platform for BI system can provide an IT support with high availability, and offers huge amount of data analysis and mining capability, and therefore enables BI system to explore a broader stage. In the near future, cloud computing platform can further assist Business Intelligent in variety area.

Acknowledgments. We thank Bill.Huang for his guide and inspiration, and thank the following people for their contributions to this work: Wenhui Zhou, Zhihong Zhang, Hongwei Sun, Xu Wang, and Leitao Guo.

References

1. Ghemawat, S., Gobioff, H., Leung, S.-T.: The google file system. In: Proceedings of 19th ACM Symposium on Operating Systems Principles (October 2003)
2. Hadoop, an open source implementing of MapReduce and GFS,
   http://hadoop.apache.org
3. Dean, J., Ghemawat, S.: Mapreduce: Simplified data processing on large clusters. In: Proceedings of OSDI 2004: Sixth Symposium on Operating System Design and Implementation (December 2004)
4. Ramaswamy, S.: Extreming Data Mining, Google Keynote speech in SIGMOD (2008)
5. Ranger, C., et al.: Evaluating MapReduce for Multi-core and Multiprocessor Systems,
   http://video.google.com/videoplay?docid=5795534100478091031
6. Chu, C.-T., et al.: MapReduce for Machine Learning on Multicore. In: NIPS 2006 (2006)
7. Mahout, open source project on data mining algorithms based MapReduce,
   http://lucene.apache.org/mahout/

Composable IO: A Novel Resource Sharing Platform in Personal Clouds

Xiaoxin Wu, Wei Wang, Ben Lin, and Kai Miao

Intel China
(xiaoxin.wu,vince.wang,ben.lin,kai.miao)@intel.com

Abstract. A fundamental goal for Cloud computing is to group resources to accomplish tasks that may require strong computing or communication capability. In this paper we design specific resource sharing technology under which IO peripherals can be shared among Cloud members. In particular, in a personal Cloud that is built up by a number of personal devices, IO peripherals at any device can be applied to support application running at another device. We call this IO sharing composable IO because it is equivalent to composing IOs from different devices for an application. We design composable USB and achieve pro-migration USB access, namely a migrated application running at the targeted host can still access the USB IO peripherals at the source host. This is supplementary to traditional VM migration under which application can only use resources from the device where the application runs. Experimental results show that through composable IO applications in personal Cloud can achieve much better user experience.

1 Introduction

The primary goal for Cloud computing is to provide services that require resource aggregation. Through good resource management/assignment scheme Cloud resources for computation, storage, and IO/network can be efficiently grouped or packaged to accomplish jobs that can't be handled by individual devices (e.g., server, client, mobile device). Cloud may also help to accomplish tasks with a much better QoS in terms of, e.g., job execution time at a much lower cost in terms of, e.g., hardware investment and server management cost.

Most Cloud research focuses on data center, e.g., EC2 [3], where thousands of computing devices are pooled together for Cloud service provision. The Cloud usage, however, may also be applied to personal environment, because today an individual may have multiple computing or communication devices. For example, a person may have a cellular phone or a Mobile Internet Device (MID) that he always carries with him. He probably also has a laptop or a desktop that has a stronger CPU/GPU set, a larger MEM/disk, a friendly input interface, and a larger display. This stronger device may probably be left somewhere (e.g.,office or home) due to inconvenience of portability. Once the owner carries a handheld and approaches to the stronger devices, e.g., when he is set at the office or at home, he can jointly use smart phone/MID and laptop/desktop through different network connections to form a personal Cloud. Under proper resource

M.G. Jaatun, G. Zhao, and C. Rong (Eds.): CloudCom 2009, LNCS 5931, pp. 232–242, 2009.

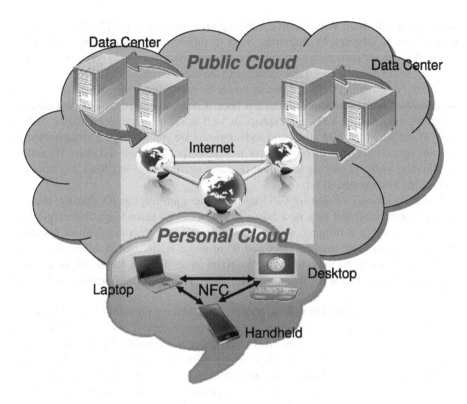

Fig. 1. A Future Person-Centralized Cloud World

management scheme, resources in such a Cloud can be grouped or shared in the most efficient way to serve this person for his best user experience.

Our vision for future person-centralized Cloud environment where a personal hand-held device, e.g., MID, is probably the center of a person's IT environment, is shown in Figure 1. There are public Clouds that are managed by big data center providers. A Cloud user can access such Clouds through Internet, and enjoy different services that may take advantage of the super computing power and intensive information/data that data centers provide. There are also personal Clouds that are built up by a personal hand-held device and its surrounding computing or costumer electronic (CE) devices. The inter-connection for the components in a personal Cloud may be, for example through near field communication (NFC) technology, under which the underlying networks can be direct cable connection or wireless networks (e.g., WLAN, WPAN, Bluetooth, etc.).

Efficient management for resource aggregation, clustering, and sharing is required for both data center Cloud and personal Cloud. Virtualization has been so far the best technology that may serve this goal. Based on virtualization, computing and storage re-sources can be shared or allocated by generating and allocating virtual machines (VM) that run part of or entire applications. In particular, when an application has been par-titioned and run in a number of VMs and each of the VMs runs at different physical machines, we can say that computing resources at these machines are aggregated to serve that application. With the live VM migration capability [1] [2], the pool of resources can be adjusted by migrating VMs to different physical machines. In other words, through virtualization resources at different devices can be aggregated for single user in a flexible way without any extra hardware requirements.

Sharing or grouping CPU computing power by managing VMs for a large work, as we described in the previous section, has been widely studied in typical virtualization technologies including VMware Vsphere as well as open source technologies such as Xen [4] and KVM [5]. VM allocation and migration are applied for, e.g., load balancing and hot spot elimination. However, how to efficiently aggregate and share IO and its peripherals, which is another important resource sharing issue in Cloud, has not been thoroughly investigated so far.

The methodology of sharing CPU through migration implies IO sharing, because an application migrated to a new host can use local IO resources at the target host machine. However, a resource sharing case that a simple migration cannot handle is that the required computing resource and IO resource are located at different physical machines. This may happen, for example, when an application has to utilize a strong CPU on a laptop while at the mean time, it relies on handheld IO functions such as 3G access.

In this work we address the above IO peripheral sharing problem by enabling a process running on a physical machine to access IO peripherals of any other physical machines that are networkly connected. In particular, we consider the highly dynamic nature of personal Cloud where Cloud components and topology may change frequently. We cover the case of IO sharing in the context of VM migration, under which the physical IO that has been accessed by an application will be maintained during and after this application has been migrated to different physical machines.

This remote IO access, or IO composition, is required when the target host for migration does not have the same IO environment as the original host, or the equivalent IO part has been occupied by some other applications. Such a pro-migration IO access also implies that a user can use aggregated IO peripherals from different devices, e.g., it can use IO from both original and target host. Although in this work we use personal Cloud as our primary investigated scenario, the work can be extended to data center as well. As a first step, we design software solution for sharing USB, because it is one of the most commonly used IO peripherals.

In summary, our major contributions are as follows:

- We design the first software solution for seamless pro-migration USB IO peripheral access. Such a virtual composable IO provides a much more convenient way for applications to share Cloud resources especially IO peripherals.
- We implement composable IO into a real personal Cloud and carry on extensive experiments for performance evaluation and bottleneck identification. We prove that the concept works, and can greatly improve user experience.

The paper is organized as follows. In section 2 we present detailed design for composable USB. In section 3 we show major performance measurements. Finally in section 4 we conclude and list future works.

2 Composable USB for IO Sharing

2.1 State of Arts for Resource Sharing

In a personal Cloud the resources may be shared or aggregated in different ways based on how applications require. There is a need for computation resource sharing. More than one device may collaborate and do the computing work together through, e.g., parallel computing that has been extensively studied for Grid Computing [7]. Another scenario for computation resource sharing is that a weak device utilizes resources from a stronger device. This has been shown in previous works [8][9]. Graphic applications running at a small device can be rendered at a device with a stronger GPU and a larger display, through capturing graphic commands at small device and sending them to the larger one.

Resource within a Cloud can be shared through either direct physical resource allocation or virtual resource allocation. Physical sharing is straightforward. Cloud members are connected together through networks and assign their disk or memory an uniform address for access, as what has been done in [10]. The challenges are that existing network bandwidth between any two Cloud members is much smaller than the intra-device IO bandwidth, and the network protocol stack results in extra latency for data or message move among devices. This dramatically degrades the application performance, in particular for real-time services. Even if the new generation CPU chip architecture and networks may mitigate such a problem by making the communication between devices equally fast as within a device, due to the dynamic nature of personal Cloud caused by mobility of the centralized user, the Cloud topology and membership may continuously change. Since any change will cause a re-configuration for pooling the overall resources in a Cloud and such a configuration not only takes time but also has to stop all the active applications, hard resource allocation may not work well in personal Cloud environment.

To address the above problem, virtualization [4][5] can be applied and the migration based on virtualization can be used for resource sharing or re-allocation by migrating applications among different devices. An application can be carried in a VM and migrated to a different physical machine that best supports it, probably because that physical machine has the required computing, network, or storage resources. Virtualization causes performance and management overhead. However, the flexibility it brings to resource management makes it by far the most promising technique for Cloud resource management. More importantly, VM can be migrated while keeping applications alive [11]. This advantage makes the resource sharing through VM allocation/migration even more appealing in particular for applications that cannot be interrupted.

2.2 Composable IO: Virtual Platform for IO Sharing

Traditional migration enables a certain level of IO sharing between the origination and destination of a migration. For example, a migrated process can still access the disk image at its original host. Technology for pro-migration access for other IO peripherals such as 3G interface and sensors, which are probably more pertinent to applications, has not been provided. In personal Cloud, pro-migration access is highly desired because

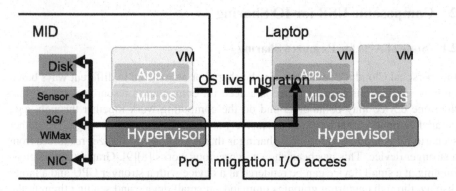

Fig. 2. Pro-migration IO access in personal Clouds

of large difference in computing capability and broad variety of IO peripherals among personal devices.

The required IO peripheral remote access capability in a personal Cloud is illustrated in Figure 2. An application running on laptop can access the IO peripherals on MID. In this scenario, the application needs the joint utilization of computing resource on the laptop and IO peripherals on the MID. In other words, the overall computing and IO resources are aggregated and assigned to an application that requires. Note that the application can also use IO peripherals at the laptop. As in this case all IO peripherals at both devices are composed to serve the application, we call this IO sharing platform composable IO. In the rest of the text, we use pro-migration IO access and composable IO interchangeably.

Composable IO enables a much richer resource sharing usage, which helps to achieve easy CPU and IO sharing in a virtualized Cloud environment. Through composable IO an application should be able to switch among IO peripherals at different devices without interrupting applications.

Below is a typical usage scenario that may happen in personal Cloud and will need pro-migration IO access. A handheld device, i.e., MID, has a lot of personal IO peripherals such as wireless broadband interface (3G, WiMAX) or sensors that traditional laptop and desktop don't have. When the MID user is running an application on the MID through, e.g., 3G interface and approaches another available device such as a laptop, a personal Cloud can be formed by connecting the two devices. The application can then be migrated from MID to laptop to take hardware advantage (e.g., stronger CPU or GPU) there. However, as the laptop does not have 3G interface, a live connection between the migrated application and the original 3G interface should be kept.

2.3   Composable USB

USB is the most commonly used IO peripherals, in particular on handheld devices. USB supports different IO usage such as 3G, WiMax, Camera, and sensors. In this subsection we give the detailed design for composable USB, which enables an application to seamless switch between USB peripherals at different physical devices in personal Cloud.

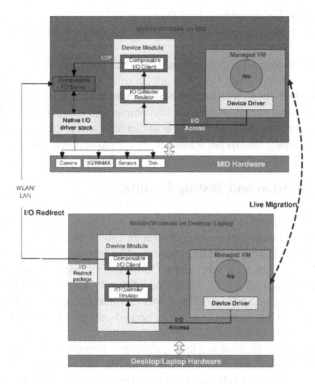

Fig. 3. Composable USB

Composable USB Architecture. The general architecture of composable USB is shown in Fig. 3. It consists of a Composable USB client and a Composable USB server. The Composable USB client, located at migration target host, packages all the USB requests from USB controller emulator in the hypervisor and then delivers the data to the server that is located at migration source host, e.g., through standard network connections such as UDP/IP over a cable connection or wireless network. Composable USB server processes all the requests from the client. It is responsible for processing incoming USB requests and building connection between the remote application and local USB peripherals. In our prototype USB command and data deliveries use the similar technology as [6], where USB data flow runs on top of IP.

We use a basic data delivery workflow to further explain how composable USB works. EHCI/UHCI block, working as I/O controller emulator, sends out USB device DATA TRANSFER request to the USB redirect server. Composable USB server checks the incoming request and dispatches it as following:

1. Check whether the message is valid by looking at its descriptor, and parse file descriptor from incoming message.
2. If the message descriptor is available, build control, bulk or isochronous transfer message according to the received message. Otherwise, return "Non Existing" error code.

3. Call local USB bus driver to deliver the request.
4. Return status code and data if operations succeed and forward the data to the caller.

Seamless IO Switching. Live migration of OS has been adopted in our platform to support resource sharing. Once OS (with application) has been migrated from MID to the laptop, the USB client will keep the connection with the USB server by talking with it using the same virtual IP address. This connection is supported by KVM VMM so that the client on the migration target host can still access the server located at the original host. To a user, the overall IO switching is both seamless and transparent.

3 Implementation and Testing Results

We build KVM composable USB in a mini personal Cloud and test its performance. In personal Cloud two devices connected through cable network. One of the device is MID and the other is laptop. For MID, it has Intel Menlow platform, with an Atom CPU Z520 (1.33 GHz), a 512K L2 Cache, and a 533 MHz FSB. Memory size is 2G. In MID host OS runs Linux Kernel 2.6.27, while Guest OS is Windows XP SP3. For laptop, it is HP DC 7700 CPU, with a Core 2 Duo E6400 2.13GHz processor, a 2MB L2 Cache, and a 1066MHz FSB. Memory size is 4G. In laptop host OS is Linux Kernel 2.6.27 and Guest OS is Windows XP SP3.

The investigated application is video conference through a 3G wireless network. USB is used for MID to receive video data from the 3G card carried on MID. The evaluating usage case is as follows. Video conference originally runs on MID, then is migrated to laptop. The application has continuous access to MID 3G card before, during, and after migration through composable USB. Through the experiments we will find out whether migration through virtualization works for MID, whether and why composable USB improves video conference performance, and what are the key factors for further improving application performance in Cloud with composable USB.

Over 100M Ethernet (Swap on)		Pre-copy			Stop and transfer remain state			Resume VM
		Time (mS)	Copy quantity (MB)	Throughput (Mbps)	Time (mS)	Copy quantity (KB)	Throughput (Mbps)	Time (mS)
Cache Warm	Empty OS	14633.58	148.37	81.11	47.38	31.50	5.32	0.022
	MS office	16079.73	169.24	84.20	61.79	38.57	4.99	0.024
	Web browsing	16891.56	176.05	83.38	69.53	31.63	3.64	0.022
Cache Cold	Empty OS	13356.48	133.60	80.02	65.33	37.09	4.54	0.030
	MS office	15783.55	162.81	82.52	61.31	35.75	4.66	0.029
	Web browsing	17131.60	182.28	85.12	63.31	31.17	3.94	0.030

Fig. 4. Migration time under 100M network

Over **Gigabit** Ethernet (Swap on)		Pre-copy			Stop and transfer remain state			Resume VM
		Time (mS)	Copy quantity (MB)	Throughput (Mbps)	Time (mS)	Copy quantity (KB)	Throughput (Mbps)	Time (mS)
Cache Warm	Empty OS	7551.56	146.95	155.68	48.60	33.78	5.56	0.019
	MS office	8266.95	174.67	169.03	48.47	42.07	6.94	0.019
	Web browsing	8488.92	187.57	176.77	55.68	39.95	5.74	0.019
Cache Cold	Empty OS	7631.51	140.38	147.16	53.83	32.54	4.84	0.025
	MS office	7753.56	152.01	156.84	63.84	40.48	5.07	0.029
	Web browsing	8240.56	178.83	173.61	67.18	30.39	3.62	0.035

Fig. 5. Migration time under 1G network

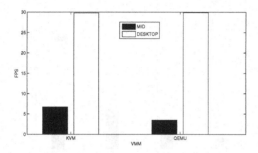

Fig. 6. FPS under replay: MID vs. Cloud with composable IO

We first test feasibility and performance for migration from a MID to a laptop. The memory assigned to MID VM is $512MB$. As shown in Fig. 4, we migrate an empty OS, an OS with MS office application, and an OS with Web browsing application through a $100Mb$ cable network. Live migration with a memory pre-copy is enabled and tested. It has been observed that MID has no problem to proceed live migrations. The service downtime is extremely low, and cannot be aware by users. The difference caused by either using warm cache (continuous testing without system reboot) and cold cache (continuous testing with system reboot) is not significant. In Fig 5 we increase the cable network speed to $1Gb$. The overall migration time can be greatly reduced because a higher bandwidth helps to reduce the pre-copy time.

Fig. 6 compares the video replay frame rate when running video conference application locally on MID's virtual machine with the rate when running the application in a personal Cloud with composable USB capability. The figure shows when migrating such an application to a stronger device while fetching data through Composable USB, significant performance (frame per second (FPS)) improvement has been made. The main reasons are as follows. First, MID has limited power to efficiently support KVM,

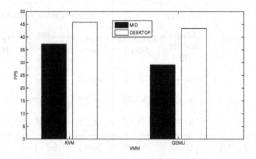

Fig. 7. FPS without replay: MID vs. Cloud with composable IO

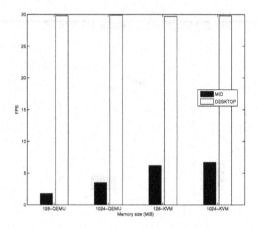

Fig. 8. Impact of MID VM memory size

in particular when such an application require large number of IO emulations, which in turn requires strong CPU power. When playing video in the VM running on the MID, the CPU of MID is not strong enough to support video replay. Therefore, the achievable frame rate is very low. On the other hand, when such an application runs in a personal Cloud, the bottleneck on MID video replay emulator does no longer exist, as the replay has been migrated to laptop that has a much stronger CPU. The achieved replay FPS then is much higher. Second, USB client power somehow determines performance in the client-server mode composable USB. Because the client on the laptop is stronger than the client on the MID, when USB upper bound is not reached, a stronger client results in a faster data delivery. The impact of client power has been shown in Fig. 7, where we compare the USB data collection speed without video replay in the two cases. The improvement contributed by the strong USB client, however, is not much, because USB data delivery is not computing intensive.

In both of the experiments we compare the video conference performance when using KVM and QUMU for virtualization. QEMU is a widely used emulator that does

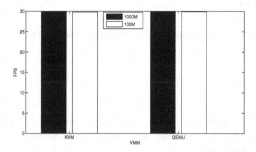

Fig. 9. Impact of network bandwidth

not require any VT support and can be adopted by other architectures such as ARM. It is observed that although KVM has a better performance, Qemu based composable IO can also help the Cloud application to reach a reasonable quality of service. In this case it reaches 30 FPS, the maximum FPS for video conference.

In Fig 8 we show the impact of changing MID VM memory size on application performance. It is observed that for KVM the impact is trivial. However, for QUMU that has to process a lot of computation for IO emulation, a larger memory size leads to a better application performance. When running the application in Cloud, increasing memory size does not lead to any performance improvement. In other words, in Cloud environment a very small memory size $128Mb$ for MID VM is enough for video conference running over composable USB.

In Fig. 9 we compare the video conference performance in personal Cloud when network has different bandwidth. An obvious observation is that if the interconnected network bandwidth is more than 100M (as most networks such as Ethernet, cable, 802.11n can support), the network bandwidth will not be a performance bottleneck.

4   Conclusions and Future Works

In this work we design and evaluate composable USB for personal Cloud applications. USB access is kept alive after live migration. Such a pro-migration IO sharing helps Cloud to more flexibly arrange and allocate resources, in particular when an application may require computing resources and IO peripherals at different physical machines. Experimental results from testing video conference over a real Cloud system that consists of a MID and a laptop shows that using composable USB the FPS can be greatly improved. This means for existing devices with a limited hardware power through our design user experience can be enhanced.

Future work will be designing a general composable IO function block that enables sharings among IOs besides USB. In particular, when newly VT such as VT-d is provided, it will be challenging to share such IO because CPU may not be able to handle this kind of IO redirections. We will investigate the possibility of providing software composable IO solution considering VT-d support and recommend hardware composable IO solutions if necessary.

Acknowledgement

We thank Xuezhao Liu for his support in testing migration performance and collecting data.

References

1. Wood, T., Shenoy, P., Venkataramani, A., Yousif, M.: Black-box and Gray-box Strategies for Virtual Machine Migration. In: Proc. 4th Symposium on Networked Systems Design and Implementation, NSDI (2007)
2. Sapuntzakis, C.P., Chandra, R., Pfaff, B., Chow, J., Lam, M.S., Rosenblum, M.: Optimizing the Migration of Virtual Computers. In: Proc. 5th Symposium on Operating Systems Design and Implementation, OSDI (2002)
3. EC2: Amazon Elastic Compute Cloud, http://aws.amazon.com/ec2/
4. Barham, P., Dragovic, B., Fraser, K., Hand, S., Harris, T., Alex Ho, R.N., Pratt, I., Warfield, A.: Xen and the Art of Virtualization. In: Proceedings of ACM Symposium on Operating Systems Principles, SOSP 2003 (2003)
5. KVM Forum, http://www.linux-kvm.org/page/KVM_Forum
6. Hirofuchi, T., Kawai, E., Fujikawa, K., Sunahara, H.: USB/IP - a Peripheral Bus Extension for Device Sharing over IP Network. In: Proc. of 2005 USENIX Annual Technical Conference (2005)
7. Krauter, K., Buyya, R., Maheswaran, M.: A taxonomy and survey of grid resource management systems for distributed computing. Software Ractice And Experience 32, 135–164 (2002)
8. Wu, X., Pei, G.: Collaborative Graphic Rendering for Improving Visual Experience. In: Proc. of Collabratecomm (2008)
9. Yang, S.J., Nieh, J., Selsky, M., Tiwari, N.: The Performance of Remote Display Mechanisms for Thin-Client Computing. In: Proceedings of the General Track of the Annual Conference on USENIX Annual Technical Conference (2002)
10. Barak*, A., Braverman, A.: Memory ushering in a scalable computing cluster. Microprocessors and Microsystems 22(3-4), 175–182 (1998)
11. Clark, C., Fraser, K., Hand, S., Hanseny, J.G., July, E., Limpach, C., Pratt, I., Warfield, A.: Live Migration of Virtual Machines. In: NSDI 2005 (2005)

SLA-Driven Adaptive Resource Management for Web Applications on a Heterogeneous Compute Cloud

Waheed Iqbal[1], Matthew Dailey[1], and David Carrera[2]

[1] Computer Science and Information Management, Asian Institute of Technology, Thailand

[2] Technical University of Catalonia (UPC) Barcelona Supercomputing Center (BSC) Barcelona, Spain

Abstract. Current service-level agreements (SLAs) offered by cloud providers make guarantees about quality attributes such as availability. However, although one of the most important quality attributes from the perspective of the users of a cloud-based Web application is its response time, current SLAs do not guarantee response time. Satisfying a maximum average response time guarantee for Web applications is difficult due to unpredictable traffic patterns, but in this paper we show how it can be accomplished through dynamic resource allocation in a virtual Web farm. We present the design and implementation of a working prototype built on a EUCALYPTUS-based heterogeneous compute cloud that actively monitors the response time of each virtual machine assigned to the farm and adaptively scales up the application to satisfy a SLA promising a specific average response time. We demonstrate the feasibility of the approach in an experimental evaluation with a testbed cloud and a synthetic workload. Adaptive resource management has the potential to increase the usability of Web applications while maximizing resource utilization.

1 Introduction

Cloud providers such as Google and Amazon offer computational and storage resource rental services to consumers. Consumers of these services host applications and store data for business or personal needs. The key features of these services, on-demand resource provisioning and pay-per-use, mean that consumers only need to pay for the resources they actually utilize. In this environment, cloud service providers must maximize their profits by fulfilling their obligations to consumers with minimal infrastructure and maximal resource utilization.

Although most cloud providers provide Service Level Agreements (SLAs) for availability or other quality attributes, the most important quality attribute for Web applications from the user's point of view, *response time*, is not addressed by current SLAs. The reason for this is obvious: Web application traffic is highly unpredictable, and response time depends on many factors, so guaranteeing a particular maximum response time for any traffic level would be suicide for the

M.G. Jaatun, G. Zhao, and C. Rong (Eds.): CloudCom 2009, LNCS 5931, pp. 243–253, 2009.

cloud provider unless it had the ability to dynamically and automatically allocate additional resources to the application as traffic grows.

In this paper, we take steps toward eliminating this limitation of current cloud-based Web application hosting SLAs. We present a working prototype system running on a EUCALYPTUS-based [1] heterogeneous compute cloud that actively monitors the response time of the compute resources assigned to a Web application and dynamically allocates the resources required by the application to maintain a SLA that guarantees specific response time requirements.

There have been several efforts to perform adaptive scaling of applications based on workload monitoring. Amazon Auto Scaling [2] allows consumers to scale up or down according to criteria such as average CPU utilization across a group of compute instances. [3] presents the design of an auto scaling solution based on incoming traffic analysis for Axis2 Web services running on Amazon EC2. [4] demonstrate two software systems, Shirako [5] and NIMO [6]. Shirako is a Java toolkit for dynamic resource allocation in the Xen virtualization environment that allocates virtual resources to guest applications from a pool of available resources. NIMO creates an application performance model using active learning techniques. The authors use NIMO to build performance models by capturing resource requirements, data characteristics, and workload statistics for a guest application. They then use Shirako to allocate the necessary resources to the application. [7] use admission control and dynamic resource provisioning to develop an overload control strategy for secure Web applications hosted on SMP (Symmetric MultiProcessing) platforms. They implement and experiment with a global resource manager for the Linux hosting platform that is responsible for allocating resources to application servers running on it and ensuring desired QoS in terms of performance stability during extreme overload. The server machines in their system are able to automatically adapt to changes in workload.

To the best of our knowledge, our system is the first SLA-driven resource manager for compute clouds based on open source technology. Our working prototype, built on top of a EUCALYPTUS-based compute cloud, provides adaptive resource allocation and dynamic load balancing for Web applications in order to satisfy a SLA that enforces specific response time requirements. We evaluate the prototype on a heterogeneous testbed cloud and demonstrate that it is able to detect SLA violations from individual computational resources and perform adaptive resource management to satisfy the SLA.

There are a few limitations to this preliminary work. We only address the application server tier, not the database tier or network. Our prototype is only able to scale up, although it would also be easy to enable the system to scale down by detecting the ends of traffic spikes. Finally, cloud providers using our approach to response time-driven SLAs would need to protect themselves with a detailed contract (imagine for example the rogue application owner who purposefully inserts delays in order to force SLA violations). We plan to address some of these limitations in future work.

In the rest of this paper, we describe our approach, the prototype implementation, and an experimental evaluation of the prototype.

2   System Design and Implementation

To manage cloud resources dynamically based on response time requirements, we developed two components, VLBCoordinator and VLBManager, in Java. We use Nginx [8] as a load balancer because it offers detailed logging and allows reloading of its configuration file without termination of existing client sessions.

VLBCoordinator interacts with the EUCALYPTUS cloud using Typica [9]. Typica is a simple API written in Java to access a variety of Amazon Web services such as EC2, SQS, SimpleDB, and DevPay. Currently, Typica is not able to interact with EUCALYPTUS-based clouds, so we patched it to allow interaction with EUCALYPTUS. The core functions of VLBCoordinator are instantiateVirtualMachine and getVMIP, which are accessible through XML-RPC.

VLBManager monitors the logs of the load balancer and detects violations of response time requirements. It reads the load balancer logs in real time and calculates the average response time for each virtual machine in a Web farm over intervals of 60 seconds. Whenever it detects that the average response time of any virtual machine exceeds the required response time, it invokes the instantiateVirtualMachine method of VLBCoordinator with the required parameters and obtains a new instance ID. After obtaining the instance ID, VLBManager waits for 20 seconds (the maximum time it takes for a VM to boot in our system) then obtains the new instance's IP address using an XML-RPC call to VLBCoordinator. After receiving the IP address of the newly instantiated virtual machine, it updates the configuration file of the load balancer then sends it a signal requesting it to reload the configuration file.

VLBManager executes as a system daemon. Nginx's proxy log entries record among other information the node that serves each specific request. VLBManager reads these log entries for 60 seconds and calculates the average response time of each node. If it finds that the average response time of any node is greater then required response time, it makes an asynchronous call to VLBCoordinator that adaptively launch a new virtual machine and add that virtual machine to the Web farm controlled by the Nginx load balancer. Following is the pseudocode for the main use case of VLBManager.

1: set $SLA_{rt} = 2.0$ {Maximum Response time (seconds) allowed in SLA}
2: set $isScaling = false$
3: **while** $true$ **do**
4:     vlbManager.ReadNginxLogEnteries(60)
5:     **for** each $node$ in $nginxWebFarm$ **do**
6:         $vlbManager.calculateAvgRT(node)$
7:     **end for**
8:     **if** Avg_{rt} of any node $> SLA_{rt}$ and $isScaling == false$ **then**
9:         $isScaling = true$
10:        $instanceId = VLBCoordinator.instantiateVirtualMachine()$
11:        $vmip = vlbCoordinator.getVMIP(instanceId)$
12:        $vlbManager.addVMtoNginxWebFarm(vmip)$

13:     $isScaling = false$
14:   **end if**
15: **end while**

The Boolean *isScaling* is used to prevent concurrent invocations of the scale-up procedure. VLBManager creates a child thread to interact with VLBCoordinator after detection of response time requirements violation at Line 8.

3   Experiments

In this section we describe the setup for an experimental evaluation of our prototype based on a testbed cloud, a sample Web application, and a synthetic workload generator.

3.1   Testbed Cloud

We built a small heterogeneous compute cloud using four physical machines. Table 1 shows the hardware configuration of the machines.

Table 1. Hardware configuration of physical machines used for the experimental compute cloud

Node	Type	CPU	RAM
Front end	Intel Pentium	2.80 GHz	2 GB
Node1	Intel Pentium	2.66 GHz	1.5 GB
Node2	Intel Celeron	2.4 GHz	2 GB
Node3	Intel Core 2 Duo	1.6 GHz	1 GB

We used EUCALYPTUS to establish a cloud architecture comprising one Cloud Controller (CLC), one Cluster Controller (CC), and three Node Controllers (NCs). We installed the CLC and CC on a front-end node attached to both our main LAN and the cloud's private network. We installed the NCs on three separate machines (Node1, Node2, and Node3) connected to the private network.

3.2   Sample Web Application and Workload Generation

The CPU is normally the bottleneck in the generation of dynamic Web content [10]. We therefore built a simple synthetic Web application consisting of one Java servlet that emulates the real behavior of dynamic web applications by alternating between a CPU intensive job and idle periods, simulating access to non-compute resources such as network connections and local I/O. The servlet accepts two parameters, a baseline time and the number of iterations to perform, and performs a matrix calculation up to the baseline time for the given number of iterations. We used httperf to generate synthetic workload for our experiments. We generate workload for a specific duration with a required number of user sessions per second.

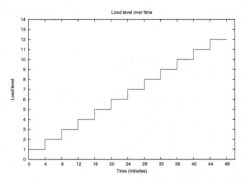

Fig. 1. Workload generation for both experiments. We linearly step the load level from load level 1 through load level 12 every four minutes. Each load level represents the number of user sessions per second, and each session involves 10 requests to the sample Web application.

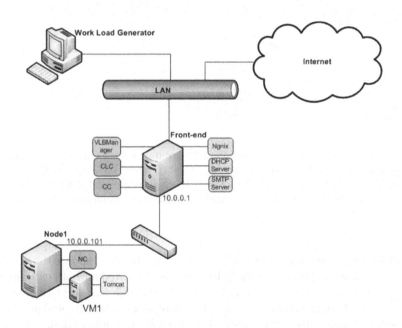

Fig. 2. Experimental setup for Experiment 1 (static resource allocation). The Nginx-based Web farm consists of one virtual machine (VM1) running the Web application. **VLBManager** is only used to obtain the average response time by actively monitoring the Nginx logs.

Each user session makes 10 requests to the application including 4 pauses to simulate user think time. We performed two experiments based on this application. Experiment 1 profiles the system's behavior with static allocation of resources to the application. Experiment 2 profiles the system's behavior under adaptive

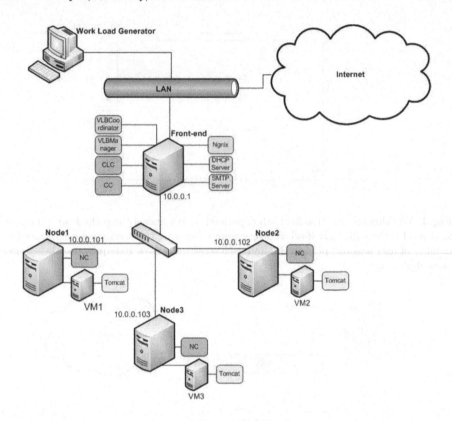

Fig. 3. Experimental setup for Experiment 2 (dynamic resource allocation). The Web farm is initialized with one virtual machine (VM1), while VM2 and VM3 are cached using EUCALYPTUS. **VLBManager** monitors the Nginx logs and detects violations of the SLA. **VLBCoordinator** adaptively invokes additional virtual machines as required to satisfy the SLA.

allocation of resources to the application to satisfy specific response time requirements. The same workload, shown in Figure 1, is generated for both experiments.
We linearly step the load level from load level 1 through load level 12 every four
minutes. Each load level represents the number of user sessions created per second,
and each session involves 10 requests to the sample Web application.

3.3 Experiment 1: Static Allocation

In this experiment, we established the experimental setup shown in Figure 2, in
which only one virtual machine (VM1) hosts the Web application. We installed
the Nginx load balancer on our front-end node and the Apache Tomcat application server on the virtual machine. The Nginx-based Web farm thus consists of
only one virtual machine (VM1). **VLBManager** is only used to obtain the average
response time by actively monitoring the Nginx logs.

3.4   Experiment 2: Adaptive Allocation

In this experiment, we used our proposed system to prevent response time increases and rejection of requests by the Web server. Figure 3 shows the experimental setup we established for this experiment. The Nginx-based Web farm is initialized with one virtual machine (VM1), while VM2 and VM3 are cached using EUCALYPTUS. In this experiment, we try to satisfy a Service Level Agreement (SLA) that enforces a two-second maximum average response time requirement for the sample Web application regardless of load level. We use `VLBManager` to monitor the Nginx logs and detect violations of the SLA. We use `VLBCoordinator` to adaptively invoke additional virtual machines as required to satisfy the SLA.

4   Results

4.1   Experiment 1: Static Allocation

This section describes the results we obtained in Experiment 1. Figure 4 shows the CPU utilization of VM1 during Experiment 1. After load level 5, the CPU is almost fully utilized by the Tomcat application server. We observe downward spike in the beginning of each load level because all user sessions are cleared between load levels and it takes some time for the system to return to a steady state.

Figure 5(a) shows the number of requests served by our system. After load level 6, we do not observe any growth in the number of served requests because the sole Web server reaches its saturation point. Although the load level increases with time, the system is unable to serve all requests, and it either rejects or queues the remaining requests. Figure 5(b) shows the number of requests rejected by our system during Experiment 1.

Figure 6 shows the average response time we observed during each load level. From load level 1 to load level 5, we observe a nearly constant response time, but

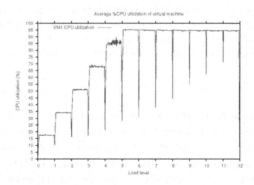

Fig. 4. CPU utilization of VM1 during Experiment 1. The duration of each load level is 4 minutes. The CPU is saturated at load level 5.

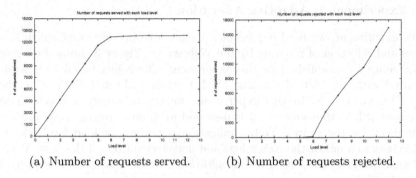

(a) Number of requests served.   (b) Number of requests rejected.

Fig. 5. Number of served and rejected requests during Experiment 1. The duration of each load level is 4 minutes. After load level 6, we do not observe any growth in the number of served requests, because the Web server reaches its saturation point. As the load level increases with time, the system is increasingly unable to serve requests and rejects more requests.

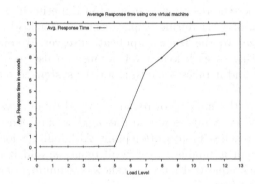

Fig. 6. Average response time for each load level during Experiment 1. The duration of each load level is 4 minutes. From load level 1 to load level 5, we observe a nearly constant response time. After load level 5, we see rapid growth in the average response time. When the Web server reaches the saturation point, requests spend more time in the queue, and the system rejects some incoming requests. From load level 6 to load level 10, some requests spend time in the queue and few requests get rejected. After load level 10, the Web server queue is also saturated, and the system rejects most requests.

after load level 5, the arrival rate exceeds the limit of the Web server's processing capability, so requests spend more time in the queue, and response time grows rapidly. From load level 5 to load level 10, requests spend more time in the queue and relatively few requests get rejected. After load level 10, however, the queue also becomes saturated, and the system rejects most requests. Therefore we do not observe further growth in the average response time.

Clearly, we cannot provide a SLA guaranteeing a specific response time with an undefined load level for a Web application using static resource allocation.

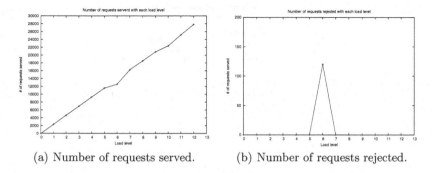

(a) Number of requests served.   (b) Number of requests rejected.

Fig. 7. Number of served and rejected requests by system during Experiment 2 with adaptive resource allocation. The number of requests served by system grows linearly with the load level while only 120 requests are rejected during the first violation of response time requirements.

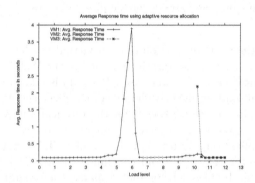

Fig. 8. Average response time for each virtual machine during Experiment 2. Whenever the system detects a violation of response time requirements in any virtual node, it dynamically creates another virtual machine and adds it to the Web farm.

4.2 Experiment 2: Adaptive Allocation

This section describes the results of Experiment 2. Figure 7(a) shows the number of requests served by the system over time. We observe linear growth in the number of requests served by the system with each load level. Figure 7(b) shows the number of requests rejected during Experiment 2. Only 120 requests are rejected during the first violation of response time requirements.

Figure 8 shows the average response time of each virtual machine as it is adaptively added to the Web farm. Whenever the system detects a violation of the response time requirement from any virtual machine, it dynamically invokes another virtual machine and adds it to the Web farm. We observe continued violation of the required response time for a period of time due to the latency of virtual machine boot-up.

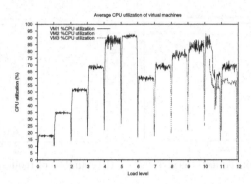

Fig. 9. CPU utilization of virtual machines during Experiment 2. The duration of each load level is four minutes. After load level 6, VM2 is adaptively added to the Web farm to satisfy the response time requirement. After load level 10, VM3 is adaptively added to the Web farm. Different load levels for different VMs reflect the use of round robin balancing and differing processor speeds for the physical nodes.

Figure 9 shows the CPU utilization of each virtual machine over the experiment. After load level 6, VM2 is adaptively added to the Web farm to satisfy the response time requirement. After load level 10, VM3 is adaptively added to the Web farm. Different load levels for different VMs reflect the use of round-robin balancing and differing processor speeds for the physical nodes.

The experiments show that adaptive management of resources on compute clouds for Web applications would allow us to offer SLAs that enforce specific response time requirements. To avoid continued violation of the SLA during VM boot-up, it would be better to predict response time requirement violations rather than waiting until the requirement is violated.

5   Conclusion and Future Work

In this paper, we have described a prototype system based on EUCALYPTUS that actively monitors the response time of a Web application hosted on a cloud and adaptively scales up the compute resources of the Web application to satisfy a SLA enforcing specific response time requirements. Adaptive resource management in clouds would allow cloud providers to manage resources more efficiently and would allow consumers (owners of Web applications) to maintain the usability of their applications.

We use the log-based approach to monitor Web applications and detect response time violations on the basis of the actual time it takes to service requests. The main benefit of this approach is that it does not require any modification of the application or adding components to the user's virtual machines. An event-based approach such as CPU utilization monitoring could be used, but this would not guarantee satisfaction of the SLA. CPU utilization or other event based approaches, while not sufficient in isolation, could be used in tandem with log-based response time monitoring to help predict future increases in response time.

We are extending our system to scale down Web applications when appropriate, and we are planning to predict VM response times in advance to overcome the virtual machine boot-up latency problem. We also plan to use fair balancing instead of round robin balancing to eliminate the need to check each VM's response time. Finally, we plan to port our system to the Amazon Web Services infrastructure.

Acknowledgments

This work was partly supported by a graduate fellowship from the Higher Education Commission (HEC) of Pakistan to WI.

References

1. Nurmi, D., Wolski, R., Grzegorczyk, C., Obertelli, G., Soman, S., Youseff, L., Zagorodnov, D.: The EUCALYPTUS Open-source Cloud-computing System. In: CCA 2008: Proceedings of the Cloud Computing and Its Applications Workshop, Chicago, IL, USA (2008)
2. Amazon Inc: Amazon web services auto scaling (2009), http://aws.amazon.com/autoscaling/
3. Azeez, A.: Auto-scaling web services on amazon ec2 (2008), http://people.apache.org/~azeez/autoscaling-web-services-azeez.pdf
4. Shivam, P., Demberel, A., Gunda, P., Irwin, D., Grit, L., Yumerefendi, A., Babu, S., Chase, J.: Automated and on-demand provisioning of virtual machines for database applications. In: SIGMOD 2007: Proceedings of the 2007 ACM SIGMOD International Conference on Management of Data, pp. 1079–1081. ACM, New York (2007)
5. Irwin, D., Chase, J., Grit, L., Yumerefendi, A., Becker, D., Yocum, K.G.: Sharing networked resources with brokered leases. In: ATEC 2006: Proceedings of the Annual Conference on USENIX 2006 Annual Technical Conference, p. 18. USENIX Association, Berkeley (2006)
6. Shivam, P., Babu, S., Chase, J.: Active and accelerated learning of cost models for optimizing scientific applications. In: VLDB 2006: Proceedings of the 32nd International Conference on Very Large Data Bases, VLDB Endowment, pp. 535–546 (2006)
7. Guitart, J., Carrera, D., Beltran, V., Torres, J., Ayguadé, E.: Dynamic CPU provisioning for self-managed secure Web applications in SMP hosting platforms. Computer Network 52(7), 1390–1409 (2008)
8. Sysoev, I.: Nginx (2002), http://nginx.net/
9. Google Code: Typica: A Java client library for a variety of Amazon Web Services (2008), http://code.google.com/p/typica/
10. Challenger, J.R., Dantzig, P., Iyengar, A., Squillante, M.S., Zhang, L.: Efficiently serving dynamic data at highly accessed web sites. IEEE/ACM Transactions on Networking 12, 233–246 (2004)

Cost of Virtual Machine Live Migration in Clouds: A Performance Evaluation

William Voorsluys[1], James Broberg[1], Srikumar Venugopal[2],
and Rajkumar Buyya[1]

[1] Cloud Computing and Distributed Systems (CLOUDS) Laboratory,
Department of Computer Science and Software Engineering,
The University of Melbourne, Australia
{williamv,brobergj,raj}@csse.unimelb.edu.au
http://www.cloudbus.org
[2] School of Computer Science and Engineering,
The University of New South Wales, Sydney, Australia
srikumarv@cse.unsw.edu.au

Abstract. Virtualization has become commonplace in modern data centers, often referred as "computing clouds". The capability of virtual machine live migration brings benefits such as improved performance, manageability and fault tolerance, while allowing workload movement with a short service downtime. However, service levels of applications are likely to be negatively affected during a live migration. For this reason, a better understanding of its effects on system performance is desirable. In this paper, we evaluate the effects of live migration of virtual machines on the performance of applications running inside Xen VMs. Results show that, in most cases, migration overhead is acceptable but cannot be disregarded, especially in systems where availability and responsiveness are governed by strict Service Level Agreements. Despite that, there is a high potential for live migration applicability in data centers serving modern Internet applications. Our results are based on a workload covering the domain of multi-tier Web 2.0 applications.

Keywords: Virtual machines, performance evaluation, migration, Xen.

1 Introduction

Virtual machine (VM) technology has recently emerged as an essential building-block of modern data centers, mainly due to its capabilities of isolating, consolidating and migrating workload [1]. Altogether, these features allow a data center to serve multiple users in a secure, flexible and efficient way. Consequently, these virtualized infrastructures are consider a key component to drive the emerging Cloud Computing paradigm [2].

Migration of virtual machines seeks to improve manageability, performance and fault tolerance of systems. More specifically, the reasons that justify VM migration in a production system include: the need to balance system load, which can be accomplished by migrating VMs out of overloaded/overheated

M.G. Jaatun, G. Zhao, and C. Rong (Eds.): CloudCom 2009, LNCS 5931, pp. 254–265, 2009.

servers; and the need of selectively bringing servers down for maintenance after migrating their workload to other servers.

The ability to migrate an entire operating system overcomes most difficulties that traditionally have made process-level migration a complex operation [3,4]. The applications themselves and their corresponding processes do not need to be aware that a migration is occurring. Popular hypervisors, such as Xen and VMWare, allow migrating an OS as it continues to run. Such procedure is termed as "live" or "hot" migration, as opposed to "pure stop-and-copy" or "cold" migration, which involves halting the VM, copying all its memory pages to the destination host and then restarting the new VM. The main advantage of live migration is the possibility to migrate an OS with near-zero downtime, an important feature when live services are being served [3].

1.1 Background

On Xen, as described by Clark et al. [3], live migrating a VM basically consists of transferring its memory image from a source server to a destination server. To live migrate a VM, the hypervisor pre-copies memory pages of the VM to the destination without interrupting the OS or any of its applications. The page copying process is repeated in multiple rounds on which dirty pages are continuously transferred. Normally, there is a set of pages that is modified so often that the VM must be stopped for a period of time, until this set is fully transferred to the destination. Subsequently, the VM can be resumed in the new server.

It has been observed that live migration of VMs allows workload movement with near zero application downtime. Nevertheless, the performance of a running application is likely to be negatively affected during the migration process due to the overhead caused by successive iterations of memory pre-copying [3]. For the duration of the pre-copying process extra CPU cycles are consumed on both source and destination servers. An extra amount of network bandwidth is consumed as well, potentially affecting the responsiveness of Internet applications. In addition, as the VM resumes after migration, a slowdown is expected due to cache warm-up at the destination [5].

Moreover, downtime and application performance are likely to be affected in different ways for different applications due to varying memory usages and access patterns. Previous studies have found that actual downtime may vary considerably between applications, ranging from as low as 60 ms when migrating a Quake game server [3] to up to 3 seconds in case of particular HPC benchmarks [5]. Regarding the overhead due to migration activity, earlier studies have shown that experienced slowdown ranged between 1% and 8% of wall-clock time for a particular set of HPC benchmarks [5].

In other scenarios using Xen, a 12% to 20% slowdown on the transmission rate of an Apache Web server running a VM with 800MB of memory and serving static content was reported [3]. In the case of a complex Web workload (SPECWeb99) the system under test could maintain the conformity to the benchmark metrics [3]. In all cases, it has been concluded that, for the particular set of applications considered, the bad effects of migration were acceptable or negligible in contrast to its potential benefits to system fault tolerance [5].

1.2 Our Contribution

The current literature lacks a practical investigation of live migration effects in the performance of modern Internet applications, such as multi-tier Web 2.0 applications. However, such a study would aid researchers and practitioners currently evaluating the deployment of this class of application in clouds. Our contribution is a case study that quantifies the effect of VM live migrations in the performance of one example, yet representative, of a modern Internet application. Our study will be potentially useful to environments where metrics, such as service availability and responsiveness, are driven by Service Level Agreements (SLAs). In such systems service providers and consumers agree upon a minimum service level and non-compliance to such agreement may incur in penalties to providers [6]. More importantly, an SLA directly reflects how end-users perceive the quality of service being delivered.

The rest of this paper is organized as follows: Section 2 positions our study among related work; Section 3 describes why modern Internet applications are different than traditional workloads; Section 4 describes our objectives, experimental testbed, workload and metrics; Section 5 presents the results of our performance evaluation; finally, we conclude the paper in Section 6.

2 Related Work

The advent of innovative technologies, such as multicore [7], paravirtualization [1], hardware-assisted virtualization [8] and live migration [3], have contributed to an increasing adoption of virtualization on server systems. At the same time, being able to quantify the pros and cons of adopting virtualization in face of such advancements is a challenging task. The impact of virtualization in a variety of scenarios has been the focus of considerable attention. A number of studies have presented individual and side by side measurements of VM runtime overhead imposed by hypervisors on a variety of workloads [1,9].

Apparao et al. [10] present a study on the impact of consolidating several applications on a single server running Xen. As workload the authors employed the vConsolidate benchmark [11] defined by Intel, which consists of a Web server VM, a database server VM, a Java server VM and mail server VM. An idle VM is also added to comply with real world scenarios, on which servers are hardly fully utilized.

The studies presented by Zhao & Figueiredo [12] and Clark et al. [3] specifically deal with VM migration. The former analyzes performance degradation when migrating CPU and memory intensive workloads as well as migrating multiple VMs at the same time; however such study employs a pure stop-and-copy migration approach rather than live migration. The later introduces Xen live migration and quantifies its effects on a set of four applications common to hosting environments, primarily focusing on quantifying downtime and total migration time and demonstrating the viability of live migration. However, these works have not evaluated the effect of migration in the performance of modern Internet workloads, such as multi-tier and social network oriented applications.

A few studies propose and evaluate the efficacy of migrating VMs across long distances, such as over the Internet. For instance, Travostino et al. [13] have demonstrated the effectiveness of VM live migration over an WAN connected by dedicated 1Gbps links; application downtime has been quantified at 5-10 times greater than that experienced on an intra-LAN set-up, despite a 1000 times higher RTT. Besides its feasibility, the concept of WAN live migration is still to be implemented in commercial hypervisors, which demands all involved machines to be in the same subnet and share storage. Our work focuses only on migrating VMs within a data center.

The Cloudstone benchmark [14] aims at computing the monetary cost, in dollars/user/month, for hosting Web 2.0 applications in cloud computing platforms such as Amazon EC2. From this work we borrow the idea of using Olio [15] and Faban [16] to compose our target workload for Web 2.0 applications. However, Cloudstone does not define a procedure to evaluate the cost of virtual machine migration and, to the best of our knowledge, no previous work has considered using this type of workload in migration experiments.

3   Characteristics of Modern Internet Applications

The domain of applications that can potentially take advantage of the Infrastructure as a Service paradigm is broad. For instance, Amazon [17] reports several case studies that leverage their EC2 platform, including video processing, genetic simulation and Web applications. In particular, such platforms are especially useful for multi-tier Web applications, generally including a Web server (e.g. Apache), an application server/dynamic content generation (e.g. PHP, Java EE), and a backend database (e.g. MySQL, Oracle). Virtual machine technology adds extra flexibility to scaling of Web applications, by allowing dynamic provisioning and replication VMs to host additional instances for one the application tiers.

Social networking websites are perhaps the most notable example of highly dynamic and interactive Web 2.0 applications which gained popularity over the past few years. Their increasing popularity has spurred demand for a highly scalable and flexible solution for hosting applications. Many larger sites are growing at 100% a year, and smaller sites are expanding at an even more rapid pace, doubling every few months [18]. These web applications present additional features that make them different from traditional static workloads [14]. For instance, their social networking features make each users' actions affect many other users, which makes static load partitioning unsuitable as a scaling strategy. In addition, by means of blogs, photostreams and tagging, users now publish content to one another rather than just consuming static content.

Altogether, these characteristics present a new type of workload with particular server/client communication patterns, write patterns and server load. However, most available performance studies use extremely simple static file retrieval tests to evaluate Web servers, often leading to erroneous conclusions [18]. In this work we have this trend into account during the workload selection process, resulting in the selection of Olio as a realistic workload.

4   Evaluation of Live Migration Cost

This study aims at achieving a better understanding of live migration effects on modern Internet applications. We have designed benchmarking experiments to evaluate the effect of live migration on a realistic Web 2.0 application hosted on networked virtual machines.

4.1   Testbed Specifications

Our testbed is a group of 6 servers (1 head-node and 5 virtualized nodes). Each node is equipped with Intel Xeon E5410 (a 2.33 GHz Quad-core processor with 2x6MB L2 cache and Intel VT technology), 4 GB of memory and a 7200 rpm hard drive. The servers are connected through a Gigabit Ethernet switch.

The head-node runs Ubuntu Server 7.10 with no hypervisor. All other nodes (VM hosts) run Citrix XenServer Enterprise Edition 5.0.0. Our choice for a commercial hypervisor is based on the assurance of an enterprise class software in accordance with the needs of target users, i.e. enterprise data centers and public application hosting environments.

All VMs run 64-bit Ubuntu Linux 8.04 Server Edition, paravirtualized kernel version 2.6.24-23. The installed web server is Apache 2.2.8 running in prefork mode. PHP version is 5.2.4-2. MySQL, with Innodb engine, is version 5.1.32.

4.2   Workload

We use Olio [15] as a Web 2.0 application, combined with the Faban load generator [16] to represent an application and workload set. Olio is a Web 2.0 toolkit that helps developers evaluate the suitability, functionality and performance of various Web technologies, devised by Sun Microsystems from its understanding of the challenges faced by Web 2.0 customers [18]. It has been successfully deployed and evaluated in a reasonably sized high-end server infrastructure [18], as well as in rented resources from Amazon EC2 [14].

The Olio Web application represents a social-events website that allows users to perform actions such as loading the homepage, logging into the system, creating new events, attending events and searching for events by date or tag. It currently provides implementations using three technologies: PHP, Ruby on Rails and J2EE. For our experiments, we have chosen to use Olio's PHP implementation, thus employing the popular LAMP stack (Linux Apache MySQL PHP).

Faban is an open-source Markov-chain load generator used to drive load against Olio; it is composed by a master program which spawns one or more load drivers, i.e. multi-threaded processes that simulate actual users. The master presents a Web interface through which it is possible to submit customized benchmark runs and monitor their results. This Olio/Faban combination was originally proposed as part of the Cloudstone benchmark [14].

The load level driven against the application may be varied by changing the number of concurrent users to be served by the application. Total time for each run is configured by adjusting three different durations, namely ramp-up, steady state and ramp-down. Resulting metrics reported by Faban only take into account the steady state period.

The main metric considered in our experiments is a Service Level Agreement defined in Cloudstone. The SLA defines minimum response times for all relevant user actions. Thus, at any 5-minute window, if a certain percentile of response times exceeds the maximum, an SLA violation is recorded. The 90th and 99th percentiles are considered in this study, representing a more relaxed and a stricter SLA, respectively. Table 1 lists the details of the SLA.

Table 1. Cloudstone's SLA: The 90th/99th percentile of response times measured in any 5-minute window during steady state should not excess the following values (in seconds):

User action	SLA	User action	SLA
Home page loading	1	User login	1
Event tag search	2	Event detail	2
Person detail	2	Add person	3
Add event	4		

4.3 Benchmarking Architecture

The architecture of our benchmarking setup is depicted in Figure 1. Based on the observation that MySQL tends to be CPU-bound when serving the Olio database, whereas Apache/PHP tends to be memory-bound [14], we have designed our system under test (SUT) by splitting the workload into two networked VMs, hosted in different servers, in order to better partition the available physical resources.

All nodes share an NFS (Network File System) mounted storage device, which resides in the head-node and stores VM images and virtual disks. In particular, a local virtual disk is hosted in the server that hosts MySQL.

The load is driven from the head-node, where the multi-threaded workload drivers run, along with Faban's master component.

4.4 Experimental Design

The overall objective of our experiments is to quantify slowdown and downtime experienced by the application when VM migrations are performed in the middle of a run. Specifically, we quantify application slowdown based on values generated by the above-mentioned SLA calculation.

In all experiments, the servers and their interconnection were dedicated to the application under test. A migration experiment consisted of migrating a single VM between two dedicated physical machines. In each run, the chosen destination machine was different from the source machine in the previous run, i.e. a series of runs did not consist of migrating a VM back and forth between the same two machines.

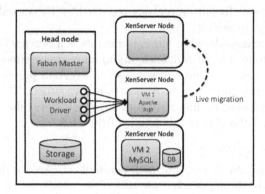

Fig. 1. Benchmarking architecture

Preliminary Experiments. Exact VM sizes were obtained by preliminary experiments, in which we have run the application without performing any VM migration. We have driven load against Olio and gradually increased the number of concurrent users between runs, in 100 users increments, while using 2 identically sized VMs with 2 vCPUs and 2GB of memory. By analyzing the SLA (both 90th and 99th percentile of response times for all user actions), we have found that 600 is the maximum number of concurrent users that can be served by our SUT. We have observed memory and CPU usage to find the minimum VM sizes capable of serving 600 users. We have then aimed at reducing the size (vCPUs and memory) of the VMs to the minimum required to serve 600 users. Thus, in the final configuration the first VM, which exclusively hosts Apache/PHP, has 1 vCPU and 2GB of memory; the second VM, which hosts MySQL, has 2 vCPUs and 1GB of memory.

In the same preliminary experiments we have noticed performance issues when hosting the MySQL server on NFS. The application would not scale to more than 400 concurrent users, which has lead us to host MySQL in a local disk, thus scaling up to 600 concurrent users. For this reason, our experiments do not include migrating the VM that hosts the database server, since XenServer requires all storage devices to be hosted in a network storage in order to perform live migrations.

Migration Experiments. In our first set experiments with Olio we have performed 10-minute and 20-minute benchmark runs with 600 concurrent users. During these experiments, live migrations of the Web server VM were performed. The goal of experimenting with this load level is to evaluate how the pre-defined SLAs are violated when the system is nearly oversubscribed, but not overloaded. Also, we aim at quantifying the duration of migration effects and the downtime experienced by the application.

Subsequently, in a second round of experiments, we have run the benchmark with smaller numbers of concurrent users, namely 100, 200, 300, 400 and 500, aiming at finding a "safe" load level on which migrations can be performed at lower risks of SLA violation, especially when considering the more stringent 99th percentile SLA.

5   Results and Discussion

Overall, our experimental results show that overhead due to live migration is acceptable but cannot be disregarded, especially in SLA-oriented environments requiring more demanding service levels.

Figure 2 shows the effect of a single migration performed after five minutes in steady state of one run. A downtime of 3 seconds is experienced near the end of a 44 second migration. The highest peak observed in response times takes place immediately after the VM resumes in the destination node; 5 seconds elapse until the system can fully serve all requests that had initiated during downtime. In spite of that, no requests were dropped or timed out due to application downtime. The downtime experienced by Olio when serving 600 concurrent users is well above the expected millisecond level, previously reported in the literature for a range of workloads [3]. This result suggests that workload complexity imposes a unusual memory access pattern, increasing the difficulty of live migrating the virtual machine.

Figure 3 presents the effect of multiple migrations on the homepage loading response times. These result corresponds to the average of 5 runs. We report the 90th and 99th percentile SLAs. We can observe that the more stringent 99th percentile SLA is violated a short moment after the first migration is performed

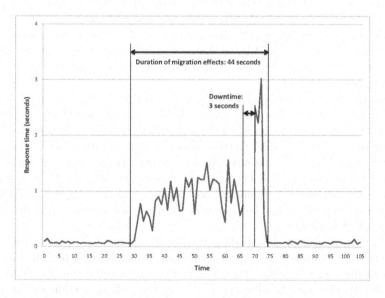

Fig. 2. Effects of a live migration on Olio's homepage loading activity

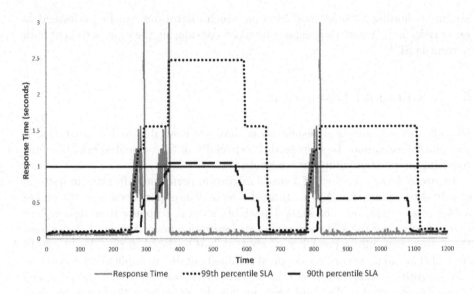

Fig. 3. 90th and 99th percentile SLA computed for the homepage loading response time with 600 concurrent users. The maximum allowed response time is 1 second.

indicating that when 600 concurrent users are being served, a single VM migration is not acceptable. The 90th percentile SLA is not violated when a single migration occurs, but is violated only when two migrations are performed in a short period of time. This figure also indicates that more than one migration might not cause violation of the 90th percentile SLA. A way of preventing such violation is allowing sufficiently spacing between migrations in order to allow the SLA formula to generate normal response time levels. Thus, it is paramount that this information is employed by SLA-oriented VM-allocation mechanisms with the objective of reducing the risk of SLA non-compliance in situations when VM migrations are inevitable.

From the above mentioned results we can conclude that, in spite of a significant slowdown and downtime caused by live migration of VMs, our SUT is resilient to a single migration when the system responsiveness is governed by the 90th percentile SLA. In other words, provided that migrations are performed at correct times, there is no cost associated with them. However, this is not the case for the 99th percentile SLA. For this reason, we have performed a new series of experiments with smaller number of concurrent users. The objective of such experiments is to gauge a safe level on which a migration could be performed with low risk of SLA violation.

Table 2 presents more detailed results listing maximum response times for all user actions as computed by the 99th percentile SLA formula when one migration was performed in the middle of a 10 minute run. In these runs the load varies from 100 to 500 users. In all cases, our SUT was able to sustain an acceptable performance even in the presence of a live migration of the Web server. For

Table 2. Maximum recorded 99th percentile SLA for all user actions when one migration is performed for 500, 400, 300, 200 and 100 concurrent users

Action	500	400	300	200	100
HomePage	0.32	0.18	0.25	0.25	0.13
Login	0.32	0.33	0.42	0.28	0.14
TagSearch	0.46	0.32	0.35	0.39	0.29
EventDetail	0.48	0.27	0.22	0.24	0.14
PersonDetail	1.53	0.62	0.69	0.61	0.32
AddPerson	2.28	1.00	1.51	1.73	0.66
AddEvent	2.26	1.02	1.30	1.81	0.98

instance, the maximum value observed for homepage loading is 0.32 seconds, which corresponds to approximately 1/3 of the maximum value allowed, i.e. 1 second. The maximum value observed for the adding a new person to the system (2.28 seconds), which is more than half of the maximum allowed, but still does not indicate risk of SLA violation. These results indicate that a workload of 500 users is the load level at which a live migration of the Web server should be carried out (e.g. to a least loaded server) in order to decrease the risk of SLA violation.

6   Conclusions and Future Work

Live migration of virtual machines is a useful capability in data centers. It allows more flexible management of available physical resources by making it possible to load balance and do infrastructure maintenance without entirely compromising application availability and responsiveness.

We have performed a series of experiments to evaluate the cost of live migration of virtual machines in a scenario where a modern Internet application is hosted on a set of virtual machines. Live migration experiments were carried out in scenarios where several levels of load were driven against the application.

Our results show that, in an instance of a nearly oversubscribed system (serving 600 concurrent users), live migration causes a significant downtime (up to 3 seconds), a larger value than expected (based on results previously reported in the literature for simpler, non Web 2.0 workloads) Also, this service disruption causes a pre-defined SLA to be violated in some situations, especially when two migrations are performed in a short period of time. On the other hand, we have found the most stringent SLA (99th percentile) can still be met when migrations are performed when the system load is slightly decreased to less concurrent users (500 in our case study).

In conclusion, we see a high potential of live migration applicability in data centers serving modern Internet services. This performance evaluation study is the first step towards the broader objective of studying the power of live migration of virtual machines for the management of data centers. We plan to use the insights of this study to develop smarter and more efficient SLA-based resource allocation systems.

We are currently planning to conduct further migration experiments with new scenarios based on different application configurations, such as: using Mem-Cached to alleviate database server load and allow for its migration. Moreover, we plan to expand our testbed to represent a large-scale clouds. As a consequence we expect to obtain a better generalization of the results, resulting in a performance model of live migration of virtual machines in clouds. This model will aid our research of market-oriented resource allocation policies in clouds.

Acknowledgements. We would like to thank Marcos Assunção, Alexandre di Constanzo, Mohsen Amini, Carlos Varela and the anonymous reviewers for their comments and assistance in improving this paper. This work is partially supported by grants from the Australian Research Council (ARC), the Australian Department of Innovation, Industry, Science and Research (DIISR) and the University of Melbourne Early Career Researcher (ECR) scheme.

References

1. Barham, P., Dragovic, B., Fraser, K., Hand, S., Harris, T., Ho, A., Neugebauer, R., Pratt, I., Warfield, A.: Xen and the art of virtualization. In: SOSP 2003: Proceedings of the 19th ACM Symposium on Operating Systems Principles, pp. 164–177. ACM, New York (2003)
2. Buyya, R., Yeo, C., Venugopal, S., Broberg, J., Brandic, I.: Cloud computing and emerging IT platforms: Vision, hype, and reality for delivering computing as the 5th utility. Future Generation Computer Systems 25(6), 599–616 (2009)
3. Clark, C., Fraser, K., Hand, S., Hansen, J.G., Jul, E., Limpach, C., Pratt, I., Warfield, A.: Live migration of virtual machines. In: NSDI 2005: Proceedings of the 2nd Conference on Symposium on Networked Systems Design & Implementation, pp. 273–286. USENIX Association, Berkeley (2005)
4. Milojicic, D., Douglis, F., Paindaveine, Y., Wheeler, R., Zhou, S.: Process migration survey. ACM Computing Surveys 32(3), 241–299 (2000)
5. Nagarajan, A.B., Mueller, F., Engelmann, C., Scott, S.L.: Proactive fault tolerance for HPC with xen virtualization. In: ICS 2007: Proceedings of the 21st Annual International Conference on Supercomputing, pp. 23–32. ACM, New York (2007)
6. Barbosa, A.C., Sauve, J., Cirne, W., Carelli, M.: Evaluating architectures for independently auditing service level agreements. Future Generation Computer Systems 22(7), 721–731 (2006)
7. Iyer, R., Illikkal, R., Zhao, L., Makineni, S., Newell, D., Moses, J., Apparao, P.: Datacenter-on-chip architectures: Tera-scale opportunities and challenges. Intel. Technology Journal 11(03) (2007)
8. Uhlig, R., Neiger, G., Rodgers, D., Santoni, A.L., Martins, F.C.M., Anderson, A.V., Bennett, S.M., Kagi, A., Leung, F.H., Smith, L.: Intel. virtualization technology. Computer 38(5), 48–56 (2005)
9. Cherkasova, L., Gardner, R.: Measuring CPU overhead for I/O processing in the Xen virtual machine monitor. In: ATEC 2005: Proceedings of the USENIX Annual Technical Conference, p. 24. USENIX Association, Berkeley (2005)
10. Apparao, P., Iyer, R., Zhang, X., Newell, D., Adelmeyer, T.: Characterization & analysis of a server consolidation benchmark. In: VEE 2008: Proceedings of the fourth ACM SIGPLAN/SIGOPS Iinternational Conference on Virtual Execution Environments, pp. 21–30. ACM, New York (2008)

11. Casazza, J.P., Greenfield, M., Shi, K.: Redefining server performance characterization for virtualization benchmarking. Intel. Technology Journal 10(3), 243–251 (2006)
12. Zhao, M., Figueiredo, R.J.: Experimental study of virtual machine migration in support of reservation of cluster resources. In: VTDC 2007: Proceedings of the 3rd International Workshop on Virtualization Technology in Distributed Computing, pp. 1–8. ACM, New York (2007)
13. Travostino, F., Daspit, P., Gommans, L., Jog, C., de Laat, C., Mambretti, J., Monga, I., van Oudenaarde, B., Raghunath, S., Wang, P.Y.: Seamless live migration of virtual machines over the man/wan. Future Generation Computer Systems 22(8), 901–907 (2006)
14. Sobel, W., Subramanyam, S., Sucharitakul, A., Nguyen, J., Wong, H., Patil, S., Fox, A., Patterson, D.: Cloudstone: Multi-platform, multi-language benchmark and measurement tools for web 2.0. In: CCA 2008: Proceedings of the 1st Workshop on Cloud Computing (2008)
15. Apache Software Foundation: Olio, http://incubator.apache.org/olio
16. Sun Microsystems: Project Faban, http://faban.sunsource.net
17. Amazon Web Services LLC: Amazon Web Services, http://aws.amazon.com
18. Subramanyam, S., Smith, R., van den Bogaard, P., Zhang, A.: Deploying web 2.0 applications on sun servers and the opensolaris operating system. Technical report, Sun Microsystems (2009)

Cloud-Oriented Virtual Machine Management with MLN

Kyrre Begnum, Nii Apleh Lartey, and Lu Xing

Oslo University College, Norway
kyrre.begnum@iu.hio.no,
niial@ifi.uio.no,
lux@ifi.uio.no

Abstract. System administrators are faced with the challenge of making their existing systems power-efficient and scalable. Although Cloud Computing is offered as a solution to this challenge by many, we argue that having multiple interfaces and cloud providers can result in more complexity than before. This paper addresses cloud computing from a user perspective. We show how complex scenarios, such as an on-demand render farm and scaling web-service, can be achieved utilizing clouds but at the same time keeping the same management interface as for local virtual machines. Further, we demonstrate that by enabling the virtual machine to have its policy locally instead of in the underlying framework, it can move between otherwise incompatible cloud providers and sites in order to achieve its goals more efficiently.

1   Introduction

Infrastructure as a service (IaaS) is becoming attractive for both researchers and technicians with the emergence of products and tools surrounding on-demand deployment of virtual machines. The main principle is that you can get computing resources (Xen-based virtual machines in the case of Amazon EC2) without investing in or setting up hardware, thereby reducing cost and power.

Being a system administrator in this era means facing a new set of management challenges. Before, it was about simply keeping systems and services running and getting enough permanent resources to survive a usage spike. Today, we are expected to *program* behavior into our systems so that they adapt and behave according to complex policies. This new paradigm means having to give our systems self-* properties, like self-configuration and self-scaling. A likely scenario is to leverage an increase in distributed server resources for temporary extra computing power or proximity to customers. One of the main challenges in achieving this from a local perspective, is the lack of tools which address both in-house virtual machine management and cloud computing through the same management interface. This is not merely a problem of learning yet another tool, but that of integrating the clouds instances into existing, local infrastructure systems, such as monitoring, user management and backup. We argue that cloud computing should be integrated into the existing management tools and

M.G. Jaatun, G. Zhao, and C. Rong (Eds.): CloudCom 2009, LNCS 5931, pp. 266–277, 2009.

practices at an organization and not having to split up management operations to span multiple provider-centric interfaces.

Consider a small company producing CGI material which may not afford to buy and maintain their own render farm. Hiring a render farm for fixed periods of time would be the alternative albeit somewhat inflexible if they fail to utilize the farm for the entire period they paid for. Cloud computing may offer a better solution where the render farm exists in a cloud such as Amazon EC2 and can be booted up only when needed. The local technicians can maintain a local version of the cluster, running entirely as virtual machines on a moderately powered computer, providing a testing ground for their software. Once they need to render a large project, the cluster is pushed into the cloud and booted up as a far more powerful version of itself. When the rendering is finished, it can be taken down again and there are no more costs associated with it.

Another example is that of a company with local web services experiencing a sudden heavy load due to increased attention from customers. Buying and installing new hardware in order to cope with the pressure has numerous drawbacks: The time to get them up will be too long and once they are up they were a wasted expense if the traffic goes down to its normal level again. Further, although they can expand their infrastructure, there might be little they can do with the capacity of their internet connection. Again, with cloud computing they could boot up web-server instances in different clouds and use load-balancing on the DNS service to direct the customers. Once the traffic dies down again, the instances can be taken down. If the load settles on a high level, the company now has time to invest in more hardware and network equipment based on their expected profits.

There are some observations to be made about these scenarios. The most important one is that the companies all have local infrastructure and the capability to run virtual machines. Further, they are cloud-aware and have the means to effectively manage instances both locally and in a cloud if necessary. As a result, they have designed their service to work with support from cloud providers when needed. Seeing cloud computing as an *addition* rather than only a replacement for local infrastructure offers many more scenarios like these.

This paper describes an effort to address the problem of cloud-aware local management by modifying the virtual machine management tool MLN to integrate cloud architectures and thereby enable seamless integration of cloud instances into local management. We showcase its usefulness today through two scenarios, an on-demand render cluster and a scaling web-scenario. Possibilities for self-management are demonstrated in a third scenario to highlight the future potential of virtualization and cloud computing.

2   Background

Amazon's elastic computing cloud (EC2) is a Xen-based IaaS product which has become a popular example of cloud computing. Users can upload custom virtual machine images and boot instances of them according to five different hardware profiles. There are several cost-metrics involved in calculating the running costs for a virtual machine, based on added services such as permanent storage partitions and network traffic. However, the most important observation is that cost is dominated by instance uptime and not CPU usage per se. The more powerful the instance, the higher the cost associated with keeping it up and running. A cost-effective utilization of Amazon's product means making sure that the instances only running when they are needed. This highlights the new paradigm of system administration where *behavior* becomes the focus rather than uptime.

An open source alternative to Amazon EC2 is Eucalyptus, a project located at the University Of California[1]. Eucalyptus is appealing because it supports the same API as Amazon EC2 and can work as a plug-in replacement for Amazon's commercial offering. This may be more attractive to research institutions, where sharing resources for experiments has been widespread. One example of such practice is PlanetLab.

An example of IaaS being used in order to enhance local infrastructure can be found in the VMplant project [9]. Here, virtual machines running on a remote infrastructure could be connected to the local area network using tunneling. The goal was the ability to dynamically expand the number of local servers.

2.1   MLN

MLN (Manage Large Networks) is an open source tool designed for management of large numbers of virtual machines. A concept of groups of virtual machines called "projects", enable atomic management operations such as building, starting and stopping entire clusters and networks. An expandable plugin framework to allow additions to MLNs configuration language and features.[10]

MLN uses a configuration language to specify how the virtual machines are to be set up. In this language both VM properties such as memory and disk size are specified along with internal system properties such as users, passwords and startup parameters. MLN supports Xen, User-Mode Linux and VMware Server and has previously been shown to work well in scenarios where large numbers of virtual machines are deployed with complex network topologies and system configurations, such as high-performance computing and virtual labs in education. [8,5,6]

2.2   Integrating Amazon EC2 and Eucalyptus

Both Amazon EC2 and Eucalyptus support by-and-large the same API for virtual machine management. For MLN, integrating support for these two cloud providers is done through the development of a plugin, which can be maintained apart from the main MLN codebase. This plugin seamlessly expands the syntax of the MLN configuration language, allowing users to include Amazon EC2 or Eucalyptus properties in the virtual machines they design. The following is a simple project consisting of only one virtual machine which is to run inside the Amazon EC2 cloud. The ec2-block inside the host specification is what is handled by the plugin and results in this virtual machine being built in the cloud.

```
global {
      project ec2example
}
host webserver {
      xen
      ec2 {
          type c1.medium
          volumes {
              2G hda1 /var/log/apache ext3 defaults
          }
      }
      network eth0 {
          address dhcp
      }
      template web.ext3
      free_space 2000M
}
```

Notice how volumes can be specified in an integrated manner, allowing MLN to coordinate which volumes belong where, letting the virtual machine always be associated with that particular volume. Associating volumes with virtual machines is of particular importance when projects of numerous virtual machines are run, where each virtual machine has its own volume. Keeping track of the volumes so that the same volume is always associated with the same virtual machine is something which is not possible with even Amazon EC2's own management console.

The management commands stay the same, which enables the user to keep managing virtual machines the exact same way regardless if they are local or in a cloud. It is even possible with projects containing both local virtual machines and cloud instances and subsequent management (starting, stopping, building, removing) of these as an atomic unit:

```
mln build -f projectfile.mln
mln < start |stop > -p projectname
```

In order to cope with long-term management of projects, MLN provides an "upgrade" command which allows modifications to running virtual machines. When upgrading, a new version of the project configuration file is submitted and MLN will attempt to enact the changes based on the difference from the previous version. The type of modification can be hardware-oriented, such as increasing disk size or memory. It can also be used to migrate the virtual machine from one server to another, so-called live migration, where it is supported. It is this upgrade mechanism which allows system administrators to migrate virtual machines which are running locally into Amazon EC2 or Eucalyptus. When doing so, the new version of the project needs to have an ec2-block inside each virtual machine which is to be migrated to a cloud. Another possibility is to add virtual machines to a running project, which leads to the possibility of a scaling site where the number of servers can be increased on demand.

3   Case: On-Demand Render Farm

In this scenario, we want to demonstrate how MLN can be used to create and manage a large cluster of virtual machines which can reside either locally or in a cloud. The case, as highlighted above,is that of a company in need for a render farm for short periods of time. The technicians maintain a local renderfarm running on a moderately powered computer, such as a modern desktop machine. The following project represents the design of the render farm in its local version:

```
global {
        project render
        autoenum {
                numhosts 5
                superclass rendernode
                hostprefix rend
        }
}
superclass common {
        xen
        memory 512
        free_space 1000M
        network eth0 {
            address dhcp
        }
        template rendernode.ext3
}
superclass rendernode {
    superclass common
    startup {
            /scripts/rendernode.pl start
    }

}
host frontend {
    superclass common
    template manager.ext3
    startup {
            /scripts/frontnode.pl start
    }
}
```

Note that some additional parameters which would have been useful, such as users and passwords have been omitted for clarity. The project consists of a frontend virtual machine and a number of render nodes which all inherit from the **rendernode** superclass. The number of render nodes (in this example 5) is defined in the **autoenum** block, which removes the complexity of adding more nodes by acting as a for-loop at parse time[6]. The project file itself will not grow based on the number of nodes, so it could just as well be 32 nodes without changing any of the management steps. The virtual machines are built from templates, which are ready-made filesystems containing the render software and libraries. The frontend node contains queueing software in order to partition the job and manage the nodes. Building and starting the cluster is done by issuing management directives on the project-level:

```
mln build -f render.mln
mln start -p render
```

Until now the render farm has been running locally while the technicians have adjusted the software to work properly with their local applications. With a low memory setting per node, this could run as local virtual machines on a moderate desktop computer using the Xen hypervisor[2]. When it is time to run the render farm as a more powerful cluster, a cloud provider will act as extra infrastructure

for the required period. The next step for the technician will be to move the
cluster into the cloud. This is achieved by using the MLN upgrade command.
First, a new version of the project file is written with the following addition to
the superclass common:

```
ec2 {
    type c1.xlarge
    volumes {
        2G hda1 /var/log
    }
}
```

By adding the ec2-block to the superclass, all virtual machines inheriting from
it will now be instances running in a cloud environment. This could be either
Amazon's EC2 framework, as the name suggests, or an Eucalyptus cloud provided by another party. There are two directives in this block. The first is a type
assignment, which will boot this VM as the most powerful hardware allocation
in terms of CPU; 8 cores and 7GB of memory. The volumes block will assign
each instance a permanent partition which will be mounted on the /var/log
folder for logging. This is useful since the EC2 frameworks do not offer permanent storage of changes made on the virtual machines while they are running.
The changes to the project are enacted using the following command:

```
mln upgrade -f render_ec2.mln
```

MLN will now bundle and transfer the images necessary to boot the project to
the cloud environment and automate the typical steps of registering the images,
creating the permanent volumes and assigning volumes to each instance. Note,
that EC2 frameworks can boot several virtual machines from the same image,
so in this case we only need to transfer two compressed images, one for a render
node and one for the frontend. This holds regardless of the size of the render
farm. Once the upgrade process is completed, the project can be started with
the same command as above on the same machine. Having 16 render nodes
of the largest type, would provide a 128 CPU cluster, which they in terms of
management can boot up and shut down as they like just like a group of local
virtual machines.

4   Case: Scaling Web Service

The ability to dynamically de- or increase it's number of resources, be it for
performance objectives or power-management, has been the focus of many in the
wake of virtualization's attention the last years. For most organizations today,
however, the technology is unavailable to them unless they invest heavily in
specialized products. Further, automatically scaling is not trivial, as it has the
potential to cost excessive amounts if the algorithm reacts to a false positives or
deliberate denial-of-service attacks.

In this scenario, MLN is used to add or remove nodes in a cloud belonging
to a web service. The service consists of a load balancer with the ability to

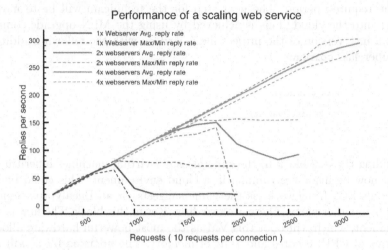

Fig. 1. The performance of a scaling website when using 1, 2 and 4 webservers running on the Amazon EC2 framework

dynamically add new nodes to be used as webservers. The system administrator can decide how many webservers to use through MLN upgrade command to the project.

Using a design similar to the render farm, a project consisting of the frontend loadbalancer and a number of webservers is declared. Different versions of that project would only differ in the number of webservers. Changing between them could then be enacted using the MLN upgrade command. Each of these commands would result in the specific number of webservers being set and can be run in arbitrary order:

```
mln upgrade -S -f webservice_x1.mln
mln upgrade -S -f webservice_x2.mln
mln upgrade -S -f webservice_x4.mln
```

The figure 1 shows the performance of the website based on the number of webservers running. The website was running on the Amazon EC2 cloud and the loadbalancer used was perlbal. The performance data was gathered using httperf. We see that the ability to withstand a high request rate increases with the number of backend webservers.

One would ask why it would be desirable to keep the website running with only one webserver when it could run with four. The answer is in essence what cloud computing is about. A system administrator, with proper monitoring, will be able to keep the site at a low-cost, low-power performance level during periods of *known* inactivity, like night-time. During the day, a scheduled job could increase the number of servers to two and four servers could be kept as a short peak-hours remedy. What is important in this scenario, is that local management commands can be used to manage cloud-based systems like we would traditionally script system behavior, and that the mechanism to control cloud-based systems is separated from the policy (or algorithm), enabling local solutions.

5 Self-management with Local Policies

This part demonstrates how cloud computing can play a role in development of advanced system policies based on ideas from agent-based behavior. A virtual machine, compared with a physical and conventional system, has the ability to be modified in ways which resemble that of traditional agents. They can increase in computing power and memory while powered on or even move between locations either while running or powered off. Virtualization provides the flexibility for agent behavior. What is needed is the individual VMs ability to enact behavior based on its own local goals.

The traditional approach of managing virtual machines is to build a framework which handles and monitors all the virtual machines combined with an algorithm for balancing the virtual machines across the physical machines. However, this approach has some drawbacks when seen from the perspective of the user:

- Cloud providers are unaware of each other, while the users more likely will have virtual machines in multiple clouds in the future. It is difficult to get homogeneous treatment of your virtual machine across the different clouds, which complicates coordinated management of all resources.
- Load balancing algorithms are very basic and limited to typical services like web applications. The customers can not decide which factors to prioritize, like accepting poor performance in order to keep costs down.
- Interfacing with a cloud is often done through a graphical application intended for humans. It is difficult to program your own algorithm on top which would give your virtual machines a specialized policy across multiple cloud providers.

The decoupling of high-level management algorithms from the infrastructure is a necessary step in order to let the virtual machines manage them selves. We will next show two examples where a virtual machine will be aware of multiple infrastructure providers and make decisions locally as to where it should be located based on its own policy. Further, we show that this can be achieved with conventional tools common in the field of configuration management.

5.1 Service Optimization through User Proximity

In [3] we let the virtual machine run a web-service and monitor the origin of its users. We introduced three location where the virtual machine could move freely based on its own local decision. The location were one in the United States and two in Norway. In order to achieve the best service to the majority of its current users, the virtual machine decided where to stay based on a short history of incoming user requests. By introducing curve-based behavior at each location

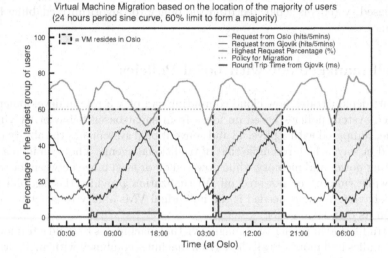

Fig. 2. The virtual machine monitors the activity from the two locations (two sine curves) and decides to migrate to the location with a majority of clients

relative to local working hours, we observed that the virtual machine moved back and forth between Norway and The United States.

The virtual machine was able to change its own location by having a local version of its own MLN project and by the ability to communicate changes down to the framework using the MLN client and issuing an upgrade with a new version of its project. The framework itself is passive and does not do any load balancing or optimization itself. The decision is made entirely inside of the virtual machine, based on its own policy. The configuration management tool Cfengine[7], was used to monitor the clients, analyze the usage and make the decision to migrate. Dynamic DNS is used to offer the same address to the clients regardless of the virtual machines current location.

The plot below shows the result from migrating a virtual machine between two norwegian cities, Oslo and Gjøvik, with induced difference in time-zones. The virtual machine uses a simple policy to decide where to stay: The desired location has more than 60% of the total current clients and their trend is rising in the last 15 minutes. The dotted line represents the threshold of 60% while the line around it depicts the current percentage of the location with the most users. The two sine curves show the activity from the two cities, normalized to fit the plot. The round-trip time, as seen from Gjøvik, is shown in the bottom line. The results show that the simple policy migrates the machine to Oslo at the beginning of their working hours. The RTT-value is lowest as seen from Oslo. Gradually, the activity increases at Gjøvik, and when Oslo is past its peak, the majority shifts and the virtual machine moves to Gjøvik. We see then that the RTT-value becomes low for Gjøvik for the remainder of their working day.

It is important to note, that the input data is something only the virtual machine can see at all times. It would be possible to see the traffic from the framework, but if Oslo and Gjøvik would represent two different providers, chances are small they would share monitoring data.

The policy used to migrate is simple but demonstrates our point that policies inside of the virtual machines can mimic those usually found in frameworks with basic resource balancing. We see from the RTT value that at some migrations, it takes time for the virtual machine to *settle* at its new location. This is because we had a level of noise in our load generators, which could impact the majority when it was still very even. However, more advanced policies with better trend analysis can take advantage of the same mechanism to use MLN in order to enforce its local policy.

5.2   Cloud-Assisted Queue Processing

In this example, we will also consider a virtual machine with a local policy. The virtual machine reads jobs from a queue and processes them in order. The jobs vary in size and could be mostly cpu-intensive, like mathematical computations or graphical rendering. The virtual machine resides at the company which issues the jobs. If the queue should become too long or a number of large jobs should reach a threshold, the virtual machine will choose to migrate into the Amazon EC2 cloud in order to become a more powerful virtual machine. The queue processing will speed up and when the number of jobs is small again, the virtual machine moves back to a physical machine at the company.

In our experiment[4], we assume a queue to be made up of different jobs of a certain type, which takes about half the time it takes to run on a local setup when processed in the cloud. It would be possible to find a length of queue for which it is more time efficient to migrate and run in the cloud. If the average time taken to migrate from the local installation to the cloud M_t, then there exists a time L_t which is the time taken for the queue to be processed locally for which $L_t = C_t + M_t$ where C_t is the time to process the queue in the cloud. For migration to be an incentive,

$$L_t >> C_t + M_t.$$

Eg. We have a queue contain units of jobs, which take 10 minutes each to complete locally, but 5 minutes complete in the cloud. Our average migration time from the local installation to the Amazon EC2 cloud was about 15 minutes, it means that there would be equilibrium when the length of queue (n) is

$$n(10) = n(5) + 15$$

This means that for an incentive for migration, $n > 3$. If $n = 10$ for example, it would take $10(10) = 100$ minutes to process the queue locally, however it would take $10(5) + 15 = 65$ minutes to process the same queue by doing a migration into the cloud first. This behavior was implemented on a virtual machine, using MLN to migrate itself into the Amazon cloud every time the queue was longer than 3. In order to control the behavior further, we introduced a maximum 6 hour allowance to be in the cloud in one day. Interestingly, migration back from Amazon is near instantaneous, since no changes are stored anyway in the cloud, we can simply boot the filesystem we sent into the cloud when we migrated last.

6 Discussion

MLN provides a familiar interface to multiple scenarios, spanning two important cloud technologies in addition to provide local virtual machine management. We believe that local, user-oriented management of virtual machines is more beneficial than todays framework-oriented approach. It is unlikely that an organization which utilizes clouds will only be a tenant at one provider, but will instead have different providers in order to gain their individual pricing advantage. A familiar tool for management will enable seamless adoption of new cloud providers without learning their particular interface.

Another important factor, is that of monitoring and detecting phase changes on services. Data centers are often criticized for having under-utilized servers which waste power. This is true, but one fails to see that for one very important moment, the servers can become fully utilized. Detecting such a change of phase from idle to active, is a prerequisite for dynamically scaling services. We have shown that such algorithms can be implemented inside of the virtual machines themselves instead of having a resource-balancing infrastructure. The most obvious case is when moving from one provider to another. It is unlikely that they will offer the same algorithms or interface for resource management. Bundling it inside of the virtual machines and moving them means keeping the operations logic across the providers. However, we do see problems with our approach as well. If the virtual machine was to be "ignorant" of other virtual machines, how should they organize themselves? If, on the other hand, all virtual machines would know about all other virtual machines, we would in effect duplicate what would be almost the same analysis on all the nodes, which could waste resources.

The field of mobile agents comes to mind in our examples. The virtual machines behavior can be characterized as that of simple, reactive agents. We find this idea intriguing, as this opens the door to use many of the established concepts of group-consensus, trust, local belief and market-place dynamics. The virtual machine as not simply an operating system instance, but rather a mobile agent with the capabilities to move about and fulfill its (or their) mission is interesting. At the same time, this agent's mission is to do real work, such as running an optimal service for its organization by being closest to its users. This brings together the field of artificial intelligence and system administration in a new way, which should be explored further. It is our concern, that over-focusing on building algorithms for frameworks and leaving the virtual machines passive may overshadow the potential of this agent-based behavior.

7 Conclusion

This paper addresses the management of virtual machines from a local system administrators perspective where IaaS-type frameworks such as Amazon EC2 and Eucalyptus are utilized for increased performance and flexibility. We show that advanced management concepts can be achieved using MLN and familiar tools in the system administration community without the need to use special web-based management consoles. Our scenarios showcase cloud-oriented management which combines both local virtual machines and cloud instances. An on-demand render farm and scaling website represent what companies would be interested in realizing today. Lastly, we consider the effect of putting the decision-making capabilities of a dynamic service inside of the virtual machine, enabling it to behave in a manner more likely to mobile agents.

References

1. Nurmi, D., Wolski, R., Grzegorczyk, C., Obertelli, G., Soman, S., Youseff, L., Zagorodnov, D.: The Eucalyptus Open-source Cloud-computing System. In: Proceedings of 9th IEEE International Symposium on Cluster Computing and the Grid, Shanghai, China
2. Barham, P., Dragovic, B., Fraser, K., Hand, S., Harris, T., Ho, A., Neugebauer, R., Pratt, I., Warfield, A.: Xen and the art of virtualization: SOSP 2003. In: Proceedings of the nineteenth ACM symposium on Operating systems principles, pp. 164–177. ACM Press, New York (2003)
3. Xing, L.: A Self-management Approach to Service Optimization and System Integrity through Multi-agent Systems. Master Thesis, University of Oslo (2008)
4. Apleh Lartey, N.: Virtual Machine Initiated Operations Logic for Resource Management Master Thesis, University of Oslo (2009)
5. Begnum, K., Koymans, K., Krap, A., Sechrest, J.: Using virtual machines in system and network administration education. In: Proceedings of the System Administration and Network Engineering Conference, SANE (2004)
6. Begnum, K., Disney, M.: Scalable Deployment and Configuration of High-Performance Virtual Clusters. In: CISE/CGCS 2006: 3rd International Conference on Cluster and Grid Computing Systems (2006)
7. Burgess, M.: Cfengine - a configuration engine. University of Oslo, Dept. of Physics report (1993)
8. Begnum, K.: Manage Large Networks of virtual machines. In: Proceedings of the 20th Large installation system administration conference. USENIX (2006)
9. Krsul, I., Ganguly, A., Zhang, J., Fortes, J.A.B., Figueiredo, R.J.: VMPlants: Providing and Managing Virtual Machine Execution Environments for Grid Computing. In: SC 2004: Proceedings of the 2004 ACM/IEEE conference on Supercomputing, IEEE Computer Society, Los Alamitos (2004)
10. Begnum, K.: Towards Autonomic Management in System Administration. PhD Thesis, University of Oslo, issn: 1501-7710, Unipup (2008)

A Systematic Process for
Developing High Quality SaaS Cloud Services*

Hyun Jung La and Soo Dong Kim

Department of Computer Science
Soongsil University
1-1 Sangdo-Dong, Dongjak-Ku, Seoul, Korea 156-743
hjla@otlab.ssu.ac.kr, sdkim777@gmail.com

Abstract. Software-as-a-Service (SaaS) is a type of cloud service which provides software functionality through Internet. Its benefits are well received in
academia and industry. To fully utilize the benefits, there should be effective
methodologies to support the development of SaaS services which provide high
reusability and applicability. Conventional approaches such as object-oriented
methods do not effectively support SaaS-specific engineering activities such as
modeling common features, variability, and designing quality services. In this
paper, we present a systematic process for developing high quality SaaS and
highlight the essentiality of commonality and variability (C&V) modeling to
maximize the reusability. We first define criteria for designing the process
model and provide a theoretical foundation for SaaS; its meta-model and C&V
model. We clarify the notion of commonality and variability in SaaS, and propose a SaaS development process which is accompanied with engineering instructions. Using the proposed process, SaaS services with high quality can be
effectively developed.

Keywords: Cloud Computing, Software-as-a-Service, SaaS, Commonality and
Variability Analysis, Development Process.

1 Introduction

Cloud Computing (CC) is emerged as an effective reuse paradigm, where hardware
and software resources are delivered as a *service* through Internet [1]. Software-as-a-
Service (SaaS) is a type of cloud services, where the whole software functionality is
run on provider' side and becomes available to consumers [2][3].

SaaS provides several benefits to consumers; no cost for purchasing, free of maintenance, accessibility through Internet, and high availability. To realize these benefits,
there should be systematic and effective processes and methods to support the development of SaaS services. Conventional methods including object-oriented modeling
would be limited in developing services, mainly due to the difference between their
computing paradigms. That is, conventional development methods do not effectively

---

* This research was supported by the National IT Industry Promotion Agency (NIPA) under the
program of Software Engineering Technologies Development and Experts Education.

M.G. Jaatun, G. Zhao, and C. Rong (Eds.): CloudCom 2009, LNCS 5931, pp. 278–289, 2009.
© Springer-Verlag Berlin Heidelberg 2009

support CC-specific engineering activities such as modeling common features and designing services. Hence, there is a great demand for effective processes for developing SaaS cloud services.

In this paper, we present a process for developing high quality SaaS. We first define criteria for designing the process model in section 3. And, we present a theoretical foundation of our work in section 4; a meta-model of SaaS and a tailored view of commonality and variability. In section 5, based on the criteria and foundation, we propose a whole life-cycle process and its instructions to develop SaaS. Using the proposed process, cloud services with high quality can be more effectively developed.

2 Related Works

A little work is known in the area of developing SaaS. We survey two related works. Javier and his colleagues present overall SaaS development process by tailoring traditional software development methodologies [4]. They first analyze how SaaS impacts each phase in the software development methodologies. Based on the analysis results, they redefine five-stage SaaS development process and a list of development artifacts. *Requirements* stage focuses on deriving business opportunities from market requirements, *Analysis* stage is also performed from a business perspective, *Design* phase is performed by using a set of technologies such as service-oriented architecture and business process modeling, *Implementation* stage is performed by considering the SaaS platform environment, and *Testing* stage focuses on validation of interaction between application and the SaaS platform, performance, and usage-metering. This work mentions a key development artifacts and essential techniques required in the development process. However, they do not cover a key characteristic of cloud services, *reusability*, in their process, and stepwise process and detailed instructions are required.

Mietzner and his colleagues present a package format for composite configurable SaaS application by considering requirements of different consumers [5]. They distinguish three key roles in SaaS environment; *SaaS consumer* using the SaaS software, *SaaS provider* selling the software as a service, and *SaaS application vendor* developing applications tha are offered as a service by SaaS provider. To be easily used by SaaS consumer, the package format contains a set of artifacts needed to provision the SaaS and customized application by using variability descriptors. This paper utilizes service component architecture (SCA) in customizing application template. This work focuses on the reusability of SaaS application by using SCA. However, they need to cover all the development process since the unique characteristics beyond the reusability can affect other stages in the process.

3 Design Criteria

Software/Service engineering processes largely depend on computing paradigms. In this section, we define two main design criteria for defining the development process for SaaS cloud services.

One criterion is to reflect the intrinsic *characteristics* of SaaS in the process. Since every well-defined development process should reflect key characteristics of its computing paradigm, this is considered as the main criterion. The other criterion is to promote developing SaaS with the *desired properties*, which are defined as the requirements that any SaaS should embed in order to reach a high level of QoS. Through our rigorous survey of literatures [4][6], we define key characteristics and desired properties of SaaS in Table 1.

Table 1. Characteristics and Desired Properties of SaaS

Characteristics	Desired Properties
◆ Supporting Commonality	◆ High Reusability
◆ Accessible via Internet	◆ High Availability
◆ Providing Complete Functionality	◆ High Scalability
◆ Supporting Multi-Tenants' Access	
◆ Thin Client Model	

We give explanation and brief justification for each characteristic given in the table. *Supporting Commonality*: As an extreme form of reuse approaches, an SaaS provides software functionality and feature which are common among and so reused by potentially a number of service consumers. Services with high commonality would yield high profits/return on the investment (ROI).

Accessible via Internet: All the current reference models of CC assume that cloud services deployed are accessed by consumer through Internet.

Providing Complete Functionality: SaaS provides the whole functionality of certain software in the form of service. This is in contrast to a *mash-up service* which provides only some portion of the whole software functionality.

Supporting Multi-Tenants' Access: SaaS deployed on providers' side is available to the public. And, a number of service consumers may access the services at the given time without advanced notices. Hence, SaaS should be designed in the way to support concurrent accesses by multiple tenants and handle their sessions in isolation.

Thin Client Model: SaaS services run on providers' side, while service consumers use browsers to access the computed results. Moreover, consumer-specific datasets which are produced by running SaaS are stored and maintained on providers' side. Hence, there will be nothing the browser-like user interaction tool installed and run on client/consumer side.

We now give explanation and brief justification for each desired property given in the table. *High Reusability*: Service providers develop and deploy cloud services and expect that the services would be reused by a large number of consumers. Services which are not much reusable by consumers would lose the justification for investment, while services that can be reused by many consumers would return high enough on the investment. Therefore, it is highly desirable for cloud services to embed a high level of reusability.

High Availability: Cloud services are not just for specific users; rather they are for any potential unknown consumers who may wish to use the services anytime and anywhere. Therefore, it is highly desirable for the service to be highly available if not always. Services with low availability would cause inconvenience and negative business impacts to consumers, and, as the result, they will suffer on reliability and reputations.

High Scalability: In CC, the amount of service requests from consumers, i.e. service load, is dynamic and hard to predict. Therefore, cloud services should be highly scalable even in the situation that an extremely high number of service invocations and so their associated resource requests are requested. Services with low scalability would suffer at the time of peak requests and so lose their reputations by consumers.

While typical web applications provide functionalities for sharing useful information and/or carrying relatively less business-intrinsic operations, SaaS is meant to substitute business-intrinsic or business logic-intensive functionality delivered by conventional software with a notion of internet-based service. Due to this observation, characteristics and properties presented above are more importantly considered in SaaS.

4 Theoretical Foundation for SaaS Services

4.1 Meta Model of SaaS

Before devising an effective SaaS development process, we need to define the key elements of SaaS. By considering general consensus on SaaS, we define its meta model in Fig. 1.

A SaaS-based system has two parties; *Client Node* is on the left, and *Provider Node* is on the right. As thin-client model, client node has only a user interface tool, typically a web browser. The provider node runs SaaS application which typically has components of three layers; *UI Component* as view, *Controller* as control, and *Entity component* as Model. Each component consists of common features and variable features which vary according to consumer.

Controller runs business logics and transactions, and hence it maintains a *Session Log* for multiple consumers. In CC, multiple consumers user the same SaaS and so their application datasets must be well maintained in isolated manner. Hence, in the figure, *Data Set* is maintained by *Entity Component*. Both *Session Log* and *Data Set* are specific to each consumer in CC.

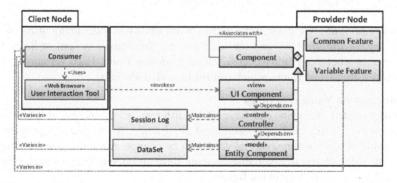

Fig. 1. Meta-Model of SaaS

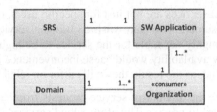

Fig. 2. Criteria on Commonality Determination

4.2 Commonality and Variability in SaaS

Reusability is a key criterion for cloud services, and commonalty is the main contributor to reusability. That is, cloud services with high commonalty will yield higher reusability. Variability is a minor difference among applications or consumers within a common feature. C&V analysis is an essential activity in component-based development (CBD) and product-line engineering (PLE). However, the some notions of C&V in SaaS are different from conventional C&V, mainly due to unique characteristics of SaaS. Hence, we provide its theoretical foundation in this section, so further sections would refer to.

Commonality in SaaS: Commonality in general denotes the amount of potential applications which need a specified feature such as a component or a service. To derive the common features which will be realized in SaaS, we define the relationships among requirement-related elements, as shown in Fig. 2.

A domain such as *finance* and *telecommunications* consists of several organizations, and an organization needs one or more software applications. Each application is associated with a SRS. Hence, a commonality of a feature can be computed as the followings;

$$\text{Commonality}(FEA_i) = \frac{\text{Number of Applications Needing } FEA_i}{\text{Total Number of Target Applications}}$$

If every application in the domain needs the given feature, the value of *Commonality* will be 1. It would be desirable to include features with high *Commonality* into the target SaaS. The range of the metric is between 0 and 1.

Variability in SaaS: We present the notion of variability in SaaS using three aspects; *persistency, variability type,* and *variability scope.* In a target system or SaaS, there can be places where variability occurs, called *Variation Point.* Each variation point is associated with a set of values which can fill in, called *Variants.*

- Persistency on Variants Settings

Variability-related elements can have three different persistencies; *no persistency, permanent persistency,* and *near-permanent persistency.* A variable in a program can hold a value at a given time, and its value can be change as a new value is assigned. Hence, the value stored in a variable does not have an intended persistency, which is illustrated as *no persistency* in the figure.

A variation point in a component in CBD or core asset in PLE is a means for users to set a valid variant, and a variant set in the variation point is persistent, i.e. 'once set not changed.' We call this level of persistency *permanent persistency*.

A variation point in SaaS adds *near-permanent persistency* in addition to the *permanent persistency*, where the variant set in a variation point may be changed over time but in limited way. SaaS is for potentially many consumers, and it has to consider the consumer-specific context and environment in running SaaS application. Consumer may change its context such as *current location/time zone* and *various units used such as currency*. Once a variant is set, its value must be stored until a new variant is set within a session or across multiple sessions. Hence, the persistency of this variant is *near-permanent*. For example, SaaS consumers using mobile-internet device (MID) often travel, and their locations get changed and noticed by SaaS application. Then, SaaS may set new variants for the new locations, and provide services with the right mobile network protocol and its associated services and contents. In SaaS, we only consider the second and third type of variant persistency.

• Variability Types
The variability embedded in a variation point can be classified into several types; *attribute*, *logic*, *workflow*, *interface*, and *persistency* in CBD and PLE [7]. In addition to these, we define two additional types for SaaS; *context* and *QoS*. Variability can occur on the consumer's current context such as *location* and *time zone*, which is called *context* variability type. For a same SaaS, different consumers may require different levels of QoS attributes. Hence, variability can also occur on QoS required by each consumer, which is called *QoS* type.

• Variability Scope
Variability scope is the range of variants which can be set into a variation point. Typically, there are three scopes; *binary*, *selection*, and *open* [7]. When a service consumer wants to customize SaaS for their requirements, they can choose a variant in *binary* or *selection* scopes. However, there is a different implication of *open* scope in SaaS. Due to the thin-client characteristic, service consumers have a limitation on implementing and containing plug-in objects as variant on their client device. To overcome this limitation, we suggest two methods.

One is for service providers to implement and deploy capability to dynamically configure the required plug-in object, and add this object to the pool of variants. The other is for service consumer to implement his or her plug-in objects (may be on a fully powered computer) and to submit the object to the service provider so that it can be added to the pool.

In summary, we identify and distinguish SaaS variability from traditional variability in terms of *persistency, variability type* and *variability scope*. Clear definitions of SaaS variability will make the SaaS process and instructions more feasible, effective in designing reusable services.

5 The Process and Instructions

We define a process for developing SaaS, which has eleven phases as shown in Fig. 3. The five phases highlighted are SaaS development-specific, while other phases are mostly generic and common among other development paradigms such as object-oriented development.

Phase, 'P1. Requirement Gathering' is to acquire a set of requirement specifications from multiple stakeholders or to define the requirements by considering marketability. Phase, 'P2. Domain Analysis' is to analyze commonality and variability in the target domain. Phase, 'P3. Functional Modeling' is to analyze the functionality in terms of use cases or business processes. Phase, 'P4. Structure Modeling' and Phase, 'P5. Dynamic Modeling' are to analyze structure and dynamic aspects of the SaaS. Phase, 'P6. Architectural Design' is to design architecture of SaaS system by considering SaaS-specific QoS attributes. Phase, 'P7. User Interface Design' is to design user interfaces of SaaS system so that the users can easily use developed SaaS through web browsers. Phase, 'P8. Database Design' is to design database schema of SaaS system including session information and data handled by the users. Phase, 'P9. Implementation' is to write source programs based on the all the design models. Phase, 'P10. Testing' is to test the developed SaaS system. And Phase, 'P11. Deployment' is to deploy all the developed SaaS onto server side.

From now, we provide detailed instructions only for SaaS-specific phases depicted with pink rectangle in subsequent sections.

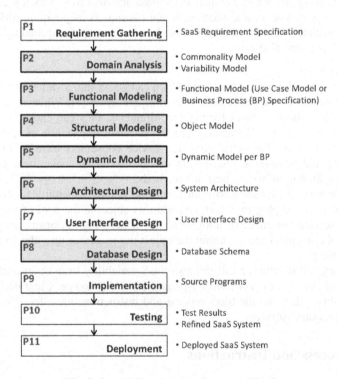

Fig. 3. Overall Development Process of SaaS

5.1 Domain Analysis

Overview: Domain Analysis is an activity to identify common and variable features which will be used in scoping and modeling SaaS [8]. Domain analysis begins with a set of acquired SRSs.

Instructions: This phase is carried out in three steps.

Step 1. Extract Commonality. A set of SRSs collected from different sources could have inconsistency in styles and terms used. Hence, we need to normalize the SRSs by defining standard terms in the domain, using techniques like [9] and [10]. Then, we compare functional and non-functional features of them by using *Commonality Analysis Table* shown in Table 2.

Table 2. Commonality Analysis Table

Feature ID & Feature Name	Feature Description	A set of SRSs				Degree of Commonality
		SRS_1	SRS_2	...	SRS_n	
F01. Generate ID	...	√	√		√	1
F02.CheckCredit	...		√		√	0.3

Step 2. Define Scope of SaaS development. This step is to choose the features which will be implemented as SaaS. We suggest the following criteria.

- A feature with a higher *Commonality(FEA_i)* tends to recruit a larger number of potential service consumers. The features with yellow color in Fig. 4 are the ones with common activities.
- A feature, FEA_i, on which other feature FEA_j depends at a relatively strong level, should be included in the SaaS scope if FEA_j is in the SaaS scope. If such FEA_i is not included, FEA_j would not fulfill its functionality. This is especially essential in SaaS which provides the whole application-level functionality.
- In addition to the two criteria, there exist other criteria for choosing the features such as ROI, marketability, degree of financial sponsorship in developing the SaaS, other essential criteria as defined in the target domain.

Based on the criteria, we now define guidelines for step 2.

- Case 1) *Commonality(FEA_i)* is zero or near-zero. If FEA_i has no other features which depend on FEA_i, exclude this feature. If there are other features which depend on FEA_i and those other features are in the SaaS scope, include this feature. These features are shown with only red color in Fig. 4.
- Case 2) *Commonality(FEA_i)* is one or near-one. Consider to include this feature unless this feature is evaluated as 'excluded' regarding other conditions. These features are shown with only yellow color in Fig. 4.
- Case 3) *Commonality(FEA_i)* is between zero and one, i.e. medium range. When this feature is evaluated as 'inclusion' regarding other conditions, include this feature. Otherwise, consider excluding this feature.

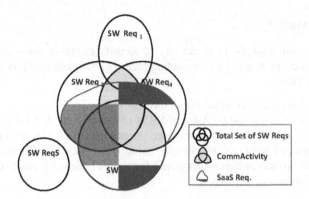

Fig. 4. Scoping the boundary of SaaS development

Table 3. Variability Analysis Table

Feature ID & Feature Name	Variation Point	Var. Type	Var. Scope	Variants for each SRS				Var. Persistency
				SRS_1	SRS_2	...	SRS_n	
F01. Generate ID	VP01	Attr.	Sel.	{a,b}	{a}	...	{b,c}	Permanent
	VP02	Logic	Bin.			...		Permanent
...	...	...	...	...	...	...		...

Step 3. Analyze Variability. For each feature in the scope of SaaS, identify its variation points and applicable variants using techniques like [11]. In addition to conventional variability types, we also identify SaaS-specific variability types as defined in
section 4.2. *Variability Analysis Table* in Table 3 can be used in this step. The first
column in the table lists features included in SaaS, the second column lists variation
points found in the feature, and subsequent columns specify variability type, variability scope, valid variants for each SRS, and variability persistency in order.

For variability analysis for SaaS, we consider the persistency of variants in addition to conventional variability types. Two kinds of persistency could occur;

- *Permanent Persistency*;
  Variants for most variability types such as workflow, logic, interface, and
  persistency are permanent, meaning the setting lasts forever once it is set.
- *Near-permanent Persistency*;
  Some types of variability types have near-permanent settings such as variants about
  user sessions, dataset recovered from service faults. Also, attribute and logic
  variabilities can have near-permanent variant settings.

Once variation points and variants are identified, subsequent phases should be carried
out by considering the variability analysis.

5.2 Functional Modeling

This phase is to model the functionality of SaaS by referring to C&V model. For each
feature in the model, we analyze detailed functionality in two *use case modeling* and
business process modeling. Use case modeling can be used when the target SaaS

embeds characteristics of conventional software applications. Business process modeling can be used when the functionality of the target SaaS largely consists of business processes as referred in service-oriented architecture and CC. This phase can be carried out by using well-established techniques such as [10]and [12].

5.3 Structural and Dynamic Modeling

These phases are to model structural and dynamic models of the SaaS based on the C&V model. Well-established techniques to design class and sequence diagrams and to define service WSDL interface can be utilized.

However, variability specified in C&V model should carefully be expressed on these diagrams and the interface. We suggest using stereotypes and/or element tags to express variability such as «variability», <*variability*>, and <*variation point*> [13].

Another consideration for this phase is to define public methods to set variants in the diagrams and interface. These methods should be defined by considering variability scopes.

5.4 Architecture Design

Architecture is an effective means for realizing non-functional requirements, i.e. quality requirements. SaaS applications also have strong requirements on QoS, representatively *scalability* and *availability* [14]. Hence, we suggest a typical architecture design practice as shown in Fig. 5.

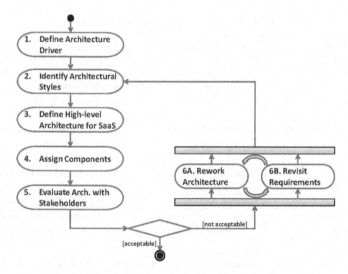

Fig. 5. Architecture Design Process

When considering *Scalability*, we can realize the following techniques in the architecture design;

- Resource Pooling with Multi-Clouds
- Dynamic Load Balancing and Migration
- On-demand Deployment

When considering *Availability*, we can realize the following techniques in the architecture design;

- Using proxy to access SaaS on Mirroring Nodes
- Downloading Lightweight Version of SaaS

5.5 Database Design

Since SaaS provides a complete application-level functionality, it typically maintains a database for strong consumer-specific data sets. Hence, in designing the database schema, two essential information should be maintained; *Session Log* and *Data Set*. Since a number of consumers may use the same SaaS, the service provider should maintain the records of all the sessions run by consumers. This is especially important for long-lasting transactions. *Data Set* is a collection of application-data specific to each consumer. Hence, SaaS should maintain multiple separate databases for the number of consumers.

6 Assessment and Conclusion

Our proposed process is evaluated by the design criterion defined in section 3, as shown in Table 4. The table shows that criteria defined in section 3 are all addressed in one or two phases. For example, *High Reusability* was addressed by *Domain Analysis* phase.

Table 4. Evaluating the Proposed Process

Design Criteria	Phase supporting Criteria	Remarks
Supporting Commonality	Domain Analysis	Proposed C&V methods.
Accessible via Internet	User Interface Design & Deployment	UI design for Browsers & Deployment for Internet Access
Providing Complete Functionality	Domain Analysis	Method to scope SaaS
Supporting Multi-Tenants' Access	Architecture Design Database Design	Architectural Consideration for this concern. DB schema design including Session and Data Sets.
Thin Client Model	Deployment	Deployed and Managed on Provider Side
High Reusability	Domain Analysis	Proposed C&V methods.
High Availability	Architecture Design	Architectural Consideration for
High Scalability	Architecture Design	these Quality concerns

SaaS provides several benefits to service consumers. To realize these benefits, it is essential to make a well-defined engineering process available. Conventional methodologies do not effectively support CC-specific engineering activities such as modeling common features, designing services and services components, and identifying variability among consumers.

In this paper, we presented a systematic process for developing high quality SaaS, and highlighted the essentiality of C&V modeling to maximize the reusability. We first defined criteria for designing the process model, and provides theoretical foundation for SaaS; its meta-model and C&V model. We clarified the notion of commonality in SaaS, and extended the conventional variability with SaaS-specific consideration. Using the proposed SaaS development process, cloud services with high quality can be more effectively developed.

As the future work, we try to define effective quality assurance guidelines for the phases, and to define a traceability framework where all the artifacts can be cross-related and the consistency can be verified.

References

[1] Weiss, A.: Computing in the Cloud. Net Worker 11(4), 16–26 (2007)
[2] Gillett, F.E.: Future View: New Tech Ecosystems of Cloud, Cloud Services, and Cloud C omputing, Forrester Research Paper (2008)
[3] Turner, M., Budgen, D., Brereton, P.: Turning Software into a Service. IEEE Computer 3 6(10), 38–44 (2003)
[4] Javier, E., David, C., Arturo, M.: Application Development over Software-as-a-Service Pl atforms. In: Proceedings of the 3rd International Conference on Software Engineering Ad vances (ICESA 2008), pp. 97–104. IEEE Computer Society, Los Alamitos (2008)
[5] Mietzner, R., Leymann, F., Papazoglou, M.P.: Defining Composite Configurable SaaS A pplication Packages Using SCA, Variability Descriptors and Multi-Tenancy Patterns. In: Proceedings of the 3rd International Conference on Internet and Web Applications and Se rvices (ICIW 2008), pp. 156–161. IEEE Computer Society, Los Alamitos (2008)
[6] Manford, C.: The Impact of the SaaS model of software delivery. In: Proceedings of the 2 1st Annual Conference of the National Advisory Committee on Computing Qualifications (NACCQ 2008), pp. 283–286 (2008)
[7] Kim, S.D., Her, J.S., Chang, S.H.: A Theoretical Foundation of Variability in Componen t-Based Development. Information and Software Technology (IST) 47, 663–673 (2005)
[8] Mili, H., Mili, A., Yacoub, S., Addy, E.: Reuse-Based Software Engineering: Techniques, Organization, and Controls. Wiley Inter-Science, Chichester (2001)
[9] Choi, S.W., Chang, S.H., Kim, S.D.: A Systematic Methodology for Developing Compon ent Frameworks. In: Wermelinger, M., Margaria-Steffen, T. (eds.) FASE 2004. LNCS, vo l. 2984, pp. 359–373. Springer, Heidelberg (2004)
[10] Her, J.S., La, H.J., Kim, S.D.: A Formal Approach to Devising a Practical Method for Mo deling Reusable Services. In: Proceedings of 2008 IEEE International Conference on e-B usiness Engineering (ICEBE 2008), pp. 221–228 (2008)
[11] Kim, S.D.: Software Reusability. Wiley Encyclopedia of Computer Science and Engineer ing 4, 2679–2689 (2009)
[12] Rumbaugh, J., Jacobson, I., Booch, G.: The Unified Modeling Language Reference Manu al, 2nd edn. Addison Wesley, Reading (2005)
[13] Chang, S.H., Kim, S.D.: A SOAD Approach to Developing Adaptable Services. In: IEEE International Conference on Services Computing, SCC 2007, July 9-13, pp. 713–714 (2007)
[14] Rozanski, N., Woods, E.: Software Systems Architecture: Working With Stakeholders Us ing Viewpoints. Addison Wesley, Reading (2005)

Cloud Computing Service Composition and Search Based on Semantic[*]

Cheng Zeng, Xiao Guo, Weijie Ou, and Dong Han

State Key Lab of Software Engineering, Wuhan University, 430072, China
zengc@whu.edu.cn, gogogxxiao@126.com, oweijie@gmail.com,
handong0610@gmail.com

Abstract. In this paper, we put forward a matching algorithm SMA between cloud computing services of multiple input/output parameters, which considers the semantic similarity of concepts in parameters based on WordNet. Moreover, a highly efficacious service composition algorithm Fast-EP and the improved FastB+-EP are presented. Then QoS information is utilized to rank the search results. At last, we show through experiment that our approach has better efficiency of service composition than traditional approaches.

Keywords: Cloud computing, Web services, Service composition.

1 Introduction

At present, cloud computing services can be provided by various forms such as public/utility computing, XaaS, MSP or others and hardwares can even been taken as services to set up scalable virtual machine. However, they all have not a unified standard and even different providers have their own patent-protected APIs, developing tools, virtualization layer, governance characteristics and so on. Thus, customers cannot easily extract their data and programs from one site to run on another. Concern about the difficulty of extracting data from the cloud is preventing some organizations from adopting cloud computing. This situation hinders the progress of cloud computing or crossing cloud applications. Another reason is most of current cloud computing services are limited to data-centered cloud storage and cloud search. These types of services are simple and their requirements for unified management and crossing cloud interaction are not urgent. However, in the near future, these requirements about how to utilize data such as data processing, data analyzing, data mining and so on will be more and more, and the complexity will be also higher. Single cloud computing service can not satisfy them and service composition will become more important.

The precondition of cloud computing service composition is to have a service description with unified standard to introduce its functionality and interface. Many manufacturers have provided cloud computing services with Web Services description language (WSDL), such as EC2, S3 of Amazon, Google Search, etc. But in cloud computing era, the traditional WSDL could not fully meet the requirement of cloud

---

[*] This work is supported by the National Basic Research 973 Program of China No.2007CB310806, Doctor Subject Fund of Education Ministry No.20070486064 and Wuhan ChenGuang Youth Sci.\&Tech. Project No. 200850731369.

M.G. Jaatun, G. Zhao, and C. Rong (Eds.): CloudCom 2009, LNCS 5931, pp. 290–300, 2009.
© Springer-Verlag Berlin Heidelberg 2009

computing services description. QoS and service price will be necessary and play more important roles in service search and service composition for cloud computing services. Most early research of web services studied how to store and search web services efficiently [1, 2]. These efforts usually focus on only a single service. Recently, the applications of web services are becoming more and more widespread, but it is often that there is no single web service which satisfies the request. Thus, the research about web service composition begins to emerge.

Ya-mei[3] adopts status evolution algorithm while LiLi[4] uses traditional work-flow technology to web service composition. [5, 6] analyze the dependency relationship between inputs and outputs extracted from operators of different services to construct Service Dependency Graph (SDG), and then transform the web service composition to related problems in graph theory. The above methods use in-memory algorithms for web service composition which will have to load lots of web services information into memory during computing service composition so that they are limited by the amount of available physical memory. When the number of web services is very large, the efficiency of these methods will greatly reduce.

Recently, many researchers begin to utilize some mature techniques in relational database to solve the service composition problem. Utkarsh[10] builds virtual tables for input/output parameters of web services to manage service interfaces, and uses multi-thread pipeline executive mechanism to improve the efficiency of web services search, so the service composition problem is transformed into query optimization in database. In [7], the web service composition is computed in advance and stored in tables of relational database system and pre-computing and searching are done by SQL statements. But it only considers the simplest status which abstracts each service as single operator and input/output parameter. The abstraction will limit the universality and practicability. Florian[8] looks service composition as a problem of selecting query plans where each service composition between any two services corresponds to a join operator. Thus, the mechanism of physical accessing plan selecting in relational database could be utilized to resolve the problem. These above methods can be applied to a large number of web services and have not additional requirement for the available amount of physical memory. However, both the efficiencies and the precision of service composition with them are not high. Though similar concepts are considered in [7], it needs to manually maintain an ontology table and the method only adapts to the simplified web service but not even slightly complicated interfaces.

Despite the fact that both cloud computing service and traditional web service currently are described with WSDL, there is risk that all systems built with the above methods will have to be rebuilt when the description standard of cloud computing service is updated. In this paper, we put forward a new storage strategy for web services which will be adaptable to flexibly extend for future cloud computing service and can greatly improve the efficiency of service composition. Moreover, we also present a service matching algorithm SMA and a service composition algorithm Fast-EP for those services of multiple input/output parameters. And SMA considers the similar concepts based on WordNet in the process of service matching. For the search results, we use QoS information to rank search results. At last, we show through experiment that our approach has better efficiency of service composition than traditional approaches. In addition, we further optimize our algorithms during the experiment to achieve higher performance.

2 Cloud Computing Services Storage and Search Framework

Traditional web services are described with semi-structured WSDL which are stored and managed in UDDI. The processing efficiency of semi-structured data is obviously lower than structured data so that current services search and service composition technology in UDDI can't adapt to the requirement of large number of web services operating. In this paper, we parse WSDL documents of web services which are automatically crawled or manually wrapped from internet, and then decompose and process main elements of WSDL to respectively store in different tables of relational database, shown in Fig.1. The main elements include service name, function description, operators and input/output parameters. This kind of storage strategy will be able to flexibly extend to adapt to new web service description standard for future cloud computing service, and improve the efficiency of service composition.

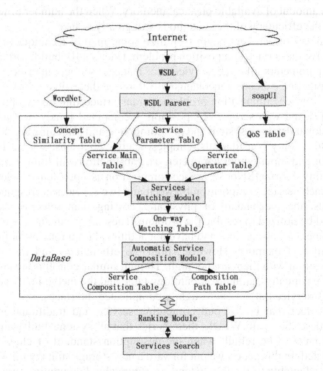

Fig. 1. Cloud Computing Services Storage and Search Framework

In fig.1, *Service Main Table (SMT)*, *Service Operator Table (SOT)* and *Service Parameter Table (SPT)* are used to store the main elements for each Web services. Concept similarity relationships are pre-computed based on WordNet (Introduced in section 3.1) and stored in *Concept Similarity Table (CST)* for improving the efficiency in the process of service matching. We can calculate the matching relationship between different web services based on their input/output parameters by using those data in the above tables, and store all results with high matching degree into *One-way Matching Table (OMT)*. Automatic service composition module analyzes all data in *OMT*, calculates all possible service composition and stores related results into *Service Composition Table (SCT)* and *Composition Path Table (CPT)*. When there is a new service search request, where system supplies 2 kinds of search modes including keywords, input/output definition and Intelligent Ranking Module will extend key concepts in search condition based on *CST* and search matched single or composite services in database. QoS Table will be used to filter or rank returned services in which QoS considers the following three elements and is recorded every time interval for long-term analysis.

- Response Time: the time interval between when a service is requested and when it is delivered;
- Availability: the percentage of time that a service is available during some time interval;
- Reliability: the probability that a request is correctly served.

3 Automatic Web Service Composition Based on Semantic

3.1 Web Service Matching Algorithm (SMA)

The matching process between any two web services is the base of service composition. The matching results will be stored in *OMT*. The principle of service matching is that output parameters of a service operator can match input parameters of another service operator. In this paper, we transform service matching problem into semantic similarity calculating between concepts of input and output parameters corresponding to different service operators.

Each web service possibly contains several operators of different functions so that the processed objects of service compositon actually are their operators. We measure the matching degree $Mat(\mathcal{P}_1, \mathcal{P}_2)$ between different service operators op1 and op2 by calculating semantic similarity between concept set $\mathcal{P}_1$ in output parameters of operator op1 and concept set $\mathcal{P}_2$ in input parameters of operator op2.

$$Mat(\mathcal{P}_1, \mathcal{P}_2) = \frac{\cap_{\mathcal{P}_1,\mathcal{P}_2} + (KM + \varrho)(\cup_{\mathcal{P}_1,\mathcal{P}_2} - \cap_{\mathcal{P}_1,\mathcal{P}_2})}{\cup_{\mathcal{P}_1,\mathcal{P}_2}} \tag{1}$$

$$where \quad KM = KM\langle Sim(C_i, C_j')\rangle \quad (C_i \in \mathcal{P}_1, C_j' \in \mathcal{P}_2)$$

In the above formula, *KM* denotes classical Kuhn-Munkres algorithm, and $Sim(C_i, C_j')$ denotes the semantic similarity between any two concepts C_i, C_j' in $\mathcal{P}_1$ and $\mathcal{P}_2$, respectively. $\cap_{\mathcal{P}_1,\mathcal{P}_2}$ represents the amount of same concept between $\mathcal{P}_1$ and $\mathcal{P}_2$ while $\cup_{\mathcal{P}_1,\mathcal{P}_2}$ represents the amount of all different concepts. ϱ is a constant between 0 to 1 when the intersection between $\mathcal{P}_1$ and $\mathcal{P}_2$ is null after deleting same concepts from them, otherwise $\varrho = 0$. Semantic similarity function [9] based on WordNet is utilized to calculate the similarity between different concept sets.

$$Sim(C_i, C_j') = \frac{\log\left(1 + 2\hat{\beta}\left(C_j', \widetilde{C_{ij}}\right)\right) - \log\left(\hat{\alpha}\left(C_i, \widetilde{C_{ij}}\right)\right)}{max\ Sim}$$

$$\hat{\alpha}\left(C_i, \widetilde{C_{ij}}\right) = APS(\widetilde{C_{ij}})/APS(C_i) \tag{2}$$

$$\hat{\beta}\left(C_j', \widetilde{C_{ij}}\right) = APS\left(\widetilde{C_{ij}}\right) - APS(C_j')$$

$$APS(C) = \frac{1}{\rho_C + 2}$$

Where $\widetilde{C_{ij}}$ is the lowest common ancestors of concept C_i and C_j' while $maxSim$ is their longest distance in WordNet. $APS(C)$ and ρ_C denote priori score and the descendant number of concept C, respectively. Priori score is like the probability that a concept is chosen. $\hat{\alpha}$ and $\hat{\beta}$ respectively correspond different processes of concept generalization and concept specialization. Detailed mathematical introduction of formula (2) can be found in [9]. Because $Sim(C_i, C_j')$ is frequently invoked during the process of calculating $Mat(\mathcal{P}_1, \mathcal{P}_2)$, we pre-compute CST for avoiding repeatedly processing.

By the above way, we calculate semantic matching degree between any two web services. Of course, the precondition is that the output parameters set of a service operator must be the subset of input parameters set of another service operator. Otherwise, the two services cannot be matched. As long as $Mat(\mathcal{P}_1, \mathcal{P}_2)$ is bigger than a certain threshold, it will be stored into OMT. It means that OMT stores all web services pairs with better semantic matching and their matching direction.

3.2 Service Composition Path Computing

We could look all data in OMT as a weighted directed graph where each node denotes a web service and each edge denotes the semantic matching degree between two web services. Thus, the service composition problem is simplified to find all reachable paths of two nodes in the graph. Concern that we don't only calculate the shortest path here, because the least services for a composite service do not imply that the QoS is the best or service price is the lowest.

In database domain, finding all reachable paths is a recursive query problem and the time complexity is $O(N^3)$ where N is the amount of tuples in OMT. EP-JOIN algorithm[7] reduces the time complexity to $O(N^2)$. In the paper, we present a Fast-EP algorithm by improving EP-JOIN and the time complexity is further reduced to $O(N*\log(N))$. The pseudo code of Fast-EP algorithm is shown as follows:

Algorithm : Fast-EP
Input: {matched services pairs in OMT}; Output: {composite services in SCT, service composition paths in CPT, new operators in SOT and new parameters in SPT}.

1. Sequentially scanning OMT, select a tuple E(i)=WS(m)→WS(n); //m, n are   operator ID
2. Insert E(i) into CPT;

3. Select all path from *CPT* where *CP_END_OPID=m*, the returned set is represented as S_1;

4. Select all path from *CPT* where *CP_START_OPID=n*, the returned set is represented as S_2;

5. If $(count(S_1) \geqq count(S_2))$ {

6.   SN=0;

7.   For each path $S_1(u)=WS(q) \to WS(m)$ {   //$0<u \leqq count(S_1)$; q is operator ID

8.   insert $WS(q) \to WS(n)$ and *SC_degree(q, n)= SC_degree(q, m)* * SC_degree(m, n)* into *SCT*;

9.   insert $WS(q) \to WS(n)$ into *CPT*;

10.   Transform $WS(q) \to WS(n)$ as a new operator, and insert relevant information into *SOT, SPT*, respectively

11.   Flag=0;

12.   For each path $S_2(v)=WS(n) \to WS(p)$ {   //$0<v \leqq count(S_2)$; p is operator ID

13.   If (Flag==0 and SN<count(S_2)+1) {   //Sn controls the times of loop

14.   insert $WS(m) \to WS(p)$ and *SC_degree(m, p)= SC_degree(m, n)* * SC_degree(n, p)* into *SCT*;

15.   insert $WS(m) \to WS(p)$ into *CPT*;

16.   Transform $WS(m) \to WS(p)$ as a new operator, and insert relevant information into *SOT, SPT*, respectively

17.   }

18.   Flag=1;SN++;

19.   insert $WS(q) \to WS(p)$ into *SCT*;

20. } }

21. } else {The inner and outer loop will exchange, the codes are omitted.

22. }

In Fast-EP algorithm, each composite service is taken as a new web service with only one operator and its relevant information is stored into *SOT* and *SPT*. Thus, when users search web services, the system can directly match input and output in *SPT*, but ignore whether the web service is a composite service. This will improve search efficiency.

4 Web Service Search and Result Ranking

4.1 Web Service Search with SQL Statements

The simplest web service search method is to use full-text index technique in traditional text search domain, where all concepts in each WSDL corresponding to a web service are extracted and concentrated on a text. The method could fast find all web services with same keywords and rank the results based on keywords matching degree. However, it ignores the input/output constraint of web services and concept semantic so that the precision ratio and the recall ratio are all very low. Thus, we present an approach with higher accuracy to realize web service search in this section.

We provide structured service search mode, namely to import keywords for service input/output, respectively. Then these keywords are extended based on concept similarity. Each keyword gains the Top(k) most similar concepts in *CST* to construct a set. We let $\Gamma(k_i)$, $\Gamma'(k_j)$ denote the similar concepts set of ith, j^{th} keyword of service input and output, respectively. The service search condition can be improved as follows:

$$\mathbb{S} = \vee_{i=1}^{I} \text{ input}: \left(\forall a \in \Gamma(k_i)\right) \text{ and } \vee_{j=1}^{J} \text{ output}: \left(\forall b \in \Gamma'(k_j)\right) \tag{3}$$

where I, J are the amounts of keywords corresponding to service input and output in initial search condition, respectively. In order to be easily understood, we give a simple example. Suppose k=1, the initial search condition is input='A_1, A_2' and output='B'. We get $\Gamma(k_1) = \{A_1, A_1{}'\}$, $\Gamma(k_2) = \{A_2, A_2{}'\}$ and $\Gamma'(k_1) = \{B, B'\}$ based on CST where $A_1{}'$, $A_2{}'$, B' is the most similar concept of A_1, A_2 and B, respectively. So the improved search condition is: (input='A_1' or input='$A_1{}''$) and (input='A_2' or input='$A_2{}'$') and (output='B' or input='B''). Thus, we could use a single SQL statement to realize service search. By this way, we could even enhance the service search mode to SQL statement with more complicated relation in the future, such as (input='A' or (input='B' and output='E')) and (output='C' and not output='D') where all customized concepts will be automatically extended.

4.2 Ranking of Service Search Results

If the system has a large number of web services, how to fast rank the returned services will be very significative. In this paper, we provide a ranking mode based on QoS. If the results contain composite services, their matching degrees will also be considered.

With the algorithm in section 3.1, it is feasible in theory that search results are ranked based on semantic similarity degree. But the response time do not satisfy the search requirement in real time. It will be the goal of our future work. In this paper, we provide the results ranking based on QoS. If the results contain composite services, their matching degrees will also be considered.

Traditional methods considered QoS in the process of web services discovery or composition [11, 12]. The reason is that they compute service composition in real time. The dynamics of QoS and the changeability of user requirement will make the problem more complicated. In fact, the possible service composition statuses are finite and static which are pre-computed and stored in our system. The approach of separable considering service composition, QoS will simplify the problem and improve the efficiency of composite service search. Moreover, QoS and service price could even be respectively stored in different tables because they play even greater roles for cloud computing services. For example, it doesn't matter for user that the QoS of invoked cloud computing services is relatively poor as long as service price is the lowest in the debug phase of web application developing. On the contrary, the importance of QoS will be more than service price after web application is released. The separable storing will increase the flexibility of web service search and returned results ranking according to user requirement.

5 Experiments

The experiment aim is to verify the feasibility and efficiency of our approach and contrast the performance of our algorithms with those in [5, 7]. We use the nearly same hardware and software environment as [7]. e.g. We ran experiments on a 3.0 GHz

Pentium IV machine with 1 GB memory running Windows XP Professional, and all algorithms are implemented in C and compiled using the Visual C++ compiler. But the used database is the free PostgreSQL 8.4.

Because the amount of current cloud computing services is small, our web services dataset uses traditional web services from seekda[1] and webxml[2]. We get the QoS information by soapUI[3] or crawling from seekda directly. And all service prices are generated with random number between 1 and 100.

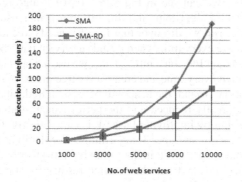

Fig. 2. The performance of SMA

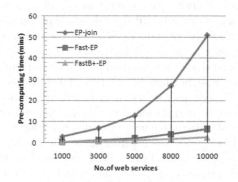

Fig. 3. The performance comparing of three service composition algorithms

At first, we test the performance of web services matching algorithm (SMA) which is ignored in [7]. Moreover, [7] suppose that each web service has only one operator, and each operator has only one input/output parameter. But in our experiment, all web service descriptions come from real WSDL so that the number of operators and input/output parameters in most of web services is more than 1 and the algorithm complexity is higher. Fig.2 shows the performance of SMA in different scales of dataset where all concept similarities in *CMT* have been pre-computed. We find that the original SMA algorithm is time-consuming because the amount of web service pairs

---

[1] http://seekda.com/
[2] http://www.webxml.com.cn
[3] http://www.soapui.org/

matched is very big. Thus, we optimize SMA algorithm, called SMA-RD algorithm, by removing those operators with same input/output parameters, storing concepts similarity relation in memory and so on. At last, the algorithm performance is improved more than doubled.

We compared the computing time of three web service composition algorithms: the EP-Join [7] and our Fast-EP, FastB$^+$-EP. The number of web services changes from 1,000 to 10,000. Because the algorithm complexity of EP-Join is $O(N^2)$ while that of Fast-EP is $O(N*logN)$, we can see in Fig.3 that Fast-EP algorithm results in better performance than EP-Join algorithm, and this difference increases as the number of web services increases. But we discover that Fast-EP needs to execute write-operator from memory to database every time when it finds a service path meeting requirement. This is actually a redundant I/O consuming. Thus, we use a heap in memory for storing those service paths found every time and create a B+ tree index in memory on the heap. When all service paths are found, the heap will be written to database one-time so that the I/O consuming is greatly reduced and the performance of algorithm is increased again. The new algorithm by improving Fast-EP is called FastB$^+$-EP. Fig.3 shows the performance comparing among the 3 algorithms. For facilitating the expression, Fast-EP is used to replace FastB$^+$-EP in the following introduction.

Fast-EP algorithm is invoked and the relevant results are stored in *SOT* and *SPT* before web service searches. Therefore, it will not affect the response time of search in real time. When a new service is registered, the system will firstly calculate the possible one-way matching relation between new service and all services in database and store them into *OMT*, and then invoke Fast-EP algorithm to supplement the new composite service paths and relevant information in *SCT* and *CPT*. The time complexity is $O(K*logN)$ where K is the amount of new tuples in *OMT* and N is sizeof(*SCT*).

Fig.4 shows the search performance comparison among In-memory system [5], PSR system [7] and our WSIS system when the numbers of web services and memory sizes change but there is only one user query. It is necessary for in-memory system to compute service composition in real time so that the execution time at large data set is longer than PSR and WSIS. But in-memory system is faster when the numbers of web services is small. And the performance gap of all systems is not big as long as the available physical memory can load all web services information, though both PSR and WSIS pre-compute the service composition, shown in Fig.4 (a). Here, we ignore the time that in-memory system loads all required web services information into memory because it needs to be executed only once. However, when the available physical memory cannot hold all web services information, in-memory system has to frequently switch data between memory and disk and the search performance will also greatly reduce. Fig.4 (b) shows that the search performance of in-memory system sharply reduces while the memory cannot hold more than about 8000 web service that leads to lots of I/O consuming. But the performance reducing for PSR and WSIS is not obvious because they only rely on SQL search speed in database. In Fig.4 (a)(b), PSR and WSIS have almost the same search performance and the former is slightly faster than the latter. The reason is both of them pre-compute the service composition so that it is enough to search by SQL statements. However, WSIS needs an additional join operator because it stores service operators and input/output parameters in different tables for improving the efficiency of service compositing and the commonality for different web service (even cloud computing service) description standards. e.g. When QoS and

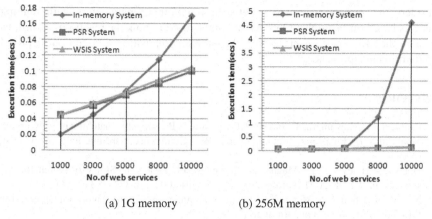

(a) 1G memory   (b) 256M memory

Fig. 4. The comparison of services search performance with different memory sizes

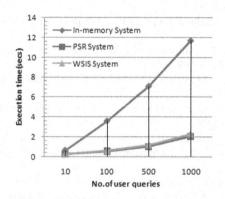

Fig. 5. The comparison of search performance with different numbers of queries

service price are added into our system, we only need to create two new tables but do not affect those data in other tables.

Fig.5 shows the similar comparison among the three systems when we fixed the number of web services to 10000 and varied the number of different user queries from 10 to 1000. We observed that the experiment result is similar as described in [7]. In-memory system does not adapt to larger number of user queries. PSR and WSIS have almost same performance but the latter is slightly low. The reason is the same as introduced in the above paragraph.

6 Conclusion

In this paper, we put forward an unconsolidated storage strategy for cloud computing services which can be flexibly extended to adapt to any new service description standard and a high efficiency of service composition algorithm Fast-EP based on the storage strategy. Moreover, a web service matching algorithm SMA is presented. The difference of SMA relative to traditional service composition algorithm is that SMA considers the semantic similarity between input/output parameters with multiple concepts based on WordNet. QoS information is used to rank the result set. At last, we compare the efficiency of service search, service composition between our approach and traditional approaches.

References

1. Paolucci, M., Kawamura, T., Payne, T.R., Sycara, K.P.: Semantic matching of web services capabilities. In: First International Semantic Web Conference, Sardinia, Italy, pp. 333–347 (2002)
2. Dong, X., Halevy, A.Y., Madhavan, J., Nemes, E., Zhang, J.: Simlarity search for web services. In: VLDB 2004, Toronto, Canada, August 2004, pp. 372–383 (2004)
3. Xia, Y.-m., Chen, J.-l., Meng, X.-w.: On the Dynamic Ant Colony Algorithm Optimization Based on Multi-pheromone. In: ICIS (2008)
4. Li, L., Chou, W., Guo, W.: Control Flow Analysis and Coverage Driven Testing for Web Services. In: ICWS (2008)
5. Hashemian, S.V., Mavaddat, F.: A graph-Based Approach to Web Services Compositon. In: SAINT (2005)
6. Gu, Z., Li, J., Xu, B.: Automatic Service Composition Based on Enhanced Service Dependency Graph. In: ICWS (2008)
7. Kwon, J., Park, K., Lee, D., Lee, S.: PSR: Pre-computing Solutions in RDBMS for Fast Web Service Composition Search. In: ICWS (2007)
8. Braga, D., Ceri, S., Danielsdf, f., Martinenghi, D.: Optimization of Multi-domain Queries on the Web. In: VLDB (2008)
9. Schickel-Zuber, V., Faltings, B.: OSS: A Semantic Similarity Function based on Hierarchical Ontologies. In: International Joint Conferences on Artificial Intelligence (2007)
10. Srivastava, U.: Query Optimization over Web Services. In: VLDB (2006)
11. Yang, S.W., Shi, M.L.: A Model for Web Service Discovery with QoS Constraints. Chinese Journal of Computer 28(04), 589–594 (2005)
12. Zeng, L., Benatallah, B., et al.: QoS-Aware Middleware for Web Services Composition. IEEE Transactions on Software Engineering 30(5) (2004)

Deploying Mobile Computation in Cloud Service*

Xuhui Li[1], Hao Zhang[1], and Yongfa Zhang[2]

[1] State Key Lab of Software Engineering, Wuhan Univ.,
Wuhan, Hubei, China
lixuhui@whu.edu.cn,
haozhang@sklse.org
[2] International School of Software, Wuhan Univ.
Wuhan, Hubei, China
yongfachang@hotmail.com

Abstract. Cloud computing advocates a service-oriented computing par- adigm where various kinds of resources are organized in a virtual way. How to specify and execute tasks to make use of the resources efficiently thus becomes an important problem in cloud computing. Mobile computation is often regarded as a good alternative to conventional RPC-based technology for situations where resources can be dynamically bound to computations. In this paper, we propose a middleware framework for cloud computing to deploy mobile computation, especially mobile agent technology, in cloud services. The major issues to enable mobile agent-based services in the service-oriented computing are discussed and the corresponding mechanisms in the framework are introduced.

1 Introduction

Recent years has witnessed the emergence of cloud computing[1], a new computing paradigm evolving from the concept of "network computer" once popular in late 1990s. A "cloud" indicates a network with resources in it. A resource in cloud can be a physical device, e.g., a storage disk or a CPU, or a software service built on other resources. Under the control of cloud environment, the resources are organized, encapsulated and managed in a virtual way. That is, a transparent service encapsulating certain resources is provided for users, and the users utilize them as a virtual resource and needn't know which resources they actually occupy. A cloud often deploys some fundamental services for organizing and utilizing the resources. For example, the infrastructure services including virtual machines and associated infrastructures lay the foundation of running cloud programs in a virtual way; the storage services including virtual data stores organize the data nodes to provide a uniform access to the data in

---

* This research is partially supported by the Wuhan ChenGuang Youth Sci.&Tech. Project under contract No. 200850731369.

M.G. Jaatun, G. Zhao, and C. Rong (Eds.): CloudCom 2009, LNCS 5931, pp. 301–311, 2009.

the cloud. Based on these fundamental services, a cloud becomes a virtual "network computer" and the computers with which users access the cloud services is thus just a terminal.

To be a virtual computer, a cloud needs more mechanisms than the ones focusing on resource management. Above all, a cloud needs to accomplish computation tasks assigned by users in a virtual way. That is, users specify their tasks in cloud as if they do in a real computer and it is the cloud's obligation to carry out the task in concrete machines in the cloud. Simple implementation of such a computation virtualization maps a task to a selected concrete machine to accomplish it. However, this doesn't comply with the original purpose of cloud which is to make use of resources efficiently. For example, for a task processing a large number of data located at computer node A, if the task is located at node B other than A, it would lead to lots of data exchange. Therefore, an ideal implementation of computation virtualization would dynamically assign the task to concrete machines for efficiency. Since a task usually involves multiple resources located diversely, there is a natural requirement for the task execution to take place here and there from time to time. This situation is similar to "mobile computation"[2], another concept popular in late 1990s.

Mobile computation is a computing paradigm which enables code mobility in network. Simple form of code mobility can be transferring codes to a remote machine for evaluation and collecting the results. Common code mobility is known as mobile agent[3], which is a software entity autonomously migrating in network during its execution. Mobile computation, especially mobile agent technology, was once treated promising in large-scale network computing. Code mobility can greatly enhance the flexibility of load balancing and reduce communication costs in network. However, security problem hinders its application in practice because malice might exist within both codes and hosts in a public area. In the cloud computing era, the security problem of mobile computation can be effectively reduced because both mobile codes and hosts in cloud can be restricted to be provided by trusted companies through certain authentication. Therefore, deploying mobile computation, especially mobile agent technology, in cloud computing environment is a promising and feasible approach to enhancing the overall performance of cloud.

In this paper, we propose a framework of mobile agent-enabled cloud computing named MCF, and discuss the major issues of deploying mobile computation in cloud services. The rest of the paper is arranged as follows: in Section 2, we introduce the related works on mobile computation, service-oriented computing and grid computing. In Section 3 we describe the mobile cloud computing framework MCF and address some key issues on designing cloud services based on mobile computation. Section 4 concludes the paper.

2   Related Works

Studies on mobile computation started in early 1990s. Early studies tried to use mobile codes for remote evaluation, and then researchers show much interest in developing software entity running in different hosts. The entity, often written in interpretative languages like Tcl and executed by certain interpreters, can migrate during execution and is known as mobile agent later. With the wide spread of Java, many mobile agent systems, e.g., IBM Aglets [4], Mole, Voyager were developed, and mobile agent technology was studied in many fields of distributed computing.

Since the early of this century, service-oriented computing[5] has become the representative direction of distributed computing and some service-oriented computing products such as Jini and .NET were released. Lots of studies have worked on establishing efficient and flexible service-oriented network computing paradigm, e.g., grid computing[6] and ubiquitous computing. Grid computing was proposed as an ideal computing paradigm which can transparently utilize the resources with services in the network. After years of research on grid computing in academic circles, cloud computing, an industrial adaption of grid computing, was proposed and advocated as the next generation of network computing.

Recently some studies began to attempt introducing mobile agent technology into grid computing. Among these studies, AgentTeamwork[7] and MAGDA[8] are representatives. AgentTeamwork is a grid-computing middleware system that dispatches a collection of mobile agents to coordinate a user job over remote computing nodes in a decentralized manner. Its utmost focus is to maintain high availability and dynamic balancing of distributed computing resources to a parallel computing job. MAGDA is also a grid computing middleware with an architecture designed according to the layered Grid model. The main purpose of MAGDA is to support parallel programming over distributed platforms through a middleware which implements the needed services of classical parallel programming environment, revisited within the mobile agent based approach. These studies concentrate on utilizing mobile agent technology in the grid to solve distributed problems in a more flexible way, however, they don't present a thorough combination of mobile agent and grid since they seldom care about the service provided by mobile agents, say, mobile services.

As to the services based on mobile agents, some studies have tried to explore the program language features of mobile agent-based services. For example, Mob[9] is a service-oriented scripting language for programming mobile agents in distributed systems. The main feature of Mob is the integration of the service-oriented and the mobile agent paradigms. However, there is still a lack of implementation of these languages in concrete mobile agent-based services.

3   MCF: A Mobile Cloud Framework

Cloud computing aims at providing services all over the Internet and thus adopts a service-oriented paradigm. As mentioned above, mobile computation can bring great efficiency to resource utilization in cloud. Therefore, building cloud services on mobile computation is beneficial to both cloud and end-users with more prompt and efficient request processing. A cloud service can deploy mobile computation in two ways: a) enabling remote evaluation of code segment, or b) being implemented by mobile agents to itinerate in cloud. Here we focus on the latter one because it is more powerful and more interesting. We name cloud service deploying mobile agents as mobile cloud service or simply mobile service.

Enabling mobile service in cloud is an interesting and very challenging task. It needs comprehensive extension to existing cloud environment for a thorough support of mobility. As a primary attempt, we propose a middleware framework named Mobile Cloud Framework (MCF) for the cloud supporting mobile service. Other than existing studies in combining mobile agent technology and grid computing, MCF focus on providing a cloud core to support mobile services rather than utilizing mobile agent to accomplish certain tasks in cloud.

3.1 Architecture of MCF

The purpose of MCF is to provide a simple model for cloud services running and migrating in the cloud as smoothly as in a machine. The general idea of designing MCF is to establish an environment supporting global invocation and addressing of mobile services, and to provide a set of mechanisms to manage the services for transparent utilization. To minimize the framework structure, as illustrated in Fig. 1, MCF is composed of 3 parts: resource services, backbone services and mobile service engines.

Resource services are stationary services encapsulating infrastructural resources, especially physical resources, in the cloud. For example, a low-level storage service can be built specifically to use a local storage device like an RAID. Typical resources include computation resources, storage resources, I/O device resources, etc. In these resources, computation resources, e.g., physical computers, play a special role because they represent platforms on which other services can execute. Computation unit services encapsulate computation

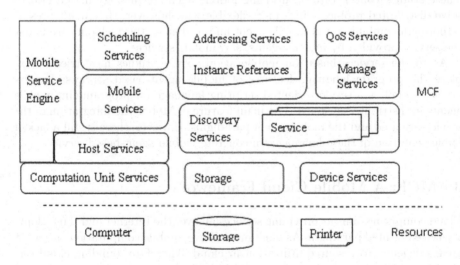

Fig. 1. Architecture of MCF

resources and provide virtual machines for running other services and softwares. Further, a computation unit service can be extended to be a host service which is equipped with the functionalities of mobile computation environment and thus allow mobile services and mobile agents executing on it. Since MCF is designed specific to mobile services, we assume that the computation unit services all be host services in MCF.

Backbone services are a set of basic services for service management and utilization. Backbone services include discovery services, addressing services, scheduling services, QoS services and manage services. Discovery services maintain a distributed service directory in cloud and take charge of service registration and lookup. Addressing services cooperate with discovery services to find real-time reference of mobile services. Scheduling services coordinate with host services, mobile services and addressing services to schedule the task to be accomplished by mobile services. QoS services consist of certain services such as monitoring and evaluation services to provide service QoS information. Manage services cooperate with QoS services to manage the cloud runtime environment. Backbone services are often implemented as stationary services running on physical machines and computation services, but it can also implemented as mobile services running on host services if necessary.

Mobile service engines enable mobile service invocation by cooperating with backbone services and computation services. Mobile service engines in MCF are implemented upon virtual machines provided by computation unit services or host services.

3.2   Service Discovery in MCF

Service discovery is a fundamental mechanism in service-oriented computing to find proper services to utilize. The mobility of service brings more problems to looking for a service than before because we need to know not only which the proper services are but also where they are and where they would be. Therefore MCF should be equipped with additional mechanisms to find mobile services.

Usually a service would register itself in the service directory to be discovered. The service registration contains service description and service reference. For a mobile service, it is not easy to maintain valid reference in service directory. On one hand, mobile service would migrate from one node to another during its lifetime. The mobility leads to volatility of service locations, and thus the reference in directory should be updated frequently. On the other hand, MCF allows a service corresponding to several service instances in the cloud to increase the concurrency of request processing. The service discovery mechanism should transparently provide a service reference to users meanwhile mapping the reference to an actual service instance.

In MCF, service discovery adopts a multi-level reference mechanism. In service directory every service corresponds to an interface rather than a stable reference to find a service instance. For a stationary service, the interface directly provides the reference to the service instance; for a mobile service, the interface is related to addressing service which would fetch an actual reference from a volatile list of references to the service instances.

To guarantee the validity of the references in addressing service, MCF adopts a proxy-based relay mechanism originating from mobile agent communication. Each mobile service instance in MCF is attached with a mobile proxy for communication and service invocation, and the reference in addressing service points to the proxy of the service instance. The proxy of a mobile service instance is invisible to users and would migrate only following the instance's commands. That means, the proxy of a service instance would not migrate without a command even the instance migrates. Therefore, the references in addressing service would not be updated frequently. Studies have shown that this relay communication mechanism for mobile agents is fairly efficient[10].

Besides reference of mobile service, the service discovery mechanism also involves the semantic description of mobile services. Common semantics in a service description might involve purpose, usage and sometimes procedures. For a mobile service, the semantics description can also concern service locations in a static way, i.e., the information of service distribution and mobility. MCF makes a primary attempt to describe service distribution and mobility. The service description contains an itinerary policy indicating the possible locations of the service. The content of the itinerary policy is extensible and its concrete syntax and semantics can be defined by the service provider. Default itinerary policy in MCF just records the possible regions of service instances, and we are now trying to adopt a simple rule-based script to represent the service migration under certain conditions.

3.3 Service Invocation in MCF

To process a service invocation involves establishing and maintaining the invocation link, transferring the invocation requests and results, and executing the service codes. For a mobile service invocation, since the invoker and the service both can be mobile, it is fundamental to maintain the invocation link. In MCF, the proxy-based communication mechanism facilitates the work. When a service invocation begins, the link between the proxies of the invoker and the service instance is established by addressing services. After that, the link is maintained by the related service engines to forward invocation requests and results. When a proxy migrates, the service engines would coordinate to reestablish the link transparently. In comparison with conventional service invocation, mobile service invocation request can have additional information about the locations to process the request. That is, the invoker can ask the service to process the invocation in preferred nodes. The scheduling services and the addressing services will try to find a service instance or create a new instance in the node to carry out the invocation.

Conventionally, service invocation is carried out by service engine, that is, service engine loads the service codes in its address space and executes them. For mobile service which is implemented by mobile agent, the service engine cannot carry out service invocation alone because mobile agent is autonomous and has its own logical address space. Usually an agent only interacts with outside through messages and thus responses requests and carries out tasks by asynchronous message handling. Therefore, in MCF mobile service engines and host services work together to carry out service invocation based on asynchronous message-handling with the assistance of the proxies. A proxy not only handles communication, but also provides a service interface which can be invoked by local service engine. Once a service instance is determined to process an invocation, the service engine invokes its proxy which will encapsulate the invocation request in a message and forward it to the service instance. The agent underlying the service instance and the agent runtime system in the host service will carry out the message and return the results to the proxy and further to the invoker. Since the proxies are mobile, the invoker and the service can negotiate to place the proxies in proper hosts to facilitate the invocation.

A practical service often processes the invocation requests concurrently with certain multi-task mechanism. MCF enables two kinds of multi-task request processing. Firstly, for a mobile service, the host service and the agent often deploy a multi-threaded mechanism underlying the agent runtime system; therefore the service can handle multiple messages concurrently. Secondly, MCF allows a service correspond to multiple service instances, and thus the requests can be transparently distributed to different service instances to deal with.

MCF adopts a flexible and powerful multi-instance mechanism to enhance the performance of multi-task processing. As mentioned above, a service can be discovered by discovery service, but its actual instances are managed by addressing services. Homogeneous service entities, i.e., implemented with same programs, can autonomously become instances of one service by registering itself in addressing services. Another kind of service instances is service clones. Usually a mobile agent can autonomously clone itself, thus a mobile service can clone itself and dispatch the clones to other nodes. MCF treats the clones of a mobile service as new instances of the service and manages them with addressing services and scheduling services. The mobile service instances would autonomously decease or be killed by manage services or scheduling services. Since mobile agent-based service can be dynamically created and deceased, the multi-instance mechanism in MCF is more flexible and powerful than conventional multi-task ones.

When a service corresponds to multiple instances, its invocation requests can be scheduled by scheduling services and addressing services to a service instance to process. Besides the one-to-one request processing, MCF also allows a service invocation request be processed by multiple instances in parallel. The general idea is that the request can be split into multiple sub-requests and handled by the instances in parallel, and the results would be collected and merged to final result to return. In fact, in mobile agent computing, it is common for a master agent to dispatch slave agents across the network to accomplish the task in parallel. This master/slave model is not fit for service-oriented computing because a) frequent creation and migration of slave agents would incur high costs and b) the slaves are not properly defined services and only work for the master. In MCF we prefer to use a P2P-like model undertaken by multiple instances of a service. That is, once a service instance is invoked for handling the request, it can notify other instances in proper places to handle the request together, meanwhile it may clone new instances in proper place for handling the request if necessary. MCF currently defines some basic interfaces to specify the requirements for splitting requests, and it is service provider's duty to ensure the soundness and consistency of the splitting and concurrency. Now we are trying to introduce into MCF Google's Map/Reduce mechanism as a standard style of parallel request processing for multiple service instances.

3.4   Service Composition in MCF

Complicated services can be composed of simpler ones. Composition can be a static one built on certain profile or programs invoking the underlying services, or be a dynamic one based on model-driven or request-driven mechanisms. Since MCF focuses on enabling mobile service in cloud computing, it only concerns static composition which is well studied and easy to implement.

MCF concentrates on supporting service composition transparently rather than providing an engine to resolve and execute composite services. For a composite service which is hard coded as service programs, it is treated as a common service and thus needs not special support from MCF. For the composite service described in certain profile, e.g., a BPEL script, it is third party's duty to provide the engine for processing the profile. In MCF, an invoker service is provided specific to support processing the composition profile. The invoker service is a mobile one whose purpose is to manage service invocations in a composite service. It can migrate to a proper location to carry out a service invocation and then collect the results. The processing engine can flexibly utilize the invoker service to process the service invocations in the composite service profile. Generally, each service invocation in the profile is managed by an invoker service instance. These instances ask the addressing services to find proper services to be invoked, interact with those services to launch the invocation, and cooperate with each other to process the composite service.

3.5   Service Programming and Execution in MCF

Mobile service programs are rather different from conventional service programs. As previously mentioned, conventional services are driven by service engine and thus the program seldom need care about the execution. As for mobile service, it is mobile agent which carries out the service tasks. Therefore, a mobile service program should concern the agent features such as reactivity, autonomy and mobility as well as carry out the task.

MCF deploys a script language SMSL (Simple Mobile Service Language) for programming mobile services. This language originates from a script language named SMAL (Simple Mobile Agent Language) which aimed at describing mobile agent-based algorithms [11], integrating service-oriented programming based on our previous studies on mobile agent-based service language. In SMSL, a service program is declared to implement a service interface and the program body consists of implementation codes of service methods and message-handling codes. Besides common imperative statements such as assignment, loop, conditional statements, several primitives are introduced into SMSL program. The primitives include *send_message* for asynchronous message sending, *lock* and *unlock* for mutual exclusive locking, *request_migrate* and *migrate* for migration, *create_agent* and *clone* for creating new agent or service instances, *find_sevice* and *invoke_service* for service invocation, *regain_messages* and *remove_messages* for internal message management, etc. The details of SMSL would be described in another paper and thus omitted here. As previously mentioned, in MCF each mobile service instance is associated with a proxy who behaves as an interface for service engine to invoke and communicates with the service instance through messages. That is, a proxy handles the service invocation action with the service engine and the mobile service instance processes the invocation request with the host service. Based on concrete host services, MCF transforms a mobile service script in SMSL to a concrete mobile service program and instantiate it as a service instance with a proxy.

Our previous studies have described that there might be ambiguity in mobile agent programs if its execution is not clearly specified. We also proposed a mobile agent execution model named SMA [11] which deploys a multi-thread message-handling mechanism. In MCF we also assume that the host service deploys this model for executing mobile agent codes. In the SMA model, each message is handled by a single thread, and the agent has full control of their message-handling. That means each mobile service invocation is handled within a single thread. For mobile services in MCF, we have to restrict the behaviors of service methods otherwise there might exist conflicts. For example, for a mobile service processing two invocations concurrently, conflict exits if one invoker prefers the service to execute in node A but the other prefers in node B. That is because the invoker's behaviors violate the principles of agent's autonomy. Therefore, MCF requires that in the mobile service program the implementation of service methods cannot directly use the primitives which would violate agent's autonomy. Instead, some primitives such as request_migrate can be used for service methods to send the migration request to agent for final decision. Generally, when migration conflict exists, the service instance can clone itself and split the conflicted requests.

3.6 Prototype of MCF

Now we are working on the implementation of MCF. A prototype named Cloud-Drift is being built following the outlines listed above.

CloudDrift is a rudiment to present basic features of mobile services in cloud computing. To simplify the implementation, CloudDrift directly deploys Jini as the underlying SOA and extends it with the backbone services in MCF. In our previous research in mobile agent simulation platform [12], we have already modified the IBM Aglets runtime system to support SMA model. Therefore, in CloudDrift we adopt the SMA Aglets runtime system as the host services.

A mobile service in CloudDrift is implemented as a pair of proxy and an SMA Aglet, as indicated previously. The service is scripted in SMSL and a parser would transform the SMSL program into an SMA Aglet program and a proxy program. A mobile service in CloudDrift is associated with a service description indicating not only the service interface but also the distribution policy of the service instances. When a service is deployed, the service engines will instantiate the programs according to the original distribution. CloudDrift deploys a federated discovery service and a federated addressing service to look up service instances. The service description would be maintained and updated by addressing service and discovery service during the service lifetime.

CloudDrift is built specifically for parallel processing. A parallelizable service profile is provided in CloudDrift for specifying the parallelization policy of the service. The profile contains the information on interface and deployment. The former is used for service and the invokers to trigger and utilize the parallelization, and the latter is used for service engines and backbone services to instantiate the service instances. A parallelizable service provide interface for users to specify that how the request to be processed in parallel, and the request can be automatically processed in parallel by the service instances in CloudDrift. Once a parallelizable service is deployed, the service engines and the addressing service would collect its distribution information and the interface information. Service engines will cooperate with the host services to transfer the parallel request to other service instances and the new service instance would be created dynamically if necessary. As previously mentioned, the parallelization policy specific to data processing like Map/Reduce is to be designed for a more flexible data processing mechanism in CloudDrift.

The implementation of CloudDrift is still in progress. Currently we focus on enabling mobile service invocation and basic functionalities to support service parallelization and composition. Other services such as the QoS services and the manage services are being implemented. We are improving the prototype to be a full-fledged middleware for mobile cloud computing.

4   Conclusion

Cloud computing advocates a service-oriented computing paradigm where various kinds of resources are organized in a virtual way. How to specify and execute tasks to make use of the resources efficiently thus becomes an important problem in cloud computing. Mobile computation is often regarded as a good alternative to conventional RPC-based technology for situations where resources can be dynamically bound to computations to enhance performance. Therefore, combining the features of mobile computation, especially mobile agent technology, and cloud computing is a promising and feasible approach to enhancing the overall performance of cloud.

In this paper, we studied deploying mobile computation in cloud services and proposed a middleware framework named MCF for mobile agent-enabled cloud computing. The major issues of enabling mobile services in MCF, e.g., service discovery, service invocation, service composition, are discussed and the service programming in MCF is briefly introduced. The ongoing prototype of MCF is also mentioned.

This paper is just a very primary trial to study the features of mobile services. As mentioned previously, MCF is just a simple model to enable mobile service in cloud. We are working on many interesting issues to improve MCF. For example, most mobile agent systems only support weak migration, i.e., the agent would not retain current execution state when migrates. To guarantee the consistency of service invocation, mobile services have to resort to mutual exclusive primitive such as lock and unlock. However, this naive mechanism is far from enough for designing services in practice. Therefore, we will explore more powerful transaction mechanisms in mobile service programming. Further, there is still much work to do in multi-clones invocation processing and workflow engines for service composition.

References

1. Hayes, B.: Cloud computing. Communications of ACM 51(7), 9–11 (2008)
2. Cardelli, L.: Mobile computation. In: Tschudin, C.F., Vitek, J. (eds.) MOS 1996. LNCS, vol. 1222, pp. 3–6. Springer, Heidelberg (1997)
3. Kotz, D., Gray, R.S.: Mobile Agents and the Future of the Internet. ACM SIGOPS Operating Systems Review 33(3), 7–13 (1999)
4. Lange, D.B., Mitsuru, O.: Programming and Deploying Java Mobile Agents Aglets. Addison-Wesley Longman Publishing Co., Amsterdam (1998)
5. Papazoglou, M.P., Georgakopoulos, D.: Service-oriented computing. Communications of the ACM 46(10), 25–28 (2003)
6. Berman, F., Fox, G., Hey, A.J.G.: Grid computing: making the global infrastructure a reality. Wiley Press, Chichester (2003)
7. Fukuda, M., Kashiwagi, K., Kobayashi, S.: AgentTeamwork: Coordinating grid-computing jobs with mobile agents. Applied Intelligence 25(2), 181–198 (2006)
8. Aversa, R., Di Martino, B., Mazzocca, N., Venticinque, S.: Magda: A mobile agent based grid architecture. Journal of Grid Computing 4(4), 395–412 (2006)
9. Paulino, H., Lopes, L.: A mobile agent service-oriented scripting language encoded on a process calculus. In: Lightfoot, D.E., Szyperski, C. (eds.) JMLC 2006. LNCS, vol. 4228, pp. 383–402. Springer, Heidelberg (2006)
10. Cao, J., Feng, X., Lu, J., Chan, H., Das, S.K.: Reliable message delivery for mobile agents: push or pull? IEEE Transactions on Systems, Man and Cybernetics 34(5), 577–587 (2004)
11. Li, X., Cao, J., He, Y.: A Language for Description and Verification of Mobile Agent Algorithms. In: Proc. of CIT 2004, pp. 546–553 (2004)
12. Li, X., Cao, J., He, Y., Chen, Y.: MADESE: a simulation environment for mobile agent. In: Proc. of CIT 2006, pp. 86–91 (2006)

A Novel Method for Mining SaaS Software Tag via Community Detection in Software Services Network

Li Qin[1,2], Bing Li[1,3,*], Wei-Feng Pan[1], and Tao Peng[1]

[1] State Key Laboratory of Software Engineering, Wuhan University, Wuhan, 430072, China
[2] School of Science , Huazhong Agricultural University , Wuhan , 430070 , China
[3] School of Computer , Wuhan University , Wuhan , 430072, China
qinli0606@sina.com, bingli@whu.edu.cn

Abstract. The number of online software services based on SaaS paradigm is increasing. However, users usually find it hard to get the exact software services they need. At present, tags are widely used to annotate specific software services and also to facilitate the searching of them. Currently these tags are arbitrary and ambiguous since mostly of them are generated manually by service developers. This paper proposes a method for mining tags from the help documents of software services. By extracting terms from the help documents and calculating the similarity between the terms, we construct a software similarity network where nodes represent software services, edges denote the similarity relationship between software services, and the weights of the edges are the similarity degrees. The hierarchical clustering algorithm is used for community detection in this software similarity network. At the final stage, tags are mined for each of the communities and stored as ontology.

Keywords: software service tag; text parsing; software similarity network.

1 Introduction

As a new business model, cloud computing and SaaS (Software-as-a-Services) are attracting more and more attention worldwide. In 1999, Salesforce.com was established by Marc Benioff, Parker Harris, and their associates. This website was the first to provide the concept of SaaS with real business and made a success in attracting customers [1]. Nowadays there is a tendency of using SaaS. Many industry giants, such as GM, AMD, have already adopted SaaS. In 2007, Google, IBM, and a number of universities embarked on a large scale cloud computing research project [1]. The industrial partners have a strong business interest in this new model, where computing chores increasingly move off individual desktops and out of corporate computer centers as services over the Internet. Google, the Internet search giant, is one of the leaders in this technology transformation. Companies like Yahoo, Amazon, eBay and Microsoft have built Internet consumer services like search, social networking, Web based e-mail and online commerce that are based on cloud computing. In the corporate market, IBM and others have built Internet services to predict market trends,

---

* Corresponding author. Tel.: +86-027-87653491, fax: +86-027-68754590.

M.G. Jaatun, G. Zhao, and C. Rong (Eds.): CloudCom 2009, LNCS 5931, pp. 312–321, 2009.
© Springer-Verlag Berlin Heidelberg 2009

tailor pricing and optimize procurement and manufacturing, etc. [2]. Ranjit Nayak, Founder and President of Marketing at eVapt, said that SaaS was a paradigm where softwares were delivered using cloud computing infrastructure [3]. Jin Zhu, Item CEO of IBM Cloud Labs & HiPODS, argued that SaaS was a part of cloud computing. she said, "cloud computing can be divided into three layers: 1) the bottom is the infrastructures, including hardware, host, etc; 2) the second layer is the intermediate platforms; 3) the upper layer is applications and services which are SaaS". She also pointed out that "through the flexible hardware allocation, cloud computing can resolve the problem of shortage of hardware or bandwidth and also can reduce the cost of SaaS" [4]. The IT customers simply regard SaaS as a form of cloud computing [5]. In brief, an upsurge in cloud computing will promote the employment of SaaS. Meanwhile, SaaS will also provide more applications and resources to cloud computing.

Many web sites, such as Google App Engine, Alisoft.com, Ophone SDN (Software Developer Network), etc, have provided platforms, by which, new software services can be developed, and developers can publish their software services as well. As a result, the number of SaaS software services is increasing dramatically. This leads to the difficulty of finding a required software service from the user's perspective. Nowadays, tags are widely used to annotate SaaS software services and are also used to facilitate the searching of specific software services. Currently, most of tags are generated by manual methods. For example, when submitting a new application to the Google App Engine Gallery, developers are requested to provide several tags to annotate the software service. In such way, the contents of these tags tend to be arbitrary and ambiguous, even meaningless, and sometimes confusing for users. To resolve this problem, this paper proposes a method for mining SaaS software service tags by parsing text documents.

2 Approach

The approach proposed for mining tags from the help documents can be described in the following six steps.

1. **Term extraction**: firstly, lexical analysis is performed to parse the help documents, after which terms (noun) are extracted from the documents.
2. **Term similarity computation**: the similarity between terms is calculated.
3. **Document similarity computation**: similarity of documents is calculated based on the numbers of the similar terms shared in the documents.
4. **Software similarity network construction**: a software similarity network is constructed, where the nodes represent software services, edges denote similarity relationship between software services, and the weights of the edges are the similarity degrees between software services.
5. **Community Detection**: a hierarchical clustering algorithm is used to cluster software in the constructed software similarity network.
6. **Tag mining**: the characteristic terms in each of software communities are mined, and the result is stored in the form of ontology. The process for mining tags is shown in Fig1.

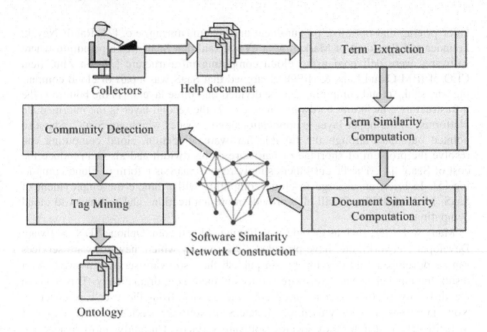

Fig. 1. The process for mining tag knowledge

2.1 Term Extraction

Currently, there are many existing lexical analysis systems which can be used for basic text parsing, such as ICTCLAS, IRLAS, etc. In this work, we use ICTCLAS3.0 [6] to parse the software help documents into words and tag POS (Part of Speech) for the words. Single word cannot express domain terms since most of the noun terms in the text are composed with multiple words. Related research also showed that 85% of the terms in text were multi-word terms [7,8,9,10]. Therefore, our research mainly focuses on multi-word terms extraction. Through the analysis of the text, we propose four rules for terms extraction which are presented as follows (the abbreviations used in the rules are: NP for noun phrase, N for noun, u for auxiliary).

1. Since each concept is a noun in the text, only words with the N tag are extracted.
2. In the case of s nouns Ni (i=1,2,...,s) linking to each other one by one in the form of N1N2...Ns, we consider the s nouns together as a noun phrase.
3. In the case of two nouns linked by an auxiliary word, as N u N, we eliminate the auxiliary word, and link the nouns together (i.e. NN) as a noun phrase.
4. In the case of a noun and a noun phrase are linked by an auxiliary word, as NP u N or N u NP, we also eliminate the auxiliary word, and link the remaining words together as a noun phrase.

2.2 Term Similarity Computation

The objective of word similarity computation is to resolve the duplicated representation of synonym in the tags. There have been various approaches in the field of word similarity computation. Tran and Smith proposed an information theoretic measure to assess the similarity of two concepts on the basis of exploring a lexical taxonomy (e.g., WordNet) [11]; Liu proposed a method for Chinese word similarity computation base on HowNet [12]; etc. But as we mentioned above, most of the multi-word terms, which we have extracted as noun phrase, are OOV (Out-Of-Vocabulary) terms in HowNet [13], thus the way of computing the similarity degree of each pair of them is the key issue in this study. The following steps are the algorithm we proposed to calculate the similarity degree between multi-word terms.

1. Take the noun phrase as a collection of nouns, like $NP1(N11, N12,...,N1n)$, $NP2(N21, N22,...,N2n)$;
2. Extract the last noun in each collection, i.e., $N1n$, $N2n$ and describe the similarity between them as $Sim_1(NP_1,NP_2)$.
3. Calculate the similarity of the remaining part of two collections, and describe the similarity between two collections as $Sim_2(NP_1,NP_2)$.
4. The overall similarity of two noun phrases can be defined as :

$$sim(NP_1, NP_2) = \sum_{i=1}^{2} \beta_i sim_i (NP_1, NP_2) . \tag{1}$$

where $\hat{a}_i$ is a constant, and $\hat{a}_1 + \hat{a}_2 = 1, \hat{a}_1 > 0.5$. $\hat{a}_1$ is used for the transferring of semantic focus in Chinese language.

We use word similarity computation method proposed in [12] to calculate $Sim_1(NP_1,NP_2)$. The steps for computing $Sim_2(NP_1,NP_2)$ is described as following.

1. Select a noun from one collection, and retrieve the corresponding noun, which has the maximum similarity in the other collection;
2. Remove this pair of nouns selected in step 1 from the collections;
3. Repeat step 1 and step 2 until one of the collections is empty. The remaining nouns in the other collection correspond to NULL and the similarity of them is zero.
4. Finally, $Sim_2(NP_1,NP_2)$ is the average of the similarity of each pair of nouns.

2.3 Document Similarity Computation

The similarity degree between every pair of the help documents is the key data in a software similarity network; therefore, how to compute the similarity between documents is another topic of our study. A considerable amount of research has been done on the document similarity computation in the last decades. Salton proposed the method to express text character by vector space model, in which document was transformed into vector by TFIDF (Term-Frequency Inverse-Document-Frequency) weights, and the similarity of documents was calculated in vector space. Salton and Buckley used it in automatic text retrieval [14]. But this method didn't take the term similarity into account, which consequently decreases the accuracy of calculation.

Peng proposed a text similarity computation formula based on inner product space model of semantic [15]. But this algorithm ignored similarity computation between multi-word terms. Based on the analysis of these methods, we adopt the following method to calculate the similarity between two documents.

1. Count the sum of terms for each document;

2. Under a given threshold, we filter out some pairs of terms whose similarities are greater than the threshold, and then count the sum of them without repetition;
3. The formula for the document similarity computation can be defined as:

$$Sim(S_A, S_B) = N / (N_A + N_B) .$$ (2)

where S_A and S_B represent document A and B respectively; N is the number of similar terms in S_A and S_B under the given threshold, N_A and N_B denote the sum of terms of S_A and S_B respectively.

2.4 Software Similarity Network Construction

In this subsection, we show the way of constructing a software similarity network. First, we give the definition of Software Similarity Network as follows.

Definition 1: Software Similarity Network (S2N). In S2N nodes represent the software services; edges between two nodes denote the similarity relationship between two software services with the weight of each edge annotating the similarity value. Therefore S2N can be described as:

$$Network_{S2N} = (Nodes, Edges, M_w) .$$ (3)

where $Network_{S2N}$ is an undirected network denoting S2N; *Nodes* are software services; *Edges* denote the similarity relationship between software services, and M_w is the similarity value.

2.5 Community Detection

There are a lot of approaches that can be used to detect community structures in complex networks. One of them is hierarchical clustering. Hierarchical clustering techniques can be divided into two categories: agglomerative techniques and divisive techniques. Our algorithm belongs to the general category of agglomerative hierarchical clustering methods. It starts with a state, in which each object is the sole member of one of n communities, and proceeds with a series of fusions of the n objects into groups according to their similarities. It can be represented by a two dimensional diagram known as dendrogram which illustrates the fusions made at each successive stage of analysis.

Similarity measurement is the key issue in controlling the iterative process of hierarchical clustering. In the following sections, we define similarity measure between sub-clusters, and presented the fast hierarchical clustering algorithm.

2.5.1 Similarity Measure

There are many different quality functions to test whether a particular division is meaningful or not, such as *MQ* introduced by Mancoridis, *EVM* function by Tucker, and modularity Q devised by Newman and Girvan. In this paper, we use the quantitative definition proposed by Newman and Girvan. It is defined as below.

$$WQ = \sum_i (We_{ii} - Wa_i^2) .$$ (4)

where WQ is the similarity of a particular division, We_{ii} is the fraction of the total weight of the edges that connect two nodes within community i, while Wa_i is the fraction total weight of the edges that have at least one endpoint within community i.

The WQ is originally devised to evaluate the effectiveness of the whole clustering, but not to evaluate the similarity of sub-clusters. To address this issue, we borrow the basic idea from Newman's fast algorithm. In this paper, we employ $\triangle WQ$ to measure the similarly between two sub-clusters. The reason is that if two communities with the maximum similarity are divided into two different communities, there will be a decrease in the modularity WQ, otherwise there will be an increase. The value of $\triangle WQ$ denotes the similarity between two sub-clusters. Hence searching for the sub-clusters with the maximum similarity means finding out the biggest $\triangle WQ$. This strategy to accelerate the speed of the algorithm is very similar to that proposed in Ref. [16] [17]. The change in WQ upon joining community i and j is defined as:

$$\triangle WQ = \begin{cases} We_{ij} + We_{ji} - 2Wa_iWa_j & i, j \text{ is connected} \\ 0 & otherwise \end{cases} \quad . \tag{5}$$

In this paper, we iteratively search for the changes $\square WQ$ resulted from the amalgamation of each pair of communities, and choose the biggest one among them, until there is only one community left.

2.5.2 A Fast Hierarchical Clustering Algorithm

In this subsection, we present the algorithm flow of the fast hierarchical clustering algorithm.

Input: S2N

Output: WQ and clustered results (software community)

1. Assign each node in S2N as a cluster
2. Calculate WQ according to formula (4), and calculate $\triangle WQ_{ij}$ from the pairs of communities according to formula (5), and store the $\triangle WQ_{ij}$ in $\triangle WQ$ matrix
3. While the number of communities > 1 do
4. Select the largest $\triangle WQ_{ij}$ from $\triangle WQ$ matrix
5. Merge the corresponding communities i and j, update $\triangle WQ$ matrix and increase WQ by $\triangle WQ_{ij}$
6. End While

2.6 Tag Mining

The final purpose of this research is to retrieve tags from help documents for annotating software services. Regarding the eligibility of a term being a tag, we argue that tags are the characteristic terms that are commonly shared in help documents of software services, so we create a collection of terms from help documents of software services in each software community, then count the number of each term's appearance in the help documents of the corresponding software community. The specific algorithm is shown as follows.

Input: S (a collection of terms)

Output: tags

1. Define each term in S with a triple (N, L, W), N is the term, L represents the document where term locates, W denotes the number of term's appearance in this group.
2. Compute the similarity between N, and filter out the pairs of terms whose similarity values are greater than a given threshold α.
3. For each term, count the number of its similar terms in all pairs of terms we have found, if two or more similar terms have the same L, they are only counted once instead of twice, then store the counting result in W.
4. Sort the terms according to W, and count K which is the sum of software services in this group.
5. Extract the terms, in which W is bigger than $K/3$.

In this algorithm, threshold α is a constant. In the following section, the effectiveness of our method will be demonstrated in a concrete experiment.

3 Experiment

In this experiment, we collected 104 help documents from alisoft.com [18]. By text parsing, we extracted 3400 terms from the help documents. Through term similarity computation, we retrieved several groups of data of document similarity under different thresholds which are presented in Table 1. Table 2 shows the software clustering results we have detected in software similarity network under different thresholds.

By comparing the data in Table 2, we find that the number of categories is relatively small when the threshold is equal or less than 0.35, and when the threshold is equal or greater than 0.65, there are many isolated software services appeared. Part of reason can be found in Table 1. When the threshold value is small, the similarity degree of documents is generally big, and the software in the software network will relatively concentrate, so the number of categories is limited. On the other hand, when the threshold value is bigger, most of document similarities decrease to zero, which results in a large number of isolated software services. Based on the analysis, it is reasonable to set the threshold in the range of [0.45, 0.55]. In this experiment, we set the threshold to 0.45.

Table 1. Document similarity under different threshold values(part of the data)

Threshold	The document similarity between two software help documents
0.35	0.79 0.73 0.72 0.63 0.54 0.41 0.40 0.39 0.32 0.30 0.30 0.26 0.25 0.20 0.12
0.45	0.60 0.53 0.44 0.32 0.32 0.19 0.21 0.23 0.17 0.17 0.18 0.14 0.08 0.13 0.08
0.55	0.56 0.45 0.38 0.28 0.27 0.18 0.19 0.19 0.16 0.17 0.14 0.14 0.06 0.09 0.07
0.65	0.18 0.10 0.09 0.06 0.07 0.05 0.03 0.05 0.03 0.05 0.03 0.04 0.00 0.03 0.02
0.75	0.15 0.09 0.06 0.04 0.07 0.02 0.00 0.04 0.01 0.05 0.03 0.01 0.00 0.01 0.00
0.85	0.14 0.09 0.06 0.04 0.07 0.00 0.00 0.02 0.00 0.02 0.01 0.00 0.00 0.00 0.00

Table 2. Software clustering results under different threshold values

Threshold	Software clustering results
0.35	3 categories, the number of software services of each category: 40, 34, 30
0.45	4 categories, the number of software services of each category: 32, 27, 24, 21
0.55	4 categories, the number of software services of each category: 33, 29, 27, 15
0.65	15 categories, the number of software services of each category: 38, 33, 13, 9, 1, 1, 1, 1, 1, 1, 1, 1, 1, 1, 1

Figure 2 shows the software similarity network where the threshold is set to 0.45, and the clustering result is also shown in Figure 2. Each concentrated software community denotes a category of software services with similar features.

In order to get the similar features of each category, we mined the tags from each category of documents, and show them in Table 3. Through the analysis of these retrieved tags, we find that the first category is about customer management and sales management. The second mainly refers to information and knowledge management. The third is concerned with user management and the fourth is about shop and product management.

The experimental results partially demonstrate the effectiveness of software clustering with our proposed method. Furthermore, the mined tags reveal the common function of each category of software services. Compared with man-picked tags, the retrieved tags can annotate the software services more effectively, reducing tag arbitrariness and ambiguity. Finally, those tags are stored in the form of ontology.

Fig. 2. The software similarity network (each node in this network represents a software service, the text note behind the node is the name of software service)

Table 3. Tags of each category

Category	Tag
First	Category Information; Demand Information; Customer Information; Sales Data; Customer Management; Customer Relationship Management; Rights Management; Business Management; Data Analysis; Sales Management; Order Information; Revenue and Expenditure Information; Information Security; Product Information; Product Management; Contact Information; Purchase Information; Edit Product; Promotion Information; Quotation Information; Advertising Information; Cost Information; Inventory Management; Goods Management; Data Backup; Project Management; E-mail Management; Customer Return Management;
Second	Plan Management; Software Management; Knowledge Management; Management Upgrade; Location Information; Altitude Information; Expenses Information; Failure Information; Network Information;
Third	User Management; Upgrading User; Treasure payment User; User Interface; User Role; User Experience; Wangwang Users; Office Users; User Requirement; User Opinion; User Agreement; Consultation for user; Anonymous User
Fourth	Product Quality; Promotion for Product; Mail Services; Shop Notice; Shop Template; Shop Location; Expenses; Overall Cost; Shop Type; Shop Address; Shop Category; Introduction of shop; Description of goods

4 Conclusion and Future Work

In most of the cases, man-picked tags cannot annotate the SaaS software services effectively. In this paper, we propose a novel method for mining tags from help documents of software services, and achieve good results in our experiment. The tags mined by this method do not only tag software services effectively, but also have the potential of describing the function, even the requirements of software services. We are planning to use the retrieved tags to construct domain knowledge model, which can be employed to define software functions and requirements. Domain knowledge model will provide more semantic information to software service tags. Furthermore, we hope domain knowledge model can act as guidance to functional designs and requirement analysis in software service development.

Acknowledgement

This work is supported by National Basic Research Program (973) of China under grant No.2007CB310801, National High Technology Research and Development Program (863) of China under grant No.2006AA04Z156, National Natural Science Foundation of China under grant No.60873083, 60803025, 60703009, 60303018, 60970017 and 60903034. Natural Science Foundation of Hubei Province for Distinguished Young Scholars under grant No. 2008CDB351. We would like to thank Ye-Yi Qin, Xiao-Yan Zhou, Kui Xiao and Ting-Ting Hou at State Key Laboratory of Software Engineering, Wuhan University and for useful conversations and thank Dr. Gan-Sen Zhao at School of Software, Sun Yat-sen University for valuable advice.

References

1. Cloud Computing From Wikipedia,
   http://en.wikipedia.org/wiki/Cloud_computing
2. Google and IBM Join in Cloud Computing Research (2007),
   http://www.nytimes.com/
3. How Are SaaS and Cloud Computing Related? (2009), http://caas.tmcnet.com/
4. Two hot technologies: Saas and cloud computing (2008), http://dev.yesky.com/
5. What is cloud computing means? (2008), http://news.csdn.net/
6. ICTCLAS3.0, Website, http://ictclas.org/
7. Nakagawa, H., Mori, T.: A simple but powerful automatic term extraction method. In: COMPUTERM 2002, pp. 1–7 (2002)
8. Jiang, X., Tan, A.-H.: Mining ontological knowledge from domain-specific text documents. In: Fifth IEEE ICDM, pp. 27–30 (2005)
9. Song, N.-R., Feng, Z.-W., Kit, C.-Y.: Automatic Chinese Multi-word Term Extraction. In: ALPIT 2008, pp. 181–184. IEEE Press, Dalian (2008)
10. Li, W., Wang, C., Shi, D.-n.: Automatic Chinese Term Extraction based on Cognition Theory. In: ICNSC 2008, pp. 170–174 (2008)
11. Hong-Minh, T., Smith, D.: Word Similarity In WordNet.: Modeling, Simulation and Optimization of Complex Processes. In: Proceedings of the Third International Conference on High Performance Scientific Computing, 2006, Hanoi, Vietnam, pp. 293–302. Springer, Heidelberg (2008)
12. Liu, Q., Li, S.-J.: A word similarity computing method based on HowNet. In: 3th Chinese Lexical Semantics Workshop, Taipei (2002)
13. Dong, Z.-D., Dong, Q.: HowNet Website, http://www.keenage.com/
14. Salton, G., Buckley, C.: Term weighting approaches in automatic text retrieval. Information Processing and Management 24(5), 513–523 (1988)
15. Peng, J., Yang, D.-Q., Tang, S.-W.: A Novel Text Clustering Algorithm Based on Inner Product Space Model of Semantic. Chinese Journal of Computers 30(8), 1354–1363 (2007)
16. Pan, W.-f., Li, B., Ma, Y.-t., Liu, J., Qin, Y.-y.: Class structure refactoring of object-oriented softwares using community detection in dependency networks. Frontiers of Computer Science in China 3(3), 396–404 (2009)
17. Newman, M.E.J.: Fast algorithm for detecting community structure in networks. Rev. E 69, 066133 (2004)
18. alisoft.com, http://mall.alisoft.com/

Retrieving and Indexing Spatial Data
in the Cloud Computing Environment

Yonggang Wang[1,*], Sheng Wang[2], and Daliang Zhou[2]

[1] Institute of Remote Sensing Applications, Chinese Academy of Sciences,
100101 Beijing, China
Phone: +86 10 64409914; Fax: +86 10 64409782
wangyg@bjgtj.gov.cn
[2] Beijing Easymap Information Technology Co., Ltd, 100080 Beijing, China

Abstract. In order to solve the drawbacks of spatial data storage in common Cloud Computing platform, we design and present a framework for retrieving, indexing, accessing and managing spatial data in the Cloud environment. An interoperable spatial data object model is provided based on the Simple Feature Coding Rules from the OGC such as Well Known Binary (WKB) and Well Known Text (WKT). And the classic spatial indexing algorithms like Quad-Tree and R-Tree are re-designed in the Cloud Computing environment. In the last we develop a prototype software based on Google App Engine to implement the proposed model.

Keywords: Spatial data; Geographic Information System; Retrieving and indexing; Cloud Computing.

1 Introduction

Currently, Geographic Information System (GIS) is now playing an important role in many areas of modern city. It is said that 80 to 90 percent of all information has a geographic component, such as an address, an area reference like a sales district, or a map coordinate [1]. Most of critical functions of modern city are relevant to geographic data such as environmental planning, disaster management, public administration and civic planning [2]. So spatial information sharing and integration service construction are being carried out and a great success have been achieved. As the development of geographic spatial information sharing service, we meet a number of new challenges such as expensive maintenance and software costs, low system performance and data, system security, which greatly hamper the deep development of spatial information service.

Today, the latest paradigm and hot topic to emerge is that of Cloud Computing. It is a new term for a long-held dream of computing as a utility, which has recently emerged as a commercial reality. Cloud Computing promises reliable services delivered through next-generation data centers that are built on computing and storage virtualization technologies [3]. Consumers will be able to access applications and data from a "Cloud" anywhere in the world on demand, making software even more

---

* Yonggang Wang, PH.D, his main interest is on the theory and application of GIS.

M.G. Jaatun, G. Zhao, and C. Rong (Eds.): CloudCom 2009, LNCS 5931, pp. 322–331, 2009.

attractive as a service and shaping the way IT hardware is designed and purchased. Cloud Computing can supply a reliable IT infrastructure to GIS effectively. Through calling those APIs of Cloud Computing platforms, GIS professionals can ignore basic maintenance job and pay more attention to designing and developing special professional functions and service. Cloud Computing have many advantages such as flexibility, scalability, security and low-cost. It neatly compliments spatial software as a service and server approaches for interacting with spatial data. It also enables many users to interact together, exchanging and collaborating with data pertaining to multiple disciplines. This means a process orientation surrounding dynamic applications can be realized. Besides we can store the spatial data in the Cloud without paying attention to details of huge volume data storage and spatial data security. In a sense, the Cloud is fertile ground for GIS and it will reach its highest potential there.

Achieving the storage and management of spatial data based on common Cloud platform is the basis of application. But currently mainstream Cloud platform don't support spatial data storage. This paper will develop and extend spatial data storage, retrieving, indexing, accessing and management model based on common Cloud Computing platform using OGC simple feature coding rules such as Well Known Binary (WKB) and Well Known Text (WKT).

2 Related Work

Before exposing our approach and introducing our study, we briefly present some studies for Cloud Computing and its application in geospatial industry. Recently, several academic and industrial organizations have started investigating and developing technologies and infrastructure for Cloud Computing. Academic efforts include Virtual Workspaces [4] and OpenNebula [5]. A lot of IT factory also put great effort to the study of Cloud Computing and many Cloud platforms are emerging.

Amazon Elastic Compute Cloud (EC2) provides a virtual computing environment that enables a user to run Linux-based applications [6]. Amazon SimpleDB is a web service providing the core database functions of data indexing and querying. This service works in close conjunction with Amazon Simple Storage Service (Amazon S3) and Amazon Elastic Compute Cloud (Amazon EC2), collectively providing the ability to store, process and query data sets except spatial data in the Cloud [7].

Google App Engine is a platform for developing and hosting web applications in Google managed data centers. It allows a user to run Web applications written using the Python programming language. Other than supporting the Python standard library, Google App Engine also supports Application Programming Interfaces (APIs) for the datastore, Google Accounts, URL fetch, image manipulation, and email services. Many projects at Google store data in Bigtable, including web indexing, Google Earth, and Google Finance [8]. BigTable is a distributed storage system for managing structured data that is designed to scale to a very large size [9].

Azure Services Platform is an application platform in the Cloud that allows applications to be hosted and run at Microsoft datacenters. It provides a Cloud operating system called Windows Azure that serves as a runtime for the applications and provides a set of services that allows development, management and hosting of managed applications off-premises [10].

It is great to be part of the excitement as the geospatial industry turns their interest to the Cloud. The Open GIS Consortium (OGC) is a not-for-profit membership organization with more than 210 Members. The goal of the OGC is the ubiquitous access and use of spatial data and spatial processing in an open marketplace [11]. The items for discussion and continuing work from OGC Web Service Phase 6 (OWS-6) include Cloud computing. Potential OWS-7 topics and related OWS are focus on emerging Cloud Computing.

The Global Earth Observation System of Systems (GEOSS) is an international program aiming to integrate space-based and terrestrial sensors from over 70 countries [12]. It will explore and investigate Cloud Computing to support processing and analysis of earth observation data in environmental scientific workflow.

WeoGeo is an innovative file management and exchange service built for the spatial data industry. Initially, WeoGeo will introduce FME's spatial ETL capabilities to the Cloud. This is the first venture to bring spatial ETL to the Cloud's infrastructure, and it promises to make spatial data even more accessible for end users [13].

3   Spatial Information System Based on Cloud

Our study aim is to build a common spatial information system based on Cloud Computing technology. At the present we are focus on the study of developing and extending spatial data storage, retrieving and indexing model based on common Cloud Computing platform. We think this work will supply the core effect with a complete spatial information system.

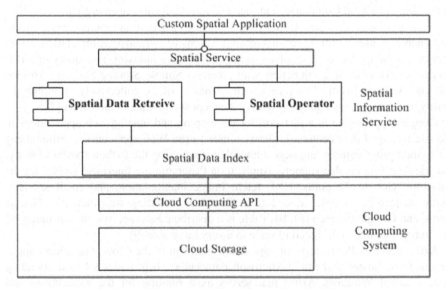

Fig. 1. Spatial information system based on the Cloud

We proposed a Cloud-based spatial information system model which is described in Figure 1. Because Cloud Computing system can provide some standard API to operate data, we can store the spatial data in Cloud. Utilizing its APIs, we can build the spatial data index, then the spatial data retrieving and the spatial data operator could be implemented. So we can achieve it like present spatial information system which can provide the standard compliant service and can be constructed applications.

Though there may be no standard data APIs for the Cloud Computing system at present, but some work has been on their way to solve this problem. The proprietary API should be replaced by standard guidelines which will benefit the widespread of the Cloud Computing technology.

4 Spatial Data Retrieving

4.1 Spatial Data Model

There are many different spatial data models which are subjected to specific applications and software such as GraphDB, Oracle Spatial, GEIS, GrassGIS, GeoOOA and others. So it leads to a lot of interoperation problems between various systems. Since late 1990s, a lot of efforts have been made to build standard spatial data model to represent, exchange and store spatial data, and the most successful achievement is the standard set by the OGC. The basic computer environments are unable to communicate in the spatial domain, so the OGC try to build the ubiquitous access and use of spatial data and spatial processing in an open marketplace. Now most of the software vendors like ESRI, Mapinfo, Oracle and IBM are implementing these standards in their products.

Because of the elegance and simplicity of the model, we have adopted the OGC Simple Feature Model in this Cloud-based spatial information system. It is also the most commonly adopted geospatial data model in the geospatial industry. The Simple Feature Model is an OpenGIS standard which specifies digital storage of geographical data with both spatial and non-spatial attributes. Simple Features are based on 2D geometry with linear interpolation between vertices. In general, 2D geometry is simple if it contains no self-intersection. The OpenGIS Simple Features Specifications define various spatial operators, which can be used to generate new geometries from existing geometries. OGC Simple Feature Coding Model is given in Figure 2.

Except the logic mode of the spatial data object, the persistent coding rules of the object have been regulated by the OGC and described in their Access and Coordinate Transformation Service Specifications. It is Well Known Text (WKT) and Well Known Binary (WKB). WKT is a text markup language for representing vector geometry objects on a map, spatial reference systems of geographic objects and transformations between spatial reference systems. WKB is used to transfer and store the same information in binary bytes. For example if we have a point object with the x coordinate and y coordinate value is 1, then the equivalent WKT and WKB formats are given in Table 1.

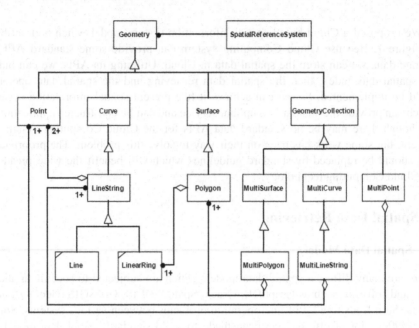

Fig. 2. OGC Simple Feature Code Model

Table 1. WKT and WKB example

OGC Service Specifications	Formats
WKT	POINT(1 1)
WKB	0101000000000000000000F03F000000000000F03F

4.2 Spatial Data Retrieving

The Cloud Computing platforms always provide APIs for access its data object. Some systems implement it with SQL-like language, and others provide functional APIs with specific language such as Java, C++ or Python. Because of the constitutionally virtualization features of Cloud Computing systems, the APIs functions interact with a virtual object. So we don't need to care about the details of the physical data storage.

Up to now, all the Cloud Computing systems can implement CRUD operation with their raw data type. Meanwhile most of them can support BLOB/CLOB data type. The BLOB/CLOB data is a collection of binary data stored as a single entity in a database, and now these data types have been moved to Cloud Computing environment. We can store the WKB object in Blob entity, and WKT object in CLOB entity. Logically the primary thought of spatial data retrieving is searching the spatial data object in a BLOB/CLOB virtual object in the Cloud, and implementing some spatial operator to manipulate the data. We have developed a spatial data retrieval model which is described as Figure 3.

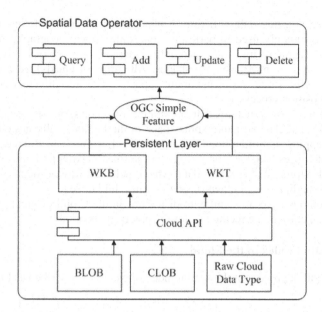

Fig. 3. Spatial data retrieval model based on the Cloud

The high level data retrieval function is the Query/Add/Update/Delete Methods. Compared to the database's CRUD operation, it can work with the spatial data object compliant with the OGC Simple Feature Specification.

All the work to access the spatial object is encapsulating in a persistent layer, through that the spatial object is encoded into WKT or WKB format. Then using common Cloud APIs to access the BLOB/CLOB virtual entity from the Cloud storage, the properties of the spatial object is treated as ordinary raw data type such as String, Number or others.

5   Spatial Data Indexing

Formerly spatial indexes are used by GIS software to optimize spatial queries. Indexes used by non-spatial models like B-Tree can't effectively handle features like that how far two points differ and whether points fall within an interest spatial area. So some specific algorithms have been developed to support the spatial indexing.

Even though we don't need to care about the indexing of physical file pointer and memory object position as before, we also need to build the index to optimize the query and operation of the spatial data stored in the Cloud.

5.1   Spatial Index Algorithm

The Cloud Storage is a collection of the virtual object. Although we can't locate its physical position, we can identify the object with the logical mark. So the problem is identical to index an object in the spatial database. And we can adopt the typical algorithm like Quad-Tree and R-Tree methods in the Cloud Computing environment.

A Quad-Tree is a tree data structure in which each internal node has up to four children. It is commonly used to partition a two-dimensional geographical space by recursively subdividing it into four quadrants or regions. The regions may be square or rectangular, or may have arbitrary shapes. All forms of Quad-Tree divide space into adaptable cells which has a maximum capacity. The tree directory follows the spatial decomposition process.

R-Trees are tree data structures that are similar to B-Trees, but are used for spatial access methods. The data structure splits space in the hierarchically nested way, and possibly overlapping minimum bounding rectangles. Each node of R-Tree has a variable number of entries which are up to some pre-defined maximum. Each entry within a non-leaf node stores two pieces of data, which include a way of identifying a child node and the bounding box of all entries within this child node.

The two methods have no significant difference in the Cloud Computing environment. So we can choose one method as for the practical situation.

5.2   Build Spatial Index in the Cloud

The implementation process of the spatial index operation is described as Figure 4.

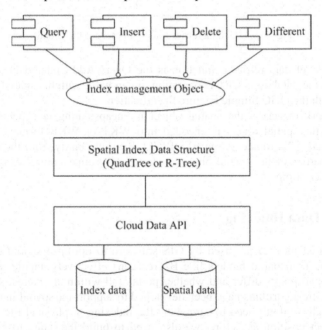

Fig. 4. Spatial index operation in the Cloud

The index is accessed by the Cloud data APIs as well as the spatial data. When spatial data has been saved into the Cloud, the index object of Quad-Tree or R-Tree can be built by an index management object in a non-volatile manner with which indexed nodes can be paged to memory if needed. So the operation of the index object could be implemented. There are some key routines which can be executed to such an indexed spatial dataset in the Cloud.

Searching includes other operations such as intersection and containment. In Quad-Tree, we can use binary search algorithm to find the element. And for R-Tree, we can use the bounding boxes to decide if searching inside a child node. In this way, most of the nodes in the tree are never touched during a search. And Log (N) complexity could be achieved.

In Quad-Tree algorithm, when a node is added or deleted, the tree should be rebalanced, but no other objects would be affected. As for R-Tree, we use the bounding boxes from the nodes to ensure that nearby elements are placed in the same leaf node. Different algorithms can be used to split nodes when they become too full, resulting in the Sub-Quadratic and linear R-tree subtypes.

6   Experiment and Result

To facilitate its use and determine its effectiveness, the spatial retrieving and indexing algorithm has been implemented based on Google App Engine. As a commercialized Cloud Computing platform, Google App Engine adds Python and Java API for the Cloud data access. The Google datastore provides persistent storage for App Engine applications, used directly or via the provided JDO or JPA interfaces. And the BLOB and Text data type which is equivalent to CLOB is completely supported. So the main components supporting spatial information system suggested by us is available.

We choose some test dataset including points, lines and polygons, which stored as ESRI shape file in the cloud. Then we upload and download the geometry object data from the Cloud in an Internet connection with 512k speed. The statistical result is given in Table 2.

Table 2. Test result of the data retrieving on the Google AppEngine

Name	Type	Record Number	Upload time	Download Time
City_PT	Point	412	120ms	43ms
River_PL	Line	25	87ms	32ms
Boundary_PY	Polygon	39	232ms	84ms
Address_PT	Point	8400	2023ms	712ms

To obtain the equivalent test results on the traditional spatial database, we employ a entry level PC server as the hardware platform, and use the oracle spatial to store and query the data. A program based on OCI interfaces has developed and executed. The results are given in Table 3.

Table 3. Test result of the data query (download) and write (upload) on spatial database

Name	Type	Record Number	Upload time	Download Time
City_PT	Point	412	92ms	50ms
River_PL	Line	25	104ms	38ms
Boundary_PY	Polygon	39	311ms	63ms
Address_PT	Point	8400	3211ms	325ms

The result shows a little difference between the two environments. And the cloud have a more quickly speed when store (upload) the geometry data. But when the number of data records increases, the spatial database has a better performance when executing query (download) operation. Considering the network factor and scalability of the cloud system, we still recognize the cloud system as a promising solution to store the spatial data.

A simple map rendering program has been developed in order to display the map image on java canvas object. We make the output result as png image file in a jsp page, through which spatial data can be retrieved real-time from the Cloud platform. The demo web page of map image is shown as Figure 5.

Fig. 5. The demo web page of map image

7   Conclusions and Future Work

It is expected that the original spatial retrieving and indexing scheme and software based on the Cloud platform can help the application of Cloud Computing in the field of geographic information system, which may contribute to the development of geo-spatial service.

However, the research in this paper just provides a preliminary framework and pro-totype software for spatial data storage and management. To reach the aim for geo-graphic information Cloud service, a lot of work need be done such as problems of mass remote sensing images storage, spatial data engine, spatial processing, 3D mod-eling and spatial analysis. These are our future interested work.

References

1. chang, K.-t.: Introduction to Geographic Information Systems. McGraw-Hill Companies, Inc., New York (2002)
2. Longley, P.A., Goodchild, M.F., Maguire, D.J., Rhind, D.W.: Geographic Information Systems and Science. John Wiley & sons, New York (2001)

3. Weiss, A.: Computing in the Clouds. Net Worker 11(4), 16–25 (2007)
4. Keahey, K., Foster, I., Freeman, T., Zhang, X.: Virtual workspaces-Achieving quality of service and quality of life in the Grid. Scientific Programming 13(4), 265–275 (2005)
5. Llorente, I.: OpenNebula Project, http://www.opennebula.org
6. Amazon Elastic Compute Cloud (EC2), http://www.amazon.com/ec2
7. Amazon web service, http://aws.amazon.com
8. Google App Engine, http://appengine.google.com
9. Chang, F., Dean, J., Ghemawat, S., Hsieh, W.C.: Bigtable: A distributed storage system for structured data. In: OSDI 2006: Seventh Symposium on Operating System Design and Implementation, pp. 15–25 (2006)
10. Windows Azure FAQ, http://www.microsoft.com/azure
11. OGC, http://www.opengis.org/techno
12. GEOSS, http://earthobservations.org/
13. WeoGeo, http://www.weogeo.com

Search Engine Prototype System Based on Cloud Computing

Jinyu Han, Min Hu, and Hongwei Sun

China Mobile Research Institute, Beijing, P.R. China, 100053

Abstract. With the development of Internet, IT support systems need to provide more storage space and faster computing power for Internet applications such as search engine. The emergence of cloud computing can effectively solve these problems. We present a search engine prototype system based on cloud computing platform in this paper.

Keywords: cloud computing, mobile internet, search engine.

1 Introduction

With the development of computer and communication technology, the number of mobile phone users increases rapidly. According to statistics in [1], there are more than 600 million mobile phone users in China by the end of 2008, and nearly 39.5 percent of overall Internet users use mobile phones to access Internet, the number of which is about 117.6 million. At the same time, with the development of 3G and mobile Internet, there is an urgent requirement for IT support systems to provide more storage space and faster computing capacity. If we build the IT support systems based on Minicomputers in mobile Internet, there exists the following drawbacks, (1) The Minicomputers are expensive and low-cost-effective, (2) Because of the use of closed-specific computer systems, procurement and maintenance costs are high, and the scalability is low. The emergence of cloud computing can effectively solve these problems. Cloud computing, which has high-performance, low-cost and high scalability features, provides processing, management and storage capabilities for mass data. Therefore, the use of cloud computing platform as Internet application infrastructure can provide a strong IT support system for the better use of the Internet. Search engine is a typical Internet application, which can use cloud computing platform.

In this paper, we present a search engine prototype system based on cloud computing platform. The organization of this paper is as follows. The advantages using cloud computing are introduced in Section 2. In Section 3, we describe the architecture and related techniques of the search engine prototype system, which is followed by a

M.G. Jaatun, G. Zhao, and C. Rong (Eds.): CloudCom 2009, LNCS 5931, pp. 332–337, 2009.
© Springer-Verlag Berlin Heidelberg 2009

presentation of the experimental results in Section 4. The discussion of this paper is concluded in Section 5.

2 Advantages Using Cloud Computing

Search engines need to deal with mass content, and the high concurrent query requests need to be handled with low-latency. The traditional centralized computing platform is not only costly, but has become increasingly inadequate to meet the demand for such applications. The cloud computing platform can be used as the core business process infrastructure, which provides high-capacity content storage, management and processing. The cloud computing platform in Google, Yahoo, Baidu, Amazon or other Internet service providers composes of hundreds or thousands or even tens of thousands of nodes, this large-scale computing systems provide mass data storage, management and processing, and are successfully used in some applications. Cloud computing has the following advantages:

Firstly, the cost is low since cloud computing platform is based on industry-standard PC. The open source software ecosystem for cloud computing platform has been relatively mature, which provides complete solutions from the distributed data storage to massive structure data management. For example, the famous Apache Hadoop project has made a major breakthrough in function, performance and reliability with the efforts of tens of thousands of open source developers. It is reasonable to believe that the open-source cloud computing platform will become the mainstream in the future.

Secondly, it is flexible. The cloud computing platform adopts distributed, loosely coupled architecture. It has good scalability and the system management cost is small. Since the cloud computing platform can be set up using heterogeneous nodes, enterprises and research institutions can reuse the existing hardware devices, which facilitates the transition from the existing systems to cloud computing platform.

Finally, it is easy to expand new business. In the era of cloud computing, multi-applications can share the cloud computing platform. For example, the e-mail application can be combined with Ad push or Fetion applications, which can improve the user stickiness and loyalty and enhance the value-added business profits.

3 Search Engine Based on Cloud Computing

The function of Search Engine (SE) includes web pages' parallel crawling, parsing, indexing, distributed search and search results display. The architecture includes 3 layers: cloud computing layer, search engine layer, service layer. The architecture of search engine is as follows.

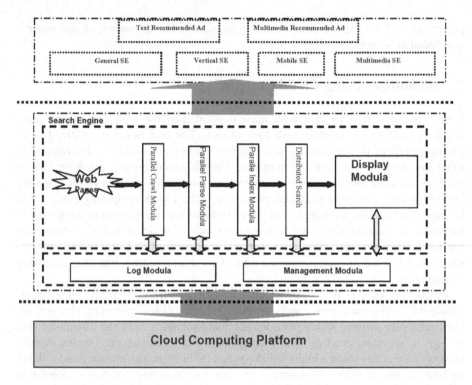

Fig. 1. Service Layer: the Mobile Service Information Search Engine, the Vertical Search Engine, the Mobile Search Engine, the Multimedia Search Engine, the (multimedia) advertisement promotion. Above all, it's necessary for the search engine abstract. Search Engine layer includes 2 parts: core part and management part.

3.1 Core Part of Search Engine

Parallel Crawl Module
It's multiple parallel computing, including the steps Injector (turn seed URL into HyperDFS, then put it into a database called CrawlDb by crawl module), Generator (scan CrawlDb database, generate a crawl list for new round), Fetcher (based on cloud computing technology, put the crawl list to all nodes, each node use multi-threading technology crawl), Updater (merge the content of original and new CrawlDb).

Crawl module also has functions of regularly updated collection. The web pages are classified according to their updating frequency. It includes 4 kinds: every hour, daily, weekly, monthly updating. Therefore, the crawl module collects web pages by their updating frequency all the time.

Parallel Parse Module
Responsible for dealing with the original page crawl data of parallel crawl module. First of all, purify the original data page, get rid of the noise content in Web pages (such as advertising, copyright information, etc.); Second, extract the theme pages and related content, including the summary page, web text, page keywords, page title,

page language type, the type of website code, web pages out-links and the corresponding text messages, and through access to web page URL to get in-links and the corresponding text; Third, according to some algorithm to get the uniquely identifies of page called DocID and web content identifies called ContentID, and in accordance with the ContentID of the web pages to eliminate the duplication; Finally, put the above information into its corresponding database, as the source data of follow-up module of the index and search.

Parallel index module

After pretreatment with the links between pages and pages of information for the input and output is inverted index file. The module achieved: with the establishment of multi-column index page (the page with multiple fields means: the website is divided into a title, text fields, etc by the pre-processing algorithm.); indexing speed reach 250M per hour; supporting the compression of index data and index swelling rate is less than 50%; loading index (compressed) time + decompression time <loading index (before compression) time; support the Chinese multi-word segment. And: the correct word segmentation rate of over 90%; part-of-speech analysis of the correct rate of 90%.

This module can distribute the index data to the search servers, and backup the indexes to ensure the reliability of the indexes data. The module also can merge the number of small indexes into a larger index to carry out the real-index.

Distributed Search modules

Use the inverted index file and the user search requests as input, according to the type of search request to generate search results. query speed at G-class data level, should be able to achieve millisecond response (average response time less than 300ms, Cache hit page response time less than 100ms).

This module provides three-tier cache. Module will cache the results of query in some commonly used to Cache, when receiving a request query, first check the cache, then query the index in the case of did not hit the cache . Thus the cache can greatly speed up the query speed and reduce the same search bring the cost of query.

Distributed module provides the search function. When distributed query servers receive a query ,first of all Web servers check the cache, if got a result of the return cache; Otherwise, the request is sent to each search query server. Improve the response query speed .

User interface modules

There are two main parts: the server side is responsible for UI features sub-module; the user's client (page in browser). These two parts coordination the display of search results.

This module get search results as the input, generate the user interface of search results; responsible for search engine users interactant: provide help document, accept user's search request.

The functions of the modules : search help documents; search results page display; multi-language support; Abstract generation; query time display; the scope of search results filters; syntax coloring; the number of query results; search results clustering.

3.2 Management Part of Search Engine

The main task is business operation and management and maintenance (such as setting permissions, data backup and disaster recovery, etc.), and record the operation of each module have a log, the log based on user feedback for the system optimization can be Parallel Data Mining using the corresponding interface.

Logging and analysis modules

The log records for log file output. Log file as a text file, each line entry, the entry format of the decision by the log type. Log includes running logs, user logs and log management.

Log analysis module, including: statistical analysis of query terms (using cloud computing statistics, first of all to check words for the key word query is mapped to the corresponding machine, the machine corresponding to the completion of the counting statistics query and output the results of the Statistics.) ; new words found (using cloud computing technology analysis the log of the user queries to determine whether word frequency of occurrence greater than a threshold); ban the word processing (to use cloud computing technology, to log every query term with the broad match ban If the query log includes the word banned word banned in the table, the query log output section); based on the log of the cache behavior analysis (based on the results of query statistics and found that relatively high frequency query .To generate the URL link of the query word through request URL realization the update of the cache.)

Maintenance and Management Module

This module includes user authority settings, data backup and disaster recovery.

4 Experimental Results

We evaluated the functionality, scalability, reliability, security, performance of the search engine prototype system. The main performance indicators are as follows:

Criteria	Test Results
Crawling web pages	300M (10-20M / day)
Crawling speed	101.3 M / node / hour
Correct content extraction rate	90.33%
Index speed	928M / node / hour
Correct word segmentation rate	90.13%
Correct part-of-speech rate	95.28%
Index Expansion Rate	0.28
Search Speed	212.48 ms (100M pages)
Correct retrieval rate	54.15% (Top20 compared with Google)

5 Conclusions

The development of various Internet applications, such as search engine, demand computing platform processing and increasing stringency of the application infrastructure bring forward a higher demand, but the traditional IT support system is cost-effective low and poor scalability, cloud computing technology with the massive information processing, management and storage capabilities, as well as its high-performance, low-cost and high scalability features, can effectively solve these problems. Cloud computing can not only support the typical application of mobile Internet search engine, but also support the new mobile Internet applications in the future, such as web disk storage and sharing, SNS, competitive intelligence analysis.

References

1. The 23rd China Internet development report. China Internet Network Information Center (CNNIC) (January 2009)
2. Hadoop project, http://hadoop.apache.org
3. Nutch project, http://www.nutch.org/
4. Mapreduce project, http://hadoop.apache.org/mapreduce/
5. Sullivan, D.: Fifth Annual Search Engine Meeting Report, Boston, MA (April 2000)

Distributed Structured Database System HugeTable

Ji Qi, Ling Qian, and Zhiguo Luo

Department of Service Support Technology, China Mobile Research Institute,
100053 Beijing, China
{QiJi,QianLing,LuoZhiguo}@chinamobile.com

Abstract. The demand of analyzing and processing mass data is increasing in recent years. Though several optimization versions developed, the traditional RDBMS still met a lot of difficulties when facing so huge volume of data. A newly designed distributed structured database HugeTable is proposed, which have the advantage of supporting very large scale of data and fast query speed. HugeTable also have a good compatibility with the standard SQL query language. The basic functions, system architecture and critical techniques are discussed in detail. The usability and efficiency are proved by experiments.

Keywords: Database Distributed.

1 Introduction

RDBMS (Relational Database Management System) technology was firstly proposed and used in practical project in the 1970's by IBM. In the following tens of years, as a result of its excellent OLTP (On-Line Transaction Processing) performance, RDBMS evolved to be the top and unique main stream data base technique.

With the fast popularization of internet and the rapid development of information technology, RDBMS met some difficulties because of the very big information scale. Facebook is one of the top SNS (Social Network Service) providers in the world. About tens of GB user data were generated every day in 2007. They use MySQL to handle all these information then. But last year, the daily data size increased to 2TB, which obviously exceeded the capacity of any RDBMS including MySQL. The latest report says that Facebook produces 15TB user data everyday now. There are a lot of similar cases, for example, phone bill data of telecommunication companies, web accessing log of internet service providers, monitoring data of sensor networks and transactional data of finance companies. All these kinds of large scale data listed above have some features in common, and so they demand analogical functions from data management tools:

1. Collecting large scale of timing related or streaming data.
2. The inner structure of data is not very flexible, and the content of historical data will rarely be updated or deleted.
3. Data don't have to be strictly available at real time, which means users don't issue queries for newly imported data.
4. The ability of querying, filtering, analyzing and aggregating data from massive data.
5. The support of simple data access interface.

M.G. Jaatun, G. Zhao, and C. Rong (Eds.): CloudCom 2009, LNCS 5931, pp. 338–346, 2009.
© Springer-Verlag Berlin Heidelberg 2009

Many systems with newly designed architecture have been proposed to meet one or more of the above requirements. Pig [1] is a parallel data processing system which is contributed to Apache Hadoop [2] project by Yahoo, whose basic idea is transforming the client side query to Map/Reduce procedures in cluster, which run on the lower level Hadoop platform. Users can execute some kind of simple queries in a way similar to SQL, however the functionality is relatively weak, and it only supports a few data types. Hive [3] is a framework of data warehouse hosted by apache Hadoop project that do-nated by Facebook. At the aspect of SQL supporting, Hive goes further than Pig and provides richer SQL grammar and more data type support. Indexing is one of the short-boards of hive, that simple query of small data scale often take minutes to get finished. HBase [4] is one of the open source implementations of Google BigTable [5]. In short words, HBase makes the key value mapping through multi-level indexing tables, and gets excellent primary key query performance. But SQL style query language is not supported by HBase, and the single Master design leads to poor availability.

HugeTable is a distributed structured database system which implements standard SQL query interface and support high performance global indexing. Especially, single point of failure is completely avoided from design. The critical techniques of Huge-Table are presented in the 2nd section. The experiment results in the 3rd section proved HugeTable has excellent performance and scalability. Finally, conclusion is given in the 4th section.

2   HugeTable System

Figure 1 describes the basic architecture of HugeTable system, which is divided into 4 levels, namely Application Level, ODBC/JDBC Driver Level, SQL Service Level and

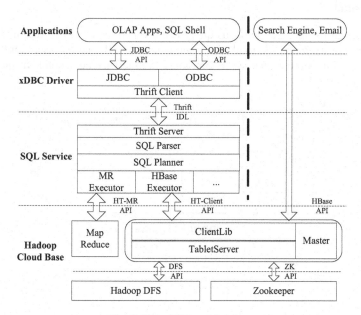

Fig. 1. HugeTable achitecture

Hadoop Cloud Base Level. HugeTable supports 2 kinds of application interfaces at the "Application Level". The first one is native application interface which enables direct access of data using batch updates. The second one is standard SQL interface. The "JDBC/ODBC Driver Level" lies right below the "Application Level", which provides JDBC/ODBC drivers to the on top SQL applications. The "SQL Service Level" analyzes all incoming SQL statements and generates corresponding parallel query procedures. The "Hadoop Cloud Base Level" includes some basic system framework components, such as MapReduce [6], DFS, Zookeeper [7] and HBase that HugeTable relies on.

2.1 ODBC/JDBC Drivers and SQL Service

The ODBC/JDBC Driver Level enables the users to INSERT, DELETE, UPDATE and QUERY data with ODBC/JDBC interface like traditional databases.

Let's take JDBC as an example to explain the overall work flow. Firstly, user Java application loads the driver, and then connects to the database with the help of JDBC Driver Manager. Query requests are sent to SQL Engine through Thrift, after which query plan is made out by SQL Engine to generate parallel procedures that execute the query on nodes inside the cluster.

The communication between JDBC/ODBC Driver and SQL Engine could not be realized by function calls for that they would not be deployed on the same node in most cases. By using Thrift as channel, part the driver code could be generated automatically, and the JDBC/ODBC drivers are then much simplified. Besides, server side code could be used by both JDBC and ODBC driver because that the two drivers use the same communication protocol to connect to server.

2.2 Indexing

In some scenarios, the user demands query result for mass data to be returned in very short time. For example, the total data scale is tens of TB, and the user wants to find all target records which have some appointed number in one second. In the design

CDR

Row	Time	UserID	SouceIP	ObjectIP	SignalType
1	20080909-12:00:00	13910001000	10.1.6.124	10.1.7.22	CreatePDP
2	20080909-12:00:00	13810001000	10.1.6.125	10.1.6.124	delPDP
3	20080909-12:00:01	13910001000	10.1.7.22	10.1.6.124	responsePDP
4	20080909-12:00:01	13910001000	10.1.7.22	10.1.6.124	CreatePDP

CDR-UserID-Index

UserID	Row
13910001000	1,3,4
13810001000	2

Fig. 2. HugeTable indexing mechanism

period of HugeTable, we found that there are no current system can satisfy the above demand. Hive is among the best ones that provide mass data processing ability, but minutes of time must be consumed for even the simplest query in TB scale of data at least. So, the global indexing table is designed for HugeTable. HBase exploited a 3-level indexing table to accelerate the look up speed for primary keys in user data tables, so HugeTable use HBase as global indexing tool for locating particular column values. Figure 2 is a simple example in which CDR is the original HugeTable data table, and CDR-UserID-Index is the assistant HBase indexing table.

The pseudo code below explains the establishing process of HugeTable global indexing table:

Pseudo code to establish global indexing table

```
Scanner = data_table.get_scanner;  /*Create scanner for
original data table*/

row = scanner.next( );      /*Get the handle of the first re-
cord in original data table*/

while (row != null){      /*Get all the following data using
the scanner*/

    value = row.get_column( target_column_name );      /*Get
    the value of target_column_name in this record*/

    if(! index_table.has_row(value)){      /*If there are no
    corresponding row for this value in the indexing table*/

        create_row(index_table, value);      /*Create one row
        for this value in the indexing table*/

    }

    append_to_row(index_table, value, row.get_rowkey( ) );
    /*Append the rowkey in the original data table for this
    value in index table*/

    row = scanner.next( );   /*Go to process the next record*/

}
```

2.3 High Availability Design

High availability is one of the basic requirements for data base systems in the area of telecommunications and finance. HugeTable have some special high availability considerations from the very start of designing work, like the multi-Master mechanism, guarantee of TabletServer durative service and the reliable Zookeeper system.

Master is the core module in HugeTable system, which mainly manages meta-data with according interfaces. The management interfaces is called whenever user create, delete tables, modify table properties, or at the time when the number of tablests changes, or when there are new TabletServer added in. There should be only one primary master taking effect in HugeTable at anytime. Several secondary masters may exist for backing up purpose. If the primary master fails, one secondary master will take its job over and become primary master instead. Figure 3 explains how it works.

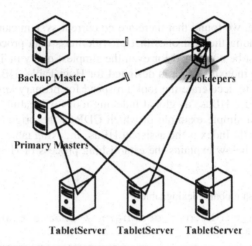

Fig. 3. Working model of HA related modules

The several secondary masters are interchangeable cold backups. If the current primary master fails, failover process will be issued and new primary master could be elected. The backup secondary masters don't have to save latest status of TabletServers. When primary master is switched, all status could be extracted from META table, and no reassignment is needed for existing tablets. With the informing mechanism of Zookeeper, all clients and TabletServers are notified right away.

HugeTable has the ability to reschedule data at the granularity of tablet. Whenever TabletServer fails, the current primary master will reassign its tablets to another TabletServer automatically according to their work loads. Thus, all data hold in HugeTable system stays available even if some of the TabletServers fail. Besides, the TabletServers keep providing data accessing service as long as the Zookeeper server could be connected, which means when masters are not in service, TabletServers can still keep its durative of service.

3 Experiments

The development of HugeTable system is done recently, and then we did some experiments to evaluate the performance and scalability.

3.1 Experiment Environment and Tools

There are 128 nodes in the experiment platform, and the total disk is 256TB totally. We use open source management tool Rocks to administrate the cluster. Centos 5.0 operating system is installed on each node. The detailed hardware information is listed below:

Table 1. Hardware configuration of experiment platform

Hardware	Functionality	Configureation
Computing Node	Master/NameNode/Tablet Server/DataNode/TaskTracker	2way 2core XEON 2.5G CPU/8G Memory/4*250G SATA 7.2K Hard Disk
Switch	3rd level routing fucntion	GE entries

All test cases are implemented in Java language, and the JDK version is SUN 1.6.0. All testing data come from the GDR table of GPRS signal monitoring system, each row of which have 21 columns and 200 bytes raw data.

3.2 Throughput

Throughput test is to evaluate the parallel access rate of HugeTable native API. There are "RandomRead", "SequentialRead", "RandomWrite", "SequentialWrite" and "Scan" five kinds of cases totally. Particular number of testing threads will be issued on each node in the testing cluster, and then certain test case will start executing the corresponding parallel data accessing operation. The sequential and scan test cases read or write continuous records from a selected position. The random test cases read or write records from randomly generated positions every time, so that the adjacent operations do not touch the same data block on hard disk.

We performed all the experiments on clusters with 8, 16, 32 nodes respectively, and the data scale is 1.7TB which is about 1 billion rows of CDR records.

Figure 4 shows the throughput of whole cluster with 8, 16 and 32 nodes respectively. The x-coordinate stands for the number nodes in cluster, and the y-coordinate stands for data operating throughput (unit: records/second). The two write experiments have an obviously higher throughput than the others. This is because that all writes operations are performed in local memory of the corresponding node, except when the memory occupation exceeds a certain threshold and disk flush happens. In all cases, we got almost linear speed up, which proved that HugeTable has good scalability.

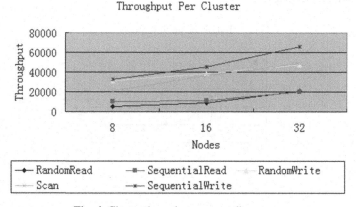

Fig. 4. Cluster throughpt contrast diagram

Figure 5 shows the throughput of each node under 3 different cluster scales. Single node processing capacity drops when the scale of cluster extends, which is because that there is only one Master node in cluster, and when the number of node increases the Master becomes the bottle neck.

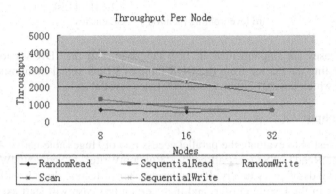

Fig. 5. Node throughput contrast diagram

3.3 Responding Time

SQL operation performance is evaluated by responding time experiments, and the SQL statements are picked from frequently used statements in GPRS signal monitoring system. Test results are the average respond time of all selected statements (every statement is executed for 3 times each).

We performed all the experiments on clusters with 6, 8, 10, 16, 20, 32, 50, 62, 126 nodes respectively, and the data scale is 1.4 TB which is about 0.8 billion rows of CDR records.

Figure 6 shows the average query responding time of all SQL statements without global index under 9 kinds of node scale. The query responding time drops almost linearly when the number of cluster nodes increases, which proved that HugeTable have good scalability when SQL Engine executes the query in the manner of MapReduce without global index.

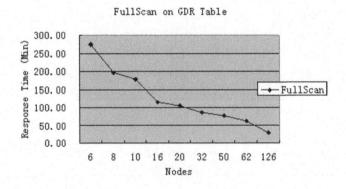

Fig. 6. SQL query responding time without index

Figure 7 shows the average query responding time of all SQL statements with global index. The responding time does not vary a lot when altering the number of nodes except the 6 nodes situation. We build up 3 column index of GDR table in this case, so considerable memory is consumed by the newly generated indexing tables. By examining the DFS NameNode portal, we found that the total disk consumption increased from 4.1TB to 4.8TB after creating global column indexes. The global indexing table of HugeTable is implemented by Hbase data table, and HBase loads all primary key indexing data into memory when the index tables are online. All memory is used up by HBase indexing data in the 6 nodes situation, so we get a much longer responding time. However, if HugeTable still have free memory, all SQL queries will be returned in stable responding time, because they are all executed with looking up HBase primary keys in the same way.

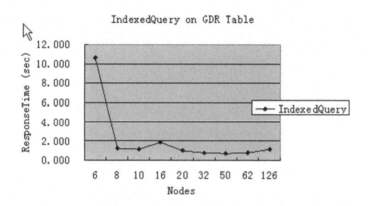

Fig. 7. SQL query responding time with index

4   Conclusions

This paper analyzed the defects of current distributed mass storage systems at first, and then proposed HugeTable, which have 4 important features as follows: (1) Support of standard SQL statement; (2) No single point of failure; (3) High performance global indexing mechanism; (4) Excellent scalability. The future work includes: (1) Promote the overall stability of HugeTable system. Although designed with failure control strategy such as multi-master and durative-TabletServer, HugeTable still do not have satisfying stability, especially in application contexts of very long time and very high load. (2) Deal with the bottle neck caused by HBase index hosted in main memory for HugeTable global column index. HBase holds all primary key indexes in memory indiscriminately which wasted a lot of memory resource, so HugeTable might not process more data because of insufficient memory even when disk occupying rate is low.

346   J. Qi, L. Qian, and Z. Luo

References

1. Hadoop Pig project, http://hadoop.apache.org/pig
2. Hadoop project, http://hadoop.apache.org
3. Hadoop Hive project, http://hadoop.apache.org/hive
4. HBase project, http://hadoop.apache.org/hbase
5. Chang, F., Dean, J., Ghemawat, S., et al.: Bigtable: A Distributed Storage System for Structured Data. In: OSDI 2006: Seventh Symposium on Operating System Design and Implementation, Seattle, WA (November 2006)
6. Dean, J., Ghemawat, S.: MapReduce: Simplified Data Processing on Large Clusters. In: OSDI 2004: Sixth Symposium on Operating System Design and Implementation, San Francisco, CA (December 2004)
7. Zookeeper project, http://hadoop.apache.org/zookeeper

Cloud Computing: A Statistics Aspect of Users

Gansen Zhao[1,2], Jiale Liu[2], Yong Tang[1], Wei Sun[2], Feng Zhang[1],
Xiaoping Ye[1], and Na Tang[1]

[1] South China Normal University, China
[2] Sun Yat-sen University, China

Abstract. Users see that cloud computing delivers elastic computing services to users based on their needs. Cloud computing service providers must make sure enough resources are provided to meet users' demand, by either the provision of more than enough resource, or the provision of just-enough resource. This paper investigates the growth of the user set of a cloud computing service from statistic's point of view. The investigation leads to a simply model on the growth of the system in terms of users. This model provides a simple way to compute the scale of a system at a given time, thus allowing a cloud computing service provider to predict the system's scale based on the number of users and plan for the infrastructure deployment.

1 Introduction

Cloud computing delivers computing services over the Internet, mostly via Web Services. Cloud computing technologies mitigate the conventional on-site computing paradigm to the current remote computing paradigm, with all computing resources be visualized as services and delivered over the Internet. This provides the benefits of the follows.

- Services can be provided at a remote site.
- Computing can be used as in a utility style by resource virtualization.
- Elastic capability according to demand.

The potential scale that a cloud may need to support will be greater than those supported by most of the conventional enterprise-wide IT systems. The large scales supported by clouds bring in new system behaviors and properties that may not be obvious in conventional IT systems with related much smaller scales.

While cloud computing is a great technology for users, which releases them from infrastructure investment, planning, and maintenance, etc, cloud computing is a much demanding technology for service providers. Service providers must invest enough infrastructure to accommodate all the users and their computing needs. This, in fact, requires that a service provider must be able to estimate approximately the amount of infrastructure needed. The amount of infrastructure needed relies on the number of users and each user's consumption of the resources at peak time.

M.G. Jaatun, G. Zhao, and C. Rong (Eds.): CloudCom 2009, LNCS 5931, pp. 347–358, 2009.

The amount of infrastructure needed is hard to model and predict, but it is relatively easy to model the growth of users. This paper presents a statistic model on the growth of users of a cloud computing service, which provides a simple and intuitive way of estimating the number of users that a service may need to support, hence the amount of infrastructure needed if the resource consumption of each user is given. The statistic model is also been compared with another model to show the benefits of the proposed model. Analysis suggests that the proposed model achieves the objective of estimating the growth of a cloud computing service.

The rest of this paper is organized as follows. Section 2 identifies the challenges of modeling user growth for cloud computing services. Section 3.2 presents a statistic model of the user growth of cloud services in terms of possibility. Section 4 reviews related work and identify the advantages and limitations of existing work. Section 5 presents the result of applying the proposed model on a set of real world data to demonstrate the performance of the proposed model. Section 6 concludes this paper with the contributions and limitations of the model, and also identifies potential future work.

2   Challenges

From a user's point of view, a good cloud computing service is a service that provides infinite amount of resource for computing. Thus a user can always request more resource according to her need. The user can always reduce her consumption of resource according to her need. The service is thus providing an elastic and on-demand service, where resource consumption is adaptive to business need.

From a service provider's point of view, the provision of elastic service is indeed a difficult target to implement for the following reasons.

- The service must provide enough resource to accommodate peak time resource consumption.
- The service must be able to grow according to the growth of the resource consumption.
- The service provider must be able to predict the growth well in advance to allow enough planning and deployment time for the change of infrastructure.

Service providers' capability in the prediction of resource consumption growth is in fact the most fundamental issue for the implementation of elastic service, unless the cost of computing infrastructure is neglectable and the amount of resource is far over sufficient. Therefore, a service provider will, in an ideal scenario, make every effort to deploy just enough amount of resource as the infrastructure to save cost and to meet users' need. It can also argue that, the service provider may trade off between the cost of infrastructure investment and the satisfaction of users. This is certainly true in most of case, but the assumption of this argument is still the same: a service provider must be able to predict the consumption growth.

The prediction of resource consumption growth is not a simple issue. Resource consumption depends on the number of users, average amount of resource needed by each user, etc. Thus predicting the resource consumption growth will involve predicting the growth of users and the growth of resource consumption per user.

In general, the amount of resource needed has a strong mathematic relationship with the number of users that a cloud service is serving. In most of the cases, the amount of resource needed to support a specific number of users for some specific tasks can be approximated if the number of users is given. Therefore, modeling the dynamic of the user set of a cloud computing service is one of the fundamental issues for the prediction of resource consumption growth.

To model the growth of users a cloud service is serving, it is necessary to capture the dynamic of the user set, such as the leaving and the joining of users. Based on the capture property, it is desirable to model the dynamic of the growth of users served by a cloud service, allowing to identify the relationship between the number of users and the time, as well as estimating the number of users at a specific time, etc. The relationship and the estimation should be straight forward and simple for practical usage.

3   Statistic Model of User Growth

Assuming there exist a strong mathematic relationship between the amount of resource a cloud service needs and the number of users the cloud is serving, a model of user growth can serve as building block to construct the model of resource consumption of a cloud. This section aims to develop a user growth model of a cloud service, which enables the approximate estimation of the number of users at any given time, as well as to illustrate the properties of user growth.

3.1   Assumptions

This paper assumes that [1], given a cloud with a large enough number of users, the joining of new users to the cloud and the leaving of existing users from the cloud both follow Poisson distribution. New joining users are independent to the leaving users. Users' joining is a Poisson process satisfying the conditions of 1, 3, and 4. Users' leaving is also a Poisson distribution with the conditions of 2, 3, and 4 held.

1. During the period of $[t, t + \delta t)$, the chance of having a new user joining the cloud is $\lambda \delta t + o(\delta t)$, where $\lambda > 0$ and λ is independent of t.
2. During the period of $[t, t + \delta t)$, the chance of having an existing user leave the cloud is $\mu \delta t + o(\delta t)$, where $\mu > 0$ and μ is independent of t.
3. For any given small enough δt, in the period of $[t, t+\delta t)$, the chance of having more than one user join or leave the cloud is $o(\delta t)$.

---

[1] For the purpose of simplicity, it is also assumed that the number of users that are not served by the cloud service is infinite.

4. Of any non-overlapped periods, the numbers of users joining are independent, and the numbers of users leaving are also independent.

Let X be the number of joining users and Y be the number of leaving users. If a cloud service satisfies all the above conditions, it is called a Double Poisson (DP) system and is denoted as $(X, Y) \sim DP(\lambda, \mu)$.

3.2   Statistic Model

With the assumptions specified in Section 3.1, the follows are obvious conclusions.

1. The number of users having joined the cloud is $p_t(n)$ in the period of $(0, t)$ where
$$p_t(n) = \frac{(\lambda t)^n}{n!} e^{-\lambda t}$$
$p_t(n)$ will be referred to as $p(n)$ in the rest of this paper when no ambiguity or misleading is caused.
2. The number of users having left the cloud is $q_t(n)$ in the period of $(0, t)$ where
$$q_t(n) = \frac{(\mu t)^n}{n!} e^{-\mu t}$$
$q_t(n)$ will be denoted by $q(n)$ in the rest of this paper when it does not cause any ambiguity or misleading.

Let a cloud have M users initially, where M is a large enough number. As the leaving and joining of users can be considered as independent, the relation between the number of users of the cloud and the time can be simplified as follows.

1. In the period $(0, t)$, the possibility of the number of users of the cloud increased from M to $M + N$ $(M \gg N)$ is $A(N)$ where
$$A(N) \approx \sum_{k=0}^{M} (p(N + k)q(k))$$

2. In the period $(0, t)$, the possibility of the number of users of the cloud decreased from M to $M - N$ $(M \gg N)$ is $D(N)$ where
$$D(N) \approx \sum_{k=0}^{M} (p(k)q(N + k))$$

3. In the period $(0, t)$, the possibility of having an increase of the number of users, by no less than N, of the cloud can be computed as below.
$$GA(N) = \sum_{m=N}^{\infty} A(m)$$
$$= \sum_{m=N}^{\infty} \sum_{k=0}^{M} (p(m + k)q(k))$$

4. In the period $(0, t)$, the possibility of having an decrease of the number of users, by no more than N, of the cloud can be computed as below.

$$LD(N) = 1 - \sum_{m=N+1}^{\infty} D(m)$$

$$= 1 - \sum_{m=N+1}^{\infty} \sum_{k=0}^{M} (p(k)q(m+k))$$

Hence, for a cloud with M users initially, the chance of having at least N users remaining in the cloud at the time t is $\varphi(M, N)$ can be computed as follows.

$$\varphi(M, N) = \begin{cases} GA(N-M) & \text{if } N \geq M \\ LD(M-N) & \text{if } N \leq M \end{cases}$$

3.3 Approximation

In order to make the statistic model more practical to use, it is better to simply the statistic model into a simpler format so that it can be computed more efficiently. The main issue for computing the statistic model presented in Section 3.2 is that the model contains infinity as the upper bound for the summation, thus requiring the addition of infinite times. This subsection presents an approximation of the statistic model, which can be calculated in a more practical way.

Let N_1, N_2 be large enough numbers, the approximation of $GA(N)$ can be computed as follows.

$$GA(N) = \sum_{m=N}^{\infty} \sum_{k=0}^{M} (p(m+k)q(k))$$

$$= \sum_{m=0}^{\infty} \sum_{k=0}^{M} (p(m+N+k)q(k))$$

$$\approx \sum_{m=0}^{N_1} \sum_{k=0}^{N_2} (p(m+N+k)q(k))$$

$$= e^{-(\lambda+\mu)t} \sum_{m=0}^{N_1} \sum_{k=0}^{N_2} \frac{(\mu t)^k (\lambda t)^{m+N+k}}{(m+N+k)!k!}$$

$$= GA'(N)$$

The absolute error between $GA(N)$ and $GA'(N)$ can be evaluated as follows.

$$\delta GA = GA(N) - GA'(N)$$

$$\leq \sum_{m=0}^{\infty} \sum_{k=0}^{\infty} (p(m+N+k)q(k)) - e^{-(\lambda+\mu)t} \sum_{m=0}^{N_1} \sum_{k=0}^{N_2} \frac{(\mu t)^k (\lambda t)^{m+N+k}}{(m+N+k)!k!}$$

$$\leq \frac{e^{-\lambda t}(\mu t)^{N_2+1}}{(N_2+1)!} \sum_{m=0}^{N_1} [\frac{(\lambda t)^{m+N+N_2+1}}{(m+N+N_2+1)!}] + \frac{(\lambda t)^{N_1+1+N}}{(N_1+1+N)!}$$

Similarly, it can be concluded that

$$LD(N) = 1 - \sum_{m=N+1}^{\infty} \sum_{k=0}^{N_2} p(k)q(m+k)$$

$$\approx 1 - \sum_{m=0}^{N_1} \sum_{k=0}^{N_2} p(k)q(m+N+1+k)$$

$$= LD'(N)$$

The difference between $LD(N)$ and $LD'(N)$ is

$$\delta LD < \frac{e^{-\mu t}(\lambda t)^{N_2+1}}{(N_2+1)!} \sum_{m=0}^{N_1} [\frac{(\mu t)^{m+N+N_2+2}}{(m+N+N_2+2)!}] + \frac{(\mu t)^{N_1+2+N}}{(N_1+2+N)!}$$

3.4 Improvement of the DP Model

The application of DP model has lots of limitations. One of the most serious limitations is the constant growth rate λ and the constant decay rate μ. The approach we use to make DP model better adapt to real world is piecewise function.

It's not reasonable to evaluate a growth rate variable by a constant value in real situation. But it is sufficiently accurate if assume that each time slice has a different growth rate (or decay rate). But during a time slice, the rate is constant. The piecewise function can be defined as follows.

$$\lambda(t) = \begin{cases} \lambda_1 & \text{if } t_1 \le t < t_2 \\ \lambda_2 & \text{if } t_2 \le t < t_3 \\ \vdots \\ \lambda_n & \text{if } t_{n-1} \le t \le t_n \end{cases} \tag{1}$$

where $\lambda_1, \lambda_2, \cdots, \lambda_n$ and $t_1, t_2, \cdots, t_n$ are constant numbers. And time sequence $\{t_i\}$ is an arithmetic sequence. Its common Difference is length of time slice.

If the property of growth can be described by T continuous functions. let $1 < N_1 < N_2 < \cdots < N_T = n$ Growth rate can be defined as:

$$\lambda_t = \begin{cases} f_1(t) & \text{if } 1 \le t < N_1 \\ f_2(t) & \text{if } N_1 \le t < N_2 \\ \vdots \\ f_T(t) & \text{if } N_{T-1} \le t \le N_T \end{cases} \tag{2}$$

In short, the DP model can describe each constant growth rate period independently. So Formula 1 and Formula 2 are applicable in DP model. But the problem for DP model is that it's not easy to predict the number of users at any time.

4   Related Work

4.1   M/M/1 Model

M/M/1 is a single server queue model that can be used for simulating a simple system. It holds the conditions where [1]:

1. Arrivals are a Poisson process where is shown at Section 3.1.
2. There is one server.
3. Service time follows negative exponential distribution.
4. The population of joining users is infinite.
5. The length of the queue where users wait at can be infinite.

The probability of queue length's (the number of waiting users) distribution function $P_n(t)$ (queue length n and time t) was found by Ledermann and Reuter with spectral theory of birth and death processes [2]. $P_n(t)$ can be described by the formula [1]:

$$
\begin{aligned}
\frac{dP_i(t)}{dt} = {} & (\frac{\mu}{\lambda})^{\frac{x_0-i}{2}} e^{-(\lambda+\mu)t}[-(\lambda+\mu)I_{x_0-i}(*) \\
& + (\lambda\mu)^{\frac{1}{2}}I_{x_0-i-1}(*) + (\lambda\mu)^{\frac{1}{2}}I_{x_0-i+1}(*) + I_{x_0+i+2}(*) \\
& + 2(\lambda+\mu)^{\frac{1}{2}}I_{x_0+i+1}(*) + \mu I_{x_0+i}(*)]
\end{aligned}
$$

where $P_{x_0}(0) = 1$, $I_n(*) = I_n(2t(\lambda\mu)^{\frac{1}{2}})$ is a n-th order bessel function.

The conclusion of M/M/1 is accurate. The advantages of M/M/1 are as follows:

1. M/M/1 model is such a simple model that it's easy for us to understand the construction of the model.
2. The transient solution of M/M/1 model is accurate. It means the conclusion can be used with no errors.

M/M/1 has the following limitations.

1. $P_n(t)$ is not an elementary function. It contains several bessel functions which make it not intuitive.
2. Its complex expression should be simplified and the bessel functions in $P_n(t)$ must be approximated before it is in service.
3. From the application's perspective, gain the accurate $P_n(t)$ formula is not complete.

The model presented in this paper is in fact an approximation and simplification of the M/M/1 model by introducing a new assumption, where the joining and the leaving of users are independent with each other.

The extra condition which is added to DP model is approximate. But if the population of users in the DP system is large enough, the approximation is acceptable. When the joining users and leaving users are far less than the users in current system, the users join in the system or not doesn't influence the number of leaving users. For example, the number of leaving users in a N users' system is much the same as that in a $N + \delta$ system, where $N \gg \delta$.

4.2   Growth Models

A number of growth rate models have been developed for system modeling [3], such as the power function model [4], the Bass model [5], and the modified Bass model [6].

The power function model [4] is defined as

$$W(t) = \frac{t^{k+1}}{k+1}$$

where $W(t)$ is the number of users in the operational phase at time t. This model is rarely used to describe the growth rate of a system. The reason for this is that the parameters of the function are not amenable to interpretation [3].

The Bass model [5] is another model that is capable of modeling the growth of users related to time. The Bass model is defined as

$$\frac{dW(t)}{dt} = (\alpha + \beta\frac{W(t)}{\overline{S}})[\overline{S} - W(t)]$$

where $\overline{S}$ is the population of all potential users excluding the existing users. The Bass model describes the process of how new products get adopted as an interaction between users and potential users. The Bass model assumes a finite set of potential users and models the user growth with respect to time.

Givon et al. [6] presents a modified version of the Bass model, which can be use to estimate the number of licensed users as well as users of pirated copies of the software.

The advantages of these models are that they are capable of modeling the user growth with respect to time. In the case of the Bass model and the modified version, they also take into account the number of potential users and the number of existing users. These allow the above models to forecast the user growth at a given time point. As some of the parameteters are environment dependent, these models can model more complicated systems with better precision than constant growth rate models.

However, One of the serious problems of these models is that they assume the system will strictly follow the mathematical formula, which is a very strong assumption. Most of the real world cases have their environments change along with time. This will incur errors in the calculation and these errors will accumulate and increase as time goes by.

In practice, most things happen in the real world are not always absolute, thus using probability to approximate the number of users is considered to be more reasonable. So instead of giving an absolute growth number of users, DP model only describe the probability of the number of users. Additionally, DP model can not only describe the increasing property, but also adapt to analyze the decreasing property. This characteristic is distinct different from power function model and Bass model.

5 Case Study

This section presents a case study on BTJunkie [7] using the DP model. BTJunkie is one of the most popular BitTorrent search engine, using a web crawler to collect information from other torrent sites. As of the time of this writing, BTJunkie has collected more than 3,000,000 torrent files, and the tracking information of around 10,000,000 p2p file sharing users.

Assuming that the system is already in a dynamic equilibrium (implies $\lambda = \mu$), it can be concluded that the proportion of user increase approximates the proportion of torrent file increase.

$$\frac{NewUsers}{TotalUsers} \approx \frac{NewTorrents}{TotalTorrents}$$

Hence,

$$\lambda = \mu = NewUsers \approx \frac{NewTorrents \times TotalUsers}{TotalTorrents} = 77705 Peers/day$$

Table 1. BTJunkie's Statistic Data

Item	Value	Remark
NewTorrents	1,498	the number of new torrents each day
TotalTorrents	3.29 Mil	the number of total of torrents
TotalUsers	170.66 Mil	the number of total of users (Seeders + Leechers)

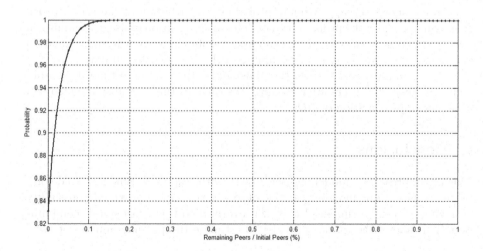

Fig. 1. Approximate User Growth Probability Distribution

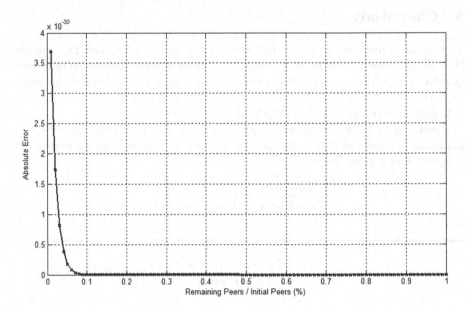

Fig. 2. Approximation Precision

where $NewTorrents, TotalUsers, TotalTorrents$ are quoted from Table 1 and $NewUsers$ is the joining rate (λ) of this system [2].

The units of μ and Peers are set with 10 M for conciseness purpose. It can be concluded that $Peers \approx 17$, $\mu t = \lambda t = 0.077705 \times t \approx 2.33$, where $t = 30$ days. And let $N_1 = N_2 = 17$ which are used for approximation.

Figure 1 shows the approximate probability distribution of the user growth. The figure provides the probabilities of different proportion of users remaining in the system after 30 days. Figure 2 shows the absolute errors of the approximation of different percentage of users remaining in the system after 30 days.

Figure 2 indicates that given the above data, there is more than 97% probability to keep 95% users after 30 days. It's obvious that the absolute errors of using the approximation of $LD(N)$.

6   Conclusions

This paper presents a model on user growth with respect to time for cloud computing services. The model is capable of forecasting the approximate possibility of having a specific number of users with respect to time with simple computation. This allows the service provider to estimate the possible number of users

---

[2] $NewUsers$ is the number of joining users. $TotalUsers$ is the number of all users. $NewTorrents$ is the number of newly collected torrent files of a day. $TotalTorrent$ is the total number of torrent files.

at a given time, thus to plan for the needed amount of resources to serve the users. A case study is given, which suggests that the approximation has achieved a high level of precision.

The contribution of this paper is as follows.

1. This paper identifies the need for user growth modeling in cloud computing. Cloud service providers need such a model to estimate system scales and the amount of resource needed. They also need such a a model to plan for the deployment of the infrastructure based on the user growth in relation to time.
2. This paper presents a user growth model that is capable to provide the approximate possibility of a given number of users at a specific time. Thus service providers can find out the possibilities of having different number of users in the future. Hence service providers can plan for the amount of resources needed and can also plan for the deployment of the infrastructure in terms of time.
3. The model is formalized in an intuitive form, which is easy to interpet. The model involves only limited computation as the benefit of approximation and simplification in the modeling.
4. This paper shows that it is actually possible to model user growth in terms of possibility in addition to modeling user growth in terms of absolute numbers. It is also argued that modeling user growth in terms of possibility is superior to modeling user growth in terms of absolute numbers.
5. This paper conducts related analysis and experiments to verify and test the proposed model, which suggest that the proposed model is capable to approximate the real world with high precision.

The model is not without its limitations. It assumes that there are infinite potential users for a cloud service. This assumption is obviously not very realistic. The model can only deal with variable growth rate systems using pairwise functions by splitting the whole time period into several smaller periods of different fixed growth rates. This introduces more complication in the modeling and more complexity in the computation. While it is more flexible to model user growth in terms of possibility, it is sometime desirable to be able to model user growth in terms of numbers, such as the models discussed inSection 4.2.

Investigation on other modeling methods on user growth and resource consumptions will be the main focus of the future work. Experiements will also be conducted to verify and test the performance of the model.

References

1. Bharucha-Reid, A.T.: Elements of the theory of Markov processes and their applications. Dover Publications, New York (1997)
2. Ledermann, W., Reuter, G.: Spectral theory for the differential equations of simple birth and death processes. Philos. Trans. Roy. Soc. London (1954)
3. Pham, H.: Springer Handbook of Engineering Statistics. Springer, London (2006)

4. Kenny, G.: Estimating defects in commercial software during operational use. IEEE Trans. Reliability 42(1) (1993)
5. Bass, F.M.: A new product growth for model consumer durables. Manage. Sci. 50(suppl. 12), 1825–1832 (2004)
6. Givon, M., Mahajan, V., Muller, E.: Software piracy: Estimation of lost sales and the impact on software diffusion. Journal of Marketing 59(1), 29–37 (1995)
7. BTJunkie: Btjunkie bittorrent website (2009), http://btjunkie.org/

An Efficient Cloud Computing-Based Architecture for Freight System Application in China Railway

Baopeng Zhang[1], Ning Zhang[1], Honghui Li[1], Feng Liu[1], and Kai Miao[2]

[1] Beijing JiaoTong University, No.3 of Shangyuan Residence Haidian District in Beijing
{bpzhang,nzhang1,hhli,fliu}@bjtu.edu.cn
[2] Intel Corporation
kai.miao@intel.com

Abstract. Cloud computing is a new network computing paradigm of distributed application environment. It utilizes the computing resource and storage resource to dynamically provide on-demand service for users. The distribution and parallel characters of cloud computing can leverage the railway freight system. We implement a cloud computing-based architecture for freight system application, which explores the Tashi and Hadoop for virtual resource management and MapReduce-based search technology. We propose the semantic model and setup configuration parameter by experiment, and develop the prototype system for freight search and tracking.

Keywords: Cloud Computing, Batch Data Process, Data Management.

1 Introduction

Cloud computing is novel distributed computing paradigm. It integrates the over-provisioning and under-provisioning computing environment for multi-user, abundant computer resources and various network communication patterns. The broadband networking and the virtualization of computing resources combined with new business models for "pay-as-you-go" resource usage leverage the development of cloud computing. Cloud computing application requirement delivers infrastructure, platform and software function as services, and cloud computing environment provides the scalable, reliable, secure and fault-tolerant supporting for user applications. China railway includes the ministry of railway and eighteen railway bureaus. Those administration parts are physically distributed, and their information system is a complex distributed system. Every railway bureau manages their computing resource and information resource individually.

The railway freight transportation system manages the freight ticket information of china railway. It includes freight ticket sub-system, confirm report sub-system and train dispatching sub-system. The freight ticket is created for describing the freight ID, source place, destination place, detail information of freight once freight is registered for transportation. When the freight is grouping to specific wagon for next railway station and the freight wagon arrive the new railway station, the confirm report information is made for affirming the freight arrival. The freight information is a

M.G. Jaatun, G. Zhao, and C. Rong (Eds.): CloudCom 2009, LNCS 5931, pp. 359–368, 2009.

distributed, mass, and dynamical information resource. For example, there are 120 thousands pieces freight ticket every day in china railway and every piece is 4k byte. The tracking period is 45 days, and the storage life is one year. That means the information to deal with is about 160G per day, and ready-search information is 1T, meantime, every piece of information need keep four to six replica in relative railway bureaus. So, the cloud computing technology can leverage the freight system of china railway over resource sharing, freight search and business integration.

Our aim is to utilize the cloud computing technology to explore the railway application mode for scalability, data backup, dynamic resource management of railway. Based on those considerations, this paper discusses the cloud computing architecture, service deployment, and data management in the distributed freight application environment of China Ministry of Railway.

2 Related Work

As the evolution of on-demand information technology services and products, cloud computing technology has been developed by industry and academic. According to difference of service provision of cloud computing implement, cloud computing incorporates three kinds of service: software as a service(SaaS), platform as a service(PaaS), and Infrastructure as a service(IaaS). Amazon(EC2)[6] played a key role in the development of cloud computing by modernizing their data center. It provides user to allocate entire virtual machines (VM) on demand, which referred to as IaaS. Google's App Engine[10] provides a language-specific APIs and libraries for user to access to computational power, storage and massive amounts of data. Salesforce.com [11] provides a number of high-level software packages for customer relationship management. In addition, Intel Tashi[9], IBM BlueCloud[14], Microsoft Azure[13] and EMC Daoli[15] explore the cloud computing technology in resource management, service application and security.

Most cloud applications support data access and process of data center. MapReduce[2] is originally proposed to optimize large batch jobs such as web index construction. Its opensource implement Hadoop[8] implements the MapReduce based on the Hadoop distributed file system(HDFS) similar to the Google File System[7]. Based on the distributed data process model, some research work is going on in job scheduling[3] and relational data processing support[4], which deals with sharing a MapReduce cluster between multiple users and related heterogeneous datasets.

3 Cloud Computing-Based Freight System Design

According to the MOR application characters and application requirement, some core issues need to deeply discussion.

3.1 Cloud Computing-Based Architecture

Multi-level user: railway user have two categories: customer and administrator user, customer is general user using the railway service. Administrator users manage the application, data, resource and infrastructure of cloud computing environment, according to different authorization in different level of MOR administration scope.

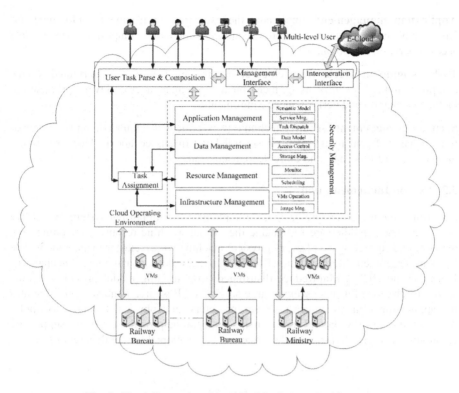

Fig. 1. Cloud Computing- based Freight System Architecture

User task parse and composition: user can utilize the application semantic model and cloud services (provided by cloud computing environment) setup the user task. Moreover, the result should conform to the semantic constraint of user task for improving efficiency and application consistency.

Interoperation Interface: implement seamless interoperation between I-cloud and E-cloud.

Infrastructure management: virtual machine management and image management. It implements resource deployment and manage physical resource and virtual resource. Such as creation, deployment, closedown of virtual machine, instance creation, deployment of computing services image.

Resource management: resource includes the physical resource (computing, storage, and network etc) and virtual resource (user-oriented resource utility management). It implement monitoring, dynamic deploying, load balancing and usage optimization with respect to cloud computing resources.

Data management: manage data storage, data access and data reliability. Data storage includes data semantic description and data distribution. Data access includes access scheduling, access control. Multi-level MOR users have different data access right. Access scheduling leverages the efficiency of data access in different location.

Application management: implement the execution environment deployment, includes application semantic relation, execution of the cloud computing services, data access operation and so on.

Task Assignment Mechanism: cloud computing application is a distributed service composition task. Its task assignment must implement a cross-level optimization, included semantic and performance requirements.

Security management: security technology is critical to cloud computing application. It has different requirement in several level discussed above. Due to it is not main content of this paper, no more deep discussion.

3.2   System Implementation

According to our architecture design, we implement the supporting system. We utilize the Tashi cloud middleware to manage the virtual machine resource, including cpu, memory and storage space of every physical machine within cluster management. The hadoop distributed files system (HDFS) provides data management mechanism. Based on the HDFS, MapReduce distributed programming model provides parallel search mechanism for processing a large-scale data. Resource management integrates the application semantic, infrastructure characters, and physical resource to implement resource allocation and deployment. With the help of those system supporting technologies, application-oriented service can be developed for the different users.

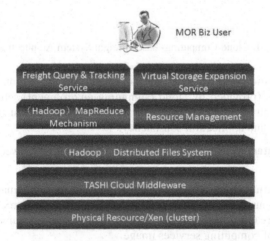

Fig. 2. Cloud Computing- based Freight System Implement.

Hadoop: Hadoop is a open framework for running applications on large clusters built of commodity hardware. The Hadoop framework transparently provides both reliability and data motion for applications. Hadoop implements a computational paradigm named MapReduce resembling the Google[2], where the application task is divided into many small fragments of work job, each of which may be executed or reexecuted on any node in the cluster. In addition, MapReduce runs on a distributed file system (HDFS) that stores data on the compute nodes, providing very high aggregate bandwidth across the cluster. Both MapReduce and the distributed file system are designed so that node failures are automatically handled by the framework. Hadoop have two kinds of node: *name node* and *data node*. Name node manages all the data nodes. Our freight query & tracking service and virtual storage expansion service is implemented on the HDFS and MapReduce mechanism.

Tashi Cloud Middleware: Tashi is a new cluster management system for cloud computing on big data. Development of Tashi is hosted by the Apache Software Foundation's (ASF) Incubator. The initial proposal and web site for this open-source software project can be found at the ASF web site. Key initial contributors include Intel Research Pittsburgh and the Parallel Data Laboratory at Carnegie Mellon University. Big Data applications, which draw from information sources such as web crawls, digital media collections, virtual worlds, simulation traces, and data obtained from scientific or medical instruments , now play a significant role in all aspects of society - from scientific study to enterprise data mining to consumer web applications. These applications, beyond simply operating on data that is big, are also typically data hungry in that the quality of their results improves with the quantity of data available. Consequently, a strong need exists for computing technologies that are scalable-to accommodate the largest datasets possible.

Fortunately, these applications are typically disk bandwidth limited (rather than seek-limited) and exhibit extremely good parallelism. Therefore, commodity cluster hardware, when employed at scale, may be harnessed to support such large dataset applications.

Tashi is designed to support cloud computing applications that operate on Big Data, and it is a virtualization-based cluster management system that provides facilities for managing virtual machines. Users of Tashi are able to create collections of virtual machines that run on the cluster's physical resources. These virtual machine collections form "virtual clusters" that operate on the Big Data stored in the cluster, and when distinctions are necessary, users who create virtual machines in Tashi are called virtual cluster owners. Virtual clusters may host services that are then consumed by clients, users that interact with, but do not own, the virtual machines managed by Tashi.

In our cluster, the configuration of Tashi is as following:

- Start one node(host node) first as it hosts nfs server, then start other nodes later.
- Go to host node, run lvdisplay to check if logic volumn image exists. If not, then install the hadoop image.
- Start Hadoop on the namenode.
- Start cluster manager on host node and input with Tashi hosts parameters.
- Start node manager on all nodes one by one.
- Create virtual machine in some physical machine according to resouce management mechanism, and automatic setup hadoop datanode image.

3.3 MapReduce-Based Freight Search Mechanism

The freight search is important mechanism for freight system to find current information of freight, analyze the freight transportation flow for optimizing the transportation scheduling. So, MapReduce-based freight search mechanism need take account of several core issue for search performance, such as block size optimization, semantic optimization and computing capability optimization.

Semantic Optimization. Freight transportation follows railway connection. Every railway bureau administrates some railway, and manages complicated data information included train, freight, scheduling and so on. According to freight application requirement, the path from the source location to the destination location is specific or limited. In this paper, two kinds of semantic relation are considered, *connection relation* (1) and *subjection relation* (2).

$$C = \{C_{ij} \mid p_i \rightarrow p_j \ i \neq j\}.$$ (1)

Where, C_{ij} defines the connection relation of railway station p_i and p_j.

$$A = \{a_{ik} \mid p_i \in B_k\}.$$ (2)

Where, a_{ik} defines railway station p_i belongs to railway bureau B_k. So the semantic mapping is shown as formula (3), which defines relative railway bureau from source station p_s to destination station p_d within constraints of connection relation and subjection relation.

$$M = \{B_i \mid p_s \xrightarrow[A]{C} p_d\}$$ (3)

For freight search, its source and destination location can determine correlated railway bureau involving the transportation flow in term of railway connection. Freight search can improve search efficiency by avoiding irrespective data set access and following *locality optimization* principle of MapReduce[2].

Based on shortest path principle in freight transportation, we construct semantic mapping model to implement data source selection of freight information. The semantic mapping model has two levels: file-level and block-level. Due to a file is divided into multiple blocks to store in HDFS, the execution level of MapReduce is block. So, the block-level is much finer mapping level. Once a query for freight comes, semantic mapping model can decide the access data set in railway bureau level, which can avoid extra network throughput and computing space. In the process of search, efficient job scheduling algorithms can be utilized to improve throughput and response time [3].

Block Size Optimization. The MapReduce expresses the computation as two functions: Map and Reduce. Map takes an input pair and produces a set of intermediate key/value pairs. Values with same key were passed to Reduce function for final result. In this process, the input data is partitioned into a set of M splits. The input splits can be processed in parallel by different machines. The MapReduce library first splits the input files into M pieces of typically 16 megabytes to 64 megabytes(MB) per piece. According to freight data character, we compare the response time in different data block size and replica number through experiment (**Fig.3.**). In our experiment, every search amount of data is 5G. Every data file size is 256M. It can see that 32M block size achieves the shortest search response time when the replica number is 1. The

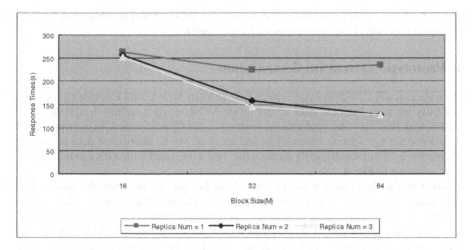

Fig. 3. Search Average Response Time Comparison with Different Block Size and Replica Number

64M block size achieves the shortest search response time when the replica number is 2. The block size of 32M and 64M achieves better response time improvement in the condition of different replica number, while the block size of 16M is not sensible to replica number. So the optimization is tradeoff of the response time and the storage requirement. In freight application, 32M block size and two replicas is optimal choice.

3.4 Virtual Storage Expansion

A geographically distributed enterprise cloud allows resources to be shared among servers at different locations. The server within the cloud can borrow storage space from other servers when it has run out of storage space locally, thereby it can overcome computing bottlenecks in a large enterprise like MOR at certain locations.

When specific railway bureau's storage become shortage, the cloud computing environment can utilize instance of IaaS – Tashi to setup the VM with definite computing, storage capacity and run image instance of hadoop datanode. The current railway bureau can transfer the some data files to the virtual space of new hadoop datanode, or provide replica space for transferring computing service to this virtual space, which lend itself to replica of dynamically increase of freight information in native bureau, and guarantee the freight search all the time.

VM-based Utility Optimization. MapReduce is FIFO mode, search task execute in sequence. In the process of freight search, multi-users and heterogeneous dataset search have low efficiency. Hadoop On Demand (HOD)[12] provides private MapReduce cluster over a large physical cluster using Torque. But HOD have poor utilization problem. Because each private cluster has a static size, some nodes in the physical cluster may be idle. Based on our architecture, we can utilize the Tashi-supported VM management technology to refine the private cluster allocation, from physical cluster to VM cluster. In the other way, the private cluster can achieve the dynamic scheduling. We compare the VM-supported cluster and physical cluster, same search can achieve similar response time, so those virtual machine can be used to support other private cluster for more freight search.

4   Prototype System Implementation

More specifically, the prototype system first showed how Cloud Computing can significantly improve business data access inside MOR, using a railway freight tracking system with real data and applications running in the Cloud testbed. In contrast to the centralized storage system currently in use today at MOR, distributed data storage in an enterprise Cloud significantly reduces the time associated with a data search operation, as shown in **Fig. 4.**

Utilizing the distributed data of each railway bureau, it can in parallel search data information conforming to specific semantic characters. Data sources that a new freight search relies on can be determined according to business routine in the railway and freight transportation. The distributed programming model – MapReduce was used to map the search job to the multiple computers for data search, and reduce the search result integrating the semantic features of freight system. Freight system involves many railway subsystems, such as freight information sub-system, train scheduling sub-system, train confirm report sub-system and so on. Through integrating those heterogeneous dataset, we can achieve more detailed freight transportation information. The freight search interface is shown as **Fig.5**.

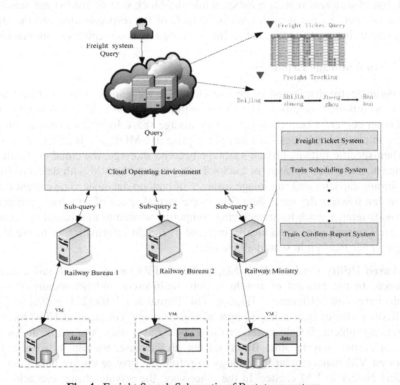

Fig. 4. Freight Search Schematic of Prototype system

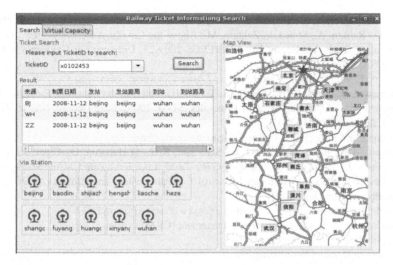

Fig. 5. Search Interface of Prototype system

5   Conclusion and Future Work

This paper introduces a novel cloud computing-based freight system application used in China Ministry of Railway. We use Tashi and Hadoop to implement the application system. Through the semantic and computing mobility optimization mechanism, the system efficiency achieves better improvement. In a word, Cloud computing-based system solution has many advantages, such as efficiency, scalability, reliability and flexibility. Its usage in MOR application has widely application future. In the next step, we will deeply research on image management, and multi-user access control to support cloud computing utility in resource management and usage security.

References

1. Rajkumar, B., Chee, S.Y., Srikumar, V.: Market oriented cloud computing: Vision, hype, and reality for delivering IT services as computing utilities. In: The 10th IEEE International Conference on High Performance Computing and Communications, Dalian, China, September 25-27 (2008)
2. Dean, J., Ghemawat, S.: MapReduce: Simplified data processing on large clusters. In: Proceedings of Operating Systems Design and Implementation (OSDI), San Francisco, CA, pp. 137–150 (2004)
3. Zaharia, M., Borthakur, D., Sarma, J.S., Elmeleegy, K., Shenker, S., Stoica, I.: Job Scheduling for Multi-User MapReduce Clusters. Technical Report No. UCB/EECS-2009-55, University of California at Berkley, USA (April 30, 2009)
4. Yang, H.-c., Dasdan, A., Hsiao, R.-L., Parker, D.S.: Map-Reduce-Merge: Simplified Relational Data Processing on Large Clusters. In: The 26th ACM SIGMOD International Conference on Management of Data (SIGMOD 2007), Beijing, China, June 12-14 (2007)

5. Armbrust, M., Fox, A., Griffith, R., Joseph, A., Katz, R., Konwinski, A., Lee, G., Patterson, D., Rabkin, A., Stoica, I., Zaharia, M.: Above the Clouds: A Berkeley View of Cloud computing. Technical Report No. UCB/EECS-2009-28, University of California at Berkley, USA, February 10 (2009)
6. Amazon Elastic Compute Cloud, http://aws.amazon.com/ec2/
7. Ghemawat, S., Gobioff, H., Leung, S.-T.: The Google File System. In: The 19th ACM Symposium on Operating Systems Principles (SOSP 2003), Lake George, NY, USA, October 2003, pp. 29–43 (2003)
8. Hadoop (2006), http://lucene.apache.org/hadoop/
9. Kozuch, M.A., Ryan, M.P., Gass, R., Schlosser, S.W., O'Hallaron, D., Cipar, J., Krevat, E., López, J., Stroucken, M., Ganger, G.R.: Tashi: Location-aware Cluster Management. In: First Workshop on Automated Control for Data centers and Clouds (ACDC 2009), Barcelona, Spain (June 2009)
10. Google App Engine, http://code.google.com/appengine/
11. Salesforce Customer Relationships Management (CRM) system, http://www.saleforce.com/
12. Hadoop on Demand Documentation, http://hadoop.apache.org/core/docs/r0.17.2/hod.html
13. Microsoft Azure, http://www.microsoft.com/azure
14. IBM Blue Cloud, http://www.ibm.com/grid/
15. EMC Daoli, http://www.daoliproject.org/

Web Server Farm in the Cloud: Performance Evaluation and Dynamic Architecture

Huan Liu and Sewook Wee

Accenture Technology Labs, San Jose, CA 95113, USA
huan.liu@accenture.com, sewook.wee@accenture.com

Abstract. Web applications' traffic demand fluctuates widely and unpredictably. The common practice of provisioning a fixed capacity would either result in unsatisfied customers (underprovision) or waste valuable capital investment (overprovision). By leveraging an infrastructure cloud's on-demand, pay-per-use capabilities, we finally can match the capacity with the demand in real time. This paper investigates how we can build a web server farm in the cloud. We first present a benchmark performance study on various cloud components, which not only shows their performance results, but also reveals their limitations. Because of the limitations, no single configuration of cloud components can excel in all traffic scenarios. We then propose a dynamic switching architecture which dynamically switches among several configurations depending on the workload and traffic pattern.

1 Introduction

When architecting a web server farm, how much capacity to provision is one of the hardest questions to answer because of the dynamic and uncertain nature of web traffic. Many new web applications start with very little traffic since they are hardly known. One day, they may become famous when they hit media (e.g., the slash-dot effect), and visitors flock to the web site, greatly driving up the traffic. Few days later, as the media effect wears off, traffic goes back to normal. Such dramatic change in traffic is often hard, if not impossible, to forecast correctly, both in terms of the timing and the peak capacity required. Thus, it is difficult to determine when and how much capacity to provision.

Even if an amount can be determined, provisioning a fixed set of capacity is not a satisfactory solution. Unfortunately, this is still a common practice today due to the difficulties in forecasting and the long lead time to procure hardware. If the capacity provisioned is less than the peak demand, some requests cannot be served during the peak, resulting in unsatisfied customers. On the other hand, if the capacity provisioned is more than the peak demand, large capacity is wasted idling during non-peak time, especially when the peak never materializes.

Fig. 1 illustrates the degree of fluctuation a web application could experience in reality. Animoto, a startup company, saw its infrastructure needs grow from 40 servers to 5000 servers in a matter of few days when it was widely publicized. Few days following the peak, its infrastructure needs followed a similar degree of

M.G. Jaatun, G. Zhao, and C. Rong (Eds.): CloudCom 2009, LNCS 5931, pp. 369–380, 2009.

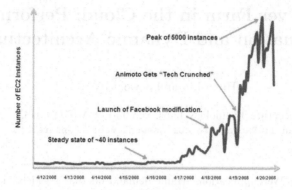

Fig. 1. Animoto's capacity change in response to fluctuation in traffic

shrinkage, eventually settling down at around 50 servers. Such a dramatic change in the infrastructure requirement would mean either gross underprovisioning or gross overprovisioning if a fixed set of capacity is provisioned.

An infrastructure cloud, such as Amazon's EC2/S3 services [1], is a promising technology that can address the inherent difficulty in matching the capacity with the demand. First, it provides practically an unlimited infrastructure capacity (e.g., computing servers, storage) on demand. Instead of grossly overprovisioning upfront due to uncertain demands, users can elastically provision their infrastructure resources from the provider's pool only when needed. Second, the pay-per-use model allows users to pay for the actual consumption instead of for the peak capacity. Third, a cloud infrastructure is much larger than most enterprise data centers. The economy of scale, both in terms of hardware procurement and infrastructure management and maintenance, helps to drive down the infrastructure cost further.

A cloud-based web server farm could dynamically adjust its size based on the user demands. It starts with as little as one web server. During traffic peak, the server farm automatically and instantaneously spawns up more web servers to serve the demand. In comparison, in a traditional enterprise infrastructure, such a scale up both takes a long time (months) and requires manual intervention. Similarly, as traffic goes away, the server farm can automatically shrink down its capacity. Again, scaling down (and stop paying for it) is very hard to achieve in a traditional enterprise infrastructure.

This paper describes how to build this cloud-based web server farm. More specifically, we present the following contributions.

1. **Performance evaluation:** Due to its business model, a cloud only provides commodity virtual servers. Compared to high-end specifically-designed web servers, their base performance and performance bottleneck points are different. We evaluate the performance of cloud components through the SPECweb2005 benchmark [2]. Through the study, we identify several performance limitations of the cloud: no hardware load balancer is available, a software load balancer has limited capacity, web-services-based load balancer

has limited scalability, and traditional techniques to design high performance web server farms do not apply in the cloud for security reasons. To the best of our knowledge, this is the first performance study of cloud from an application's perspective.

2. **Dynamic switching architecture:** Through the performance study, we identify several cloud configurations that can be used to host web applications; each has its own strength and weakness. Based on this evaluation, we propose a dynamic switching architecture which dynamically switches among the configurations based on the workload and traffic patterns. We discuss the criteria for switching, and how to switch in real time.

2 Understanding Cloud Components

Unlike in a traditional infrastructure, where an application owner can choose from any infrastructure component, a cloud only offers a limited number of components to choose from. Understanding the capabilities and limitations of cloud components is a prerequisite for migrating an existing application architecture or designing a new one. In this section, using SPECweb [2], a web server benchmark, we study the performance of several cloud components: 1) Amazon EC2 instances (virtual machines), 2) Google App Engine, 3) Amazon Elastic Load Balancing web services, and 4) Amazon S3. Then, we assess their performance as either a web server or a load balancer.

2.1 Performance Assessment Setup

To assess the performance of cloud components, we use the SPECweb2005 benchmark [2], which is designed to simulate a real web application. It consists of three workloads: *banking*, *support*, and *ecommerce*. As its name suggests, the *banking* workload simulates the web server front-end of an online banking system. It is the most CPU intensive workload amongst the three because it handles all communications through SSL for security reasons and because most of the requests and responses are short. On the other hand, the *support* workload simulates a product support website where users download large files such as documentation files and device drivers. It stresses the network bandwidth the most; all communications are through regular HTTP and the largest file to download is up to 40MB. The *ecommerce* workload simulates an E-commerce website where users browse the site's inventory (HTTP) and buy items (SSL). Therefore, in terms of workload characteristics, it is a combination of the above two. For simple comparison purpose, hereafter we will only focus on *banking* and *support* because they stress the CPU and the network bandwidth, respectively. Note that the memory capacity is often the performance bottleneck in web servers. However, through our extensive benchmark, we observe that EC2 instances have enough memory compared to other resources; a standard instance (*m1.small*, *m1.large*, or *m1.xlarge*) is usually bounded by the CPU because it has relatively more memory than CPU (1.7 GB memory per 1 GHz computing power); a high-CPU instance (*c1.medium* or *c1.xlarge*) is usually bounded by the network bandwidth (800 Mbps).

The SPECweb benchmark consists of two components: the web application and the traffic generator. The web application implements the backend application logic. All pages are dynamically generated and a user can choose from either a PHP implementation or a JSP implementation. The traffic generator generates simulated user sessions to interact with the backend web application, where each session simulates an individual browser. The traffic generator could run on several servers in order to spread out the traffic generating workload.

The performance metric for the benchmark is the number of simultaneous sessions that the web server can handle while meeting its QoS requirement. For each test, the load generator generates a number of simultaneous sessions, as specified by the user, and it collects the response time statistics for each session. A test passes if 95 % of the pages return within TIME_TOLERABLE and 99 % of the pages return within TIME_GOOD, where TIME_TOLERABLE and TIME_GOOD are specified by the benchmark and they represent the QoS requirement. To find the maximum number of sessions, we have to try a number of choices of the number of user sessions until we find one that passes the QoS requirement. The traffic generator is hosted in Amazon EC2 since our Labs' WAN network is not fast enough to support high traffic simulation.

We focus only on the larger cloud platforms – Google and Amazon – because they are currently widely used. Within Amazon, we choose to profile only a few types of EC2 instances[1] to illustrate the capabilities and limitations of these cloud components. The instances we use include the smallest EC2 instance: *m1.small*, which is the smallest and cheapest unit of scaling, thus it provides the finest elastic provisioning granularity. We also evaluate *c1.medium* which has 5 times the computing power of *m1.small*, and *c1.xlarge* which has 20 times the computing power of *m1.small*. All Amazon instances have a half-duplex Gigabit network interface and they are able to transmit at around 800 Mbps (input and output combined) according to our independent tests.

2.2   Amazon EC2 Instance as a Web Server

Table 1 shows the performance results for four different combinations of workloads and EC2 instances. The *m1.small* instance is CPU-bounded and it is not able to saturate the network interface for both the *support* and *banking* workloads. Since *support* is not CPU intensive, we are able to saturate the network with a slight increase in the CPU power by using *c1.medium*. Note that, with linear projection, the largest instance would saturate the network bandwidth for *banking* with 18,000 simultaneous sessions. However, due to a bug with the Rock web server (which they are currently fixing), the *c1.xlarge* instance became saturated with 7,000 simultaneous sessions because the requests from clients were not evenly distributed to all eight CPUs.

---

[1] *Instance* is Amazon's term for a virtual server.

Table 1. Single EC2 instance performance as a web server

	CPU load (%)	Network bandwidth (Mbps)	# of sessions
Banking on *m1.small*	90	60	1,350
Banking on *c1.xlarge*	20	310	7,000
Support on *m1.small*	90	500	1,190
Support on *c1.medium*	20	800	1,800

2.3   Amazon EC2 Instance as a Load Balancer

There are two reasons to use a load balancer for high traffic sites. First, one may want to use *m1.small* as the unit of auto-scaling to minimize the cost. As shown in the last section, *m1.small* is not able to fully utilize the network bandwidth for either workload. Second, a web application may be more CPU-hungry compared to the SPECweb benchmarks and thus may need to scale beyond a single instance's computation capacity.

Since Amazon does not offer a hardware load balancer as a building block, we have to use a software load balancer hosted on a virtual server. Beyond a virtual server's capacity limit, the cloud can further limit the scalability of a software load balancer because of security requirements. For example, for security reasons, Amazon EC2 disabled many layer 2 capabilities, such as promiscuous mode and IP spoofing. Traditional techniques used to scale software load balancers, such as TCP handoff [3] and direct web server return [4], do not work because they assume the web servers could take the same IP address as the load balancer.

There are many software load balancer implementations. Some, such as the Linux Virtual Server [5], do not work in the Amazon environment because they require the ability to spoof their IP address. We profiled several that work well in the Amazon environment including HaProxy [6], Nginx [7] and Rock [8]. Both HaProxy and Nginx forward traffic at layer 7, so they are less scalable because of SSL termination and SSL renegotiation. In comparison, Rock forwards traffic at layer 4 without the SSL processing overhead.

For brevity, we only report the performance of the Rock load balancer running on an *m1.small* instance. For the *banking* workload, an *m1.small* instance is able to process 400 Mbps traffic. Although we are not yet able to run the Rock load balancer on a bigger instance due to a bug in the software, we believe running on a *c1.medium* instance can easily saturate the full network interface speed. For the *support* workload, the requests are mostly for long file transfers. Therefore, the load balancer needs to do less work since each packet is big and there are fewer packets to relay. As a result, an *m1.small* instance is able to handle the full 800 Mbps bandwidth. Because the load balancer does not process the traffic, but rather, only forwards the packets, we expect the results to hold for other web applications.

For each incoming (outgoing) packet, the load balancer must first receive the packet from the client (web server) and then send it to the web server (client).

Therefore, the effective client throughput is only half of the network interface throughput, i.e., even if we saturate the load balancer's network interface, the client throughput is only 400 Mbps.

We must take into account the tradeoff when deciding between running a single web server versus running a load balancer with several web servers. A load balancer can only handle half the traffic because of cloud limitations; however, we can scale the number of web servers in the back end especially if the web application is CPU intensive. A single web server can handle a larger amount of traffic; however, care must be taken to ensure that the CPU does not become the bottleneck before the network interface.

2.4 Google App Engine as a Load Balancer

Because running a web presence is a common usage case for a cloud, there are dedicated cloud offerings specifically targeted at hosting web applications. For example, Google App Engine [9] promises to transparently scale a web application without limit. Although possible in theory, we found that it is not as easy to scale a web application in reality.

Again, we use SPECweb to profile App Engine's performance. Google App Engine is currently limited to the Python and Java programming languages. Java support is still in beta, where many java packages are not allowed to run for security reasons. Since the SPECweb benchmark has only PHP and JSP implementations, it is not straightforward to port to App Engine. Instead, we implemented a load balancer in App Engine. Both the load generators and the web servers run in Amazon EC2, but all web requests are first sent to the load balancer front end. Then, they are forwarded to the web servers in EC2.

Initially when we tested App Engine, even a test with 30 simultaneous sessions fails because we are exceeding the burst quota. Over the course of 5 months (since early Feb. 2009), we have been working with the App Engine team trying to increase our quota limit to enable testing. However, getting around the quota limit seems to require significant re-engineering. As of the date of the submission, we are only able to pass a *banking* test at 100 simultaneous sessions.

Beyond the performance limits, App Engine has a number of other limitations. It currently only supports the Python and Java programming languages. In addition, incoming and outgoing requests are limited to 10 MB per request (it was 1 MB until Mar. 2009), so the SPECweb *support* workload will fail. However, App Engine does have a rich programming library and an integrated persistent data store. When considering App Engine as a possible cloud component for hosting a web site, we must consider the tradeoffs. For example, we choose to design the server farm monitoring capabilities in App Engine to benefit from its rich graphic library and the persistent store for our monitoring data. Since the monitoring engine is only collecting data from a handful of servers, instead of responding to thousands of user queries, App Engine can easily handle the workload.

2.5   Amazon Elastic Load Balancing

Recently, Amazon Web Services announced the dedicated load balancing service: Elastic Load Balancing (ELB) [10]. It provides a virtual load balancer with a DNS name and the capability to add or remove backend web servers and check their health. Because the ELB interface is not inherently tied to a single server, we believe it has the potential to scale and address the performance bottlenecks of software load balancers discussed in Section 2.3. However, our evaluation shows that it currently does not scale better than a single instance Rock load balancer.

Again, we use SPECweb to evaluate the Amazon ELB service. To stress the bandwidth limit, we use the *support* workload. Recall that 1800 sessions saturate the network bandwidth of a single web server running on a *c1.medium* instance and 900 sessions saturate the network bandwidth of a Rock load balancer. Amazon ELB fails to meet the QoS requirement above 850 sessions and refuses to serve more than 950 sessions complaining that the server is too busy. Therefore, we conclude that Amazon ELB's current scalability is about the same as a single instance Rock load balancer.

Interestingly, Amazon ELB is an expensive alternative to the Rock load balancer. Rock load balancer costs $0.10 per hour (the instance cost), whereas Amazon ELB costs $0.025 per hour plus $0.008 per GB of the traffic it processes. Hence, with more than 22 Mbps of traffic, Rock load balancer is cheaper. Moreover, we do not need a load balancer with traffic smaller than 22 Mbps, unless the web application is very CPU intensive, which is not the case for all three workloads in the SPECweb benchmark.

2.6   Amazon S3 as a Web Server for Static Content

Another cloud component that can be used for hosting a web presence is Amazon S3. Although designed for data storage through a SOAP or REST API, it can additionally host static web contents. To enable domain hosting in S3, we have to perform two steps. First, we have to change the DNS record so that the domain name's (e.g., www.testing.com) CNAME record points to S3 (i.e., s3.amazonaws.com). Second, we have to create a S3 bucket with the same name as the domain (i.e., www.testing.com) and store all static web pages under the bucket. When a client requests a web page, the request is sent to S3. S3 first uses the "Host" header (a required header in HTTP 1.1) to determine the bucket name, then uses the path in the URI as the key to look up the file to return.

Since the SPECweb benchmark dynamically generates the web pages, we cannot evaluate S3 directly using the benchmark. Instead, we host a large number of static files on S3, and we launch a number of EC2 *m1.small* instances, each has 10 simultaneous TCP sessions sequentially requesting these files one by one as fast as it is able to. Figure 2 shows the aggregate throughput as a function of the number of *m1.small* instances. As shown in the graph, S3 throughput increases linearly. At 100 instances, we achieved 16 Gbps throughput. Since we are accessing S3 from EC2, the latency is all below the TIME_GOOD and TIME_TOLERABLE parameters in SPECweb.

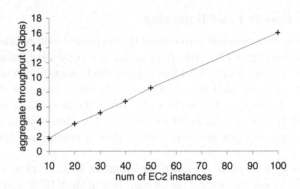

Fig. 2. Aggregate S3 throughput as a function of the number of EC2 instances who simultaneously query S3

The Amazon CloudFront offering enables S3 to be used as geographically distributed content distribution servers. One can simply enable CloudFront on a bucket by issuing a web service API call, and the content is automatically cached in geographically distributed servers. Since we do not have access to a geographically distributed set of servers, we are not able to evaluate CloudFront's performance from the end-users' perspective. But, in theory, it should offer the same scale as S3 with the additional benefits of reduced latency when accessing from remote locations.

Although highly scalable, S3 has two limitations. First, it can only host static content. Second, in order to use S3 as a web hosting platform, a client can only access the non-SSL end point. This is because S3 needs the "Host" header to determine the bucket, and SSL would hide this information.

3   Dynamic Switching Architecture

As we have seen, there is not a single cloud configuration that is able to satisfy requirements of all web applications. For CPU intensive web applications, it is beneficial to use a load balancer so that the computation could be spread across many instances. However, for network intensive applications, it is better to run them on a standalone instance, possibly one with high CPU computation capacity, to maximize the network throughput. Yet, for even more network intensive applications, it may be necessary to use DNS load balancing to get around a single instance's bandwidth limitation.

If an application's workload is mostly static or if the application cannot tolerate the slightest disruption, the performance study we performed in the last section can help to pick the best static configuration. One can pick a cloud configuration based on the peak demand, assuming the peak demand can be accurately forecasted, but the application cannot enjoy the full economical benefits of a cloud when the demand goes away.

Unfortunately, most applications' usage fluctuates over time. It is conjectured [11] that the diurnal pattern of network activity is one of the few invariant properties in Internet, which is mostly due to human-related daily activities. Many web applications exhibit even greater fluctuation, for example, during flash crowd. Moreover, web applications' workload characteristic itself is not static, but rather a mix of many. The overall workload characteristic could shift as the usage pattern shifts. Consider a sample website that hosts entertainment contents. During daytime, a majority of the traffic may be for CPU intensive content search. However, during night time, network intensive multi-media content streaming may dominate.

In this paper, we propose a dynamic switching architecture which chooses the most appropriate cloud configuration based on the application workload. This is enabled by the dynamic capabilities offered by a cloud.

3.1 Cloud Configurations

The dynamic switching architecture may employ one of the following four cloud configurations.

1. **Small instance:** A single web server running on an *m1.small* instance. This is the cheapest way to run a web presence and it is used when the web application is least loaded, such as during the night.
2. **Load balancer:** A single software load balancer running on a *c1.medium* instance. It balances traffic to a number of web servers running on *m1.small* instances (the number of them is automatically adjusted based on the traffic volume) in the backend. Having them as the smallest unit of auto-scaling means that we incur the least cost. As our performance result shows, a single *c1.medium* instance is able to load balance traffic up to its network interface speed, even when the packet size is small.
3. **Large instance:** A single web server running on a *c1.xlarge* instance. A *c1.xlarge* instance has the highest CPU power (20 times greater than *m1.small*) and it can saturate the network interface even for applications that are more CPU intensive than the *banking* workload,
4. **DNS:** For applications that may require more than 800 Mbps bandwidth or more computation capacity than a *c1.xlarge* can provide, there is currently not a single cloud component from Google and Amazon that can handle the workload. We have to resort to DNS level load balancing. In this configuration, we run several web servers on *c1.xlarge* instances (the number of them is automatically adjusted based on the traffic volume). Then, we program the DNS to point to a list of IP addresses, each one corresponding to one instance.

3.2 Switching Mechanism and Criteria

To switch between the different configurations without affecting customers' experience, we leverage a cloud's dynamic capability. Specifically, we use Amazon's

Elastic IP feature to reassign the same IP address to different configurations. When we determine that there is a need to switch, we first launch the new configuration, program the Elastic IP to point to the new configuration, then shut down the old configuration. In our experiments, re-programming Elastic IP takes less than 5 seconds to complete, thus it has a minimal impact on the application. For example, we ran SPECweb *support* workload with 100 sessions and it finished with no error even though we re-programmed elastic IP from one configuration to another. New requests during the re-programming period will be buffered, thus they may experience a longer latency than usual, and existing requests may be terminated. Although some requests may be terminated, a simple retry will fix the problem if we have the session management mechanism in place as described in Section 3.3.

We actively monitor the CPU and bandwidth usage on each instance in order to determine whether we need to switch between the different configurations. The rules for switching are shown in Fig. 3. For clarity, we only show the transition to scale up. The logic to scale down when workload reduces is exactly the opposite.

Each configuration has its own performance limit as follows.

- **Small instance:** CPU capacity is one EC2 Compute Unit, where one EC2 Compute Unit (ECU) provides the equivalent CPU capacity of a 1.0-1.2 GHz 2007 Opteron or 2007 Xeon processor. Network capacity is roughly 800 Mbps.
- **Load balancer:** CPU capacity is unlimited because we can scale an arbitrary number of web servers in the backend. Network capacity is roughly 400 Mbps client traffic. The load balancer network interface will still experience 800 Mbps traffic because it relays traffic to the backend.
- **Large instance:** CPU capacity is 20 ECU. Network capacity is roughly 800 Mbps.
- **DNS:** Unlimited CPU and network capacity. In reality, the network speed is limited by the overall bandwidth into the Amazon cloud. Unfortunately, we are not able to test this limit because we do not have access to hosts outside Amazon that are able to generate a high load.

We make the switching decision when the workload approaches the capacity of a configuration. The configuration we switch to depends on the projection whether the current workload will overload the new configuration. Note that, depending on the application characteristics, we may not switch from one configuration to the immediate next configuration. For example, let us consider a web application that is very CPU intensive. It would run fine under the **load balancer** configuration since we can unlimitedly scale the number of web servers sitting behind the load balancer. However, when the aggregate traffic exceeds 400 Mbps, we may not be able to switch to a **large instance** configuration as a *c1.xlarge* instance may not be able to handle the CPU workload. Instead, we will switch to the **DNS** configuration directly when traffic increases. We make this decision automatically based on the measured traffic consumption and CPU load, and then project the workload on the target configuration.

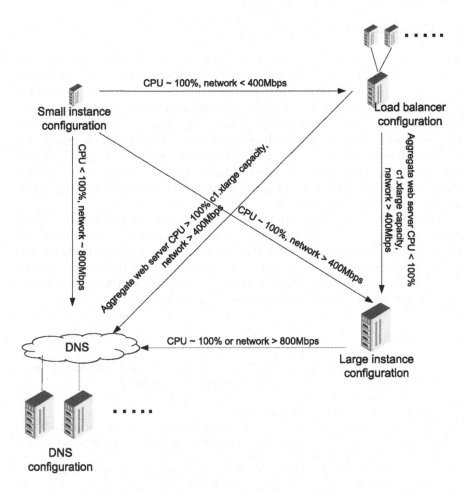

Fig. 3. Switching decision logic when switching to a higher configuration

3.3   Session Management

To avoid state replication, the dynamic switching architecture requires the session states to be stored in the client, typically in the form of a browser cookie. If the server state can be captured compactly, the server can set the entire state in a browser cookie. When the client browser makes the next request, the state is returned in the cookie in the request, so that the server (which can be different from the original server after configuration switching) can decipher the last state. If the server state is large, it can be captured in a central database and the server only needs to return a token. Since the central database will remain the same across configuration changes, a new server can still look up the complete previous state. Since the central database only captures state information, it is easier to make it sufficient scalable to handle the whole web application.

4   Conclusions

In this paper, we investigate how to build a web server farm in a cloud. We present a benchmark performance study of the various existing cloud components, which not only shows their performance results, but also reveals their limitations. First, a single web server's performance is an order of magnitude lower than the state-of-art web server hardware solutions. Second, the performance of a software load balancer based approach is limited by both a single network interface and traffic relaying, which halves its effective throughput. Third, both Google App Engine and Amazon's Elastic Load balancing fall short of their promise of unlimited scalability. Finally, Amazon S3 scales the best, but it is only a viable option for static content.

Due to these limitations, there is not a single configuration that can satisfy all traffic scenarios. We propose a dynamic switching architecture which can switch between different configurations based on detected workload and traffic characteristics. We discuss the switching criteria and how we use the cloud's dynamic capability to implement the architecture. The dynamic switching architecture achieves the highest scalability while incurring the least cost.

References

1. Amazon Web Services: Amazon Web Services (AWS), http://aws.amazon.com
2. SPEC: Specweb2005 benchmark, http://spec.org/web2005/
3. Hunt, G., Nahum, E., Tracey, J.: Enabling content-based load distribution for scalable services. Technical report (1997)
4. Cherkasova, L.: Flex: Load balancing and management strategy for scalable web hosting service. In: Proceedings of the Fifth International Symposium on Computers and Communications, ISCC 2000, pp. 8–13 (2000)
5. LVS: Linux virtual server project, http://www.linuxvirtualserver.org/
6. HaProxy: HaProxy load balancer, http://haproxy.1wt.eu/
7. Nginx: Nginx web server and load balancer, http://nginx.net/
8. Accoria: Rock web server and load balancer, http://www.accoria.com
9. Google Inc: Google App Engine, http://code.google.com/appengine/
10. Amazon Web Services: Elastic Load Balancing,
    http://aws.amazon.com/elasticloadbalancing/
11. Floyd, S., Paxson, V.: Difficulties in simulating the internet. IEEE/ACM Trans. on Networking 9(4), 392–403 (2001)

SPECI, a Simulation Tool Exploring Cloud-Scale Data Centres

Ilango Sriram

University of Bristol, Department of Computer Science,
Merchant Venturers Building, Woodland Road, Bristol BS81UB, United Kingdom
isriram@cs.bris.ac.uk

Abstract. There is a rapid increase in the size of data centres (DCs) used to provide cloud computing services. It is commonly agreed that not all properties in the middleware that manages DCs will scale linearly with the number of components. Further, "normal failure" complicates the assessment of the performance of a DC. However, unlike in other engineering domains, there are no well established tools that allow the prediction of the performance and behaviour of future generations of DCs. SPECI, Simulation Program for Elastic Cloud Infrastructures, is a simulation tool which allows exploration of aspects of scaling as well as performance properties of future DCs.

Keywords: Cloud computing, data centre, middleware, scaling of performance, simulation tools.

1 Introduction

The current trend towards cloud computing drives the demand for IT resources provisioned from data centres (DCs). Economies of scale accelerate the growth in the size of DCs, and over the coming decades are very likely to lead to DCs several orders of magnitude larger than the biggest ones today. IBM's project Kittyhawk already has the vision of one day building a DC for high performance computing that is big enough to host a single application as big and powerful as today's entire internet [1].

However, not all properties are expected to scale linearly when adding more components and increasing the scale of DCs. Further, the number of components will be so large as to impose "normal failure". For example with 500,000 servers in the DC, if the average life expectancy of a server is three years and the time to a temporary failure a few months [2], then on average 650 servers will need to be replaced every day with multiple temporary failures every minute. The state of near permanent hardware failures has to be taken into account by the DC's resilience mechanisms. Furthermore, load-balancing of virtual machines will cause continuous dynamics in the system. These constant changes have to be taken into consideration when assessing the overall performance capabilities of a data centre.

In most engineering fields there are predictive tools that allow simulation of engineered products that are not yet built. While in other domains these can model the following generations of technology with high precision given the computing

M.G. Jaatun, G. Zhao, and C. Rong (Eds.): CloudCom 2009, LNCS 5931, pp. 381–392, 2009.

resources, such as SPICE for circuits on microchips [3], there is only limited under-standing, and there are no well-established predictive tools for data centres. We pro-pose SPECI, Simulation Program for Elastic Cloud Infrastructures, a simulation tool that enables exploration of scaling properties of large data centres. The aim of this project is to simulate the performance and behaviour of data centres, given the size and middleware design policy as input.

The rest of this paper is organised as follows. Section 2 discusses cloud computing and its current state which forms the motivation for this work and introduces middle-ware of data centres. Section 3 introduces the related work in the field of cloud com-puting, and introduces Simkit, the simulation framework that was used. Section 4 explains how scalable middleware will be executed at the node level, and that the method used to communicate with the nodes will partially determine the performance overhead of the data centre: in this section a simplified problem of communicating aliveness of components for the resilience component is introduced; this builds the basis for SPECI. Section 5 explains the current architecture of SPECI. A case study with SPECI was conducted and is presented in Section 6, before Section 7 closes with discussion of planned future work and conclusion.

2 Background

2.1 Cloud Computing

Cloud computing is a growing form of IT provision, where resources are delivered as a service from data centres. The advent of large-scale, commodity-computer data centres built at low-cost locations is a driver of this technology.

There has been a long debate about what cloud computing stands for. This is com-ing to an end, and analysts' position papers have converging definitions, such as Gartner [4], Forrester Research [5], and The 451Group [6]. Recently, further, a widely accepted working definition of Cloud Computing has been published by the American NIST institute [7]. In general an IT provision is cloud computing, if it is (1) delivered as a service (2) using Internet technologies from (3) massively scalable (elastic) re-sources which are generally (4) shared with other customers (multi-tenancy), where (5) resources are distributed dynamically and redistributed on demand. In addition to this, cloud computing is an economic model of billing resources (6) by consumption in metered quality and quantity (pay-as-you-go).

There is a differentiation between public clouds and private clouds. While public clouds are run by utility providers, private clouds are owned, operated, and under control of the company that uses them. Private clouds nevertheless use the same ser-vice technology and offer interoperability. This allows elasticity into the public cloud which is called cloudbursting, so that consumers can use public clouds if they need additional resources.

In practice, cloud computing is delivered in three forms: Infrastructure as a Service (IaaS), Platform as a Service (PaaS) and Software as a Service (SaaS). IaaS provides bare resources or Virtual Machines (VMs). PaaS goes beyond the bare provision of resources, and gives consumers a preconfigured platform for their work. With PaaS, developers can develop the software they are working on, but do not have to care about requirements such as an SDK or a database, or a framework for scaling the application to use further resources. These requirements are provided by the platform. Finally with SaaS, ready to use hosted software solutions are provided to consumers.

Industry analysts are in consent that the development of mature cloud computing is well underway. Although cloud computing is not likely to completely replace traditional IT in the near future, for some application areas it is set to replace current IT delivery from in-house DCs [9]. However precise the figures are, the turn towards cloud computing is obvious, and it will accelerate the demand for DCs of increasing scale. The more cloud computing gets adopted and standardised, the less qualitative differences between offers will exist, and the more provisions will be differentiated purely on cost. To further cut costs, economies of scale will bring in a demand for even larger DCs. As mentioned above, however, not all properties in DCs and its middleware will scale linearly and it is not known how the behaviours of following generations of DCs are going to be. There is lack of predictive simulation tools; this is something SPECI is addressing.

2.2 Normal Failure and Middleware Scalability

Cloud data centres are built using commodity hardware, and can be divided into racks, blades, and VMs. Unlike in high performance computing (HPC) where DCs are often custom-built for the purpose of the computations and a significant part of computing power is gained from graphical processing units (GPUs), cloud DCs rely on inexpensive traditional architecture with the key components being CPUs, memory, discs, and network. As economies of scale are driving the growth of these DCs, the sheer number of off-the-shelf components used in coming decades in combination with each component's average life cycle will imply that failure will occur continually and not just in exceptional or unusual cases. This expected near-permanent failing of components is called "normal failure". For cost reasons, the DC operator will leave the failed components in place and from time to time replace the blades on which failure occurred or even entire racks on which several blades have failed. The impact of failure and resilience or recovery needs to be taken into account in the overall performance assessment of the system.

The components of the DCs are tethered by a software layer called middleware, which takes care of job scheduling, load-balancing, security, virtual networks, and resilience. It combines the parts of the DC together and is the management layer of the DC. When the numbers of components in the DC increases, the middleware has to handle it. It is unlikely that all properties in middleware will scale linearly when scaling up the size of DCs. Currently, there is a lack of predictive tools or methods to estimate the performance of the middleware and thus of the DC before building it.

Therefore, there is a need for simulation tools that can help us evaluate the behaviour and performance with reproducible results, prior to designing and building such DCs. In the absence of such simulation tools one has to rely on theoretical simplified models or build the system and simply hope it performs well. The latter is undesirable and imposes financial drawbacks, if systems can't be tuned before developing and deploying.

3 Related Work

3.1 Cloud Computing

So far there are only a few scientific publications on technologies that are enabled by cloud computing, such as CloneCloud [10] which enables resource intensive computations like face recognition on smartphones by automatically and transparently cloning the context of the computations into the cloud. We expect to see an increase in academic publications describing new technologies, but at the moment the majority of publications in cloud computing are either management articles or come from practitioners of utility computing and grid computing.

In the area of performance assessment of cloud DCs, there is some preliminary work going on within the Open Cirrus project [11]. They have built a cloud research test bed running Eucalyptus [12], which is an open source implementation of the EC2 interface. However, so far they are only looking at the performance of individual virtual machines in cloud environments at Amazon EC2 in comparison to execution in local DCs, and not at the performance capabilities of the entire DCs.

Vishwanath et al. [18] have looked into performance and cost for datacenters that consist of modularized shipping containers which are not serviced for hardware faults until the entire container gets replaced. Further, the HP Cells as a Service project [13] is developing a prototype middleware and management system for cloud infrastructures that is scalable, reliable and secure. While it achieves security using virtual machines, virtual storage volumes and virtual networks, details of how they solve reliability and tolerate the continuous failures that occur in large-scale DCs, and how they solve scalability performance issues, are not yet public.

There is no known work so far on predicting scaling issues for future generations of commodity-computer DCs. However, there is CloudSim [14], a simulation framework to evaluate the performance of cloud computing infrastructure. The simulator is built on top of a grid computing simulator (GridSim) and looks at the scheduling of the execution application, and the impact of virtualisation on the application's performance. However, in this project our interest is more on the DC provider side. We assume that the cloud elasticity is big enough to not reach bottlenecks in the execution of applications, but we do want to know how the overall DC and in particular the middleware that tethers the network of virtual services can perform with increasing numbers of components. Further, we believe that grid architecture and virtualisation technique used for cloud computing are two competing technologies that will not be used in combination. Running a grid under the virtualisation layer adds significant complexity without offering any obvious advantage.

3.2 Simulation Method: Simkit

In the absence of real test beds, of alternative physical representations, or of precise formal models, simulation helps in exploring assumptions about models before building the systems. Discrete event simulations (DES) [15] are a type of simulation where events are ordered in time, maintained in a queue of events by the simulator, and each processed at given simulation time. This means the model is time based, and takes into account resources, constraints and interactions between the events as time passes.

Central to DES are a clock and an event list that tells what steps have to be executed. In order not to re-implement common features of DES, SPECI uses an existing package for DES in Java. There exist several such packages and toolkits, and we chose SimKit [16] which was one of few Java packages that were updated recently. It implements the clock using a queue of events, each of which is associated with a start time. The computation of the event then takes place with duration of zero time interval. When the computation of the event has finished, the clock advances to the time of the next event in the schedule. Simkit also offers many distributions for random-number generation.

Simulation tools are common in other domains: For example in the microelectronics industry there is the circuit simulator SPICE [3], that allows one to simulate the behaviour of future designs of chips with high precision before actually building them, given the computing resources. With the help of this simulation tool better chip designs can be found, and verified quicker and at lower cost. Similarly, SPECI is intended to give us insights into the expected performance of DCs when they are designed, and well before they are built.

4 SPECI Example: Scalable Middleware

DCs are managed by middleware which provides functionality such as job scheduling, load-balancing, security, virtual networks, and resilience. Because many of these settings change very frequently, it needs to continuously communicate new policies to the nodes. Scalable middleware can either manage its constituent nodes using central control nodes, which is a poorly scaling hierarchical design, or it can manage the DC using policies, which are broken into components that can be distributed using peer-to-peer (P2P) communication channels and executed locally at each node. This better scalable solution can cause a problem of timeliness of how quickly updated policies will be available at every node, and of consistency whether the same policies are available and in place everywhere. A certain overhead load for the management will be generated in either case, which will determine the performance loss when scaling the DC by adding more components. [17]

As a first step, we have built a simulator to observe the behaviour of part of the middleware that recognises failed components across the network of systems. This failure communication mechanism can be seen as a simplified substitution for the policy distribution problem.

We were interested in the behaviour of a system with a large number of components, where each component can be working correctly or exhibiting a temporary or permanent failure. Failures occur frequently in large DCs given the number of components and the expected lifetime of each of them. Any one component cooperates with some of the other components, is thus interested in the aliveness of these and performs queries to find this out. As the number of components increases, the number of states that have to be communicated over the network increases. We need to know what happens with our system in terms of how well in time can the states be communicated and at the cost of what load. This setup is of interest to any computing facility with such a large number of components where some will be near permanently failing or other changes need to be communicated frequently. To find out how various protocols may scale, and how quickly or whether at all a consistent view of the state of cooperating nodes can be achieved under certain conditions, a set of simulation experiments was set up, as described in the following paragraphs.

There is a number (n) of nodes or services connected through a network. Each of these nodes can be functioning (alive) or not (dead). To discover the aliveness of other nodes, each node provides an arbitrary state to which other nodes can listen. When the state can be retrieved the node is alive, otherwise it is dead. The retrieval of aliveness of other components is called "heartbeat". Every node is interested in the aliveness of some of the other nodes, the amount of "some" being configurable. Each node maintains a subscription list of nodes in whose aliveness it is interested. We are interested in how the implementation of the heartbeat retrieval affects the system under given configurations, when the total number of nodes n increases.

Several architectures of heartbeat retrieval could be possible. First, there could be central nodes that collect the aliveness of all other nodes and then inform any node interested in any particular state. Second, there could be a hierarchical design where depending on the number of hierarchy levels certain nodes would gather the information of some other nodes, and make them available to their members and to the node next higher in the hierarchy. Third, there could be a simple P2P mechanism where any node simply contacts the node of interest directly. Then, there could be a smarter P2P protocol where a contacted node would automatically reply with all aliveness information it has available of other relevant nodes.

The investigation reported here was set up to observe the behaviour of the overall system under these protocols and various change rates when the number of nodes involved scales up. The simulations address a number of questions. The first question of interest is, what the overall network load is for each of the above protocols under given settings and size, and how much data has to be sent over the network in a given time period. Second, there is significant interest in how the "time-for-consistency" curve of the system looks like. This means, after simultaneous failure or recovery of a number of nodes, after how many time-steps changes are propagated through the entire system, and if there are continuous failures appearing, how many nodes have a consistent view of the system over time? It is of further interest to see how many time-steps and how much load it takes until new or recovered nodes have a consistent view of the system, and how many time-steps it takes to recover after failure of a large number n of nodes, or for recovery of the entire network. There is also interest in the trade-off between timeliness and load for each of the protocols in the sense of how much extra load will be required to retrieve a better or more consistent view. In other words, for how much load can one get what degree of timeliness?

5 Simulator Architecture

The implementation of SPECI is split in two packages, one represents the data centre layout and topology, and the other one contains the components for experiment execution and measuring.

The experiment part of the simulator builds upon SimKit, which offers event scheduling as well as random distribution drawing. SimKit has preconfigured pseudo random classes for common distributions, which return the same value for repeated executions. This makes it possible to execute repeated runs with modified settings, and in each run to receive the same random draws, and thus the same scheduling sequence and scheduling times for events.

The simulation entry class is a wrapper class that contains the configurations of all runs. It triggers the Simkit engine to start the simulations and handles the statistical analysis of the output once the runs have terminated. The Simkit engine always starts simulations by calling the method doRun() of all existing objects in the project where implemented. These are used to start the experiments, and need to trigger accordingly configured parameter change listeners or place new events on the scheduling engine. In this simulator, there is only one doRun() method in the singleton handler. This method creates the DC setup from the data centre layout package with the specifications provided. It then adds three types of events to the event scheduler: probing events, update events, and failure events. The first probing event is generated at 2.0 seconds simulation time to allow instantiation before measuring potential inconsistencies in the system. When this event is triggered, all subscriptions are tested for inconsistencies against the real state and the total number passed on to a class for collecting tally statistics of the simulation model. Before the probing event terminates, it reschedules itself for the next execution 1.0 seconds later than the current simulation time. Thus, every second a monitoring probe is passed on for an evaluation after termination of the simulation. Further, the handler generates one update event for every node in the data centre. This event triggers the node to update the list of its subscriptions. These heartbeat retrieval events are drawn from a uniform distribution with a delay between 0.8 and 1.2 seconds and reschedule themselves with a delay from the same distribution. Similarly, the handler schedules the occurrence of the first failure. The time to the next failure is variable in our experiments and has to be specified in form of a parameterised random function. When the failure event is triggered, it picks a node at random which it will set to have failed. If the failure function picks a node that is already failed, it will act as repair event and bring the component back alive. Alternatively, failed components are not repaired, and kept until the entire shipping container is replaced, as proposed in Vishwanath's [18] DC model.

The data centre layout package contains classes for each type of component in the data centre, such as nodes and network links. These components mimic the operations of interest in the observed data centre, such as the transfer of network packets, maintaining subscriptions to other nodes, and keeping subscriptions up to date using the policy chosen for the experiment. The components have monitoring points that can be activated as required by the experiment. As simplification the network topology assumes a one hop switch, as this work is not interested in routing and the load on parts of the network, but rather on individual network links associated to a node and the entire network. The data centre package further contains a component that maintains a global view of the data centre to deal with the connection and referral logic, which is only used when the topology chosen is a centralised heartbeat retrieval or policy distribution, such as the central or hierarchical one. In the central case this is a list of providers, which pass on information to all other nodes. In the hierarchical case, the global view knows of the hierarchy levels, and which node ought to request information from which other node, as described in Section 4. If the setup configuration uses the simple P2P or transitive P2P communication channel, then the communication logic is dealt by the nodes, as in this case only a local view of the system is required.

Depending on the used policy, some, none or all nodes can act as providers and pass on information they have about other nodes. In reality this passing on can cause delayed information, as the information stored and passed on is not necessarily real time. In this simulator there is a configurable threshold of say one second, which is the maximum permitted age information can have to still be passed on. If the information is older, the providing node will not pass on this data, but instead retrieve newer data by the respective mechanism. If nodes are provider nodes, they have the option to only accept a maximum number of requests per time interval.

In the initialisation phase at runtime, the simulator creates an object for each node and network link in the data centre, subscribes all nodes to some other ones with a distribution as specified in the configuration, and loads the communication policy for the setup. The rest of the runtime is entirely driven by the event queue. The model terminates when the specified simulation time has expired. The simulator will then calculate statistics collected by tally statistics classes. Further more detailed monitoring data is written to files. Therefore, while each object is retrieving the heartbeat of its subscriptions, the load generated is monitored, and aggregated access counts per component over a configurable duration stored to a file. Similarly, when a failure occurs, the time and the number of nodes which have become inconsistent with the actual state of the landscape gets saved to another file. After the simulations are executed these data files can be visualised independent of the simulator.

6   Case Study

In this section, we present a case study made using SPECI in which we observe the number of nodes that have an inconsistent view of the system. This is the case if any of the subscriptions a node has contains incorrect aliveness information. We measure the number of inconsistencies by probing the count every second. After an individual failure occurs, there are as many inconsistencies as there are nodes subscribed to the failed node. Some of these will regain a consistent view before the following observation, and the remaining ones will be counted as inconsistent at this observation point. If the recovery is quicker than the time to the next failure at the following observations less nodes will be inconsistent until the curve drops to zero, and the inconsistency curve could look like Figure 1. This probing was carried out while running SPECI with increasing failure rates and scale. Runs were carried out for DC sizes of 10^2, 10^3, 10^4, and 10^5 nodes. Assuming the number of subscriptions grow slower than the number of nodes in a DC, we set the number of subscriptions fixed to the square root of the number of nodes.

For each of these sizes a failure distribution was chosen such that on average in every minute 0.01%, 0.1%, 1%, and 10% of the nodes would fail. Because this work is essentially exploratory, a gamma distribution and a pair of coefficients that would result in the desired number of failures were picked. For each pair of configurations 10 runs, each lasting 3600 simulation time seconds, were carried out and the average number of inconsistencies along with its standard deviation, maximum, and minimum number were observed. The half width of the 95% confidence intervals (95% CI) was then calculated using the Student's t-distribution for small or incomplete data sets.

Figure 2 shows that the average number of inconsistencies increases when the failure rate increases, and also when the number of nodes increases. Figure 3 shows the same data as Figure 2, but the first few data points are plotted on a linear scale. This makes the confidence intervals visible, and one can see for small DCs or small failure rates the two protocols differ insignificantly. But as these numbers increase, the mean of one protocol moves out of the other protocol's confidence interval, and when the sizes get bigger the confidence intervals get distinct as can be seen for 1000 nodes and 1% failure rate. This shows that with growing size and failure rates, the choice of the protocol becomes more significant, and also that the P2P protocol scales better for the objective of low inconsistencies under the given simplifications. The surprising result here is, given there were identical polling intervals, that the transitive P2P was expected to be the protocol with the biggest delay due to the fact that delays would accumulate with forwarding. However, for such an accumulating of age for aliveness data to be observable it is necessary to have larger numbers of subscriptions or to generate the subscriptions with a structure so that the chance of subscribing to a node is higher if the node has similar subscriptions, because only then enough transitive subscription sharing is available. Figure 4 shows inconsistencies grouped by failure rates. To compare the values of different DC sizes, the number of inconsistencies is normalised by the number of nodes. At the same time, the number of inconsistencies still grows with the size of the DC. This suggests that none of the protocols scale linearly. On the other hand, when grouping by DC sizes, these normalised values increase by one order of magnitude when the failure rate increases by such. This suggests that the failure tolerance of both protocols appears robust.

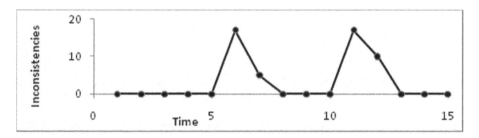

Fig. 1. Inconsistency probes during recovery from failures

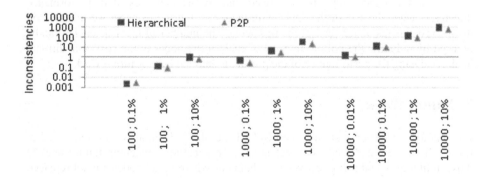

Fig. 2. The mean of Inconsistencies increases with the failure rate

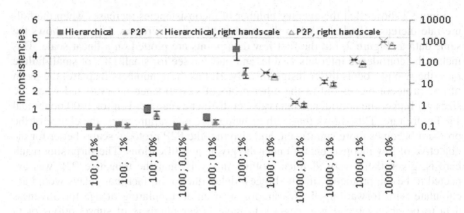

Fig. 3. Mean of Inconsistencies and their confidence intervals, linear vertical scale for smaller and logarithmic scale for larger values. With increasing size differences become significant.

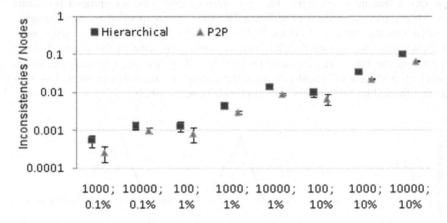

Fig. 4. Inconsistencies normalized by number of nodes. Both protocols scale linearly with the failure rates, but not with the number of nodes.

The careful reader might have noticed that we were interested in performance drawbacks when the size of the data centre increases, but in this paper we focussed on the inconsistencies under each of the protocols. The number of inconsistencies can be reduced by reducing the polling interval of each of the nodes at the cost of additional load. Analysing the performance of the protocols shall be left for future work.

7   Future Work

Imminently, further case studies with SPECI are planned. First, we are interested in using other failure and recovery mechanisms. This includes matching failure rates to those in literature and using recovery mechanisms where failed nodes are not replaced until the entire building unit gets replaced. Second, runs for larger DC sizes are to be carried out. In addition it should be observed how the system behaves when using different numbers of subscriptions. In combination with the transitive P2P this could show whether any benefits or differences from node cliques can be found. Further, correlated failure and conditions where a huge amount of nodes or the entire DC fail at the same time need to be simulated. Then, it is necessary to combine the simulation's load measurements with measurements of inconsistencies during varying failure rates. This can show what the failure and load thresholds which prevent the system from ever reaching a consistent status are, and what settings make it impossible for the system to recover. These simulations can also be used to suggest a load and consistency trade-off for middleware mechanisms.

The following step is to look for alternative models to verify the findings. These could be mathematical or formal models, and for smaller DCs comparison with values that can be measured. For medium term future work, it is necessary to expand SPECI. At the moment it looks at one dimensional state communication problems. Real middleware has to distribute several policies over the network. It needs to account for VMs and load-balancing, security, and job scheduling. SPECI must become capable of modelling such multidimensional problems that middleware is facing in order to access the scaling properties of future cloud-scale DCs.

8 Conclusion

When designing scalable middleware, centralised orchestration will not be feasible; instead it will be necessary to have the system orchestrate itself with just the given local view and without knowledge of the entire system. Even then, it is expected that DCs do not scale linearly when they get larger and contain more components. Practitioners need to know about the scaling properties before building these DCs. In this paper we have presented SPECI, a simulation tool which allows exploration of aspects of scaling as well as performance properties of future DCs. SPECI was then used to look at inconsistencies that arise after failures occur, and it could be shown at the example of the communication of failures, that when the size and failure rate of the DC increases, a distributed DC management becomes favourable.

Acknowledgements

This project is part of a PhD funded by Hewlett-Packard Labs' Automated Infrastructure Lab. We thank Hewlett-Packard for the interest in this topic and support.

References

1. Appavoo, J., Volkmar, U., Waterland, A.: Project Kittyhawk: building a global-scale computer: Blue Gene/P as a generic computing platform. SIGOPS Oper. Syst. Rev. 42(1), 77–84 (2008)
2. Failure Rates in Google Data Centers,
   http://www.datacenterknowledge.com/archives/2008/05/30/
   failure-rates-in-google-data-centers/

3. Nagel, L.W.: SPICE2: A Computer Program to Simulate Semiconductor Circuits. Technical Report No. ERL-M520, University of California, Berkeley (1975)
4. Cloud, SaaS, Hosting, and Other Off-Premises Computing Models. Gartner Research (2008)
5. Gillett, F.E.: The New Tech Ecosystems of Cloud, Cloud Services, and Cloud Computing. Forrester Research (2008)
6. The 451 Group: Partly Cloudy: Blue Sky Thinking about Cloud Computing (2008)
7. Mell, P., Grance, T.: Draft NIST Working Definition of Cloud Computing. National Institute of Standards and Technology, Information Technology Laboratory (2009)
8. Clearwater, S.H., Huberman, B.A.: Swing Options: a Mechanism for Pricing IT Peak Demand. In: International Conference on Computing in Economics (2005)
9. Gillett, F.E.: There are Three IT Architectures, Not One. Forrester Research (2007)
10. Chun, B., Maniatis, P.: Augmented Smart Phone Applications Through Cloud Clone Execution. In: HotOS XII (2009)
11. Baun, C., et al.: Elastic Cloud Computing Infrastructures in the Open Cirrus Testbed Implemented via Eucalyptus. In: ISGC 2009 (forthcoming 2009),
    http://bit.ly/2Ck3tv
12. Nurmi, D., Wolski, R., Grzegorczyk, C., Obertelli, G., Soman, S., Youseff, L., Zagorodnov, D.: The eucalyptus open-source cloud-computing system. In: CCGrid, 9th IEEE/ACM International Symposium on Cluster Computing and the Grid, pp. 124–131 (2009)
13. HP Labs: Cells as a Service,
    http://www.hpl.hp.com/open_innovation/cloud_collaboration/projects.html
14. Buyya, R., Ranjan, R., Calheiros, R.N.: Modeling and Simulation of Scalable Cloud Computing Environments and the CloudSim Toolkit: Challenges and Opportunities. In: Proceedings of the 7th High Performance Computing and Simulation (HPCS 2009) Conference, Leipzig, Germany (2009)
15. Ferscha, A.: Parallel and Distributed Simulation of Discrete Event Systems. In: Zomaya, A.Y. (ed.) Parallel and Distributed Computing Handbook, pp. 1003–1041. McGraw-Hill, New York (1996)
16. Buss, A.: Simkit: Component based simulation modeling with Simkit. In: 34th Conference on Winter Simulation, pp. 243–249 (2002)
17. Isard, M.: Autopilot: automatic data center management. SIGOPS Oper. Syst. Rev. 41(2) (2007)
18. Vishwanath, K.V., Greenberg, A., Reed, D.: Modular data centers: how to design them? In: Proceedings of the 1st ACM Workshop on LSAP (2009)

CloudWF: A Computational Workflow System for Clouds Based on Hadoop

Chen Zhang[1] and Hans De Sterck[2]

[1] David R. Cheriton School of Computer Science, University of Waterloo, Canada
[2] Department of Applied Mathematics, University of Waterloo, Canada

Abstract. This paper describes CloudWF, a scalable and lightweight computational workflow system for clouds on top of Hadoop. CloudWF can run workflow jobs composed of multiple Hadoop MapReduce or legacy programs. Its novelty lies in several aspects: a simple workflow description language that encodes workflow blocks and block-to-block dependencies separately as standalone executable components; a new workflow storage method that uses Hadoop HBase sparse tables to store workflow information internally and reconstruct workflow block dependencies implicitly for efficient workflow execution; transparent file staging with Hadoop DFS; and decentralized workflow execution management relying on the MapReduce framework for task scheduling and fault tolerance. This paper describes the design and implementation of CloudWF.

1 Introduction

Cloud computing is receiving more and more attention in both the commercial and academic arenas. Cloud resource services provide on-demand hardware availability for dedicated usage. Cloud computing software frameworks manage cloud resources and provide scalable and fault tolerant computing utilities with globally uniform and hardware-transparent user interfaces. Hadoop [5] is a popular open source cloud computing framework that has shown to perform well in various usage scenarios (*e.g.*, see [10]). Its MapReduce framework offers transparent distribution of compute tasks and data with optimized data locality and task level fault tolerance; its distributed file system (DFS) offers a single global interface to access data from anywhere with data replication for fault tolerance; its HBase sparse data store allows to manage structured metadata on top of DFS. Due to the scalability, fault tolerance, transparency and easy deployability inherent in the cloud computing concept, Hadoop and other cloud computing frameworks have proven highly successful in the context of the processing of very large data sets that can be divided easily in parts that can be processed with limited inter-task communication. However, Hadoop does not support workflow jobs and there exist no well-established computational workflow systems on top of Hadoop for automatic execution of complex workflows with large data sets in a cloud environment.

CloudWF is a computational workflow system for clouds based on Hadoop. The main objective of computational workflows is to streamline and automate

M.G. Jaatun, G. Zhao, and C. Rong (Eds.): CloudCom 2009, LNCS 5931, pp. 393–404, 2009.

complex computational processes that require multiple interdependent computing steps and data staging in between the steps. CloudWF accepts from the
user workflow description XML files having workflow blocks and connectors as
workflow components, stores the component information in Hadoop HBase, and
processes the components using the Hadoop MapReduce framework with workflow data and processing programs stored in DFS.

CloudWF can run workflows composed of both MapReduce and legacy programs (existing programs not built by using the MapReduce API). In CloudWF,
each workflow block contains either a MapReduce or a legacy program; each
workflow connector contains a block-to-block dependency which may involve file
copies between connected blocks. DFS is used as an intermediary for staging
files between blocks that may execute on different cloud nodes. Both blocks and
connectors can be executed independently with no concern of which workflow
they belong to, while each of the workflow-wise block dependency trees is maintained and reconstructed implicitly based on the HBase records of the workflow
components. As a result, the workflow executions are decentralized, in the sense
that there is no separate execution control for each workflow instance to keep
track of dependencies: blocks and connectors of all workflows that are being
executed at a given time are scheduled by the CloudWF system in a uniform
way. This allows for highly parallel and scalable execution of multiple workflows
at the same time. With CloudWF and a Hadoop cloud environment, users can
easily connect MapReduce or general unix command-line program invocations
into workflows with almost no need to rewrite any commands to adapt to the
workflow description language used. The details of file staging between blocks
are hidden for the user: files used in the workflow command descriptions can be
assumed to have already been staged to the local machine with no worries about
file path and access protocol heterogeneity.

Compared with other scientific workflow systems on grids [6,7,8] and dataflow
systems such as cascading [3] that have recently emerged, CloudWF is easy to
use and highly scalable with fault tolerance: it directly inherits the scalability
and fault tolerance provided by Hadoop.

The novelty of CloudWF mainly lies in the following aspects.

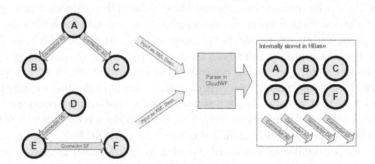

Fig. 1. Breaking up the components of two workflows into independent blocks and
connectors. The HBase tables store the dependencies between components implicitly.

1. It adopts a simple prototype workflow description language that encodes workflow blocks and block-to-block dependencies separately as standalone executable components, as illustrated in Figure 1. As a result, there is no need for centralized execution control per workflow instance to explicitly direct the dataflow, which enhances scalability.
2. It adopts a new workflow storage method that uses HBase sparse tables to store workflow information internally and reconstruct workflow block dependencies. The directed acyclic graphs (DAGs) of the workflows are encoded in the sparse HBase tables, which are a natural data structure for encoding graphs and allow for efficient querying of the graph connections.
3. It adopts DFS for transparent file staging between connected blocks. Because of employing DFS, users and the workflow system have a globally accessible file repository. Using DFS to store and relay files is convenient and reduces the complexity of handling files in a distributed environment: the uniformity of the cloud environment allows for simple file handling solutions.
4. It uses Hadoop's MapReduce framework for simple scheduling and task level fault tolerance. This avoids conflicting schedules as described in [9].
5. It enables easy step-by-step execution steering as well as real-time dataflow change with little influence on existing workflow components. These features are important for scientists to perform multiple trial-and-error experiments.

The remaining sections of the paper are organized as follows. Section 2 describes the design and implementation of the CloudWF system in detail. Section 3 briefly introduces proposed advanced features of CloudWF. Related work is discussed in Section 4, and Section 5 gives conclusions and describes future work.

2   System Design and Implementation

2.1   Overview

As show in Figure 2, CloudWF puts all essential functionalities inside a cloud, while leaving the user with a very simple interface for submitting workflow XML description files for specification of workflows, and commands to start workflows and monitor their execution. The user also has to place any input and program files into the user area of the cloud DFS, and can retrieve workflow output from the DFS as well. (Note that the DFS is divided into two parts, a system part that is used by CloudWF to relay files between workflow blocks, and a user part that users employ for workflow input and output.)

When the cloud Front End receives a user workflow description file, it parses the file into independent workflow components and stores the components into three HBase tables. In the workflow table ("WF"), we store workflow metadata, such as workflow IDs. In the workflow block table ("WFBlock"), we store block metadata such as ID and execution status. In the workflow connector table ("WFConnector"), we store block-to-block dependency information, including any file transfers that are required from the origin block to the destination

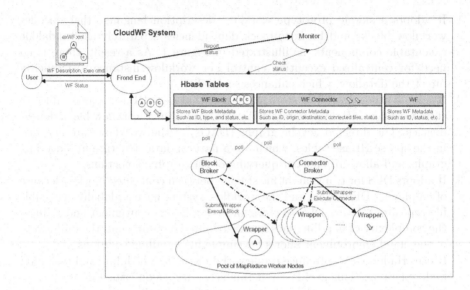

Fig. 2. CloudWF system overview

block. The Block Broker polls the "WFBlock" table at small time intervals, submits Wrappers to execute ready-for-execution blocks, and manages some block status changes. The Connector Broker polls the "WFConnector" table, submits Wrappers to execute ready-for-execution connectors, and manages connector status changes. The pool of MapReduce worker nodes executes submitted blocks and connectors using the MapReduce framework and updates the corresponding block/connector status in the "WFBlock" and "WFConnector" tables so that Block Broker and Connector Broker can easily detect the results of the Wrappers' execution by HBase queries. Real-time workflow execution status is obtained by the Monitor. When the Front End receives commands to retrieve workflow status, it calls the Monitor which in turn obtains information from the three HBase tables and sends back the results through the Frond End to users.

2.2   Expressing Workflows: CloudWF Description Language

CloudWF uses its own prototype workflow description language. The design objective of the language is to allow users to easily and quickly construct cloud workflows from existing MapReduce and legacy unix command line program invocations with minimum changes. The motivation for creating this new language is threefold. First, we find that there exist few very lightweight languages that are straightforward to use and not much more complicated than scripting languages like bash scripts. Second, we want to develop a language to deal specifically with both legacy and MapReduce program invocations. Third, we want to design a language that describes workflows in a scalable way so that no extra overhead resulting from processing the language would be added when workflow executions are to be massively scaled up in Hadoop cloud environments.

To make the discussion specific, we consider two example command line invocations, one each of the two types of commands (MapReduce and legacy unix command line) that we want to embed in our workflows:

1. legacy unix command line: cat inC1 inC2 > outC
2. MapReduce command line:
   /HadoopHome/bin/hadoop jar wordcount.jar org.myorg.WordCount
   /user/c15zhang/wordcount/input /user/c15zhang/wordcount/output

The first example is a simple unix cat with two input files and one output file that are stored in the working directory on the unix local file system (LFS) of the cloud node on which it executes, and the second is a simple Hadoop wordcount with one DFS input file and one DFS output file (DFS files are always referenced by their absolute DFS path, since there is no concept of 'working directory' in DFS or Hadoop.). Note that, in the second example, the "hadoop" executable resides on the LFS of the cloud node on which it executes, and "wordcount.jar" (which contains org.myorg.WordCount) resides in the unix current working directory on the LFS of the cloud node on which the hadoop invocation executes.

In the rest of this paper, we will explain CloudWF based on two simple example workflows, presented in Figures 3 and 4. The first example workflow (Figure 3) is composed of legacy blocks (type "legacy" in the XML file). Blocks A, B and C perform simple unix commands, and output files from blocks A and B are used as input for block C. CloudWF automatically stages these files from the cloud nodes on which A and B are executed, to the cloud node on which C executes, using DFS as an intermediary. To this end, the user designates these files as outputs in their origin blocks in the XML file (blocks A and B), and as inputs in the XML description of block C. The user then describes connector

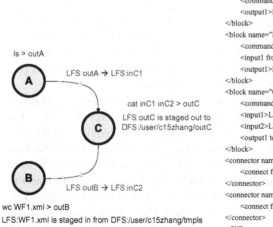

```
<WF ID="exWF">
<block name="A" type="legacy">
    <command>ls > outA</command>
    <output1>LFS:outA</output1>
</block>
<block name="B" type="legacy">
    <command>wc WF1.xml > outB</command>
    <input1 from="DFS:/user/c15zhang/tmpls">LFS:WF1.xml</input1>
    <output1>LFS:outB</output1>
</block>
<block name="C" type="legacy">
    <command>cat inC1 inC2 > outC</command>
    <input1>LFS:inC1</input1>
    <input2>LFS:inC2</input2>
    <output1 to="DFS:/user/c15zhang/outC">LFS:outC</output1>
</block>
<connector name="connector1" origin="A" dest="C">
    <connect from="output1" to="input1"/>
</connector>
<connector name="connector2" origin="B" dest="C">
    <connect from="output1" to="input2"/>
</connector>
</WF>
```

Fig. 3. First example workflow and XML file (legacy blocks)

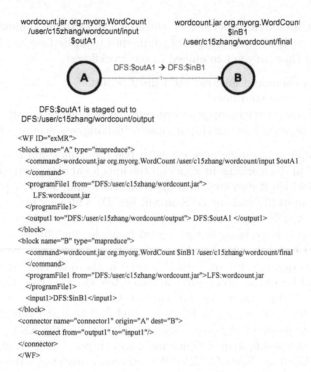

Fig. 4. Second example workflow and XML file (MapReduce blocks)

components in the XML file that describe the order of execution in the workflow (C depends on A and C depends on B) and the files that have to be 'connected' between the blocks. The input file of block B is staged into the workflow system from the user DFS area, and the output file of block C is staged out from the workflow system to the user DFS area. The precise mechanisms by which file staging is accomplished are described in Section 2.4, together with a more detailed explanation of the entries in the XML description file. For now we can just point out that the workflow ID of the first example workflow is "exWF", and that blocks and connectors in this workflow will be referred to as, for example, "exWF.A" and "exWF.connector1" in the HBase tables.

The second example workflow (Figure 4) is similar, but has blocks of MapReduce type. In block A a simple MapReduce wordcount is executed on a file that resides in the DFS user directory (/user/c15zhang/wordcount/input), and the result is stored in a DFS file in a system location (referred to by $outA1 in block A). This result file is also staged out to a file in the user DFS area (/user/c15zhang/wordcount/output). Note that the first part of the full Hadoop command is omitted in the XML command description such that the CloudWF user does not need to know the details about where Hadoop is installed on the cloud nodes. The user specifies in a connector in the XML file that $outA1 will also serve as input to block B, and CloudWF then makes the files accessible to block B (by a mechanism to be explained in Section 2.4). Block B performs a wordcount on the output file of block A, and puts the result in file /user/c15zhang/wordcount/final in the DFS user area. Note that the DFS files that have to be passed from block A to block B in Figure 4 are parametrized by placeholders $outA1 and $inB1, and CloudWF replaces these placeholders by absolute DFS paths at execution time. It is explained in Section 2.4 why and how this is done, and why this is not necessary when files are passed between legacy blocks.

2.3   Storing Workflows: HBase Tables

CloudWF uses HBase to store workflow component information. There are three main reasons to use HBase. First, we need a database-like reliable metadata store to manage various types of workflow information that is important for workflow execution control, as well as to save intermediate results for fault tolerance and future reuse. Second, we have designed a set of sparse tables and find them very suitable for easily expressing and searching for workflow information and connectivity, which results in efficient processing without invoking complex database-like queries, thus voiding the need for specialized relational database systems. Finally, HBase is tightly coupled with the Hadoop framework and can be scaled and deployed more easily than mainstream database systems.

In HBase, we use three tables: the "WF" table, the "WFBlock" table and the "WFConnector" table (Figure 5). CloudWF relies on these tables to store workflow metadata and control execution. Additionally, the block dependency tree of a workflow is implicitly stored within the "WFBlock" and "WFConnector" tables and is used for fast discovery of the next block/connector ready for execution. The following explains how we achieve that.

Figure 5 shows the HBase tables that correspond to the first example workflow (Figure 3) before execution is started. In WFBlock, every block has one entry. There are three HBase column families: ID, Program and Status. The first column in the ID column family, ID:blockID, gives the block ID. The second column indicates that the blocks belong to workflow exWF. Note that, every time a workflow is added, an additional sparse column is created for that workflow (for example, ID:exWF2): the sparse columns ID:exWF and ID:exWF2 can be used for fast querying of the columns of workflows exWF and exWF2, respectively. The third column lists the dependency count of the blocks. Block C depends on A and B, so its count is 2. The dependency count will be reduced as blocks finish (see Section 2.5), and when it reaches 0 the block is detected as being ready for execution. The first column in the Program column family gives the commands, and the next two contain the lists of input and output files that have to be passed between blocks (specified by the <input> and <output> blocks in the XML file in Figure 3.) The Status column family is used during execution (see Section 2.5).

Similarly, the WFConnector table has one entry per connector in the workflow, with ID, Link, Origin and Status column families. The ID and Status families function as above. The Link family lists the origin and destination block of each connector, and the descriptors for the files that need to be connected. The

WFBlock Table

ID: blockID	ID: exWF	ID: blockType	ID: dependencyCount	Program: command	Program: input	Program: output
exWF.A	Y	legacy	0	ls > outA		(output1,LFS:outA)
exWF.B	Y	Legacy	0	wc WF1.xml > outB	(input1,DFS: /user/c15zhang/tmpls)	(output1,LFS: outB)
exWF.C	Y	legacy	2	cat inC1 inC2 > outC	(input1,LFS:inC1) (input2,LFS:inC2)	(output1,LFS:outC)

Status: readyForExecution	Status: inExecution	Status: readyForConnectors	Status: done

WFConnector Table

ID:connectorID	ID:exWF	Link:origin	Link:destination	Link:fromToList
exWF.connector1	Y	exWF.A	exWF.C	(output1, input1)
exWF.connector2	Y	exWF.B	exWF.C	(output1, input2)

Origin: exWF.A	Origin: exWF.B	Status: readyForExecution	Status: inExecution	Status: readyForBlock	Status: done
Y					
	Y				

WF Table

ID:WFID	ID:exWF	Status: readyForExecution	Status: inExecution	Status: done
exWF	Y			

Fig. 5. HBase tables for the example workflow of Figure 3

Origin column family appears redundant but is crucial for good performance: every workflow block that has a connector originating from it has its own (sparse) column in this family, thus allowing for very fast searching of which connectors have to be activated when a given workflow block finishes. This is important for performance when very large amounts of blocks and connectors are stored in the tables. Indeed, the sparse table concept of HBase allows us to create sparse columns for every block without much storage overhead (each column will only have one "Y" entry), and HBase provides a very fast mechanism to return all records in a table that are non-null in a given column. These features of HBase sparse tables allow us to store and query the connectivity of the workflow DAG in a natural and efficient way.

The third Table, WFTable, is used to store workflow information.

2.4   Staging Files Transparently with DFS

File staging is a major issue in workflow management. CloudWF makes this easy by using DFS as a globally accessible file repository so that files that appear on workflow component commandlines can be staged between any two cloud machines by relaying through DFS. In CloudWF, we consider two types of file staging. The first type of file staging is between blocks, as described by the connector components in Figures 3, 4 and 5. The second type is staging files in from the user DFS area into the workflow, and staging files out from the workflow to the user DFS area. As already discussed before, the DFS is divided into a user area and a CloudWF system area, and similarly, a CloudWF system area is also created on the local file system (LFS) of each cloud node.

During workflow execution, CloudWF creates two working directories for each block that is executed: one DFS working directory in the system part of the globally accessible DFS, and one LFS working directory in the system part of the LFS of the cloud node on which the block executes. The MapReduce Wrapper and its command line invocation (which itself is legacy or MapReduce) are executed from the LFS working directory. The DFS working directory is used for staging files between blocks, and for staging files in or out. For example, the DFS and LFS paths to the DFS and LFS working directories for block A in workflow exWF are given by

- DFS working directory: /DFSHomePrefix/exWF/exWF.A/
- LFS working directory: /LFSHomePrefix/exWF/exWF.A/

The file staging for the workflows in Figures 3 and 4 then works as follows. As we said before, files that appear on command lines and have to be staged between blocks have to be specified in <input> and <output> blocks in the XML file, and are tagged as LFS files or DFS files depending on their nature (consistent with their use in the command line). Inside the <input> and <output> blocks, only relative paths can be used. These relative paths refer to the working directory of the block for which the <input> or <output> is specified. For unix legacy command lines, the file names in the command lines can simply be given relative to the unix working directory of the block, and command lines need no change.

Let us consider the connector from block A to C in Figure 3. The block-to-block staging works as follows: after the commandline execution of block A, the CloudWF Wrapper copies outA to the DFS working directory of block A. When connector 1 is executed, it copies outA from the DFS working directory of block A to the DFS working directory of block C. When block B starts, the CloudWF Wrapper copies the file from the DFS working directory of block C to the LFS working directory of block C (with name inC1), and then C's command line can be invoked. This mechanism is transparent to the user, who only has to provide the 'connectors' in the XML file. The use of this connector mechanism allows highly parallel execution of multiple workflows at the same time, see Section 2.5.

For workflows with MapReduce blocks (see Figure 4) the situation is somewhat more complicated. Let us consider the connector from blocks A to B, which connects the DFS output file from A to the DFS input file of B. CloudWF again uses the DFS working directory of block A and the DFS working directory of block B to relay the file, but the problem is now that the MapReduce command line requires absolute paths for DFS files (because MapReduce does not have a DFS working directory concept). We want to hide the system absolute paths to the DFS working directories of blocks A and B from the user (because in practice they may not be known in advance, and it is not desirable that the user would have to know the details of paths used by the system), and to this end we provide placeholders like $outA1, which are to be used for DFS files on command lines and in <input> and <output> blocks, and which CloudWF replaces by absolute DFS paths to the block's DFS working directory at runtime. In this way, the user can stage DFS files block-to-block in a way that is similar to staging LFS files: the only difference is that DFS files are referred to using placeholders. Note also that the overhead in copying multiple DFS files in order to get them from one block to another is small, since Hadoop DFS uses copy-on-write, and most large DFS input files are not written to. Note that users can also relay files themselves via the user section of DFS, but then the user has to do all the bookkeeping and has to make sure that all necessary directories are available at runtime, which is cumbersome, so the transparent block-to-block file staging mechanism that CloudWF provides is attractive.

The mechanism for staging files into and out of the workflow is the same for Figures 3 and 4: the 'from' and 'to' fields in <input> and <output> blocks can contain absolute DFS or LFS paths, and inside the <input> and <output> blocks the files are tagged as DFS or LFS depending on their use on the commandline, and placeholders are used for DFS files.

In short, CloudWF uses DFS to achieve transparent file staging in the background. For large and frequently used files, users can choose to populate the files to all cloud nodes beforehand to optimize system performance.

2.5   Executing Workflows

CloudWF executes blocks and connectors whenever they are ready for execution. For example, for the workflow of Figures 3 and 4, the user initiates execution through the Front End, after which blocks A and B (which have dependency count 0) are set to 'readyForExecution' in the WFBlock table. Upon polling, the Block broker (Figure 2) finds the blocks that are ready for execution and submits Wrappers to the cloud pool. When block A finishes, the connectors that originate from A (obtained by a fast query of WFConnector) are set as 'readyForExecution', and are then picked up by the Connection broker and submitted for execution. Upon completion of the connector from A to C, the dependency count of C is decreased by one. When both connectors have executed, C then becomes ready for execution. If any Wrapper fails, it is restarted by the MapReduce framework automatically for six times by default. If all retries fail, the task (block or connector) fails and thus the entire workflow fails. If the Wrapper is alive and the submitted component execution fails, the Wrapper detects this failure and restarts the failed component command once. If the command fails again, the Wrapper marks the component status to fail and thus the entire workflow fails. In the future, more advanced failure handling mechanisms will be introduced to better cope with workflow failures.

3   Advanced Features

The CloudWF design supports several advanced features. Prototype implementations of these features already exist, but will be described in future work.

1. Virtual start and end blocks: CloudWF creates one virtual start and one virtual end block for each workflow instance, which are connected to all blocks without incoming or outgoing connectors, respectively. The workflow is started by setting the virtual start block to 'readyForExecution', and workflow completion is easily detected when the virtual end block completes.
2. Workflow templates and nested workflows: CloudWF supports workflow composition by reusing existing workflows or workflow components as templates to avoid duplicated coding. Nested workflows are also supported.
3. Steering and runtime workflow structure change: Workflow steering enables step-by-step interactive workflow execution, which is very useful for performing experiments, and can be done easily because blocks and connectors are decoupled. Runtime structural change is also necessary for modifying parts of large complex workflows while other parts are already in execution.

4   Related Work

Many scientific workflow systems on clusters and grids exist for various usage needs such as [2,6,7,8], see also the review paper [11]. Use of public clouds for scientific computing has been explored in [4]. A major concern with workflow systems is always the complexity of usage. With the advent of clouds, it is possible to develop easy-to-use lightweight systems that can take advantage of the desirable properties clouds can provide, such as scalability, fault tolerance, transparency and easy deployment. Our CloudWF system tries to achieve this goal. We are only aware of one other effort in this direction, namely Cascading [3] which also makes use of cloud features. However, it serves a different purpose: it is intended for expert programmers and lets them build workflows as monolithic programs (each workflow instance gets executed separately). This makes it more complicated for users to reuse existing programs directly and it is harder to parallelize the execution of multiple workflows (each workflow instance needs its own scheduler). In comparison, CloudWF is intended for application users who are not programming specialists: it provides a simple way to run workflows composed of existing MapReduce or legacy programs. In terms of general workflow organization, our system is different from existing workflow systems in that it encodes workflow blocks and block-to-block dependencies separately as standalone executable components which enables decentralized workflow execution management, in a way that is naturally suitable for cloud environments.

5   Conclusions and Future Work

CloudWF is a computational workflow system specifically targeted at cloud environments where Hadoop is installed. It uses Hadoop components to perform job execution, file staging and workflow information storage. The novelty of the system lies in its ability to take full advantage of what the underlying cloud computing framework can provide, and in its new workflow description method that separates out workflow component dependencies as standalone executable components. Decentralization in space and time is achieved in workflow execution. Thus the system is highly scalable compared to existing workflow solutions. Future work includes designing and implementing advanced policy management to better handle workflow faults automatically, as well as adding a web-based graphical user interface for better user interaction. The system is also being used for large-scale biological image processing workflows [12].

References

1. Ailamaki, A., Ioannidis, Y.E., Livny, M.: Scientific Workflow Management by Database Management. In: 10th Intl. Conf. on Scientific and Statistical Database Management (SSDBM), Capri, Italy (1998)
2. Bowers, S., Ludaescher, B.: Actor-Oriented Design of Scientific Workflows. In: Delcambre, L.M.L., Kop, C., Mayr, H.C., Mylopoulos, J., Pastor, Ó. (eds.) ER 2005. LNCS, vol. 3716, pp. 369–384. Springer, Heidelberg (2005)
3. Cascading, http://www.cascading.org/ (retrieval date: September 25, 2009)
4. Deelman, E., Singh, G., Livny, M., Berriman, B., Good, J.: The cost of doing science on the cloud: the Montage example. In: Proceedings of the ACM/IEEE conference on Supercomputing (SC), Austin, USA (2008)
5. Hadoop, http://hadoop.apache.org/ (retrieval date: September 25, 2009)
6. Ludscher, B., Altintas, I., Berkley, C., Higgins, D., Jaeger, E., Jones, M., Lee, E., Tao, J., Zhao, Y.: Scientific Workflow Management and the Kepler System. In: Concurrency and Computation: Practice and Experience, vol. 18, pp. 1039–1065 (2006)
7. Majithia, S., Shields, M., Taylor, I., Wang, I.: Triana: A Graphical Web Service Composition and Execution Toolkit. In: Proc. IEEE Intl. Conf. Web Services (ICWS), pp. 514–524 (2004)
8. Oinn, T., Greenwood, M., Addis, M.J., Alpdemir, M.N., Ferris, J., Glover, K., Goble, C., Goderis, A., Hull, D., Marvin, D.J., Li, P., Lord, P., Pocock, M.R., Senger, M., Stevens, R., Wipat, A., Wroe, C.: Taverna: Lessons in Creating a Workflow Environment for the Life Sciences. J. Concurrency and Computation: Practice and Experience 18, 1067–1100 (2002)
9. Ranjan, R., Rehman, M., Buyya, R.: A Decentralized and Cooperative Workflow Scheduling Algorithm. In: Proc. 8th Intl. Conf. on Cluster Computing and the Grid (CCGrid). IEEE Computer Society Press, Los Alamitos (2008)
10. TeraByte Sort on Apache Hadoop, http://www.hpl.hp.com/hosted/sortbenchmark/YahooHadoop.pdf (retrieval date: September 25, 2009)
11. Yu, J., Buyya, R.: A Taxonomy of Scientific Workflow Systems for Grid Computing. SIGMOD Record 34, 44–49 (2005)
12. Zhang, C., De Sterck, H., Djambazian, H., Sladek, R.: Case Study of Scientific Data Processing on a Cloud Using Hadoop. In: High Performance Computing Symposium (HPCS), Kingston, Canada (2009)

A Novel Multipath Load Balancing Algorithm in Fat-Tree Data Center

Laiquan Han, Jinkuan Wang, and Cuirong Wang

Information Science and Engineering, Northeastern University,
110004 Shenyang, China
likesea@163.com, {wjk,wangcr}@mail.neuq.edu.cn

Abstract. The rapid development of CPU technology, storage technology and bandwidth improvement have given rise to a strong research interest in cloud computing technology. As a basic infrastructure component of cloud computing, data center becomes more and more important. Based on the analysis of transmission efficiency, a novel hierarchical flow multipath forward (HFMF) algorithm is proposed. HFMF can use adaptive flow-splitting schemes according to the corresponding level in the three-tier fat-tree topology. NS2 simulations prove that HFMF reduces the packet disorder arrival and achieves a better performance of load balancing in the data center.

Keywords: fat tree, load balancing, data center, multipath forwarding.

1 Introduction

Cloud computing is a new computing model and the computing is based on the Internet. Cloud computing also has the name of on-demand computing, software as a service, distributed computing or utility computing, etc. Cloud computing fuses distributed computing, parallel computing and grid computing with Internet computing. Computing is very important in this technology, traditional expensive computing resources become relatively cheap commodity resources today. Every one can use the computing resources for their own just with a cheaper price.

Cloud computing can be viewed from two different aspects [1]. One is the cloud infrastructure and the other is cloud application. GFS (Goggle File System) and MapReduce are applications of cloud computing in Goggle company. BlueCloud have been used in IBM. Elastic compute cloud is a platform of Amazon. Determining how to migrate the application is an important issue when an enterprise wants to deploy these technologies. However, how much maintenance cost will be reduced with the use of cloud computing is not clear to the budget of an enterprise.

Besides the deployment problems, however, there are a lot of technology problems required to be addressed, such as requirements of storage, security of information, upgrade of hardware and installment of numerous softwares. Cloud computing is a new merging technology to address these questions.

In cloud computing, the partition function of server and client will be migrated into the data center which provides the support for hardware maintenance, software upgrade, and system security and so on. With the rapid development of virtual

M.G. Jaatun, G. Zhao, and C. Rong (Eds.): CloudCom 2009, LNCS 5931, pp. 405–412, 2009.

technology, and distribution technology, the packets which want to transmit in the data center become more and more. As a basic infrastructure component of cloud computing, data center becomes more and more important.

The rest of the paper is organized as follows. In section 2, related work is described briefly for the related research of load balancing and multipath transmission. Fat tree data center and HFMF (hierarchical flow multipath forward) algorithm implement are discussed in section 3. In section 4, the scenarios setting and performance analysis are presented. Finally the conclusion is described in section 5.

2   Related Work

According to the categories of aggressive traffic and the normal traffic and applying different scheduling schemes, Shi [2] proposed adaptive methods to balance the traffic and obtained both the load balancing and resources utilization. Kencl [3] proposed a novel load sharing algorithm by a feedback control mechanism that minimizes the probability of flow reordering. Kandula [4] proposed a new approach FLARE that operated on bursts of packets (flowlets) carefully chosen to avoid reordering, and allowed a finer forwarding granularity.

Appropriate use of CMP will improve throughput, reduce packet-loss and delay, and obtain a better system performance [5] [6]. In order to send the packets to the available path, forwarding overhead of data-plane will be higher for traditional schemes. Kvalbein [7] and Feamster [8] used multiple implementations of the same protocol to obtain different forwarding table. A random perturbation will be set to the weight of different link. The perturbation makes the forwarding tables converge to different states, so these schemes can obtain different forwarding results for different applications.

Some previous work about CMP done by us is presented in literature [9-11]. Using dynamic list to increase certain connection-oriented function, connection oriented CMP forwarding algorithm [9] can classify different flows and forward those flows to different available paths. For CMP forwarding in multi-homed host, we proposed a novel Single-hop Delay Probe algorithm [10], which can avoid the performance degradation of different paths. Based on the analysis of flow relation and forwarding granularity, CCRF [11] can forward packets in the same categories path concurrently but it will cause certain overhead for router CPU.

3   Fat Tree Model and Algorithm Implementation

3.1   Fat Tree Model

Typical architectures today consist of three-level trees of switches or routers. As illustrated in Figure 1, a three-tiered design has a core tier in the root of the tree, an aggregation tier in the middle and an edge tier at the third level of the tree [12]. In the edge level or aggregation level, every device has two outlets for the connection of high level devices. Traditional, one outlet is for the purpose of data transmission and the other one is for the purpose of backup. The backup link is also called duplicate link or alternative link.

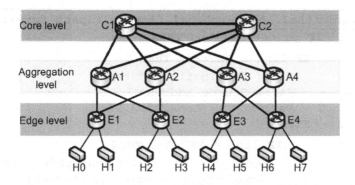

Fig. 1. Fat tree topology is a common architecture model for a large number of enterprise networks

How to utilize these alternative paths to transmit traffic, how to obtain higher transmission efficient and how to optimize the relation of different available paths, these interests become more and more important, which have been the research hotspots of a lot of literatures. Recently, two novel data center schemes, DCell [13] and FiConn [14], are proposed to obtain more available expanded features, a lower cost and higher performance.

With the rapid development in links upgrade and reliability improvement for these years, link failure becomes fewer and fewer. Furthermore, with the tolerance development for both hardware and software, the backup link has become a left unused link almost all the time. So in order to use the idle link and obtain a better performance of link utilization, we use the backup link to transmit data concurrently.

3.2 Algorithm Implementation

The pseudo code of HFMF algorithm is shown in algorithm 1. The algorithm consists of two parts. One is the flow forwarding in aggregation level; the other is multipath forwarding in core level.

The *SET E-A* in line 2 stands for the link from edge link to aggregation link (not the reverse direction). The *SET A-C* in line 7 stands for the link from aggregation link to core link. In the implementation of line 5, the next-hop will be obtained from the destination address (*DA*) and source address (*SA*). This is different from the traditional routing technology. If the link is towards the core link, however, the next-hop will be obtain from different available paths depending on whether the link is used or not in the previous time. The function '*lookup*' , which occurs in line 5, line 9 and line 13, is most important in this algorithm. It is an overload function. In line 8 and line 9, *next-path* belongs to one of the unused available paths. It is another parameter for this overload function. At last, the *lookup* function in line 13, which uses the parameter *DA*, is the traditional implementation of general router.

Algorithm1. hierarchical flow multipath forward
1: **IF** packet arrived **THEN**
2:    **IF** link ∈ *SET E-A* **THEN**
3:      *DA* := Destination Address
4:      *SA* := Source Address
5:      *Next-hop* := Lookup(*DA,SA*)
6:    **ELSE**
7:        **IF** link ∈ *SET A-C* **THEN**
8:          *Next-path* := unused available path
9:          *Next-hop* := Lookup (*Next-path*)
10:          Set-Used-Path*(Next-path)*
11:        **ELSE**
12:          *DA* := Destination Address
13:          *Next-hop* := Lookup (*DA*)
14:        **END IF**
15:    **END IF**
16: **END IF**

4 Simulation and Performance Analysis

NS2 simulation tool is used in algorithm implement. Because the support for concurrent multipath is fewer in NS2.31, we modify and add some source codes corresponding to concurrent multipath, and then NS2 is recompiled for these changing. Only in this way can NS2 forward the packet as HFMF algorithm.

4.1 Scenarios Introduction

We design five scenarios, which have the same topology, just like the topology of Fig. 1.There are three level in the simulation scripts and each level has the same bandwidth and delay parameters. With the same topology, the traffic request is also the same in every scenario. Node 0 (H0) connects node 4 (H4) for data transmission. For ease of exposition, we denote this transmission as red flow. Node 1 (H1) connects node 5 (H5) for another data transmission, and we denote this transmission as blue flow. These two flows have the same network address (prefix).

The specific simulation implement of these five scenarios elaborates in subsection 4.2, 4.3 and 4.4. Subsection 4.2 depicts single path forwarding with different queue types. Subsection 4.3 analyzes flow-based forwarding and subsection 4.4 describes the ECMP forwarding. Finally, HFMF scheme is simulated in subsection 4.5.

4.2 Single Path Forwarding

As illustrated in figure 2, H0 establishes data transmission with H4 in red flow, while H1 has data transmission with H5 in blue flow. Analyzing the simulation phenomenon, we can see that when using traditional OSPF routing with drop-tail queue, blue flow has severe packet loss and almost all packet loss happens with blue flow. As illustrated in figure 3, after using the RED (Random Early Detection) queue, we can

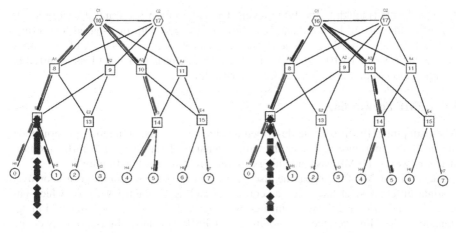

Fig. 2. Drop-tail queue   **Fig. 3.** RED queue

find that red and blue flow both have a reasonable packets loss. Due to the concerning on the unfair characteristics of drop-tail, RED queue has obtained better queue performance. Furthermore, from the simulation results, we can see that both the blue flow and the total packet loss have been reduced because of the using of RED queue.

4.3 Flow-Based Forwarding

Under the same scenario of topology and traffic requirements, without conflicting and colliding for the same path of 12-8-18-10-14 in previous implementation, red flow use the path of 12-8-16-11-14 and blue flow use the path of 12-9-17-10-14. As illustrated in figure 4, there is no packet loss during these two transmissions when employing flow-based scheme [11]. However, because of the lower utilization rate of the core link, for example, link 8-17 and 9-16 are not used, the data packet transmission rate in flow-based scheme is relatively low.

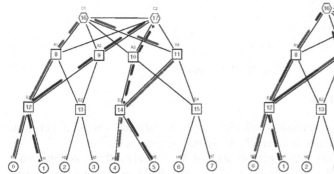
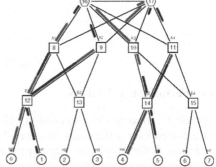

Fig. 4. Flow-based multipath forwarding   **Fig. 5.** ECMP forwarding

4.4 ECMP Forwarding

For the same traffic request just like the scenario above, when we use the ECMP (Equal Cost Multi-Path) scheme to implement multipath transmission, nodes in different levels (including the Edge level, the Aggregation level and the Core level) can split and transmit both red and blue flow. Compared with flow-based forwarding in figure 4, the forwarding efficiency has been increased with the use of core links such as 8-17, 9-16, 16-10 and 17-11. Furthermore, there is no packet loss occurred in the simulation implementation of ECMP forwarding.

4.5 HFMF Forwarding

When adopting HFMF scheme described as algorithm 1, the simulation phenomenon can be found in figure 6. Under the same scenario of topology and traffic requirements, however, HFMF has something different from figure 4 and figure 5.

Packets in ECMP will appear the disorder problems for the random transmission over multiple different level link, such as core level and aggregation level link, which has different bandwidth and delay. Compared with figure 5, HFMF is not disordered in aggregation level. However, the flow-splitting for HFMF will cause almost no delay deviation for the same performance of bandwidth and delay characteristics in core level link.

Although there is no disorder problem, flow-based forwarding also has poor link utilization in core level. Compared with figure 4, HFMF scheme makes more use of core link, so that the utilization rate of core level has been enhanced. After being split, blue flow and red flow are transmitted in different link in core level. Therefore, we can come to the conclusion that using the HFMF scheme can relieve packet loss and achieve a higher data transmission rate.

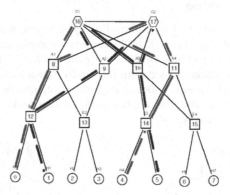

Fig. 6. HFMF forwarding

4.6 Performance Analysis

Though the five specific simulation implements, the throughput and delay performance comparison is illustrated in figure 7 and figure 8 respectively.

Figure 7 shows the throughput performance of the five algorithms. Because only one path is used, OSPF (both drop-tail queue and RED queue) has the lowest throughput. Because these links transmit traffic at almost full bandwidth utilization, these two routing technologies achieve almost the same throughput. Flow-based strategy is in the middle of the throughput. By making full use of available bandwidth of core link, ECMP and HFMF have the best throughput because of more paths in transmission than flow-based and OSPF scheme.

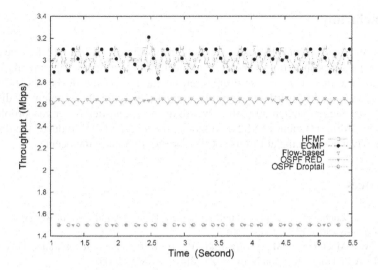

Fig. 7. Throughput comparison

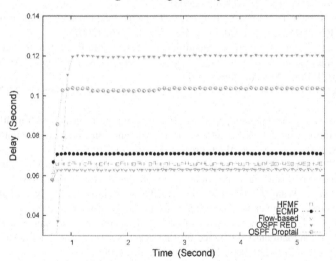

Fig. 8. Delay comparison

Figure 8 shows the delay comparison of the five algorithms; OSPF has the largest end-to-end delay because the forwarding paths have been in a state of congestion and a large amount of packets wait in the queue for sending. Flow-based strategy has the best performance of delay. Through the using of hierarchical and flow-splitting forwarding, HFMF reduces the delay greatly than OSPF and obtain almost the same performance with Flow-based scheme.

In summary, considering throughput and delay as the performance measures, the traditional single-path has the worst performance, the performance of flow-based strategy is in the middle, and HFMF has the best performance among the five.

5 Conclusion

Study on the disorder problem and backbone forwarding efficiency of fat-tree topology, this paper proposed a novel hierarchical flow multipath forward algorithm. HFMF can use different flow-splitting strategy due to different level of data center. The source address forwarding in first-tier of fat-tree is for the problem of disorder packets. The hierarchical multipath forwarding in second-tier is for the problem of higher forwarding efficiency. NS2 simulations prove that HFMF reduces the disorder packets arrival and can make full use of the core bandwidth of data center.

References

1. Chen, K., Zheng, W.: Cloud Computing: System Instances and Current Research. Journal of Software 20(5), 1337–1348 (2009)
2. Shi, W., MacGregor, M., Gburzynski, P.: Load Balancing for Parallel Forwarding. IEEE/ACM Transactions on Networking 13(4), 790–801 (2005)
3. Kencl, L., Boudec, J.: Adaptive Load Sharing for Network Processors. IEEE/ACM Transactions on Networking 16(2), 293–306 (2008)
4. Kandula, S., Katabi, D., Sinha, S., Berger, A.: Dynamic load balancing without packet reordering. SIGCOMM Comput. Commun. Rev. 37(2), 51–62 (2007)
5. Li, Y., Zhang, Y., Qiu, L., Lam, S.: Smarttunnel: Achieving Reliability in the Internet. In: 26th IEEE International Conference on Computer Communications (INFOCOM 2007), pp. 830–838. IEEE Press, Los Alamitos (2007)
6. He, J., Rexford, J.: Toward internet-wide multipath routing. IEEE Network 22(2), 16–21 (2008)
7. Kvalbein, A., Cicic, T., Gjessing, S.: Post-failure routing performance with multiple routing configurations. In: 26th IEEE International Conference on Computer Communications (INFOCOM 2007), pp. 98–106. IEEE Press, Los Alamitos (2007)
8. Motiwala, M., Elmore, M., Feamster, N., Vempala, S.: Path splicing. In: ACM SIGCOMM 2008 conference on Data communication, pp. 27–38. ACM, New York (2008)
9. Han, L., Wang, J., Wang, C.: Connection-oriented concurrent multipath forward algorithm. Journal of Southeast University (Natural Science Edition) 38, 12–16 (2008)
10. Han, L., Wang, J., Wang, C.: A novel single-hop delay probe algorithm in multi-homed host. In: First International Conference on Intelligent Networks and Intelligent Systems, Wuhan, China, pp. 217–220. IEEE Press, Los Alamitos (2008)
11. Han, L., Wang, J., Wang, C.: A crosslayer concurrent multipath random forward algorithm. In: 9th International Conference for Young Computer Scientists, Zhangjiajie, China, pp. 270–275. IEEE Press, Los Alamitos (2008)
12. Al-Fares, M., Loukissas, A., Vahdat, A.: A Scalable, Commodity Data Center Network Architecture. In: ACM SIGCOMM 2008 conference on Data communication, pp. 63–74. ACM, New York (2008)
13. Guo, C., Wu, H., Tan, K., Shi, L., Zhang, Y., Lu, S.: DCell: A Scalable and Fault-Tolerant Network Structure for Data Centers. In: ACM SIGCOMM 2008 conference on Data communication, pp. 75–86. ACM, New York (2008)
14. Li, D., Guo, C., Wu, H., Tan, K., Zhang, Y., Lu, S.: FiConn: Using Backup Port for Server Interconnection in Data Centers. In: 28th IEEE International Conference on Computer Communications (INFOCOM 2009), pp. 2276–2285. IEEE Press, Los Alamitos (2009)

Scheduling Active Services in Clustered JBI Environment

Xiangyang Jia[1], Shi Ying[1], Luokai Hu[1], and Chunlin Chen[2]

[1] State Key Lab of Software Engineering , Wuhan University, Hubei, China
[2] Yuanguang Software Co.,Ltd, Guangdong, China
jiaxiangyang@163.com, yingshi@whu.edu.cn, luokaihu@gmail.com,
ccl@ygsoft.com

Abstract. Active services may cause business or runtime errors in clustered JBI environment. To cope with this problem, a scheduling mechanism is proposed. The overall scheduling framework and scheduling algorithm is given, to guarantee the conflict-free and load balance of active services. The scheduling mechanism is implemented in SOAWARE, a SOA-based application integration platform for electric enterprises, and the experiment proves the effectiveness of scheduling algorithm.

Keywords: Active services, scheduling framework, load balancing, JBI.

1 Introduction

Java Business Integration (JBI)[1,2] is an java-based, service-oriented enterprise application integration standard. It is developed under the Java Community Process (JCP) as an approach to implementing a service-oriented architecture for enterprise application integration. JBI defines a plug-in architecture that enables dynamically installing and uninstalling components. The components in JBI play the role of service provider, consumer or both, and allow publishing heterogeneous applications as services. Therefore JBI is able to be utilized as SOA-based SaaS technology to support cloud computing.

In most cases, the services in JBI environment work in passive mode, i.e. the service's job is to answer the requests from client side, and without request, no work. However, in JBI environment, the active services are also allowed. The active services can do jobs by themselves without outside request. For example, there could be an "ftp service" which can download or upload files from ftp servers every 5 minutes, or a "report service" which generates daily business report at 6 o'clock PM every day. The "publish/subscribe service" based on WSN (Web Services Notification) is another typical example of active service. Active service is an important design pattern of SOA [3, 4], and is useful to develop software based on event-driven or publish/subscribe modes.

Since the active services do jobs by themselves rather than be activated by outside requests, they may cause some problems in clustered environment. For example, when the "ftp service" mentioned above is deployed to multiple nodes of cluster and run as multiple instances, error will happen when they upload same files concurrently. Similarly, the "report service" mentioned above in clustered environment may cause duplicate reports of the day.

M.G. Jaatun, G. Zhao, and C. Rong (Eds.): CloudCom 2009, LNCS 5931, pp. 413–422, 2009.
© Springer-Verlag Berlin Heidelberg 2009

The JBI environments we have known, like Apache Servicemix[5] or SUN OpenESB[6], still have no good solutions for this problem, and they push this problem to JBI components. For example, the Servicemix-file and Servicemix-ftp components allow developers to write lock manager to avoid concurrency conflict. However, lock manager is not the best solutions either. They can avoid runtime error, but is useless for business error. For example, the "report service" mentioned above will generate same report twice when they run on two nodes of a cluster, this is not what the developer expects.

The reason of this problem is that most (not all) active services must run as single instance in cluster, otherwise, they will do duplicate jobs, either concurrently or in an uncertain order. This paper proposes a new approach for this issue: the active services , if they has to run in singleton mode, are scheduled from a global view in clustered JBI environments, and each of them are arranged on one single node to execute, so as to avoid the runtime and business errors.

2 JBI Components, Service Unit and Service Assembly

The JBI components are software units designed to provide or consume specific kinds of services. They are divided into two distinct groups: *service engine* and *binding component*. Service engines provide business logic and transformation services to other components, as well as consume services of other components. Binding components provide connectivity to services which is external to a JBI environment.

Each type of JBI component needs specific application artifacts to configure how the component provides and consumes services. These application artifacts are called *service units (SU)*. Service units are component-related. It is deployed into specific component, and defines services the component provides and consumes.

The artifact package that includes a collection of related service units is called a *service assembly (SA)*. A service assembly can be deployed or un-deployed in JBI environment. When it is deployed, the service units it includes will be automatically deployed into corresponding components.

The services units and service assemblies can be started or stopped in JBI environment to enable or disable the related services the components provide.

3 Scheduling Mechanism

We propose a scheduling mechanism for active services in clustered JBI environment. The scheduling mechanism schedule the active services by controls the lifecycle of services units (SUs) which define these services. We called these services units *singleton SUs*. Each singleton SU is arranged to be executed upon one node in cluster, so as to guarantee active service only has one single running instance in cluster.

3.1 Overview of Scheduling Framework

Figure 1 shows the overview of scheduling framework for active services.

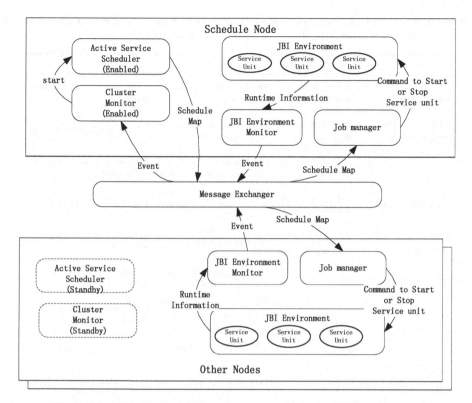

Fig. 1. Scheduling framework for active services in clustered JBI environment

The Schedule Node. In our approach, there exists a schedule node in cluster, which monitors the cluster and schedules the singleton SUs. The schedule node is not pre-defined. It is automatically chosen at runtime. If the schedule node is down, one of other nodes will replace its role immediately. Every node in cluster has cluster monitor and active service scheduler, but only the schedule node activate them.

Monitors and Events. The cluster monitor on schedule node continuously listens the events from cluster, and start the service scheduler when specific events happen. The event may be a request for starting or stopping service unit from administrator, or a runtime error from one node's JBI environment monitor when exception happens, or a notification from cluster when one node is down.

The JBI environment monitor is responsible for monitoring the running state of JBI environment. When the JBI container is started and stopped, or a SU is started and stopped, it will send the event to schedule node. Table 1 shows the main events in our scheduling framework.

Scheduler and Job Manager. Active service scheduler is responsible for scheduling the singleton SUs according to nodes' load. The scheduling algorithm is detailed in section 3.2. The scheduling result is schedule map, a hash-map which use singleton SUs' names as key set, and use nodes' identities as value set. The key-value pair <singleton SU' name, node's identity> indicates which node is responsible for starting the singleton SU.

Table 1. The events in scheduling framework. The event source could be JBI enviorment monitor, Client , or Cluster itself. Event are handled based on its type.

Event	Event Source	Notes	Handle Action
JBI_CONTAINER _STARTED	JBI environment monitor	The JBI container on one node is started	mark node as schedulable node
JBI_CONTAINER _SHUTDOWN	JBI environment monitor	The JBI container on one node is shutdown	Re-schedule the active service unit the node used to start.
SU_START_ERROR	JBI environment monitor	One singleton service unit is not started successfully.	Try another node to start this service unit.
SU_STOP_ERROR	JBI environment monitor	One singleton service unit is not stopped successfully.	Retry to stop the service unit.
USER_SCHEDULE _ALL	Client	User's request for schedule all active service units	Schedule all the singleton SUs
USER_START_SA	Client	User's request for starting a service assembly	Schedule the singleton SUs included by SA.
USER_STOP_SA	Client	User's request for stopping a service assembly	Stop the singleton SUs included by SA
NODE_ONLINE	Cluster	One node is added to cluster	Mark node as online node.
NODE_OFFLINE	Cluster	One node is down and removed from cluster	Re-schedule the singleton SUs the node used to start.

The schedule map will be multicast to every node in cluster. After the node receives the schedule map, the job manager on the node will be put into work, which checks the local state of singleton SUs, and compares them with schedule map, so as to decide which SU in JBI container should be started and which one should be stopped. Then, a list of "start SU" or "stop SU" jobs is created to start or stop the SUs in JBI environment. If error accrues in the process of starting or stopping SU, the JBI environment monitor will sends "SU_START_ERROR" or "SU_STOP_ERROR" event to the schedule node.

3.2 Scheduling Algorithm

The aim of scheduling algorithm is to guarantee that each singleton SU only run on exactly one node, as well as keep the load balance between nodes. The outline of scheduling algorithm is as following.

Algorithm 1. scheduling algorithm for singleton SUs in clustered JBI environment
The Schedule Node:
1. Gets load information of every node from cluster;
2. Creates a load-table.
3. For each singleton SU that is to be scheduled
4.   Calculates and choose the least-load node;
5.   Sets the node as the executing node of SU

```
6.            in schedule-map;
7.   Adds the SU's weight to the node's load
8.            in load-table.
9. End For
10. Multicasts schedule-map to every node in cluster;
```

Every node in cluster:
```
1. Receives the schedule-map;
2. Gets running state of all SUs in local JBI container;
3. For each SU
4.   If SU is expected to be started on this node in
5.      schedule-map, but is not started,
6.   then creates "start SU" job;
7.   If SU is not expected to be started in schedule-map,
8.            but is started,
9.   then creates "stop SU" job;
10. End For
11. If error accrues while starting or stopping SU,
12.   then sends SU_START_ERROR or SU_STOP_ERROR event
13.            to Schedule node
```

Calculate Nodes' Load. The algorithm is not complex, but the central problem is how to calculate and evaluate the load of every node. We propose an approach based on the singleton SUs' load weights.

Different singleton SU may have different influence on the load of node. Some SU may occupy more CPU time, while other SUs may need a wider network bandwidth. In our approach, every singleton SU has three pre-defined load weights: CPU weight, memory weight and network weight. The weight is an integer number between 0 and 100, indicating the relative resource occupied degree for CPU, memory and network.

For the SU need more CPU time, we should choose the node which has the less CPU load. Similarly, for the SU that need a wider network bandwidth, we should choose the node that has the less network load. Therefore, the load of every node should be calculated considering the current SU's requirement. We call it *relative load*.

Given an active service unit su, let its CPU weight as C_{su}, memory weight as M_{su} and network weight as N_{su}. If one node is executing n active service units, then the relative load of this node for su is:

$$L_{node-su} = (\sum_{i=1}^{n} C_i) \times \frac{C_{su}}{C_{su}+M_{su}+N_{su}} + (\sum_{i=1}^{n} M_i) \times \frac{M_{su}}{C_{su}+M_{su}+N_{su}} + (\sum_{i=1}^{n} N_i) \times \frac{N_{su}}{C_{su}+M_{su}+N_{su}} \qquad (1)$$

In the formula, $\sum_{i=1}^{n} C_i$ is the sum of CPU weight of executing active SUs on the node, indicating the CPU load of the node. Similarly, $\sum_{i=1}^{n} M_i$ and $\sum_{i=1}^{n} N_i$ are memory load and network load of the node.

The relative load takes current SU's requirement into consideration, so it is a reasonable method to calculate the load for singleton SUs on nodes. After calculate the relative load of every node, the node that has the least relative load will be the most suitable one to be scheduled for current SU.

4 Case Study

We implement our scheduling mechanism recently in SOAWARE, a SOA-based application integration platform for electric enterprises. The SOAWARE project is initiated by Wuhan University and Yuanguang Software Co., Ltd in Januuary, 2009 and is ongoing by now.

SOAWARE adopts JBI as application integration standard to enable heterogeneous applications connecting and interoperating with each other, and adopts BPEL as business process standard to (re)construct enterprises' business process, which coordinates the enterprises' applications, and makes them work together for given business goals.

SOAWARE is build based on open-source software. Its JBI enviornment is based on Apache Servicemix, and its BPEL engine is based on Apache ODE. SOAWARE provides the extended features like cluster, security, system monitor and administration, improving the reliablity, scalbility, performance of the platform to support the complex requirement of application integration for electric enterprises.

4.1 Cluster and Load Balancing of SOAWARE Platform

SOAWARE platform is developed as a web application, and is able to be deployed into application servers, like tomcat, jboss, websphere, weblogic. Therefore it is possible to utilize the cluster feature of application servers, e.g. load balancing and failover. The load-balancing of HTTP message can be done by clustered application servers. Also, SOAWARE platform use Apache ActiveMQ as its reliable messaging transport infrastructure, and load-balancing of JMS message can be done by clustered activeMQ servers. SOAWARE platform has an administration system to monitor and manage the cluster. The administration system adopts JGroup to support the communication between nodes in cluster.

4.2 Active Services Scheduling Mechanism in SOAWARE Platform

Active services are very common requirements in application integration practice of electric enterprises. For example, the service that automatically provides business report to higher-up department every day, the service periodically transports finance-related data from business management system to financial system or the service continuously monitors the device data, and notifies the administrator when error happens.

SOAWARE platform manage the cluster based on JGroup[7]. Every node in cluster can send or receive messages with each other on *JGroup channel*. When one node is started or halted, other nodes can receive the notification from the channel.

The channel has a *view* object which records the sequence of cluster members. The first member in the view plays the schedule node in our scheduling mechanism. When the schedule node is down, one of the other nodes will become the first member; therefore become the new schedule node.

The cluster monitor of schedule node will receive schedule event messages from JGroup channel. Once the event message arrives, the cluster monitor will start the corresponding handling process. If it is need to schedule the active services, the scheduler will be put into action. The JBI environment monitor can query runtime information from ServiceMix, the JBI environment of SOAWARE, through administration API, and sends event message when error happens.

The scheduler enacts the scheduling process according the scheduling algorithm. It can multicast request and receive response message through channel to query current state of singleton SUs on every nodes, and multicast schedule map to every node through channel after scheduled.

The job manager is implemented based on Quartz[8], a job scheduling tools. The commands to start or stop a SU will be implemented as *jobs*. When a job is created, it will put into job pool, and scheduled by Quartz scheduler.

5 Experiment and Discussion

5.1 Experiment

We use an experiment to test whether our scheduling algorithm works well. The experiment simulates such a situation: a cluster that has 5 nodes, and 300 active service units to be scheduled. The aim of experiment is to check whether the algorithm can keep the load balance of cluster after scheduled.

The CPU weight, memory weight and network weight of these service units are assigned random values between 0 and 100. The test program gets the service unit one by one, and schedules it to the node which has the least relative load. We record the nodes' loads when every service unit is scheduled. The result is as shown in table 2.

Table 2. The experiment's result of scheduling algorithm. The five numbers within square brackets is the loads of five nodes after certain number of SU is scheduled.

Amount of SU	CPU load	Memory load	Network load
5	[43 36 62 67 24]	[77 98 35 85 64]	[56 33 24 95 51]
10	[95 120 105 138 89]	[140 105 89 174 148]	[132 127 44 122 150]
20	[250 171 216 232 204]	[247 191 219 267 253]	[245 204 202 187 233]
50	[518 534 457 518 462]	[527 522 495 533 495]	[602 514 579 509 579]
80	[798 818 829 824 758]	[824 885 904 949 898]	[841 805 915 894 811]
100	[1040 1014 1034 1007 1066]	[1088 1060 1099 1098 1104]	[1096 1020 1118 1047 1009]
150	[1511 1486 1466 1461 1486]	[1623 1674 1574 1654 1653]	[1485 1573 1529 1554 1465]
200	[2001 1973 2018 1993 1994]	[2221 2112 2172 2131 2224]	[1996 2017 1942 2072 2099]
300	[2955 3027 2989 3082 2985]	[3245 3197 3186 3216 3222]	[3041 2947 2988 3069 3025]

The result shows that the CPU load, memory load and network load of five nodes will increase proportionately as the amount of scheduled SU increases. Especially when the load is heavy, the five nodes keep load balance quit well.

5.2 Discussion

JBI is a new thing in SOA community. Improved by SUN, Apache and other companies and open source organizations, it makes great progress in the past two years. The JBI platform Apache Servicemix and SUN openESB has attracted much attention from the industrial and academic circles.

However, the software infrastructure of JBI is still far from maturity. For example, the cluster feature of Servicemix is still incomplete [5], and openESB relies on its application server Glassfish to support clustering [6]. In addition, many JBI components are not cluster aware, and will results errors in clustered environment, especially the one which can provides active services, e.g. the Servicemix-quartz component, Servicemix-file component, Servicemix-wsn2005 component , etc.

The common solution for active services problem of clustered JBI component is lock mechanism, which controls the access right of resource, to avoid the access error while multiple nodes running same active service concurrently. However, the lock mechanism cannot avoid business errors of duplicate works, which results from multiple instances of same service.

Our approach resolves this problem from a new perspective. By scheduling the active services from a global view, it makes sure every active service only has one running instance in cluster, therefore avoids the runtime and business errors. The approach is suitable for all the JBI components which have active services problems, without writing complex lock managers for specific components.

We propose a load balancing algorithm for active services, which is different from that of passive services. The passive services are invoked by outside HTTP, JMS requests, and the load balancing algorithm is always based on the current state of cluster node, e.g. Round Robin algorithm, least connection algorithm, least loaded algorithm[9,10]. The active service's load press on node is uncertain, they may very busy in this second, but very idle in another second. Load balancing algorithm based on the current state of cluster is unsuitable. So, we provide an algorithm based on the load weight of SUs. The load weights of SU are experiential values, indicating SU's overall load press on nodes.

In our scheduling algorithm, the accuracy of load weights of SU is very important. In present time, this value is pre-defined by developer. In the next step, we will develop tool that monitors and records the load press of SU, and dynamically adjust the value to enable more accurate load distribution. In addition, the developer of active service should follow one best practice: let the passive services do heavy works and the active service invoke it. In this way, the heavy work will not always be done on one node, avoiding the potential overload problems.

In fact, the "singleton service" problem also exists in middlewares. Weblogic and Jboss application server all provide mechanism for singleton service in cluster environment. For example, In Jboss, every singleton service (as MBean) has a Controller named HASingletonController to control its lifecycle, On each node in the cluster where these MBeans are deployed, the controller will work with all of the other controllers with the same MBean name deployed in the same cluster partition to oversee the lifecycle of the singleton. The controllers are responsible for tracking the cluster topology. Their job is to elect the master node of the singleton upon startup, as well as to elect a new master should the current one fail or shut down. In the latter case, when the master node shuts down gracefully, the controllers will wait for the singleton to stop before starting another instance on the new master node [11].

The differences between our approach and Jboss' includes: (1) though active services in JBI environment and the singleton service in application server have some similarity, they are inherently different things with different execution and lifecycle management mechanism. (2)our approach has only one "controller", the active service scheduler, for all the singleton services in cluster. The merit is obviously. The active service scheduler knows all the allocation information of singleton services, and this makes it possible to keep the load balance of all the active services.

6 Conclusion

JBI environment allows developer to define and publish active services. However these active services may lead to business or runtime error in clustered environment. Aimed at this problem, a scheduling mechanism for active services in cluster environment is proposed. We give the overall framework of scheduling mechanism, along with the scheduling mechanism for load balancing of active services. The approach is implemented in SOAWARE, a SOA-based application integration platform for electric enterprises, and an experiment is done to check the effectiveness of scheduling mechanism.

In the next step, we will try this approach in cloud computing environment, where cluster is the inherent feature and the active service problems inevitably exist.

References

1. Vinoski, S.: Java Business Integration. IEEE Internet Computing 9(4), 89–91 (2005)
2. Java Community Process: JSR 208: Java Business Integration (JBI),
   http://www.jcp.org/en/jsr/detail?id=208
3. Rotem-Gal-Oz, A.: SOA Patterns. Manning Publications, MEAP Release (June 2007)
4. Haldor, S., Rolv, B.: Describing Active Services for Publication and Discovery. In: Software Engineering Research, Management and Applications, vol. 150, pp. 173–187. Springer, Heidelberg (2001)
5. Apache Software Foundation: Apache Servicemix Project Home,
   http://servicemix.apache.org
6. SUN : OpenESB: the open enterprise service bus,
   https://open-esb.dev.java.net/

422   X. Jia et al.

7. Montresor, A.: Jgroup Tutorial and Programmer's Manual. Technical report: BOLOGNA#UBLCS-2000-13, University of Bologna (2000)
8. Cavaness, C.: Quartz Job Scheduling Framework: Building Open Source Enterprise Applications. Prentice Hall PTR, Englewood Cliffs (2006)
9. Cardellini, V., Colajanni, M., Yu, P.S.: Dynamic load balancing on web-server systems. IEEE Internet Computing 3(3), 28–39 (1999)
10. Teo, Y.M., Ayani, R.: Comparison of load balancing strategies on cluster-based web servers, Simulation. The Journal of the Society for Modeling and Simulation International 77(5-6), 185–195 (2001)
11. Ivanov, I.: J2EE Clustering with JBoss,
    http://onjava.com/pub/a/onjava/2003/08/20/
    jboss_clustering.html?page=1

Task Parallel Scheduling over Multi-core System*

Bo Wang

Department of Computer Science and Technology,
Tsinghua National Laboratory for Information Science and Technology
Tsinghua University Beijing 100084, China
bo-wang06@mails.tsinghua.edu.cn

Abstract. Parallel scheduling research based on multi-core system become more and more popular due to its super computing capacity. Scheduling fairness and load balance is the key performance indicator for current scheduling algorithm. The action of scheduler can be modeled as this: accepting the task state graph, task scheduling analyzing and putting the produced task into scheduling queue. Current algorithms involve in the action prediction according to the history record of task scheduling. One disadvantage is that it becomes little efficient when task cost keeps great difference. Our devotion is to rearrange one long task into small subtasks, then form another task state graph and parallel schedule them into task queue. The final experiments show that 20% performance booster has been reached by comparison with the traditional method.

Keywords: task, parallel scheduling, multi-core.

1 Introduction

Multi-core system becomes more and more popular with the CPU frequency reaching the summit. In future, common desktop CPU can possess more than 8 cores and some server can reach from 64 to 128 cores. Hardware has provided so powerful computing capacity that more research work is currently focusing on the parallel application such as parallel scheduling, parallel task partition, parallel communication and parallel accessing policies. As far as the parallel scheduling is concerned, this question is NP-Hard. First, our target is to reduce the whole task running time to minimum duration; second, the difficulties are how to optimally partition the task into different processors the incoming tasks which have different parameters such as beginning time, executing time and ending time. The common way to solve this is to adopt some approximate algorithm such as Fixed Parameter Algorithm.

One whole process of task scheduling can be described likes this: first, programmers write one parallel program using the parallel programming language such as

---

* This Work is co-sponsored by Natural Science Foundation of China (60673152,60773145, 60803121), National High-Tech R&D (863) Program of China (2006AA01A101, 2006AA01A106, 2006AA01A108, 2006AA01A111, 2006AA01A117), National Basic Research (973) Program of China (2004CB318000), and Tsinghua National Laboratory for Information Science and Technology (TNLIST) Cross-discipline Foundation.

M.G. Jaatun, G. Zhao, and C. Rong (Eds.): CloudCom 2009, LNCS 5931, pp. 423–434, 2009.
© Springer-Verlag Berlin Heidelberg 2009

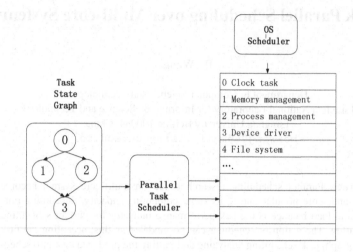

Fig. 1. This shows the relation between task parallel scheduler and operating system scheduler

OpenMP or TBB. Through the controlling over the task partition using the special marking, programmers tell the scheduling which parts can be executed parallel and which parts must be executed serial. Second, based on the initial task logical partition proposed by programmers, the scheduling will take the bridge role between the logical tasks and real processors. One way, it accepts the input tasks and strands some of them to form one string of pearls which means that these must be scheduled serial, meanwhile, it also it can organize them to form the independent subtasks which means that they can be scheduled parallel.

We simple decompose the action of parallel task scheduler as follows: acquiring the task state graph, analyzing it with certain algorithm, producing the executing order and putting them into the tasks queue. Based on multi-core system, our work is exploiting some parallel running on each step. And our proposed algorithm is trying to partition one task into many subtasks which some of them can be parallel executed, and immediately put them into the task queue without predicating the future conditions.

2 Related Work

Much research work assumes that some tasks need more execution time. The algorithm GFB, RHS, Dhall shows bad performance when at least one task with large execution requirements. [1][2].James H. Anderson proposes one scheduling method for real-time systems implemented on multi-core architecture that encourages certain groups of tasks to be scheduled together while ensuring real-time constraints [3][4]. The current Linux scheduler is Completely Fair Scheduler (CFS) scheduler which was introduced into the Linux kernel in version 2.6.23[6]. Some research imposes certain requirements that may limit its practical implementation and address such limitation which requires processor time to always be allocated in units of fixed-sized quanta that are synchronized across processors and determine the impact of relaxing it [5]. Finding a schedule of minimal length is in general a so difficult problem that people begin to realize that optimal schedule is a trade-off between high parallelism and low processor communication. In fact, the general decision problem associated with the scheduling problem is NP-complete [8]. The parallel iterator allows the structure of the program to remain unchanged, it may be used with any collection type and it supports several scheduling schemes which may even be decided dynamically at run-time. Along with the ease of use, the results reveal negligible overhead and the expected inherent speedup [9].

The paper is organized as follows: section 3 includes a detailed account of multi-processor parallel scheduling; section 4 evaluates the system performance and experimental results. Section 5 and 6 are future work and conclusion.

3 Task Scheduling

Task scheduling can be separated into static and dynamic scheduling. Static scheduling usually means that the scheduling will run at compile time, as opposed to dynamic scheduling, which is scheduled during the execution of the program. Fig.2 shows current Linux scheduler and fig.3 shows the common task state graph which can be decomposed into several subtasks and executed parallel.

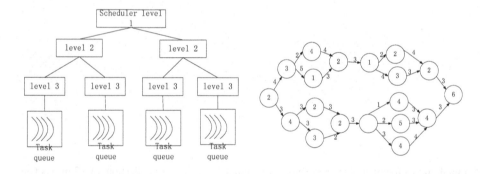

Fig. 2. the hierarchy scheduler in Linux 2.6 based on multi-core system

Fig. 3. This figure shows one special task graph. It includes in the node whose value shows the computation cost and the edge whose value stands for communication cost.

3.1 Task Scheduling Definition

Processor Allocation: A processor allocation A of the task graph $G=(V,E,w,c)$ on a finite set P of processors is the processor allocation function proc: $V{\rightarrow}P$ of nodes of G to the processor of P.

Scheduling: A schedule S of the task graph $G = (V,E,w,c)$ on a finite set P of processor is the function pair (ts,proc), WHERE

w: is the computation cost function of the edge $n \in V$. The communication cost $w(n)$ of node n is the time the task represented by n occupies a processor of P for its execution.

c: is the communication cost function of the edge $e \in E$. The communication cost $c(e)$

Ts: is the start time function of the nodes of G.

Proc: $V \rightarrow P$ is the processor allocation function of the nodes of G to the processor of P.

The two functions ts and proc describe the spatial and temporal assignment of tasks which reflect the feature of the task graph.

3.2 Concurrent Model Definitions for Scheduling

In Figure 4: the incoming task is submitted to the scheduler which decides which sub-scheduler can acquire it; during this process, there exists one basic principle: try to allocate the dependent tasks into the same physical package unit in order to reducing the communication overhead and saving the processor power consumption. Different processors can access the task queue at the same time.

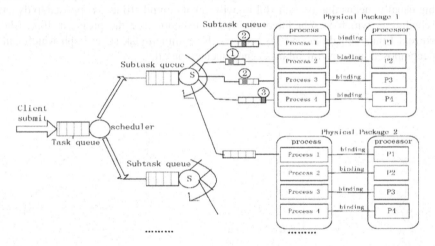

Fig. 4. in this figure, 1, 2, 3 represent the execution order for one application, two 2 means two tasks can be executed parallel

4 Parallel Algorithm Implements in the Multi-core System

In figure 5, it shows several algorithms to access the concurrent queue; different algorithms need the support of certain protocols for data consistency [11]. Using some locks and doing some traverse are required to ensure they are deadlock-free and starvation-free. One method is deadlock-free if this phenomenon is not happened in any case that two or more threads are waiting each other to release their locked resources. One method is starvation-free if in the finite steps each call will finish executing.

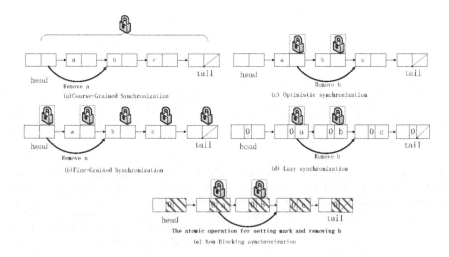

Fig. 5. five different synchronization algorithms. In (a) shows one coarse-grained algorithm and others show fine-grained or improved fine-grained algorithm. In (e) shows the non-blocked algorithm and others show blocked algorithm.

Below are some introducing about these algorithms. As far as the performance as a whole is concerned, more factors should be considered such as the fairness principle, asymmetry architecture, thread migration and repeatability, etc [12]. Fairness means that threads with the same priority should receive about the same share of core processing power [13].

4.1 Synchronization Algorithm Introduction

4.1.1 Coarse-Grained Synchronization
Each method locks the object to avoid contention happening on the different threads. The disadvantage is when many threads access it at the same time, it will reduce the throughput.

4.1.2 Fine-Grained Synchronization
This method splits object into pieces and each of them has its own lock; more than one thread can access the disjoint pieces not damaging the queue integrity and consistency. In figure 5, b is the operation for removing node a. To be safe, remove function must lock both previous node and current node until finding the correct location to remove. Comparing current key value with node's hash value, deciding if find the right place.

4.1.3 Optimistic Synchronization
This method tries to reduce synchronization costs. Take an example for remove operation. When it traverses the queue and does not find the correct node, it does not lock previous and current node; and when it find the correct node, it will lock the current and previous nodes and then it need to validate that these two nodes are in the

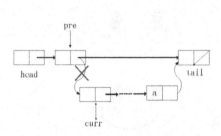

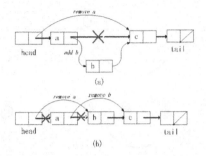

Fig. 6. One node is removed by another thread, but if current thread does not traverse the queue and verify that current node is reachable, then this bad scenario will happen

Fig. 7. (a) Shows one thread wants to remove node a; another wants to add node b, in the end node a is correctly added while b is not added into the queue. (b) Shows one wants to remove a; another wants to remove b. In the end, a is removed and b not.

current queue by traversing from the head until the current node is reachable. If current is unreachable, this operation will be failed. The main reason for validating is that traversing any dynamically changing lock-based queue, sometimes if the nodes what you are operating are removed by other threads, still you think these nodes are well keeping in the queue. For a clear description, fig.6 is the figure for this scenario:

4.1.4 Lazy Synchronization
During the end of optimistic method operation such as add, remove, one thing must be done that the current node must be reachable from the head node. This is acquired by traversing the whole queue. So this method works better if the cost of traversing the queue twice (first finding the correct node) without locking is evidently less than the cost of traversing the queue once with locking.

4.1.5 Non-blocking Synchronization
It is one good idea to mark nodes as logically removed before physically removing them from the queue. It will bring about the some disadvantages we speak of above. The main reason resulting in it lies in not atomic for logical and physical operations. In this method, we use one operation to verify that they are atomically executed. In Figure 7, the scenario (a) and (b) are not successful for all operations. If so, it will need more re-traversing and make the call delayed.

4.1.6 Dual-Accessing Synchronization
All the above methods illustrate the parallel accessing the queue without destroying the data consistency. One disadvantage for them is that when the data length becomes long, more work will be done on the traversing the queue and one replaceable parallel structure is parallel hash table and another application scenario for above parallel algorithm is data sorting. Our proposed applied parallel accessing method is dual-accessing and dynamic changeable length of queue structure whose operation is pushing data into the front of the queue and popping data from the tail of the queue when data length is dynamic changing with the operation keeping.

4.2 Several Algorithm Implementations for Parallel Adding Operation

input:*A:one value;Q:one queue which will be inserted by A*

ouput:*Q*

begin

   {initialize pred,curr,key;}

    *Lock Q;/** it can be blocked***/*

   while *curr.key<key*

     do *{ pred=curr;curr=curr.next;}*

   if *key==curr.key* **then**

    return false

   else then

     {initialize node ;}

     node.next=curr;

     pred.next=node;

     return true;

   end if

   Unlock Q;

end begin

(a)*Coarse-Grained Synchronization*

input:*A:one value;Q:one queue which will be inserted by A*

ouput:*Q*

begin

   {initialize head,pred,curr,key;}

   lock head; curr=pred.next;lock curr;

    */*lock can be blocked*/*

   while *curr.key<key* **do**

    {unlock pred;pred=curr;

    curr=curr.next;unlock curr;}

   if *key==curr.key* **then**

    return false

   else then

    {Initialize node ;}

    node.next=curr;

    pred.next=node;

    return true;

   end if

   Unlock curr;Unlock pred;

end begin;

(b) *Fine-Grained Synchronization*

Fig. 8. code description for *add* function in these parallel algorithms. The lazy, non-blocking and dual-accessing algorithms are not list here.

5 Experiment Evaluation

To demonstrate the multi-core architecture, serials of case studies are performed to evaluate the multi-core effectiveness of system. Some instances in task scheduling will run between 10s and several hours, depending on the type of application and allocation of resources. Here we simulate the action of the task scheduler and design the experiments under the multi-core system.

The scheduler handle the tasks in multi-core system like this way: when it queues the tasks in the order they arrive it schedules one of them into optimal nodes according to the dependency of tasks. So the common action is this: the queue of tasks is changing dynamically with the tasks' increment and decrement. Several processors can concurrently access the tasks and under with different load of task number, these algorithms show different performance. Below are the details about them.

First experiment reflects the algorithm execution time under different data size from 1024 to 262144, keeping 8 threads accessing these data during thread is alive. From (a), fine-grained algorithm has the longest running time and steep variation trend, on the other side, coarse-grained algorithm keep the lowest running time and good performance. One main reason why the result is so is that during sequential operations, including add, contain and remove, thread number is small, meanwhile operation does not frequently acquire the lock. So coarse-grained can get the best performance in this scenario. By comparison, parallel algorithm in (d) shows the lazy acquires best performance, meanwhile, fine-grained get worst. In sequential and parallel algorithm, fine-grained always keep worst performance. From the algorithm, even if it can let more threads concurrently access the queue, it must lock the two other objects from the head until it finds the correct object. So during this it spends more time locking and releasing useless object. With the data size bigger and bigger, the overhead on this becomes more obvious. One serious result is its memory overflow when the data size reaches 128*64.

When data size is kept constant at the value of 128*256, thread number is changed from 128 to 128*1024. (b) and (d) reflect the execution time of 5 algorithms. During sequential operation (add, contain, and remove), even if thread number become bigger, each of them can finish all operations without waiting for anytime. All 5 algorithms spent same time on different thread number; by comparison, parallel operation does not keep level and show certain increment with the growing of thread number. The lazy algorithm acquires best performance, while fine-grained does worst.

In another group experiment, we simulate the action of LSF which is used to analysis the off-instrument SOLiD data. SOLiD belongs to one of next-generation sequencing technologies. It expands the boundaries of traditional genetic analysis and enables applications such as whole genome and targeted resequencing, whole transcriptome analysis, de novo sequencing, ChIP-Seq, and methylation analysis. The action of LSF in the application of SOLiD can be reduced to this: extract the command and corresponding parameters from the input file and schedule it to one of node. After the execution of the command, the other node will return the result to the initial node. In traditional task scheduling, one task for job manager is to deciding which

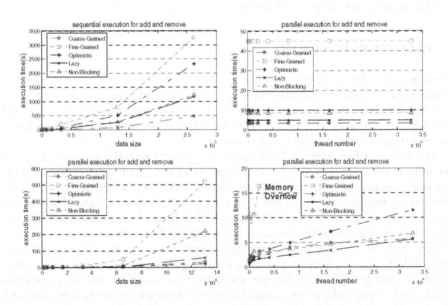

Fig. 9. Algorithms execution efficiency in different data size or thread number. In (a) and (c), keeping thread number is one constant value for 128*256, meanwhile, in (b) and (d), constant value is data size. This experiments show that using different algorithm, execution performance exist evident difference.

node is optional for scheduling according to the certain algorithm. In future multi-core system will possess more cores such as 64,128 or more. Letting each core positive acquires tasks will save more time and resource. In traditional method, maybe scheduler produces many tasks which can not be removed timely because others nodes can not finish related job. But it still keeps many connections with different nodes. The main reason is that scheduler greedily works and does not care if so many threads can congestion the system and take up lots of resources. In our experiments, if each thread needs much space to save arrays or other objects, too many threads will result in the heap overflows. The main reason for this is that thread takes up some memory space but CPU has not chances to handle it timely. Even if multi-threads will cover up some waiting time during threads interrupt, too many threads will result in the improvement of the thread switching load and sacrifice the time of real execution of thread.

The experiments are done like this: one file keeps the list of gene data and matching parameters which are used as one sub-string to find if it is existed in the gene data. The scheduler will one by one dispatch the task and run it as one thread. As far as OS is concerned, the object of its managing is process or thread according to different concrete operating system.

Experiment Environment
Operating system: Linux el5xen
CPU: SMP Intel(R) Xeon(R) 8CPU E5310 @ 1.60GHz
Cache size on each core: 4096KB
Memory size: 8GB

In figure 10 and 11, we compare the sequential and multi-thread based on multi-core system. In figure 10, sequential method is better than latter. The main reason is that each thread is allocated with less time which improves the overhead in managing and switching threads. Here we give the function:

$$t_{total} = t_{realwork} + t_{auxiliary}$$

The total execution is partitioned into two parts: one is real work and another is auxiliary. If each thread works less time, the auxiliary work will improve accordingly. So we should give appropriate execution time for each thread. From the experience, each thread should execute the instruction from 10,000 to 100,000. In Figure 11, with the increase of execution time, parallel algorithm shows better than sequential.

In figure 12 and 13, we compare the traditional and our method, even if the traditional scheduling allocates one task which will be executed as one thread, the main disadvantage is that in one internal thread, opening file and data computing are executed together. Between them, there need some interruption invoke instruction and thread switching which will result in cache flush and thread waiting. The result illustrates that given certain workload (source code available through our email), 20% performance booster has been reached by comparison with the initial method.

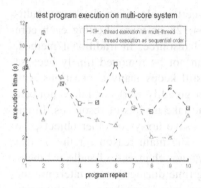

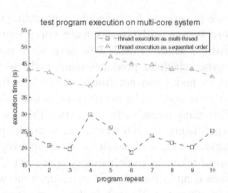

Fig. 10. The number is 2000 files, 5000 strings and 100 sub-strings. Each file includes one string and sub-string. The operation is looking for sub-string in one string.

Fig. 11. The number is 2000 files, 5000 strings and 100 sub-strings. Each file includes one string and sub-string.

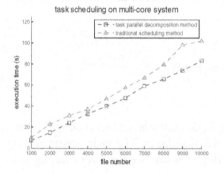

Fig. 12. In this figure, two scheduling methods are executed on multi-cores (8)

Fig. 13. we compare the traditional method with our proposed method when the data length changes

6 Future Work

Our future work will focus on the performance research given different length of task not subtask in order to fulfill more fairness policy and shorten the penalty time wasted by the small subtask execution time. Another puts forward requirement specification method based on a sliding constraint, which model the problem as an extension of the multiple-choice knapsack problem [15]. Batch mode methods provide fast planning by exploring characteristics of distributed and highly heterogeneous systems [16]. Most of parallel scientific applications have demand on simultaneous exploitation of tasks and data parallelism for efficient and effective utilization of system and other resources [17]. Some mixed-parallel applications arise for instance in image processing applications that consist of the scheduling of image filters, where some of these filters can be themselves implemented as data-parallel applications [18]. To acquire the maximal throughput for accessing the computer resources, batch scheduler is used as a common resources management system in some production [19].

7 Conclusion

In this paper, one rearranging task method is presented based on the gene matching application. Comparing with traditional method, more work should be done to decompose the task into equal length of subtasks rather than predict the future task characteristic. Another work that we have done is to design one concurrent queue which can be parallel accessed by multi-core system. Comparing with the traditional design method, our method is more pragmatic and more close to the real application which shows good efficiency in different conditions.

References

[1] Baruah, S.K., et al.: Proportionate progress: a notion of fairness in resource allocation. In: Proceedings of the twenty-fifth annual ACM symposium on Theory of computing. ACM, San Diego (1993)

[2] Bertogna, M., Cirinei, M., Lipari, G.: Schedulability Analysis of Global Scheduling Algorithms on Multiprocessor Platforms. IEEE Trans. Parallel Distrib. Syst. 20(4), 553–566 (2009)

[3] Anderson, J.H., Calandrino, J.M.: Parallel task scheduling on multicore platforms. SIGBED Rev. 3(1), 1–6 (2006)

[4] Carpenter, J., Funk, S., Holman, P., Srinivasan, A., Anderson, J., Baruah, S.: A categorization of real-time multiprocessor scheduling problems and algorithms. In: Leung, J.Y. (ed.) Handbook on Scheduling Algorithms, Methods, and Models, pp. 30.1–30.19. Chapman Hall/CRC, Boca Raton (2004)

[5] Devi, U.C., Anderson, J.H.: Desynchronized Pfair Scheduling on Multiprocessors. In: Proceedings of the 19th IEEE International Parallel and Distributed Processing Symposium (IPDPS 2005) - Papers, vol. 01. IEEE Computer Society, Los Alamitos (2005)

[6] Kumar, A., http://www.ibm.com/developerworks/linux/library/l-cfs/index.html

[7] Anderson, J.H., Calandrino, J.M.: Parallel Real-Time Task Scheduling on Multicore Platforms. In: Proceedings of the 27th IEEE International Real-Time Systems Symposium. IEEE Computer Society, Los Alamitos (2006)

[8] Sinnen, O.: Task Scheduling for Parallel Systems. Wiley Series on Parallel and Distributed Computing. Wiley-Interscience, Hoboken (2007)

[9] Giacaman, N., Sinnen, O.: Parallel iterator for parallelising object oriented applications. In: Proceedings of the 7th WSEAS International Conference on Software Engineering, Parallel and Distributed Systems. World Scientific and Engineering Academy and Society (WSEAS), Cambridge (2008)

[10] Ali, A., Johnsson, L., Subhlok, J.: Scheduling FFT computation on SMP and multicore systems. In: Proceedings of the 21st annual international conference on Supercomputing. ACM, Washington (2007)

[11] Herlihy, M.: The art of multiprocessor programming. In: Proceedings of the twenty-fifth annual ACM symposium on Principles of distributed computing. ACM, Denver (2006)

[12] Feitelson, D.G., Rudolph, L., Schwiegelshohn, U.: Parallel Job Scheduling — a Status Report. In: Feitelson, D.G., Rudolph, L., Schwiegelshohn, U. (eds.) JSSPP 2004. LNCS, vol. 3277, pp. 1–16. Springer, Heidelberg (2005)

[13] Li, T., Baumberge, D., et al.: Efficient and scalable multiprocessor fair scheduling using distributed weighted round-robin. In: Proceedings of the 14th ACM SIGPLAN symposium on Principles and practice of parallel programming, ACM, Raleigh (2008)

[14] Chatzigiannaki, I., Giannouli, G., et al.: Scheduling tasks with dependencies on asymmetric multiprocessors. In: Proceedings of the twenty-seventh ACM symposium on Principles of distributed computing. ACM, Toronto (2008)

[15] Sonnta, R., et al.: An Efficient Weighted-Round-Robin Algorithm for Multiprocessor Architectures. In: Proceedings of the 41st Annual Simulation Symposium (ANSS-41 2008). IEEE Computer Society, Los Alamitos (2008)

[16] Wieczore, M., Podlipni, S., et al.: Bi-criteria Scheduling of Scientific Workflows for the Grid. In: Proceedings of the 2008 Eighth IEEE International Symposium on Cluster Computing and the Grid. IEEE Computer Society, Los Alamitos (2008)

[17] Xhaf, F., Baroll, L., et al.: Batch mode scheduling in grid systems. Int. J. Web Grid Serv. 3(1), 19–37 (2007)

[18] Bansa, S., Kuma, P., et al.: An improved two-step algorithm for task and data parallel scheduling in distributed memory machines. Parallel Comput. 32(10), 759–774 (2006)

[19] Aid, K., Casanova, H.: Scheduling mixed-parallel applications with advance reservations. In: Proceedings of the 17th international symposium on High performance distributed computing. ACM, Boston (2008)

Cost-Minimizing Scheduling of Workflows on a Cloud of Memory Managed Multicore Machines

Nicolas G. Grounds[1], John K. Antonio[2], and Jeff Muehring[1]

[1] RiskMetrics Group, 201 David L. Boren Blvd, Suite 300, Norman, OK, USA
[2] School of Computer Science, University of Oklahoma, Norman, OK, USA

Abstract. Workflows are modeled as hierarchically structured directed acyclic graphs in which vertices represent computational tasks, referred to as requests, and edges represent precedent constraints among requests. Associated with each workflow is a deadline that defines the time by which all computations of a workflow should be complete. Workflows are submitted by numerous clients to a scheduler that assigns workflow requests to a cloud of memory managed multicore machines for execution. A cost function is assumed to be associated with each workflow, which maps values of relative workflow tardiness to corresponding cost function values. A novel cost-minimizing scheduling framework is introduced to schedule requests of workflows so as to minimize the sum of cost function values for all workflows. The utility of the proposed scheduler is compared to another previously known scheduling policy.

1 Introduction

The service-oriented architecture (SOA) framework is a viable approach to cloud computing in which computational requirements of a user are represented by basic service requests. In this framework, the computational requirements of a user are modeled as a workflow graph (WFG), which is a directed and acyclic graph that defines precedence constraints among service requests required by the user. WFGs can vary greatly in size and structure. For example, a small WFG may contain just a few requests (i.e., vertices) while a large WFG may contain thousands of requests. Regarding structure, at one extreme a WFG may represent a single chain of requests in which no two requests may be executed in parallel. At another extreme, the structure of a WFG may contain numerous independent chains of requests in which requests belonging to distinct chains may be executed in parallel.

For the purposes of this paper, the SOA is supported by a collection of memory-managed multicore machines. Each machine supports one or more services, and associated with each service are a number of supporting operations. A service request involves the execution of an operation provided by a service. Each multicore machine in the assumed platform can concurrently execute multiple service requests because each request is executed as an independent thread on the machine. The instantaneous performance efficiency of each machine is assumed to depend on an aggregate measure of CPU loading and heap memory loading

M.G. Jaatun, G. Zhao, and C. Rong (Eds.): CloudCom 2009, LNCS 5931, pp. 435–450, 2009.

of all requests executing on the machine. An efficiency-based performance model for memory-managed multicore machines is adopted in this paper.

In the framework considered here, WFGs are assumed to be submitted by multiple clients to a scheduler. Associated with each submitted WFG is a deadline that defines the time by which all requests of the WFG should complete execution. A cost function is assumed to be associated with each workflow, which maps values of workflow tardiness to corresponding cost function values. A novel cost-minimizing scheduling approach is introduced to schedule requests of workflows so as to minimize the sum of cost function values for all workflows.

The remainder of the paper is organized in the following manner. Section 2 includes an overview of related work. Section 3 describes the assumed cloud environment, including models and descriptions for the workflow graphs and the machines that support the cloud's SOA. Section 4 describes the new cost-minimizing scheduler. Section 5 provides the results of simulation studies, followed by concluding remarks in the final section.

2   Background and Related Work

Previous related work is reviewed in three broad areas: (1) machine modeling and simulation environments; (2) automatic memory management; and (3) scheduling and load balancing.

Considerable work has been published related to modeling of machines in distributed environments. Much of the past research in this area has focused on modeling and predicting CPU performance, e.g., [1, 2]. The machine model described in the present paper (refer to Section 3.3) relies on assumed knowledge of the characteristics of the requests (i.e., computational tasks); it is similar in a sense to the SPAP approach proposed in [1].

In memory managed systems, the effect of long and/or frequent garbage collections can lead to undesirable – and difficult to predict – degradations in system performance. Garbage collection tuning, and predicting the impact of garbage collections on system performance, are important and growing areas of research, e.g., [3, 4, 5, 6, 7]. To estimate the overhead associated with various garbage collectors, experiments were designed and conducted in [4, 5] to compare the performance associated with executing an application assuming automatic memory management versus explicit memory management. The machine model proposed here accounts for the overhead associated with automatic memory management.

Formulations of realistic scheduling problems are typically found to be NP-complete, hence heuristic scheduling policies are generally employed to provide acceptable scheduling solutions, e.g., refer to [7, 8, 9, 10, 11, 12]. The scheduling evaluations conducted in the present paper account for the impact that garbage collection has on a machine's performance. Examples of other memory-aware scheduling approaches are described in [7, 13].

Load balancing involves techniques for allocating workload to available machine(s) in a distributed system as a means of improving overall system performance. Examples of both centralized and distributed load balancing approaches are described in [8]. The scheduling framework developed in the present paper incorporates load balancing in the sense that the scheduler only assigns requests to machines if doing so is beneficial relative to minimizing a desired cost function. For simplicity the algorithm assumes every machine can service any request although relaxing this assumption is a straight-forward extension to the approach described here.

3   Cloud Environment

3.1   Overview

Fig. 1 illustrates the major components of the assumed system in which clients submit workflow graphs (WFGs) to a cloud environment for execution. Clients purchase computing services from the cloud, which implements a service-oriented architecture. Associated with each WFG is a service-level agreement (SLA) [9] that defines a deadline for finishing all computations of the WFG. An SLA generally defines cost penalties in the event that the terms of an SLA are not met, e.g., a deadline is missed. For instance, a cost penalty value increases as a function of increasing WFG tardiness. The precise terms of an SLA are carefully constructed for business applications in which timely delivery of computational results are a critical component of a client process — and not having these results delivered to the client by the deadline incurs costs.

The next two subsections provide descriptions and models for the WFG and machine components shown in Fig. 1. Variants of the material presented in Subsections 3.2 and 3.3 were originally introduced in [14]. A primary contribution of the present paper is the introduction of the new cost-minimizing scheduler, which is described in Section 4 and evaluated through simulation studies in Section 5.

3.2   Workflow Graph (WFG) Model

A WFG is a directed acyclic graph with a hierarchical structure composed of parallel and sequential combinations of request chains (RCs). An example WFG is shown in Fig. 2(a). The vertices of the graph represent requests and the directed arcs denote precedence constraints that exist between requests, e.g., request 2 in Fig. 2(a) cannot begin executing until request 1 finishes executing.

The hierarchical nature of the WFG of Fig. 2(a) is illustrated by the tree structure in Fig. 2(b). The leaf nodes of the tree represent the requests of the WFG. Traversing the tree in a depth-first order defines the structure of the associated WFG; non-leaf tree nodes are labeled "S" or "P," which defines whether that node's children must be executed sequentially (S) or may be executed in parallel (P). The children nodes (sub-trees) of a node labeled P are assumed to represent independent and identical computational structures executed with distinct input data. Although all of the children sub-trees of a P node could potentially be executed in parallel, it may not be possible (or effective) to fully

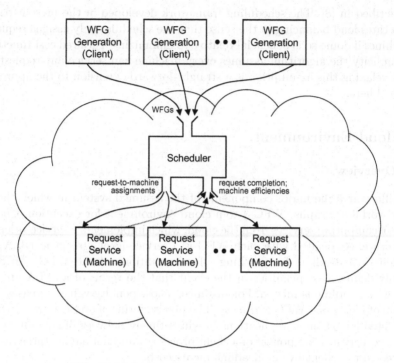

Fig. 1. Major components of the system model

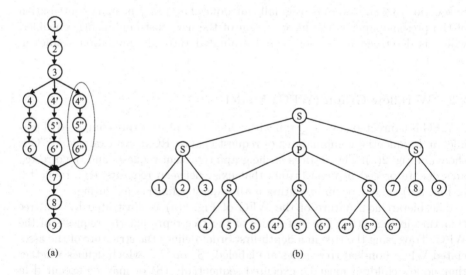

Fig. 2. (a) Sample WFG with one of five RCs encircled. (b) Hierarchical structure of the WFG shown in (a).

exploit all available parallelism associated with all currently executing WFGs due to resource limitations and/or loading.

When a WFG arrives at the scheduler, it is placed in a pool that holds all WFGs that have not yet finished execution. Once all requests of a WFG have finished execution, the entire WFG is defined as finished and removed from the scheduling pool. The scheduler tracks the status of individual requests according to the following states: "blocked," "ready," "executing," or "finished."

The time instant that the state of a request r transitions from "blocked" to "ready" is defined as r's birth time and is denoted by b_r. The finish time of a request is denoted by f_r. The birth time of a request r is defined as the maximum of all finish times of r's precedence requests. For example, in Fig. 2(a), $b_7 = \max\{f_6, f_{6'}, f_{6''}\}$. The time instant that the state of a request transitions from "ready" to "executing" is defined as the request's start time and is denoted by s_r. The start time of a request must be greater than or equal to its birth time, i.e., $s_r \geq b_r$. The function of the scheduler is to determine the start time s_r for each request r as well as determine r's machine assignment, denoted by M_r.

The time instant when WFG w arrives at the scheduling pool is defined as w's birth time, denoted by b_w. The birth time of a WFG is also the birth time of all requests in the WFG that have no precedence constraints, e.g., the birth time of the WFG in Fig. 2(a) equals the birth time of request 1. The start time of a WFG is defined as the minimum start time value of all requests associated with the WFG. Thus, the start time of w is defined by $s_w = \min_{r \in w}\{s_r\}$. The finish time of w, denoted f_w, is defined as the maximum finish time of all requests in w, i.e., $f_w = \max_{r \in w}\{f_r\}$.

Associated with each WFG w is a known deadline d_w, which defines the point in time by which w should finish execution. If $f_w \leq d_w$, then w is not tardy; otherwise (if $f_w > d_w$) w is declared to be tardy. By making judicious choices for request start times and machine assignments, the scheduler attempts to minimize the cost associated with workflow tardiness. Because each machine has a finite capacity, assigning too many concurrent requests to the same machine can degrade the efficiency of that machine, thus extending the finish times of all requests assigned to that machine. Extending the finish times of requests can ultimately extend the finish time of the corresponding WFGs, possibly leading to one or more being tardy.

3.3   Efficiency-Based Machine Model

Each request is assumed to require a fraction of two basic resources available on each machine of the cloud: CPU cycles and heap memory. Table 1 summarizes the notation and definitions of basic computational and heap memory requirements for request r.

The CPU utilization factor of r, U_r, can be no greater than unity and no less than zero. A request having a CPU utilization factor of unity is typically referred to as a CPU-bound request, e.g., refer to [1].

The efficiency value for a machine depends on the aggregate CPU and heap memory loading due to all requests executing on the machine. The CPU and heap

Table 1. Definitions of CPU and heap memory requirements for request r

$C_r > 0$	C_r is the number of CPU cycles required to complete r.
$I_r \geq C_r$	I_r is the execution time duration of r on an ideal machine.
$U_r = C_r/I_r$	U_r is the CPU utilization factor of r.
$H_r > 0$	H_r is the maximum reachable heap memory requirement of r.

memory loading of a given machine changes with time only when new requests are assigned and start executing on the machine, or when existing requests finish execution on the machine. Generally, The efficiency value of a machine generally decreases when new requests begin executing on the machine, and increases when request(s) complete execution on that machine.

The machine to which request r is assigned is denoted by M_r. The efficiency of machine M_r from time instance t_i to time instance t_{i+1}, denoted by $e(M_r, t_i)$, has a value between zero and unity. The number of CPU cycles remaining to complete execution of request r at time instance t_i is denoted by $c_r(t_i)$. The value of $c_r(t_{i+1})$ is calculated based on $c_r(t_i)$ according to the following equation:

$$
c_r(t_{i+1}) = \begin{cases} C_r, & t_{i+1} < s_r \\ \max\left\{0, c_r(t_i) - (t_{i+1} - t_i)e(M_r, t_i)U_r\right\}, & t_{i+1} \geq s_r \end{cases} \tag{1}
$$

For time instants less than r's start time, the value of $c_r(t)$ remains constant at C_r (see Table 1) because the request has not yet started executing. For time instants greater than the request's start time, the value of $c_r(t)$ decreases according to the difference equation defined by the second case of Eq. 1. The value deducted from the CPU cycles remaining to complete execution of request r is proportional to the product of the efficiency of the machine on which the request is assigned and that request's CPU utilization factor. Thus, the maximum possible deduction is $t_{i+1} - t_i$, which corresponds to a situation in which the request is executing on a machine with an efficiency of unity and the request has a CPU utilization factor of unity. The application of the max function in the equation ensures that the number of CPU cycles remaining to complete execution of request r is non-negative.

Fig. 3 illustrates how changes in a machine's efficiency value affects the time required to execute a request on that machine. From the figure, notice that request r starts executing on the assigned machine at $t = s_r$. Near the beginning of the request's execution, note that the efficiency of the machine is relatively high, and the slope of the curve for $c_r(t)$ is correspondingly steep (refer to Eq. 1). Throughout the execution of request r, other requests start executing on the machine (corresponding to decreases in the machine's efficiency value) and complete execution on the machine (corresponding to increases in the machine's efficiency value). The finish time of r is defined as the first point in time when $c_r(t) = 0$, indicated by f_r in Fig. 3.

The following discussion describes how the value of a machine's efficiency is modeled. Throughout this discussion, it is understood that the efficiency value is related to a particular machine for a particular time instant. Thus, the value

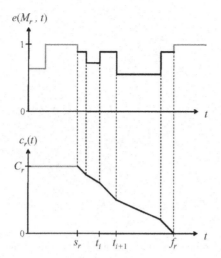

Fig. 3. Illustration of how a machine's efficiency value affects the time required to execute a request on the machine

of efficiency is often referred to as simply e, instead of $e(M, t)$, to ease notational burden.

CPU loading and heap memory loading are the two primary factors used to characterize a machine's relative efficiency. In the machine model, the overall efficiency of a machine is defined by the product of two terms:

$$e = e_c e_h. \tag{2}$$

The terms on the right hand side of Eq. 2 are defined as the CPU efficiency and heap efficiency, respectively. The values of e_c and e_h represent the relative impact on a machine's overall efficiency due to loading of the machine's CPU and heap resources, respectively. The specific functions assumed in the present paper are given by Eq. 3 and Eq. 4.

$$e_c = \begin{cases} 1, & \ell_c < 4 \\ (4/\ell_c), & \ell_c \geq 4 \end{cases} \tag{3}$$

$$e_h = \frac{10}{10 + \frac{1}{(1/\ell_h)-1}} \tag{4}$$

Derivations of these two functions are provided in [14]. The CPU efficiency function of Eq. 3 models a quad-core machine with a CPU loading factor of $\ell_c \geq 0$. The value of ℓ_c is assumed to equal the sum of the U_r's (CPU utilization factors) of all requests executing on the machine. The heap efficiency function of Eq. 4 models the efficiency of the machine's memory managed system as a function of a normalized heap loading factor, $0 < \ell_h < 1$. The specific function of Eq. 4 assumes the time required for a single (full) garbage collection is 10 times less than the execution time of the typical request execution time.

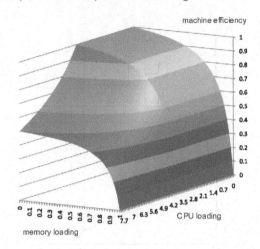

Fig. 4. Derived machine efficiency surface based on the functions for e_c in Eq. 3 and e_h in Eq. 4

Fig. 4 shows a two-dimensional surface plot of $e = e_c e_h$, which is the product of the formulas given in Eqs. 3 and 4. This efficiency function surface is assumed for each machine for the simulations conducted in Section 5.

4   Cost-Minimizing Scheduler

4.1   Notation

Let $\mathcal{W}$ denote the set of all WFGs to be scheduled for execution. For each $w \in \mathcal{W}$ there is assumed to be a cost function, $F_w(\tau_w)$, which maps a normalized measure of w's tardiness, τ_w, to a cost value. The total cost of the system, denoted by $F(\tau)$, is defined by summing the costs of all WFGs:

$$F(\tau) = \sum_{w \in \mathcal{W}} F_w(\tau_w), \qquad (5)$$

where $\tau = [\tau_w]_{w \in \mathcal{W}}$.

The normalized tardiness of WFG w is defined by the follow equation:

$$\tau_w = \frac{f_w - d_w}{d_w - b_w}. \qquad (6)$$

The numerator of the expression, $f_w - d_w$, represents the actual tardiness of w. The denominator of the expression, $d_w - b_w$, represents the maximum desired amount of time allocated for executing w, and is by definition positive. The numerator can be either positive or negative. Thus, $\tau_w \leq 0$ indicates that w is not tardy and $\tau_w > 0$ indicates w is tardy.

Because τ_w is normalized, it is straightforward to compare the relative tardiness values of WFGs of different sizes and/or expected durations. For instance, an actual tardiness of $f_w - d_w = 10$ seconds is relatively insignificant if the overall allocated duration is $d_w - b_w = 1$ hour, i.e., $\tau_w = \frac{10}{3600} = 0.0028$. However, a tardiness of 10 seconds could be quite significant if the overall allocated duration is defined to be 40 seconds, i.e., $\tau_w = \frac{10}{40} = 0.25$.

In order to derive an effective cost-minimizing scheduler, it is convenient to assume that the WFG functions $F_w(\tau_w)$ are non-decreasing functions. This is a reasonable assumption in practice because a sensible SLA should not allow greater tardiness to be less costly than any lesser tardiness.

4.2   Cost-Minimizing Scheduling Algorithm (CMSA)

The function of CMSA is to decide which, if any, of the "ready" requests present in the scheduling pool should be assigned to a machine to begin execution. Scheduling decisions are implemented only at discrete points in time defined as *scheduling instances.* Two events can trigger a scheduling instance: (1) when a request finishes execution or (2) when a new WFG arrives in the scheduling pool. During the time period between two consecutive scheduling instances, the currently executing requests continue executing and the states of the requests in the scheduling pool do not change. Also, based on the machine model described in the previous section, the efficiency value, e, of each machine does not change during the time period between consecutive scheduling instances.

At each scheduling instance, and for each ready request in the scheduling pool, CMSA decides whether to start a request on a machine, based on the outcome of cost function analysis. Specifically, the scheduler estimates the cost associated with starting a ready request now (at the current scheduling instance) or holding the request in the pool until a future scheduling instance. Central to the algorithm's decision-making process is the ability to estimate the costs associated with competing scheduling options. A primary source of uncertainty in estimating a WFG's cost, $F_w(\tau_w)$, is estimating the finish time, f_w, of the WFG. Recall from Eq. 6 that τ_w is directly proportional to f_w.

Predicting the exact value of f_w (before w has finished execution) is generally not possible because all scheduling decisions, including those yet to be made, ultimately affect the values of f_w for all WFGs. As is apparent from Fig. 3, the issue of how to best estimate the finish time of even a single request is not obvious because the value of f_r depends on factors in addition to the request's start time s_r, including how the efficiency of the machine on which it is executing varies with time.

For the purposes of the present discussion, an estimate is assumed to be available for w's finish time at scheduling instance t_i, and this estimate is denoted by $\tilde{f}_w(t_i)$. A description of the particular method used to calculate $\tilde{f}_w(t_i)$ in the simulation studies is provided in Section 5.

Let $\mathcal{M}$ denote the set of machines and $M(t_i)$ denote the set of requests currently executing on machine $M \in \mathcal{M}$ at scheduling instance t_i. Let $R(t_i)$ denote the set of ready requests in the scheduling pool at scheduling instance t_i, and let $w(r)$ denote the WFG associated with request r.

Basic Scheduling Decision: A basic decision made by the scheduling algorithm involves deciding whether to start executing a ready request at a current scheduling instance or to wait until a future scheduling instance. This basic decision assumes a candidate ready request and a candidate machine are specified.

> For ready request $r \in R(t_i)$ and machine $M \in \mathcal{M}$, determine whether it is less costly to start r on M at the current scheduling instance t_i or wait until a future scheduling instance $t_M > t_i$.

The value of t_M is defined to be the next scheduling instance generated by machine M due to the completion of one of M's executing requests. The value of t_M is itself dependant upon whether a particular ready request r^* is started at instance t_i. The formulas for the two possible values of t_M, denoted t_M^{wait} and t_M^{start}, are given by:

$$t_M^{\text{wait}} = t_i + \min_{r \in M} \left\{ \frac{c_r(t_i)}{U_r} \frac{1}{e^{\text{wait}}} \right\} \tag{7}$$

$$t_M^{\text{start}} = t_i + \min_{r \in M \cup \{r^*\}} \left\{ \frac{c_r(t_i)}{U_r} \frac{1}{e^{\text{start}}} \right\}, \tag{8}$$

where $e^{\text{wait}} = e(M(t_i), t_i)$ and $e^{\text{start}} = e(M(t_i) \cup \{r^*\}, t_i)$.

For convenience, define $\Delta t^{\text{wait}} = t_M^{\text{wait}} - t_i$ and $\Delta t^{\text{start}} = t_M^{\text{start}} - t_i$. The cost associated with waiting until t_M^{wait} to begin executing r^* on M is defined by:

$$F_{r^*,M}^{\text{wait}} = F_{w(r^*)} \left(\frac{\tilde{f}_{w(r^*)} + \Delta t^{\text{wait}} - d_{w(r^*)}}{d_{w(r^*)} - b_{w(r^*)}} \right) + \sum_{r \in M} F_{w(r)} \left(\frac{\tilde{f}_{w(r)} - d_{w(r)}}{d_{w(r)} - b_{w(r)}} \right). \tag{9}$$

The cost associated with starting r^* on M at time t_i is defined by:

$$F_{r^*,M}^{\text{start}} = \sum_{r \in M \cup \{r^*\}} F_{w(r)} \left(\frac{\tilde{f}_{w(r)} + \Delta t^{\text{start}} \left(\frac{1}{e^{\text{start}}} - \frac{1}{e^{\text{wait}}} \right) - d_{w(r)}}{d_{w(r)} - b_{w(r)}} \right). \tag{10}$$

For each ready request $r \in R(t_i)$ and each machine $M \in \mathcal{M}$, the cost-minimizing algorithm computes the difference in costs $\Delta F_{r,M} = F_{r,M}^{\text{start}} - F_{r,M}^{\text{wait}}$. If $\Delta F_{r,M} > 0$ for all $r \in R(t_i)$ and for all $M \in \mathcal{M}$, then the scheduler will not start any request now (at scheduling instance t_i). However, if there exists one or more combinations of requests and machines for which $\Delta F_{r,M} \leq 0$, then the scheduler will start the request on the machine having the smallest starting penalty, defined as follows:

$$F_{r,M}^{\text{penalty}} = \Delta F_{r,M} + F_{w(r)} \left(\frac{\tilde{f}_{w(r)} + \Delta t^{\text{wait}} - d_{w(r)}}{d_{w(r)} - b_{w(r)}} \right). \tag{11}$$

Fig. 5 provides the precise description of CMSA. For a given scheduling instance t_i, CMSA first performs computations for all combinations of ready requests and machines, refer to lines 3 through 11. After completing this phase of computation, CMSA then determines whether there exists a request that can be started on a machine. If the answer is no, then the algorithm exits, refer to lines 12 and 13. However, if the answer is yes, then the selected request is assigned to the selected machine (line 14), the selected request is removed from the set of ready requests (line 15), and the algorithm again performs computations for all combinations of ready requests and machines (line 16). The complexity associated with performing computations for all combinations of ready requests and machines is $O(|R(t_i)||\mathcal{M}|)$. Because it is possible that these computations may be performed up to $|R(t_i)|$ times, the worst case computational complexity of CMSA is $O(|R(t_i)|^2|\mathcal{M}|)$.

Note that if the system is highly loaded, then $|R(t_i)|$ will tend to be large. This is because a highly loaded system implies there are limited machine resources available to assign ready requests, thus ready requests will tend to accumulate in the scheduling pool. Because of this, it is likely that CMSA will exit soon under the highly loaded assumption, meaning that while $|R(t_i)|$ is large, the actual complexity of CMSA may be closer to $O(|R(t_i)||\mathcal{M}|)$ than $O(|R(t_i)|^2|\mathcal{M}|)$. On the other hand, if the system is lightly loaded, then $|R(t_i)|$ will tend to be small. This is because a lightly loaded system implies there are ample machine resources available to assign ready requests, thus ready requests will tend to be removed quickly from the scheduling pool. Thus, in the lightly loaded case, the complexity of CMSA tends to be characterized by $O(|R(t_i)|^2|\mathcal{M}|)$. However, because $|R(t_i)|$ is relatively small, the actual complexity for the lightly loaded case may be comparable to, or even less than, the complexity of CMSA under high loading.

```
1      for scheduling instance t_i
2          minPenalty ← ∞, r_min ← ∞, M_min ← ∞
3          for each r ∈ R(t_i)
4              for each M ∈ M
5                  compute ΔF_r,M = F_r,M^start − F_r,M^wait
6                  compute F_r,M^penalty
7                  if ΔF_r,M ≤ 0
8                      if F_r,M^penalty < minPenalty
9                          minPenalty ← F_r,M^penalty
10                         r_min ← r
11                         M_min ← M
12         if minPenalty = ∞
13             exit
14         assign request r_min to machine M_min
15         R(t_i) ← R(t_i) − {r_min}
16         goto line 2
```

Fig. 5. Pseudocode for CMSA

5 Simulation Studies

CMSA is evaluated through simulation studies for a realistic scenario in which different types of WFGs are submitted to the cloud (refer to Fig. 1) by clients from three primary regions: Americas; Europe; and Asia. Furthermore, WFGs of three different types are submitted by clients: Batch, Webservice, and Interactive. Batch WFGs generally have a larger number of requests and requests with greater CPU and memory heap requirements compared to the other two WFG types. The Webservice WFGs generally have more requests than and requests with more requirements than Interactive WFGs.

In addition to differences in number and sizes of requests, the different WFG types are characterized by different arrival rates. The studies conducted were modeled from a typical 24 hour period observed in a live system. Webservice WFGs arrive uniformly over the 24 hours. Interactive WFGs arrive at constant rates only during three 8 hour periods that are partially overlapping. These periods represent interactive use by clients during normal working hours for the three client regions. The bulk of Batch WFGs arrive at hour seven and the arrival rate exponentially decays afterward. The arrival rates over a 24 hour period for the three types of WFGs are illustrated graphically in Fig. 6.

The parameter value ranges and distributions associated with the simulation studies are summarized in Table 2. The table defines parameters related to the structural characteristics for each type of WFG, which are all assumed to have a level of depth as the example in Fig. 2. Also provided in the table are CPU and heap memory characteristics of the requests associated with each WFG type. In all cases, a parallelization factor of two is used in determining a base deadline for each generated WFG; it defines the degree of parallelism assumed for executing parallel RCs from a common WFG. Once a base deadline is determined for a WFG, it is multiplied by the Deadline Factor (last row in the table) to define actual deadline for the WFG.

In making assignment decisions, the Scheduler can make use of computational and heap memory requirements assumed to be known and available for each request. Having access to such information is realistic in the assumed environment in which off-line profiling and/or historical logging can be performed to collect/estimate these data. Also associated with each WFG is a single timing deadline, and the Scheduler can also make use of WFG deadline requirements in making request scheduling decisions.

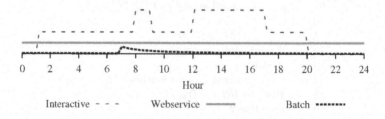

Fig. 6. Arrival rate of WFGs by type over a 24-hour period

Table 2. WFG parameter value ranges, [Min, Max], taken from uniform distributions for simulation studies

Parameter	Interactive WFG	Webservice WFG	Batch WFG
Compound Nodes	[1, 1]	[1, 3]	[3, 5]
Parallel RCs	[1, 2]	[2, 3]	[5, 20]
Requests in RCs	[5, 8]	[5, 8]	[3, 8]
Request Ideal Duration (secs), I_r	[1, 5]	[10, 30]	[50, 250]
Request CPU Utilization, U_r	[0.5, 1.0]	[0.5, 1.0]	[0.5, 1.0]
Request Heap Memory, H_r	[0.05, 0.1]	[0.05, 0.1]	[0.05, 0.15]
WFG Deadline Factor	[1.1, 1.2]	[1.3, 1.5]	[1.3, 1.5]

As described in Section 4, an estimate of each WFG's finish time, denoted as $\tilde{f}_w(t_i)$, is necessary for the CMSA. The following formula is used to estimate WFG finish time in the simulation studies:

$$\tilde{f}_w(t_i) = t_i + (t_i - s_w) \left(\sum_{r \in w} C_r - \sum_{\substack{r \in w \\ f_r < t_i}} C_r \right) \Bigg/ \left(\sum_{\substack{r \in w \\ f_r < t_i}} C_r \right). \qquad (12)$$

The CMSA is evaluated against a previously known algorithm, proportional least laxity first (PLLF) [14], which prioritizes scheduling requests with the least estimated proportional laxity, which is equivalent to the greatest normalized tardiness defined in Eq. 6. PLLF does not make use of any cost function, but only defines the order in which requests are considered for scheduling and relies on a separate policy to decide what machine to start the request on or when to forego scheduling ready requests. In the studies presented PLLF is combined with an algorithm that selects the machine based on the one that will have the largest values of e^{start}, which is defined as the efficiency that results if the request is started on that machine at the current time instance. PLLF elects to forego scheduling requests if all machines' values of e^{start} are below a prescribed threshold value.

Two sets of simulation studies were conducted, one with a sigmoid cost function and the other with a quadratic cost function. Fig. 7 shows the percentage of workflows whose normalized tardiness is at or below the given value of normalized tardiness. For example, only about 30% of workflows scheduled using PLLF had a normalized tardiness of zero or less (met their deadline or were early). In contrast, over 90% of the workflows scheduled by CMSA (using the sigmoid cost function) met their deadline. Also illustrated for reference are the sigmoid and quadratic cost functions. Fig. 8 shows the cumulative running cost of workflows by born time across the 24 hour simulated study period for both cost functions. Although PLLF does not explicitly use a cost function, it was evaluated using the same cost function used by CMSA. The cumulative running cost of both algorithms coincide during the zero to seven hour period, which represented a period when the system is lightly loaded. However, after this point the PLLF algorithm makes very different scheduling decisions than CMSA.

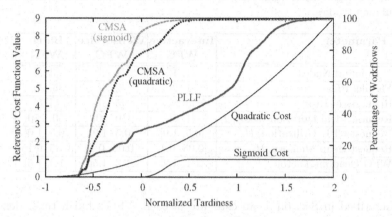

Fig. 7. Percentage of workflows as a function of normalized tardiness for PLLF and CMSA. Also shown are the reference sigmoid and quadratic cost functions.

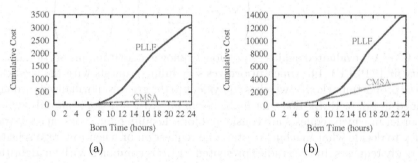

Fig. 8. The cumulative running cost of all WFGs by born time for PLLF and CMSA assuming: (a) sigmoid and (b) quadratic cost functions

Table 3. Summary of results of simulation studies

Measure	Sigmoid		Quadratic	
	PLLF	**CMSA**	**PLLF**	**CMSA**
Cumulative Cost	3,121.7	135.8	13,935.7	3,432.5
% Workflows Late	70.7	8.4	70.7	22.2
% Interactive WFGs Late	74.9	14.0	74.9	37.6
% Batch WFGS Late	96.6	41.5	96.6	57.6
% Webservice WFGs Late	64.3	0.1	64.3	2.3
Normalized Tardiness 95th percentile	1.45	0.10	1.45	0.35
Normalized Tardiness 99th percentile	1.73	0.61	1.73	0.75
Maximum Normalized Tardiness	2.09	5.10	2.09	1.85

Table 3 gives a quantitative summary of all results. From the table, the scheduling produced by PLLF is relatively closer to CMSA for the case of a quadratic cost function $(13, 935.7/3, 432.5 \approx 4 < 3, 121.7/135.8 \approx 23)$. This is because PLLF elects to work on WFGs that are estimated to be most tardy and CMSA ultimately does as well due to the unbounded increasing nature of the quadratic cost function.

In the case study using the sigmoid cost function the CMSA achieves lower normalized tardinesses for the vast majority of WFGs due to the fact that the sigmoid cost function limits the cost of WFGs with normalized tardiness values greater than 0.5. Refer to the table data for the normalized tardiness values of the 95th and 99th percentiles, as well as the maximum normalized tardiness for each policy.

6 Conclusions

A new cost-minimizing scheduling algorithm (CMSA) is introduced for scheduling requests of multi-level workflows of various types and degrees of complexity. The algorithm assumes a cost function is provided, and operates by making scheduling decisions in order to minimize the estimated value of cumulative cost. The performance of the new algorithm is evaluated through realistic simulation studies and compared to a previously best-known scheduling heuristic named PLLF, which is a priority-based scheduler that attempts to minimize maximum normalized tardiness. The simulation studies show that for both sigmoid and quadratic cost functions, CMSA results in maximum normalized tardiness values less than those for PLLF for over 99% of the workflows. Using the sigmoid cost function with CMSA, only about 8% of the workflows were tardy; in contrast, for the same scenario, over 70% of the workflows were tardy using the PLLF policy.

References

[1] Beltrán, M., Guzmán, A., Bosque, J.L.: A new cpu availability prediction model for time-shared systems. IEEE Transactions on Computers 57(7), 865–875 (2008)
[2] Zhang, Y., Sun, W., Inoguchi, Y.: Predicting running time of grid tasks on cpu load predictions. Proceedings of the 7th IEEE/ACM International Conference on Grid Computing, 286–292 (September 2006)
[3] Appel, A.W.: Garbage collection can be faster than stack allocation. Information Processing Letters 25(4), 275–279 (1987)
[4] Hertz, M.: Quantifying and Improving the Performance of Garbage Collection. Ph.D. Dissertation, University of Massachusetts, Amherst (2006)
[5] Hertz, M., Berger, E.D.: Quantifying the performance of garbage collection vs. explicit memory management. In: Proceedings of the Object-Oriented Programming Systems, Languages and Applications (OOPSLA 2005) (October 2005)
[6] Jones, R., Lins, R.: Garbage Collection: Algorithms for Automatic Dynamic Memory Management. John Wiley & Sons, New York (1996)

[7] Koide, H., Oie, Y.: A new task scheduling method for distributed programs that require memory management. Concurrency and Computation: Practice and Experience 18, 941–945 (2006)

[8] Dhakal, S., Hayat, M.M., Pezoa, J.E., Yang, C., Bader, D.A.: Dynamic load balancing in distributed systems in the presence of delays: A regeneration-theory approach. IEEE Transactions on Parallel & Distributed Systems 18(4), 485–497 (2007)

[9] Dyachuk, D., Deters, R.: Using sla context to ensure quality of service for composite services. IEEE Transactions on Computers 57(7), 865–875 (2008)

[10] Kim, J.K., Shivle, S., Siegel, H.J., Maciejewski, A.A., Braun, T., Schneider, M., Tideman, S., Chitta, R., Dilmaghani, R.B., Joshi, R., Kaul, A., Sharma, A., Sripada, S., Vangari, P., Yellampalli, S.S.: Dynamic mapping in a heterogeneous environment with tasks having priorities and multiple deadlines. In: 12th Heterogeneous Computing Workshop (HCW 2003), Proceedings of the 17th International Parallel and Distributed Processing Symposium (IPDPS 2003) (April 2003)

[11] Oh, S.H., Yang, S.M.: A modified least-laxity-first scheduling algorithm for real-time tasks. In: Proceedings of the 5th International Workshop on Real-Time Computing Systems and Applications (RTCSA 1998), October 1998, pp. 31–36 (1998)

[12] Salmani, V., Naghibzadeh, M., Habibi, A., Deldari, H.: Quantitative comparison of job-level dynamic scheduling policies in parallel real-time systems. In: Proceedings TENCON, 2006 IEEE Region 10 Conference (November 2006)

[13] Feizabadi, Y., Back, G.: Garbage collection-aware utility accrual scheduling. Real-Time Systems 36(1-2), 3–22 (2007)

[14] Shrestha, H.K., Grounds, N., Madden, J., Martin, M., Antonio, J.K., Sachs, J., Zuech, J., Sanchez, C.: Scheduling workflows on a cluster of memory managed multicore machines. In: Proceedings of the International Conference on Parallel and Distributed Processing Techniques and Applications, PDPTA 2009 (July 2009)

[15] Dertouzos, M.L., Mok, A.K.-l.: Multiprocessor on-line scheduling of hard-real-time tasks. IEEE Transactions on Software Engineering 15(12), 1497–1506 (1989)

Green Cloud on the Horizon

Mufajjul Ali

Orange Labs, Chiswick, London
Mufajjul.ali@orange-ftgroup.com

Abstract. This paper proposes a Green Cloud model for mobile Cloud computing. The proposed model leverage on the current trend of IaaS (Infrastructure
as a Service), PaaS (Platform as a Service) and SaaS (Software as a Service),
and look at new paradigm called "Network as a Service" (NaaS). The Green
Cloud model proposes various Telco's revenue generating streams and services
with the CaaS (Cloud as a Service) for the near future.

Keywords: Telco, Virtualization, Architecture, NaaS, CaaS, Web Services.

1 Introduction

Cloud computing is deemed to be the next era of the Internet evolution. It adheres to
the principle from service computing [1, 2], utility computing [4] and grid computing
[5]. Cloud computing relies on running/managing service/application remotely, allowing the scope of dynamic scaling, remote management and diversity.

The current high speed broadband connectivity on wired network and faster 3G [3]
network data transfer on the mobile devices forms a hybrid network topology of interconnected devices, which can deliver on demand services on the move. The ever
growing service market for mobile devices such as the iPhone's service catalogue
store has generated a great deal of interest from the network operators.

Mobile Cloud computing can be seen as the launching pad for the ever demanding
resource intensive and computationally high mobile service to become a reality. The
network operator's existing pricing model can be seen as complementary to the Cloud
computing model for next generation of mobile services.

Currently, there is a limited presence of major mobile network operators providing
Cloud services, but there is a general interest leaping toward the Cloud computing.

2 Background

Cloud computing is defined as "A large-scale distributed computing paradigm that is
driven by economies of scale, in which a pool of abstracted, virtualized, dynamically-
scalable, managed computing power, storage, platforms, and services are delivered on
demand to external customers over the Internet" [6]. There are three main models of
Cloud computing paradigm in existence today, these are: Infrastructure as a Service
(IaaS)[13], Platform as a Service (PaaS)[12] Software as a Service (SaaS)[11]. IaaS
allows a customer to host the complete IT infrastructure remotely, on the virtual network

M.G. Jaatun, G. Zhao, and C. Rong (Eds.): CloudCom 2009, LNCS 5931, pp. 451–459, 2009.

of the provider. The PaaS allow organizations to develop and deploy application/service remotely, and SaaS are the services provided by the Cloud host. At present, the leading Cloud service providers are the likes of Google [12], Amazon, and IBM [14].

3 Green Cloud

The current trend for Telco is to embrace the service market with the promise of an all encompassing IP based network, (IMS [15]) has attracted greater interest in the field of Cloud computing. Telco such as Orange, not only provide voice and messaging service but they also have a large presence in the Broadband sector, with a broader vision of converged services. In order for this vision to become a fruitful venture, a new innovative architectural model is required to support computational/storage needs, being more economical and environmentally friendly.

The core principle of the Green Cloud is to bring new business opportunities to Telco and in the same time be as economically/ energy efficient as possible.

Energy efficiency can be achieved by adhering to energy reduction principles such as replacing the high powered terminal with using low powered devices since most of the processing will be done by the Cloud.

The virtualized servers will ensure that only the required servers are operational. Using optimal cooling system and applying other energy saving techniques, which can ultimately reduce the operational and maintenance cost.

Green Cloud can be seen as a massive IT infrastructure with the mobile and physical line as the core interconnected network, partitioned logically, physically and geographically. This enables the Green Cloud to model other sub-Clouds (see fig 1) which can be seen as Cloud as a Service (CaaS). Each Cloud encapsulates a particular business need in order to meet the requirement of the end users/businesses. Each of the Cloud can interface with each other based on a trust model.

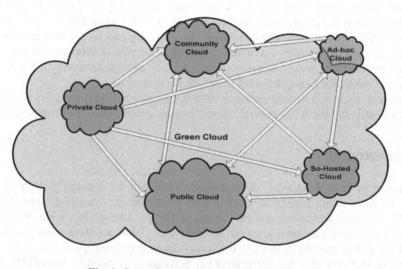

Fig. 1. Green Cloud Interaction Business Model

3.1 Ad-Hoc Cloud

It was estimated that there are more than 2.6 billion mobile devices in existence globally [16] and the handset sales for first quarter of 2009 was 515.5m [17]. The wide use of mobile broadband from a particular network operator can be grouped and considered as a larger cluster of resources, with each device seen as a resource node in the inter-connected network. This essentially forms the base of the Ad-hoc Cloud. Each device acts as a spare resource provider to the resource pool. The control of the availability of resources on the devices is handled and monitored by the network operator. High computational and resource intensive applications such as games and multimedia can acquire additional resources via the Ad-hoc Cloud.

A dynamic pricing structure can be applied where credit is gained and deducted based on the resource usage and shared, in essence, a form of a machine to machine (M2M) pricing model can be established. Telco operators can generate revenue by increase data packet usage. It may also be possible that devices do not belong to the particular mobile network to be part of an Ad-hoc Cloud, but the pricing model may vary based on the device contribution.

3.2 So-Hosted Cloud

The So-Hosted Cloud differs from the traditional Cloud to an extent that a 3rd party company can lease part of the Green Cloud as having their own; this can be seen as a traditional franchise model. This model provides agility and flexibility, as it is based on an on-demand hiring of segment of the Cloud. The revenue model for Telco operator can be based on a franchise license, and a total share of the net revenue generated.

The trust model amongst the Clouds restricts the So-hosted access; it can only interface with the Public and Community Cloud.

3.3 Community Cloud

Community groups such as the Glassfish Community [7]) and other open source community have contributed tremendously in recent years for proving innovative product and services. Community Cloud can be seen as a resource pool that is confined in space to allow Telco based communities collaborate to achieve common goals, such as enhancing the mobile Cloud services, advance converged Cloud applications, etc. Revenues can be generated from shared ownership of the final innovation/product released from the community. This model has slightly higher restricted trust model, this is due to possible 3rd party collaboration.

3.4 Private Cloud

The large presence of mobile operators such as Orange with over 180,000 employees requires high level of content sharing and resource management between divisions. Each division can deploy a private Cloud.

This model can reduce the overall operational cost and management cost of a Telco operator's internal projects by rapid allocation of resources, on-demand platform set-up, quick development and test deployment environment. Once the project has terminated, the resources can be released back to the Cloud, reducing the long term maintenance cost. The model can increase the time to market time, this can be achieved by migrating the test deployment platform to the commercial production environment on the public Cloud.

The private Cloud conceals any outside exposure to its data. The trust model is purely unidirectional, only private Cloud can access the other Clouds.

3.5 Public Cloud

Public Cloud is the main gateway of Telco exposing their APIs and services. It is publicly accessible and can be seen as the main dominant Cloud. This model provides a unified deployment platform for common service development. Highest level of security is required to ensure the SLA (Service Level Agreement) is fulfilled, and QoS (Quality of Service) is maintained for normal and converged Telco services.

4 Green Cloud Architecture

The architecture of the Green Cloud consists of a total of seven layers as opposed to the six (see fig 2 below) layers provided by the traditional Cloud model. The advantage of this model is that there is a separate of concerns amongst the layers; each of the layers provides certain level of functionality that is complimentary to the layer below. There is also a degree of flexibility amongst layers and in some cases it may not need to directly interface with the layer below. It also models the Telco's biggest asset which is the physical network topology as the core superset layer of the architecture. This enables the Telco operators to guarantee the QoS and adhere to SLA, which may not be possible with the existing Cloud architecture. The functionalities of each layer as follows:

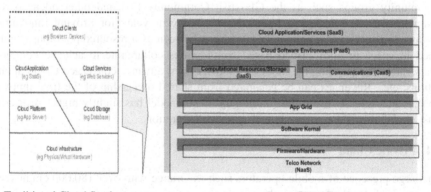

Traditional Cloud Stack   Green Cloud Stack

Fig. 2. Extended Cloud Stack

4.1 Layer 1 – Telco Network (NaaS)

Telco operator Orange is currently the number one Broadband provider in France, and has a large presence globally. The Network as a Service (NaaS) is the concept of dynamic bandwidth consumption and quality of server based on the application/service requirement.

The operator allocates and de-allocates bandwidth at close to real-time as required by the application/services. This ensures that consumer will only pay for their actual usage of the bandwidth, rather than a fixed amount monthly. NaaS is the corner stone for the Cloud as a Service (CaaS). At present the SLA (Service Level Agreement) cannot be guaranteed since Cloud provides little or no control of the network traffic. The NaaS can ensure that a certain level of SLA can be met with adequate QoS (Quality of Service).

4.2 Layer 2 – Firmware/Hardware

The actual physical hardware is located in this layer. Through virtualization the hardware can also be considered as a service. The on-demand resource can be accommodated by merely allowing the hypervisor [10] to access larger capacities of the existing hardware. Additional hardware can be added with minimal impact on the overall stack.

4.3 Layer 3 – Software Kernel

The Software kernel is the host Operating system, where the software environment will reside. The kernel will utilise the virtual resources to optimize the performance. Typically, the most common kernel is used in such architecture as Linux based.

4.4 Layer 4 – App Grid

This layer is essential for providing highly scalable and on-demand services with high availability. It allows the parallel process of executing tasks for computationally high applications.

4.5 Layer 5 – Computational Resource/ Storage and Communication

Computational resources and storage is referred to as Infrastructure as a Service. These are the virtualized nodes in the Cloud. It ensures that the hardware is logically separated from the OS, making it more portable and easier to manage. The VM (Virtual Machine) can dynamically allocate and de-allocate resources required for developing/running of applications. The storage can be an integrated part of the computational resource or as a separate entity.

4.6 Layer 6 – Cloud Software Environment

The Cloud software environment is based on SOA [18] architecture. It provides the backbone for developing services, it can be seen as a Platform as a Service (PaaS).

The traditional model of Cloud is typically based on Web service architecture; this restricts availability of the many services provided by Telco. The SOA stack extends the Cloud communication stack to enable session protocol such as SIP, and other protocols, which are fundamental to telephony/Telco services. This is to ensure that there are certain levels of quality of service and reliability maintained.

4.7 Layer 7 – Cloud Application/Services

The Cloud application/service layer can be seen as Software as a Service (SaaS). This is this main layer of user interfacing with the Cloud. This layer exposes the services and applications that can be used by the users.

Any internet enabled device supporting Web runtime environment should be able to access this layer. The physical representation of the content of the service may vary based on the Web runtime engine running on the device.

5 Green Cloud Benefits

Green Cloud can bring several benefits to Telco operator, their enterprise businesses and end users. Telco operators primarily focus is on providing service based solutions to the consumer. This is based on the Software as a Service model (SaaS). The service may range from typical general purpose Web based services to more specialized Telco based converged services. The enterprise generally requires an IT infrastructure for delivering their business contents; this can be achieved by Telco providing the IaaS model. It may also use the Platform as a Service (PaaS) model to offer additional services to their customer.

Fig 3 below represents possible trend for the service demand and revenue growth for Green Cloud. There is a potential growth for the service market using Telco assets by businesses, in turn Telco making larger revenue.

It is predicted that by 2015, the Cloud computing revenue projection is about 200bn [19]. As the service growth increases, it is likely to generate more revenue for Telco. Telco being the resource supplier may be able to maintain a sustainable revenue growth.

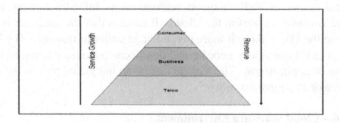

Fig. 3. Green Cloud Service & Revenue Model

5.1 Benefits for Telco

- Sustainable revenue –Public, So-hosted and Ad-hoc Clouds are potentially new revenue generating model for Telco.
- Simplistic model – The various types of sub-Clouds provides the agility required by business to meet their day to day demand.
- Cost reduction – This can be achieved from to lower to higher granularity, it may include from small to large project, R&D to commercial, local to regional to global unit.
- Extensibility – Can provide additional resource with minimal impact.

5.2 Benefits for Businesses

- Cost reduction – Can reduce the overall OPEX (operational expenditure) and CAPEX (capital expenditure) cost by adapting to the required sub-Green Cloud model.
- Highly automated – Technical complexity is handled by the Cloud.
- Ease of use – Based on Web interface, minimal technical expertise/training required to operate
- High availability – Dynamic resource availability to meet the customer's demand
- Simplified operation – Icon based operations simplifies HCI with the system.
- More mobility – Can operate from any location

5.3 Benefits for Consumer

- Potential revenue – The Ad-hoc model could potentially generate revenue for the consumers if the resource allocation sustained competitively.
- QoS – Likely to receive uninterrupted service, and always available.

6 Conclusion

The proposed Green Cloud tries to model the needs for different types of consumers, communities and organizations, with the vision of being "Greener" on the environment and being simple and agile. However, the Network as a Service (NaaS) model has several challenging factors that require addressing, the likes of: interaction between the Clouds, physical network/operation required to enabler dynamic NaaS model, and appropriate pricing model.

The interface between different Clouds has not been fully defined and may be a stumbling point for inter-operability between different Clouds. The lack of defined standardization for Cloud computing is a major concern as each vendor providing their custom Cloud solution may restrict the flexibility of the consumer and danger of vendor lock-in.

The NaaS model may require major upgrade on the network in order to provide dynamic bandwidth, and other challenges lie in providing unified end to end broadband speed at a constant rate, network congestion and security threats such as denial of service are also a concern.

The existing Telco's pricing structure may not be sufficient to model the needs for Green Cloud as it is mainly static. A flexible pricing model is required that is not only beneficial to the customers, but a good return in revenue is generated. There is also a greater need for a balance between competitiveness and a quality of service provided.

To conclude, the Green Cloud model offers a new viable revenue generating model that can be sustainable over a long period; it is agile enough to provide the right level of service required by the customer, and simple enough to attract a broad range of consumer for various sectors. However, in-depth research is required for investigating the challenges stated above to lay the building blocks of the Green Cloud.

These views and opinions are solely of the writer, and do not necessarily reflect any way or form of the organization.

References

[1] Yan, Y.: When Service Computing Meets Software Engineering, services. IEEE Congress on Services - Part I, 49–52 (2008)

[2] Zhang, L.-J., Li, H., Lam, H.: Services Computing: Grid Applications for Today. IT Professional 6(4), 5–7 (2004)

[3] Hoikkanen, A.: Economics of 3G Long-Term Evolution: the Business Case for the Mobile Operator. In: 2007 IFIP International Conference on Wireless and Optical Communications Networks, WOCN 2007 (2007)

[4] Llorente, I.M., Montero, R.S., Huedo, E., Leal, K.: A Grid Infrastructure for Utility Computing. In: Proceedings of the 15th IEEE International Workshops on Enabling Technologies: Infrastructure for Collaborative Enterprises, pp. 163–168 (2006)

[5] Leong, P., Miao, C., Lee, B.-S.: Agent Oriented Software Engineering for Grid Computing. In: Proceedings of the Sixth IEEE International Symposium on Cluster Computing and the Grid, p. 2 (2006)

[6] Foster, I., Zhao, Y., Raicu, I., Lu, S.: Cloud Computing and Grid Computing 360-Degree Compared. In: IEEE Grid Computing Environments (GCE 2008) 2008, co-located with IEEE/ACM Supercomputing (2008) (to appear)

[7] http://java.sun.com/javaee/community/glassfish/

[8] Newport-Networks Sip Security and the Ims Core,
http://www.newport-networks.co.uk/cust-docs/
88-Security-and-IMS.pdf

[9] Aymerich, F.M., Fenu, G., Surcis, S.: An Approach to a Cloud Computing Network. In: Applications of Digital Information and Web Technologies, ICADIWT 2008, pp. 113–118 (2008)

[10] Vouk, M.A.: Cloud Computing – Issues, Research and Implementations. In: ITI 2008 30th Int. Conf. on Information Technology Interfaces (June 23-26, 2008)

[11] Erdogmus, H.: Cloud Computing: Does Nirvana Hide behind the Nebula? IEEE Software 26(2), 4–6 (2009)

[12] Google (2009),
http://code.google.com/appengine/docs/python/gettingstarted/
uploading.html

[13] Grossman, R.L.: The Case for Cloud Computing. IT Professional 11(2), 23–27 (2009)

[14] IBM (2008), http://www.ibm.com/ibm/cloud/

[15] Panwar, B., Singh, K.: IMS Sip core server test bed: IP Multimedia Subsystem Architecture and Applications. In: 2007 International Conference, December 6-8, pp. 1–5 (2007)

[16] 2.6 Billion Mobile Phone Users in the World (2006),
http://www.esato.com/news/article.php/id=1365

[17] mobileisgood.com (2009),
http://www.mobileisgood.com/statistics.php#current

[18] Castro-Leon, E., He, J., Chang, M.: Scaling Down SOA to Small Businesses. In: IEEE International Conference on Service-Oriented Computing and Applications, SOCA 2007 (2007)

[19] Coda Research Consultancy Ltd., Cloud computing: An assessment (2009),
http://www.codarc.co.uk/cc2009/
Cloud%20Computing%20An%20assessment%20-%20opening%20pages.pdf

Industrial Cloud:
Toward Inter-enterprise Integration

Tomasz Wiktor Wlodarczyk, Chunming Rong, and Kari Anne Haaland Thorsen

Department of Electrical Engineering and Computer Science, University of Stavanger,
N-4036 Stavanger, Norway
{tomasz.w.wlodarczyk,chunming.rong,kari.a.thorsen}@uis.no

Abstract. Industrial cloud is introduced as a new inter-enterprise integration concept in cloud computing. The characteristics of an industrial cloud are given by its definition and architecture and compared with other general cloud concepts. The concept is then demonstrated by a practical use case, based on Integrated Operations (IO) in the Norwegian Continental Shelf (NCS), showing how industrial digital information integration platform gives competitive advantage to the companies involved. Further research and development challenges are also discussed.

Keywords: cloud computing, integrated operations.

1 Introduction

The increasing amount of industrial digital information requires an integrated industrial information platform to exchange, process and analyze the incoming data, and to consult related information, e.g. historic or from other connected components, in order to obtain an accurate overview of the current operation status for a consequent decision. Collected information may often cross disciplines where it originated from. The challenge is to handle it in an *integrated*, *cost effective*, *secure* and *reliable* way. An enterprise may use the existing organizational structure for their information classification. However, as collaborations often exist across enterprises, information flow that crosses enterprise boundaries must be facilitated. Earlier attempts have been made within one enterprise. An industry wide collaboration poses more challenges. Existing general solution such as information grid [1] are not adequate to deal with the complexity in the challenges.

Recently, there have been many discussions on what cloud is and is not [2-14]. Potential adopters were also discussed [4, 7]. However, most solutions mainly focus on small and medium size companies that adopt what is called a public cloud. Adoption of public cloud by large companies was discussed, but there were significant obstacles in it, mainly related with security. Some of them were answered by what is called a private cloud. In this paper, industrial cloud is introduced as a new inter-enterprise integration concept in cloud computing to solve the stated problem. Both definition and architecture of an industrial cloud are given and compared with the general cloud characteristics. By extending existing cloud computing concepts, we propose a solution that may provide convenient, integrated and cost effective adaptation. These

M.G. Jaatun, G. Zhao, and C. Rong (Eds.): CloudCom 2009, LNCS 5931, pp. 460–471, 2009.

advantages are recognized in a large scale industrial collaboration project Integrated Operations (IO) [16], where a central element is to establish an inter-enterprise digital information integration platform for members of OLF in Norwegian Continental Shelf (NCS) [15].

The paper consists of five sections. After a short introduction in Section 1, a brief survey of the recent efforts on cloud computing is given in the Section 2. A categorization of cloud is proposed to reflect actual business models and to facilitate more precise definition.

In Section 3 the concept of industrial cloud is precisely defined. Generic architecture is proposed and explained. Further, a practical use case, based on Integrated Operations in NCS, is provided to show how this industrial digital information integration platform gives a competitive advantage to companies involved. Existing technologies that are essential parts of industrial cloud are named and described. In the end of this section further research and development challenges are also discussed. In Section 4 compact comparison of the three types of clouds: public, enterprise and industrial, is provided. Paper concludes with summary of main points.

2   Categories of Clouds

The general goals of cloud computing are to obtain better resource utilization and availability. The concept of cloud computing is presented sometimes as a grouping of other various concepts, especially SaaS, IaaS and HaaS [17], but the concept has also been defined differently from paper to paper in [2-14], indicating different models of cloud. The differences in organization and architecture of a cloud are often influenced by different business models cloud computing concept is applied to. Division between public and private (also hybrid between them) can be seen in several publications [8]. In this paper, public and enterprise cloud are identified by business models they are applied to, viewed from a global perspective.

2.1 Public Cloud

Public cloud is the most common model of cloud, with popular examples such as Amazon Web Services [18] and Google App Engine [19]. One definition of public cloud, given by McKinsey [3], states that:

> *Clouds are hardware-based services offering compute, network*
> *and storage capacity where:*
> *1. Hardware management is highly abstracted from the buyer*
> *2. Buyers incur infrastructure costs as variable OPEX*
> *3. Infrastructure capacity if highly elastic (up or down)*

Public cloud is used mainly by small and medium size companies, very often start-ups. That is because it offers effortless hardware management and flexibility without any significant entrance costs. Access to public cloud is realized through internet. Hardware is owned and managed by an external company. Hardware issues are of no interest for companies using it. High degree of hardware utilization is achieved by means of virtualization (other examples also exist [20]). Platform is generic, usually providing one of application frameworks or access to standard computing resources.

There is no particular focus on collaboration between applications and no facilitation of reusing data between them. Public cloud features OpEx (Operational Expenditure) type of billing based on actual usage or on per month fee. There is small to usually none CapEx (Captial Expenditure).

Security and privacy might be an issue as data is stored by en external entity. On the other hand, cloud providers might have better focus and bigger resources to address those issues than a small company [21]. Companies have no control over cloud provider. Therefore, it is important that there are clear policies on data handling and possibly external audit [22]. Public cloud also might raise geopolitical issues because of physical data placement. That is currently solved by separate data centers in different parts of the world [18]. However, it is a questionable solution in longer term. There is vendor lock-in threat, resulting in problems with data transfer between cloud vendors. However, that is a bigger issue for users of cloud-based applications than for companies providing services over the cloud.

2.2 Enterprise Cloud

Enterprise cloud focuses not only on better utilization of computer resources, but also on integrating services crucial to company's operations and thereof their optimization. Good example here is Cisco vision [17].

Access to enterprise cloud is realized mainly through intranet, but internet might also be used. Hardware is owned and managed by the enterprise itself. Therefore, hardware issues are still present, however, to lesser extent. Hardware utilization can be improved by means of virtualization; however it might cover only some parts of company's datacenter. Platform is designed for the specific purpose and capable of supporting company's key operations. There is strong focus on collaboration between applications and facilitation of reusing and integrating data between them. Enterprise cloud can be economically beneficial to the company however it requires up-front investment and does not offer OpEx-type of billing.

Control, security and privacy is not an issue (beyond what is required currently) as data are stored by the company itself. What is more, thanks to centralization security level might significantly increase [23]. There might be some geopolitical issues in case of centralization of international operations. There is no significant vendor lock-in threat. Dependence on software vendors providing cloud functionalities is more or less the same as on currently used software.

Adoption of public cloud by large companies or enterprises was also discussed [3]. There are already some examples of such adoptions [24]. At the same time many companies do not even consider such step. In their case benefits of public cloud are too small to counterbalance security, privacy and control risks.

2.3 Beyond Enterprise Cloud

Enterprise cloud seems to be a good solution for integration inside a large company. However nowadays, enterprises face additional challenges which result from collaboration with other enterprises in the industry. Such collaboration is necessary to stay competitive, but it requires introduction of new technological solutions.

Some of integration and provisioning challenges have already been discussed in the concept of Information Grid. Notably, Semantic Web solutions were proposed to unify all the data in the company and to view them in a "smooth continuum from the Internet to the Intranet" [1]. Some authors proposed also integrating resources provisioning [25]. However, Information Grid model, that focuses on one enterprise only, did not offer convenient, seamless and integrated approach to practically solve inter-enterprise challenges. It is not only information data that are involved, but also work processes, and definition, operation and service models that need to be reconciled and collaborated in a seamless way. Hence, information grid is only a beginning. Finally, Information Grid model does not lead to new opportunities in the industry in the way cloud computing does e.g. lowering entrance costs for start-ups that leads to increased competition and innovation level.

Therefore, in the next section industrial cloud is introduced as a new inter-enterprise integration concept in cloud computing. A precise definition is given and then explained by a practical use case.

3   Industrial Cloud

3.1   Definition and Architecture

Industrial cloud is a platform for industrial digital information integration and collaboration. It connects unified data standards and common ontologies with open and shared architecture in order to facilitate data exchange and service composition between several companies. It should be controlled by an organization in form of e.g. special interest group (SIG) consisting of industry representatives to ensure development, evolution and adoption of standards. SIG should cooperate with international standardization body.

In Fig. 1. industrial cloud is presented. It binds together enterprises in the industry and also service companies. Enterprises are the core of the industry. Service companies usually provide services to those enterprises and very often participate in more than industry.

In traditional business-to-business (B2B) systems metadata and semantics are agreed upon in advance and are encapsulated in the systems. However, the trend is moving towards more open environment where communicating partners are not given at prior. This demands solutions where the semantics are explicit and standardized [26]. Information management, information integration and application integration require that the underlying data and processes can be described and managed semantically.

Collaboration and communication within an industrial cloud depend on a shared understanding of concepts. Therefore, the basic elements of industrial cloud are unified data standards, common ontolgies, open and shared architecture and secure and reliable infrastructure. Unified data standards allow easy data exchange between companies. Common ontologies ensure shared point of view on meaning of data. Metadata need to be shared among applications, and it should be possible to semantically describe applications within the cloud. Open and shared architecture is a way to efficiently interconnect participants in industrial cloud.

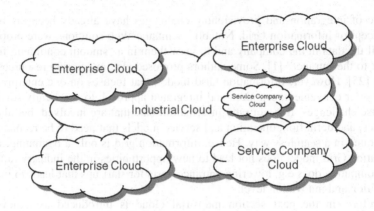

Fig. 1. Industrial Cloud

An ontology is a structure capturing semantic knowledge about a certain domain, by describing relevant concepts and the relations between these concepts [27, 28]. With a shared ontology it is possible to communicate information across domains and systems, independent of local names and structuring. This enables an automatic and seamless flow of data, where information can be accessed from its original location in the same way as if it was stored locally. In [29] Noy et al point out several reasons to construct and deploy ontologies, e.g.: ease of information exchange, easier for a third party to extract and aggregate information from diverse systems, easier to change assumptions of the world and analyze domain knowledge.

The ontology creation should be mainly industry focused process. There is current and stable trend of moving construction of meta-data from enterprise to industrial level. Cross-industry approach might be useful; however, it is not probably on larger scale. In our current work we see that those ontologies have to be hierarchically organized depending on their detail level. The more general ones will be common in the industry. More detailed ones might stay specific to a particular company or consortium. However, they will still have reference to the more general ontologies.

Data standards together with ontologies acting on open and shared architecture allow for easy service composition from multiple providers. Secure and reliable infrastructure builds trust for the platform and between all participants.

It should be easy to add new applications to the cloud and applications should be easy to be found based on the services and they provide. By providing applications as semantically described web services [30], based on the commonly agreed ontology, it would be easy to search for particular service within them. Domain-knowledge is extracted from the applications; not hard-coded within the systems. It is then easier to provide new services, and automatically interpret the operations provided by these services.

Industry can form an industrial cloud in order to enable on-the-fly and automatic outsourcing and subcontracting, lower operation costs, increase innovation level and create new opportunities for the industry. Cloud approach can be used as a way to ensure abstraction layer over all underlying technological solutions and integration patterns. Industrial cloud is the lacking element that binds and structures existing

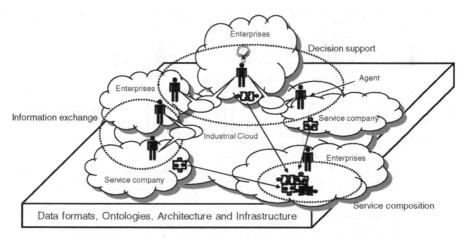

Fig. 2. Integration, collaboration and composition in industrial cloud

technologies on the way to practical implementation. Fig. 2. summarizes main goals of industrial cloud, that is: information exchange, decision support and service composition.

As for now, industrial cloud was defined in terms of its general purpose and technologies used. Further, it is important to place it in comparison with already existing types of clouds. In Fig. 3. all three types of cloud are presented in a form of a stack of functionalities they provide.

Looking at current providers of public cloud like Google Apps Engine[19] or AWS[18] one can see that they offer two basic functions: provisioning (mainly of processing time and storage space), and metering and billing systems for resources they provide. Public cloud is realized through hardware virtualization (or similar technologies). Cloud provider supplies an API that is later utilized by cloud adopters.

Enterprise cloud builds on fundament of public cloud. Further, it adds possibility of administrating workflows in the cloud, managing workload and monitoring which goes further than simple metering in public cloud. In this way enterprise cloud is less general but at the same time provides better support of large business users.

Industrial cloud is created on the base of public and enterprise cloud. It features easier hardware provisioning by virtualization, it offers workflows administration, workload management and monitoring. However, it further facilitates integrational tasks like policies, reliability management, security and trust, outsourcing and subcontracting. It adds support for semantic interpretation of data, mapping, data fusion and service discovery and composition.

Fig. 3. visualizes why the inter-enterprise integration concept introduced in this paper forms part of cloud computing. It builds on already existing cloud models and introduces extensions to them based on actual needs of industries. With time some of new functions in industrial cloud may migrate into the lower level clouds.

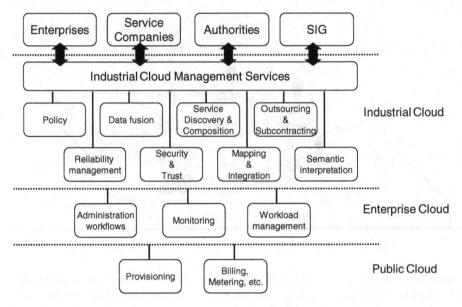

Fig. 3. Industrial Cloud stacked on Enterprise and Public Cloud

3.2 Example from the Integrated Operations in Oil and Gas

The oil and gas industry on NCS has for some years now been working on the concept of Integrated Operations (IO). Integrated operations aim at supporting the industry in "reaching better, faster and more reliable decisions", and is expected to have a great impact on information flow between different sub-domains. IO is planed to be implemented in two steps: Generation 1 and Generation 2 (G1 and G2). G1 focuses on integration of offshore and onshore, real-time simulation and optimizing of key work processes. G2 integrates operation centers of operators (enterprises) and vendors (service providers), focuses on heavy automation of processes and optimization of processes across domains. There are several ongoing research project related to IO. The biggest, *Integrated Operations in the High North* (IOHN) [16], embraces several sub-projects focusing on different aspects of IO G2. The suggested technologies rely on an underlying architecture to build upon. The industrial cloud may provide such architecture solution

The oil and gas industry is an information and knowledge industry. Data exist for decades and needs to be shared across different businesses, domains and applications. By combining data from several sources it is possible to gain more information than if the information was separated. This relies on the ability to semantically recognize the content of data. At present, data are isolated in information silos. Communicating and sharing information often result in man-hours and expenses on mapping data from one structure to another. By example, within the sub-domain of drilling and completion alone there are more than five different communication standards to relate to e.g. WITSML or OPC-UA. Much of the knowledge and logic is hard-coded within the different applications. It is difficult to share and transfer data to new or other systems without information loss. In the recent years, ISO15926 was being developed as an upper-level data integration standard and ontology that could enable data sharing among several companies. It proved to be successful in initial tests. With the use of a shared ontology metadata are extracted from the applications and presented in a way that can be more easily shared among partners.

Data are often stored in several places and over time these data tend to be inconsistent. Barriers between isolated information domains need to be broken down. There is a need for solutions where data can be accessed directly from the source. The industrial cloud focuses on cross-company application collaboration, and will ease communication and access of data across company and application boundaries.

The oil and gas industry has already developed SOIL, an industrial communication network that provides high reliability and independence of other solution like internet. However, SOIL does not offer any kind of collaboration and integration facilities apart from secure network connection. The industry consists of many, both small and large, companies. Service companies providing services to several operators spend much time on integration with operators' systems. With an underlying cloud architecture service provides can offer new services to the cloud as a whole, without the need for tailored integration with all the different operators.

Industrial cloud could serve as a platform for actual delivery of Integrated Operations on NCS. Industrial cloud is capable of providing easy, abstracted access to all aforementioned technological solution integrating them in one efficient and simple product.

3.3 Challenges and Further Work

Industrial cloud can be the solution to the problem of inter-enterprise digital information integration and collaboration. However, there are a few challenges that should be a subject of research and industrial effort while practically implementing the industrial cloud concept.

Integration and collaboration requires inter-enterprise standardization. To do that different definitions or names on the same concept, different data formats, different work procedures have to be reconciled. This is usually easier said than done. For example, the ISO15926 is still far from completion after over ten years effort with participation of major actors in the domain.

The biggest challenge is security. How to secure each companies data, but at the same time do not impede collaboration? Multi-level authentication could be a solution to this. However, more development in this field has to done as proper security solutions will be a key element of industrial cloud.

Other challenges consist of dealing with many versions of truth for reasoning purposes, what is result of shared environment and integration of data in many formats. This topics are subject of current research in Semantic Web field [31].

Enabling old data to be used in the new environment is also a challenge. It is important as companies want to use all the data they already have. There already have be interesting attempts to do that [32].

Communication and possibly synchronization between industrial cloud and enterprise clouds is not yet solved. Similar but not exactly the same problems are already investigated in form of synchronization between private and public cloud [8].

As outsourcing can be automatic there is a need for automated contracting solutions, which have been topic of recent research [33].

4 Cloud Categories Comparison

Industrial cloud should also be compared with other types of cloud in terms of: how it is implemented, who is using it and what are problematic issues. This is summarized in Table. 1. In contrast with public cloud, industrial cloud is used by large companies together with smaller companies and in contrast with enterprise cloud it focuses on collaboration between several companies. Access to industrial cloud is realized

Table 1. Cloud categories comparison

	Public	Enterprise	Industrial
Who and why	Small and medium companies; to lower hardware maintenance costs	Large companies; to integrate internal services	Large and other companies in one industry; to integrate inter-enterprice collaboration
Network	Internet	Intranet (and internet)	Extranet (and internet)
Hardware	External owner; aggressive virtualization	Owned by the enterprise; some virtualization	Many owners; some individual virtualization; cross company virtualization not probable
Platform	programming and resources access	supporting integration of operations	focused on integration and collaboration
Applications	Various; no collaboration	Company specific; collaboration	Enterprise specific; collaboration and composition
Economics	OpEx	CapEx	CapEx, some OpEx possible
Security and privacy	Might be higher in some aspects; but privacy is a significant problem	Security will increase as a result of central enforcing of policies	Crucial issue; need of top-level security while preserving collaboration
Control	Problem; need of open policies and external audits	Not an issue; everything controlled by one company	Not an issue; controlled by SIG (collaborating with international standard authority)
Geopolitics	Problem; geographically dependent data centers only a temporary solution	Some issues; but company should be ready to deal with them	Some issues; but industry should be ready to deal with them
Vendor lock-in	Problem; open standards should help	Not a problem; everything owned by the company	Not a significant problem; issue controlled by SIG

through extranet or internet. Hardware is owned and managed independently by many companies, though, some part of hardware in each company will follow shared standard of open architecture. Basing on that, some companies can provide access to its data centers to other companies. This will improve hardware utilization and also facilitate agent mobility.

Platform is designed for the specific purpose and capable of supporting industry's key operations. There is strong focus on collaboration between applications and facilitation of reusing and integrating data between them. Security and privacy are crucial issue as data must be shared and protected at the same time. Because of security and reliability needs extranet implementation might be very often advised. Some geopolitical issues might appear, however, industries are probably already aware of them. Vendor lock-in threat is not a significant issue as long as industrial cloud is wisely managed by SIG. Actually, it might be much smaller than currently. SIG should be organized on industrial level. Cross-industrial approach would most probably create many SIGs that would jeopardize standardization process. It should possible to avoided on industrial level, even though, that is definitely a challenge.

5 Summary

In this paper, industrial cloud is introduced as a new inter-enterprise integration concept in cloud computing. Both definition and architecture of industrial cloud are given in comparison with the general cloud characteristics. The concept is then demonstrated by a practical use case, based on IO in the NCS, showing how industrial digital information integration platform gives competitive advantage to the companies involved. The oil and gas industry in NCS recognizes the great potential value in full implementation and deployment of industrial cloud, where integration and collaboration are the key.

References

1. Alonso, O., Banerjee, S., Drake, M.: The Information Grid: A Practical Approach to the Semantic Web,
   http://www.oracle.com/technology/tech/semantic_technologies/
   pdf/informationgrid_oracle.pdf
2. Mitra, S.: Deconstructing The Cloud (2008),
   http://www.forbes.com/2008/09/18/
   mitra-cloud-computing-tech-enter-cx_sm_0919mitra.html
3. Forrest, W.: McKinsey & Co. Report: Clearing the Air on Cloud Computing (2009),
   http://uptimeinstitute.org/images/stories/
   McKinsey_Report_Cloud_Computing/
   clearing_the_air_on_cloud_computing.pdf
4. Buyya, R., Chee Shin, Y., Venugopal, S.: Market-Oriented Cloud Computing: Vision, Hype, and Reality.... In: 10th IEEE International Conference on High Performance Computing and Communications, HPCC 2008 (2008)
5. Douglis, F.: Staring at Clouds. IEEE Internet Computing 13(3), 4–6 (2009)
6. Grossman, R.L.: The Case for Cloud Computing. IT Professional 11(2) (2009)

7. Hutchinson, C., Ward, J., Castilon, K.: Navigating the Next-Generation Application Architecture. IT Professional 11(2), 18–22 (2009)
8. IBM. IBM Perspective on Cloud Computing (2008),
   http://ftp.software.ibm.com/software/tivoli/brochures/
   IBM_Perspective_on_Cloud_Computing.pdf
9. Lijun, M., Chan, W.K., Tse, T.H.: A Tale of Clouds: Paradigm Comparisons and Some Thoughts on Research Issues. In: Asia-Pacific Services Computing Conference 2008, APSCC 2008, IEEE, Los Alamitos (2008)
10. Lizhe, W., et al.: Scientific Cloud Computing: Early Definition and Experience. In: 10th IEEE International Conference on HPCC 2008 (2008)
11. Youseff, L., Butrico, M., Da Silva, D.: Toward a Unified Ontology of Cloud Computing. In: Grid Computing Environments Workshop, GCE 2008 (2008)
12. Rayport, J.F., Heyward, A.: Envisioning the Cloud: The Next Computing Paradigm (2009),
    http://www.marketspaceadvisory.com/cloud/
    Envisioning_the_Cloud_PresentationDeck.pdf
13. Weinhardt, C., et al.: Business Models in the Service World. IT Professional 11(2), 28–33 (2009)
14. Open Cloud Manifesto (2009), http://www.opencloudmanifesto.org/
15. Map of the Norwegian continental shelf (2004),
    http://www.npd.no/English/Produkter+og+tjenester/
    Publikasjoner/map2003.htm
16. Integrated Operations in the High North,
    http://www.posccaesar.org/wiki/IOHN
17. Gore, R.: The experience of Web 2.0 Communications and collaboration tools in a global enterprise - The road to 3.0 (2009),
    http://www.posccaesar.org/svn/pub/SemanticDays/2009/
    Session_1_Rich_Gore.pdf
18. Amazon Web Services, http://aws.amazon.com
19. Google App Engine, http://code.google.com/appengine/
20. Perilli, A.: Google fires back at VMware about virtualization for cloud computing (2009),
    http://www.virtualization.info/2009/04/
    google-fires-back-at-vmware-about.html
21. Have You Adopted Small Business Cloud Computing? (2009),
    http://www.smallbusinessnewz.com/topnews/2009/02/04/
    have-you-adopted-small-business-cloud-computing
22. Gartner: Seven cloud-computing security risks (2008),
    http://www.infoworld.com/d/security-central/
    gartner-seven-cloud-computing-security-risks-853
23. Should an organization centralize its information security division? (2006),
    http://searchsecurity.techtarget.com/expert/
    KnowledgebaseAnswer/0,289625,sid14_gci1228539,00.html
24. Google Apps makes its way into big business (2009),
    http://www.computerweekly.com/Articles/2008/06/24/231178/
    google-apps-makes-its-way-into-big-business.htm
25. Taylor, S., Surridge, M., Marvin, D.: Grid Resources for Industrial Applications. In: IEEE International Conference on Web Services (2004)
26. Aassve, Ø., et al.: The SIM Report - A comparative Study of Semantic Technologies (2007)

27. Antoniou, G., Harmelen, F.v.: A Semantic Web Primer, 2nd edn. MIT Press, Cambridge (2008)
28. Grobelnik, M., Mladeni, D.: Knowledge Discovery for Ontology Construction. In: John Davies, R.S.P.W. (ed.) Semantic Web Technologies, pp. 9–27 (2006)
29. Noy, N.F., McGuinness, D.L.: Ontology Development 101: A guide to.., in Stanford Knowledge Systems Laboratory Technical Report, p. 25 (2001)
30. Roman, D., et al.: Semantic Web Services - Approaches and Perspectives. In: Davies, J., Studer, R., Warren, P. (eds.) Semantic Web Technologies: Trends and Research in Ontology-based Systems, pp. 191–236. John Wiley & Sons, Chichester (2006)
31. W3C Semantic Web Activity (2009), http://www.w3.org/2001/sw/
32. Calvanese, D., Giacomo, G.d.: Ontology based data integration (2009), http://www.posccaesar.org/svn/pub/SemanticDays/2009/Tutorials_Ontology_based_data_integration.pdf
33. Baumann, C.: Contracting and Copyright Issues for Composite Semantic Services. In: Sheth, A.P., Staab, S., Dean, M., Paolucci, M., Maynard, D., Finin, T., Thirunarayan, K. (eds.) ISWC 2008. LNCS, vol. 5318, pp. 895–900. Springer, Heidelberg (2008)

Community Cloud Computing

Alexandros Marinos[1] and Gerard Briscoe[2]

[1] Department of Computing, University of Surrey, United Kingdom
`a.marinos@surrey.ac.uk`
[2] Department of Media and Communications, London School of Economics and
Political Science, United Kingdom
`g.briscoe@lse.ac.uk`

Abstract. Cloud Computing is rising fast, with its data centres growing at an unprecedented rate. However, this has come with concerns over
privacy, efficiency at the expense of resilience, and environmental sustainability, because of the dependence on Cloud vendors such as Google,
Amazon and Microsoft. Our response is an alternative model for the
Cloud conceptualisation, providing a paradigm for Clouds in the community, utilising networked personal computers for liberation from the
centralised vendor model. Community Cloud Computing (C3) offers an
alternative architecture, created by combing the Cloud with paradigms
from Grid Computing, principles from Digital Ecosystems, and sustainability from Green Computing, while remaining true to the original
vision of the Internet. It is more technically challenging than Cloud
Computing, having to deal with distributed computing issues, including
heterogeneous nodes, varying quality of service, and additional security
constraints. However, these are not insurmountable challenges, and with
the need to retain control over our digital lives and the potential environmental consequences, it is a challenge we must pursue.

Keywords: Cloud Computing, Community Cloud, Community Cloud
Computing, Green Computing, Sustainability.

1   Introduction

The recent development of Cloud Computing provides a compelling value proposition for organisations to outsource their Information and Communications
Technology (ICT) infrastructure [1]. However, there are growing concerns over
the control ceded to large Cloud vendors, especially the lack of information
privacy [2]. Also, the data centres required for Cloud Computing are growing
exponentially [3], creating an ever-increasing *carbon footprint* [4].

The distributed resource provision from Grid Computing, distributed control
from Digital Ecosystems, and sustainability from Green Computing, can remedy
these concerns. Cloud Computing combined with these approaches would provide a compelling socio-technical conceptualisation for sustainable distributed
computing, utilising the spare resources of networked personal computers collectively to provide the facilities of a virtual *data centre* and form a Community
Cloud.

M.G. Jaatun, G. Zhao, and C. Rong (Eds.): CloudCom 2009, LNCS 5931, pp. 472–484, 2009.

2   Cloud Computing

Cloud Computing is the use of Internet-based technologies for the provision of services [1], originating from the *cloud* as a metaphor for the Internet, based on depictions in computer network diagrams to abstract the complex infrastructure it conceals. It offers the illusion of infinite computing resources available on demand, with the elimination of upfront commitment from users, and payment for the use of computing resources on a short-term basis as needed [2]. Furthermore, it does not require the node providing a service to be present once its service is deployed [2]. It is being promoted as the cutting-edge of scalable web application development [2], in which dynamically scalable and often virtualised resources are provided as a service over the Internet [5], with users having no knowledge of, expertise in, or control over the technology infrastructure of the Cloud supporting them. It currently has significant momentum in two extremes of the web development industry [2]: the consumer web technology incumbents who have resource surpluses in their vast *data centres* and various consumers and start-ups that do not have access to such computational resources. Cloud Computing conceptually incorporates Software-as-a-Service (SaaS), Web 2.0 and other technologies with reliance on the Internet, providing common business applications online through web browsers to satisfy the computing needs of users, while the software and data are stored on the servers.

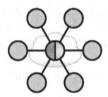

Fig. 1. Cloud Computing

Figure 1 shows the typical configuration of Cloud Computing at run-time when consumers visit an application served by the central Cloud, which is housed in one or more data centres [6]. *Green* symbolises resource *consumption*, and *yellow* resource *provision*. The role of *coordinator* for resource provision is designated by *red*, and is centrally controlled. Providers, who are the controllers, are usually companies with other web activities that require large computing resources, and in their efforts to scale their primary businesses have gained considerable expertise and hardware. For them, Cloud Computing is a way to resell these as a new product while expanding into a new market. Consumers include everyday users, Small and Medium sized Enterprises (SMEs), and ambitious start-ups whose innovation potentially threatens the incumbent providers.

2.1   Layers of Abstraction

While there is a significant *buzz* around Cloud Computing, there is little clarity over which offerings qualify or their interrelation. The key to resolving this

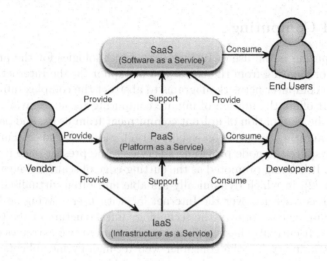

Fig. 2. Abstractions of Cloud Computing

confusion is the realisation that the various offerings fall into different levels of abstraction, as shown in Figure 2, aimed at different market segments.

Infrastructure-as-a-Service (IaaS). At the most basic level of Cloud Computing offerings, there are providers such as Amazon and Mosso, who provide *machine instances* to developers. These instances essentially behave like dedicated servers that are controlled by the developers, who therefore have full responsibility for their operation. So, once a machine reaches its performance limits, the developers have to manually instantiate another machine and scale their application out to it.

Platform-as-a-Service (PaaS). One level of abstraction above, services like Google App Engine provide a programming environment that abstracts machine instances and other technical details from developers. The programs are executed over data centres, not concerning the developers with matters of allocation. In exchange for this, the developers have to handle some constraints that the environment imposes on their application design, for example the use of *key-value stores* instead of *relational databases*.

Software-as-a-Service (SaaS). At the consumer-facing level are the most popular examples of Cloud Computing, with well-defined applications offering users online resources and storage. This differentiates SaaS from traditional websites or web applications which do not interface with user information (e.g. documents) or do so in a limited manner.

To better understand Cloud Computing we can categorise the roles of the various actors. The *vendor* as resource provider has already been discussed. The application *developers* utilise the resources provided, building services for the *end users*. This separation of roles helps define the stakeholders and their differing interests. However, actors can take on multiple roles, with *vendors* also developing services for the *end users*, or *developers* utilising the services of others to build their own services. Yet, within each Cloud the role of provider, and therefore controller, can only be occupied by the *vendor* providing the Cloud.

2.2   Concerns

The Cloud Computing model is not without concerns, as others have noted [2], and we consider the following as primary:

Failure of Monocultures. The uptime of Cloud Computing based solutions is an advantage, when compared to businesses running their own infrastructure, but often overlooked is the co-occurrence of downtime in vendor-driven *monocultures*. The use of globally decentralised *data centres* for vendor Clouds minimises failure, aiding its adoption. However, when a Cloud fails, there is a cascade effect crippling all organisations dependent on that Cloud, and all those dependent upon them. So, failures are now system-wide, instead of being partial or localised. Therefore, the efficiencies gained from centralising infrastructure for Cloud Computing are increasingly at the expense of the Internet's resilience.

Convenience vs Control. The growing popularity of Cloud Computing comes from its convenience, but also brings vendor control, an issue of ever-increasing concern. The even greater concern is the loss of information privacy, with vendors having full access to the resources stored on their Clouds. In particularly sensitive cases of SMEs and start-ups, the provider-consumer relationship that Cloud Computing fosters between the owners of resources and their users could potentially be detrimental, as there is a potential conflict of interest for the providers. They profit by providing resources to up-and-coming players, but also wish to maintain dominant positions in their consumer-facing industries.

Environmental Impact. The other major concern is the ever-increasing *carbon footprint* from the *exponential growth* [3] of the *data centres* required for Cloud Computing. The industry is being motivated to address the problem by legislation [7], the operational limit of power grids [8], and the potential financial benefits of increased efficiency [4]. Their primary solution is the use of *virtualisation* to maximise resource utilisation, but the problem remains [9].

While these issues are endemic to Cloud Computing, they are not flaws in the Cloud conceptualisation, but the vendor provision and implementation of Clouds. There are attempts to address some of these concerns, such as a portability layer between vendor Clouds to avoid lock-in. However, this will not alleviate issues such as inter-Cloud latency. An open source implementation of the Amazon (EC2) Cloud, called Eucalyptus, allows a data centre to execute code compatible with Amazon's Cloud. Allowing for the creation of *private internal* Clouds, avoiding vendor lock-in and providing information privacy, but only for those with their own data centre and so is not really Cloud Computing. Therefore, vendor Clouds remain synonymous with Cloud Computing [5].

Our response is an alternative model for the Cloud conceptualisation, created by combining the Cloud with paradigms from Grid Computing, principles from Digital Ecosystems, and sustainability from Green Computing, while remaining true to the original vision of the Internet.

3   Grid Computing: Distributing Provision

Grid Computing is a form of distributed computing in which a *virtual super computer* is composed from a cluster of networked, loosely coupled computers, acting in concert to perform very large tasks [10].

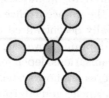

Fig. 3. Grid Computing

What distinguishes Grid Computing from *cluster computing* is being more loosely coupled, heterogeneous, and geographically dispersed [10]. Also, grids are often constructed with general-purpose grid software libraries and middleware, dividing and apportioning pieces of a program to potentially thousands of computers [10]. However, what distinguishes Cloud Computing from Grid Computing is being web-centric, despite some of its definitions being conceptually similar [11].

4   Digital Ecosystems: Distributing Control

Digital Ecosystems are distributed adaptive open socio-technical systems, with properties of self-organisation, scalability and sustainability, inspired by natural ecosystems [12, 13]. Emerging as a novel approach to the catalysis of sustainable regional development driven by SMEs. The community focused on the deployment of Digital Ecosystems, REgions for Digital Ecosystems Network (REDEN), is supported by projects such as the Digital Ecosystems Network of regions for (4) DissEmination and Knowledge Deployment (DEN4DEK). This thematic network that aims to share experiences and disseminate knowledge to let regions effectively deploy of Digital Ecosystems at all levels (economic, social, technical and political) to produce real impacts in the economic activities of European regions through the improvement of SME business environments.

Digital Ecosystems aim to support network-based economies reliant on next-generation ICT that will extend the Service-Oriented Architecture (SOA) concept with the automatic combining of available and applicable services in a scalable architecture, to meet business user requests for applications that facilitate business processes. So, the realisation of their vision requires a form of Cloud Computing, but with their principle of community-based infrastructure where individual users share ownership [12].

5 Green Computing: Growing Sustainably

Green Computing is the efficient use of computing resources, with the primary objective being to account for the *triple bottom line* (*people, planet, profit*), an expanded spectrum of values and criteria for measuring organisational (and societal) success [14]. It is systemic in nature, because ever-increasingly sophisticated modern computer systems rely upon people, networks and hardware.

One of the greatest environmental concerns of the industry is their data centres [15], which have increased in number over time as business demands have increased, with facilities housing a rising amount of evermore powerful equipment [16]. To the extent that data centre efficiency has become an important global issue, leading to the creation of the Green Grid, an international non-profit organisation mandating an increase in the energy efficiency of data centres. Their approach, virtualisation, has improved efficiency [9], but is optimising a flawed model that does not consider the whole system, where resource provision is disconnected from resource consumption. So, we would argue that an alternative more systemic approach is required, where resource consumption and provision are connected, to minimise the environmental impact and allow sustainable growth.

6 Community Cloud

C3 arises from concerns over Cloud Computing, specifically control by vendors and lack of environmental sustainability. Replacing vendor Clouds by shaping the under-utilised resources of user machines to form a Community Cloud, with nodes potentially fulfilling all roles, *consumer, producer*, and most importantly *coordinator*, as shown in Figure 4.

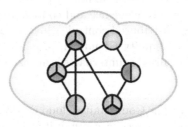

Fig. 4. Community Cloud

6.1 Conceptualisation

The conceptualisation of the Community Cloud draws upon Cloud Computing [6], Grid Computing [11], Digital Ecosystems [12], Green Computing and Autonomic Computing [17]. A paradigm for Cloud Computing in the *community*, without dependence on Cloud vendors, such as Google, Amazon, or Microsoft.

Openness. Removing dependence on vendors makes the Community Cloud the open equivalent to vendor Clouds, and therefore identifies a new dimension in the open versus proprietary struggle that has emerged in code, standards and data, but has yet to be expressed in the realm of hosted services.

Community. The Community Cloud is as much a social structure as a technology paradigm [18], because of the community ownership of the infrastructure. Carrying with it a degree of economic scalability, without which there would be diminished competition and potential stifling of innovation as risked in vendor Clouds.

Individual Autonomy. In the Community Cloud, nodes have their own utility functions in contrast with data centres, in which dedicated machines execute software as instructed. So, with nodes expected to act in their own self-interest, centralised control would be impractical, as with consumer electronics like game consoles [19]. In the Community Cloud, where no concrete vendors exist, it is even more important to avoid antagonising the users, instead embracing their self interest and harnessing it for the benefit of the community with measures such as a *community currency*.

Graceful Failures. The Community Cloud is not owned or controlled by any one organisation, and therefore not dependent on the lifespan or failure of any one organisation. It therefore ought be robust and resilient to failure, and immune to the system-wide cascade failures of vendor Clouds, because of the diversity of its supporting nodes. When occasionally failing doing so gracefully, non-destructively, and with minimal downtime, as the unaffected nodes mobilise to compensate for the failure.

Convenience and Control. The Community Cloud, unlike vendor Clouds, has no inherent conflict between convenience and control, resulting from its community ownership providing distributed control, which would be more democratic. However, whether the Community Cloud can provide technical quality equivalent or superior to its centralised counterparts is an issue that will require further research.

Community Currency. The Community Cloud would require its own currency to support the sharing of resources, a *community currency*, which in economics is a medium (currency), not backed by a central authority (e.g. national government), for exchanging goods and services within a community. It does not need to be restricted geographically, despite sometimes being a local currency [20].

Quality of Service. Ensuring acceptable quality of service (QoS) in a hetero-geneous system will be a challenge. Not least because achieving and maintaining the different aspects of QoS will require reaching *critical mass* in participating nodes and available services. Thankfully, the *community currency* could support long-term promises by resource providers and allow the higher quality providers, through market forces, to command a higher price for their service provision. Interestingly, the Community Cloud could provide a better QoS than vendor Clouds, utilising time-based and geographical variations advantageously in the dynamic scaling of resource provision.

Environmental Sustainability. We expect the Community Cloud to have a smaller *carbon footprint* than vendor Clouds, on the assumption that making use of under-utilised user machines will require less energy than the dedicated data centres required for vendor Clouds. The server farms within data centres are an intensive form of computing resource provision, while the Community Cloud is more organic, growing and shrinking in a symbiotic relationship to support the demands of the community, which in turn supports it.

6.2 Architecture

The method of materialising the Community Cloud is the distribution of its server functionality amongst a population of nodes provided by user machines, shaping their under-utilised resources into a *virtual data centre*. While straightforward in principle, it poses challenges on many different levels. So, an architecture for C3 can be divided into three layers, dealing with these challenges iteratively. The most fundamental layer deals with distributing *coordination*, which is taken for granted in homogeneous data centres where good connectivity, constant presence and cen-tralised infrastructure can be assumed. One layer above, *resource* provision and consumption are arranged on top of the coordination framework. Easy in the ho-mogeneous grid of a data centre where all nodes have the same interests, but more challenging in a distributed heterogeneous environment. Finally, the *service* layer is where resources are combined into end-user accessible services, to then them-selves be composed into higher-level services.

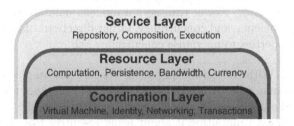

Fig. 5. Community Cloud Computing

Coordination Layer. To achieve coordination, the nodes need to be deployed as isolated *virtual machines*, forming a fully distributed P2P network that can provide support for distributed identity, trust, and transactions.

Virtual Machines (VMs): Executing arbitrary code in the machine of a resource-providing user would require a *sandbox* for the guest code, a VM to protect the host. The role of the VM is to make system resources *safely* available to the Community Cloud, upon which Cloud processes could be run safely (without danger to the host machine). Regarding deployment, users would be required to maintain an active browser window or tab, or install a dedicated application. While the first would not require installation privileges, the later would with the benefit of greater functionality.

Distributed Identity: In distributed systems with variable node reliability, historical context is logically required to have certainty of node interactions. Fundamental to this context is the ability to identify nodes and therefore reference previous interactions. However, current identification schemes have *identity providers* controlling provision. Identity in the Community Cloud has to arise naturally from the structure of the network, based on the relation of nodes to each other, so that it can scale and expand without centralised control. We can utilise the property that a large enough identifier-space is unlikely to suffer collisions. So, assuming each node independently produces a private-public key pair, the probability of public key collision is negligible. Also, from the human identification of nodes we can utilise the property that each node, despite formal identity, possesses a unique position in the network, i.e. set of connections to other nodes. Therefore, combining these two properties provides reasonable certainty for a *distributed identity model* where universal identification can be accomplished without centralised mediation, but this is still an active area of research.

Networking: At this level, nodes should be interconnected to form a P2P network. Engineered to provide high resilience while avoiding single points of control and failure, which would make decentralised super-peer based control mechanisms insufficient. Newer P2P designs [21] offer sufficient guarantees of distribution, immunity to super-peer failure, and resistance to enforced control.

Distributed Transactions: A key element of distributed coordination is the ability of nodes to jointly participate in transactions that influence their individual state. Appropriately annotated business processes can be executed over a distributed network with a transactional model maintaining the ACID properties on behalf of the initiator. Newer transaction models maintain these properties while increasing efficiency and concurrency. Other directions of research include relaxing these properties to maximise concurrency [22].

Resource layer. With the networking infrastructure now in place, we can consider the first consumer-facing uses for the *virtual data centre* of the Community Cloud. Offering the usage experience of Cloud Computing on the PaaS layer and above, because Cloud Computing is about using resources from the Cloud. So, Utility Computing scenarios, such as access to raw storage and computation, should be available at the PaaS layer. Access to these abstract resources for service deployment would then provide the SaaS layer.

Distributed Computation: The field has a successful history of centrally controlled incarnations. However, C3 should also take inspiration from Grid Computing and Digital Ecosystems to provide distributed coordination of the computational capabilities that nodes offer to the Community Cloud.

Distributed Persistence: The Community Cloud would naturally require storage on its participating nodes, taking advantage of the ever-increasing surplus on most personal computers. However, the method of information storage in the Community Cloud is an issue with multiple aspects. First, information can be file-based or structured. Second, while constant and instant availability can be crucial, there are scenarios in which recall times can be relaxed. Such varying requirements call for a combination of approaches, including distributed storage, distributed databases and key-value stores [23]. Information privacy in the Community Cloud should be provided by the encryption of user information when on remote nodes, only being unencrypted when accessed by the user, allowing for the secure and distributed storage of information.

Bandwidth Management: The Community Cloud would probably require more bandwidth at the user nodes than vendor Clouds, but can take advantage of the ever-increasing bandwidth and deployment of broadband. Also, P2P protocols such as BitTorrent make the distribution of information over networks much less bandwidth-intensive for content providers, accomplished by using the downloading peers as repeaters of the information they receive. C3 should adopt such approaches to ensure the efficient use of available network bandwidth, avoiding fluctuations and sudden rises in demand burdening parts of the network.

Community Currency: An important theme in the Community Cloud is that of nodes being contributors as well as consumers, which would require a *community currency* (redeemable against resources in the community) to reward users for offering resources [24]. This would also allow traditional Cloud vendors to participate by offering their resources to the Community Cloud to gather considerable *community currency*, which they can then monetise against participants running a *community currency* deficit (i.e. contributing less then they consume). The relative cost of resources (storage, computation, bandwidth) should fluctuate based on market demand, not least because of the impracticality of predicting or hard-coding such ratios. So, a node of the network would gather *community currency* by performing tasks for the community, which its user could then use to access resources of the Community Cloud.

Resource Repository: Given that each node providing resources has a different location in the network and quality characteristics, a distributed resource repository would be required that could respond to queries for resources according to desired performance profiles. Such a query would have to consider historical performance, current availability, projected cost and geographical distribution of the nodes to be returned. A constraint optimisation problem, the results returned would be a set of nodes that fit the required profile, proportionally to the availability of suitable nodes.

Service Layer. Cloud Computing represents a new era for SOAs, making services explicitly dependent on other resource providers instead of building on self-sufficient resource locations. C3 makes this more explicit, breaking down the stand-alone service paradigm, with any service by default being composed of resources contributed by multiple participants. So, the following sections define the core infrastructural services that the Community Cloud would need to provide.

Distributed Service Repository (DSR): The service repository of the Community Cloud must provide persistence, as with traditional service repositories, for the pointers to services and their semantic descriptions. To support the absence of service-producing nodes during service execution, there must also be persistence of the executable code of services. Naturally, the implementation of a distributed service repository is made easier by the availability of the distributed storage infrastructure of the Community Cloud.

Service Deployment and Execution: When a service is required, but is not currently instantiated on a suitable node, a copy should be retrieved from the DSR and instantiated as necessary, allowing for flexible responsiveness and resilience to unpredictable traffic spikes. As nodes are opportunistically interested in executing services to gather *community currency* for their users, so developers should note the resource cost of their services in their descriptions, allowing for pre-execution resource budgeting, and post-execution *community currency* payments. Being in a developer's own interest to mark resource costs correctly, because over-budgeting would burden their users and under-budgeting would cause premature service termination. Remote service execution would need to be secured against potentially compromised nodes, perhaps through encrypted processing schemes [25]. Since delivering a service over large distances in the network comes at a potentially high cost, the lack of a central well-connected server calls for a fundamental paradigm shift, from *pull*-oriented approaches to hybrid *push/pull*-oriented approaches [13].

7   In the Community Cloud

While we have covered the fundamental motivations and architecture of the Community Cloud, its practical application may still be unclear. So, this section discusses the case of YouTube, where the application of C3 would yield significant benefits, because it has an unstable funding model, requires increasing scalability, and is community oriented.

YouTube requires significant bandwidth for content distribution, significant computational resources for video transcoding, and is yet to settle on a profitable business model. In the Community Cloud, websites like YouTube would have a self-sustaining scalable resource provision model, which would significantly reduce the income required for them to turn a profit. Were YouTube to adopt C3, it would also be distributed throughout the Community Cloud alongside other services. Updates such as commenting on a YouTube video, would similarly need to propagate through the distributed persistence layer. So, the community would provide the bandwidth for content distribution, and the computational resources for video transcoding, required for YouTube's service. Also, YouTube's streaming of live events has necessitated the services of bespoke content distribution networks, a type of service for which the Community Cloud would naturally excel.

We have discussed YouTube in the Community Cloud, but other sites such as Wikipedia, arXiv and Facebook would equally benefit. As C3's organisational model for resource provision moves the cost of service provision to the user base, effectively creating a micro-payment scheme, which would dramatically lower the barrier of entry for innovative start-ups.

8 Conclusions

We have presented the Community Cloud as an alternative to Cloud Computing, created from blending its usage scenarios with paradigms from Grid Computing, principles from Digital Ecosystems, self-management from Autonomic Computing, and sustainability from Green Computing. So, C3 utilises the spare resources of networked personal computers to provide the facilities of data centres, such that the community provides the computing power for the Cloud they wish to use. A socio-technical conceptualisation for sustainable distributed computing.

References

1. Haynie, M.: Enterprise cloud services: Deriving business value from Cloud Computing. Technical report, Micro Focus (2009)
2. Armbrust, M., Fox, A., Griffith, R., Joseph, A., Katz, R., Konwinski, A., Lee, G., Patterson, D., Rabkin, A., Stoica, I., Zaharia, M.: Above the Clouds: A Berkeley view of Cloud Computing. University of California, Berkeley (2009)
3. Hayes, J.: Cred - or croak? Technical report, IET Knowledge Network (2008)
4. Kaplan, J., Forrest, W., Kindler, N.: Revolutionizing data center energy efficiency. Technical report, McKinsey & Company (2008)
5. Gruman, G., Knorr, E.: What Cloud Computing really means. Technical report, Info World Inc. (2008)
6. Buyya, R., Yeo, C., Venugopal, S.: Market-oriented cloud computing: Vision, hype, and reality for delivering it services as computing utilities. In: Conference on High Performance Computing and Communications. IEEE, Los Alamitos (2008)
7. Environmental Protection Agency: EPA report to congress on server and data center energy efficiency. Technical report, US Congress (2007)
8. Miller, R.: NSA maxes out Baltimore power grid. Technical report, Data Center Knowledge (2006)
9. Brill, K.: The invisible crisis in the data center: The economic meltdown of Moore's law. Technical report, Uptime Institute (2007)
10. Foster, I., Kesselman, C.: The grid: blueprint for a new computing infrastructure. Morgan Kaufmann, San Francisco (2004)
11. Foster, I., Zhao, Y., Raicu, I., Lu, S.: Cloud Computing and Grid Computing 360-degree compared. In: Grid Computing Environments Workshop, pp. 1–10 (2008)
12. Briscoe, G., De Wilde, P.: Digital Ecosystems: Evolving service-oriented architectures. In: Conference on Bio Inspired Models of Network, Information and Computing Systems. IEEE Press, Los Alamitos (2006)
13. Briscoe, G.: Digital Ecosystems. PhD thesis, Imperial College London (2009)

14. Williams, J., Curtis, L.: Green: The new computing coat of arms? IT Professional, 12–16 (2008)
15. Brodkin, J.: Gartner in 'green' data centre warning. Techworld (2008)
16. Arregoces, M., Portolani, M.: Data center fundamentals. Cisco Press (2003)
17. Kephart, J., Chess, D., Center, I., Hawthorne, N.: The vision of autonomic computing. Computer 36(1), 41–50 (2003)
18. Benkler, Y.: Sharing nicely: on shareable goods and the emergence of sharing as a modality of economic production. The Yale Law Journal 114(2), 273–359 (2004)
19. Grand, J., Thornton, F., Yarusso, A., Baer, R.: Game Console Hacking: Have Fun While Voiding You Warranty. Syngress Press (2004)
20. Doteuchi, A.: Community currency and NPOs- A model for solving social issues in the 21st century. Social Development Research Group, NLI Research (2002)
21. Razavi, A., Moschoyiannis, S., Krause, P.: A scale-free business network for digital ecosystems. In: IEEE Conf. on Digital Ecosystems and Technologies (2008)
22. Vogels, W.: Eventually consistent. ACM Queue 6 (2008)
23. Bain, T.: Is the relational database doomed? (2008), http://ReadWriteWeb.com
24. Turner, D., Ross, K.: A lightweight currency paradigm for the p2p resource market. In: International Conference on Electronic Commerce Research (2004)
25. Gentry, C.: Fully homomorphic encryption using ideal lattices. In: Symposium on Theory of computing, pp. 169–178. ACM, New York (2009)

A Semantic Grid Oriented to E-Tourism

Xiao Ming Zhang

College of Computer and Communication, Hunan University, 410082 Changsha, China
School of Hospitality & Tourism Management, Florida International University,
33181 Miami, USA
zhangxm19712003@yahoo.com.cn

Abstract. With increasing complexity of tourism business models and tasks, there is a clear need of the next generation e-Tourism infrastructure to support flexible automation, integration, computation, storage, and collaboration. Currently several enabling technologies such as semantic Web, Web service, agent and grid computing have been applied in the different e-Tourism applications, however there is no a unified framework to be able to integrate all of them. So this paper presents a promising e-Tourism framework based on emerging semantic grid, in which a number of key design issues are discussed including architecture, ontologies structure, semantic reconciliation, service and resource discovery, role based authorization and intelligent agent. The paper finally provides the implementation of the framework.

Keywords: e-Tourism; Semantic Grid; Semantic Web; Web service; Agent

1 Introduction

Tourism has become the world's largest industry, composing of numerous enterprises such as airlines, hoteliers, car rentals, leisure suppliers, and travel agencies. The World Tourism Organization predicts that by 2020 tourist arrivals around the world would increase over 200% [1]. In this huge industry, e-Tourism representing almost 40% of all global e-Commerce [2] is facing a need of the next generation infrastructure to support more innovative and sophisticated tasks like dynamic packaging, travel planning, price comparison, travel route design, and multimedia based marketing and promotion. Fig. 1 shows an e-Tourism task scenario which can illustrate several use cases and aid in capturing feature requirements for the future e-Tourism infrastructure.

- **Use case 1:** A travel agency receives a tourist's request of travel plan for the holiday (step 1), so it enters a VO (Virtual Organization) which is able to organize necessary, rich and authorized tourism services and resources in a cross-institutional way. Then the travel agency forwards tourists' travel plan task to an agent (step 2). Next, the agent coordinates other agents and assigns them smaller branch tasks (step 3). In fig. 1, one branch task is to design travel route which performs complex calculations based on GIS and Traffic database, and the other two branch tasks are queries of related air fare and hotel room rates through GDS (Global Distribution Framework) and CRM (Central Reservation Management). Finally the first agent processes the results from its partners and returns travel plans to the travel agency (step 4) and the tourist (step 5).

M.G. Jaatun, G. Zhao, and C. Rong (Eds.): CloudCom 2009, LNCS 5931, pp. 485–496, 2009.
© Springer-Verlag Berlin Heidelberg 2009

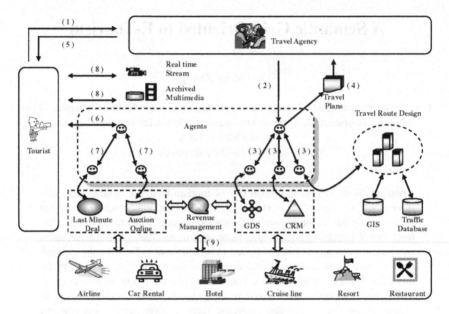

Fig. 1. An e-Tourism Task Scenario

- **Use case 2**: The authorized tourist directly enters the VO and search required services. In this situation, the system needs to trace and analyze user's preferences and requirements, then compare them with services' functionalities. In fig. 1, the system discovers and returns Last Minute Deal and Auction Online services to the tourist who interests in the best room rates of hotel (step 6, 7).
- **Use case 3**: To promote the products or services, some services providers conduct a multimedia marketing, allowing tourists watch large amount of archived photos and live streaming video on line (step 8).
- **Use case 4**: The services are able to access other services and resources owned by different service providers seamlessly. For example, some advanced service providers prefer to use Revenue Management service (step 9), which is able to interact with other sales online systems (e.g. GDS) and maximize business profit through differentiating the prices of different products in those online systems.

From the above use cases, several feature requirements for the future e-Tourism infrastructure can be identified:

- Personalization and intelligent agent. The individual intention and tasks should be able to be personalized and represented in intelligent agents who can interact with other agents and objects, perform various tasks, deal with events timely and seek solutions to the targets autonomously.
- Knowledge service. It includes discovering resource and services through inference, annotating the contributed resource, combining content from multiple sources, and scheduling the agents and workflow to the tasks.
- High degree of automation. It refers to describe the services, resources and even workflow in a machine understandable manner, and thus different tasks like

travel planning could be performed in an automatic way with a good performance, without or with very limited human support.

- Seamless integration. Various resources, services and relevant users should be integrated in a uniform and seamless manner, realizing the dynamically and semantically enhanced information processing.
- Computations. The distributed, extensible and transparent computation resource is required by the computing intensive services like travel route design.
- Storages. The system should be able to store and process potentially huge volumes of multimedia content, user information and business data in a timely and efficient fashion.
- VO and collaborations. VO is required to make users share resources, access services and collaborate in a cross-institutional way.

To meet the above requirements, currently several enabling technologies like semantic Web [3], Web services, grid and agent have been adopted in the different e-Tourism applications, however there is no an unified framework to be able to seamlessly integrate all of them. Inspired by UK e-Science program, the paper focuses on the solution from a promising infrastructure, semantic grid [4][5]. Semantic grid is able to provide an Internet centered interconnection environment that effectively organize, share, cluster, fuse, and manage globally distributed versatile resources based on the interconnection semantics [6]. In this paper, we research an e-Tourism framework based on semantic grid, which conforms to the S-OGSA architecture [7] and enhanced by several customizations and extensions such as the ontologies, intelligent agent, unified service and resource discovery, etc.

The remainder of this paper is structured in the following manner. Section 2 provides framework overview. Section 3 discusses several design issues including architecture, ontologies structure, agent, etc. Section 4 presents the implementation. Section 5 introduces the related work and section 6 gives out the conclusion.

2 Framework Overview

The e-Tourism framework proposed in this paper is designed based on semantic grid, which conforms to three layered views: service view, content view and technological view (fig. 2).

Firstly, from the service view, the framework takes the notion of service-oriented, in which any users including tourist, travel agency, hotel, restaurant, airline and resort should be considered as either service consumer or service provider. VOs organize services and relevant resources and users in a virtual administrative domain, allowing the access of services in a cross-institutional way.

Secondly, content view refers to the objects that the framework can process from simple data to meaningful information, then to higher abstract knowledge. This view has been widely accepted since it is presented by David, Nicholas and Nigel [8]. In this view, the data is concerned with the way how it is obtained, shipped, processed and transmitted by services, resources and even some special equipments like camera; then, the information is the data equipped with meaning, which is related to the way how it is represented, annotated, achieved, shared and maintained. For example, the number can be annotated as distance between a hotel and an airport; finally, the knowledge is the information aiding users to achieve their particular goals, which is concerned with the way how it is acquired, inferred, retrieved, published and maintained. For instance, a piece of knowledge can be stated like this: 20 minutes driving is needed from the airport to a hotel if the distance is about 20 miles.

Thirdly, technological view considers the state of the art technological components which implement the e-Tourism semantic grid. For instance, grid supports VO, computation, storage and collaboration management; agent and workflow facilities provide personalization and intelligent automation; semantic Web and Web services enable the seamless integration and knowledge inferring.

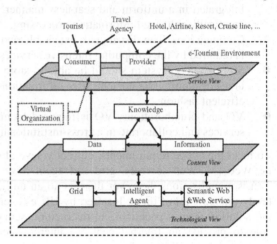

Fig. 2. Overview of E-Tourism Framework

3 Design Issues

In this section, some detailed design issues are discussed mainly focusing on e-Tourism specific requirements, which include framework architecture, ontologies structure, semantic reconciliation, service and resource discovery, role based authorization and intelligent agent.

3.1 Architecture

To avoid the reinvention of the wheel, our framework takes S-OGSA as the start point for architecture design, which is widely considered as the first reference architecture for semantic grid by extending the current OGSA (Open Grid Services Architecture) [9] with semantics. S-OGSA integrates the grid, semantic Web and semantic Services together, supports many important knowledge services. For example, ontology and reasoning services are designed for the conceptual models of representing knowledge, while metadata and annotation services are invented to implement semantic binding for different types of information sources, like documents, databases, provenance information, credentials, etc. However, as a basic and common architecture, S-OGSA can't be directly applied to all different applications, so according to the specific requirements of e-Tourism, we extend or enhance S-OGSA as followings:

● Extending ontologies structure with tourism domain requirements
● Introducing semantic reconciliation to solve the interoperability of ontologies
● Unifying the service and resource discovery
● Establishing role based authorization
● Integrating intelligent agent facility.

3.2 Ontologies Structure

In the e-Tourism semantic grid, ontologies are the fundamental blocks to capture the expressive power of modeling and reasoning with knowledge [8].

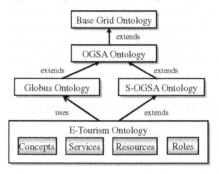

Fig. 3. Ontologies Structure

From the ontologies structure illustrated in Fig. 3, e-Tourism ontology is obtained through extending the S-OGSA ontology and using part of the Globus [10] ontology. To meet the specific requirements in tourism domain, e-Tourism ontology is composed of four parts: Concepts ontology provides basic definitions and standard terms based on WTO (World Tourism Organization) Thesaurus [11], which is an international standardization and normalization guide to tourism terminology;

Roles ontology contains descriptions of user roles like tourist, travel agency and service provider; Resources ontology states the capability of the hardware, software and communication resources which support the services, for example, CPU performance and network bandwidth; Services ontology defines the uniform service interfaces and functionalities conforming to the OTA specification [11], which includes air services, cruise services, destination services, dynamic package services, golf services, hotel services, insurance service, loyalty services, tour services and vehicle services. Fig. 4 gives out hierarchical structure of OTA-Compliant services ontology and an example interface description of TourSearchRQService.

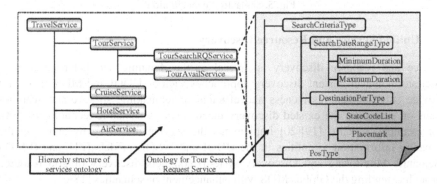

Fig. 4. OTA-Compliant E-Tourism Services Ontology

3.3 Semantic Reconciliation

Although e-Tourism ontology is helpful in establishing the new semantically interoperable services, it's impractical to reinvent all legend services and make them complaint to a global ontology in the tourism domain. Some different ontologies mentioned at the related work of this document have been adopted by several legend

tourism systems or services, so there is a need of semantic reconciliation which typically implemented through ontology mediation or mapping in some projects
[12][13][14].

In this framework, semantic reconciliation is solved mainly by stub service
[15][16] and ontology service. Stub service encapsulates the details of translating
between OTA-Compliant messages and Provider-Specific messages. In translation,
stub services collaborate with ontology service which supports ontologies mapping
besides the storage capability. Upon completing transformation of messages, stub
services forward them to the target Provider-Specific services. In fig. 5, an OTA-
Compliant request to TourSearchRQService is converted into Amadeus-specific and
Sabre-specific requests in the different stub services through the ontology mapping.

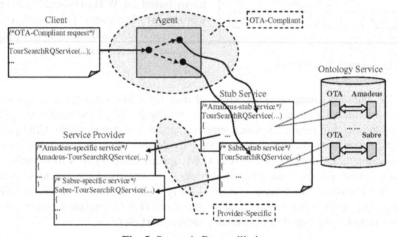

Fig. 5. Semantic Reconciliation

3.4 Unified Service and Resource Discovery

Service and resource discovery is critical to the dynamic and heterogeneous e-
Tourism, however current discovery approaches such as UDDI and MDS [17] can't
provide sufficient expressiveness and efficient matchmaking, so several researches
focus on extending the existed discovery mechanism by semantic technologies [18].
For example, myGrid [19][20] implements the service discovery by attaching the
semantic information to entities in the UDDI and WSDL models [21], and S-MDS
(Semantic Monitoring and Discovery system) conducts discovery of grid resource
through extending the Globus MDS with enhancement of semantics [18].

Based on the above achievements, our discovery solution strives to unify semantic
discovery of service and resource together, because the service discovery in the grid is
not only relied on the requirements of functionalities and features, but also the availability and performance of associated underlying resources [22]. As illustrated in fig.
6, the information of service and its respective stub service is stored in UDDI; the
relied resource information with property of related service name and UDDI index is
stored in MDS; the association among capability, service and its stub service is

described in OWL-SR language [22] and stored in Mediator. At runtime clients or agents send semantic query to Mediator, for example "find a tour search service on a resource with CPU utilization less than 10%". Then Mediator infers a list of services which meet the service capability description through contacting ontology service and reasoning service. Next, Mediator infers and sends a query to the MDS based on this service list and the resource requirement. Upon receipt of resources from MDS, Mediator is able to narrow down the service list by kicking out the services without required resources. Finally Mediator forms a list composing of the stub services corresponding to the previously narrowed service list, and returns it to the clients or agents. This last step is critical to the system integration in the heterogeneous e-Tourism, because the OTA-Compliant interfaces provided by stub services are able to hide the interface difference of specific providers, which in turn simplifies and unifies the client and agent programming.

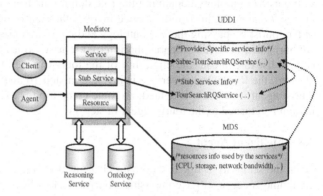

Fig. 6. Unified Service and Resource Discovery

3.5 Role Based Authorization

VO provides an effective way for cross-institutional services and resources accessing in the e-Tourism system. However, the authorization of the users from the different administrative domain cannot be pre-determined statically until at runtime. So we make a role based access control policy that conforms to the OGSA-AuthZ framework and is able to determine the users' eligibility dynamically [23] [24]. Under this policy, users' roles can be inferred from their properties during runtime. For example, EcnomicTourist role is assigned to a tourist whose consuming points in the past 12 months are below 5000, and he can be

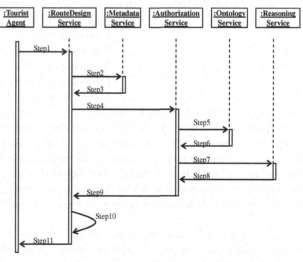

Fig. 7. Authorization Process Based on Roles

upgrades to VipTourist role when his consuming points in the past 12 months reach 5000 or above.

The fig. 7 illustrates the authorization process for a tourist to access RouteDesign service which is only authorized to VipTourist users. Initially Authorization service maintains an access control list based on roles. In step 1, a tourist entering the VO requests the RouteDesign service through his agent. Then the RouteDesign service collects the properties of the tourist through Metadata service in step 2, 3. Next, in step 4 RouteDesign service generates an Authorization request which contains the RDF based property regarding consuming points. In step 5 and 6, Authorization service gets VO ontology containing the role definitions from the ontology service. And in step 7 and 8, Authorization service invokes the Reasoning service to infer the role of the tourist by passing the VO ontology and the tourist property as parameters. Then Authorization service compares the inferred tourist's roles and the role based access control list to evaluate the eligibility of the tourist in step 9. Finally, if the access is allowed, the RouteDesign service is invoked in step 10 and returns the travel route to tourist agent in step 11. If denied, no route computing is executed and the deny information is returned to the tourist agent in step 11.

3.6 Intelligent Agent

From the scenario in fig. 1, there is a clear need of agents to perform some flexible, autonomous actions to accomplish e-Tourism tasks [25]. Some agents act as the representative of the tourists or travel agencies to forward the requests, monitor the status and receive the responses. While some other agents are capable of mining preference, which aids in precise and timely targeting, and personalization of tourism products. To achieve this, the agent need to trace the user's requests, analyze his preferences, and continually refresh the dynamic part of user profile like interests. In the following example, an Interests-Value array IV_{ij} $(i=1...n$ items of interests, $j=0, 1)$ is used by the agent to represent relevant tourist's interests.

   when j=0, IVij={items of interests};
   when j=1, IVij={1,2,3,4,5}. /*value of interests:
                    1, invokes of service in a month <5;
                    2, invokes of service in a month <10 and >=5;
                    3, invokes of service in a month <15 and >=10;
                    4, invokes of service in a month <20 and >=15;
                    5, invokes of service in a month >=20 */

From the above definition, *items of interests* is a set of requests invoked by the tourist in the past month. *Value of interests* reflects the frequency of requests invokes by the tourist in the past month. More frequently a request is invoked by a user, the higher the *value of interests* is. If the *value of interests* of a request, for example "Request (op: airFare, source: Beijing, destination: Newyork)", is greater than a threshold, then this request will be added to a preference list and invoked by the agent periodically, thus the updated air fare from Beijing to Newyork will be automatically returned to the tourist.

For complex e-Tourism business, the agent need to be enhanced by workflow and rule based reasoning engine. Workflow engine enables multiple agents to collaborate in a customizable way, while reasoning engine can assign agents the capacity to infer knowledge through declarative rules. There have been lots of discussions on reasoning and workflow of agents[26] [27] [28] [29].

4 Implementation

The framework is implemented on two layers: application and infrastructure. Application layer contains semantic aware e-Tourism grid services (e.g. RouteDesign service), which solve the business problems in e-Tourism domain and are deployed in the containers supported by the lower semantic grid infrastructure. The infrastructure layer conforms to the S-OGSA and is implemented by OntoGrid framework [30]. It deploys Globus Toolkit 4 as basic grid platform, integrates Jena [31] to support semantic Web functionalities (for example, RDF based metadata storage and reasoning), and uses Apache Axis [32] and WSRF [33] to declare Web services and execute SOAP requests. Moreover, several customizations and enhancements like ontologies, Mediator and intelligent agent have been applied on OntoGrid framework to better serve the e-Tourism requirements. Specially, the agent facilities are set up through JADE (Java Agent Development Evnironment) [34] with extensions of reasoning and workflow engines: JESS (Java Expert System Shell) [29] and Wade (Workflow and Agent Development Environment) [26]. Additionally, integration between agent facilities and S-OGSA framework is completed through a service oriented manner in which the communication is realized via Web services.

5 Related Work

The semantic Web and semantic Web service has substantial effects on next generation e-Tourism infrastructure, which enhances existing tourism Web resources and services through semantic way, makes them "smarter" and capable of carrying out intelligent reasoning behind the scenes. Some typical projects include:

● Harmonise [35] is an EU Tourism Harmonisation Network established by eCTRL, IFITT and others. It creates an electronic space for tourism stakeholders to exchange information in a seamless, semiautomatic manner, independent from geographical, linguistic and technological boundaries. It defines an Interoperability Minimum Harmonisation Ontology for modeling and saving concepts of transaction data.

● Hi-Touch project [36] is to develop semantic Web methodologies and tools for intra-European sustainable tourism. It makes use of the WTO Thesaurus on Tourism and Leisure Activities as an authoritative source for its ontology.

● OnTour project [37] developed by e-Tourism Working Group at Digital Enterprise Research Institute, designs an advanced e-Tourism semantic Web portal connecting the customers and virtual travel agents, and an e-Tourism ontology using OWL and WTO Thesaurus.

● SATINE project [13] realizes a semantic based infrastructure which allows the Web services on well-established service registries like UDDI or ebXML to seamlessly interoperate with Web services on P2P Networks. The travel ontologies are developed based on standard specifications of Open Travel Alliance (OTA).

Despite contributing a lot for the e-Tourism infrastructure, semantic Web and semantic Web services have the weakness in flexible computation, storage, VO and collaboration which are critical to next generation e-Tourism. Semantic grid, however, is able to compensate these lacks by seamlessly integrating grid facilities with semantic Web and Web services. Currently several pioneering applications based on semantic grid have been developed in the following:

- GRISINO project aims to develop an experimental test-bed combining advanced prototypes of each of the three technologies: Knowledge Content Objects as a model for the unit of value, WSMO/L/X as a framework for the description and execution of semantic Web services and Globus as the grid infrastructure for managing resources and hosting services.
- UK e-Science program has reinforced the practical need for the semantic grid, and funded many e-Science projects based on various semantic grid solutions, like CombeChem/eBank, CoAKTinG, MIAKT and Medical Devices.
- There are still more significant efforts to provide an architecture like S-OGSA for the development of semantic grid applications or simply semantic aware grid Services, such as projects InteliGrid [38] and myGrid, showing how explicit metadata can be used in the context of existing grid applications.

6 Conclusion

This paper has discussed the semantic grid as the next generation e-Tourism infrastructure, which supports high degree automation, seamless integration, knowledge services, intelligent agent, flexible collaboration, and sharing of computation and storage resources on a global scale. It's not difficult to imagine a lot of innovative e-Tourism applications on this promising infrastructure. However, the semantic grid is still in its early experimentation phase of pioneering applications and far away from the mature [23]. To make it a reality, there are still many research challenges, for example, performance, scalability, reliability and security problems.

References

1. Cardoso, J.: E-Tourism: Creating Dynamic Packages using Semantic Web Processes. In: W3C Workshop on Frameworks for Semantics in Web Services. Innsbruck (2005)
2. Keun, H.K., Jeong, S.H., Pilsoo, S.K.: Modeling for Intelligent Tourism E-Marketplace Based on Ontology. In: Proc. of the 2007 International Conference on Recreation, Tourism, and Hospitality Industry Trends, Taiwan, pp. 56–65 (2007)
3. Berners-Lee, T., Hendler, J., Lassila, O.: Semantic Web. J. Scientific American 284(5), 34–43 (2001)
4. Murphy, M.J., Dick, M., Fischer, T.: Towards the Semantic Grid. J. Communications of the IIMA 8(3), 11–24 (2008)
5. Roure, D.D.: Future for European Grids: GRIDs and Service Oriented Knowledge Utilities. In: Vision and Research Directions 2010 and Beyond,
   http://www.semanticgrid.org/documents/ngg3/ngg3.html

6. Zhuge, H.: Semantic Grid: Scientific Issues, Infrastructure, and Methodology. J. Communications of The ACM 48(4), 117–119 (2005)
7. Corcho, O., Alper, P., Kotsiopoulos, I., Missier, P., Bechhofer, S., Goble, C.: An overview of S-OGSA: A Reference Semantic Grid Architecture. J. Web Semantics 4, 102–115 (2006)
8. Roure, D.D., Jennings, N.R., Shadbolt, N.R.: The Semantic Grid: A Future e-Science Infrastructure. In: Grid Computing - Making the Global Infrastructure a Reality, pp. 437–470. John Wiley and Sons Ltd., Chichester (2003)
9. Foster, I., Kishimoto, H., Savva, A., Berry, D., Djaoui, A., Grimshaw, A., Horn, B., Maciel, F., Siebenlist, F., Subramaniam, R., Treadwell, J., Reich, J.V.: The Open Grid Services Architecture, Version 1.0. Technical report, Global Grid Forum (2005)
10. Foster, I.: A Globus Toolkit Primer (2005), http://www.globus.org/primer
11. Prantner, K., Ding, Y., Luger, M., Yan, Z., Herzog, C.: Tourism Ontology and Semantic Management System: State-of-the-arts Analysis. In: IADIS International Conference WWW/Internet 2007. Vila Real, Portugal (2007)
12. Maedche, A., Motik, D., Silva, N., Volz, R.: MAFRA-A MApping FRAmework for Distributed Ontologies. In: Gómez-Pérez, A., Benjamins, V.R. (eds.) EKAW 2002. LNCS (LNAI), vol. 2473, pp. 235–250. Springer, Heidelberg (2002)
13. Dogac, A., Kabak, Y., Laleci, G., Sinir, S., Yildiz, A., Tumer, A.: SATINE Project: Exploiting Web Services in the Travel Industry. In: eChallenges 2004, Vienna (2004)
14. Dogac, A., Kabak, Y., Laleci, G., Sinir, S., Yildiz, A., Kirbas, S., Gurcan, Y.: Semantically Enriched Web Services for the Travel Industry. J. ACM Sigmod Record 33(3) (2004)
15. Zhang, X.M.: High performance virtual distributed object. J. Journal of Computer Research and Development suppl., 102–107 (2000)
16. Zhang, X.M.: A Dynamic Scalable Asynchronous Message Model Based on Distributed Objects. J. Computer Engineering and Science 3, 48–50 (2002)
17. GT 4.0 WS MDS Index Service: System Administrator's Guide, http://www-unix.globus.org/toolkit/docs/development/4.0-drafts/info/index/admin/
18. S-MDS: semantic monitoring and discovery system for the Grid. J. Grid Computing 7, 205–224 (2009)
19. Sharman, N., Alpdemir, N., Ferris, J., Greenwood, M., Li, P., Wroe, C.: The myGrid Information Model. In: UK e-Science programme All Hands Conference (2004)
20. myGrid: The myGrid project (2008), http://www.mygrid.org.uk/
21. Miles, S., Papay, J., Payne, T.R., Decker, K., Moreau, L.: Towards a protocol for the attachment of semantic descriptions to Grid services. In: European Across Grids Conference, pp. 230–239 (2004)
22. Lee, F., Garg, S., Garg, S.: OWL-SR: Unified Semantic Service and Resource Discovery for Grids. In: Franconi, E., Kifer, M., May, W. (eds.) ESWC 2007. LNCS, vol. 4519. Springer, Heidelberg (2007)
23. Alper, P., Corcho, O., Parkin, M., Kotsiopoulos, I., Missier, P., Bechhofer, S., Goble, C.: An authorisation scenario for S-OGSA. In: Sure, Y., Domingue, J. (eds.) ESWC 2006. LNCS, vol. 4011, pp. 7–8. Springer, Heidelberg (2006)
24. Brooke, J.M., Parkin, M.S.: Enabling scientific collaboration on the Grid. J. Future Generation Computer Systems (2008)
25. Wooldridge, M.: Agent-based software engineering. IEE Proc. on Software Engineering 144(1), 26–37 (1997)

26. Caire, G., Gotta, D., Banzi, M.: WADE: a software platform to develop mission critical applications exploiting agents and workflows. In: Proc. of the 7th international joint conference on Autonomous agents and multiagent systems, Estoril, pp. 29–36 (2008)
27. Buhler, P.A., Vidal, J.M.: Towards Adaptive Workflow Enactment Using Multiagent Systems. J. Information Technology and Management 6(1), 61–87 (2005)
28. Negri, A., Poggi, A., Tomaiuolo, M.: Dynamic Grid Tasks Composition and Distribution through Agents. J. Concurrency and Computation 18(8), 875–885 (2006)
29. JESS: the Rule Engine for the JavaTM Platform (2009),
    http://herzberg.ca.sandia.gov/jess/
30. Goble, C., Kotsiopoulos, I., Corcho, O., Missier, P., Alper, P., Bechhofer, S.: S-OGSA as a Reference Architecture for OntoGrid and for the Semantic Grid. In: GGF16 Semantic Grid Workshop (2006)
31. Carroll, J.J., Dickinson, I., Dollin, C., Reynolds, D., Seaborne, A., Wilkinson, K.: Jena: implementing the semantic web recommendations. In: Proc. of the 13th international World Wide Web conference, New York (2004)
32. Axis Architecture Guide,
    http://ws.apache.org/axis/java/architecture-guide.html
33. Czajkowski, K., Ferguson, D., Foster, I., Frey, J., Graham, S., Sedukhin, I., Snelling, D., Tuecke, S., Vambenepe, W.: Web Services Resource Framework (WSRF). Technical report, Globus Alliance and IBM (2005)
34. Bellifemine, F., Poggi, A., Rimassa, G.: Jade: a fipa2000 compliant agent development environment. In: Proceedings of the fifth international conference on Autonomous agents, pp. 216–217. ACM Press, New York (2001)
35. Missikoff, M., Werthner, H., Hopken, W., et al.: Harmonise-Towards Interoperability in the Tourism Domain. In: Proc. of the 10th International Conference on the Information and Communication Technologies in Travel & Tourism, Helsinki, Finland (2003)
36. Hi-Touch project,
    http://icadc.cordis.lu/fepcgi/
    srchidadb?CALLER=PROJ_IST&ACTION=D&RCN=63604&DOC=20&QUERY=3
37. Bachlechner, D.: OnTour - The Semantic Web and its Benefits for the Tourism Industry (2005), http://e-tourism.deri.at/ont
38. Dolenc, M., Turk, Ž., Katranuschkov, P., Krzysztof, K.: D93.2 Final report of the InteliGrid. Technical report, The InteliGrid Consortium and University of Ljubljana (2007)

Irregular Community Discovery for Social CRM in Cloud Computing

Jin Liu[1,2], Fei Liu[1], Jing Zhou[3], and ChengWan He[4]

[1] State Key Lab. Of Software Engineering, Wuhan University, China 430072
[2] State Key Lab. for Novel Software Technology, Nanjing University, China 210093
[3] School of Computer, Communication University of China, 100024
[4] School of Computer Science and Engineering, Wuhan Institute of Technology, 430073
mailjinliu@yahoo.com

Abstract. Social CRM is critical in utilities services provided by cloud computing. These services rely on virtual customer communities forming spontaneously and evolving continuously. Thus clarifying the explicit boundaries of these communities is quite essential to the quality of utilities services in cloud computing. Communities with overlapping feature or projecting vertexes are usually typical irregular communities. Traditional community identification algorithms are limited in discovering irregular topological structures from a CR networks. These uneven shapes usually play a prominent role in finding prominent customer which is usually ignored in social CRM. A novel method of discovering irregular community based on density threshold and similarity degree. It finds and merges primitive maximal cliques from the first. Irregular features of overlapping and prominent sparse vertex are further considered. An empirical case and a method comparison test indicates its efficiency and feasibility

Keywords: Cloud computing; Irregular community discovery; Social CRM.

1 Introduction

The distinctive traits of cloud computing are its efforts on providing value-added trustee services, maximizing flexible integration of computing resource, as well as advancing cost-saving IT service. To provide value-added trustee services, the "cloud" should be capable of identifying the customer relationship communities and answering for users' innovation strategy. To maximize flexible integration of computing resource, the "cloud" should integrate both human computing resources and electronic computing resources. Many computing tasks are usually more suitable for human to process than for electronic computing machines. Integrating the Human computing ability or crowd computing ability into the "cloud" can enhance its processing capabilities with the help of vast human brains dispersed on the Internet [22, 23]. This means that the "cloud" should be competent for tracking customer information and understanding the interaction way of its users.

Accordingly, customer relationship management CRM is critical in utilities services provided by cloud computing. Fig 1 illustrates that social CRM plays an important role in supporting value-added trustee service and exploiting human computing resources in

M.G. Jaatun, G. Zhao, and C. Rong (Eds.): CloudCom 2009, LNCS 5931, pp. 497–509, 2009.
© Springer-Verlag Berlin Heidelberg 2009

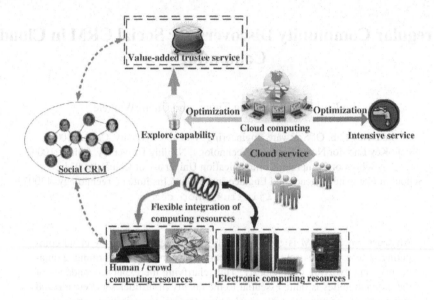

Fig. 1. Social CRM as an important components in cloud computing

cloud computing. CRM involves in attracting new profitable customers and forming tighter bonds with existing ones [1, 3]. Since online social communities and conversations carry heavy consequences for companies, social CRM integrates social network into the traditional CRM capabilities [4]. Information gained through social CRM initiatives can support the development of marketing strategy by developing the organization's knowledge in areas such as identifying customer relationship community, improving customer retention, improving product offerings by better understanding customer needs [4, 8]. Customer relationship network as a kind of social network, with CR network for short, uses a vertex for a customer and a link for the relationship between two vertexes. Many online cloud computing services rely on virtual communities that spontaneously emerge and continuously evolve. Thus clarifying the explicit boundaries of these communities is quite essential to ensure service qualification.

Communities with overlapping feature or projecting vertexes are usually typical irregular communities. Traditional community identification algorithms are limited in discovering irregular topological CR network that is very important in CRM [1, 7, 9, 12, 13, 14, 16, 17, 18, 19]. With an uneven shape, these communities usually play a prominent role in finding prominent customer which is usually ignored in social CRM [20]. For this reason, this paper proposes a novel approach of irregular community identification based on density threshold and similarity degree. With a polymerization approach, maximal complete cliques in a CR network are identified from the beginning. These primitives are further assembled into larger combinations. For overlapping cases, processes of merging these combinations or repartitioning them are executed according to corresponding rules. And communities with prominent parts are also considered in irregular identification.

2 Essential Elements

A CR community is a special sub-graph in a CR network (a graph), where vertexes within community are densely connected to each other while links are sparse between communities. An irregular community as a kind of special community with some bizarre vertexes contains the general community characteristics. Several concepts and knowledge are introduced to explain irregular community in CR network.

A clique is a complete sub-graph. A maximal clique is a set of vertices that induces a complete sub-graph, and that is not a subset of the vertices of any larger complete sub-graph [5, 10, 11]. Let $G=(V, E)$ be a CR network with $|V(G)|=n$ vertexes and $|E(G)|=m$ links, C be a community of CR network, the density of C is defined as :

$$density \ (C) = |E(C)| \Big/ \binom{|V(C)|}{2} = \frac{|E(C)|}{|V(C)|(|V(C)|-1)/2} \tag{1}$$

where $|V(C)|$ is the number of vertexes in C and $|E(C)|$ is the number of links in C.

The density of a graph reflects the interaction degree among vertexes within the graph. As a community, there are high interactions among vertexes in the community. Therefore, the graph with high density usually can be regarded as a community.

Graph H is a sub-graph of CR network G. Let be a vertex $v \in H$ and the degree of v be $D(v)$, then $D(v)$ comes from two parts such that

$$D(v)= D_{in}(v)+ D_{out} (v) \tag{2}$$

In equation (2), $D_{in}(v)$ is the number of links where v is adjacent to vertexes in H and $D_{out} (v)$ is the number of links where v is adjacent to vertexes in $V(G)-V(H)$.

The close degree between two sub-graphs H_1 and H_2 in G is defined as follows, with CD for short. CD relies on the number of relation links between H_1 and H_2.

$$CD(H_1,H_2) = \sum_{v_i \in H_1, v_j \in H_2} C(v_i,v_j) \tag{3}$$

where $C(v_i,v_j) = \begin{cases} 1, & (v_i,v_j) \in E(G) \\ 0, & (v_i,v_j) \notin E(G) \end{cases}$.

The following intermediate theorem can be deduced from the definition of density.

Lemma 1. Considering CR network G, let $H \subset G$, v_1, v_1,..., $v_n \in V(G)-V(H)$, denote link(v_i) as the number of links that v_j connect to the H vertexes and v_i with the maximal link value as v. H can maximally increase the density or minimally decrease the density if v is added to the graph.

Proof. Suppose that the graph $H=(V, E)$ is extended into a new graph H' after a vertex v adds to the graph.

$$H'=(\{V \cup v\},\{E \cup E'\}) \tag{4}$$

where E' contains the all links which v is adjacent to $V(H)$.

The number of links is represented as $link(v)$. We denote

$$\Delta d = density(H') - density(H) = \frac{|E(V)| + link(v)}{(|V(H)| + 1) \cdot |V(H)|/2} - \frac{|E(H)|}{|V(H)| \cdot (|V(H)| - 1|)/2} \tag{5}$$

where $link(v) = \max\{ link(v_1), link(v_2), \ldots, link(v_n)\}$, $link(v_i) \notin H$, i $=1,2,\ldots$, n.

It is apparent that the density of the graph H increases maximally when $\Delta d > 0$ and decreases minimally when $\Delta d < 0$.   ∎

Lemma 2. For a graph H with its density greater than threshold α, if the density of newly formed graph H' keeps steady or increase after a vertex v adds to H, it holds that:

$$link(v) \geq \alpha|V(H)|^2 - 2|E(H)| \tag{6}$$

Proof. It is known that

$$density(H) = \frac{|E(H)|}{|V(H)|(|V(H)| - 1)/2} \geq \alpha \tag{7}$$

and

$$density(H') = \frac{|E(H)| + link(v)}{(|V(H)| + 1) \cdot |V(H)|/2} \geq \alpha \tag{8}$$

Hence

$$0.5 * \alpha|V(H)| \geq 0.5\alpha|V(H)|^2 - |E(H)| \tag{9}$$

and

$$link(v) \geq 0.5\alpha|V(H)|^2 + 0.5\alpha|V(H)| - |E(H)| \tag{10}$$

It can deduce that $link(v) \geq \alpha|V(H)|^2 - 2|E(H)|$.   ∎

3 Irregular Community Identification

Since irregular community construction is different from traditional community and cannot be identified with traditional methods, a new approach denoted as the graph extension algorithm is proposed. The basic idea of graph extension algorithm is as follows. Firstly, all maximal cliques are identified from an initial CR network. Then all maximal cliques are merged or extended into a new structure by adding several special vertexes to these maximal cliques. Finally, the combined graph is processed to produce irregular communities in accordance with rational criterions.

3.1 Maximal Clique Combination

Identification of irregular community is premised on maximal cliques. Process 1 recognizes maximal cliques from a CR network to the DFS algorithm in graph theory. With a recursive manner, function fcg in process 1 explores a vertex v in CR network and checks whether it and its adjacent vertexes could constitute a clique until all cliques that include v are identified.

```
Process 1. idenfiticationMaximalClique()
 1: put graph data into vertexHouse;
 2:  for(int I = 0;i<vertexHouse.size(); i++){
 3:      Vertex n = vertexHouse.get(i);
 4:      fcg("", -1 , n  , n.neighnorList);
 5:  }
 6: Function fcg(String cg,int degree,Vertex n,List<Vertex>list)
 7:  cg += n.ID;
 8:  degree ++;
 9:  if(list.size() = = 0 ){
10:      if(degree < = 1)  return;
11:      cgList.add(cg);
12:      return;
13:  }
14: while(list.size()>0){
15:  Vertex n1 = list.get(0);
16:  list.remove(0);
17:  List<Vertex> L = new List<Vertex>();
18:  for( int i = 0; i<list.size(); i++){
19:  Vertex n2 = list.get(i);
20:  if(n1.neighborHash.containsKey(n2.getId()))L.add(n2);
22:  }
23:  }
24:  fcg(cg , degree, n1, L);
25: }
```

To merge overlapping maximal cliques, similarity is introduced to estimate the similar degree among sub-graphs. It takes account for the mutual vertexes among cliques and the size of cliques.

$$similarity(H_1, H_2, ..., H_t) = \lambda_1 \frac{|V(H_1 \cap H_2 \cap ... \cap H_t)|}{\min\{|V(H_1)|,|V(H_2)|,...,|V(H_t)|\}}$$

$$+ \lambda_2 \frac{\min\{|V(H_1)|,|V(H_2)|,...,|V(H_t)|\}}{\max\{|V(H_1)|,|V(H_2)|,...,|V(H_t)|\}} \tag{11}$$

where $\lambda_1 + \lambda_2 = 1$, $H_1, H_2, ..., H_t$ are compete graphs and $|V(H_i)| \geq 3$, $i = 1, 2, ..., t$.

The combination condition of overlapping maximal cliques can be as follows.

$$similarity(H_1, H_2, ..., H_t) \geq \beta \geq \alpha \tag{12}$$

where β is a threshold that can be determined later in the light of the specific case. If the similarity of $H_1, H_2, ..., H_t$ satisfies the restriction of formula (12), then the graphs $H_1, H_2, ..., H_t$ can be merged, denoted as $H = H_1 \cup H_2 \cup H_3 \cup ... H_t$.

Fig 2. illustrates a combination example of maximal cliques. The maximal cliques H_1, H_2, H_3 and H_4 share a common vertex "ahfylxy". The maximal cliques H_1, H_2 and H_3 share a common vertex set {"ahfylxy", "aimee6", "akhanjiang", "andydiana"}. Without loss of generality, if the value of λ_1 is taken as 0.5 and β as empirical threshold value 0.6, similarity (H_1, H_2, H_3) is 0.9, with $\max\{|V(H_1)|, V(H_2)|,V(H_3)|\}$ 5, $\min\{|V(H_1)|,V(H_2)|, V(H_3)|\}$ 5 and $|V(H_1 \cap H_2 \cap H_3)|$ 4. Since similarity (H_1, H_2, H_3) exceeds β, H_1, H_2 and H_3 are merged into a new combination, or M-graph for short. In another case, similarity (H_1,H_2,H_3, H_4) is 0.5, with $\max\{|V(H_1)|,V(H_2)|, V(H_3),V(H_4)|\}$ 5, $\min\{|V(H_1)|,V(H_2)|, V(H_3), V(H_4)|\}$ 4 and $|V(H_1 \cap H_2 \cap H_3 \cap H_4)|$ 1. Due to the lower similarity (H_1, H_2, H_3, H_4) value than β, H_4 can not be absorbed into M-graph. The merge process of maximal cliques can be rendered as follows.

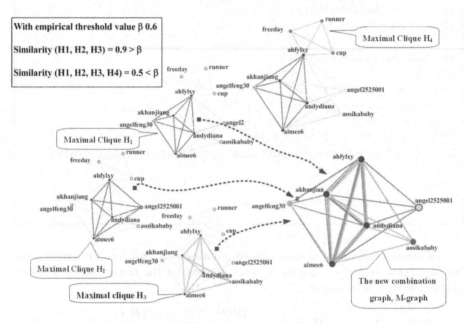

Fig. 2. A combination demonstration of maximal cliques

Process 2.   mergeMaximalClique()
1: If the similarity of the maximal cliques H_i and H_j satisfy the empirical combination threshold β,attaching a label combination marker between H_i and H_j (i,j=1,2,...,t, and i≠j);
2: Repeat this remarking operation on any two the maximal cliques, it gets a mark network G' =(V', E').
3: Scan G' and identify all connected components in G';
4: Merge each connected component into the M-graph and form the initial community.

For sub-graphs that are not maximal cliques in a CR network, the k-degree graph approach may be used to identify the maximal k-degree *(k>2)* graph. In a graph H at least contains three vertexes, if each vertex is adjacent to at least other k vertexes in H, H is a k-degree graph. Further, a maximal k-degree graph H is a k-degree graph where each vertex belongs to the k-degree graph rather than to a $(k+1)$-degree graph. A clique C with $|V(C)|= n$ is a maximal $(n-1)$-degree graph.

3.2 Irregular Overlapping Community

Several communities may be overlapped with several vertexes located in multiple communities. Since each community is adhesive graph, the combination of these communities may more often than not result in a newly formed community with irregular shape, where several vertexes are located in the multiple original communities. To combine two communities or repartition them into disjoint components, the operation should comply with the following rules, as illustrated in Fig. 3. Before perform these rules, vertexes with "multiple roles" should be identified from the first.

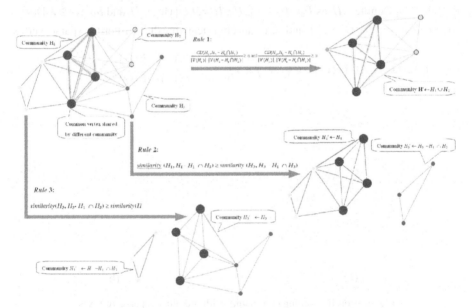

Fig. 3. Processing rules of irregular overlapping community

For two community H_1 and H_2 with common vertexes,

Rule 1. If $\dfrac{CD(H_2, H_2 - H_1 \mathrm{I} H_2)}{|V(H_1)| \cdot |V(H_2 - H_1 \mathrm{I} H_2)|} \geq \alpha$ and $\dfrac{CD(H_1, H_1 - H_1 \mathrm{I} H_2)}{|V(H_2)| \cdot |V(H_1 - H_1 \mathrm{I} H_2)|} \geq \alpha$,

H_1 and H_2 are merged into one community, denoted as $H_1 \cup H_2$;

Rule 2. If it does not hold the condition of *Rule* 1 and $similarity(H_1, H_1 - H_1 \cap H_2) \geq similarity(H_2, H_2 - H_1 \cap H_2)$, $H_1' \leftarrow H_1$ and $H_2' \leftarrow H_2 - H_1 \cap H_2$;

Rule 3. If it does not hold the condition of *Rule* 1 and *similarity*(H_2, H_2- $H_1 \cap H_2$) ≥ *similarity*(H_1, H_1- $H_1 \cap H_2$), $H_1 \leftarrow H_1$ -$H_1 \cap H_2$ and $H_2 \leftarrow H_2$.

3.3 Community with Sparse Vertex

Considering two type vertex in a CR network, one is the vertex that can not combine with its adjacent neighbor vertexes to form a clique; the other is the vertex with low link value so that it can not be merged into a cohesive sub-graph. These vertexes are usually sparse. If these sparse vertexes are merged into a cohesive sub-graph in a CR network, the density of the newly formed sub-graph will decrease and even less than the threshold α in formula (6). But there are some vertexes in reality very important to the community by analyzing the actual interaction between a user vertex and this community. This vertex cannot be arbitrarily excluded from this community. If there are sparse vertexes exist around cohesive communities $H_1, H_2, \ldots, H_n$, these vertexes should be examined the possibility of merging into a community.

Suppose community H_i' is the result of combination of H_i and sparse vertexes, where i = 1,2,…, n. Denote $\cup H_i$ as $H_1 \cup H_2 \cup \ldots \cup H_n$, $H_i'=H_i \cup \{v|v \notin \cup H_i$ and $link(v) \geq \lambda \cdot D(v)\}$, where $link(v) = \sum\limits_{v_k \in H} C(v,v_k)$ and λ is an empirical threshold filtering sparse vertex

$$v, i = 1,2,\ldots,n. \text{ For } C(v,v_k), \; C(v,v_k) = \begin{cases} 1, & \text{if } (v,v_k) \in E(G) \\ 0, & \text{if } (v,v_k) \notin E(G) \end{cases}, \; v_k \in H_i.$$

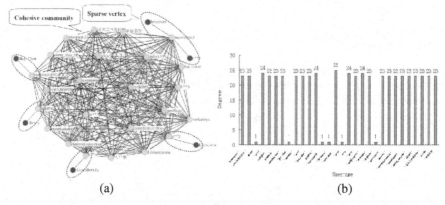

Fig. 4. A on-line selling community with prominent sparse vertexes

Fig.4 demonstrates a community with sparse vertexes. It is an information slice drawn from a tea store in TaoBao e-commence market, which is the biggest online auction market in China. The highlighted circles in Fig.4(a) are connected sparse vertexes, in five different positions around the cohesive main body with a high graph density. These connected sparse vertexes compose projecting parts of this community and form an uneven shape. Fig.4(b) indicates that the main body of this community is almost a clique. In this community, 23 out of total 30 vertexes are with vertex degree 19, 6 vertexes with degree 6, 4 vertexes with degree 4 and 1 vertex with degree 25. The percentage of projecting vertexes in the whole community is 20%.

4   Empirical Case

4.1   Co-buying CR Network

A CR community identification for an online book selling service is discussed herein. The CR network $G = (V, E)$ denotes the customer network of online shop with V for customers and E for selling relationship among these customers. If any two customers A and B buy the same product, there may be a product-buying relationship between them. The products bought by a customer is *purchase* {$purchase_1$, $purchase_2$, ..., $purchase_n$}, with the price and quantities of *purchase* as {P_1, P_2,..., P_n} and { C_1, C_2,..., C_n } respectively. The count-price strength two customers is $CPW = \sum_{i=1}^{t} P_i \cdot C_i$, where t is the number of the same product bought by both customers. When CPW is more than the

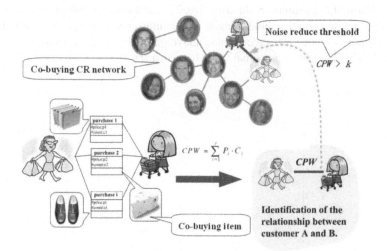

Fig. 5. The process of identifying customer relationships and constructing CR network

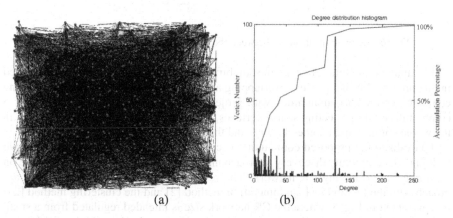

Fig. 6. The co-buy CR network of the on-line selling service in Taobao and its Pareto chart that indicates the vertex number with each degree value and the percentage accumulation trend

noise-reduce threshold k, the co-buying relationship between two customers is identified. A link between customer A and B is added into the CR network, as illustrated in Fig.5.

The CR network of the online shop is established by iterating this identification operation between any two customers. In the e-commence case, 1975 customers and 35 types of products are involved in constructing a CR network according to live business records of the online shop. Fig. 6 indicates that the result of noise reduce process is a CR network G with 490 vertexes and 7807 co-buying links.

4.2   Community Identification and Evaluation

The process idenfiticationMaximalClique() recovers 241 maximal cliques from the co-buying CR network. The process mergeMaximalClique() further unifies intersecting maximal cliques into bigger cohesive combinations with high graph density. The quality of these combinations is examined with Q value that is introduced by [18, 21] to estimate rationalization of community modularity. Fig. 7 is the analysis result of the relationship of Q value and division threshold β under the circumstance of the co-buy CR network. The modularity Q value takes ideal value above 0.5 with β ranging from 0.55 to 0.64. Especially, Q value takes it maximal value 6.4 when β is 0.578.

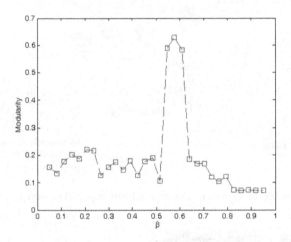

Fig. 7. The relationship carve between the threshold β and modularity Q value

12 initial communities, that are the combinations of maximal cliques, are discovered in this process. Further process overlapping and sparse features, it gets 10 overlapping communities and 3 communities with projecting sparse vertexes in Table 1. For 3 communities with projecting sparse vertexes, one takes the spare percentage 3.12% in the whole community, another 17.39% and the last 12.5%.

To evaluate the proposed community discovery approach, it is compared with two well known community discovery approach under exponent the modularity Q value on the foregoing co-buying CR network. The result comparing our polymerization approach with the hierarchical agglomeration method [2] and the clustering method [24] is represented in Fig. 8, where the CR network size is intended regulated from a small size to the full one. In most situations, our proposed approach takes a higher modularity Q value than its contrasts.

Table 1. Community discovered in the co-buying CR network

Community			Irregular Feature		
NO	Vertex Number	Density	Overlapping	Sparse	Sparse percentage
1	11	1.0000	√		
2	321	0.1344	√	√	3.12%
3	18	0.4575	√		
4	13	1.0000	√		
5	19	1.0000			
6	23	0.3126	√	√	17.39%
7	9	1.0000	√		
8	21	0.4286	√		
9	10	0.6667			
10	8	0.6786	√	√	12.5%
11	30	0.5977			
12	7	0.8571	√		

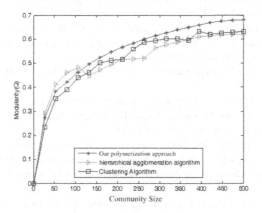

Fig. 8. A comparative test of our proposed polymerization approach, the hierarchical agglomeration method and the clustering method

5 Conclusions

Many communities with irregular topology exist in social CRM service under cloud computing environment. Irregular community identification can be transferred into the research issuer of irregular topological sub-graph identification from a CR network graph. Most well known algorithm of community discovery ignore this truth and impair the service quality ground on CR analysis.

The proposed approach serves to discover irregular community from the CR networks with essential knowledge and techniques such as maximal clique, graph similarity, combination of maximal clique and close degree, which makes for enhancing the quality of utilities services in cloud computing. More positive analysis should be carried out to perceive the application characteristics of social CR networks and improve the suggested method.

Acknowledgments

The authors would like to thank Hainan Zhou for his selfless programming work. This work was under the financial support of National Natural Science Foundation of China (60703018; 60873024), 973 Program (2007CB310800), 863 Program (2008AA01Z208; 2006AA04Z156) and Open Fund Project of State Key Lab. for Novel Software Technology, Nanjing University.

References

1. Capocci, A., Servedio, V.D.P., Caldarelli, G.: Detecting communities in large networks. Physica A 352, 669–676 (2005)
2. Clauset, A., Newman, M.E.J.: Finding community structure in very large networks. Physical Review. E 70 (2004)
3. Cloud Computing, Wikipedia (2009),
   http://en.wikipedia.org/wiki/Cloud_Computing
4. Social CRM, Wikipedia (2009),
   http://en.wikipedia.org/wiki/Oracle_CRM#Social_CRM
5. Cazals, F., Karande, C.: An algorithm for reporting maximal c-cliques. Theoretical Computer Science 349(3), 484–490 (2005)
6. Cazals, F., Karande, C.: Reporting maximal cliques: new insights. Rapport de recherché. 5615, INRIA (2007)
7. Radicchi, F., Castellano, C., Cecconi, F., Loreto, V., Parisi, D.: Defining and identifying communities in networks. In: Proceedings of the National Academy of Science of the United State of America, vol. 101, pp. 2658–2663 (2004)
8. Avlonitis, G.J., Panagopoulos, N.G.: Antecedents and consequences of CRM technology acceptance in the sales force. Industrial Marketing Management 34, 355–368 (2005)
9. Zhou, H.: Distance, dissimilarity index and network community structure. Physical Review. E 67 (2003)
10. Koch, I.: Fundamental study: Enumerating all connected maximal common sub-graphs in two graphs. Theoretical Computer Science 250, 1–30 (2001)
11. Koch, I., Wanke, E., Lengauer, T.: An algorithm for finding maximal common subtopologies in a set of protein structures. Journal of Computational Biology 3(2) (1996)
12. Pujol, J.M., Béjar, J., Delgado, J.: Clustering algorithm for determining community structure in large networks. Physical Review. E 74 (2006)
13. Duch, J., Arenas, A.: Community detection in complex networks using extremal optimization. Physical Review E 72 (2005)
14. Kumpula, J.M., Saramäki, J., Kaski, K., Kertész, J.: Limited resolution in complex network community detection with Potts model approach. The European Physical Journal B 56, 41–45 (2007)
15. Liu, J., Liu, B., Li, D.: Discovering Protein Complexes from Protein-Protein Interaction Data by Local Cluster Detecting Algorithm, pp. 280–284. IEEE Computer Society, Los Alamitos (2007)
16. Danon, L., Duch, J., Diaz-Guilera, A., Arenas, A.: Comparing community structure identification. Journal of Statistical Mechanics (2005)
17. Newman, M.E.J.: Finding community structure in networks using the eigenvectors of matrices. Physical Review E 74 (2006)

18. Newman, M.E.J., Girvan, M.: Finding and evaluating community structure in networks. Physical Review E 69 (2004)
19. Rosvall, M., Bergstrom, C.T.: An information-theoretic framework for resolving community structure in complex networks. In: Proceedings of the National Academy of Science of the United State of America, vol. 18, pp. 7327–7331 (2007)
20. Zhang, S.H., Wang, R.S., Zhang, X.S.: Identification of overlapping community structure in complex networks. Physical A 374, 483–490 (2007)
21. Newman, M.E.J.: Mixing patterns in networks. Phys. Rev. E 67, 026126 (2003)
22. reCAPTCHA, Wikipedia (2009), http://en.wikipedia.org/wiki/ReCAPTCHA
23. Crowd computing, Wikipedia (2009),
http://en.wikipedia.org/wiki/Crowd_computing
24. Pujol, J.M., Béjar, J., Delgado, J.: Clustering algorithm for determining community structure in large networks. Phys. Rev. E 74, 016107 (2006)

A Contextual Information Acquisition Approach Based on Semantics and Mashup Technology

Yangfan He[1], Lu Li[2], Keqing He[1], and Xiuhong Chen[1]

[1] State Key Lab of Software Engineering, Wuhan University, 430072, Wuhan, Hubei, China
heyangfan927@163.com
[2] International School of Software, Wuhan University, 430072, Wuhan, Hubei, China
lulu.li1989@gmail.com

Abstract. Pay per use is an essential feature of cloud computing. Users can make use of some parts of a large scale service to satisfy their requirements, merely at the cost of a little payment. A good understanding of the users' requirement is a prerequisite for choosing the service in need precisely. Context implies users' potential requirements, which can be a complement to the requirements delivered explicitly. However, traditional context-aware computing research always demands some specific kinds of sensors to acquire contextual information, which renders a threshold too high for an application to become context-aware. This paper comes up with an approach which combines contextual information obtained directly and indirectly from the cloud services. Semantic relationship between different kinds of contexts lays foundation for the searching of the cloud services. And mashup technology is adopted to compose the heterogonous services. Abundant contextual information may lend strong support to a comprehensive understanding of users' context and a bettered abstraction of contextual requirements.

Keywords: context acquisition, mashup, context ontology.

1 Introduction

Pay per use is an important feature of cloud computing[1]. Users wouldn't bother to install a bunch of software which have complicated functions. They can enjoy cloud services selected from the Internet according to their personal needs. Salesforce represents a trend of cloud service, which means providing a fairly complete solution pertinent to a specific problem[2]. For a specific user, some parts of the service would suffice, making it necessary to tailor the large scale service like Salesforce according to the user's personal requirements. Therefore, precisely capturing user's requirements from various aspects is key to the success of "on-demand service provision" and "pay per use".

Users' requirements can be divided into two categories: those expressed explicitly and those expressed implicitly. Users' context conveys their potential requirements [3]. In the past, contextual requirements research was usually carried out in some fixed contexts and under the presumption that these contexts could be attained directly by sensors[4]. In cloud computing, capturing and analyzing contextual

M.G. Jaatun, G. Zhao, and C. Rong (Eds.): CloudCom 2009, LNCS 5931, pp. 510–518, 2009.
© Springer-Verlag Berlin Heidelberg 2009

information will be a common practice. So context awareness realized by means of deploying all kinds of sensors will be too expensive to be adopted. Methods are needed to obtain users' context in a cheaper way and thus lower the threshold of context awareness.

Among the plentiful contextual information, time and space, which can be easily acquired with the aid of services like GPS, are two most fundamental types. Via the dependency between different kinds of context and the services reside in the cloud, we can also get some other contextual information, such as temperature, illumination, and feasibility for exercises etc, based on time and space. There may be difference in the types of the contextual information provision services. So some methods should be taken to fuse these heterogonous services.

Mashup is a new technology for information fusion[5]. It takes the calls of different services' API to mix up the services. Well-known mashups include applications based on Google and those based on Amazon, etc[6][7]. With the information sharing spirit of mashup, users can enjoy bundles of services within one site. This gives a ray of hope to resolve the problem of contextual provision services fusion.

This paper presents a semantics and mashup technology based approach to establish context space. In this approach, a context ontology is employed to express the dependency between different kinds of context. Then a context mining algorithm could be used to obtain context provision services from the cloud based on context ontology. Those services take available context as input and produce other contextual information as output. The two kinds of context services , already available ones and those reside in the cloud are then combined by mashup technology to enrich the context categories in the context space. This searching and mashup process continues until all the available services have been collected or the context space has reached the preset utmost. Thus, a refined context space, which can provide rich contextual information for contextual requirements acquisition, can be set up. Compared with methods in use, the most conspicuous characteristics of this approach are the analysis of the dependency between different kinds of context in context ontology and the application of mashup technology.

The content of this paper is organized as follows. Section 2 provides an introduction of the approach. Section 3 discusses the construction and management of context ontology. Section 4 is an analysis of the algorithm for context mining. Section 5 introduces a tool named "Context Box" which is used to set up the context space. Section 6 is related works and finally is the conclusion.

2　The Approach

Figure 1 illustrates a typical application scenario of this approach. Users can get their location information from GPS service of mobile phone, and mobile phone can also provide current time. Knowledge of context ontology tells that contexts like temperature and ultraviolet intensity depend on time and location. However, the surrounding has no sensors besides mobile phone, to provide information about temperature and ultraviolet intensity directly.

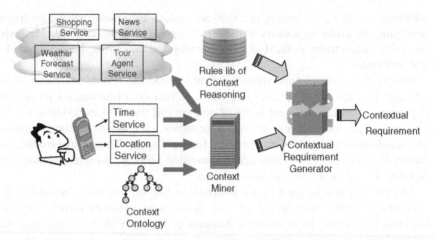

Fig. 1. A Typical Application Scenario

At the same time, there are many kinds of services, including various weather fore-cast services, in the cloud. These services take time and location of mobile phone service as input and output temperature and ultraviolet intensity information at speci-fied time and location. Context miner can check the available cloud services to get context which directly or indirectly depends on location and time. With the help of context miner, a context space can be set up gradually. The time and location service and services from cloud may differ in many aspects. At run time, mashup technology can be employed to connect the heterogonous context provision services.

Context requirement generator may reason out users' contextual requirement based on the contextual information provided by context mashup and the rules set for con-text reasoning. The content of the rules set will be changed when different application scenarios are considered.

3   Building and Managing Context Ontology

The context mining process explained in section 2 implies that context ontology acts as the basis for context provision service searching, and provides foundation for the gradually formed context space. Figure 2 shows a simple example of context ontology.

Context ontology can be divided into two levels: low level context and high level context. Low level context can be expressed in fundamental physical parameters. For instance, temperature, humidity and illumination belong to low level context. High level context is an integration of low level contexts. For example, " It is a fine day" is a high level context.

So far, there have been a lot of literature discussing context modeling. From a gen-eral perspective, there can hardly be any general context ontology which fits all appli-cations. It is the need of the application that decides the most relevant contextual information.

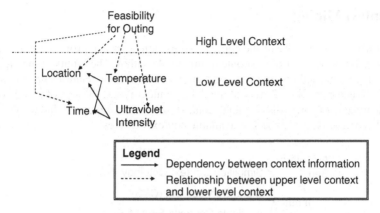

Fig. 2. An Example of Context Ontology

According to the long term vision of cloud computing, cloud service will become an infrastructure just like water, electricity and telecommunication[8]. Contextual information conveys user's potential requirement. Effective capturing and analysis of contextual information contributes to a better understanding of user's require-ment, and thus paves way for "on-demand service provision" and "pay per use". Therefore, contextual information will hopefully be a first class factor for cloud computing. Reuse of high-quality context ontology will streamline the process of context ontology construction and service fusing based on common context. So effective management of context ontology will be of great importance.

ISO/IEC 19763-3 suggests tailoring and composing elements from reference on-tology, which fits for general utilization, to form local ontology which is more quali-fied for specific applications[9]. Figure 3 illustrates how to employ ISO/IEC 19763-3 to manage context ontology. ISO/IEC 19763-3 helps to retain the association between context ontology, facilitating service fusion based on context.

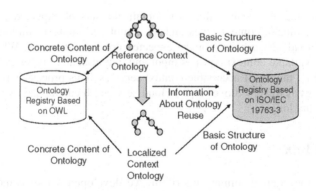

Fig. 3. Context Ontology Management Based on ISO/IEC 19763-3

4 Context Mining

Context Mining is the core of the context acquisition approach proposed in this paper. Figure 4 is the flow chart of the context mining algorithm. The inputs of the algorithm include: (1) simplified context ontology, in which concepts' relationships are simplified into directed graphs, (2) sets of available context types, (3) sets of cloud services to be searched, (4) sets of available context services. Outputs include: (1) sets of available context types; (2) sets of available context services.

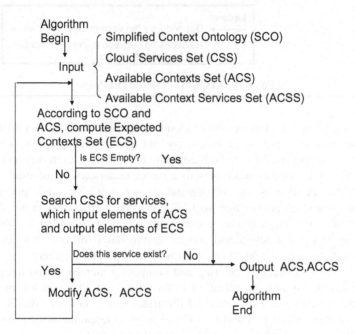

Fig. 4. Flow Chart of Context Mining Algorithm

The central idea of the algorithm is to obtain the sets of expected context types from the sets available context types and the simplified context ontology, and then searched the cloud services sets for the expected context types sets. When a certain service takes available context types as input and output context types in expectation, it can be put into the set of accessible context services. This process is repeated until context ontology is traversed over or the cloud service lib cannot satisfy the expected context types any longer.

5 Context Box

According to the context mining algorithm, we developed a tool named "Context Box" which can be used to collect context provision services from the cloud. Figure 5 takes an example to show the information produced after each step of the algorithm.

Based on the time and GPS services in mobile phones, temporal and spatial information will be available. Then with the guidance of context ontology, there will be a chain of searches for more context going on. The first round of search can be carried out with time and location as input. Output includes information about weather and the famous places around, which will be provided by some web services. The information produced after the first run of search is illustrated in figure(a).

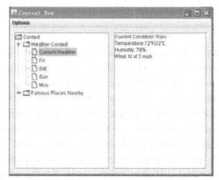

(a) Information produced after the first round of search

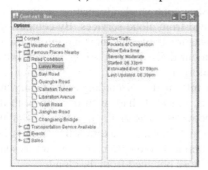

(b) Information produced after the   (c) Information produced after the
second round of search   third round of search

Fig. 5. Interface of Context Box

All the information above can be integrated as the input for the second round. The context space after the second round is illustrated in figure (b). According to the current location and the location of a place nearby, we can know the real time traffic information in these places and available transportation back and forth. The location information of places around can also be combined with current time to have big events happening there found out by services like news service. If a shopping mall is around, it is possible to have some information about sales in some store at present. Films on show recent days will also be attained in case there is a cinema nearby. Since the context provision services may differ in the way they are accessed, mashup technology will be employed in the service fuse process.

Similarly, all the contexts obtained in the second round may help to invoke the third one. The available transportation in the last search can be used to search for the running condition of a certain bus or subway, like whether it is crowded. The available seats for a certain film can also be queried based on the film information acquired in the second round. The information produced after the third search is illustrated in figure (c).

6 Related Work

In context aware computing research, contextual information is usually supposed to be acquired through sensors. Hence, most literature focus on how to get information from specific sensors, how to guarantee the compatibility of contextual information from different sensors, and how to implement context aware web services[10][11].

[12][13][14][15] have done some research work similar with ours. [12] refers to the concept of software sensor, but lacks in a detailed explanation of it. [12] suggests to implement communication interface between sensors and information gathered with sensor widget. These widgets register in sensor yellow page service to enable the interaction between sensor and different subsystems. So the idea of reusing sensors' information in [12] is similar with the idea of contextual information sharing in our approach. However, our approach distinguishes contextual information acquired directly from physical sensors from that obtained from cloud services. By comparison, [12] doesn't cover any content about the association between contextual information.

[13][14] suggest using common objects in our daily life as a source for contextual information. In their experiment, they get information, such as object's location and events happening on the objects from gravity information, according to the theory that gravity is the inherent property of all objects. [13][14] share with our approach the emphasis on making use of relationship between contextual information. But the difference is that we adopt context ontology as a means to express the relationship between contextual information and use mashup technology to combine various sensing services, including the physical ones and those obtained from the cloud.

[15]'s discussion about context acquisition concentrates on how to take advantages of sensors. As for the relationship between the contextual information and Internet, [15] emphasizes that context acquisition services should comply with some criteria, which is a guarantee for the interoperation between context-aware services. Compared to [15], our approach considers contextual provision services from the cloud as well. Moreover, we adopt web service to express context acquisition services, laying a consolidated foundation for the interoperation with the other types of services in the cloud.

7 Conclusion

In cloud computing, capturing user's requirements as completely as possible is a premise for on-demand service provision. Efficient methods to obtain user's context, an important source for potential requirements, contribute to a better understanding of user's requirement. Most of the current context acquisition methods emphasize the physical deployment of sensors to acquire users' contexts, which costs dearly and hence proves impractical for cloud computing.

This paper provides a novel approach to acquire user's context. Context ontology is employed to express the relationship between different kinds of context, which acts as basis for searching context provision services in the cloud. In order to handle the differences of these services, mashup technology is adopted to ease the context fusion process. Detailed explanation of the approach and an example to show its usage are provided in the paper.

Future work includes the refinement of context ontology and the enhancement of the context mining tool. Besides, some effort will be devoted to integrating the tool with mobile computing platform. Some complex real world scenarios will be tried to test the efficiency of the approach introduced in this paper.

Acknowledgement

The Project ISO/IEC 19763-3 Second Edition was approved by ISO/IEC JTC1 SC32. The Project number is 1.32.22.02.03.00.

This work was supported by the National Basic Research Program of China (973) under Grant 2007CB310801, the National Natural Science Foundation of China under Grant No.60970017 and 60903034, the National High Technology Research and Development Program of China (863) under Grant No.2006AA04Z156 and the Eleventh Five-Year Plan for National Key Technology R&D Program under grant 2006BAK04A20-7.

References

1. Armbrust, M., Fox, A., Griffith, R., Joseph, A., Katz, R., Konwinsi, A., Lee, G., Patterson, D., Rabkin, A., Stoica, I., Zaharia, M.: Above the Clouds: A Berkeley View of Cloud Computing, http://www.eecs.berkeley.edu/Pubs/TechRpts/2009/EECS-2009-28.html
2. Boujena, O., Johnston, W.J., Merunka, D.R.: The Benefits of Sales Force Automation: A Customer's Perspective. Journal of Personal Selling and Sales Management 29(2), 137–150 (spring 2009)
3. He, Y., He, K., Wang, J., Wang, C.: Toward a context driven approach for semantic web service evolution. In: Proceedings of the 3rd International Conference on Convergence and Hybrid Information Technology, Korea, pp. 1089–1094 (2008)
4. Fujii, K., Suda, T.: Semantics-based Context-aware Dynamic Service Composition. ACM Transactions on Autonomous and Adaptive Systems 4(2), article 12, 1–31
5. Fischer, T., Bakalov, F., Nauerz, A.: An Overview of Current Approaches to Mashup Generation. Wissensmanagement, 254–259 (2009)
6. Ennals, R., Gay, D.: User Friendly Functional Programming for Web Mashups. In: ACM ICFP (2007)
7. Tuchinda, R., Szekely, P.A., Knoblock, C.A.: Building Mashups by example. IUI 2008, 139–148 (2008)
8. Erdogmus, H.: Cloud Computing: Does Nirvana Hide behind the Nebula? IEEE Software (SOFTWARE) 26(2), 4–6 (2009)
9. ISO/IEC 19763-3 Metamodel for Ontology Registration (2007)

10. Li, Y., Fang, J., Xiong, J.: A Context-aware Services Mash-up System. In: Proceedings of 2008 Seventh International Conference on Grid and Cooperative Computing, pp. 707–712. IEEE Press, Los Alamitos (2008)
11. Daniel, F., Matera, M.: Mashing Up Context-Aware Web Applications: A Component-Based Development Approach. In: Bailey, J., Maier, D., Schewe, K.-D., Thalheim, B., Wang, X.S. (eds.) WISE 2008. LNCS, vol. 5175, pp. 250–263. Springer, Heidelberg (2008)
12. Costa, P., Botelho, L.: Generic Context Acquisition and Management Framework. In: First European Young Researchers Workshop on Service Oriented Computing (2005)
13. Matthews, T., Gellersen, H.-W., Van Laerhoven, K., Dey, A.K.: Augmenting Collections of Everyday Objects: A Case Study of Clothes Hangers As an Information Display. In: Ferscha, A., Mattern, F. (eds.) PERVASIVE 2004. LNCS, vol. 3001, pp. 340–344. Springer, Heidelberg (2004)
14. Schmidt, A., Strohbach, M., Van Laerhoven, K., Friday, A., Gellersen, H.-W.: Context Acquisition Based on Load Sensing. In: Borriello, G., Holmquist, L.E. (eds.) UbiComp 2002. LNCS, vol. 2498, pp. 333–350. Springer, Heidelberg (2002)
15. Zhdanova, A.V., Zoric, J., Marengo, M., van Kranenburg, H., Snoeck, N., Sutterer, M., Rack, C., Droegehorn, O., Arbanowski, S.: Context Acquisition, Representation and Employment in Mobile Service Platforms. In: Proceedings of Mobile IST Summit 2006 Workshop on Capturing Context and Context Aware Systems and Platforms (June 2006)

Evaluating MapReduce on Virtual Machines: The Hadoop Case[*]

Shadi Ibrahim[1], Hai Jin[1], Lu Lu[1], Li Qi[2], Song Wu[1], and Xuanhua Shi[1]

[1] Cluster and Grid Computing Lab
Services Computing Technology and System Lab
Huazhong University of Science & Technology, Wuhan, 430074, China
{shadi,hjin}@hust.edu.cn
[2] Operation Center
China Development Bank, Beijing, China
quick.qi@gmail.com

Abstract. MapReduce is emerging as an important programming model for large scale parallel application. Meanwhile, Hadoop is an open source implementation of MapReduce enjoying wide popularity for developing data intensive applications in the cloud. As, in the cloud, the computing unit is virtual machine (VM) based; it is feasible to demonstrate the applicability of MapReduce on virtualized data center. Although the potential for poor performance and heavy load no doubt exists, virtual machines can instead be used to fully utilize the system resources, ease the management of such systems, improve the reliability, and save the power. In this paper, a series of experiments are conducted to measure and analyze the performance of Hadoop on VMs. Our experiments are used as a basis for outlining several issues that will need to be considered when implementing MapReduce to fit completely in the cloud.

Keywords: Cloud Computing, Data Intensive, MapReduce, Hadoop, Distributed File System, Virtual Machine.

1 Introduction

The computing world is undergoing a significant transformation from traditional non-centralized distributed system architecture, typified by distribute data and computation on different geographic areas to a centralized cloud computing architecture, where the computations and data are operated somewhere in the cloud, data centers owned and maintained by third party. However, in term of resources, the three main characteristics of cloud are: (1) On-demand unlimited data storage, (2) on-demand computation power with no lock, mainly represented as VMs, and (3) using internet, limited bandwidth connection, to access, use and process these resources.

[*] This work is supported by National 973 Key Basic Research Program under grant No.2007CB310900, Information Technology Foundation of MOE and Intel under grant MOE-INTEL-09-03, and National High-Tech 863 R&D Plan of China under grant 2006AA01A115.

M.G. Jaatun, G. Zhao, and C. Rong (Eds.): CloudCom 2009, LNCS 5931, pp. 519–528, 2009.
© Springer-Verlag Berlin Heidelberg 2009

The new surge and interest of cloud computing in accompanied with exponentially growing of data size generated from digital media (images/audio/video), web authoring, scientific instruments, and physical simulations. Thus, how to effectively process these immense data sets is becoming a challenging issue in the cloud. While, the traditional data intensive system, typified by moving data to computing, design and programming models are, due to the bottleneck of the internet when transferring large amount of data to the computing nodes, to be not efficient for cloud [1]. Data-aware approach is proven to be efficient and robust, where data and computation are collocated. This approach has been widely used and studied, especially after the great success of Google version, namely Google File System (GFS) [2] and MapReduce [3] (e.g. Google uses its MapReduec framework to process 20 petabytes of data per day [3]). Recently, many projects are exploring ways to support MapReduce on various types of distributed architecture (e.g. Hadoop [4] for data intensive applications, Phoenix [5] for multi-core programming), and for wider applications [6, 7].

Hadoop [4] is an open source implementation of MapReduce sponsored by Yahoo. It has been widely used and experienced for large scale data applications in the clouds [6, 7]. Furthermore, Hadoop is advocated by industry's premier web players - Google, Yahoo, Microsoft, and Facebook - as the engine to power the cloud [8]. As in the cloud, the computing unit is mostly VM-based (Amazon Elastic Cloud Computing [9] and GoGrid [10] are providing VM-based computing infrastructure as a service), it is feasible to demonstrate the applicability of MapReduce in virtualized data center. Although the potential for poor performance and heavy load undoubtedly exists, virtual machine can instead be used to help to fully utilize the system resources, ease the management of such systems as well as improve the reliability, and power saving (i.e. virtual machines have been a promising approach for various distributed systems [11-14]). More recently, Amazon added a new service, called Amazon Elastic MapReduce [15], enables customers easily and cost-effectively process vast amounts of data. It utilizes a hosted Hadoop framework running on the web-scale infrastructure of Amazon Elastic Compute Cloud (EC2) and Simple Storage Service (S3) [16].

To practically introduce the challenges and the opportunities of combining MapReduce and VM technologies, in this paper, a series of experiments are conducted to measure the performance of Hadoop on VMs in different scenarios. First, we comparatively evaluate the performance of Hadoop Distributed File System (HDFS) on both physical and virtual cluster. Then we analyze the performance of the Hadoop MapReduce framework in virtualized cluster. In summary, the main contributions of our work are:

- We are first in the cloud community to carry out detail performance evaluations when deploying Hadoop on virtualized cluster.
- We elaborate several issues that can be used for better fit of MapReduce in the cloud.

The rest of this paper is organized as follows. Section 2 provides the background knowledge related to this work including an overview of the MapReduce programming model and why deploying MapReduce on virtual machines. In section 3, we take an overview on our experimental methodology, platform and benchmarks. We then present our results in section 4. While section 5 discusses some open issues and the lessons learned from our experiments. Finally, we conclude the paper and propose our future work in section 6.

2 Background and Motivations

In this section, we briefly introduce MapReduce model and its widely used implementation, Hadoop. Then we propose some aspects when using VMs with MapReduce.

2.1 MapReduce

MapReduce [3] is a programming model for data intensive computing inspired by the functional programming. It is simply represented in two functions:

- The map function, written by the user, processes a key/value pair to generate a set of intermediate key/value pairs.

$$map\ (key_1,\ value_1) \rightarrow list\ (key_2,\ value_2)$$

- The reduce function, also written by the user, merges all intermediate values associated with the same intermediate key.

$$reduce\ (key2,\ list\ (value2)) \rightarrow list\ (value2)$$

The MapReduce model allows programmers to easily design parallel and distributed applications, simply by writing Map/Reduce components, while the MapReduce runtime is responsible for parallelization, concurrency control and fault tolerance.

2.2 Hadoop

Hadoop [4] is java open source implementation of MapReduce sponsored by Yahoo. The Hadoop project is a collection of various subprojects for reliable, scalable distributed computing [4]. The two fundamental subprojects are the Hadoop MapReduce framework and the HDFS.

HDFS is a distributed file system that provides high throughput access to application data [4]. It is inspired by the GFS. HDFS has master/slave architecture. The master server, called NameNode, splits files into blocks and distributes them across the cluster with replication for fault tolerance. It holds all metadata information about stored files. The HDFS slaves, the actual store of the data blocks called DataNodes, serve read/write requests from clients and propagate replication tasks as directed by the NameNode.

The Hadoop MapReduce is a software framework for distributed processing of large data sets on compute clusters [4]. It runs on top of HDFS. Thus data processing is collocated with data storage. It also has master/slave architecture. The master, called *Job Tracker* (JT), is responsible for : (a) querying the NameNode for the block locations, (b) considering the information retrieved by the NameNode, JT schedules the tasks on the slaves, called *Task Trackers* (TT), and (c) monitoring the success and failures of the tasks.

2.3 Why MapReduce on VMs

Currently, driven by the increasing maturity of virtualization technology in general, virtual machine in particular, VMs have been experienced in various distributed systems such as grid [11], HPC application [12-14]. To this end, in this section we discuss the main factors contributing to the interests of MapReduce on virtual machines:

1. Driven by the increasing popularity of cloud computing in which VMs are the main computation units, and the widely adoption of MapReduce, due to its magnificent features, as the programming model for data intensive applications. Consequently, combining theses two technologies is promising approach for large scale data cloud computing. Moreover, VMs can be effectively used to utilize the cluster resources; especially those equipped with multi-core processors and can greatly benefit cluster computing from aspects of ease of management, customized OS and security [11].

2. Recently, MapReduce is using speculative tasks approach to provide reliable performance. Speculative tasks are normally performed by re-execute the task on different DataNodes. Executing two copies of the same tasks can cause waste of the cluster resources. Thus, benefiting of the recent advances of VM checkpointing and live migration [17, 18], it is feasible to use these techniques to improve the reliability of MapReduce performance. Moreover, VM checkpointing and migration can be used to improve the reliability of the MapReduce master node as it is single point of failure.

3 Methodology and Hardware Platform

Our experimental hardware consists of seven nodes cluster. Each node in the cluster is equipped with two quad-core 2.33GHz Xeon processors, 8GB of memory and 1TB of disk, runs RHEL5 with kernel 2.6.22, and is connected with 1 Gigabit Ethernet. In VM-based environments, we use Xen 3.2 [19]. The VMs are running with RHEL5 with kernel 2.6.22. VM is configured with 1 VCPU and 1GB memory. The same cluster is used to obtain performance results for both the VM-based environment and the native, non-virtualized environment. All results described in this paper are obtained using Hadoop version 0.18.0, while the data is stored with 2 replicas per block in HDFS. We perform five jobs per experiment and compute the average across jobs.

3.1 Experiments Design and Motivations

This section reports on several experiments designed to evaluate the MapReduce performance on virtual machines. First, as the HDFS playing a big role during the MapReduce process, we comparatively evaluate the performance of the HDFS when writing/reading data in both physical and virtual cluster. Second, we report on the feasibility of using VM to enhance the performance of MapReduce by increasing the resource utilization as CPU cycles. Third, we conduct the experiments to evaluate the execution time and the number of the lunched speculative tasks with different VMs load per physical machine.

3.2 Benchmarks

In all our experiments, we use two different and widely used benchmarks, sort and wordcount benchmarks, which are sample programs in the Hadoop distribution.

- Sort Benchmark. The sort benchmark [20] simply uses the map/reduce framework to sort the input directory into output directory (two replica by default), both the input and output must be sequence files. The map function extracts the key from each record and emits a <key, record> pair, the reduce function emits all pairs unchanged. All the input data are generated using the Random Writer sample application in the Hadoop distribution.
- WordCount Benchmark. The wordcount [20] counts the number of occurrences of each word in a file and writes the output to local disk. The map function emits each word plus an associated count of occurrences. The reduce function sums together all counts emitted for a particular word. In addition, a combiner function is used to fold redundant <word, _> pairs into a single one, which magnificently reduces the network I/O. All the input data are generated by duplicating the text file used by Phoenix [5].

4   Experiment Results

In this section, we evaluate the performance impact of using virtualization for the two specific benchmarks on our cluster system.

4.1   Hadoop Distributed File System

MapReduce programming model strongly depends on the underlying storage system, namely GFS for Google MapReduce and HDFS in Hadoop. We evaluate the HDFS performance in both physical cluster (PH-HDFS for short) and virtual cluster (VM-HDFS for short) when transferring data to and from the DFS, using the *put* and *get* command respectively. In particular, we conduct our experiments using three different scenarios (different data size, different cluster size, and different throughput when multi requests). In all our experiments one VM has been uniquely deployed on each physical node.

First, we evaluate the performance when transferring different data size (1.5GB, 3GB, 6GB, and 12 GB). As shown in Fig. 1, the PH-HDFS performs better than VM-HDFS in terms of reading and writing capacities. Moreover, the performance gap is markedly increases as the data size is increasing in both cases writing data to or reading data from the DFS.

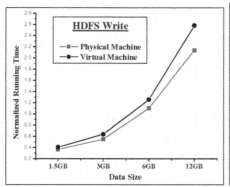 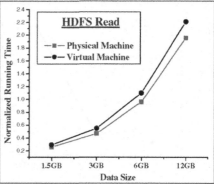

Fig. 1. PH-HDFS *vs* VM-HDFS with different data scale and 7 nodes cluster

Second, we fix the data distribution per node to 512MB. Accordingly, if there are 2, 4 and 6 DataNodes, 1, 2 and 3GB of data are transferring respectively. The PH-HDFS also performs better than the VM-HDFS as the number of data node increases as shown in Fig. 2.

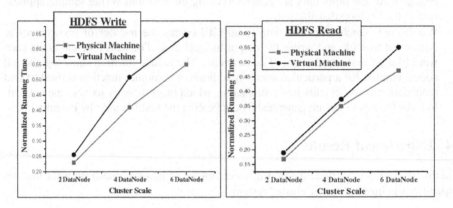

Fig. 2. PH-HDFS *vs* VM-HDFS with different cluster scale, with the same data distribution (512MB per DataNode)

Third, we evaluate different throughputs by starting 1, 2, and 3 requests simultaneously and measuring the time needed for data transfer, the average in the case of two and three requests. As shown in Fig. 3, the PH-HDFS performs better than VH-HDFS. In addition the performance gap is markedly increasing when writing data in, while it is slightly increasing in case of reading data from the DFS.

4.2   VMs Feasibility

Driven by the advent of multi-core, it is feasible to study the opportunities of utilizing the multi-core processor and memory management of the cluster while processing large scale data using Hadoop.

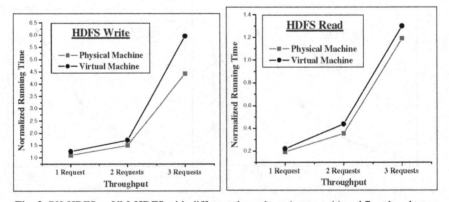

Fig. 3. PH-HDFS *vs* VM-HDFS with different throughput (requests/s) and 7 nodes cluster

In our experiment, we choose the wordcount benchmark because the data transfer during the copy phase is small and this will reduce the effects of data transfer in our experimental results. We evaluate the performance among four homogenous clusters as shown in Table 1, physical cluster (Ph-Cluster) and three virtual clusters (V-Cluster, V2-Cluster, and V4-Cluster with one, two, and four VMs running on each physical machine, respectively).

Table 1. Four Homogeneous Testbed Clusters

	Ph-Cluster	V-Cluster	V2-Cluster	V4-Cluster
VM Load	-	1 VM/Node	2 VM/Node	4 VM/Node
Cluster Size	7 Physical nodes	7 VM nodes	13 VM nodes	25 VM nodes

As shown in Fig. 4, the wordcount job in Ph-Cluster costs less time than in V-Cluster. In particular, when computing 1GB, the performance gap is small. While for data set of 8GB, this gap is obviously big. This is because: (1) HDFS performing better in physical cluster than in virtual one as shown in section 4.1, and (2) the increasing number of speculative tasks causing inefficient utilize of the resources. On the other hand, as expected, V2-Cluster and V4-Cluster are performing faster than the Ph-Cluster. This is because more computing cycles are available and more slots are free.

4.3 MapReduce on Virtual Machines Performance Analyze

In this section we report on different experiments with different VM load per physical node as shown in Table 1, and different data distribution on each data node.

As shown in Fig. 5, when running the sort benchmark, the execution time of the jobs for the same data distribution increases with the increment of VMs deployed on each physical node. Moreover, the performance gaps among these three different

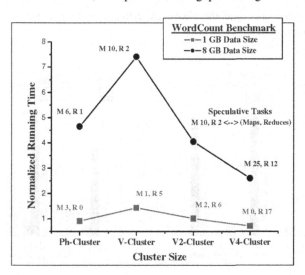

Fig. 4. Wordcount execution: physical cluster *vs* virtual clusters with different VM load per node (1, 2, and 4), and two data sets (1GB and 8 GB)

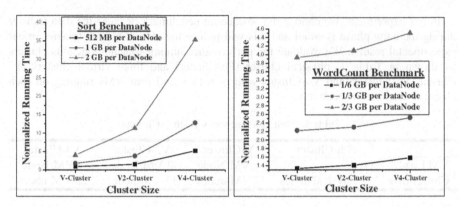

Fig. 5. Sort and wordcount execution with different VM load per node, and different data size

clusters markedly increase as the size of data distribution increases. This is due to three reasons: (a) the bad performance of HDFS on VMs when reading/writing the data blocks from/to the HDFS; (2) the increasing number of speculative tasks as shown in Fig. 6, and (3) more importantly, the large amount of data transferred during the copy of the intermediate data, especially that VMs are competing for the node I/O resources.

For the wordcount benchmark this gap is slightly increasing for different data distribution, caused by the same aforementioned reasons with less emphasize on the third reason as the data transfer is small.

5 Discussion and Open Issues

Based on the experience and the above experiments with MapReduce on VMs, we draw several open issues:

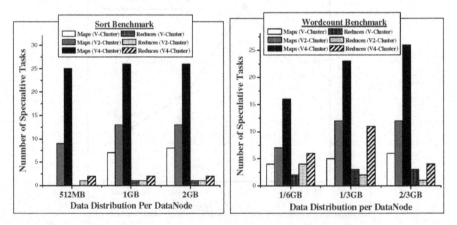

Fig. 6. Sort and wordcount launched speculative tasks with different VM load per node, and different data distribution

- Motivated by our experiments results in section 4.1, as well as VM being highly prone to error, it is useful to separate the permanent data storage (DFS) from the virtual storage associated with VM. In addition, using VM as execution unit only will allow us to study the possibilities of using VM migration as a replacement of the existing fault tolerance mechanism represented as speculative tasks, resulting with better performance and reduce the wasted resources caused by the increased number of speculative tasks in VM-based cluster [21] as shown in section 4.3.
- As shown is section 4.2, it is feasible to use VM in data intensive computing systems to fully utilize the physical node resources, using VM only as a computation unit for the data located on its physical node. More importantly, VM should be configured to perfectly suit the running data intensive applications.
- VMs within the same physical node are competing for the node I/O, causing poor performance. Therefore, many possibilities could be studied to improve it such as starting reduce tasks after all the map tasks are successfully finished and make the data transfer physical machine-based by collecting all the maps output within one physical node, from different VMs, and check new scheduling algorithms to reduce the data transferred.
- Finally, as the master node is a single point of failure for the Map/Reduce infrastructure, if it goes down, all running jobs are lost. Therefore, VM being highly prone to failure, it is not highly recommended to keep the master node physical based or use the VM checkpointing to implement more reliable master.

6 Conclusion and Future Work

Driven by the new trend in distributed system towards cloud computing and the increasing popularity and adoption of cloud storage services, processing this large data has become big challenge. Data-aware based data intensive approach is proven to be efficient and robust, where data and computation are collocated. This approach has been widely used and studied, especially after the huge success of Google version, namely GFS and MapReduce. Meanwhile, through the recent improvement and maturity of virtual machine, cloud community is strongly adopting VMs as the computation units in the cloud. Lots of research have been carried out about VM-based HPC application, while up to date, no paper has introduced and evaluated the integration of VM and MapReduce based data intensive application, mainly the challenges and the opportunities.

Based on our experiments with MapReduce, Hadoop in particular, we have elaborated a number of issues when running data intensive applications using Hadoop in virtual cluster. This is intended as an invitation to cloud researchers to influence these important technologies in a constructive manner by drawing on research and experience.

Current and future research efforts include developing MapReduce framework on VMs, namely Cloudlet [22], and experimenting with scheduling and migrating the VMs within a cluster to improve high performance, reliability, manageability, and power management.

References

1. Szalay, A., Bunn, A., Gray, J., Foster, I., Raicu, I.: The Importance of Data Locality in Distributed Computing Applications. In: Proceedings of the NSF Workflow Workshop (2006)
2. Ghemawat, S., Gobioff, H., Leung, S.T.: The Google file system. In: Proceedings of 19th ACM Symposium on Operating Systems Principles, pp. 29–43. ACM Press, New York (2003)
3. Dean, J., Ghemawat, S.: Mapreduce: simplified data processing on large clusters. In: Proceedings of 6th Conference on Operating Systems Design & Implementation (2004)
4. Hadoop, http://lucene.apache.org/hadoop
5. Ranger, C., Raghuraman, R., Penmetsa, A., Bradski, G., Kozyrakis, C.: Evaluating MapReduce for Multi-core and Multiprocessor Systems. In: Proceedings of 13th International Symposium on High Performance Computer Architecture, pp. 13–24. ACM Press, New York (2007)
6. Bryant, R.E.: Data-Intensive Supercomputing: The Case for DISC. CMU-CS-07-128, Technical Report, Department of Computer Science, Carnegie Mellon University (May 2007)
7. Chen, S., Schlosser, S.W.: Map-Reduce Meets Wider Varieties of Applications, IRP-TR-08-05, Technical Report, Intel. Research Pittsburgh (May 2008)
8. CNET news, http://news.cnet.com/8301-13505_3-10196871-16.html (accessed September 2009)
9. Amazon Elastic Cloud Computing, http://aws.amazon.com/ec2/
10. GoGrid Cloud Hosting, http://www.gogrid.com/
11. Figueiredo, R., Dinda, P., Fortes, J.: A Case for Grid Computing on Virtual Machines. In: Proceedings of 23rd International Conference on Distributed Computing Systems, pp. 550–559. IEEE CS Press, Los Alamitos (2003)
12. Mergen, M.F., Uhlig, V., Krieger, O., Xenidis, J.: Virtualization for High Performance Computing. ACM SIGOPS Oper. Syst. Rev. 40(2), 8–11 (2006)
13. Huang, W., Liu, J., Abali, B., Panda, D.K.: A Case for High Performance Computing with Virtual Machines. In: Proceedings of 20th ACM International Conference on Supercomputing, pp. 125–134. ACM Press, New York (2006)
14. Nagarajan, A.B., Mueller, F., Engelmann, C., Scott, S.L.: Proactive Fault Tolerance for HPC with Xen Virtualization. In: Proceedings of 21st ACM International Conference on Supercomputing, pp. 23–32. ACM Press, New York (2007)
15. Amazon Elastic MapReduce, http://aws.amazon.com/elasticmapreduce/
16. Amazon Simple Storage Service, http://aws.amazon.com/s3/
17. Clark, C., Fraser, K., Hand, S., Hansen, J.G., Jul, E., Limpach, C., Pratt, I., Warfield, A.: Live Migration of Virtual Machines. In: Proceedings of USENIX Symposium on Networked Systems Design and Implementation (2005)
18. Zhao, M., Figueiredo, R.J.: Experimental Study of Virtual Machine Migration in Support of Reservation of Cluster Resources. In: Proceedings of 2nd International Workshop on Virtualization Technology in Distributed Computing (2007)
19. XenSource (2008), http://www.xensource.com/
20. Hadoop Wiki (2008), http://wiki.apache.org/hadoop/
21. Zaharia, M., Konwinski, A., Joseph, A.D., Katz, R., Stoica, I.: Improving mapreduce performance in heterogeneous environments. In: Proceedings of 8th USENIX Symposium on Operating Systems Design and Implementation (2008)
22. Ibrahim, S., Jin, H., Cheng, B., Cao, H., Wu, S., Qi, L.: Cloudlet: Towards MapReduce implementation on Virtual machines. In: Proceedings of 18th ACM International Symposium on High Performance Distributed Computing, pp. 65–66. ACM Press, New York (2009)

APFA: Asynchronous Parallel Finite Automaton for Deep Packet Inspection in Cloud Computing

Yang Li, Zheng Li, Nenghai Yu, and Ke Ma

MOE-Microsoft Key Laboratory of Multimedia Computing and Communication,
University of Science and Technology of China
{Yang Li,Zheng Li,Nenghai Yu,Ke Ma}liyangwj@mail.ustc.edu.cn

Abstract. Security in cloud computing is getting more and more important recently. Besides passive defense such as encryption, it is necessary to implement real-time active monitoring, detection and defense in the cloud. According to the published researches, DPI (deep packet inspection) is the most effective technology to realize active inspection and defense. However, most recent works of DPI aim at space reduction but could not meet the demands of high speed and stability in the cloud. So, it is important to improve regular methods of DPI, making it more suitable for cloud computing. In this paper, an asynchronous parallel finite automaton named APFA is proposed, by introducing the asynchronous parallelization and the heuristically forecast mechanism, which significantly decreases the time consumed in matching while still keeps reducing the memory required. What is more, APFA is immune to the overlapping problem so that the stability is also enhanced. The evaluation results show that APFA achieves higher stability, better performance on time and memory. In short, APFA is more suitable for cloud computing.

Keywords: Cloud computing, Deep packet inspection, Asynchronous parallel finite automaton.

1 Introduction

Cloud computing is becoming more and more popular in IT industry and academe recently. Vendors such as Amazon, IBM, HP, Google, and Microsoft are starting to create and deploy Clouds in various locations around the world to realize cloud computing [1]. Although there are many cloud computing definitions, none of them are widely accepted [2]. Generally, it delivers infrastructure, platform, and software as services, which are available to customers in a pay-per-use model. In this way, cloud computing gains many advantages, such as cost savings, high availability, and easy scalability, which really attract customers [3], [4].

Nonetheless, the technology is still immature and has not yet been widely adopted. Cloud can be seen as a huge Internet data center, in which all the customers store their private data and perform their tasks. However, relinquishing physical control of the datacenter infrastructure and information increases the risk of data compromise considerably [5]. [3] shows a recent survey of chief information officers and IT executives, and they rated security as their main cloud-computing concern.

M.G. Jaatun, G. Zhao, and C. Rong (Eds.): CloudCom 2009, LNCS 5931, pp. 529–540, 2009.
© Springer-Verlag Berlin Heidelberg 2009

As a public data center, the cloud is very sensitive to intrusion, virus, attacks and malicious application-layer data, so it requires total situational awareness of the threats to the network, infrastructure and information [6]. Ordinary passive defense like encryption is not adequate, so it is necessary to actively monitor, detect and defense the traffic flow in real time. As described in many research [11]-[21], DPI is the most effective mechanism to realize active monitoring, inspection and defense. Nonetheless, as a technology that detects the payload by regular expression matching, DPI is implemented by either DFA (Deterministic Finite Automata) with infeasible huge memory or NFA (Nondeterministic Finite Automata) with low speed. Many recent works reduced the memory usage of DFA, but at the cost of much additional time. Moreover, they are not stable enough while encountering overlapping problem. As a result, most of recent improvements of DPI are insufficient for the requirements of high speed and stability, which originate from huge numbers of customers and high concurrence in cloud computing.

In order to speed up and enhance the stability of the DPI in cloud computing, an asynchronous parallel finite automaton named APFA is proposed in this paper. By introducing the asynchronous parallelism and heuristically forecast mechanism, it decreases the time effectively, even much less than DFA in some occasions. What is more, it also reduces memory to much less than XFA (extended FA) and DFA, while solving the overlapping problem for enhancing stability in the mean time. The evaluation results show that APFA could implement DPI with much less memory, higher speed and stability, and it is more suitable for cloud computing.

This paper is organized as follows: after related works, motivation of our proposal is described in section 3. Section 4 presents main concept of APFA and section 5 analyzes the time and memory performance, as well as the overlapping problem. Evaluation results are given in section 6, and finally section 7 is the conclusion.

2 Related Works

Cloud computing is relatively new to academe, and most of the published works research about the description, advantages, challenges, and future of it [1]-[5]. So far there has been little research published on cloud computing security, and they almost investigate the security infrastructure, such as the Private Virtual Infrastructure in [6] and the architecture that cryptographically secures each virtual machine in [7]. Besides these, it is necessary to use DPI for defense against intrusions and virus in cloud computing, but few of the existing literatures focus on this. In fact, DPI is popularly researched recently while regular expression matching is widely adopted by well known tools and devices, such as Snort [8], Bro [9] and Cisco [10]. DFA is typically used for regular expression matching with a deterministic line speed, but state explosion emerges when complex regular expressions are met. In order to reduce the memory of states in DFA, many improvements are proposed.

The most typical proposal to optimize the constructed DFA is D^2FA (Delayed Input DFA) [11], which reduced the states' identical edges and obtained a 95% reduction in space at the expense of additional time consumed in searching through the default path. Some improvements were proposed to reduce the additional time, such as work [12], [13]. Research [14] proposed a technique that allows nonequivalent states to be merged. Instead of optimizing the constructed DFA, Kumar et al. proposed H-cFA (History-based counting Finite Automata) [15] to construct optimized DFA by using signs to record matched closures and counters to keep track of counts. Similarly, R.Smith brought forth XFA (extended FA) [16] which retrieved the idea of adding some auxiliary variables to remember past partial matched information [17], [18]. They achieved better space performance than other proposals; however, the additional time and vulnerability make them unsuitable for cloud. Beyond that, the pattern rewriting idea [20], Hybrid Finite Automata [19] and δFA [21] also proposed some methods to reduce the memory cost.

The improvements described above all reduced the memory of finite automata to some extent, however, the expense of much additional time and the vulnerability to overlapping problems restricted their applications in cloud computing.

3 Motivation

It can be seen from above that the problem is how to keep high speed and stability while eliminating the state explosion. In this section, state explosion is analyzed firstly, and then the solution of XFA and main observations of APFA are described.

3.1 State Explosion

As recent research described, state explosion emerges not only from transforming regular expressions to single DFA, but also from combining numbers of DFA into a synthesized DFA. The different number of states from different k-characters patterns is showed in Fig.1A, which is summarized in [20]. In addition, Fig.1B described an example of synthesized DFA which also introduced state explosion [16].

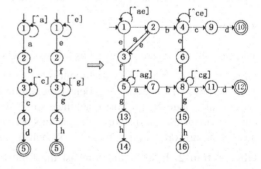

Patterns	#of states
ˆABCD .*ABCD	k+1
ˆAB.*CD .*AB.*CD	k+1
ˆAB.{j}CD ˆAB.{0, j}CD	O(k*j)
ˆA+[A-Z].{j}D	O(k+j²)
.*AB.{j}CD .*A[A-Z]{j, }CD	O(k+2ʲ)

A. states of single DFAs   B. a synthesized DFA for {ab.*cd, ef.*gh}

Fig. 1. State explosion in DFA

It can be concluded from the figure that length restriction in regular expressions, such as the ".{j}" in the regular expression ".*AB.{j}CD", is the most influential element for the state explosion. It could even induce state explosions of exponential size while combining with closures, which is also named "dot-stars" conditions.

3.2 Handle the Length Restriction

Objectively, length restriction is the most serious problem for state explosion. And subjectively, there is also the Amnesia problem in DFA. It only remembers a single state of parsing and ignores everything about the earlier parse. The intuitional method is to count the occurrences of certain sub-expressions, such as in H-CFA and XFA, some variables are used to record matched closures and count for length restriction.

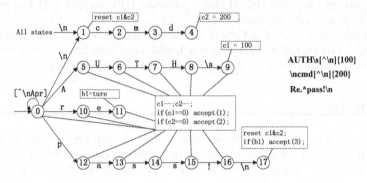

Fig. 2. An example of XFA

As can be seen in Fig.2, XFA uses sign $b1$ to notify whether the prefix *"re"* has been matched or not, and employs the counters *{c1,c2}* to count the occurrence of *"not \n"* character. As a result, XFA reduces the states to 18 while encountering length restrictions of 100 and 200. However, the time and memory consumed in maintaining variables is considerable. What is more, if the flow *"AUTH\sAUTH\s...."* is input, counters explosion would also arise and not stable enough.

3.3 Observations

Three observations are proposed as follows, and our mechanism is based on that.

Observation 1: Preliminary treatment is possible before matching.

Generally, DPI is applied to detect the application layer data of the received packets in router, gateway or host machines, so DFA's input is not a real character stream but a segment of data packet. The packets are buffered in off-chip memory and it is possible to do some pretreatment works before matching.

Observation 2: If we could forecast the following characters, the instable and burdensome work to maintain the counters can be avoided.

If the string *"AUTH\sAUTH\s....."* is input, XFA would activate lots of counters to count after every *"AUTH\s"*. However, if we could foresee and check the following characters when the counter should be initialized, the matching result could be heuristically predicted without maintaining counters.

Observation 3: The length restrictions in Snort rules are predominantly concerned with the character '\n'.

It is not difficult to discover that most of the length restrictions in Snort rules are associated with the character '\n', and this simplifies the pretreatment and the matching mechanism by only considering the occurrence of character '\n'.

4 Main concept of APFA

As can be seen from the observations above, the essential part of our mechanism is to predict whether the following characters match the length restriction or not, and this goal is accomplished by the preprocessing and asynchronous parallelism.

4.1 Preprocessing Module

The preprocessing module is the foundation of asynchronous parallel mechanism. As shown in Fig.3, the first $N-1$ characters of the packet are put into a circular array firstly, which is located in on-chip cache. In order to adapt to every length restriction, the number N, which means the size of the array, must be bigger than the maximum number of length restriction. By considering the cost, number N can be formulized as:

$$N = 2 + \max\{a, b \mid \{a\}, \{a, b\}, \{b\} \in ruleset\} \tag{1}$$

The first $N-1$ characters must also be compared to character '\n' one after another, and locations of the character '\n' are recorded in a queue. After all the characters are checked, the counter in which the value means the distance to next '\n' is initialized. The pseudo code of the pretreatment process is also showed in Fig.3.

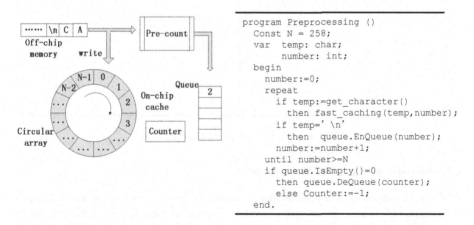

Fig. 3. The preprocessing module of APFA

4.2 Asynchronous Parallelism

After the preprocessing works, APFA upgrades the original matching process to two parallel processes: pre-count and FA matching, which is showed in Fig.4. The FA matching process is responsible for pre-storing the packet contents left by preprocessing in the circular array, as well as getting and matching characters from the array. On the other hand, the pre-count process prejudges the new-stored characters and updates the counter. The pre-count process must run N characters ahead of the FA matching process to realize the prediction, so the parallelism is asynchronous. The pseudo code of the two processes is also listed.

As the pre-count process does not write any data into the circular array and the two processes access the array in a clockwise direction, the management of the circular array is not difficult. By carefully managing two access pointers: *old* and *new*, which can be seen in Fig.4, the two threads can run in parallel without collision. The maintaining of the counter is similar to this, and the asynchronous parallelism can be executed successfully in multi-core or multi-processor environments.

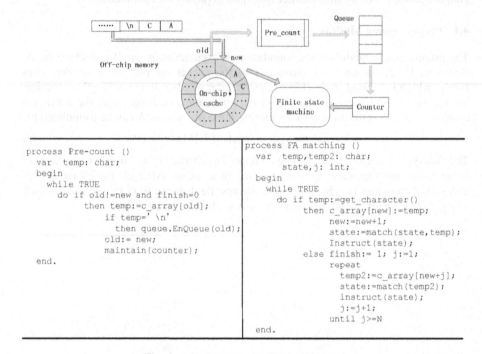

```
process Pre-count ()                │ process FA matching ()
  var  temp: char;                  │   var  temp,temp2: char;
  begin                             │        state,j: int;
    while TRUE                      │   begin
      do if old!=new and finish=0   │     while TRUE
        then temp:=c_array[old];    │       do if temp:=get_character()
          if temp=' \n'             │         then c_array[new]:=temp;
            then queue.EnQueue(old); │           new:=new+1;
          old:= new;                │           state:=match(state,temp);
          maintain(counter);        │           Instruct(state);
  end.                              │         else finish:= 1; j:=1;
                                    │           repeat
                                    │             temp2:=c_array[new+j];
                                    │             state:=match(temp2);
                                    │             instruct(state);
                                    │             j:=j+1;
                                    │           until j>=N
                                    │   end.
```

Fig. 4. Asynchronous parallel mechanism

4.3 Heuristically Forecast Mechanism

While pre-count process is maintaining a counter in which the value means the length of the explored longest "no \n suffix" of the current character, FA matching process is also reading the counter's value to match the length restriction, and this is done in function *instruct* by using the heuristically forecast mechanism. A detailed description of the mechanism is given in Fig.5.

When APFA transferred to a new state, it took out all the patterns for which the new state is one of the final states. After that, the corresponding number in length restriction of the pattern is compared with the counter's value. If the value is bigger than the number in length restriction, APFA can heuristically ascertain that the pattern is matched without considering the following characters could meet the requirements of the length restriction or not, and the result is equivalent to forecasting.

```
Program instruct (int state)
{Assuming strUct pattern has two elements: paTTern_id(int) and
next(point)};
   var    ptr: pattern *;
          r_number: int;
   begin
     if ptr := get_pattern(state)
        then repeat
                  r_number :=restrict_number_array[ptr->pattern_id];
                  if counter > r_number
                    then Output(ptr->pattern_id);
                  ptr := ptr->next;
            until ptr = NULL
   end.
```

Fig. 5. Heuristically forecast mechanism

For instance, suppose that state i is one of the final states for pattern *"/AUTH\s[^\n]{100}/"*. When APFA gets into state i, which means that string *"AUTH\s"* is matched. Without delay for considering the following 100 characters, APFA compares the counter's value with the number 100 immediately, if the value is bigger than 100, then APFA can heuristically forecast that the pattern is matched.

5 Analysis and Optimization

In this section, the time and memory performance of APFA is analyzed, as well as the overlapping problem. Optimizations are proposed at last.

5.1 Time and Memory Performance

As described above, preprocess is the foundation of our APFA, however, the time consumed in it is pivotal to the efficiency of APFA. According to the procedure of preprocess, the whole preprocess-time $t\_preprocess$ and each character's preprocess-time $t\_precheck$ can be formalized as follows.

$$t\_preprocess = (N-1) * t\_precheck \qquad (2)$$

$$t\_precheck = t\_offread + t\_write + t\_compare + t\_enqueue \qquad (3)$$

The variable $t\_precheck$ consists of the time to read from off-chip memory, the time to write in the circular array, the time to compare with character '\n' and the time to update the queue if it is exactly character '\n'. As known, the time to compare is much less than the time to write or read, if we suppose the distribution of characters is entirely uniform, then the variable $t\_preprocess$ can be denoted as:

$$t\_preprocess \approx (N-1) * (t\_offread + t\_write + t\_write / 256) \qquad (4)$$

Work [25] demonstrated that one access to the on-chip memory takes $t\_on = 4T$ and to an external memory $t\_off = 10T$. So $t\_preprocess$ can be expressed as:

$$t\_preprocess \approx (N-1) * (10T + 4T + 4T / 256) \approx (N-1) * 14T \qquad (5)$$

It seems that APFA consumes much time in preprocess works; however, the time spent in matching is largely reduced in APFA due to its higher cache-hit rate, as DFA is so huge that it is not practical to store the whole DFA into on-chip cache. Furthermore, APFA needn't run the pre-process twice. The pre-count process can pre-check the following packet when current packet is checked yet but still in matching.

On the other hand, APFA and XFA both construct the simple finite automaton which is much smaller than DFA. However, as APFA needs stable memory due to the deterministic length of queue and circular cache, it has better actual memory performance than XFA in which variables are dynamically increased.

Consequently, if asynchronous parallelism is implemented well in multi-core environment instead of running by turns, APFA need not much more time than DFA and even much less in some occasions. In addition, APFA has better actual memory performance than XFA. The experiments in section 6 also prove this.

5.2 Optimizations

As can be seen from section 4, the counter's maintaining work is pivotal to the success of heuristically forecast mechanism. However, if the flow "\n\n\n…" is input, the update operation in the queue and the counter would be repeated again and again, affecting the stability and speed of APFA. In order to solve this problem, we use the minimum of the numbers in length restrictions as the threshold for updating the counter, and the value can be described as:

$$n = \min\{a, b \mid \{a\}, \{a, b\}, \{b, \} \in ruleset\} \qquad (6)$$

When the counter decreased to zero, if the new value is smaller than n, APFA needn't update the counter as it wouldn't satisfy the length restriction. It would be at the cost of some additional variables or defining special value of the counter.

Besides the semantic problem, APFA is proposed on the observation that most length restrictions in Snort rules are concerning the character '\n'. However, it is still possible to meet other length restrictions which are related with other characters, like '\s'. In that case, APFA is not efficient to cope with the situation. Actually, it is easy for APFA to accommodate the new situation by adding a queue and a counter to record and update the key character's information.

5.3 Overlapping Problem

Ordinarily, the overlapping problem is that current matching overlaps with the subsequent matching, and it is not easy to eliminate performance degradation resulted from semantic assaults. Take the pattern"/AUTH\s[^\n]{100}/" for example, if the flow "AUTH/sAUTH/s…" is input, numbers of matching against the same pattern would overlaps with each other and many counters would be updated simultaneously in XFA. Pattern rewriting idea [20] eliminates the redundancy by simplifying the patterns, which is only suitable for some occasions. Moreover, it is not valid for a more complex overlapping problem, while most informed researches ignore it. The problem can be illustrated with the pattern ".*A[^\n]{20}B", in which the length restriction is restricted both by prefix and suffix. If the string "AAA…." is put in, we must consider every prefix 'A' met due to the uncertainty of the suffix 'B', then overlapping emerges again.

It is encouraging that APFA can solve the problem, because the asynchronous parallel mechanism can realize the prediction to a certain degree. When a prefix is matched, APFA can access to the circular array to judge whether the corresponding characters equal to the suffix or not. It only needs a simple offset calculation and comparison. As a result, APFA can immediately confirm whether the rule is matched or not, then the current matching is over and would not overlaps with the others.

6 Experiment Evaluation

We evaluate APFA on the patterns from the open source Snort, which has rule sets consist of more than a thousand regular expressions for deep packet inspection. It is not necessary to match the rules in Snort simultaneously, as the packets would be classified before they are parsed. Therefore, we select four subsets from Snort rules by their default applications and evaluate APFA on them separately. In the evaluations, not only the stable memory performance comparison is carried out, but also the real runtime and memory performance contrast is realized.

6.1 Stable Space Performance

First of all, we evaluated APFA on the required memory of the finite automata. Four simplified Finite Automatons were constructed from the Snort rule sets on different protocols, such as ftp, imap, pop and web, with the regex tools [22].

Table 1. Memory required of the finite automata

Snort Rule set	#of rules	#of closures	#of length restriction	#of automata	Total # states DFA APFA	# memory(KB) DFA APFA
FTP	20	2	7	1	585 147	13,900 11
IMAP	26	2	15	1	97,765 3739	121,893 375
POP	13	0	10	1	48,603 79	66,080 4
WEB	12	4	5	1	12862 229	16,222 17

As shown in Table 1, by comparing to DFA, the total states numbers of the automatons are largely reduced by 97.8% averagely, and the memory reduction could reach 99.85% averagely as well. What is more, the numbers in the length restrictions had been reduced in order to drop the complexity to construct the original DFA, which already reduced the space that is not considered.

Table 2. The static memory size of XFA and APFA

Snort Rule set	Total #of states	#of final states	#of states (re)set sign Set Reset	states' average instructions XFA APFA	additional memory (B) XFA APFA	Program size (KB) XFA APFA
FTP	147	49	17 20	11.66 2.45	≥208 =188	277 326
IMAP	3739	310	80 78	18.67 2.10	≥356 =204	291 339
POP	79	23	20 14	13.32 2.54	≥212 =144	227 326
WEB	229	46	12 4	10.41 2.25	≥160 =172	299 347

As APFA is build on the basis of XFA, both of them acquire the similar simplified automaton by segmenting the regular expressions with closures and length restrictions. The key difference is the operations in states. As shown in Table 2, APFA decreases the states' average instructions by 81.7% averagely. Of course, the program size of APFA is a bit larger than XFA, as we need to maintain the parallel threads carefully.

6.2   Real Space and Runtime Performance

In order to compare the real memory and runtime performance between XFA and APFA, we first construct the pseudo-random semantic assaults flow which is against the regular expression in the rule sets. The actual space occupied in running and time cost of each automaton are recorded in Table 3, and the preload time in the table means the time to load the finite automata into the system memory.

Table 3. Runtime performance against artificial flows

Snort Rule set	Space occupied(KB)			Burst variables	Preload time(ms)			Match time(s)		
	DFA	XFA	APFA	XFA	DFA	XFA	APFA	DFA	XFA	APFA
FTP	14,126	30,756	1,808	540,965	1,703	15.8	8.0	5.1	10.1	3.4
IMAP	124,832	96,108	5,620	1,675,592	15,296	242.6	264.2	3.6	9.6	3.7
POP	75,480	39,488	1,736	769,656	8,904	9.4	4.2	3.6	4.2	2.4
WEB	17,612	132,732	1,892	2,646,038	2,391	10.5	12.3	4.2	197.3	4.8

As can be seen in Table 3, DFA takes up large mounts of memory due to the huge size of the automata, and XFA also occupies huge size of memory due to the huge numbers of burst variables when the special flow is met, which is even 6.5 times more than DFA in Snort WEB. By contrast, the space required in APFA is much less than DFA and XFA, which only needs 17.5% of the space required by XFA averagely. Besides the preload time, the time cost in match comparison can be also found in the table. Our mechanism costs much less time than XFA in this evaluation, the maximum reduction rate is 97.6%, and the average timesaving can also reach 67.1%. What is more, the time cost in POP and FTP are even much less than DFA, it results from the low cache-hit rate of the big-size DFA, and our parallelism in multi-core environments is also crucial.

After the semantic assaults evaluation, we also test the three automatons on the real internet traffic traces which is provided by shmoo group [23]. As the packet traces downloaded consist of more than twenty cap files, we choose 5 packet traces of different size. We test the Snort FTP and WEB on the traces, and the space and time cost can be found in Table 4.

Table 4. The space and time performance against real traffic traces

	Snort FTP						Snort WEB					
	Space occupied(KB)			time cost(ms)			Space occupied(KB)			time cost(ms)		
	DFA	XFA	APFA	DFA	XFA	APFA	DFA	XFA	APFA	DFA	XFA	APFA
1	15,568	3,200	3,112	47	63	46	15,244	3,324	3,140	62	47	47
2	15,140	3,500	3,112	141	156	78	11,724	3,556	3,140	109	141	78
3	15,548	7,116	3,112	782	1,422	796	15,628	4,236	3,140	782	1,219	828
4	15,548	5,668	3,112	2,532	4,656	2,656	17,044	6,572	3,304	2,532	4,407	2,672
5	15,548	9,408	3,112	8,703	15,750	8,922	17,044	14,316	3,304	8,625	13,213	9,016

As shown in Table 4, XFA's space performance is comparatively improved to be much better than DFA; however, our APFA still reduces the memory of XFA averagely by 36.4% in FTP and 34.0% in WEB. Besides the space performance improvements, APFA also improves the time performance, the time cost in match of APFA is equal to DFA on the whole, while it only accounts for 58.5% of the time in XFA with Snort FTP and 70.4% of the time with Snort WEB.

It can be concluded from the evaluations above that our APFA acquires better time and memory performance than XFA and DFA indeed, and has higher stability for semantic assaults. In a word, it is more suitable for cloud computing.

7 Conclusion

It is necessary to use DPI for actively monitoring and defense in cloud computing security, but most recent research of DPI can not satisfy the requirements of high speed and stability in the cloud. In this paper, an asynchronous parallel finite automaton named APFA is proposed to solve the problem. While inheriting the ideology of using variables to record the past partial matched information, APFA introduces the asynchronous parallelism and heuristically forecast mechanism in multi-core environment. From the theoretical analysis and evaluation, the results all indicate that APFA is more suitable for cloud computing, as it acquires less and stable memory cost, better runtime performance and higher stability.

We are confident in cloud computing, which is a new technology trend and is expected to change the IT processes and market in the future. The key would be whether cloud computing can overcome the challenges, such as security, reliability, and so on. This paper is expected to make a further step to address the security in the cloud.

References

1. Buyya, R.: Market-Oriented Cloud Computing: Vision, Hype, and Reality of Delivering Computing as the 5th Utility. In: 2009 9th IEEE/ACM International Symposium on Cluster Computing and the Grid (2009)
2. Vaquero, L.M., et al.: A Break in the Clouds: Towards a Cloud Definition. ACM SIG-COMM 39(1) (January 2009)
3. Leavitt, N.: Is cloud computing really ready for prime time? IEEE Computer Society, Los Alamitos (2009)

4. Armbrust, M., Fox, A., Griffith, R., et al.: Above the Clouds: A Berkeley View of Cloud Computing. University of California, Berkeley (2009)
5. Heiser, J., Nicolett, M.: Accessing the Security Risks of Cloud Computing. Gartner Inc., Stamford (2008)
6. Krautheim, F.J.: Private Virtual Infrastructure for Cloud Computing. University of Maryland, hotcloud (2009), http://usenix.org
7. Krautheim, F.J., Phatak, D.S.: LoBot: Locator Bot for Securing Cloud Computing Environments. In: ACM Cloud Computing Security Workshop, Chicago, IL (submitted 2009)
8. Snort: Lightweight Intrusion Detection for Networks, http://www.Snort.org/
9. Bro, http://www.bro-ids.org/
10. Cisco Systems, http://www.cisco.com/
11. Kumar, S., et al.: Algorithms to Accelerate Multiple Regular Expressions Matching for Deep Packet Inspection. In: ACM SIGCOMM 2006, Pisa, Italy (September 2006)
12. Kumar, S., et al.: Advanced Algorithms for Fast and Scalable Deep Packet Inspection. In: ACM ANCS 2006, San Jose, California, USA (December 2006)
13. Becchi, M., Crowley, P.: An improved algorithm to accelerate regular expression evaluation. In: Proc. of ANCS 2007, pp. 145–154 (2007)
14. Becchi, M., Cadambi, S.: Memory-efficient regular expression search using state merging. In: Proc. of INFOCOM 2007 (May 2007)
15. Kumar, S., et al.: Curing Regular Expressions Matching Algorithms from Insomnia, Amnesia, and Acalculia. In: ACM ANCS 2007, Orlando, Florida, USA (December 2007)
16. Smith, R., Estan, C., Jha, S., Kong, S.: Deflating the Big Bang: Fast and Scalable Deep Packet Inspection with Extended Finite Automata. In: ACM SIGCOMM 2008, Seattle, Washington, USA (August 2008)
17. Smith, R., Estan, C., Jha, S.: Xfa: Faster signature matching with extended automata. In: IEEE Symposium on Security and Privacy (May 2008)
18. Smith, R., Estan, C., Jha, S.: Xfas: Fast and compact signature matching. Technical report, University of Wisconsin, Madison (August 2007)
19. Becchi, M., Crowley, P.: A Hybrid Finite Automaton for Practical Deep Packet Inspection. In: ACM CoNEXT 2007, New York, NY, USA (December 2007)
20. Yu, F., Chen, Z., Diao, Y.: Fast and Memory-Efficient Regular Expression Matching for Deep Packet Inspection. In: ACM ANCS 2006, San Jose, California, USA (December 2006)
21. Ficara, D., Giordano, S., Procissi, G., et al.: An Improved DFA for Fast Regular Expression Matching. ACM SIGCOMM Computer Communication Review 38(5), 29–40 (2008)
22. Becchi, M.: regex tool, http://regex.wustl.edu/
23. Internet traffic traces, http://cctf.shmoo.com/
24. Eatherton, W., Dittia, Z., Varghese, G.: Tree bitmap: Hardware/software ip lookups with incremental updates. ACM SIGCOMM Computer Communications Review 34 (2004)
25. Varghese, G.: Network Algorithmics: An Interdisciplinary Approach to Designing Fast Networked Devices. Morgan Kaufmann Publishers Inc., San Francisco (2004)

Secure Document Service for Cloud Computing[*]

Jin-Song Xu[1,2], Ru-Cheng Huang[2], Wan-Ming Huang[1], and Geng Yang[1]

[1] College of Computer Science,
Nanjing University of Posts and Telecommunications, Nanjing, 210003, China
[2] TongDa College,
Nanjing University of Posts and Telecommunications, Nanjing, 210003, China
xujs@njupt.edu.cn, rafa.huang@gmail.com, huangwm999@gmail.com,
yangg@njupt.edu.cn

Abstract. The development of cloud computing is still in its initial stage, and the biggest obstacle is data security. How to guarantee the privacy of user data is a worthwhile study. This paper has proposed a secure document service mechanism based on cloud computing. Out of consideration of security, in this mechanism, the content and the format of documents were separated prior to handling and storing. In addition, documents could be accessed safely within an optimized method of authorization. This mechanism would protect documents stored in cloud environment from leakage and provide an infrastructure for establishing reliable cloud services.

1 Introduction

Cloud computing is a new variation of traditional distributed computing and grid computing. The development of cloud computing is still facing enormous challenges. A major concern is about data security, that is, how to protect data from unauthorized users and leakage. In order to reduce operation costs on client-end and boost the efficiency of collaboration, the cloud undertook the majority of jobs. From the view of users, losing control of the executions of jobs may increase the risk of being hacked especially when the security of entire task highly depend on the trustworthiness of the cloud.

As can be seen, for both individual user and large-scale enterprises, it is an important issue to protect key data within cloud pattern. This issue, to some extent, has a great impact on the development of cloud computing. This paper has designed a secure document service mechanism for the document service based on cloud environment. We highlight that the major threats against the safety of document service and the privacy of user documents focus on two concept: 1)documents would be intercepted and captured during transferring from client-end to the cloud and 2)access control for documents stored in the cloud.

---

[*] This work has been partially funded by National Natural Science Foundation Project (60873231), Natural Science Foundation for Colleges and Universities in Jiangsu Province (08KJB520006) and "The Six Major Peak Talent" Foundation Project in Jiangsu Province (06-E-044)

M.G. Jaatun, G. Zhao, and C. Rong (Eds.): CloudCom 2009, LNCS 5931, pp. 541–546, 2009.
© Springer-Verlag Berlin Heidelberg 2009

To guarantee the privacy of document, on the one hand, the content and the format of document were separated prior to handling and storing, because most of private information was stored in the content of documents. An optimized authorization method was proposed to assign access right for authorized users on the other hand.

2   Related Work

Cloud computing derived from traditional distributed computing where existed two main methods to satisfy the requirements of reliable data storage service. The first one heavily relied on a trusted third-party. A successful example in business is eBay [1], in which all of users' transaction information were stored at official center server. In this pattern, the most important component for data access control–authorization was deployed in the center server. The second one often used in P2P context. In decentralized P2P environment, authority did not exist and reputation-based trust relation were emphasized [2][3][4]. The weak point of their works was that they could not give full privacy just a part of it, which determined that the above methods cannot be directly applied in cloud environment. Within another distributed patterngrid computing community, there is no consensus that how data authentication should be done within virtual organizations [5].

Thus, cloud environment needs new models to handle potential security problems. This new model should allow an information owner to protect their data while not interfering with the privacy of other information owners within the cloud [6]. From the view of client, the remote service deployed in cloud was hardly to be regarded as trustworthy in default situation. In recent studies, [7] focused on the lower layer IaaS cloud providers where securing a customers virtual machines is more manageable. Their work provided a closed box execution environment. [6] proposed Private Virtual Infrastructure that shares the responsibility of security in cloud computing between the service provider and client, reducing the risk of them both. Our aim is to provide an efficient methodology to guarantee privacy of user data in cloud computing environment.

3   Secure Document Service Mechanism

Guaranteeing full privacy of user's document was an important concept for security document service. For ideal distributed document service based on cloud computing, document handling and storing were not executed by local system in client-end but by remote cloud server that provide document service. Since the work on remote cloud server cannot be considered as trustworthy in default setting, we propose a novel mechanism to protect the privacy of user's document, which correspond with cloud computing fashion.

3.1   Separation of Content and Format

This paper has focused on document service in cloud and the term "data" refer to document file in general.

Document. A data stream that consist of content and format. The content of
document can be browsed and handled in a specified manner that determined
by its format.

For example,

```
<B> hello </B> <BR/> <B> world !</B>
```

In this fragment of an HTML file, the strings "hello" and "world !" are content which can be browsed in browser. The tags like "<***>" are format, while
the couple "<B>" and "</B>" make the strings "hello" and "world !" bold
and "<BR/>" gives a line break between the two words. We identify any documents with content-format combinations. For example, above HTML file can be
seen as B(hello)BR()B(world !).Therefore, document handling could be seen as
combination of content handling and format handling.

Actually, most of private information was not stored in format but content.
Making the procedure of content handling secure was essential for guaranteeing
document privacy. In our design, we separated content from document and then
content should be encrypted (by several sophisticated cryptographic algorithms,
e.g., RSA [8], DES [9], etc.) before document being propagated and stored in
remote server.

3.2   Document Partition

Usually, document handling often did not cover the whole content and format
but a part of them. It is not necessary to re-store the whole document, but just
its partition that were handled. It is believed that partitioning the document
prior to handling and only updating the modified partition could reduce the
overhead of document service and the possibility of the whole document being
damaged and hacked.

If the size of document partition were rather large, the possibility of this partition being updating were somewhat high than of a smaller partition. Because
Because it was more possible that handling happened in a larger partition. Unfortunately, if the handling that only changed punctuation or a letter happened
in a very large partition, the efficiency of transferring and storing document
would be affected.

3.3   Document Authorization

Data authorization can be implemented by public-key cryptography in traditional network environment. Correspondingly, cloud computing environment was
lacking in nature pre-trusted party that was responsible for authentication and
authorization.

1. **General Authorization Method (Method 1).** In general practice, the
   document owner had charge of authorizing other users for accessing

documents. We denoted the public and private key of $Owner_I$ as B_I, P_I and the public and private key of $User_J$ as B_J, P_J, respectively. $B_I(c)$ depicted that content c was encrypted with $Owner_I$'s public key and the procedure of decryption could be written as $P_I(B_I(c))$. If $Owner_I$ wanted to authorize $User_J$ for accessing document, $Owner_I$ required encrypt the content by $User_J$'s public key, namely $B_J(P_I(c))$. This method could be implemented relatively easily. Document owners overhead of encrypting content, however, would be in conformity with the number of users who were authorized.

2. **Optimized Authorization Method (Method 2)**
   (a) Construct two encryption functions $f(x)$, $g(x)$, both of them have the following properties:
       i. It is hard to find inverse functions for both functions.
       ii. For any M, when $f(M) = N$, there must be $g(N) = M$. Also, for any M, when $g(M) = N$, there must be $f(N) = M$. As summarize, $g(f(M)) = f(g(M)) = M$.
       iii. It is hard to find inverse function for $f(g(x))$ and to decompose $f(g(x))$ as the combination of $f(x)$ and $g(x)$. Denote $f(g(x))$ as $H(x)$.
       iv. It is hard to find inverse function for $f(g(g(x)))$ and to decompose $f(g(g(x)))$ as the combination of $f(x)$ and $g(x)$. Denote $f(g(g(x)))$ as $I(x)$.
       v. For any M, when $f(M) = N$, there is $H(N) = f(M)$.
       vi. For any M, when $f(M) = N$, there is $I(N) = f(g(M))$.
   (b) Suppose $H(x)$ existed and encrypted document $B_I(c)$ stored in cloud server, when $Owner_I$ authorized $User_J$ for access to $B_I(c)$, $H(x)$ would be submitted to cloud server. Cloud server would then automatically compute $H(B_I(c))$ and send it to $User_J$. $H(B_I(c))$ could be generated as $B_J(c)$ by $User_J$. It is easy for $User_J$ to decrypted $B_J(c)$ by using P_J.
   (c) Suppose $I(x)$ existed, when $User_J$ obtained encrypted content $B_J(P_I(c))$, content c could be generated by computing $B_I(P_J((B_J(P_I(c)))))$.

4 Secure Document Service Archetype

We provided the model of our mechanism, as follows:

As Fig.1 depicted, Documents were stored in "Cloud Document Warehouse". The handling involved document format was completely done by "Document Service", while owner in client-end was responsible for encryption and decryption of document content. To save document, client must re-encrypt partitioned content and then send it to "Document Service".

There were two kinds of authorization procedures (Fig.2). For Method 1, by decryption, client can get the access to documents from "Document Service". There was a pre-requirement, for Method 2, of the existence of $H(x)$ and $I(x)$. Using Method 2 can significantly reduce the overhead of authorization of Client H and the complexity of procedure of sharing documents among clients.

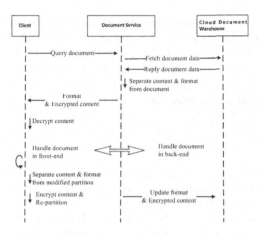

Fig. 1. Separation of Content and Format

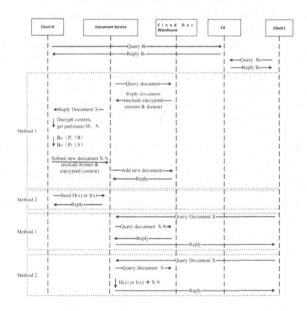

Fig. 2. Procedure of Authorization

5 Conclusion and Future Work

The mechanism of security document service for cloud computing environment has been proposed and an archetype has been given. In this mechanism, content and format were separated from document to keep their privacy. Also, an optimized authorization method has been proposed for assigning access right of document to authorized users.

In the near future, we will highlight several fields where new approaches for implementing secure document service are required, particularly in constructing appropriate functions of $H(x)$ and $I(x)$ for authorization. Also, the authors will explore sophisticated partition strategies suitable for files in different formats. In this direction, the most significant result would be a novel file format that can perfectly keep privacy of content.

References

[1] Resnick, P., Zeckhauser, R.: Trust among strangers in Internet transactions: Empirical analysis of eBay's reputation system. Advances in Applied Microeconomics: A Research Annual 11, 127–157 (2002)
[2] Kamvar, S., Schlosser, M., Garcia-Molina, H.: The eigentrust algorithm for reputation management in p2p networks. In: Proceedings of the 12th international conference on World Wide Web, pp. 640–651. ACM, New York (2003)
[3] Xiong, L., Liu, L.: Peertrust: Supporting reputation-based trust for peer-to-peer electronic communities. IEEE transactions on Knowledge and Data Engineering 16(7), 843–857 (2004)
[4] Rahbar, A., Yang, O.: Powertrust: A robust and scalable reputation system for trusted peer-to-peer computing. IEEE Transactions on Parallel and Distributed Systems 18(4), 460–473 (2007)
[5] Antonioletti, M., Atkinson, M., Baxter, R., Borley, A., Hong, N., Collins, B., Hardman, N., Hume, A., Knox, A., Jackson, M., et al.: The design and implementation of Grid database services in OGSA-DAI. Concurrency and Computation: Practice & Experience 17(2), 357–376 (2005)
[6] Krautheim, F.J.: Private virtual infrastructure for cloud computing. In: HotCloud, USNIX (2009)
[7] Nuno Santos, K.P.G., Rodrigues, R.: Towards trusted cloud computing. In: HotCloud, USNIX (2009)
[8] Rivest, R., Shamir, A., Adleman, L.: A method for obtaining digital signatures and public-key cryptosystems (1978)
[9] Biham, E., Shamir, A.: Differential cryptanalysis of DES-like cryptosystems. Journal of Cryptology 4(1), 3–72 (1991)

Privacy of Value-Added Context-Aware Service Cloud

Xin Huang[1], Yin He[2], Yifan Hou[2], Lisi Li[2], Lan Sun[2], Sina Zhang[2], Yang Jiang[2],
and Tingting Zhang[1]

[1] ITM, Mid Sweden University, Sundsvall, SE 85170, Sweden
{xin.huang,tingting.zhang}@miun.se
[2] School of Electronics and Information Engineering, Beijing Jiaotong University,
Beijing, CN 100044, P. R. China
{yihe0800,yiho0800,lili0807,lasu0801,sizh0800,
yaji0800}@student.miun.se

Abstract. In the cloud computing era, service provider cloud and context service cloud store all your personal context data. This is a positive aspect for value-added context-aware service cloud as it makes that context information collection are easier than was the case previously. However, this computing environment does add a series of threats in relation to privacy protection. Whoever receives the context information is able to deduce the status of the owners and, generally owners are not happy to share this information. In this paper, we propose a privacy preserved framework which can be utilized by value-added context-aware service cloud. Context data and related services access privileges are determined by context-aware role-based access control (CRAC) extended from role-based access control (RAC). Privacy preserved context service protocol (PPCS) is designed to protect user privacy from exposed context information. Additionally, user network and information diffusion is combined to evaluate the privacy protection effect.

Keywords: Cloud computing, Privacy.

1 Introduction

Gartner defines cloud computing as "a style of computing where massively scalable IT-enabled capabilities are delivered 'as a service' to external customers using Internet technologies." [1] In the cloud computing era, all your personal context data are stored in service provider cloud and context service cloud. This is a positive aspect for value-added context-aware service cloud as it makes that context information collection are easier than was the case previously. In our project, context information is mainly collected from a system using distributed context exchange protocol (DCXP) [2, 3]. Users in DCXP system can capture, process, and store a variety of context information, e.g., location information, temperature.

However, a value-added context-aware cloud does add a series of threats to privacy protection. The manner in which context information is handled then becomes a critical question. The information may be sensitive and users are not prepared to share this with others. However, the user context information is always collected and analyzed when this user is engaged in a service in value-added context-aware service cloud. In

M.G. Jaatun, G. Zhao, and C. Rong (Eds.): CloudCom 2009, LNCS 5931, pp. 547–552, 2009.
© Springer-Verlag Berlin Heidelberg 2009

addition, the service provider is able to use user data without the user being aware of this situation [4, 5]. Increasingly, a simple service may be involved in a chain of service clouds; each cloud is able to access data in its cloud without the control of any technology [1]. So, access control is definitely necessary and another important issue involves how to protect user privacy from exposed context information.

In this paper, a privacy protection framework for value-added context-aware service cloud is described. There are two fundamental construction parts: Context-aware Role-based Access Control (CRAC) and Privacy Preserved Context Service Protocol (PPCS). CRAC is for protecting personal context information and related services from unauthorized persons. CRAC is more reasonable and has better privacy protection than the role-based access control model (RAC) [6, 7, 8]. Meanwhile, PPCS protocol is used to protect user privacy from exposed context information. PPCS is based on the K-anonymity model [9-14].

To evaluate the effect, information diffusion models are developed. In these models, information is diffused in a user network which is scale-free [15, 16, 17]. A scale-free network is a network whose fraction of nodes with connections k follows a power law degree distribution $P(k) \sim k^{(-r)}$. The parameter r is a constant and this value typically falls within the range $2 < r < 3$. The implication of this is that a few nodes show high connectivity while the others are poorly connected.

Our paper is organized as follows. Section 2 describes the framework, the scenario and message flow; Section 3 shows the privacy protection elements; Section 4 contains the results. Finally some important conclusions are made in Section 5.

2 Framework

The framework for value-added context-aware service cloud is shown in Fig. 1. There is a context service cloud which supplies the context information, e.g., location information. The service provider cloud provides services, for example, Google Calendar. The value-added context-aware service cloud is the core of this framework. It contains context-aware service, privacy service and security service.

The standard scenario is as follow. The first page is the login page. Then Tom requests service in a service request page. After both the PPCS and CRAC procedures, a permission decision page is displayed. Tom can then choose any permitted way to communicate with Jerry in order to make an appointment.

Security service supplies basic security functionalities, e.g., authentication, message encryption, key management and message authentication code (MAC).

The core modules for protecting privacy are CRAC and PPCS and the effect that they have is tested in user networks in which information diffusion is considered.

2.1 CRAC

CRAC is a combination of RAC and the context aware role. A context aware role is a job function selected and based on the changing context of communication parties with some associated semantics regarding the authority and responsibility conferred on the user assigned to the role. In CRAC, a value-added service cloud is treated as an agent user.

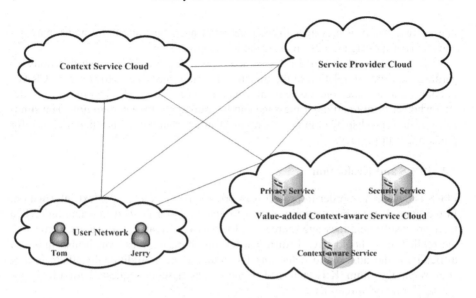

Fig. 1. System Topology

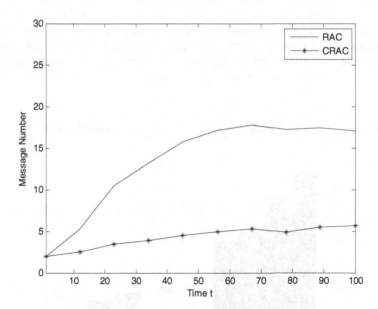

Fig. 2. Message number in CRAC and RAC

An information diffusion model is used to verify the effect. In this simulation, a 100 nodes scale-free network is used to model the behavior of the users. Each user is viewed as a node. Each node has several friends with whom the node may communicate and the number of friends follows a power-law distribution. Two messages are generated in the source node and are diffused to others in this network. All the nodes may diffuse received messages to their neighboring nodes; and these nodes may delete received messages and stop diffusing at each time step.

In RAC, links are assigned roles statically, which are used to make decisions regarding the rights in relation to the transfer of certain messages. However, in CRAC, in addition to a static role, context information must also be checked in order to decide whether or not particular message can be transferred by a certain link. The simulation results are displayed in Fig. 2 and it illustrates that CRAC is a better choice for protecting user privacy.

2.2 PPCS and Evaluation

PPCS is designed in order to protect user privacy from exposed context information. In the main, it uses K-anonymity model to generate blur context information. When there are insufficient message sources, L-diversity is activated. L-diversity means that the replied area should have L different terrain characteristics, which also makes it difficult for the attacker to determine the actual source. Additionally, there is a K adjustment algorithm. K is increased if one requester sends requests with a high frequency for no clear reasons.

Now, combining the idea of information relation with the diffusion in a user social network, a multi-message diffusion model is built in order to simulate the effect of PPCS. In this simulation, the same scale-free network is used. The hop distance is used to represent the relations between the nodes and the source. 10 messages are generated in the source node and are diffused to others in this network. All these messages are related to private data of the source to some degree R. After a time, some nodes may accumulate enough messages to deduce the private information. This

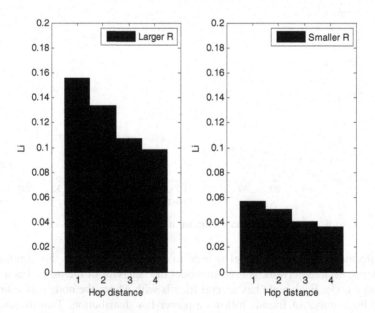

Fig. 3. Message leakage degrees for different R and hop distance

chance is measured by the leakage degree Li, which is the sum of all the relation degrees of messages accumulated in node i. PPCS blurs the context information and K adjustment increases K in order to decrease the R of the messages for one requester with a high request frequency.

The averaged results of the 100 independent simulations are shown in Fig. 3: a smaller R makes Li smaller. This means that PPCS can reduce a person's privacy leakage.

3 Conclusion

A privacy preserved framework of value-added context-aware service cloud is proposed. CRAC and PPCS protocol are the two main elements which are used in order to support privacy protection. CRAC is used to protect personal context data and related services from parties without proper privileges. It is more flexible than the traditional RAC; it can provide a better privacy protection. PPCS is designed to protect user privacy from exposed context information. Additionally, user network and information diffusion model are used together to evaluate the privacy protection effect. To our best knowledge, this is the first method which has simulated the privacy protection effect.

In future, we intend to delve more deeply into the information diffusion model. This model is useful to design privacy preserved cloud computing services.

Acknowledgement

We would like to thank Sensible Things That Communicate (STC) research, regional EU target 2, regional public sector, and industries such as Ericsson Research and Telia for their funding.

References

[1] Heiser, J., Nicolett, M.: Assessing the security risks of cloud computing. Technical report, Gartner (2008)
[2] Angeles, C.: Distribution of context information using the session initiation protocol (SIP). Master Thesis, Royal Institute of Technology, Stockholm, Sweden (2008)
[3] Vidal, S.Q.: Context-aware Networks Design, Implementation and Evaluation of an Architecture and a Protocol for the Ambient Networks Project. Master Thesis, Linköping University, Linköping, Sweden (2006)
[4] Horrigan, J.B.: Use of cloud computing applications and services. Pew Internet & American Life project memo (2008)
[5] Greenberg, A.: Cloud Computing's Stormy Side. Forbes Magazine (2008)
[6] Hakkila, J., Kansala, I.: Role based privacy applied to context-aware mobile applications. In: IEEE International Conference on Systems, Man and Cybernetics, vol. 6, pp. 5467–5472. IEEE Press, New York (2004)

[7] Damiani, M.L., Bertino, E.: Access Control and Privacy in Location-Aware Services for Mobile Organizations. In: 7th International Conference on Mobile Data Management, MDM 2006, p. 11. IEEE Computer Society, Los Alamitos (2006)

[8] Ardagna, C.A., Cremonini, M., De Capitani di Vimercati, S., Samarati, P.: A Privacy-Aware Access Control System. Journal of Computer Security (JCS) 16(4), 369–392 (2008)

[9] Ghinita, G., Kalnis, P., Skiadopoulos, S.: PRIVE: Anonymous Location-based Queries in Distributed Mobile Systems. In: Proc. 16th Int'l World Wide Web Conf (WWW 2007), pp. 371–380. ACM, New York (2007)

[10] Bamba, B., Liu, L., Pesti, P., Wang, T.: Supporting anonymous location queries in mobile environments with privacygrid. In: Proceedings of 17th International World Wide Web Conference (WWW 2008), pp. 237–248. ACM, New York (2008)

[11] Chow, C., Mokbel, M.F., Liu, X.: A peer-to-peer spatial cloaking algorithm for anonymous location-based service. In: Proceedings of the 14th annual ACM international symposium on Advances in geographic information systems, pp. 171–178. ACM, New York (2006)

[12] Samarati, P.: Protecting respondents' identities in microdata release. IEEE Transactions on Knowledge and Data Engineering 13, 1010–1027 (2001)

[13] Sweeney, L.: K-anonymity: a model for protecting privacy. International Journal on Uncertainty, Fuzziness and Knowledge-based Systems 10(5), 557–570 (2002)

[14] Machanavajjhala, A., Gehrke, J., Kifer, D., Venkitasubramaniam, M.: L-diversity: Privacy beyond k-anonymity. In: 22nd IEEE International Conference on Data Engineering (2006)

[15] Newman, M.E.J.: The Structure and Function of Complex Networks. SIAM Review 45, 167–256 (2003)

[16] Albert, R., Barabási, A.-L.: Statistical Mechanics of Complex Networks. Rev. Mod. Phys. 74, 47–97 (2005)

[17] Huang, X., Zhang, T.: Information Diffusion and Privacy. Unpublished, Mid Sweden University, Sundsvall, Sweden (2009)

A Simple Technique for Securing Data at Rest Stored in a Computing Cloud

Jeff Sedayao, Steven Su, Xiaohao Ma, Minghao Jiang, and Kai Miao

Intel Corporation
999 YingLun Rd,
Shanghai 200131, China
{jeff.sedayao,steven.su,xiaohao.ma,minghao.jiang,
kai.miao}@intel.com

Abstract. "Cloud Computing" offers many potential benefits, including cost savings, the ability to deploy applications and services quickly, and the ease of scaling those application and services once they are deployed. A key barrier for enterprise adoption is the confidentiality of data stored on Cloud Computing Infrastructure. Our simple technique implemented with Open Source software solves this problem by using public key encryption to render stored data at rest unreadable by unauthorized personnel, including system administrators of the cloud computing service on which the data is stored. We validate our approach on a network measurement system implemented on PlanetLab. We then use it on a service where confidentiality is critical – a scanning application that validates external firewall implementations.

Keywords: Cloud Computing, PlanetLab, Security, Encryption, Data at Rest Storage.

1 Introduction

"Cloud Computing" offers many potential benefits, including cost savings, the ability to deploy and scale applications and services quickly. We define "Cloud Computing" as Computing infrastructure that is highly scalable, managed, and abstracted as a service available through the Internet. Cloud Computing services are billed by consumption and are used by multiple customers. Well known examples like Amazon's Elastic Computing Cloud (EC2) [1] and Scalable Storage Service (S3) [2] allow users to buy virtual machines and storage accessed over the Internet. Infrastructure shared by multiple customers allows Cloud service providers to spread out costs over many users. When combined with consumption based billing, service abstraction, and scalability, Cloud Computing can offers compelling value to organizations deploying services.

While sharing infrastructure lowers costs, it is a major barrier blocking enterprise adoption of Cloud Computing, as organizations are concerned about retaining the confidentiality of their data. The administrators of a Cloud Computing service could read data stored at the service. In this paper, we describe how we solved this problem by using open source and public key encryption to render stored data at rest

M.G. Jaatun, G. Zhao, and C. Rong (Eds.): CloudCom 2009, LNCS 5931, pp. 553–558, 2009.

unreadable by unauthorized parties. The first section of this paper outlines the problem that we are trying to solve. The second section talks about our solution architecture, and the third talks about our implementation experiences. The next section cover related work, and the last discusses our conclusions and plans for future work.

2 Problem Scope

Our goal is to ensure the confidentiality of data at rest. By "data at rest", we mean that the data that is stored in a readable form on a Cloud Computing service, whether in a storage product like S3 or in a virtual machine instance as in EC2. Figure 1 illustrates this definition. In a cloud computing service instantiation, be it a virtual machine instance or an instance of virtual storage, some process generates data to be stored on disk. To protect data at rest, we want to prevent other users in the cloud infrastructure who might have access to the same storage from reading the data our process has stored. We also want to prevent system administrators who run the cloud computing service from reading the data.

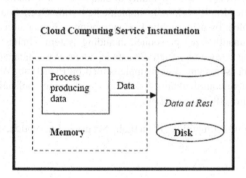

Fig. 1. Process in a Cloud Computing Infrastructure producing Data at Rest

We assume that it is unlikely for an adversary to snoop on the contents of memory. If the adversary had that capability, it is unlikely that we could trust the confidentiality of any of the data that we generated there. While the administrative staff of the cloud computing service could theoretically monitor the data moving in memory before it is stored in disk, we believe that administrative and legal controls should prevent this from happening. We also do not guard against the modification of the data at rest, although we are likely to be able to detect this.

3 Solution Design

Our approach is to use public key encryption to insure the confidentiality of our data at rest. The process producing data also encrypts the data with the public key of a separate collection agent, as shown in Figure 2.

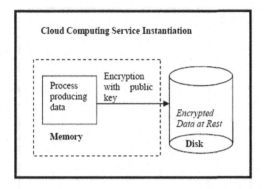

Fig. 2. Process in a Cloud Computing Infrastructure producing Encrypted Data at Rest

On a trusted host, we collect the encrypted data, as shown in Figure 3, and decrypt it with the collection agent's private key which stays on that host. Note that in this case, we are in exclusive control of the private key, which the cloud service provider has no view or control over. We will discuss this feature of our solution later.

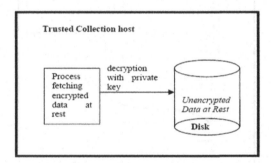

Fig. 3. Process in a Cloud Computing Infrastructure producing Encrypted Data at Rest

4   Implementation Experiences

In this section, we describe our implementation experiences and use cases for our technique. Our first implementation encrypted data from web site performance monitoring. Our second implementation involves encrypting data from doing security scans.

4.1   Web Performance Measurement Implementation

Intel needed a service that could give us an idea of end users' experiences with the corporate website from different regions of the globe and contrast that experience to other comparable websites. We wanted to compare the end-user experiences using different services for providing web content from a global perspective – how the different providers would do in different regions of the world. Intel is a member of the PlanetLab consortium [3] and has access over 1039 systems at more than 485 sites

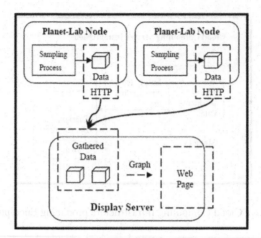

Fig. 4. Web performance data gathering and display methodology

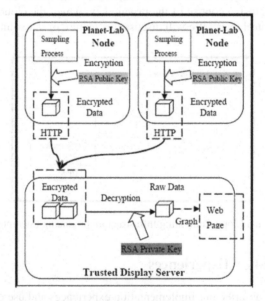

Fig. 5. Secured Web Performance Monitoring Application with Data Encryption and Decryption

across the globe. While we could have purchased a similar service, we decided to implement our monitor on PlanetLab. Figure 4 shows how the first implementation of the monitoring service [4] functioned. Each PlanetLab node in the appropriate geography took samples of the URLs we specified and made the data available through PlanetLab's sensor interface [5]. The display service grabbed the data from the sensor via HTTP, and shows the data to users of the display server as web pages.

Some departments within Intel preferred that the performance information gathered on the PlanetLab nodes not be widely available. PlanetLab nodes have many of the characteristics of Cloud Computing hosts, with multiple users' virtual machines sharing individual hosts. We decided to encrypt the data on the PlanetLab nodes that gather the data. We designated a trusted host as a collection agent, and encrypted the performance data that was stored on the nodes with the public key. The corresponding private key was put on the trusted host and used to decrypt incoming data. The correction is depicted as Figure 5.

The availability of public key open source implementations made this simple and convenient to implement. Using OpenSSL [6], the encryption process can take place in a filter in a single shell command line. Also, only the public key is resident on the cloud storage. If someone, including a cloud service administrator, looks at the files and finds the keys, they will only have the public key, which will not give them access to the encrypted content.

4.2 Scanner Implementation

Intel invests significant resources in creating a security perimeter around Intel but has trouble verifying that the policies created are implemented correctly. With PlanetLab, we could scan Intel's firewalls from multiple external points and compare the results to the policies. These external points can also scan the public services of Intel which are not behind the firewall or servers from other companies.

The scanner is much like the web performance monitor as they work under the same model of result data generation and collection. We set up NMAP [7] on the external Planet-Lab nodes and defined scan scenario there. Output was periodically generated and saved as encrypted file available for pickup with HTTP. Later, a collecting server inside Intel downloads the data and decrypted it for subsequent application to get it analyzed. As with the web performance monitor, we used OpenSSL to quickly and conveniently implement public key encryption.

5 Related Work

There are a number of efforts to make storage of data in clouds more secure. Amazon Virtual Private Cloud (VPC) [8] creates a VPN between virtual machines in the Amazon cloud and an organization's network. Amazon VPC protects data in transit, but does nothing for data at rest. Piworx [9] and Mozy [10] are services that offer data storage. Piworx uses its own proprietary public key implementation, and apparently can access user data, although they promise that will only be done with user permission. Piworx is implemented on top of Amazon EC2. Mozy uses public key encryption, but typically handles both generating and storing the public and private keys. Mozy also warns their users that if they forget their own custom generated private key, they will not be able to access their own data. Our solution differs from these two public cloud storage implementations in that we are always in charge of our own private keys. Our use of open source enables anyone to quickly and easily implement it on any cloud infrastructure. Tahoe [11] is a distributed file system that also incorporates public key encryption to provide confidentiality. It adds many other features that may or may not be of interest, such as being a true file system and been fault tolerant. Tahoe is currently used in the Allmydata [12] backup service.

6 Conclusions

Our technique protects data at rest while being easy and cheap to implement. It does have some notable limitations. As mentioned previously, this model works only for a process that produces data on a host (virtual or real) that is collected for use by some other host. No other process on that real or virtual host that produced the data can use it without somehow exposing the private key. Still, our model can be used for a number of applications of which we have presented two. While we guard against casual browsing of files by system administrators and others, we need to ensure that the programs that produce data don't leave around key data in any temporary files. A process might leave copies of data in some temporary storage directory before writing encrypting the final output. Finally, we found that PlanetLab has been a very useful testbed for trying out Cloud Computing concepts. Advertising this capability may lead more enterprises to join PlanetLab.

References

1. Amazon. Elastic Computing Cloud, http://aws.amazon.com/ec2
2. Amazon. Simple Storage Service, http://aws.amazon.com/s3
3. Peterson, L., Anderson, T., Culler, D., Roscoe, T.: A blueprint for introducing disruptive technology into the Internet. SIGCOMM Comput. Commun. Rev. 33(1), 59–64 (2003)
4. Sedayao, J.: Implementing and operating an internet scale distributed application using service oriented architecture principles and cloud computing infrastructure. In: Kotsis, G., Taniar, D., Pardede, E., Khalil, I. (eds.) Proceedings of the 10th international Conference on information integration and Web-Based Applications & Services, iiWAS 2008, Linz, Austria, November 24 - 26, pp. 417–421. ACM, New York (2008)
5. Roscoe, T., Peterson, L., Karlin, S., Wawrzoniak, M.: A Simple Common Sensor Interface for PlanetLab. PlanetLab Design Note PDN 03-010 (2003)
6. OpenSSL, http://www.openssl.org/
7. NMAP, http://nmap.org/
8. Amazon Virtual Private Cloud, http://aws.amazon.com/vpc/
9. Piworx, http://www.piworx.com/
10. Mozy, http://mozy.com/
11. Wilcox-O'Hearn, Z., Warner, B.: Tahoe: the least-authority filesystem. In: Proceedings of the 4th ACM international Workshop on Storage Security and Survivability, StorageSS 2008, Alexandria, Virginia, USA, October 31 - 31, pp. 21–26. ACM, New York (2008)
12. Allmydata, http://www.allmydata.com/

Access Control of Cloud Service Based on UCON

Chen Danwei, Huang Xiuli, and Ren Xunyi

Nanjing University of posts & Telecommunications, New Model Street No.66,
210003, Nanjing, China
chendw@njupt.edu.cn, juliehxl@163.com, renxy@njupt.edu.cn

Abstract. Cloud computing is an emerging computing paradigm, and cloud service is also becoming increasingly relevant. Most research communities have recently embarked in the area, and research challenges in every aspect. This paper mainly discusses cloud service security. Cloud service is based on Web Services, and it will face all kinds of security problems including what Web Services face. The development of cloud service closely relates to its security, so the research of cloud service security is a very important theme. This paper introduces cloud computing and cloud service firstly, and then gives cloud services access control model based on UCON and negotiation technologies, and also designs the negotiation module.

Keyword: Cloud Service, Access Control, UCON, Negotiation.

1 Introduction

Cloud Computing is a large-scale distributed computing paradigm that is driven by economies of scale, in which a pool of abstracted, virtualized, dynamically-scalable, managed computing power, storage, platforms, and services are delivered on demand to external customers over the Internet[1]. Cloud is the network which is constructed through cloud computing model, and cloud service is the service provided in cloud. Now, Cloud Computing has become the hottest technology in IT, and is also the research focus in academic.

The goal of cloud computing is to realize "the network is a high performance computer", that is to allow users to put all data and services into cloud and get all kinds of services from cloud only by their Internet terminal equipment. What users see is a virtual view when they use cloud service, and the data and services are actually distributed at different locations in cloud. The tendency that services and data will be transferred to web is inevitable, and more and more services and data will be in cloud.

Cloud service is based on Web Services [2], and Web Services are based on Internet. Internet has many its own inherent security flaws because of its openness, and it also has many other attacks and threats. Therefore, cloud services will face a wide range of security issues. At present, there are already many security specifications and technologies about Web Services, so it is of great significance for us to resolve security issues of cloud service using these existed security knowledge.

M.G. Jaatun, G. Zhao, and C. Rong (Eds.): CloudCom 2009, LNCS 5931, pp. 559–564, 2009.

Access control is one of the most important security mechanisms in cloud service, and Cloud service can not apply the traditional access control model to achieve access control because of its characteristics. But cloud services need to face the same security problems and Security requirements; and we also can't be divorced from the traditional access control model ideas.

For Unauthorized Access problems, it often built on fragile ID authentication and authorization. The mainly causes include: ①No authentication or fragile authentication; ②To send the password and authentication information in plaintext. The system should adopt a strong authentication system and make encryption transmission to prevent unauthorized access.

2   Cloud Services Access Control Based UCON

2.1   UCON Model

The usual traditional access control models include DAC, MAC and RBAC. New access control models have TBAC [3], ABAC [4], and UCON [5]. Cloud service usually has the following features: large amounts of resources, highly dynamic and flexible construction, lots of dynamic users, and so on. UCON can easily implement the security strategy of DAC, MAC and RBAC, and also includes security strategy of trust and DRM management covering security and privacy which are two important issues in the demand of Modern business information systems. As the next generation access control technology, besides taking ABC conception, UCON also inherits all the merits of traditional access control technologies, and can be established various access control model under every kinds of complex situation, and among them $UCON_{ABC}$ is the most integrated model.. UCON provides very superior decision-making ability, and will be a better choice to be used to establish cloud service access control model.

UCON is just a conceptual model, and no concrete realization specification, so there is still much work to do for establishing access control model based on UCON. UCON model is composed of six parts: Subjects, Rights, Objects, Authorization, oBligation, Conditions.

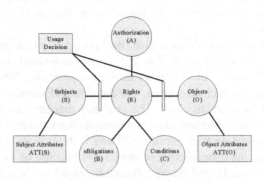

Fig. 1. UCON model

(1)Subject and Subject Attribute

Subject is an entity which has some rights of using object, marked as S. Subject means widely, it may be the user group, the user himself, or may also be a computer terminal, card machine, hand-held terminal (wireless), and even may be a program or process application.

Subject Attribute identifies the main capabilities and features of subject, and is the important parameter in the decision-making process, marked as ATT (S). The common subject attributes include: identity, user group, role, membership, and capacity list and security level.

(2)Object and Object Attribute

Object is an entity which accepts the visit of Subject, marked as O. Object also has a wide meanings, and it may be information, documents and records used in workflow system, or may be hardware on the network and wireless communication terminals.

Object Attribute identifies the important information of object, marked as ATT (O). Object attributes include security label, relations, type and access control lists and so on.

(3) Rights

Rights are a set of actions that subject visits object, marked as R. And the set also defines some conditions restriction that object request of subject. There are many types of rights.

(4) Authorization the principal,

Authorization is the only decision-making factor in the traditional access control model, and also is also an important part in UCON model, marked as A. Authorization is based on subject attributes, object attributes, as well as the right to request (for example: read or write privileges, etc.) and in accordance with the permission rules set to determine the operation of the authority. Implementation of authorization may lead to some changes to subject attribute or object attribute value, which will also impact on the decision-making process of this visit and the next.

(5) Obligation

Obligation is the function that must be implemented before visiting or during visiting, marked as B. What obligation should be fulfilled will be not statically set up by the system administrator in advance, and it is dynamically selected according to subject attributes and object attributes. The implementation of obligation may also update the variable attributes of the entities, which will also impact on the decision-making process of this visit and the next.

(6) Condition

Condition is the decision-making factor objected-condition and system, marked as C. Condition assesses the current hardware environment or relevant system limitations to decide whether or not to meet the user request. Conditions assessment doesn't change any subject attributes or object attributes.

2.2 Cloud Services Access Control Based UCON

2.2.1 Nego-UCON$_{ABC}$ Model

In UCON$_{ABC}$, authorization bases on attributes, obligations and conditions. Attributes are often provided in form of the digital certificate by which issuer declares the

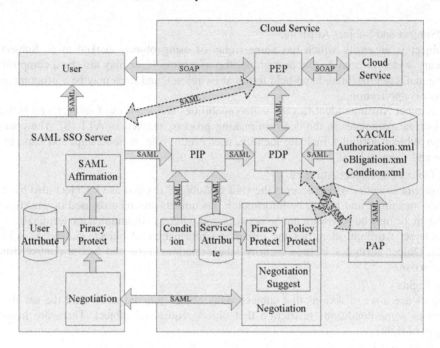

Fig. 2. Nego-UCON$_{ABC}$ model

attributes that an entity has. Obligations are storage in policy DB as rules in XACML [6]. Conditions will be obtained through the operating environment and be storied in policy DB as rules in XACML.

Besides, negotiation module is applied in model in order to enhance flexibility of cloud service access control. When access request mismatches with access rules, it allows user to get a second access choice through negotiation in certain circumstances, in stead of refusing access directly. That is, user can get chance to access through changing certain parameters and attributes in the negotiation process.

Authorization of UCON model bases on entity's attributes and access policies, but sometimes these attributes and policies are sensitive and need to be protected. And we need consider the protection of these sensitive attributes and policies in negotiation. Figure 2 is Nego-UCON$_{ABC}$ model bases on UCON$_{ABC}$ and negotiation.

Figure 2 includes three parts: Cloud user, SAML server and Cloud service. Cloud user is the initiator in service request. And SAML Server part includes three modules: SAML assertion module, sensitive attributes protection module and negotiation module. SAML assertion module mainly issues assertions and responses to assertions requests. Sensitive attributes protection module used to protect user's sensitive attributes and will be called when SAML issues assertion, and then attributes will be exposed according to the privacy polices. Negotiation module is used to negotiate with cloud server for attributes, obligations and conditions.

Cloud service part includes seven modules: Cloud service, PEP, PDP, PIP, PAP, XACML policy DB and negotiation module. Cloud service is the service provider. PEP is the policy enforcement point, and it accepts user's requests, and then executes decision of PDP. PDP is the policy decision point, it make authorization decision based on ABC policies according to the entity attributes, obligations, conditions. PIP is the policy information point, it get entity attributes and conditions and provides them to PDP for making decision. PAP is policy administration point, and it makes and manages polices. XACML policy DB stores ABC polices, and polices are expressed in extensible access control markup Language in it. Negotiation module is used to negotiate with cloud user for attributes, obligations and conditions.

2.2.2 Nego Module

Nego module is added for enhancing flexibility of access control model. When user attributes are insufficient or condition parameters are inconsistent, the negotiation module will run. Nego module is shown in Figure 3. The whole module running process is divided into three negotiation levels: attributes query, attributes automatic negotiation [7] and artificial negotiation. Attribute query will start querying user's attribute when attributes are insufficient, and negotiation will end if getting the wanted attributes. Otherwise attribute automatic negotiation will run, this negotiation level will help get the wanted attributes according to attributes privacy polices of both sides, and negotiation will end if getting the wanted attributes. And if attribute automatic negotiation even has no result, cloud service will want user to participate in artificial negotiation, and cloud service will send negotiation suggestions to user firstly, then user will adjust his privacy policy for providing his attributes or change his conditions requests to meet demand of visit cloud service.

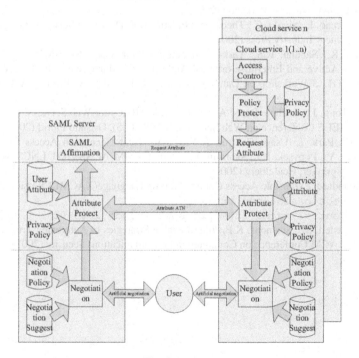

Fig. 3. Nego module

Nego module mainly includes two parts: SAML server and Cloud service.

SAML server part has three modules: SAML assertion, attribute protect and negotiation. SAML module response the requests of user attribute from cloud service, and attribute protect module protects privacy attribute during attributes automatic negotiation, and negotiation module provides the third way to visit cloud service by artificial negotiation.

Correspondingly, Cloud service part has three modules: Policy Protect, Attribute Protect and negotiation. Policy protect module protects privacy policy which decides the safe query sequence of attribute, and attribute protect module and negotiation modules have the same function to those of SAML server part.

3 Summary

This paper gives the cloud service security solution, and makes a research on cloud service access control model based UCON and negotiation. The next work that we will do is to realize the cloud service security prototype system.

References

1. Foster, I., Zhao, Y.: Cloud Computing and Grid Computing 360-Degree Compared. In: Grid Computing Environments Workshop (2008)
2. ning, G., jiamao, L., xiaolu, C.: Theory and Practice R & D of Web Services, January 2006, p. 10. Machinery Industry Press (2006)
3. Thomas, R.K., Sandhu, R.S.: Task-based Authorization Controls(TBAC): A Family of Models for Active and Enterprise-oriented Authorization Management. In: Proceedings of the IFIP WG11.3 Workshop on Database Security, Lake Tahoe, California, August 11-13 (1997)
4. Yuan, E., Tong, J.: Attribute Based Access Control (ABAC) for Web Services. In: Proceedings of the IEEE Conference on Web Services (ICWS 2005). Orlando Florid (2005)
5. Sandhu, R., Park, J.: Usage Control: A Vision for Next Generation Access Control. In: Gorodetsky, V., Popyack, L.J., Skormin, V.A. (eds.) MMM-ACNS 2003. LNCS, vol. 2776, pp. 17–31. Springer, Heidelberg (2003)
6. OASIS Standard. eXtensible Access Control Markup Language(XACML) Version 2.0[OL], http://docs.oasis-open.org/xacml/2.0/ access_control-xacml-2.0-core-spec-os.pdf,2005-02
7. Yu, T., Winslett, M., Seamons, K.E.: Interoperable Strategies in Automated Trust Negotiation. In: 8th ACM Conference on Computer and Communications Security (2001)

Replica Replacement Strategy Evaluation Based on Grid Locality

Lihua Ai and Siwei Luo

School of Computer and Information Technology, Beijing Jiaotong University, China
{lhai,swluo}@bjtu.edu.cn

Abstract. It is highly needed on grid environment to have a high degree of data reuse to increase the performance of grid computing. We present a measure of grid locality to identify the degree of data reuse. The measure of grid locality unifies composite factors such as hit ratio, storage buffer size, and network transmission rate. The measure is applied to the evaluation of replica replacement strategy utilized in grid environment. Experiments show that the grid locality measure can evaluate the influence conducted by replica replacement strategy effectively.

Keywords: data grid, grid locality, evaluation, replica replacement strategy, data reuse.

1 Introduction

With the increasing performance of network infrastructures, high performance computing and distributed resources sharing have obtained a promising development prospects. Grid computing [1] is trying to combine all above to solve the related internet ranges of services, computing, and data share. Data grids have been adopted as the next generation platform by many scientific communities that need to share, access, transport, process, and manage large data collections distributed worldwide [2].

In data grids application, the degree of data reuse could affect grids performance significantly. The higher degree of data reuse, the less network traffic is consumed. And the better assurance is to performance enhancement. Besides the potential data reusability of applications specific, replica replacement strategies also play a great role in affecting the degree of data reusability. Therefore, it is necessary to find a measure appropriate for grid environment to evaluate the degree of data reuse, and apply it to evaluate replica replacement strategy in further.

In this paper, we focus on the degree of data reuse and present a concept of grid locality to characterize that degree. We use grid locality to reflect the mixed impact invoked by buffer size, network bandwidth, file size, replica replacement strategy and job scheduling rule. In further, we propose a metric of grid locality to quantify the degree of data reuse. To our best knowledge, no such measure has been presented yet.

M.G. Jaatun, G. Zhao, and C. Rong (Eds.): CloudCom 2009, LNCS 5931, pp. 565–570, 2009.

2 Related Works

Locality of reference has long been observed that each time a page is referenced by a program, the next page to be referenced is very likely to come from some small set of pages. P.J. Denning [3] proposes a working set idea to assist in exploiting the locality degree of a program. This enables operating system to decide which information is in use by processes and which is not. Such knowledge is vital for dynamic management of paged memories. Further, P.J. Denning points that the chief problem in memory management of computers is deciding which pages ought to be removed or replaced. It is known that LRU (Least Recently Used) has been historically utilized as replacement algorithm because it exploits the property of locality in references.

As we can see that locality is exploited on program level involving in instructions and operands. Recently, researchers are trying to construct a virtual computing platform based on grid. The computing platform is migrating from host to grid environment. However, the properties of grid environment are much different from those of host environment. Therefore, it needs new solutions to exploit the locality and the metric evaluating the locality degree appropriate the changed environment.

Funded under the European DataGrid and UK GridPP projects, Bell W.H. et al. [4] propose a replacement algorithm based on economic model (referred to as Eco) for grid environment. They use a prediction function for estimating the future revenue of data files. That value predicts the number of times the data file will be requested in a time window in future. It is assumed that the file access history can be represented by a random walk in the space of files. In the random walk, the identifier of the next requested file is obtained from the current identifier by the addition of a step, the value of which is given by a binomial distribution. This Eco model defines a rule for data files replacement and is compared with traditional LRU (Least Recently Used) algorithm by OptorSim (Bell W.H. et al [5]).

To some extent, Bell W.H. et al. propose a strategy to exploit the locality among data files required by a grid job, which represents the locality degree of data files level. And that is a part of the grid locality we define in this article.

As for the program locality measure research, Richard B. Bunt et al. [6] consider the mean number of consecutive references to a page and a derived value from the Bradford-Zipf distribution as the program locality metric. Where, the two parameters reflect the persistence and concentration aspect of locality respectively.

Cherkasova.L et al. [7] introduce a measure of temporal locality, the scaled stack distance, which captures the impact of short-term correlation in web requests. They combine this quantity with file frequency and size to generate synthetic web traces for web server performance analysis studies.

Our contribution is to present a measure of locality in grid environment so that the intrinsic locality can be quantitative. It is important to evaluate the replica replacement strategy and job scheduling rule. Even though the grid locality is impacted by synthesized factors such as buffer size, network bandwidth, file size, replica replacement strategy and job scheduling rule. In this paper, we focus on the evaluation of the replica replacement strategy.

3 Grid Locality and Measure

Grid locality is different from program locality explored in both instruction and data level. Grid locality is explored among job, file, and network level.

3.1 Grid locality Concept and Influence Analysis

Definition 1. Grid locality consists of grid jobs assignment locality, files access locality and network locality.

In grid environment, each grid job may require some data files labeled as $\{f_1, f_2, ..., f_n\}$. During execution, job X generates a file reference stream of $r_1, r_2, ... , r_{t-1}, r_t, r_{t+1} ,...$ where $r_t = f_i$, t is the start time. And $\{r_i; i=1, 2,...\}$ could be assumed as i.i.d. random variables sequence. Further,

$$\Pr(r_t = f_i) = \beta_i \ and \ \sum_{i=1}^{n} \beta_i = 1$$

Here, β_i is the probability value of accessed file f_i.

Definition 2. A job j assigned to grid node q occurred at time t, which qualifies as grid job assignment locality if there is a job j assignment to the same grid node q again at time t', where $t' \le t+\delta$, and δ is a preset small time value.

The job level locality should be highly considerate during job schedule.

Definition 3. A file f referenced occurred at time t, which qualifies as files access locality if there is a reference to f again at time t', where $t' \le t+\varepsilon$, and ε is a preset small time value.

The file locality should be cared for when replica is replaced.

Definition 4. The fact that files are always fetched from the alternative grid node with the maximum network bandwidth is called network locality.

When there is a miss fault invoked by a file requirement of a grid job, network level locality should be considered of fetching a replica from alternative grid nodes.

Data grids would be benefit at good grid locality. With good grid locality, there would be lower data files miss ratio, less network traffic to get data replica, even approximate to zero time of local file accessed. Grid locality is influenced by composite factors including the application specific intrinsic locality, storage buffer size, network bandwidth, file size, replica replacement strategy and job scheduling rule. Next, the hit probability analysis will be given.

The storage files set S of a grid node is made up of recently used files set U and potentially replaced files set R, where $S=U \cup R$. The number of files in set U is $k=|f_i \in U|$, while the number of files in set R is $m=|f_i \in R|$. The probability of file access hit for grid job j at time t is:

$$P_h(r_t \mid (X(t) = j)) = \sum_{i=1}^{k} \beta_i \cdot \overline{(X_i \oplus j)} + \sum_{i=k+1}^{k+m} \left(\frac{m-1}{m}\right)^{i-k} \cdot \beta_i \overline{(X_i \oplus j)} \tag{1}$$

Here $\beta_i=Pr(f_i)$ and f_i is one of data files required by job X_i. Both the storage buffer size and file size impact the value of k and m. If having good file access locality, job X could get the hit probability during execution as follow:

$$P_h\big(r_t\mid(X(t-1)=j)\wedge(X(t)=j)\big)=\sum_{i=1}^{k}\beta_i+\sum_{i=k+1}^{k+m}\left(\frac{m-1}{m}\right)^{i-k}\cdot\beta_i\overline{(X_i\oplus j)}\tag{2}$$

Both the intrinsic locality of application specific and replica replacement strategy will contribute to this higher hit probability. At the shift of grid job for a grid node, such as from job j to job j', file access locality could be significantly affected if files set F_j required by job j is wholly different from files set $F_{j'}$ required by job j', that is $F_j\cap F_{j'}=\varnothing$. In such case, the hit probability could be:

$$P_h\big(r_t\mid(X(t-1)=j)\wedge(X(t)=j')\big)=\sum_{i=k+1}^{k+m}\left(\frac{m-1}{m}\right)^{i-k}\cdot\beta_i\overline{(X_i\oplus j)}\tag{3}$$

In order to avoid penalty time of files loaded at grid job shift as possible, job schedule should be designed carefully. At the same time network bandwidth should be considered in fetching of the miss file from alternative grid nodes.

3.2 Measure of Grid Locality

We use the degree of grid locality (DoGL) as a metric of grid locality. DoGL is expressed as the product of *hitRatio* and *averageTransRate*, which are file hit ratio and average transmission rate for fetching the miss file, respectively. That is:

$$DoGL = hitRatio\times averageTransRate\tag{4}$$

The *hitRatio* results from the interaction among the application specific intrinsic locality, storage buffer size, replica replacement algorithm, file size and job schedule. The higher *hitRatio*, the more local access instead of remote access is. On the other hand, the *averageTransRate* for fetching the miss file relates to available network bandwidth. The bigger network bandwidth, the less miss penalty spends. Therefore, the better DoGL is.

We can further replace *averageTransRate* with average miss file size, marked as *averageMissFileSize*, divided by the correspondent miss penalty, written as *missPenalty*. We then transform the above (4) to (5):

$$DoGL = hitRatio\times\frac{averageMissFileSize}{missPenalty}\tag{5}$$

As the *averageMissFileSize* is proportional to miss ratio, we can obtain the ratio of grid locality for the same application in two synthetic environments as follow:

$$\frac{DoGL_1}{DoGL_2}=\frac{missRatio_1}{missRatio_2}\times\frac{hitRatio_1}{hitRatio_2}\times\frac{missPenalty_2}{missPenalty_1}\tag{6}$$

The measure of grid locality is very important for evaluation of the impact by strategies such as replica replacement.

4 Experiment and Conclusion

We evaluate replica replacement strategy based on grid locality. Two parameters, Mean Job Time of all Jobs and data files miss ratio, can be obtained by Optorsim.

4.1 Simulation Configuration and Results

The grid topology is that of the CMS testbed which consists of 8 routers and 20 grid nodes. In the CMS configuration, each grid site is allocated a computing element and a storage element with capacity of 50GB. In our test, CERN acts as storage repositories: a master copy of each file is stored. Each job process time is 100000ms. The categories of users available are CMS DC04 users.

As we focus on replica replacement strategy, the scheduling algorithm affecting on job locality is fixed on the access cost plus queue cost scheduler. However, the files access patterns affecting on file locality intrinsically is alternative in sequential(SEQ), random walk unitary(WALK), and random walk Gaussian(GAUSS) access generator. The choice of file replacement rule influencing grid locality is alternative in LRU and Eco.

As 1000 jobs are submitted to grid nodes and the size of each accessed file is 1GB, we get Mean Job Time of all Jobs on Grid and file miss ratio as figure1, including both (a) and (b). The *missPenalty* can be calculated from the difference between Mean Job Time and job process time. According to (6), $DoGL_{LRU}/DoGL_{Eco}$ can be obtained as table1. If the $DoGL_{LRU}/DoGL_{Eco} = 1$, that means the compared replica replacement strategy have the same performance. The higher it is, the better LRU is.

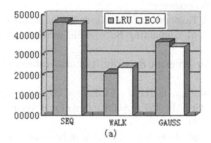 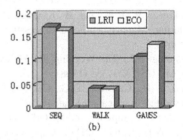

Fig. 1. For 1000 jobs (a) Mean Job Time of all jobs on Grid (Time (s)); (b) File miss ratio

Table 1. $DoGL_{LRU}/DoGL_{Eco}$ (for 1000 jobs)

	SEQ	WALK	GAUSS
$DoGL_{LRU}/DoGL_{Eco}$	1.0156	1.2266	0.7833

4.2 Performance Evaluation

An ordinary grid user would want the fastest possible turnaround time for his jobs and thus consider Mean Job Execution Time the most important evaluation metric. However, the file miss ratio, defined as the ratio of the number of remote file accesses to the number of total file access, may be a puzzle to evaluation. As the miss ratio is not always proportional to the Mean Job Execution Time. Luckily enough, the grid locality measure $DoGL_{LRU}/DoGL_{Eco}$ can unify them and give a reasonable rank for LRU and Eco.

As table1 shows, Eco has a better performance when the application specific file reference trends to random walk Gaussian distribution. Both LRU and Eco have similar performance as the application file access sequentially. And when the application specific locality is good enough, as it conforms to random walk unitary, LRU performs better than Eco.

4.3 Conclusion

Grid locality affects the performance of grid computing. File access pattern embodies the potential locality of application specific. Either LRU or Eco exploits files level locality. The measure of grid locality can evaluate replica replacement strategies, thus an appropriate replica replacement strategy could be adopted corresponding to the environment. Although we only focus on the replica replacement strategy evaluation in the paper, the impact to grid locality invoked by job schedule can be also be evaluated.

References

[1] Foster, I., Kesselman, C., Nicl, J., et al.: The Physiology of the Grid: An Open Grid Services Architecture for Distributed Systems Integration (January 2002),
   http://www.globus.org/research/papers/ogsa.pdf
[2] Srikumar, V., Rajkumar, B., Kotagiri, R.: A Taxonomy of Data Grids for Distributed Data Sharing, Management, and Processing. ACM Computing Surveys 38, article 3 (March 2006)
[3] Denning, P.J.: The Working Set Model for Program Behavior. Communications of the ACM 11(5), 323–333 (1968)
[4] Bell, W.H., Cameron, D.G., Carvajal-Schiaffino, R., et al.: Evaluation of an Economy-Based File Replication Strategy for a Data Grid. In: IEEE/ACM International Symposium on Cluster Computing and the Grid, pp. 661–668 (2003)
[5] Bell, W.H., Cameron, D.G., Capozza, L., et al.: Optorsim: A Grid Simulator for Studying Dynamic Data Replication Strategy. International Journal of High Performance Computing Applications 17(4), 403–416 (2003)
[6] Bunt, R.B., Murphy, J.M., Majumdar, S.: A Measure of Program Locality and Its Application. In: Proceedings of the 1984 ACM SIGMETRIC Conference on Measurement and Modeling of Computer Systems, January 1984, pp. 28–40 (1984)
[7] Cherkasova, L., Ciardo, G.: Characterizing Temporal Locality and its Impact on Web Server Performance. In: Proceedings of ICCCN (October 2000)

Performance Evaluation of Cloud Service Considering Fault Recovery

Bo Yang[1], Feng Tan[2], Yuan-Shun Dai[3], and Suchang Guo[2]

[1] Collaborative Autonomic Computing Laboratory, University of Electronic Science and Technology of China, Chengdu, China
yangbo@uestc.edu.cn
[2] Department of Industrial Engineering, University of Electronic Science and Technology of China, Chengdu, China
tf.uestc@gmail.com, schguo@uestc.edu.cn
[3] Innovative Computing Laboratory, Department of Electrical Engineering & Computer Science, University of Tennessee, Knoxville, USA
ydai1@eecs.utk.edu

Abstract. In cloud computing, cloud service performance is an important issue. To improve cloud service reliability, fault recovery may be used. However, the use of fault recovery could have impact on the performance of cloud service. In this paper, we conduct a preliminary study on this issue. Cloud service performance is quantified by service response time, whose probability density function as well as the mean is derived.

Keywords: Cloud service, performance evaluation, fault recovery.

1 Introduction

In recent years, new computing paradigms have been proposed and adopted such as cloud computing. Cloud computing refers to both the applications delivered as services over the Internet and the hardware and systems software in the datacenters that provide those services [1].

For cloud service, two issues are of great importance, the reliability and the performance of cloud service. Cloud service reliability is concerned with how probable that the cloud can successfully provide the service requested by users. Cloud service performance, on the other hand, is concerned with how fast the cloud can provide the requested service.

In cloud computing, fault recovery, one of the fault tolerance techniques, may be used to improve cloud service reliability [2]. Nevertheless, the use of fault recovery could have impact on the performance of cloud service. In this paper, we study this issue in detail, and we consider only the situation where the cloud can successfully provide the requested service, because research on cloud service reliability is out of the scope of this paper.

M.G. Jaatun, G. Zhao, and C. Rong (Eds.): CloudCom 2009, LNCS 5931, pp. 571–576, 2009.
© Springer-Verlag Berlin Heidelberg 2009

2 Service Response Time Modeling

When a user submits a service request to the cloud, the request will first arrive at the *cloud management system* (CMS) which maintains a request queue. If the queue is not full, the request will enter the queue; otherwise it will be dropped and the requested service fails. A request that successfully enters the queue will then reach a *scheduler* which will divide the request into several subtasks and assign the subtasks to different processing nodes (nodes). Generally there are multiple schedulers which are homogeneous with similar structures, schemes and equipments, to serve the requests.

After all subtasks are assigned to corresponding nodes, they will be executed on the nodes. During the execution of subtasks, there may be exchange of data through communication channels. After all subtasks are completed, the results are returned and integrated into a final output, which is sent to the user.

It is thus clear that the *service response time*, T_{SRT}, is given by

$$T_{SRT} = T_{SUB} + T_W + T_S + T_E + T_R, \tag{1}$$

where T_{SUB} is the *submission time* (the time period from the user's initiating a service request until the request arrives at the CMS); T_W is the *waiting time* (the time period from a request's arrival at the CMS until it begins to be served); T_S is the *service time*; T_E is the *total execution time* of the service (which will be explained in detail later); and T_R is the *return time* (the time spent in obtaining results from subtasks, integrating them, and sending the final output to the user).

In this paper, we assume that T_{SUB} and T_R are negligible. Thus (1) can be rewritten as

$$T_{SRT} = T_W + T_S + T_E. \tag{2}$$

We further assume T_W, T_S and T_E are statistically independent (*s*-independent).

2.1 Waiting Time and Service Time

Assume that the service requests arrive at the CMS according a Poisson process with arrival rate λ_a, and the service times of the requests are identical independently distributed (i.i.d.) random variables (r.v.'s) following exponential distribution with parameter μ_r (service rate). Assume that there are S ($S \geq 1$) homogeneous schedulers. Denote by N ($N \geq S$) the system capacity, i.e., the maximum allowed number of requests in the queueing system (including the ones waiting in the queue).

Denote by p_j ($j = 0,1,\cdots,N$) the steady-state probability that there are j requests in the system, then from standard queueing theory we have

$$p_j = \left[\sum_{i=0}^{S-1} \frac{\rho^i}{i!} + \sum_{i=S}^{N} \frac{\rho^i}{S!S^{i-S}} \right]^{-1} (j=0); \frac{\rho^j}{j!} p_0 (1 \leq j < S); \frac{\rho^j}{S!S^{j-S}} p_0 (S \leq j \leq N), \tag{3}$$

where $\rho \equiv \dfrac{\lambda_a}{\mu_r}$.

When a new request arrives, it may or may not enter the queue. For those requests which actually enter the queue, the steady-state probability that a request finds j requests (excluding itself) in the system, denoted by q_j, is

$$q_j = \frac{p_j}{1 - p_N}, \quad j = 0, 1, \cdots, N - 1. \tag{4}$$

When a request enters the system, if there are j ($0 \le j \le S - 1$) requests in the system, then it will be served immediately, thus the waiting time $T_W = 0$. If there are j ($S \le j \le N - 1$) requests in the system, then the waiting time T_W follows gamma distribution of order $j - S + 1$ with scale parameter $\mu_r S$. Therefore, the cumulative distribution function (c.d.f.) of T_W is

$$F_{T_W}(t) \equiv \Pr\{T_W \le t\} = 0(t < 0); \sum_{j=0}^{S-1} q_j (t = 0); \sum_{j=0}^{S-1} q_j + \sum_{j=S}^{N-1} q_j \frac{\Gamma(j - S + 1, \mu_r St)}{\Gamma(j - S + 1)} (t > 0), \tag{5}$$

where $\Gamma(\eta) \equiv (\eta - 1)!$ for any positive integer η; and $\Gamma(\eta, u) \equiv \int_0^u x^{\eta-1} \exp(-x) dx$.

The probability density function (p.d.f.) of T_W is

$$f_{T_W}(t) = \sum_{j=S}^{N-1} q_j \frac{\mu_r S(\mu_r St)^{j-S}}{\Gamma(j - S + 1)} \exp(-\mu_r St), t \ge 0. \tag{6}$$

The mean of T_W is

$$E[T_W] = \sum_{j=S}^{N-1} q_j \frac{j - S + 1}{\mu_r S}. \tag{7}$$

The service time, T_S, follows exponential distribution with parameter $\mu_r S$.

2.2 Total Execution Time

Suppose a service request is divided into M ($M \ge 1$) subtasks, which are assigned to N ($N \ge 1$) nodes for execution. Suppose the i:th subtask is assigned to the j:th node. Denote by wp_i the workload of the i:th subtask, and denote by ps_j the processing speed of the j:th node, then the *required execution time*, denoted by τ_{ij}, is

$$\tau_{ij} = \frac{wp_i}{ps_j}, \quad i = 1, 2, \cdots, M, \quad j = 1, 2, \cdots, N. \tag{10}$$

However, when fault recovery is adopted, the *actual execution time*, denoted by T_{ij}, is different from τ_{ij}. When the subtask fails during execution, if the failure is recoverable, then after some time (recovery time), the node will resume the execution of this subtask. In this paper, we only consider the case in which all the failures are recoverable, since if there occurs any unrecoverable failure, the subtask will fail and thus the service fails, which is out of the scope of this paper.

Assume that the j:th node has a constant failure rate of λ_j. Denote by $N_j(t)$ the total number of failures that occurs on the j:th node during time interval $(0, t]$, then

$$\Pr\{N_j(t) = n\} = \frac{(\lambda_j t)^n}{n!} \exp(-\lambda_j t), \ n = 0,1,\cdots. \tag{11}$$

Denote by $TR_j^{(k)}$ the k:th recovery time on node j, and we assume that $TR_j^{(k)}$'s are i.i.d. exponential r.v.'s with parameter μ_j. The *total recovery time*, $TR_j(t)$, is

$$TR_j(t) = \sum_{k=1}^{N_j(t)} TR_j^{(k)}. \tag{12}$$

It can be seen that $TR_j(t)$ is a compound Poisson Process, whose mean is:

$$E[TR_j(t)] = \lambda_j t \cdot E[TR_j^{(k)}] = \frac{\lambda_j t}{\mu_j}. \tag{13}$$

Since the required execution time is τ_{ij}, we have

$$T_{ij} = \begin{cases} \tau_{ij} & N_j(\tau_{ij}) = 0 \\ \tau_{ij} + TR_j(\tau_{ij}) & N_j(\tau_{ij}) = 1,2,\cdots \end{cases} \tag{14}$$

To derive the distribution of T_{ij}, we need first obtain the distribution of $TR_j(\tau_{ij})$. If $N_j(\tau_{ij}) = n$ ($n = 1,2,\cdots$), then from (12) we know that $TR_j(\tau_{ij})$ follows gamma distribution of order n with scale parameter μ_j. Thus the c.d.f. of $TR_j(\tau_{ij})$ is

$$F_{TR_j(\tau_{ij})}(t) \equiv \Pr\{TR_j(\tau_{ij}) \le t\} = \sum_{n=1}^{\infty} \Pr\{N_j(\tau_{ij}) = n\} \frac{\Gamma(n, \mu_j t)}{\Gamma(n)}, t \ge 0. \tag{15}$$

From (11), we have

$$F_{TR_j(\tau_{ij})}(t) = \exp(-\lambda_j \tau_{ij}) \sum_{n=1}^{\infty} (\lambda_j \tau_{ij})^n \frac{\Gamma(n, \mu_j t)}{\Gamma(n+1)\Gamma(n)}, t \ge 0. \tag{16}$$

Therefore, from (14), the c.d.f. of T_{ij} is

$$F_{T_{ij}}(t) \equiv \Pr\{T_{ij} \le t\} = \Pr\{T_{ij} - \tau_{ij} \le \kappa_{ij}\} = \exp(-\lambda_j \tau_{ij}) \left[1 + \sum_{n=1}^{\infty} (\lambda_j \tau_{ij})^n \frac{\Gamma(n, \mu_j \kappa_{ij})}{\Gamma(n+1)\Gamma(n)} \right], t \ge \tau_{ij} \tag{17}$$

where $\kappa_{ij} \equiv t - \tau_{ij}$. The p.d.f. of T_{ij} is

$$f_{T_{ij}}(t) = \frac{\exp(-\lambda_j \tau_{ij} - \mu_j \kappa_{ij})}{\kappa_{ij}} \sum_{n=1}^{\infty} \frac{(\lambda_j \mu_j \tau_{ij} \kappa_{ij})^n}{\Gamma(n+1)\Gamma(n)}, t \ge \tau_{ij}. \tag{18}$$

From (13) and (14) we can obtain the mean of T_{ij}, which is

$$E[T_{ij}] = \tau_{ij}\left(1 + \frac{\lambda_j}{\mu_j}\right) - \tau_{ij}\frac{\lambda_j}{\mu_j}\exp(-\lambda_j\tau_{ij}).$$ (19)

During subtasks' execution, a subtask may need to exchange data with other subtasks being executed on remote nodes, thus communication time is involved. We assume that during the execution of a subtask, if the subtask needs to exchange data with another node for further execution, the subtask has to be paused and wait for the completion of data exchange. During the communication with the remote node, the subtask is idle. After data exchange is completed, the subtask resumes its execution.

Denote by $D(i)$ the set of communication channels that the i:th subtask uses to exchange data with remote nodes. Denote by c_{ik} the amount of data that the i:th subtask exchanges through the k:th communication channel which has a bandwidth of bw_k. Assume that during data exchange, communication channels will not fail, then the communication time of the i:th subtask through the k:th communication channel is

$$s_{ik} = \frac{c_{ik}}{bw_k}, \quad i = 1,2,\cdots,M, \quad k \in D(i).$$ (20)

The *total communication time* of the i:th subtask, denoted by y_i, is

$$y_i = \sum_{k \in D(i)} s_{ik}.$$ (21)

The *total execution time* of the i:th subtask, denoted by Z_{ij}, is thus given by

$$Z_{ij} = T_{ij} + y_i.$$ (22)

From (17), the c.d.f. of Z_{ij}, denoted by $F_{Z_{ij}}(t)$, can be easily derived. Its mean can also be easily derived from (19)

Since all subtasks are executed in parallel, the *total execution time* of the service, T_E, is the maximum of Z_{ij}'s. Assume that Z_{ij}'s are s-independent, then T_E has a maximum extreme-value distribution, whose c.d.f. and p.d.f. are respectively

$$F_{T_E}(t) = \prod_{i=1}^{M} F_{Z_{ij}}(t), \quad f_{T_E}(t) = \sum_{k=1}^{M} f_{Z_{kj}}(t) \prod_{1 \leq i \leq M, i \neq k} F_{Z_{ij}}(t).$$ (23)

The mean of T_E is

$$E[T_E] = \int_0^\infty \left[1 - \prod_{i=1}^{M} \int_0^x f_{Z_{ij}}(t)dt\right]dx.$$ (24)

2.3 Service Response Time

From (2), the mean of the service response time, T_{SRT}, is

$$E[T_{SRT}] = E[T_W] + \frac{1}{\mu_r S} + E[T_E],$$ (25)

where $E[T_W]$ and $E[T_E]$ are given by (7) and (24), respectively.

By the assumption that T_W, T_S and T_E are s-independent, the p.d.f. of T_{SRT} is

$$f_{T_{SRT}}(t) = f_{T_W}(t) \otimes f_{T_S}(t) \otimes f_{T_E}(t). \tag{26}$$

3 Conclusion

In this paper, we conduct a preliminary study on cloud service performance considering fault recovery. Cloud service performance is quantified by the service response time, whose probability density function as well as the mean is derived.

However, we have made several assumptions which may not be realistic, e.g., the s-independence. Moreover, fault recovery may be adopted for communication channels as well. We shall address these issues in our future work.

Acknowledgments. This work is supported by National Natural Science Foundation of China (No. 50805018) and Key Project of Chinese Ministry of Education (No. 109138).

References

1. Armbrust, M., Fox, A., Griffith, R., et al.: Above the clouds: A Berkeley view of cloud computing. Technical Report No. UCB/EECS-2009-28, University of California at Berkeley (2009)
2. Guo, S., Yang, B., Huang, H.Z.: Grid service reliability modeling on fault recovery and optimal task scheduling. In: Proceedings of the 55th Annual Reliability & Maintainability Symposium (RAMS 2009), Fort Worth, Texas, USA, January 2009, pp. 471–476 (2009)

BlueSky Cloud Framework: An E-Learning Framework Embracing Cloud Computing

Bo Dong[1,2], Qinghua Zheng[1,2], Mu Qiao[1,2], Jian Shu[3], and Jie Yang[1,2]

[1] MOE KLINNS Lab and SKLMS Lab, Xi'an Jiaotong University, China
[2] Department of Computer Science and Technology, Xi'an Jiaotong University, China
[3] IBM China Software Development Lab, China
dong.bo@mail.xjtu.edu.cn, qhzheng@mail.xjtu.edu.cn,
qiaomuf@gmail.com, shujian@cn.ibm.com, xtyangjie@gmail.com

Abstract. Currently, E-Learning has grown into a widely accepted way of learning. With the huge growth of users, services, education contents and resources, E-Learning systems are facing challenges of optimizing resource allocations, dealing with dynamic concurrency demands, handling rapid storage growth requirements and cost controlling. In this paper, an E-Learning framework based on cloud computing is presented, namely BlueSky cloud framework. Particularly, the architecture and core components of BlueSky cloud framework are introduced. In BlueSky cloud framework, physical machines are virtualized, and allocated on demand for E-Learning systems. Moreover, BlueSky cloud framework combines with traditional middleware functions (such as load balancing and data caching) to serve for E-Learning systems as a general architecture. It delivers reliable, scalable and cost-efficient services to E-Learning systems, and E-Learning organizations can establish systems through these services in a simple way. BlueSky cloud framework solves the challenges faced by E-Learning, and improves the performance, availability and scalability of E-Learning systems.

Keywords: cloud computing, E-Learning framework, virtualization, service orientation, automatic provision, data fabric.

1 Introduction

E-Learning is the acquisition and use of knowledge distributed and facilitated primarily by electronic means [1]. It is an innovative approach for delivering well-designed, learner-centered, interactive and facilitated learning environments to anyone, anyplace and anytime [2]. In recent years, E-Learning has grown into a widely accepted way of learning.

With the huge growth of users, services, education contents and resources, E-Learning systems become more and more large-scale. Massive machines are demanded to deal with the computation, storage and communication requirements. As a typical Internet application, an E-Learning system is facing challenges of optimizing resource management and provisioning, dealing with dynamic concurrency requests, meeting scalable storage demands and cost controlling.

M.G. Jaatun, G. Zhao, and C. Rong (Eds.): CloudCom 2009, LNCS 5931, pp. 577–582, 2009.
© Springer-Verlag Berlin Heidelberg 2009

Cloud computing has attracted significant attention over the past years. Cloud computing is a style of computing where massively scalable IT-related capabilities are provided "as a service" [3]. It reduces the coupling between resources and applications, improves resource utilization and enhances the availability and scalability of applications.

The main contribution of this paper is to introduce BlueSky cloud framework - a generic E-Learning framework based on cloud computing. In BlueSky cloud framework, technologies of cloud computing, load balancing and data caching are integrated to dynamically delivery massively reliable, scalable and cost-efficient IT enabled services for education purposes. This makes it realized to solve the troubles of low resource utilization and lack of scalability of E-Learning systems.

This paper is organized as follows. Section 2 describes the challenges of current E-Learning systems. Section 3 demonstrates the architecture and core components of BlueSky cloud framework, and Section 4 is the summary.

2   Challenges of Current E-Learning Systems

Currently, E-Learning systems are still weak on scalability at the infrastructure level. Most resources are deployed and assigned for some specific tasks or applications, and physical machines are usually stacked simply and exclusively. When receiving high workloads, an E-Learning system mainly deals with them by adding new resources. With the growth of resources, the overhead of resource management becomes a key issue with unacceptable increasing costs.

Moreover, the utilization of those resources is another problem. E-Learning systems often hold resources as many as those at their peak hours, even when some of them are idle. Meanwhile, education contents are various and grow rapidly in amount, requiring scalable storage capacity. Specifically, the requests to education contents follow highly dynamic rule. These issues affect the resource utilization to a great extent. Today servers typically achieve only 20%-40% processor utilization on a daily basis [4], and in the E-Learning domain the utilization is even worse.

Cloud computing has been a hot topic of computing paradigm. Cloud computing provides dynamically scalable infrastructure supplying computation, storage and communication capabilities as services. It renders users/applications with service interfaces to access those resources without knowing the detailed information. Cloud computing is the promising infrastructure which can provide tremendous values to E-Learning [5]. E-Learning organizations do not have to establish their own IT infrastructures, but build E-Learning systems through cloud services in a simple way.

3   BlueSky Cloud Framework

The aim of BlueSky cloud is to provide an E-Learning platform based on cloud computing for basic education throughout China. It combines cloud computing with traditional middleware features, and delivers reliable, scalable IT services, so as to enhance the performance, availability and scalability of E-Learning systems.

3.1 Design of BlueSky Cloud Framework

BlueSky cloud framework orients its aims at the following designs.

1. Virtualization of hardware and middleware

Virtualization technology is used to dispose hardware resources in fine granularity. Resources are virtualized as a resource pool, and are managed and maintained as a whole. Furthermore, uniform interfaces are supplied. Middleware are also virtualized.

2. Automatic deployment and resource provisioning

Resources are allocated to E-Learning systems according to the real-time demands. BlueSky cloud framework provides rapid and efficient resource provisioning automatically in response to the demand changes both up and down.

3. Dynamic cluster of runtime

E-Learning applications are deployed into dynamic clusters. At the runtime level, BlueSky cloud framework monitors the real-time workloads of applications, according to which, applications automatically obtain the required runtime environment (such as J2EE container and database) from BlueSky cloud.

4. Smart load balancing

Load balancing is introduced into cloud computing platform in BlueSky cloud framework. Load balancing routes the requests according to the real-time workloads. Different form traditional load balancing, when the load balancing component itself makes full use of its resources, it will apply more resources from the infrastructure smartly and automatically to ensure the efficiency of load balancing.

5. Data fabric

BlueSky cloud framework provides scalable and flexible data fabric. Data fabric disposes various data and provides effective management. When disposing structured data, data fabric constructs distributed data caching on the basis of cloud distributed environment to boost accesses. For unstructured data, it deals with storage tasks with distributed file systems. The data management policy is easy to extend.

3.2 Architecture of BlueSky Cloud Framework

BlueSky cloud framework is designed following the principles of SOA, and functions are encapsulated in the form of services. In detail, BlueSky cloud framework is composed of six layers, as is shown in Fig. 1.

User interface layer is the entry-point into BlueSky cloud. It provides function interfaces and interaction interfaces, including Web UIs and clients.

Application layer focuses on the logical presentation of education processes, and supplies a set of available E-Learning applications serving particular functional needs.

Common service layer provides reusable common services for higher layers, such as provision services, monitoring services, information services, account management services, and log management services. Services are encapsulated from the components of the capability layer.

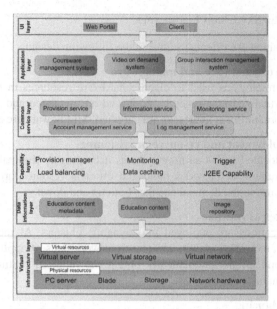

Fig. 1. The architecture of BlueSky cloud framework

Capability layer is made up of core components that provide specific types of capabilities. Those components include provision manager, monitoring, trigger and so on. They jointly manage and maintain the resource pool in the virtual infrastructure layer. Traditional middleware are also provided in this layer, including load balancing component and data caching component.

Data information layer provides functions of data fabric for persistence. It manages the storage of VM images and education contents (education content entities, metadata and so on).

Virtual infrastructure layer enhances the transparency of hardware by virtualization, and realizes fine-grained management of resources. There are two sub-layers in this layer. Physical machines are in the lower and virtualized as a resource pool in the upper. This layer eliminates the differences among physical machines and offers a basis to provision resources dynamically.

3.3 Core Components of BlueSky Cloud Framework

Capability layer, data information layer and virtual infrastructure layer are the core layers of BlueSky cloud framework. The relations between the constituent parts of the three layers are shown in Fig. 2.

Virtual resource pool is the core component in the virtual infrastructure layer. There are large numbers of physical machines, such as blades, storage equipments and network equipments in BlueSky cloud. Hypervisors [6] are deployed onto each physical node, and those machines are virtualized as a resource pool. Virtual resource pool supplies uniform management method and interfaces, supporting the of computation, storage and communication capabilities.

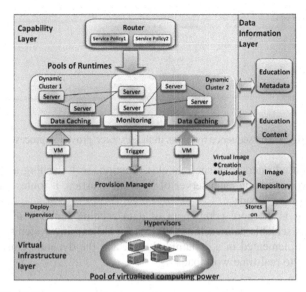

Fig. 2. The relations of the constituent parts in the three core layers

Image repository is one core component in the data information layer. There are various VM (virtual machine) images in the "requirement list" of E-Learning systems. Those images are stored and managed in the image repository.

Monitoring takes charge of monitoring the runtime status of E-Learning systems and setting up the thresholds of scheduling policy. Those thresholds are configured by specified response times, parameters of the runtime environment (CPU, memory percent utilization and so on). Once the thresholds are reached, monitoring will call trigger to start specified operations.

Trigger is one core component in the capability layer. On some specified conditions, E-Learning systems should be triggered to take certain operations. For example, once reaching its threshold of response time, an E-Learning system claims that more resources are needed, and certain operation should be triggered to apply for new resources. The operations are initiated by trigger in BlueSky cloud.

Provision manager takes charge of resource provisioning. E-Learning systems are deployed into servers of dynamic clusters. BlueSky cloud dynamically allocates resources for dynamic clusters in the form of VM image from image repository. Provision manager maintains the configuration, deployment information and runtime environment of images, and is invoked to apply or give back images. For instance, when allocating new VMs, provision manager chooses the right VM image according to the required configuration and deployment environment. Then the image is deployed to one or multiple hypervisors and configured as servers. After VMs join into the dynamic cluster as servers, systems will be deployed onto them. The whole progress takes place automatically, as shown in Fig.3. Furthermore, provision manager also provisions software and applications.

Router is the load balancing component in the capability layer. According to the features in the E-Learning domain, administrators institute service priorities and strategies for E-Learning systems on the router. On the basis of these strategies, router

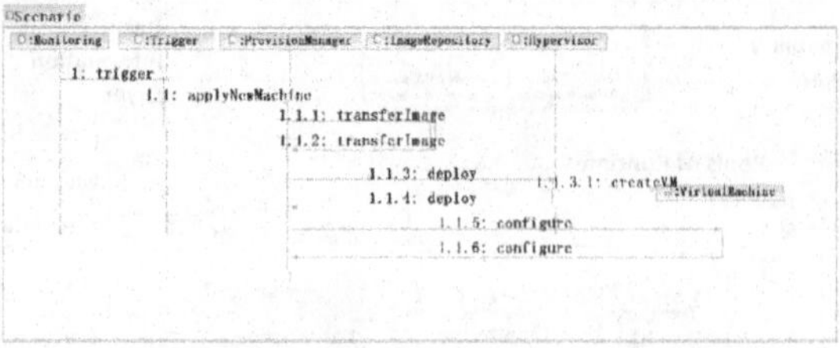

Fig. 3. The sequence relations in the resource provision process

carries out specified operations such as classification, sort, caching and forwarding. Based on the workloads on each server of dynamic clusters, it routes the requests to get the balance of workloads.

Data caching is the core component of data caching function in the capability layer. It provides scalable data caching services for E-Learning systems. Data caching component is implemented in a dynamic cluster, and the dynamic cluster expand or shrink according to real-time workloads.

4   Conclusion

In this paper, BlueSky cloud framework is proposed. It offers reliable and scalable IT services for E-Learning systems. E-Learning organizations can build systems through those services, and don't have to worry about issues such as system scalability and resource management. Specially, BlueSky cloud framework allocates resources on demand, which solves the dynamic workload problem of E-Learning systems. These improve the performance, availability and scalability of E-Learning systems.

Acknowledgements. This paper is supported by the NSFC (60825202, 60633020), the National High-Tech R&D Program of China (2008AA01Z131), and IBM SUR Project (Research on Transferring BlueSky System to Cloud Computing Platform).

References

1. Wentling, T., Waight, C., Gallaher, J., La Fleur, J., Wang, C., Kanfer, A.: E-Learning - A review of literature,
   http://learning.ncsa.uiuc.edu/papers/elearnlit.pdf
2. Khan, B.H.: Learning Features in an Open, Flexible, and Distributed Environment. AACE Journal 13(2), 137–153 (2005)
3. Gartner says cloud computing will be as influential as E-business,
   http://www.gartner.com/it/page.jsp?id=707508
4. EMC Corporation: Deploying a Virtual Infrastructure for SAP with EMC and VMware Technologies,
   http://www.vmware.com/files/pdf/
   deploying_vi_sap_emc_vmware_tech.pdf
5. Dong, B., Zheng, Q., Yang, J., Li, H., Qiao, M.: An E-learning Ecosystem Based on Cloud Computing Infrastructure. In: 9th IEEE International Conference on Advanced Learning Technologies, pp. 125–127. IEEE Press, Latvia (2009)
6. Hypervisor wiki, http://en.wikipedia.org/wiki/Hypervisor

Cloud Infrastructure & Applications – CloudIA

Anthony Sulistio, Christoph Reich, and Frank Doelitzscher

Department of Computer Science
Hochschule Furtwangen University, Germany
{anthony.sulistio,christoph.reich,
frank.doelitzscher}@hs-furtwangen.de

Abstract. The idea behind Cloud Computing is to deliver Infrastructure-as-a-Services and Software-as-a-Service over the Internet on an easy pay-per-use business model. To harness the potentials of Cloud Computing for e-Learning and research purposes, and to small- and medium-sized enterprises, the Hochschule Furtwangen University establishes a new project, called Cloud Infrastructure & Applications (CloudIA). The CloudIA project is a market-oriented cloud infrastructure that leverages different virtualization technologies, by supporting Service-Level Agreements for various service offerings. This paper describes the CloudIA project in details and mentions our early experiences in building a private cloud using an existing infrastructure.

1 Introduction

Although Cloud Computing is a popular trend, it is difficult to get a clear definition of it. Ian et al. [1] discuss the basic concepts of Cloud Computing and show the differences compared to Grid Computing. The key of Cloud Computing lies in its component-based nature, i.e. reusability, substitutability (e.g. alternative implementations, specialized interfaces and runtime component replacements), extensibility, customizability and scalability [2]. In addition, Armbrust et al. [3] give a good overview of Cloud Computing by highlighting obstacles and proposing several opportunities to solve them.

From our point of view, Cloud Computing delivers Infrastructure- and Software-as-a-Service (IaaS and SaaS) on a simple pay-per-use basis. For small- and medium-sized enterprises (SMEs), Cloud Computing enables them to avoid over-provisioning of IT infrastructure and training personnel. Thus, SMEs can take advantage of using a cloud when the IT capacity needs to be increased on the fly. Typically, more resources are needed for services that are available only for a certain period. For example, AF83, a company specializing in social networking and live web solutions, uses Amazon IT infrastructure to deliver a live concert via the web and mobile devices [4]. The concert attracted 7,000 simultaneous users. By using Cloud Computing, AF83 avoids purchasing new hardware for this special event, and delivers this successful event in a short amount of time.

For companies with large IT infrastructure, such as Amazon and Google, becoming a cloud provider allow them to offer their resources to SMEs based on pay-as-you-go and subscription models, respectively. Because not all services need the full resources at the same time for a long period of time, these companies can still use and lease their existing infrastructure with a relatively small cost. Hence, they can reduce the total cost of ownership (TCO) and increase hardware utilization [3].

M.G. Jaatun, G. Zhao, and C. Rong (Eds.): CloudCom 2009, LNCS 5931, pp. 583–588, 2009.
© Springer-Verlag Berlin Heidelberg 2009

In a typical university scenario, PC labs and servers are under-utilized during the night and semester breaks. In addition, these resources are on high demands mainly towards the end of a semester. With the aforementioned motivations and scenarios, the Hochschule Furtwangen University (HFU) acknowledges the potential benefits of Cloud Computing. As a result, HFU establishes a new project called Cloud Infrastructure and Application (CloudIA). The targeted users of the CloudIA project are SMEs and HFU staff and students, running e-Science and e-Learning applications. Such use case scenarios are analyzing third party software, software testing and offering a custom-made SaaS. Therefore, in this paper, we introduce our work in building a private cloud in order to support various Quality of Service (QoS) objectives, such as availability, reliability, and security.

The rest of this paper is organized as follows. Section 2 explains the CloudIA project and its architecture. Section 3 shows the potential usage of the CloudIA project, by providing several use case scenarios, whereas Section 4 describes a servlet container application, running on our cloud infrastructure and Amazon. Section 5 mentions our early experiences in building a private cloud. Finally, Section 6 concludes the paper and gives future work.

2   The CloudIA Project

To harness the potentials of Cloud Computing for internal usages, and to SMEs, the CloudIA project is established. The main objective of this project is to build a private cloud for the purpose of running e-Science and e-Learning applications. The overview of the CloudIA architecture is shown in Figure 1.

CloudIA leverages various virtualization technologies, such as Xen [5] and KVM [6], and supports Service-Level Agreements (SLAs) as IaaS and SaaS models, as shown in Figure 2. In this figure, the Cloud Management System (CMS) of CloudIA is divided into several layers for extensibility and maintainability. The descriptions of each layer are as followed:

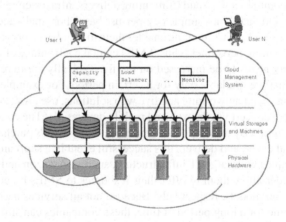

Fig. 1. Overview of the CloudIA architecture

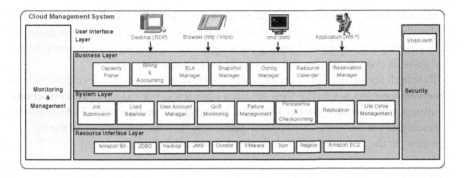

Fig. 2. Cloud Management System of CloudIA

- **User Interface Layer:** This layer provides various access points to users and/or an administrator of the CMS in accessing our cloud system.
- **Business Layer:** This layer aims to regulate resource supply and demand through the use of economy and SLA. In addition, this layer enables users to reserve VMs in advance and manage their personal VMs.
- **System Layer:** This layer is responsible for daily operation of the CMS, such as submitting jobs, managing user accounts and monitoring QoS.
- **Resource Interface Layer:** This layer deals with the physical hardware and hosts many interfaces and plugins to various virtualization, database, distributed system and other technologies, such as Xen, Amazon EC2 and S3, and Nagios [7].
- **Monitoring & Management Component:** To ensure the reliability of each layer in the system, a monitoring and management component is needed. Thus, this component allows system administrator to monitor and to initiate activities of each layer, in case of failures, conflicts with SLA objectives, under- or over-utilized resources.
- **Security Component:** To ensure the privacy, recovery, integrity and security of user data and transactions, a security feature on all layers is required. Besides the technical solutions, issues in areas such as regulatory compliance and data auditing are important. Therefore, this component is also addressing these issues.

3   Use Case Scenarios

To show the potential of the CloudIA project, use case scenarios for SMEs, e-Learning and research purposes are described below:

- **SME scenario:** There are many opportunities and advantages for SMEs in using Cloud Computing. For example, SMEs can leverage the CloudIA project for system and application testing. Software developers must test their software with different configurations on various operating systems. However, this scenario requires a huge machine farm to satisfy the testing environment. Therefore, SMEs can utilize Cloud Computing by acquiring various resources with different specifications on demand.
- **E-Learning scenario:** Many programming courses at HFU require students to have their own Java servlet environment for experimentation. In order to reduce a high

learning curve for students, a VM image containing MySQL, Tomcat, PHP, and Apache web server is created. With this approach, students can focus more on developing, deploying and testing their applications in a servlet container. More details on this servlet container can be found in Section 4.

– **Research scenario:** HFU works together with many research and development labs or companies in achieving their research objectives. For example, HFU offers its infrastructure to run parallel jobs of a holographic memory model. As a result, researchers at Thomson, a company specializing in communication and media, can minimize the running time of their simulation model significantly [8].

4   Cloud Application: Servlet Container for e-Learning Purposes

As mentioned earlier, many programming courses at HFU require students to have their own Java servlet environment for experimentation. With a cloud-enabled infrastructure, students are able to reserve VMs, e.g. for 100 hours with pre-defined packages and software for their courses. Since these VMs are running in isolation, IT administrator only need to develop a web front-end embedded in FELIX [9], a Learning Management System (LMS), for authentication purposes. Thus, to access these VMs, students only need to login to FELIX, as shown in Figure 3.

After authentication, the students are able to use servlet container VMs with the following functionalities:

– enables to start and stop servlet container instances, since they can only use these instances for a limited amount of time, e.g. 100 hours.
– saves and deletes snapshots of their work. A snapshot refers to the Tomcat and MySQL configuration details and data, such as war files and database tables.
– runs a VM with one of the saved snapshots.
– downloads snapshots to a local hard disk. Thus, students only need to send their snapshots for the project submission.

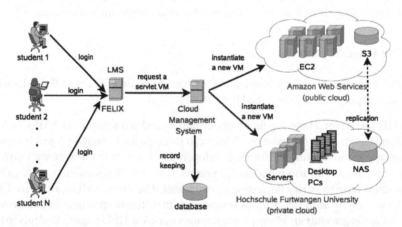

Fig. 3. High level overview of running the servlet container application on the cloud

By default, servlet container instances are running on HFU. However, if there are no servers or PCs available, then instances will be running in the public cloud, i.e. using Amazon's small EC2 instances, as shown in Figure 3. Once the students stop or shutdown their instances, only their snapshots are being saved. The VMs and/or Amazon Machine Images (AMIs) are deleted to save storage. Therefore, these snapshots are replicated between Amazon S3 and our internal network area storage (NAS). In addition, Amazon S3 stores a template AMI for the servlet container with the same basic configurations as the VM hosted on HFU.

By having a servlet container on the cloud, students can start working on their projects, instead of spending time on installing Apache web server, Tomcat and MySQL on their computers. The same scenario can also be applied to a tutor or lecturer for marking the projects. In addition, students can start a basic VM if they misconfigure the Tomcat and/or MySQL configuration details. Thus, for this application, Cloud Computing provides a fool-proof environment and enhances an e-Learning experience.

5   Early Experiences in Building a Cloud Infrastructure

Currently, many organizations are building their own private clouds from their existing infrastructure [3]. Our experiences and difficulties of building a cloud infrastructure are as followed:

- **Internal IT policies:** Our university has two departments which are responsible in maintaining and managing IT resources, i.e. IT and Computer Science departments. Each department has its own PC pools, data centers and secured network. Thus, with this separation, each department has their own firewall rules and IP subnets. We found that this is obstructive for building a cloud computing infrastructure using heterogeneous resources in the university. We later faced a problem of running out of IP addresses, due to the dynamic creation of virtual instances on the host PCs that belong to same subnet. As the network plays a critical role in the whole concept of Cloud Computing, an organization wanting to create a Private Cloud needs to be wary of the IT policies and practices deployed across internal divisions.
- **Running appropriate services and applications on the Cloud:** Hosting a particular service or running a legacy application on the Cloud can be counterproductive, i.e. slowing the application down. In addition, it consumes the whole physical resource. Thus, preventing other VMs running on the same resource. For example, our university's time table and room management software, TimeEdit [10] was tested on a VM on the HP ESX server. Although the hardware specification meets the requirement of running several virtual instances, TimeEdit was constantly consumed the available resource. This is because the underlying database of TimeEdit could not be efficiently run on a VM. Hence, it is important to monitor VM consumption periodically, and to run resource-intensive services and applications on dedicated machines.

6 Conclusion and Future Work

The idea behind Cloud Computing is to deliver Infrastructure-as-a-Services (IaaS) and Software-as-a-Service (SaaS) over the Internet on an easy pay-per-use business model. To harness the potentials of Cloud Computing for internal usages, and to small- and medium-sized enterprises, the Hochschule Furtwangen University establishes a Cloud Infrastructure & Application (CloudIA) project – a cloud infrastructure targeted towards e-Science and e-Learning applications. To show the potential of CloudIA, we describe several use case scenarios and early experiences in building a cloud infrastructure.

As for future work, a DNS server to enable the mapping of dynamic IP addresses to public names will be considered. In addition, we will examine the feasibility of moving existing services and e-Learning applications hosted on dedicated servers into the Cloud. Finally, a rule-based cloud monitoring component to control virtual machines' connection and interaction with other CloudIA components will be considered. In addition, the CloudIA project is in its early stages. Implementation and evaluation of the components described in this paper are work in progress. Thus, presentation of these results are considered as future work.

References

1. Foster, I., Zhao, Y., Raicu, I., Lu, S.: Cloud Computing and Grid Computing 360-Degree Compared. In: Proceedings of the Grid Computing Environments Workshop (GCE 2008), Austin, Texas, USA (November 16, 2008)
2. Vouk, M., Averritt, S., Bugaev, M., Kurth, A., Peeler, A., Schaffer, H., Sills, E., Stein, S., Thompson, J.: Powered by VCL – Using Virtual Computing Laboratory (VCL) Technology to Power Cloud Computing. In: Proceedings of the 2nd International Conference on the Virtual Computing Initiative (ICVCI 2008), May 16-17 (2008)
3. Armbrust, M., Fox, A., Griffith, R., Joseph, A.D., Katz, R., Konwinski, A., Lee, G., Patterson, D., Rabkin, A., Stoica, I., Zaharia, M.: Above the Clouds: A Berkeley View of Cloud Computing. Technical Report UCB/EECS-2009-28, Univ. of California at Berkeley (February 2009)
4. Amazon Web Services: AF83 Case Study (May 2009),
   http://aws.amazon.com/solutions/case-studies/af83/
5. Barham, P., Dragovic, B., Fraser, K., Hand, S., Harris, T., Ho, A., Neugebauer, R., Pratt, I., Warfield, A.: Xen and The Art of Virtualization. In: Proceedings of the 19th ACM Symposium on Operating Systems Principles (SOSP 2003), New York, USA, October 19-22 (2003)
6. Qumranet: KVM: White Paper (2006), http://www.linux-kvm.org/
7. Nagios (May 2009), http://www.nagios.org/
8. Eckhardt, M., Garwers, S., Ruebsamen, T., Stoeffelmaier, T., Zehnder, J., Reich, C.: Windows Desktop Grid. Technical Report CRL-2009-01, Hochschule Furtwangen University (January 2009)
9. HFU: Furtwangen E-Learning & Information eXchange (FELIX) (May 2009),
   https://felix2.hs-furtwangen.de
10. TimeEdit (May 2009), http://www.timeedit.com/

One Program Model for Cloud Computing

Guofu Zhou and Guoliang He

The State Key Laboratory of Software Engineering,
Wuhan University, Wuhan, Hubei 430072, China
gfzhou@whu.edu.cn

Abstract. Cloud computing is dynamically virtual scalable in which neither a central computing nor a central storage is provided. All resources are virtualized and provided as a service over the Internet. Therefore different to the traditional program, the cloud program shall be expressed in a new style. Based on one presented architecture of cloud computing, characteristics of program in "cloud", control, variable and operation, are discussed respectively. Accordingly, one program model for cloud computing is presented for the future formalization.

1 Introduction

Cloud computing is a style of computing in which dynamically scalable and often virtualized resources are provided as a service over the Internet[1,2]. Users need not have knowledge of, expertise in, or control over the technology infrastructure in the "cloud" that supports them[3]. The term "cloud" is used as a metaphor for Internet, based on how the Internet is depicted in computer network diagrams and is an abstraction for the complex infrastructure it conceals[4].

With the development of Internet, more and more applications[5,6] that rely on internet to satisfy the computing needs of users. And the application and data are stored on the servers behind "cloud".

Prof. Ramnath K. Chellappa thinks cloud computing is determined by economic rationale rather than technical limits[7]. And InfoWorld roughly presents what cloud computing is all about[5]: Software as a Service(SaaS), Utility Computing (UC) , Web service(WS), Platform as a Service(PaaS), Management service provider(MSP), Service commerce platforms(SCP), and Internet integration(II).

The idea of cloud computing is not new, In 90's, Oracle presented an architecture of Network Computer, and also supported by Apple, Sun, IBM and Netscape. Later in 1997, Microsoft and Intel together presented NetPC concept, and which is supported by Intel,HP,Dell,Compaq.

Furthermore, the form of cloud computing is getting new life from Amazon.com, Sun, IBM, and others who now offer storage and virtual servers that IT can access on demand. Cloud computing is different to both NetPC and NC in theory level. NetPC or NC is a computing entity, but cloud computing emphasize particularly on service.

Cloud computing create a new software mode based on the individual web-based service by collecting and integrating the internet sources. Therefore, cloud

M.G. Jaatun, G. Zhao, and C. Rong (Eds.): CloudCom 2009, LNCS 5931, pp. 589–594, 2009.

computing has a special features, principles and rules[8] different to the traditional computing model. Cloud computing has a clear boundary, economic or physical, which is a pool of resources, e.g., computing power or data center.

In the paper, we will present one framework for cloud computing in section 2. Control flow of program in cloud computing is discussed in section 3. Variable, operation and interaction are discussed in section 4. And in the last section, we will summarize the program model on the cloud computing framework.

2   System Model

The traditional computing model is on Turing. CPU, RAM, data and I/O device are connected through local high speed bus. However, the model of cloud computing is not based on Turing. In other words, in cloud computing, CPU, RAM and other I/O device are not integrated but distributed in the physical space.

Clouds can be classified into two basic group, computing (cloud) and data storage (cloud)(figure 1), which can be analogous to CPU and DISK respectively in the traditional PC .

In computing cloud, each CPU and RAM execute instruction as that in the traditional PC. Data storage cloud is a self-governing unit which is not passive as DISK(data storage device) of the traditional PC. Data storage cloud can do something for data, e.g., split the data and composite the data. Moreover, Computing cloud can communicate with data storage cloud through Internet.

Furthermore, cloud computing can fulfil a task by two models . one is the whole task is assigned to one single server, similar to the traditional computing model. The other one is the task is parallelized and assigned respectively to serval servers.

In the first model, Any task will be fulfilled finally in one single server. The task of cloud computing is only balance the computing workload and dispatch the the task to one server completely. Therefore, the architecture of program remains unchanged(see figure 2).

However, in the second model, a special architecture shall also be provided. Compared with the presented cloud ontology in [8], the five layers framework for cloud computing in figure 3 is more encapsulated .

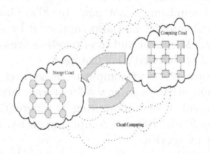

Fig. 1. Inside cloud

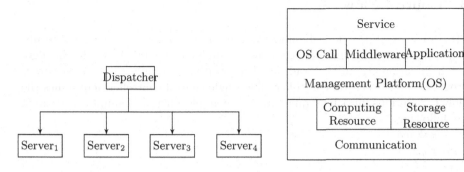

Fig. 2. Task balance   **Fig. 3.** Five layers Model

Where,

Computing Resource is independent and self-governing unit which can fulfil completely one computing task.

Storage Resource is independent and self-governing unit which can store data. And, this unit can process independently tasks on data.

Communication provides an interaction way between computing resource and storage resource, and management platform interacts with computing resource and storage resource.

Management Platform will decompose a task into some subtasks and allocate the resource for subtasks, such as computing resource and storage resource.

Cloudware will provide functions for user called directly, such as APIs provided by google.

Application is the special software system residing on the server and delivered to users by internet.

OS Call is interfaces of management platform functions.

Service is the last layer in cloud computing. The provider will release a usage and renting principles for users.

This model supports a virtual encapsulated system for cloud computing. Boundaries of model layers are clear and independent. In fact, this mode looks more like a virtual network computer, the CPU is composed by nodes of network and the storage is also composed by nodes of network.

There are two layers in a cloud program, an implementation layer and a logic layer. The implementation layer describes the basic function of program and deploys the control flow(logic level in figure 4). The logic layer describes the workflow of business(implementation level in figure 4).

In the implementation layer, M_i is code which describes the computing how to work together.

In the logic layer, $Service_i$ focus on the business workflow and can't know the implementation detail .

The model, the logic layer and the implementation layer, can guarantee more platform-independent .

3   Control Flow

Program control flow describe how the computer works for the expected result. When design a program, engineers always imply the control flow into the algorithm intentionally. In the traditional imperative program, the control flow is processed by the central controller. The single central controller determines the global operations must be sequential. For example, there is a simple program in the following:

void foo()
{ *int x,y,z;*
x:=1;
y:=2;
z:=x+y; }

For the above code, one kind of control flow of program can be described as in figure 5.

The program also can be described as figure 6. Based on the interleaving assumption, the semantic of figure 6 is equivalent to that of figure 5 .

Meanwhile, when design a traditional program, engineers have to map the control flow in different time and space into the sequent control flow in the same time and space, such as either in figure 5 or in figure 6, although $x := 1$ and $y := 1$ can be concurrent. As discussed as above, cloud computing is platform-free and no interleaving assumption. Therefore, to suite for the situation, the

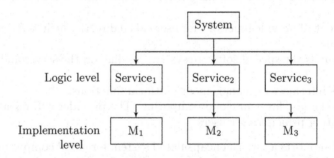

Fig. 4. Two levels of cloud computing

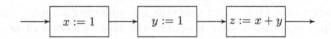

Fig. 5. One kind of control flow

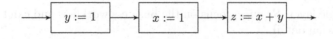

Fig. 6. Another kind of control flow

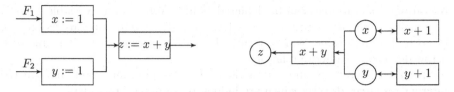

Fig. 7. Control flows without a central controller

Fig. 8. Relations between operations and variabes

control flow must be described explicitly. Another control can be described as in figure 7.

The reason that there are two or more kinds of control flows in one program is the controls are determined by the platform limits. The platform-related control also can be further grouped into the absolute control and the relative control. The absolute control is that platform determines unconditionally how to run a program can ,e.g. , the platform will determine only one must be choose, either figure 5 or figure 6. The relative control affects indirectly a program run through allocating resources, such as allocating RAM, CPU time and etc.

4   Variable, Operation and Interaction

Any program can be regarded as a set of variables and operations by the viewpoint of Turing machine. However, the traditional program always contains implicitly the platform control .

Cloud program focus on the business function and specially hide the detail of computing implementation. Therefore operations of cloud program is business operation but not the traditional algorithm operations.

To suit cloud computing situation, a cloud program (as well as module, pointer, function) is a description of variables, operations, control flows and resources. Essentially speaking, the basic parts of program still are data and process on the data. Variables are basic data units through which programs can be observed[9].

Generally speaking, Operations is processes on variables and which includes assigning, logic comparing and value computing.

The semantics of assignment statement is read a value out from a variable, then do process on the value, finally the computing result is written into the variable. Contrast to the local addresses in RAM, In cloud computing, variables are resided in network (internet), and variables are accessed through internet addresses.

Variables in cloud computing are real physical spaces with addresses where store values. Accordingly, operations on variables are read and write through communication. Any operation of program can be decomposed into a set of primitive reads-writes on variables (through internet address).

Programs are running can be observed through variables which record the trace of values change , either stored, read or write. Therefore variables are undertaker of changing and observing windows of program . The relations between operations and variables can be depicted as in 8. Where every variable , x or y ,is resided in a node of Internet. $x + 1, y + 1$ and $x + y$ are operations on x, y or both. The final values will be returned to x and y respectively. The line with arrow denotes a readwrite relation.

Specially, operations and interactions of cloud program don't manage the internet resources directly which are hidden by resources' providers.

5   Conclusion

Cloud computing is a hot topic in recent. However, there is no a common definition of cloud computing yet.

We know the platform of program is transforming from desktop to internet. Internet-based is the most important characteristic of cloud computing. Different to the desktop, internet can not hold one single central control unit, e.g. one single CPU.

Therefore, in cloud computing, computing units are located in different places. Accordingly, a exact global time can not be hold. The number of objective entities in the universe is unaccountable and the space of universe is grand. It is rather difficult to hold a global time under such a situation. In fact, it is unnecessary to hold a global time for the objective universe.

Limited by the space of paper, these characteristics can't be further discussed. We will continue these topics in the other papers. In the paper, we only present one five-level model for cloud computing. Furthermore, control flow, variable, operation and interaction in cloud program are specially discussed. Based on the model, cloud program can be designed as a service. In the future, we will further study the features of "cloud" respectively.

References

1. Armbrust, M., Fox, A., Griffith, R., Joseph, A.D., Katz, R.H., Konwinski, A., Lee, G., Patterson, D.A., Rabkin, A., Stoica, I., Zaharia, M.: Above the clouds: A berkeley view of cloud computing. Technical report, Electrical Engineering and Computer Sciences University of California at Berkeley, February 10 (2009)
2. Foster, I., Zhao, Y., Raicu, I., Lu, S.: Cloud computing and grid computing 360-degree compared. In: IEEE Grid Computing Environments (2008)
3. Gartner: Gartner says cloud computing will be as influential as e-business (2008)
4. Liu, H., Orban, D.: Gridbatch: Cloud computing for large-scale data-intensive batch applications. In: Eighth IEEE International Symposium on Cluster Computing and the Grid, pp. 295–305 (2008)
5. Knorr, E., Gruman, G.: What cloud computing really means (2008)
6. Lawton, G.: Moving the os to the web. Computer 41(3), 16–19 (2008)
7. Vaquero, L.M., Rodero-Merino, L., Caceres, J., Lindner, M.: A break in the clouds: Toward a cloud definition. ACM SIGCOMM Computer Communication Review 39(1), 50–55 (2009)
8. Youseff, L., Butrico, M., Silva, D.D.: Toward a unified ontology of cloud computing. In: Grid Computing Environments Workshop, pp. 1–10 (2008)
9. Hoare, C.A.R.: Communicating Sequential Processes. Prentice Hall, NewYork (1985)

Enterprise Cloud Architecture for Chinese Ministry of Railway

Xumei Shan and Hefeng Liu

Intel IT Flex
Shanghai, China
theresa.shan@intel.com

Abstract. Enterprise like PRC Ministry of Railways (MOR), is facing various challenges ranging from highly distributed computing environment and low legacy system utilization, Cloud Computing is increasingly regarded as one workable solution to address this. This article describes full scale cloud solution with Intel Tashi as virtual machine infrastructure layer, Hadoop HDFS as computing platform, and self developed SaaS interface, gluing virtual machine and HDFS with Xen hypervisor. As a result, on demand computing task application and deployment have been tackled per MOR real working scenarios at the end of article.

Keywords: Cloud Computing, Hadoop, Map Reduce, HDFS, Tashi.

1 Background

Railway freight data are critical basic information in railway transportation. It's tremendously bulky, including the whole freight tracing information.

The freight tracing system is a highly distributed dynamic information system that spans across approximately 100,000 kilometer railways in China. There are about 120,000 transactions per day, up to 160G data volume. These data are dispersed in certain servers in different bureaus. The same data record is replicated among different railway bureaus. The overall data volume is expected to grow exponentially in the coming 5 years. How to take full advantage of the storage space and to store these large-sized data is an urgent topic.

The freight transportation status (eg. transportation path, property info, shipment status etc.) are required by query system. MOR requires centralized federated data management to meet the complex query requirements. How to get rich real-time freight transportation data from distributed bureaus is a big challenge.

Moreover, error recovery and dynamic scalability are also ad hoc problems for MOR freight tracing system, which ensures data integrity and stability.

Cloud computing [1] is an emerging technology which promises to revolutionize software and business life-cycles. By making data available in the cloud, it can be more easily and ubiquitously accessed, often at much lower cost, increasing its value by enabling opportunities for enhanced collaboration, integration, and analysis on a shared common platform.

M.G. Jaatun, G. Zhao, and C. Rong (Eds.): CloudCom 2009, LNCS 5931, pp. 595–600, 2009.
© Springer-Verlag Berlin Heidelberg 2009

In this paper, we introduce an enterprise cloud architecture to resolve the critical TCO issue in PRC MOR IT infrastructure and address compute resource sharing challenges across geographically distributed MOR railway bureaus. The cloud architecture for MOR develops specific mechanisms for Manageability and intensive computing. This paper is structured as follows. In section 2, we introduce hadoop and Tashi's architectures and frameworks. In section 3, we describe our approach and architecture. In section 4, we outline the result and advantage of our architecture. We conclude with a section on our future work.

2 Hadoop and Tashi

In this section, we have a brief idea of hadoop and tashi's framework and architecture.

2.1 Hadoop

The ability to process enormous quantities of data efficiently, through strategies such as the map-reduce programming model, has become an essential ingredient for the success of many prominent enterprises, including the search giants Google and Yahoo!. Hadoop [2-3] provides a distributed file system (HDFS) that can store data across thousands of servers, and a means of running work (Map/Reduce jobs) across those machines, running the work near the data.

2.1.1 Hadoop Map/Reduce

MapReduce is a programming model for processing large data sets. It uses a map algorithm that processes a key/value pair to generate a set of intermediate key/value pairs, and a reduce algorithm that merges all intermediate values associated with the same intermediate key.

Figure 1 describes the dataflow of the map reduce process. The figure shows the task split into four nodes running map algorithm and three nodes running reduce algorithm. The persistent data are input and output data respectively. The transient data is the output of map stage, which are key-pair sets for reduce stage.

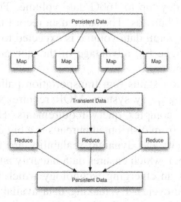

Fig. 1. Map Reduce Dataflow

2.1.2 Hadoop DFS (HDFS)

Hadoop implements MapReduce, using the HDFS. Typical file size in HDFS is in the order of terabytes with a block size of 128MB. Blocks are replicated for reliability and rack-aware placement is used to improve bandwidth. The HDFS operates in a master-slave mode with one master node called the NameNode that holds the meta-data and manages the system and a number of slave nodes called DataNodes.

2.2 Tashi

The Tashi [4] project builds a software infrastructure for cloud computing on massive internet-scale datasets (what we call Big Data). It is a cluster management system that enables the Big Data that are stored in a cluster/data center to be accessed, shared, manipulated, and computed on by remote users in a convenient and efficient manner.

User could request Virtual Machines (VM) from Tashi. These VMs could be batched from various images in Tashi's image repository. Tashi returns hostnames, ips and VM status to client. Then user's able to access the VM directly for operation.

Tashi is still under development and will support more VM hypervisors besides KVM/Xen and implement security mechanism for VM monitor in the future.

3 Enterprise Cloud Architecture and Implement

In our approach, depicted in figure 2, our cloud has also been divided into three components: IaaS (Infrastructure as a Service), PaaS (Platform as a Service) and SaaS (Software as a Service) [5].

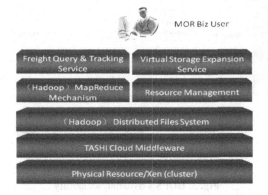

Fig. 2. Enterprise Cloud Conceptual Architecture

3.1 IaaS

IaaS products provides computational and storage infrastructure in a centralized, location-transparent service. There are tens of thousands of servers in 18 railway bureaus, which consist of our cloud test bed.

Tashi, as a management system, manipulates, balances and assigns these computing and storage resources in MOR's cloud. Cloud resources are uniform infrastructure available for computing whose physical location is irrelevant. There are several virtu-alization packages available for Linux, some of which take advantage of processor-level virtualization support. We choose the open-source Xen [6] hypervisor, which supports both full virtualization and para-virtualization. It enables us to share these resources for map-reduce computing and HDFS storage.

3.2 PaaS

PaaS products offer a full or partial application development environment that users can access and utilize online, even in collaboration with others. We setup Hadoop above IaaS as MOR's platform level, which boasts for its fault tolerance, low cost, large data sets, scalability and portability across heterogeneous hardware or software platforms.

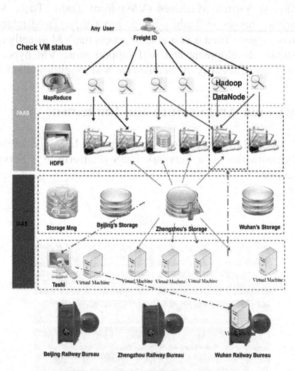

Fig. 3. HDFS's dynamic scalability

Each VM is a data node of HDFS, contributing computing and storage capability.

All the freight tracing data are stored and replicated as blocks on VM nodes with Map Reduce job.

Once a VM fails, data on this node will be automatically proliferated to other data nodes. End user won't deceive anything wrong and data will still keep integrity.

If system storage reaches its maximal capacity, some new devices would be ap-pended to the system. HDFS assesses the load balance of each node and put the new blocks onto VM nodes in new appending machines. System scales to larger storage capacity smoothly. Here we bind Tashi and Hadoop together. We inject scripts in VM image, which will be executed each time it runs. Once a new VM is setup, it would be automatically included into HDFS by scripts.

Figure 3 depicts the situation when Zhengzhou railway Bureau's storage is full. A new VM is created by Tashi on Wuhan railway bureau which is then added into the HDFS as a new data node. Then the new freight tracing information will be stored on the new VM node. HDFS's expansion is totally transparent to end user. Moreover, it does not impact the whole data storage at all.

3.3 SaaS

SaaS products provide a complete, turnkey application—including complex programs such as those for CRM or enterprise-resource management via the Internet. MOR provides freight tracing service and virtual storage expansion service.

Freight tracing service execute queries with map reduce algorithm [7] on top of HDFS. Since all data are stored on the shared cloud platform, user could get real-time geographical data from any of the 18 railway bureaus. Map-reduce mechanism moves query computation onto each data nodes rather than moving data together, which increases query efficiency.

Virtual storage expansion service supports dynamic scalability. In figure 4, Wuhan railway bureau added a new server. Tashi will take charge of the physical machine and creates VM on it. Then these new VMs will be included in HDFS automatically, namely, system storage's expanded easily.

4 Results

MOR's enterprise cloud architecture provides an enterprise perspective and solves most freight tracing problems. Tashi centralizes, manipulates all hardware recourses and takes full use of physical devices. Instead of purchasing large volume machines, our IaaS layer provides massive cluster/data center for resource sharing and map reduce computing. With hadoop's powerful replication, data recovery and scalability functions, our PaaS layer ensure MOR freight tracing system's data integrity, data reliability and resource scalability. Freight tracing service and virtual storage expansion service in SaaS layer makes real-time query and virtual expansion workable. Table 1 illustrates key challenges we met and the solution we use to overcome them.

Table 1. How cloud architecture solve MOR's problems

No.	MOR's problems	Solutions in Cloud Environment
1	Real-time geographic information query	Freight tracing and query service
2	Storage expansion	Virtual storage expansion service
3	Error recovery	Automatic failover
4	Data Replication	Data block replication in HDFS

The freight tracing system is also highly improved in performance by our solutions:

1. Location irrelevant: Getting rid of high hierarchical query structure, our solution distributes the workload to each data node. Thus, MOR's headquarter won't be the bottle neck of the whole system.
2. Real-time query and sharing: Cloud framework avoids IT island situation. Freight tracing data could be shared and queried throughout the MOR's bureaus.
3. Service-based application: Without expensive installation, software maintenance fee and costly upgrades, SaaS-based application provides global access and no installation is required.
4. Redundancy free: Instead of repeating data replication, HDFS only makes essential backup for data recovery, which helps to reduce redundancy and free unnecessary storage.

5   Conclusion and Future Work

In summary, three layers (IaaS, PaaS and SaaS) Cloud computing solution could help enterprise like PRC MOR to improve HW system utilization, provide on demand, flexible computing capability to meet scalable requesting. As for next step work, easy deployment and reliability could be worthy topic; also, security consideration is another must-have feature for enterprise implementation.

References

1. Lohr, S.: Google and IBM join in cloud computing research. New York Times (October 8, 2007)
2. The Hadoop Project, http://hadoop.apache.org/ (last visited July 2009)
3. Lämmel, R.: Google's Map Reduce programming model - Revisited. Sci. Comput. Program. 70(1), 1–30 (2008)
4. The Tashi Project, http://incubator.apache.org/tashi/
5. Cloud Computing: An Overview. P1. ACM, New York (2009)
6. Xen Community, http://www.xen.org/
7. Dean, J., Ghemawat, S.: MapReduce: Simplified data processing on large clusters (2008), http://labs.google.com/papers/mapreduce.html (retrieved August 22, 2008)

Research on Cloud Computing Based on Deep Analysis to Typical Platforms

Tianze Xia, Zheng Li, and Nenghai Yu

MoE-Microsoft Key Laboratory of Multimedia Computing and Commucation
University of Science and Technology of China
{Tianze Xia,Zheng Li,Nenghai Yu}Zenith@mail.ustc.edu.cn

Abstract. Cloud Computing, as a long-term dream of turning the computation to a public utility, has the potential to make IT industry great changed: making software more charming as a service and changing the way hardware designed and purchased. Along with the rapid development of Cloud Computing, many organizations have developed different Cloud Computing platforms, expressing their different understandings of the Cloud. Based on these facts, this paper has analyzed these understandings, introduced and tested several typical kinds of Cloud Computing platforms, and contrasted among them. The purpose of the study is to give a deep insight to the trend of Cloud Computing technology and to provide reference on choosing Cloud Computing platforms according to different needs.

Keywords: Cloud computing, Hadoop, Enomaly, Eucalyptus, trends.

1 Introduction

With Cloud, developers worked for new Internet services no longer need the large capital outlays in hardware to deploy their service. They do not have to worry about over-provisioning for a service whose popularity does not meet predictions, or under-provisioning for one that then becomes popular. Since the concept of Cloud Computing has been made, it gets rapid development. Not only Google, Microsoft, Amazon, such commercial companies launched their own Cloud Computing products, but there are also many open-source software groups published their attractive platforms.

The first part of this paper has studied the principle and structure of Hadoop then tested. The second part studied and tested two Iaas Cloud platforms—Eucalyptus and Enomaly. Finally some issues about the tendency of the Cloud Computing will be raised in this paper.

2 Studies on Cloud Computing Platforms

2.1 Hadoop

Hadoop is a distributed computing framework provided by Apache[4]. It is a Cloud service similar to PaaS. The core of Hadoop is MapReduce[8] and Hadoop Distributed

M.G. Jaatun, G. Zhao, and C. Rong (Eds.): CloudCom 2009, LNCS 5931, pp. 601–608, 2009.
© Springer-Verlag Berlin Heidelberg 2009

File System (HDFS).[5][9] The idea of MapReduce is from a Google's paper and is now widely circulated[8]. HDFS provided underying support for distributed storage.

Hadoop is most suitable for mass data analysis. Mass data is divided and sent to a number of nodes. And then by each node's parallel computing the output result will be integrated.

2.2 Eucalyptus

Eucalyptus is developed by University of California (Santa Barbara) for Cloud Computing research[2]. It is compatible with the EC2's API system. Although it supports for Amazon in the syntax of interfaces and achieve the same functionality (with some exceptions), but is almost completely different inside. The design goal for Eucalyptus is easy to expand, and easy to install and maintain. Eucalyptus will become an integrated part of Ubuntu Linux. Ubuntu users will be able to easily use Eucalyptus building private clouds.

2.3 Enomaly's Elastic Computing Platform (ECP)

Enomaly's Elastic Computing Platform (ECP) is an open source web-based virtual infrastructure platform.[3] It is also an IaaS platform. Its design goal is to manage the Distributed Virtual Server environment that is complicated.

2.4 Conclusion

From the introduction of each platform, we can see that Hadoop might be the most proper for processing data; Eucalyptus might be good for Linux users to build their private IaaS Cloud; And ECP may be suitable for IT managers to supervise their Clouds. However, all these are just the official introduction given by each of them, the real features and performances of them need to be dug and evaluated by experiments and tests. In the following parts, we will perform tests to give a deep analysis for each of these platforms.

3   Research on Hadoop

3.1   Architecture of Hadoop

There are many elements in Hadoop. At the bottom there is Hadoop Distributed File System (HDFS)[5].It stores all the data in Hadoop system. On top of HDFS is MapReduce engine that consists of JobTrackers and TaskTrackers.

HDFS using master /slave architecture. HDFS is a cluster of one Namenode and numbers of Datanodes[7]. Namenode is a central server that is responsible for managing the file system namespace, and controls the access of files. From the internal perspective, a file is divided into one or more data blocks, these blocks are stored in a group of Datanodes. Namenode executes the operation of namespace,such as open, close, rename files or directories. It is also responsible for map a certain data block to a certain Datanode. Datanode is responsible for handling file system requests.

Namenode usually runs independently in a machine. It is responsible for the management of file system name space and controls the access to external clients. NameNode decide how to map files to data blocks in Datenodes. The actual I / O stream does not go through it. When an external client sent a request to access a file, Namenode responds a Datanode's IP address that contains the file's copy. Then the Datanode responds for the client's request. This feature of hadoop is very important. It does not move data to a certain location to process, but move processing to data. So use hadoop to process data is very efficient.

3.2 Test on Hadoop

During the test of hadoop, we run WordCount[10] for a pdf text file on different numbers machines. The pdf's size is 300MB. Table 1 shows the results. The advantage of hadoop mentioned above can be clearly seen.

Table 1. The result of Hadoop test

Number of Datanodes	1	3	7	15
Time cost(seconds)	931	511	274	153

Also we do a file write test. The test system has 16 machines (15 machines are configured as datanode) and connected with 1000M Ethernet. The results are shown in Table 2.

Table 2. The result of HDFS test

fileSize (byte)	118147302	12340000	708002	82545	50193
Time cost(ms)	28432	13	63	15	16

3.3 Current Deployment of Hadoop and Some Issues

The feature of Hadoop's map/reduce and the HDFS make it very easy to handle vast amounts of data[12]. Because of this and other features like easy to extend, reliable, Yahoo! has chosen Hadoop as its cloud computing platform[6], built the world's largest Hadoop platform—Yahoo! Search Webmap[11]. In addition, Yahoo! And Carnegie - Mellon University launched the Open Academic Clusters-M45 that has more than 500 machines today and has completed many valuable projects. [13]The index of Amazon's search portal—a9.com is also accomplished by Hadoop. The Facebook.com use Hadoop to build the entire site's database,which currently has more than 320 machines for log analysis and data mining.

During the use and the test of hadoop, we found some issues.

a)   The performance of hadoop is not stable. Some application might cost different times. This problem makes hadoop OK to process offline data but unsafe to handle real-time tasks.

b)   Hadoop is based on Java. This makes it compatible on different systems but limit its performance. In a test from Open Cloud Consortium[10], Sector[18] which is written in C++ is about twice as fast as Hadoop. To build a Hadoop C++ version is a hopeful way.

4   Research on Eucalyptus and ECP

4.1   Eucalyptus

Eucalyptus will be soon integrated into Ubuntu. Ubuntu users can easily use Eucalyptus building private clouds, just like Amazon Web Services LLC (AWS).And more this private cloud can work together with AWS to create a "composite cloud". [14] Eucalyptus has three components [17]:

a)   Cloud Manager (CM) : The CM is responsible for processing incoming user-initiated or administrative requests, making high-level VM instance scheduling decisions, processing service-level agreements(SLAs) and maintaining persistent system and user metadata.

b)   Instance Manager (IM): The IM executes on the physical resources that host VM instances and is responsible for instance start up, inspection, shutdown and cleanup.

c)   Group Manager (GM): The GM is responsible for gathering state information from its collection of IMs, scheduling incoming VM instance execution requests to individual IMs, and managing the configuration of public and private instance networks.

Communications between these three components is "SOAP with WS-security". In every cluster there will be only one node operating as Cluster Controller. Every node has a node controller.

4.2   Enomaly's Elastic Computing Platform (ECP)

Compared with Eucalyptus, ECP has these features:

a)   A number of server entities can be managed as a virtual cluster

b)   Support a wide range of virtualization environments。 It has a long history of complete KVM support.

c)   Provide an easy-to-use web management. After deployment, almost all operations can be completed by the web interface.

d)   Support python language. That makes the expansion and maintenance are simple.

e)   Valet feature is quite handy when building clusters of VM's.

f)   Use KVM as the virtualization hypervisor, by VM Creator in ECP, virtual machines that OS is pre-installed can be produced in less than 1 minute.

The specific performance of ECP will be described below.

4.3   Test of Eucalyptus and ECP

Eucalyptus and Enomaly's Elastic Computing Platform (ECP) are also IaaS platforms and both provide the use of virtual machines. So we made a Comparison test between them.

In the test, Eucalyptus adopts Xen and takes ubuntu 8.04LTS as the VM's OS. ECP adopt KVM and Debain 4.0. We also made an original OS that runs on real machine to be the comparison platform. It is fedora Core 6.

Eucalyptus and ECP's VM both have 512MB RAM, single virtual CPU, 10GB system image + 20GB supplementary storage. The comparison platform is also build as this.

Gzip Compression tests the efficiency of virtual CPUs. The shorter time costs the more effective CPU is virtualized.

Lame Compilation tests the cloud VMs' overall performance. The RAMspeed batch copy and batch run tests the cloud VMs' memory speed.

Table 3 to Table 6 gives the results.[16]

Table 3. Gzip Compression Test Result

Platforms	Fedora Core 6	Eucalyptus	ECP
Time (seconds)	67.73	103.30	97.72

This test runs "time gzip –c test.tar > test.tar.gz" The size of test.tar is 801MB.

Table 4. Lame Compilation Test Restlt

Platforms	Fedora Core 6	Eucalyptus	ECP
Time (seconds)	9.24	35	43.27

This test runs "time make –j 5".

Table 5. RAMspeed Batch Copy Test Result

Platforms	Fedora Core 6	Eucalyptus	ECP
Speed(MB/s)	1201.45	1124.36	622.20

This test runs as INTEGER BatchRun Copy.

Table 6. RAMspeed Batch Run Test Result

Platforms	Fedora Core 6	Eucalyptus	ECP
Speed(MB/s)	1345.50	1298.84	783.39

This test runs as INTEGER BatchRun Add.

Test Conclusion:
We can see from the test that the performance of VM that the two IaaS platform provided has a gap between the actual system there. This should be the cost of network communication and VM scheduling. But for these two types of cloud computing platform, the computing power of the VM is similar. In the VM memory speed test, Eucalyptus leads significantly. The reasons for this result may be caused by different virtualization technologies. And it is also possible that because of different mechanisms of these two platforms, such as scheduling. We shall study this problem in future work.

4.4 Comparison of EC2 Eucalyptus and ECP and Some Issues

Finally we compared some key features of Eucalyptus ECP and Amazon EC2. List as Table 7.

Table 7. The comparison of EC2 Eucalyptus & ECP

	EC2	Eucalyptus	ECP
Flow control in data transport	O	O	O
Billing Mechanism	O	X	X
Storage Mechanism	O(s3[15])	O(Walrus)	O
Block Storage Mechanism	O(EBS)	O(Walrus)	O
Load Balance & Live Migration	O(SQS)	X	X
Target Customers	Users	Administrators&Users	Administrators

a) Both Eucalyptus and ECP do not support virtualization technology from commercial company such like VMware or Hyper-V.

b) Eucalyptus will be contained in Ubuntu 9.10. This makes it easy to be employed. However it lacks a method like appzero[19] that can inosculate itself to other public clouds. This can help people in this scene: employ Eucalyptus as a development platform to build applications and then run these applications on AWS seamlessly.

c) The Web management of ECP is a special feature. It is better if the Web system can provide management on not only VMs but virtual networks, virtual applications and storage just by drag and clicks.

5   Predictions and Suggestions

At the basis of research for the developing states on Cloud Computing in different companies, we have made predictions for the possible developing directions of Cloud Computing. What is more, from the experiments and tests results described above, we made an analysis for the performances of the typical existing Cloud Computing platforms, as well as given some suggestions for choosing proper platforms based on different needs.

5.1   Predictions for Trend of Cloud Computing

1. Most clouds today are designed to work just within one data center. An interesting research direction is to develop appropriate network protocols, architectures and middleware for wide area clouds that span multiple data centers.

2. To investigate how different clouds can interoperate. That is, how two different clouds, perhaps managed by two different organizations, can share information. And how the "composite cloud" can be build.

3. A practical question is to develop standards and standard based architectures for cloud services. And thus develop a way to benchmark clouds.

4. Neither of the two IaaS platforms discussed in this paper support VM's Live Migration. When and how to migration VMs from one server to another shall be a key problem.
5. There are lots of open-source Cloud Computing platforms in the level of IaaS and PaaS but few in SaaS. More platforms like 10GEN[1] is needed.
6. Almost all open-source Cloud Computing platforms are based on Linux. A useful research direction is to make open-source platforms to support multiple operating systems such like Microsoft Widows. This can make the Cloud Computing more popular in everyone's life.
7. Nowadays the ability of Cloud Computing cannot fully meet the requirements of entertainment. Image this Scene: a user adopted Amazon EC2 and wants to play 3D games in the VM. Of course the experience he gets will not be good today. The virtualization technologies have not covered GPU yet. This is another charming direction. GPU has more Floating-point computing power than CPU. If GPUs can be virtualized, it is also benefit for Scientific Computing.

5.2 Suggestions for Choosing the Proper Platforms

As shown above, Hadoop suits when the ability of intensive data processing is required, like data mining, Target Recognition on remote-sensing image and so on. Eucalyptus is a good choice when you are using Ubuntu. It makes a simple way to build up private Cloud and can work with Amazon EC2 smoothly. So it also suits to the companies or groups that deployed Amazon EC2 but want to process private data in their own Cloud. Also the Appscale[20] can run on Eucalyptus. This means people who want to deploy Google App Engine can choose Eucalyptus. And for Enomaly's Elastic Computing Platform, Python support and management of servers as virtual clusters are its strengths.

References

1. 10gen, http://www.10gen.com/
2. Rich, W., Chris, G., Dan, N.: Eucalyptus: An Open-source Infrastructure for Cloud Computing,
   http://open.eucalyptus.com/documents/
   eucalyptus-slides-wolski-cloud_expo_apr08.pdf
3. Enomaly, http://www.enomaly.com/Product-Overview.419.0.html
4. Hadoop, http://hadoop.apache.org/core/
5. Hadoop DFS User Guide, http://hadoop.apache.org/core/docs/r0.17.2/
   hdfs_user_guide.html
6. Yahoo! Developer Network Blog (2008),
   http://developer.yahoo.net/blogs/hadoop/2008/02/
   yahoo-worlds-largest-production-hadoop.html
7. Doug, Cutting. Hadoop: Funny Name, Powerful Software (2008),
   http://www.tuxme.com/
   index2.php?option=com_content&do_pdf=1&id=27470
8. Hadoop Wiki, http://wiki.apache.org/hadoop/PoweredBy

9. Michael, N.: Running Hadoop on Ubuntu Linux (Multi-Node Cluster),
   http://wiki.apache.org/hadoop/
   Running_Hadoop_On_Ubuntu_Linux_(Single-Node_Cluster)
10. Open Cloud Testbed,
    http://www.opencloudconsortium.org/testbed.html
11. Scott, D.: Yahoo's Doug Cutting on MapReduce and the Future of Hadoop (2007),
    http://www.infoq.com/articles/hadoop-interview
12. Robert, L., Grossman, Yunhong, G.: On the Varieties of Clouds for Data Intensive Computing. IEEE Computer Society Technical Committee on Data Engineering (2009)
13. Open Cloud Consortium (2008), http://www.opencloudconsortium.org
14. Michael, A., Armando, F., et al.: Above the Clouds: A Berkeley View of Cloud Computing, http://nma.berkeley.edu/ark:/28722/bk000471b6t
15. Amazon Simple Storage Service, https://s3.amazonaws.com
16. Ramspeed, http://www.alasir.com/software/ramspeed/
17. Daniel, N., Rich, W.: The Eucalyptus Open-source Cloud-computing System,
    http://open.eucalyptus.com/documents/nurmi_et_al-
    eucalyptus_open_source_cloud_computing_system-cca_2008.pdf
18. Sector-Sphere, http://sector.sourceforge.net/
19. Appzero, http://www.trigence.com/
20. Appscale, http://code.google.com/p/appscale/

Automatic Construction of SP Problem-Solving Resource Space

Jin Liu[1,2], Fei Liu[1], Xue Chen[3], and Junfeng Wang[4]

[1] State Key Lab. Of Software Engineering, Wuhan University, China 430072
[2] State Key Lab. for Novel Software Technology, Nanjing University, China 210093
[3] Digital Content Computing and Semantic Grid Group, Key Lab of Grid Technology, Shanghai University, China 200072
[4] College of Computer Science, Sichuan University, China 610065
mailjinliu@yahoo.com

Abstract. The automation and adaptability of software systems to the dynamic environment and requirement variation is quite critical ability in cloud computing. This paper tends to organize vast stacks of problem solution resources for software processes into a structured resource space according to their topic words. The Resource Space model is well-developed by continuously adapting to its surroundings, expanding example group and refining model information. Resource topics are extracted with TDDF algorithm from document resources. Topic networks are established with topic connection strength. Then these topic networks are transformed into maximum spanning trees that are divided into different classification parts with pruning operation. This work may promotes automation of RS-based software service and development of novel software development in cloud computing environment.

Keywords: Networked software, Resource space, Problem-solving resource, Software automation.

1   Introduction

Cloud computing occurs in a highly open computing environment, where various information processing units interacting with each other. More requirements are produced during these interaction processes, where the cycle of system evolution is shorten compared with the same one in the relative close environment. Accordingly, the adaptability of software systems to the dynamic environment and requirement variation is quite critical, i.e., the evolution ability of online software system. It is also an underlying driving force for "X" as-a-service ("X"AAS) [2].

The motivation of this paper is that vast stacks of problem solution resources for software processes are deposited on the open interconnected environment. These resources possess prolific empirical knowledge and design knowledge for problem solutions. The huge mass of knowledge resources can be organized into a structured resource space according to their topic words. And personalized resource services may further be provided to deliver suggestive reference empirical knowledge in software process, which may improve reuse of legacy knowledge resources, reduce cost

M.G. Jaatun, G. Zhao, and C. Rong (Eds.): CloudCom 2009, LNCS 5931, pp. 609–614, 2009.

of higher-value design and speed product delivery cycles in the interconnected environment. Our work focuses on investigate a way of automatic construction and online evolution of Resource Spaces for sharing SP problem-solving resources.

The primitive idea is that priori knowledge about the structure of resource organization or the resource space model is limited. It becomes progressively explicit during the running time of the resource space. The model of the web resource space is well-developed by continuously adapting to its surroundings, expanding example group and refining model information.

2 The Web Resource Space

The resource space model is used to organize, specify and share versatile web resources with orthogonal classification semantics, which provides a universal resource view for conveniently discovering and consuming these resources [3]. It is applicable to managing versatile problem-solving resources that are produced in software processes and deposited on the Web. Document topics produced in requirement acquisition can be extracted and organized into a web resource space. The digested resources can be found and consumed with corresponding topics in the web resource space. Figure 1 indicates that problem-solving documents produced in requirement acquisition are organized into a web resource space. The orthogonal classification scheme shown bottom left in this figure prescribes the resource organizing solution. As a semantic coordinate system with independent coordinates and mutual-orthogonal axes in normal forms, the Web resource space is an ideal approach to eliminate redundant, disorder and useless resources so as to guarantee the correctness and accuracy of resource operations. A resource-coordination is denoted as a resource point that contains a resource set with the same classification feature. The orthogonal classification semantics is accordance with human's cognitive habit.

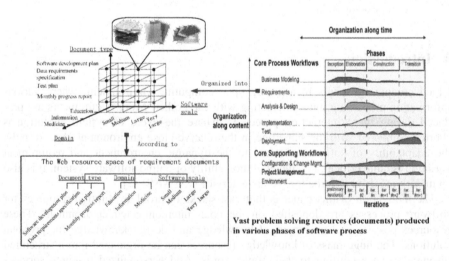

Fig. 1. A web resource space of problem-solving resources produced in requirement acquisition

3 Domain Topic Extraction

Domain topic words of a document are benefit to identifying problem solving resources. Approaches of topic extraction includes term frequency inverse document frequency (TFIDF), as well as mutual information, information gain, relevancy score, chi-square, NGL coefficient and odds ratio [1]. Since TFIDF is effective in extracting textual keywords from single text, it is more often used in text analysis [1]. And yet it is difficult to extract domain keywords from multi-texts using TFIDF [1]. TDDF (TFIDF direct document frequency of domain), proposed by Digital Content Computing and Semantic Grid Group from Shanghai University, is introduced herein to extract desired domain topic set from problem solving documents produced in software process [1]. TDDF enhances TFIDF in domain keyword extraction from multi-texts by taking document frequency of domain into account and evaluating topic word frequency in related documents belonging to the same domain.

Definition 1 (Domain Document Frequency): Domain Document frequency $ddf(t, \vec{D})$, is the number of documents where the word c appears in a domain set $\vec{D}$.

Definition 2 (Word Common Possession Rate): The rate of word common possession $ddf(t, \vec{D})/M$, denoted as c, is the rate of the document frequency of the domain with the document number in $\vec{D}$, where M is the document number in $\vec{D}$. Word common possession rate is almost proportional to the possibility of a word t being a domain keyword.

The primitive definition of TDDF can be expressed with equation (1).

$$W(t, \vec{d_i}, \vec{D}) = \frac{W_{\vec{d_i}}^t(t, \vec{d_i}) + 0.01 \times \beta \dfrac{ddf(t, \vec{D})}{M}}{\sqrt{\sum_{t \in \vec{D}}\left[W_{\vec{d_i}}^t(t, \vec{d_i}) + 0.01 \times \beta \dfrac{ddf(t, \vec{D})}{M}\right]^2}} \tag{1}$$

where $W_{\vec{d_i}}^t(t, \vec{d_i}) = \dfrac{tf(t, \vec{d_i}) \times \log(N / n_t^{\vec{d_i}} + 0.01)}{\sqrt{\sum_{t \in \vec{d_i}}\left[tf(t, \vec{d_i}) \times \log(N / n_t^{\vec{d_i}} + 0.01)\right]^2}}$ is the weight of word

t in document $\vec{d_i}$; $tf(t, \vec{d_i})$ is the frequency of word t in document $\vec{d_i}$; N is the number of unrelated documents; $n_t^{\vec{d_i}}$ is the document frequency in unrelated documents; $ddf(t, \vec{D})$ is the document frequency of word t in $\vec{d_i}$; β is the impact degree of $ddf(t, \vec{D})$ on domain topics; denominator is a standardization factor, and the value 0.01 prevents the denominator from becoming zero.

If β is very large, the impact of $ddf(t, \vec{D})$ on the extraction of keywords is significant. TDDF with fixed word common possession rate c can be expressed as:

$$W(t, \vec{d}_i, \vec{D}) = \begin{cases} \dfrac{W_{\vec{d}_i}^t(t, \vec{d}_i) + 0.01}{\sqrt{\sum_{t \in \vec{D}}\left[W_{\vec{d}_i}^t(t, \vec{d}_i) + 0.01\right]^2}} & \text{if } ddf(t, \vec{D})/M \ge c \\ \\ 0 & \text{if } ddf(t, \vec{D})/M < c \end{cases} \qquad (2)$$

The empirical study indicates that the appropriate c value from 0.2 to 0.4 induces an acceptable correct extraction rate and the number of domain topics [1, 4].

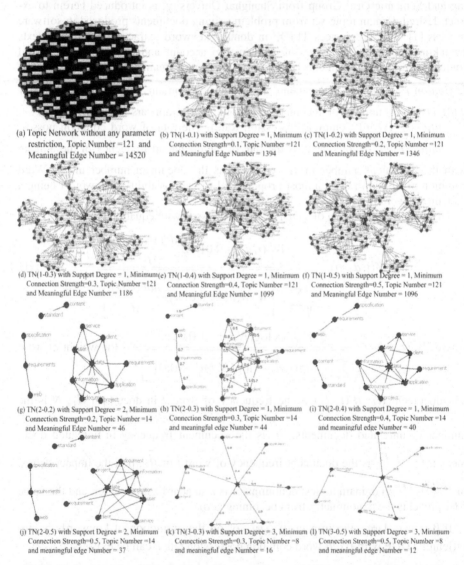

(a) Topic Network without any parameter restriction, Topic Number =121 and Meaningful Edge Number = 14520

(b) TN(1-0.1) with Support Degree = 1, Minimum Connection Strength=0.1, Topic Number =121 and Meaningful Edge Number = 1394

(c) TN(1-0.2) with Support Degree = 1, Minimum Connection Strength=0.2, Topic Number =121 and Meaningful Edge Number = 1346

(d) TN(1-0.3) with Support Degree = 1, Minimum Connection Strength=0.3, Topic Number =121 and Meaningful Edge Number = 1186

(e) TN(1-0.4) with Support Degree = 1, Minimum Connection Strength=0.4, Topic Number =121 and Meaningful Edge Number = 1099

(f) TN(1-0.5) with Support Degree = 1, Minimum Connection Strength=0.5, Topic Number =121 and Meaningful Edge Number = 1096

(g) TN(2-0.2) with Support Degree = 2, Minimum Connection Strength=0.2, Topic Number =14 and Meaningful Edge Number = 46

(h) TN(2-0.3) with Support Degree = 1, Minimum Connection Strength=0.3, Topic Number =14 and meaningful edge Number = 44

(i) TN(2-0.4) with Support Degree = 1, Minimum Connection Strength=0.4, Topic Number =14 and meaningful edge Number = 40

(j) TN(2-0.5) with Support Degree = 2, Minimum Connection Strength=0.5, Topic Number =14 and meaningful edge Number = 37

(k) TN(3-0.3) with Support Degree = 3, Minimum Connection Strength=0.3, Topic Number =8 and meaningful edge Number = 16

(l) TN(3-0.5) with Support Degree = 3, Minimum Connection Strength=0.5, Topic Number =8 and meaningful edge Number = 12

Fig. 2. Topic networks of SP resource solving resources with different restriction parameters

4 Topic Clustering

4.1 Topic Network

Definition 3 (Connection Strength): The connection strength of any two topics p and q, denoted as $CS(p, q)$, is expressed as equation (3).

$$CS(p, q) = \log \frac{(N \times N(q \mid p))}{N(p) \times N(q)} \Big/ \log N \tag{3}$$

where N is the number of all documents in domain $\vec{D}$; $N(p)$ is the total number that the topic p presents in documents in $\vec{D}$; $N(q)$ is the number that the topic q presents in documents in $\vec{D}$; $N(q \mid p)$ is the number that the topic p occurs when the topic q presents in the same document in $\vec{D}$. In general, $CS(p, q)$ is not equal to $CS(q, p)$.

Definition 4 (Topic Network) A topic network is a directed graph that takes topics as its vectors and the connection length between two vectors as the weight on the edge connecting these two vectors, denoted as $G_{TN} = (V, E)$, where V is a vector set and E is a directed edge set, with the connection strength as the edge weight of any two vectors. An example of a topic network with 5 vectors is demonstrated in figure 2.

4.2 Topic Classification

A spanning tree of a connected graph is a minimal connected graph that includes all vectors in a graph and n-1 edges that only constitutes one tree. And a topic network can be transformed into a maximum spanning tree that the sum of all edge weights is max in all spanning trees with n vectors. An example of maximum spanning tree that is deduced from aforementioned case is demonstrated in Fig 3.

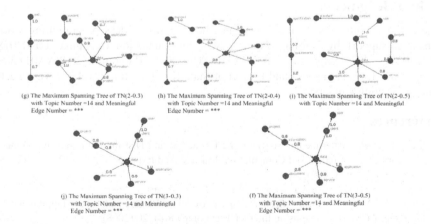

(g) The Maximum Spanning Tree of TN(2-0.3) with Topic Number =14 and Meaningful Edge Number = ***

(h) The Maximum Spanning Tree of TN(2-0.4) with Topic Number =14 and Meaningful Edge Number = ***

(i) The Maximum Spanning Tree of TN(2-0.5) with Topic Number =14 and Meaningful

(j) The Maximum Spanning Tree of TN(3-0.3) with Topic Number =14 and Meaningful Edge Number = ***

(f) The Maximum Spanning Tree of TN(3-0.5) with Topic Number =14 and Meaningful Edge Number = ***

Fig. 3. Maximum spanning trees deduced from topic networks of SP resource solving resources

Fig 4. is the classification of a topic set that can be performed by pruning on its maximum spanning tree with a threshold value 0.4. Fig 4(k) is chosen as the core topic classification that is extended to ensure each resource can be found through this core topic classification with the measurement of shortest graph paths. The automatically produced Resource Space is at the right hand in this picture.

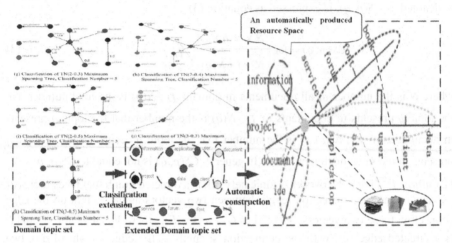

Fig. 4. Topic set classification and automatically produced Resource Space

5 Discussion and Conclusions

The procedure and critical techniques of the proposed automatic construction of SP problem-solving Resource Space is sketchily explained due to the page limitation. More complex empirical cases will further investigated. Relative research points of on-line evolution and automatic deployment are being carried out recently.

Acknowledgments

The authors would like to thank Hainan Zhou for his selfless programming work. Financial support by National Natural Science Foundation of China (60703018; 60873024), 973 Program (2007CB310800), 863 Program (2008AA01Z208; 2006AA04Z156) and Open Fund Project of State Key Lab. for Novel Software Technology, Nanjing University.

References

1. Luo, X., et al.: Experimental Study on the Extraction and Distribution of Textual Domain Keywords. Concurrency And Computation: Practice And Experience 20, 1917–1932 (2008)
2. SAAS, Wikipedia (2009),
   http://en.wikipedia.org/wiki/Software_as_a_service
3. Zhuge, H., Xing, Y., Shi, P.: Resource Space Model, OWL and Database: Mapping and Integration. ACM Transactions on Internet Technology 8(4), 20 (2008)
4. Zhuge, H., Luo, X.: Automatic generation of document semantics for the e-science. The Journal of Systems and Software 79, 969–983 (2006)

An Idea of Special Cloud Computing in Forest Pests' Control

Shaocan Jiang, Luming Fang, and Xiaoying Huang*

School of Information Engineering, Zhejiang Forestry University,
Lin'an 311300, Zhejiang, China
shaocan.jiang@gmail.com, ahxyhn@yahoo.com.cn

Abstract. Forest pests, fires and deforestation, are known as the three forest disasters. And the severity of forest pests infection has increased in recent decades. Therefore, it's becoming more important to have strategic approach toward forest pests control.

In the face of increasingly serious forest pests control work, the existing forest management systems are no longer applicable. We are in urgent need of a new management model. After examining a variety of techniques and models, we settled on the concept and application of Cloud Computing.

In this paper, we put forward an idea of Special Cloud Computing in forest pests' control. It is a strong professional cloud computing service which applies to forest pests' control. It is provided by cloud computing provider and forest pests' management.

Keywords: Forest Pests, Cloud Computing, Special Cloud, Data Center, SAAS.

1 Introduction

China, which has total forest area of 150 million hm², is one of the countries that suffer most serious forest pests infection in the world. At the present time, the scourge to the forest by forest pests is far more severe than that by forest fires. During the ninth "Five Years Plan" (From 1996 to 2000), the forest pests arose in China was 7333 thousand hm² annually on average. And among that was an area of 42,670 thousand hm² that suffered more than moderate, which was roughly equal to 80% of the area of artificial afforestation every year. This was far higher than the average level compare to other part of the world.[1, 2, 7]

Forest pests forecasting is not only important to forest pests control work, but also a basis for effectively preventing pests from arising and developing [3, 4]. It combines mathematical analysis with other natural subjects. After decades of research, we have accumulated and summed up a wealth of forest pests data. However, the data information is growing so fast that currently we meet an increasingly large amount of pests' control work. And there are many disadvantages difficult to overcome in the existing forest pests MIS, such as the high cost and low utilization. So we have to seek a

---

* Corresponding Author.

M.G. Jaatun, G. Zhao, and C. Rong (Eds.): CloudCom 2009, LNCS 5931, pp. 615–620, 2009.

newer technology, use a newer management and protection platform to solve the existing key problems of forest pests' control.[6, 7]

After examining a variety of techniques and models, we settled on the concept and application of Cloud Computing, which is a revolution in IT.[5, 10, 13] Being contrary to the present IT deployment and operating mode, it enhances business management and resource utilization efficiently.

2 Overview of Cloud Computing

Cloud computing, which is developed from Virtualization, Utility Computing, IAAS (Infrastructure as a Service), SAAS (Software as a Service), etc, sets Parallel Computing, Distributed Computing and Grid Computing all in one.[8, 10]

We can regard cloud computing as a kind of computing method that integrates the free scattered resources into a big pool and takes it as a service to the customers through the Internet. The resources that customers are using, such as data, server, software, R&D platform, etc, are all from the virtualization center in the cloud [10, 13]. A cloud is a data center architecture that automates the allocation and reallocation of IT resources to end-user applications in order to dynamically respond to changing business demands and priorities, while billing users for consumption [13].

Cloud computing is growing extremely fast. And there are numerous providers succeeded in this field. Here are some clouds provided by commercial entities.

➤ Amazon EC2 is a web service that provides resizable compute capacity in the cloud. It is designed to make web-scale computing easier for developers.[14]

➤ Google App Engine offers a complete development stack that uses familiar technologies to build and host web applications.[15]

➤ Microsoft Azure Services Platform provides a wide range of Internet services that can be consumed from either on-premises environments or the Internet.[16]

➤ IBM Blue Cloud is to provide services that automate fluctuating demands for IT resources.[17]

3 The Idea of Special Cloud Computing

3.1 Choice of Cloud

Forest pests control work differs from the operations and management of general enterprises. It involves forestry administration from national to local levels, large and small natural and artificial forest throughout our country. With tens of thousands of species and the complex management computation, ordinary cloud computing may appear weak in dealing with the strong professional problems of forest pests control.

Cloud computing can be roughly divided into two broad categories. Public Cloud (or External Cloud) is offered to every paying customers by a service provider, while Private Cloud (or Internal Cloud) is deployed by the IT department of an enterprise to its internal users.[12]

However, neither of these two clouds suits our pests' control and can not solves the professional problems. The IT requirements in public cloud are not well-defined, while the resources in private cloud are underutilized.[11, 12, 13]

After comparing these two clouds, we attempt to build a new cloud which differs from the public cloud and private cloud--Special Cloud in Forest Pests' Control.

3.2 Special Cloud Computing

We come up with such an idea: a special forestry administration (in this paper, we give it a code name "C") cooperates with the cloud computing provider (code name "P") in setting up the Special Cloud Computing in Forest Pests' Control.

We define that Special Cloud Computing is a strong professional cloud computing service for a particular field, and co-provided by professional cloud computing provider and special administrations in this field.

In our idea, C will be the Chinese State Forestry Administration--the most senior administration section in China. And the model of special cloud is shown in Figure 1.

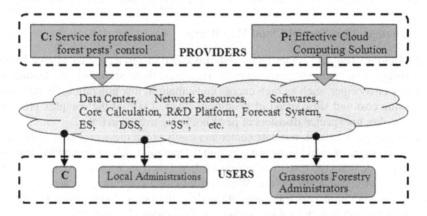

Fig. 1. The model of special cloud computing in forest pests' control

In this special cloud, C provides service mostly for professional pests' control, while P provides an effective cloud computing solution. Specifically, the functions of C and P could be allocated as Table 1 shows at the time of building this special cloud.

Table 1. Functions of C & P

	Underlying Structure	**Services**	**Management & Maintenance**
C	Data center	Majority is for forest pests' control (Software, Core Calculation, R&D Platform, Forecast System, ES, DSS, "3S", etc.)	Data, Software, etc.
P	Original resources of cloud (Server, Virtualization Components, Monitoring & Management Technology, etc.)	Majority is for cloud (Software, Core Calculation, R&D and Other Platforms, Network Resources, etc.)	Software, Overall framework

On the other hand, we can figure out from figure 1 that C has a dual identity, is both a provider of special cloud computing, and its user. This is also one of the most important characteristics of special cloud. As a provider, C plays a decisive role in setting up and perfecting the special cloud computing service and protecting data information security and privacy.

In special cloud computing, the identities of all participants are very important. The matter of identity is also the basis for the distinction between special cloud and other clouds. The identities of all participants can be shown in Table 2.

Table 2. The identities of all participants in three different clouds

	Public Cloud	**Private Cloud**	**SpecialCloud**
Provider	cloud computing provider	IT department of an enterprise	cloud computing provider & special administrations in a particular field (Co-provider)
User	paying customers	Enterprise's internal users	administrators in the field

3.3 Changes That Special Cloud May Bring

Data Center. The data center can supply information services, data storage backup, core calculation for forest pests' control. However, there are many shortcomings in ordinary data center, such as high energy consumption, low utilization, limited space, increasing cost and slow speed of operation, etc.[5, 13] And the complex prediction model makes unexpected disasters of pests not being treated in time.

Now, in special cloud, our data center can easily solve these problems. And one of the key features of cloud computing is Super Operation. Cloud computing just integrates the free scattered resources in the cloud, and then endows the users with operating power as it had never before. With special cloud computing, experts can create prediction models in real time notwithstanding the dense forest and miscellaneous pests and non-linear relationships between pests ecological groups.

SAAS & PAAS. During the process of forestry informatization, modern information technologies have been applied to the work of forest pest control. ES and "3S" technology are very practical. But as the causes of strong professional, complex operation, high cost, etc, these high and new technologies can not be popularized in grassroots forest management.

In our idea, we attempt to combined server, network and various kinds of high and new technologies into special cloud computing platform by virtualizing them seamlessly. And then supply them to all forestry administrators through SAAS and PAAS (Platform as a Service). This mode of lease or pay-as-you-go is an ideal model to the grassroots forestry administrators. Meanwhile, it helps them omit the heavy and annoying work to maintain all kinds of softwares. On the other hand, PAAS offers an integrated environment to design, develop, test, deploy and support custom applications [9, 11]. As for the outbreaking pests disasters, forest pests' experts can explore some systems aiming at the disasters in real time by PAAS and then supply them to all forestry administrators.

Resource Sharing. The forest pests reporting is in great quantity and cluttered. And the process from primary statistics to final reporting is extremely trivial. It not only wastes a lot of resources and material, but also delays the reporting. What's worse, some unexpected disasters cannot be dealt with in time. And grassroots administrators can't communicate effectively, which will result in breakdown of information flow.

Through special cloud computing service, we can easily make resource sharing possible. In the special cloud, there will be a communal space, and both the upper and lower levels (the State Forestry Administration and all local administrations and grassroots administrators) can get the information and data resources they need in real time. The efficiency of pests' control will increase greatly by this convenient and rapid way to access resources.

In addition, special cloud computing can also easily make the resources sharing between different devices possible. When the forestry administrators carry on a on-the-spot investigation in pests' control, they can easily access to data and use all the resources in cloud just by connecting to the cloud through some web devices, like laptops, mobile phones or PDA.

4 Security in Special Cloud

While deploying cloud computing, the primary problems to take into account are data information security and privacy. And it is the key issue to governments and enterprises to enhance data information security and privacy.

The main security problem of cloud computing exists not in the invasion by hackers and network worms, but in the cloud computing providers. Providers hold the root permissions for all machines in their cloud computing platforms. That is to say, providers hold all the information and data of users.

Thus, after the special cloud computing in forest pests' control being set up, the application processes the following advantages:

➢ The forest pests control work is different from business activities of enterprises. And the security level of its information and data is lower than that of governments and public safeties'. So the data information security demands in pests' control is much smaller.
➢ In our idea, C plays a key role in supervision and restraint of P as well as all users. This will greatly enhance the data information security level.
➢ In this idea, C and P together hold the root permissions for all machines and the resources of pests' control in the special cloud. This lets them supervise mutually, and then efficiently prevents careless disclosure by either P or C.
➢ There are not only professional IT maintenance personnel, but also pests control experts in special cloud. This makes the risk of data loss to minimum.

5 Conclusion

Not only general cloud computing service, special cloud computing in forest pests' control can provide necessary and professional service for forest pests' control. First, it gives all forestry administrations and grassroots administrators the ultra-large-scale computing power to enable them to efficiently collect, process data information of pests, then analyze and forecast the cycles of pests arise. Second, it provides a R&D platform for pest control management. Experts at forest pests can develop a variety of different systems that aim at different plants and pests, and make these systems available to other forest managers through resource sharing. And third, there's an effective pests management standard in special cloud to improve the interoperability of the system and the environment of collaboration within the pests control community. Last but not least, it supports flexible autonomy, so that all forest managers can acquire resources on demand, and make it easier to overcome the period of high rising of forest pests. What's more, it largely heightens the security and privacy of information and data resources.

However, cloud computing is still in its early stages, the relevant tools and techniques are being continually perfected. And the special cloud computing in forest pests' control is still just an idea. We need considerable effort to make it into a reality.

References

1. Pan, H.: Problems and Countermeasures in Forest Pests Prevention in China. J. Forest Pest and Disease 21(1) (2002)
2. Pan, H., Wu, J.: Occurrence Dynamics of Important Forest Pests in the Period of the Ninth-Five-Year Plan and Analysis on the Causes. J. Forest Pest and Disease 20(4) (2001)
3. Wang, Z., Cheng, J., Jiang, M.: Expert System and Its Application in Integrated Pest Management. J. Acta Agriculturae Jiangxi 12(1) (2000)
4. Ding, S., Cheng, S., Su, B.: The Multiple Fuzzy Regression Forecasting Model and Its Application. J. Fuzzy Systems and Mathematics 14(3) (2000)
5. Nathuji, R., Schwan, K., Somani, A., Joshi, Y.: VPM Tokens: Virtual Machine-aware Power Budgeting in Datacenters. J. Cluster Computing 12(2), 189–203 (2009)
6. Wen, L.: Construction of Forest Disease and Pest Consultation Diagnosis Expert System Based on Network. Master's Dissertation, Beijing Forestry University (2006)
7. Zhang, P.: Forest Pests MIS Development. Master's Dissertation, Nanjing Forestry University (2002)
8. Minoli, D.: Grid Computing for Commercial Enterprise Environments. In: Handbook on Information Technology in Finance. International Handbook on Information Systems. Pt. I, pp. 257–289. Springer, Heidelberg (2008)
9. Ma, D., Seidmann, A.: The Pricing Strategy Analysis for the "Software-as-a-Service" Business Model. In: Altmann, J., Neumann, D., Fahringer, T. (eds.) GECON 2008. LNCS, vol. 5206, pp. 103–112. Springer, Heidelberg (2008)
10. Foster, I., Zhao, Y., Raicu, I., Lu, S.: Cloud Computing and Grid Computing 360-Degree Compared. In: IEEE Grid Computing Environments (GCE 2008), Texas, pp. 1–10 (2008)
11. Li, H., Sedayao, J., Hahn-Steichen, J., Jimison, E., Spence, C., Chahal, S.: Developing an Enterprise Cloud Computing Strategy (2009),
   http://download.intel.com/it/pdf/320566.pdf
12. IT Modernization: From Grid to Cloud in Financial Services. (2009),
   http://www.platform.com/resources/brochures/
   FSCloud-MarketBrochure-web.pdf
13. Arista Networks, http://www.aristanetworks.com/
14. Amazon EC2, http://aws.amazon.com/ec2/
15. Google App Engine, http://code.google.com/appengine/
16. Microsoft Azure Services,
   http://www.microsoft.com/azure/default.mspx
17. IBM Blue Cloud, http://www.bluecloud.org/

IBM Cloud Computing Powering a Smarter Planet

Jinzy Zhu, Xing Fang, Zhe Guo, Meng Hua Niu,
Fan Cao, Shuang Yue, and Qin Yu Liu,

Abstract. With increasing need for intelligent systems supporting the world's businesses, Cloud Computing has emerged as a dominant trend to provide a dynamic infrastructure to make such intelligence possible. The article introduced how to build a smarter planet with cloud computing technology. First, it introduced why we need cloud, and the evolution of cloud technology. Secondly, it analyzed the value of cloud computing and how to apply cloud technology. Finally, it predicted the future of cloud in the smarter planet.

Keywords: Cloud Computing, Smarter Planet.

1 Why Cloud?

The world is increasingly interconnected, instrumented and intelligent, creating unprecedented opportunities for business and society. We need think about more intelligent ways to handle the 15 petabytes of new information we generate each day, and the massive increase of connected devices we use to work with that data. It's time for a platform designed for efficient, effective computing in wide open spaces. In other words, we need a smarter planet.

Success in the new smarter planet demands reduced capital and operating expense, greater collaboration, and flawless execution when responding to rapidly changing market conditions. Using a dynamic infrastructure that adapts to changing requirements, IBM Service Management helps clients create and deliver new services like cloud computing - to improve service quality, reduce costs, and manage risk. As a complement to your existing enterprise, IBM Cloud is a complete IBM Service Management package of hardware, software and services, which simplifies cloud computing acquisition and deployment.

2 Evolution of Cloud Computing Technology

As a new computing model, cloud computing has been in the making for a long time - - it embodies the development and evolution of existing computing styles such as grid computing and utility computing. Some traces of grid computing and utility computing can be found in cloud computing use cases. However, cloud computing distinguishes itself from previous technology with its combination of the latest in technical developments and emerging business model, creating remarkable commercial value in new use scenarios.

Taking IT capability as a service may be a simple idea, but to realize it, many problems remain to be solved. Different types of cloud computing services (IaaS, PaaS,

M.G. Jaatun, G. Zhao, and C. Rong (Eds.): CloudCom 2009, LNCS 5931, pp. 621–625, 2009.

SaaS) are faced with different problems. The following table shows the different technologies used in different cloud computing service types.

Table 1. Different technologies used in IaaS, PaaS and SaaS services

Service Type	IaaS	PaaS	SaaS
Service Category	VM Rental, Online Storage	Online Operating Environment, Online Database, Online Message Queue	Application and Software Rental
Service Customization	Server Template	Logic Resource Template	Application Template
Service Provisioning	Automation	Automation	Automation
Service Accessing and Using	Remote Console, Web 2.0	Online Development and Debugging, Integration of Offline Development Tools and Cloud	Web 2.0
Service Monitoring	Physical Resource Monitoring	Logic Resource Monitoring	Application Monitoring
Service Level Management	Dynamic Orchestration of Physical Resources	Dynamic Orchestration of Logic Resources	Dynamic Orchestration of Application
Service Resource Optimization	Network Virtualization, Server Virtualization, Storage Virtualization	Large-scale Distributed File System, Database, Middleware etc	Multi-tenancy
Service Measurement	Physical Resource Metering	Logic Resource Usage Metering	Business Resource Usage Metering
Service Integration and Combination	Load Balance	SOA	SOA, Mashup
Service Security	Storage Encryption and Isolation, VM Isolation, VLAN, SSL/SSH	Data Isolation, Operating Environment Isolation, SSL	Data Isolation, Operating Environment Isolation, SSL, Web Authentication and Authorization

At the IaaS level, what cloud computing service provider offer is basic computing and storage capability, such as the cloud computing center founded by IBM in Wuxi Software Park and Amazon EC2. Taking computing power provision as an example, the basic unit provided is the server, including CPU, memory, storage, operating system and some software. In order to allow users customize their own servers, server template technology is resorted to, which means binding certain server configuration and the operating system and software together, and providing customized functions as required at the same time. Service provision is crucial since it directly affects the service efficiency and the IaaS maintenance and operation costs. Automation, the core technology, can make resources available for users through self-service without getting the service providers involved. Additionally, virtualization is another key technology. It can maximize resource utilization efficiency and reduce cost of IaaS platform and user usage by promoting physical resource sharing. The dynamic migration function of virtualization technology can dramatically improve the service availability and this is attractive for many users.

At the PaaS level, what the service providers offer is packaged IT capability, or some logical resources, such as databases, file systems, and application operating environment. Currently, actual cases in the industry include Rational developer cloud of IBM, Azure of Microsoft and AppEngine of Google. At this level, two core technologies are involved. The first is software development, testing and running based on cloud. PaaS service is software developer-oriented. It used to be a huge difficulty for developers to write programs via network in the cloud environment, and now due to the improvement of network bandwidth, two technologies can solve this problem. The first is online development tools. Developers can directly complete remote development and application through browser and remote console (development tools run in the console) technologies without local installation of development tools. Another is integration technology of local development tools and cloud computing, which means to deploy the developed application directly into cloud computing environment through local development tools. The second core technology is large-scale distributed application operating environment. It refers to scalable application middleware, database and file system built with a large amount of servers. This application operating environment enables application to make full use of abundant computing and storage resource in cloud computing center to achieve full extension, go beyond the resource limitation of single physical hardware, and meet the access requirements of millions of Internet users.

At the SaaS level, service providers offer the industrial application directly to end users and various enterprise users. At this level, the following technologies are involved: Web 2.0, Mashup, SOA and multi-tenancy. The development of AJAX technology of Web 2.0 makes Web application easier to use, and brings user experience of desktop application to Web users, which in turn make people adapt to the transfer from desktop application to Web application easily. Mashup technology provide a capability of assembling contents on Web, which can allow users to customize websites freely and aggregate contents from different websites, and enables developers to build application quickly. Similarly, SOA provides combination and integration function as well, but it provides the function in the background of Web. Multi-tenancy is a technology that supports multi tenancies and customers in the same operating environment. It can significantly reduce resource consumptions and cost for every customer.

To sum up, important technologies used in cloud computing are: automation, virtualization, dynamic orchestration, online development, large-scale distributed application operating environment, Web 2.0, Mashup, SOA and multi-tenancy etc. Most of these technologies matured in recent years, and that's exactly why cloud computing is so different.

3   Value of Cloud Computing for Smarter Planet

With Cloud Computing, we could build a smarter planet. IBM Cloud fully demonstrated the application value of new technology and new methodology: reducing operation cost, easily and flexibly responding to business changes, building green datacenter.

Through virtualization technology, cloud computing center could increase the utilization rate of server, storage, network and so on; Automation technology could reduce labor cost. IT professionals can devote more energy to enhancing the value of using IT for their enterprises and less on the day-to-day challenges of IT.

Cloud computing liberates organizations to deliver IT services as never before. Cloud enables the dynamic availability of IT applications and infrastructure, regardless of location. More rapid service delivery results from the ability to orchestrate the tasks to create, configure, provision and add computing power in support of IT and business services much more quickly than would be possible with today's computing infrastructure.

The great majority of experts in the science community now agree that it is overwhelmingly obvious that climate change is an accelerating reality that will impact us and our children much sooner than we think. IT leaders throughout the world understand that Green IT technologies will pay a massively greater role in the coming years, and will be among the fastest growing areas in IT. Unitek Education has worked closely with Boots on the Roof to develop a boot camp that discusses a comprehensive approach to Green IT, including waste reduction, virtualization, blade technologies and cloud computing.

4   Cloud Computing Model Application Methodology

Cloud computing is a new business services model. This kind of service delivery model is based on future development consideration and can meet current development requirements. The three levels of cloud computing service (IaaS, PaaS and SaaS) cover a huge range of services. Besides computing and the service delivery mode of storage infrastructure, various modes such as data, software application, programming model etc are applicable to cloud computing. More importantly, cloud computing mode involves all aspects of enterprise transformation in its evolution, so technology architecture is only one part of it, and multi-aspect development such as organization, processes and different business modes should also be under consideration. Based on IBM Enterprise Architecture methodology and combined with best practices of cloud computing in different areas, IBM has designed a Cloud Mode Application Methodology to guide industry customer analysis and solve potential problems and risks emerged during the evolution from current computing mode to cloud computing mode. This methodology can also be used to instruct the investment and decision making analysis of cloud computing mode, determine the process, standard, interface and public service of IT assets deployment and management to promote business development. The diagram below shows the overall status of this methodology.

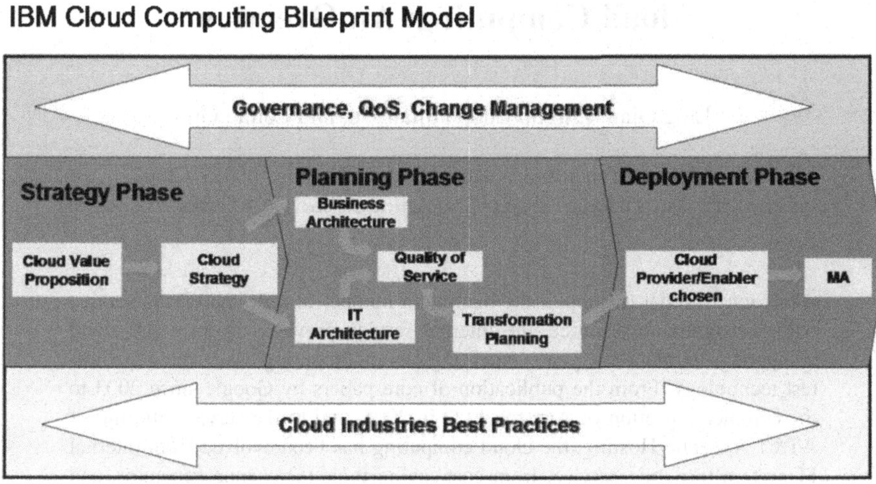

IBM Cloud Computing Blueprint Model

Fig. 1. IBM Cloud Computing Blueprint Model

5 The Outlook of Cloud Computing

Cloud computing un-tethers the applications from the underlying physical infrastructure and delivers them to the end user over the internet or intranet. Computing processes function without a direct connection to the computer or ownership of the application or infrastructure. In the 21st century, the intelligence resides in the infrastructure. Cloud computing can serve as the "connective tissue" among the foundational building blocks of technology and skills that IBM has defined and delivered for years.

Cloud Computing: An Overview

Ling Qian, Zhiguo Luo, Yujian Du, and Leitao Guo

53A, Xibianmennei Ave, Xuanwu District, Beijing 100053, China
{qianling,luozhiguo,duyujian,guoleitao}@chinamobile.com

Abstract. In order to support the maximum number of user and elastic service with the minimum resource, the Internet service provider invented the cloud computing. within a few years, emerging cloud computing has became the hottest technology. From the publication of core papers by Google since 2003 to the commercialization of Amazon EC2 in 2006, and to the service offering of AT&T Synaptic Hosting, the cloud computing has been evolved from internal IT system to public service, from cost-saving tools to revenue generator, and from ISP to telecom. This paper introduces the concept, history, pros and cons of cloud computing as well as the value chain and standardization effort.

Keywords: Cloud computing, Cloud Storage, Virtualization.

1 Definitions of Cloud Computing

Similar to e-commerce, cloud computing is one of the most vague technique terminologies in history. One reason is that cloud computing can be used in many application scenarios, the other reason is that cloud computing are hyped by lots of companies for business promotion. From the Hyper Cycle published by Gartner Group in 2008, we can see that the cloud computing is in the phase of fast growing.

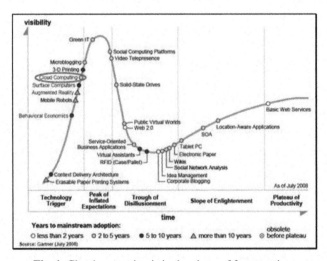

Fig. 1. Cloud computing is in the phase of fast growing

M.G. Jaatun, G. Zhao, and C. Rong (Eds.): CloudCom 2009, LNCS 5931, pp. 626–631, 2009.
© Springer-Verlag Berlin Heidelberg 2009

In the MIT Centennial talk in 1961, John McCarthy said that "... The computer utility could become the basis of a new and important industry", which implied the underlying concepts of cloud computing. However the "cloud computing" as a whole is probably first introduced by Eric Schmidt in his talk on Search Engine Strategies Conferences in 2006[15].

Now there are lots of definitions and metaphors of cloud computing. From our points of view, *cloud computing is a kind of computing technique where IT services are provided by massive low-cost computing units connected by IP networks*. Cloud computing is rooted in search engine platform design. There are 5 major technical characteristics of cloud computing: (1) large scale computing resources (2) high scalability & elastic (3)shared resource pool (virtualized and physical resource) (4)dynamic resource scheduling and (5) general purpose.

2 History and Status

With the explosion of the Internet, tight pressure is put to the existing storage and computing facilities. The Internet service providers start to use the cheap commodity PCs as the underlying hardware platform. Various kinds of software technologies are invented to make these PCs work elastically, which has led to 3 major cloud computing styles based on the underlying resource abstraction technologies: the Amazon style, Google Style and Microsoft style.

- Amazon's cloud computing is based on **server virtualization** technology. Amazon released Xen-based Elastic Compute Cloud™ (EC2), object storage service (S3) and structure data storage service (SimpleDB)[12] during the 2006 – 2007, under the name Amazon Web Service™ (AWS)[9]. On-demand and cheaper AWS becomes the pioneer of Infrastructure as a Service (IaaS) provider.
- Google's style is based on **technique-specific sandbox**. Google published several research papers from 2003 to 2006[1-5], which outline a kind of Platform as a Service (PaaS) cloud computing. The platform, which is called Google App Engine™ (GAE), is released to public as a service in 2008.
- Microsoft Azure™ [10] is released in Oct. 2008, which uses Windows Azure Hypervisor (WAH) as the underlying cloud infrastructure and .NET as the application container. Azure also offers services including BLOB object storage and SQL service.

It's hard to judge which one is better, but apparently server virtualization is more flexible and compatible with existing software and applications; while the sandboxes put more restrictions on programming languages but less abstraction overhead. Currently, server virtualization is the most popular resource abstraction technique in cloud computing.

Except these public cloud services, lots of companies has experimented and/or implemented internal cloud computing systems. Cloud computing is already key strategy for IT vendors, ISP and telecom service providers. Even further, United States of America and Japan have made cloud computing the national strategy. The following table lists some of the adopters for each style.

Table 1. Three major cloud computing styles and their adopters, based on the resource abstraction techniques

Resource Abstraction Tech.	Adopters
Server Virtualization (Amazon Style)	Amazon EC2 (Xen), GoGrid (Xen), 21vianet CloudEx (Xen), RackSpace Mosso (Xen), Joyent (Accelerator), AT&T Synaptic (Vmware), Verizon CaaS (Vmware)
Technique-specific sandbox (Google Style)	GAE (Python & JVM), Heroku (Ruby), Morph Application Platform(Ruby)
Server Virtualization & Technique-specific sandbox (Microsoft Style)	Microsoft Azure (WAH & .NET)

3 Cloud Computing Architecture

Many organizations and researchers have defined the architecture for cloud computing. Basically the whole system can be divided into the core stack and the management. In the core stack, there are three layers: (1) Resource (2) Platform and (3) Application. The resource layer is the infrastructure layer which is composed of physical and virtualized computing, storage and networking resources.

The platform layer is the most complex part which could be divided into many sublayers. E.g. a computing framework manages the transaction dispatching and/or task scheduling. A storage sub-layer provides unlimited storage and caching capability. The application server and other components support the same general application logic as before with either on-demand capability or flexible management, such that no components will be the bottle neck of the whole system.

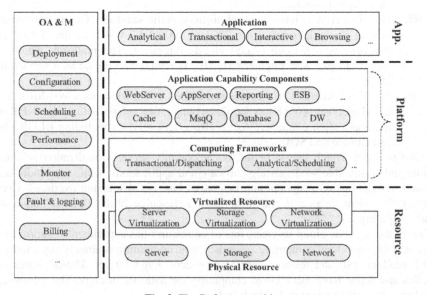

Fig. 2. The Reference architecture

Based on the underlying resource and components, the application could support large and distributed transactions and management of huge volume of data. All the layers provide external service through web service or other open interfaces.

4 Cloud Computing Categories

There are diverse dimensions to classify cloud computing, two commonly used categories are: service boundary and service type.

* From the service boundary's view, cloud computing can be classified as public cloud, private cloud and hybrid cloud. The public cloud refers to services provided to external parties. The enterprises build and operate private cloud for themselves. Hybrid cloud shares resources between public cloud and private cloud by a secure network. Virtual Private Cloud (VPC) services released by Google[8] and Amazon[9] are examples of Hybrid cloud.

* From the service type's view, cloud computing can be classified as Infrastructure as a Service (IaaS), Platform as a Service (PaaS) and Software as a Service (SaaS). SaaS provide services to end users, while IaaS and PaaS provide services to ISV and developers - leaving a margin for 3-party application developers.

5 Advantages and Risks

The cloud computing is a Win-Win strategy for the service provider and the service consumer. We summarize the advantages as below:

- ✓ **Satisfy business requirements on demand** by resizing the resource occupied by application to fulfill the changing the customer requirements.
- ✓ **Lower cost and energy-saving**. By making use of low cost PC, customerized low power consuming hardware and server virtualization, both CAPEX and OPEX are decreased.
- ✓ **Improve the efficiency of resource management** through dynamic resource scheduling.

However there are also some major challenges to be studied.

- ✓ **Privacy and security**. Customer has concerns on their privacy and data security than traditional hosting service.
- ✓ **The continuity of service**. It refers to the factors that may negatively affected the continuity of cloud computing such as Internet problems, power cut-off, service disruption and system bugs. Followed are some typical cases of such problems: In November 2007, RackSpace, Amazon's competitor, stopped its service for 3 hours because of power cut-off at its data center; in June 2008, Google App Engine service broke off for 6 hours due to some bugs of storage system; In March 2009, Microsoft Azure experienced 22 hours' out of service caused by OS system update. Currently, the public cloud provider based on virtualization, defines the reliability of service as 99.9% in SLA.
- ✓ **Service migration**. Currently, no regularity organization have reached the agreement on the standardization of cloud computing's external interface.

As a result, once a customer started to use the service of a cloud computing provider, he is most likely to be locked by the provider, which lay the customer in unfavorable conditions.

6 Value Chain of Cloud Computing

The following figure depicts the cloud computing value chain with related organizations and their functionalities.

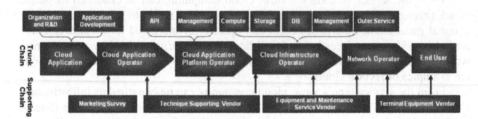

Fig. 3. The trunk and supporting value chain of cloud computing

✓ Cloud Applications: The driven force of cloud computing, which is different from traditional application module.

✓ Cloud Application Operator: Offers cloud computing products. In many cases, they are same as by application provider or platform provider.

✓ Cloud Application Platform Operator: Provides cloud application and development platform, such as GAE™ and Force.com™, etc.

✓ Cloud infrastructure operator: Provide infrastructure service, such as AWS™ and GoGrid.

✓ Network Operator: Provide network access service to the above platform operators and the end users.

✓ Technique supporting vendor: Offer technical support to players in this chain, including software development, testing, provisioning and operation.

✓ Terminal equipment vendor: Offer device maintenance service for all players in the chain.

✓ End Users: End users pays for the cloud services.

7 Standardization

Distributed Management Task Force[7] is an industry alliance composed by over 200 IT related corporations including IBM, EMC, HP, Cisco, Oracle and Microsoft, which is committed to develop, maintain and popularize the IT management system under enterprise context. DMTF has published Virtualization Management Initiative and Open Virtualization Format, and the latter is declared to be supported by major vendors. DMFT founded Open Cloud Standards Incubator at the year 2009, whose aim is to clarify the interoperability between several cloud systems.

OGF (Open Grid Forum) has started some work to discuss cloud computing related standards, which is a standardization organization like IETF aiming at promoting the standardization and best practice of distribute computing related techniques. CCI-WG (Open Cloud Computing Interface Working Group) is established to design resource management API for IaaS cloud services by OGF. Some cloud computing service providers like ElasticHosts, GoGrid, and FlexiScale have announced to adhere this API in the later developments.

Besides, SNIA (Storage Network Industry Association), CSA (Cloud Security Alliance) and OCC (Open Cloud Consortium) is now working on cloud storage, cloud security and cloud intercommunication standards respectively. In order to coordinate the work of above standardization organizations, OMG (Object Management Group) appealed that all the organizations maintain their own standards on http://cloud-standards.org.

PaaS and SaaS don't have related cloud computing standards yet. Most current systems exploit mature protocols and have variety kinds of service forms.

References

[1] Ghemawat, S., Gobioff, H., Leung, S.-T.: The Google File System. In: SOSP (2003)
[2] Dean, J., Ghemawat, S.: MapReduce: Simplifed Data Processing on Large Clusters. In: OSDI 2004 (2004)
[3] Chang, F., Dean, J., Ghemawat, S., et al.: Bigtable: A Distributed Storage System for Structured Data. In: OSDI 2006 (2006)
[4] Burrows, M.: The Chubby lock service for loosely-coupled distributed systems. In: OSDI 2006 (2006)
[5] Pike, R., Dorward, S., Griesemer, R., Quinlan, S.: Interpreting the Data: Parallel Analysis with Sawzall. Scientific Programming (2005)
[6] Open Cloud Computing Interface, http://www.occi-wg.org/doku.php
[7] Distributed Management Task Force, http://www.dmtf.org
[8] Google App Engine, http://appengine.google.com
[9] Amazon Web Service, http://aws.amazon.com
[10] Microsoft Azure, http://www.microsoft.com/azure/
[11] DeCandia, G., Hastorun, D., Jampani, M., et al.: Dynamo: Amazon's Highly Available Key-value Store. In: SOSP 2007 (October 2007)
[12] Schmidt, E.: Conversation with Eric Schmidt hosted by Danny Sullivan. In: Search Engine Strategies Conference (August 2006)

Integrating Cloud-Computing-Specific Model into Aircraft Design[*]

Tian Zhimin[1,2], Lin Qi[2], and Yang Guangwen[1]

[1] Department of Computer Science & Technology, Tsinghua University
[2] Aviation Industry Development Research Center of China
T_zhm@163.com, linqi_1999@yahoo.com.cn, ygw@tsinghua.edu.cn

Abstract. Cloud Computing is becoming increasingly relevant, as it will enable companies involved in spreading this technology to open the door to Web 3.0. In the paper, the new categories of services introduced will slowly replace many types of computational resources currently used. In this perspective, grid computing, the basic element for the large scale supply of cloud services, will play a fundamental role in defining how those services will be provided. The paper tries to integrate cloud computing specific model into aircraft design. This work has acquired good results in sharing licenses of large scale and expensive software, such as CFD (Computational Fluid Dynamics), UG, CATIA, and so on.

Keywords: Cloud Computing, Model, Aircraft Design, License Share.

1 Introduction

An important factor to the success of portals like Google[1], Yahoo[2] and MSN[3] is that often involve highly personalized solutions or even, in the case of Google, an ad hoc infrastructure. Both IBM[4] and Google have taken the latter as starting point to create the new computing paradigm, cloud computing[5], which will allow the companies to open the doors to Web 3.0.

Cloud computing, recently introduced by the media, is thought by some to be an innovative term. But behind this poetic name probably lies one of the most important new technologies in the ICT area[6]. The first to give prominence to the term of cloud computing was Google's CEO Eric Schmidt, in late 2006. The term refers to an important and long-term trend: computing over the Internet.

The birth of cloud computing is very recent, but the technology's origins can be traced to the evolution of grid computing technologies and in particular, the accomplished business way from the main search engines, which were also the first to propose cloud services on the market, such as the well-known Amazon ecommerce site[7][8]. Gartner maintains that cloud computing is one of the 10 strategic technologies for 2008 and many companies will compete in this IT sector.

---

[*] This work has been supported by 863. (NO.2006AA01A106).

M.G. Jaatun, G. Zhao, and C. Rong (Eds.): CloudCom 2009, LNCS 5931, pp. 632–637, 2009.
© Springer-Verlag Berlin Heidelberg 2009

In the aviation industry cloud computing model is exploited step by step. During the tenth five-year plan, we have already create grid computing platform for aviation industry that implemented share of license of expensive software and representative scientific computing, such as CFD, etc. However, we only resolve the problem of lack of license at the peak of application, regardless of priority. For example, the owner of the hardware and software resources may have preferential right. They may seize/order the resources that have being used. In this work, we will resolve the problem by cloud computing pattern.

2   Cloud Computing Model in Aviation Industry

A key differentiating element of a successful information technology (IT) is its ability to become a true, valuable, and economical contributor to cyberinfrastructure[9]. Cloud computing embraces cyberinfrastructure and builds upon decades of research in virtualization, distributed computing, grid computing, utility computing, and more recently networking, web and software services. It implies a service oriented architecture, reduced information technology overhead for the end user, greater flexibility, reduced total cost of ownership, on-demand services and so on[10][11].

2.1   General Framework

The framework of Cloud Computing Platform of Aviation Industry(CCPAI) includes physical resource layer, grid middleware layer, Cloud Middleware Layer and Application Service Layer. Meanwhile, the framework efficiently provides a mechanism of monitoring management and security.

The physical resource layer integrates high performance computing infrastructure, floating license, all sorts of data that every factory and institute has provided. In the grid middleware layer, the platform may implement share of hardware based on virtualization technology. The cloud middleware layer, as the core of the CCPAI, encapsulates the services such as computing resources scheduling service, data service, global floating license management service, charging service. The layer supports to create the typical application of the whole industry. In application layer, it is conceived to construct share of UG/CATIA, CFD computing, DMU(Digital Mock-up) service and so on. The application is divided into small work units, and each unit can be executed in any computational node. The framework also has a distributed file system, which stores data on the various nodes. Once the cloud services supply platform has been created, it will provide access to the grid, to those factories/institutes requesting it. Every guest may decide whether to offer cloud services or introduce its services in a general catalogue within a default cloud and in the same common administrative domain. The main features of the platform include high system reliability and transparent management of information shifting. One possible configuration of the hierarchical abstraction layers involved in this case-study is shown in the Figure 1.

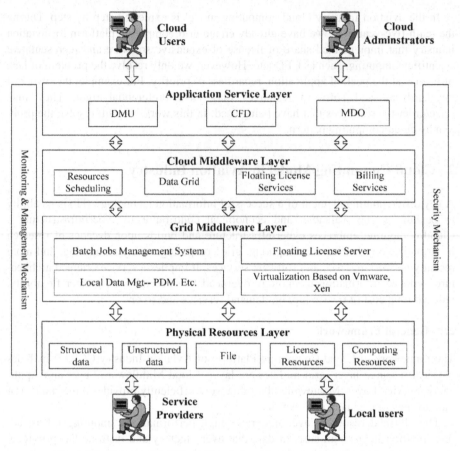

Fig. 1. The framework of Cloud Computing Platform of Aviation Industry

The mechanism of monitoring management is responsible for running of the whole cloud computing environment. In defense industry information security is of vital importance. Intellectual property protection is crucial among the facto-ries/institutes. Information security strategy is proposed to ensure confidentiality of all of the resources in CCPAI. According to responsibility and right, we divide the users into four categories: local user, cloud user, resources provider, and cloud administrators. The local users directly use the cluster and data of the companies owned, while they don't use the resources of other companies. The cloud users, as aircraft designers over cloud, use UG/CATIA floating license to design or manufac-ture the aircraft. The resources providers are the administrators of the facto-ries/institutes. They are responsible for deploying their hardware and software re-sources on the cloud. The cloud administrators monitor and configure the whole cloud platform.

2.2 Virtualization

Virtualization is another very useful concept. It allows abstraction and isolation of lower-level functionalities and underlying hardware. This enables portability of higher-level functions and sharing and/or aggregation of the physical resources.

The virtualization concept has been around in some form since 1960s. Since then, the concept has matured considerably and it has been applied to all aspects of computing – memory, storage, processors, software, networks, as well as services that IT offers. It is the combination of the growing needs and the recent advances in the IT architectures and solutions that is now bringing the virtualization to the true commodity level. Virtualization, through its economy of scale, and its ability to offer very advanced and complex IT services at a reasonable cost, is poised to become, along with wireless and highly distributed and pervasive computing devices, such as sensors and personal cell-based access devices, the driving technology behind the next wave in IT growth.

In the aerocraft design phase, the system will break the input data as so to split a big analysis job into several fairly small jobs. After the split, each small job will have its own input and output data. Job scheduling software will submit the split jobs to the computing resource pool in the grid, and conduct each analysis separately in each node, after the job is done, the analysis result will be merged by the postprocessing, and store the result in PDM data base. The analysis process in the grid is illustrated in the following figure.

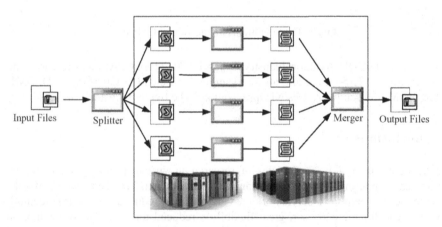

Fig. 2. The process of Flow Field Solving

3 The Simplified Architecture of CCPAI

The aims of the CCPAI range from license share of expensive software to resources scheduling, to management and share of industry experimental data and design drawings, to run of the platform, and to mechanism of security and monitoring. The platform has efficiently aggregated the resources, including hardware and software, of CAE(Chinese Aeronautical Establishment), ACTRI(Aviation Computing Technology Research Institute), FAI(The First Aircraft Institute of AVIC), and

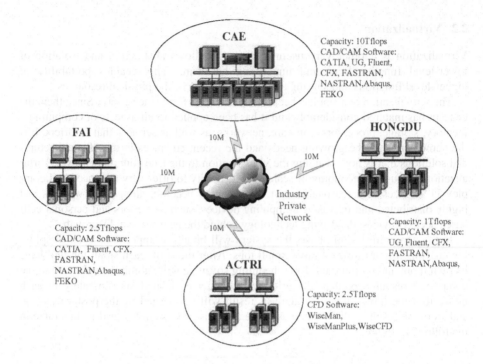

Fig. 3. The Simplified Architecture of CCPAI

HONGDU(HONGDU Aviation Industry Group LTD). The CCPAI takes research and manufacturing of L15 trainer aircraft for example to efficiently support the CFD, DMU and MDO(Multidisciplinary Design Optimization). The figure 3 illustrates the case.

4 Conclusions

Cloud computing builds on decades of research in virtualization, grid computing, distributed computing, utility computing, and more recently network, web and software services. It implies a service oriented architecture, reduced information technology overhead for the end-user, great flexibility, reduced total cost of ownership, on demand services and many other things. This paper discussed the concept of cloud computing, issues it tries to address, related research topics, and a cloud implementation in aviation industry. Our experience technology is excellent and we are in the process of addition functionalities and features that will make it even more suitable for cloud framework construction.

References

1. Google App Engine, http://code.google.com/appengine/
2. HP, Intel and Yahoo Cloud Computing Test Bed,
   http://labs.yahoo.com/Cloud_Computing

3. Microsoft Cloud Computing Tools,
   http://msdn.microsoft.com/en-us/vstudio/cc972640.aspx
4. IBM Blue Cloud,
   http://www03.ibm.com/press/us/en/pressrelease/22613.wss
5. Wikipedia, Cloud Computing (May 2009),
   http://en.wikipedia.org/wiki/Cloud_computing
6. Vaguero, L., et al.: A Break in the Clouds: Towards a Cloud Definition. ACM SIGCOMM Computer Communication Review 39(1), 1 (2009)
7. Amazon Web Services, http://aws.amazon.com
8. Palankar, M., Onibokun, A., et al.: Amazon S3 for Science Grids: a Viable Solution. In: 4th USENIX Symposium on Networked Systems Design & Implementation (NSDI 2007) (2007)
9. Vouk, M.A.: Cloud computing-Issues, research and implementations. Information Technology Interfaces, 31–40 (2008)
10. Ramakrishnan, A., Singh, G., et al.: Scheduling Data-Intensive Workflows onto Storage-Constrained Distributed Resources. In: CCGrid 2007 (2007)
11. Liu, H., Orban, D.: Gridbatch: Cloud computing for large-scale data-intensive batch applications. In: CCGRID, pp. 295–305. IEEE Computer Society, Los Alamitos (2008)

Towards a Theory of Universally Composable Cloud Computing

Huafei Zhu

I^{2}R, A*STAR, Singapore

Abstract. This paper studies universally composable Cloud computing and makes the following two-fold contributions
- In the first fold, various notions of Clouds are introduced and formalized. The security of public Cloud computing is formalized within the standard secure computations framework.
- In the second, a universally composable theorem of Cloud computing in the presence of monotone adversary structure within Canetti's universally composable framework is presented and analyzed.

Our contribution possibly bridges security gaps between the industrial views of Clouds and that of theoretical researchers.

1 Introduction

Cloud computing is a style of computing services over the Internet, usually at the scale and with the reliability of a data center (say, [3], [12] and [11]). Cloud computing is closely related to the notion of Grid computing. Grid interfaces tend to be complete and try to expose a complete set of available system capability. Cloud interfaces however, tend to be minimalistic and try to expose only a limited set of capabilities so that is enough to process a given job. There are at least two types of computing Clouds: the first category of computing Cloud is designed to providing computing instances on demand, while the second category of computing Cloud is designed to providing computing capacity on demand. As an example of the first category of computing Cloud, Amazon's EC2 service provides computing instances on demand (say [1] and [2]). As an example of the second category of computing Cloud, Google's MapReduce application provides computing capacity on demand [10]. Note that both computing clouds use similar machines, but the first is designed to scale out by providing additional computing instances, while the second is designed to support data or compute intensive applications by scaling capacity.

It is certainly welcome to distinguish between private Clouds and public Clouds. A private Cloud is designed to be used internally by a company or an organization while a public Cloud is designed to provide Cloud-based services to third party clients. For example, the Google file system [13], Mapreduce [10] and BigTable [14] are examples of private Cloud services that are designed to realize certain functionalities on demand by Google. Since private/public Cloud services serve multiple customers, there are various issues related to multiple

M.G. Jaatun, G. Zhao, and C. Rong (Eds.): CloudCom 2009, LNCS 5931, pp. 638–643, 2009.
© Springer-Verlag Berlin Heidelberg 2009

customers possibly sharing the same piece of hardware and software and having data accessible by third parties, private/public Cloud services may present security, compliance or regulatory issues. On the other side, there are economy scale advantages when security related services are provided by data centers.

Security is an area of Cloud computing that presents some special challenges. For Cloud computing applications, security is still somewhat immature. For example, the first category of Cloud [1] and [2] and the second category of Cloud [13], [10] and [14] do not support high-level security applications although they are expected in later developments.

1.1 This Work

This paper towards a theory of Cloud in the universally composable framework in the context of the standard multi-party computations. Firstly, various notions of Clouds are introduced and formalized. Secondly, a universally composable theorem of Cloud computing in the framework of Canetti is presented which is informally stated below:

A universally composable Cloud computing theorem: Let $\mathcal{A}$ and $\mathcal{B}$ be monotone adversary structures such that $\mathcal{B} \preceq \mathcal{A}$. Let f and g be two n-party functions, and ρ be an n-party protocol that non-adaptively and t-securely evaluates f in the presence of adversary structure $\mathcal{A}$. Let π be an n-party protocol that non-adaptively and t-securely evaluates g in the f-hybrid model in the presence of adversary structure $\mathcal{B}$. Then the composed protocol π^ρ non-adaptively and t-securely evaluates g in the adversary structure $\mathcal{B}$.

1.2 Applications

Our result bridges security-related gaps between industrial views of clouds and that from theoretical researchers. To demonstrate interesting applications of our result, we consider the parallel computing of MapReduce over Clouds.

MapReduce is a simple yet powerful interface that enables automatic parallelization and distribution of large-scale computations introduced and formalized by Dean and Ghemawat [10]. MapReduce is a programming model and an associated implemenation for processing and generating large data sets. In MapReduce model, users specify a map function that processes a key/value pair to generate a set of intermediate key/value pairs, and reduce function merges all intermediate values associated with the same intermediate key. Assume that the adversary structure in the first map-and-reduce is $\mathcal{A}$ and the instance implementation is secure against the adversarial structure $\mathcal{A}$ and in the second map-and-reduce is $\mathcal{B}$ and the instance implementation is secure against the adversarial structure $\mathcal{B}$, then the composition of the two map-and-reduce computations should maintain the security in the presence of the adversary structure $\mathcal{B}$, where $\mathcal{B} \preceq \mathcal{A}$.

Another example is Cloud-storage in the context of secure payment systems. Note that a payment system cannot naturally be formulated as a computation of a single function: what we want here is to continuously keep track of how much money each player has available and avoid cases where for instances people spend more money than they have. Such a system should behave like a secure general purpose computer: it can receive inputs from the players at several points in time and each time it will produce results for each player computed in a specified way from the current inputs and from previous stored values. A MapReduce computation can easily produce list of transactions, with each transaction contains payments of players. To maintain the security of transaction record in different storages, the universally composable security is essential for such an application environment.

2   A Formalization of Cloud and Cloud Computing

Secure Cloud computing can be viewed as an extension of classic secure computations of any function in the computational setting by Yao [15], Goldreich, Micali and Wigderson [8] and Goldreich, Micali and Wigderson [9] or information theoretical setting by Ben-Or, Goldwasser and Wigderson [4] and Chaum, Crépeau and Damgård [7]. Any party in a protocol is formalized as an Interactive Turing Machine (ITM). An ITM is a six-tape deterministic machine with a ready only input tape, a ready-only random type, a read/write work tape, a read-only communication tape, a write-only communication tape, and a write-only output tape. The content of the input tape is called the input, and the content of the output tape is called the output. The content of the read-only communication tape is called the received messages and the content on the write-only communication tape is called sent messages. The infinite content of the random tape is called the infinite unbiased coin tosses of the machine. Let I be a countable index set. An ensemble indexed by I is a sequence of random variables $X = \{X_i\}_{i \in I}$. An ensemble $X = \{X_i\}_{i \in I}$ is polynomial time computable (or constructible) if there exists a probabilistic polynomial time algorithm A so that for every $i \in I$, the random variables $A(1^n)$ and X_n are identically distributed (notation: $A(1^n) \equiv X_n$).

2.1   A Formalization of Cloud

Recall that the concept of Cloud computing refers to both applications delivered as services over the Internet and the hardware and software in the data centers that provide those services (hardware as a service and software as a service). We view hardware and software of a data center as ITMs, and formalize notions of Cloud and Cloud computing in the context of ITMs.

Let $\{\mathcal{F}_i\}_{i=1}^{\infty}$ be a set of functionalities provided by a service-center. Let $\mathcal{F} = \{\mathcal{F}_i\}_{i=1}^{\infty}$. Let $\{\mathcal{I}_i\}_{i=1}^{\infty}$ be a set of implementations of $\mathcal{F}$. Let $\mathcal{P}$ be a set of functionalities listed in a public bulletin board (a bulletin board is a read-only public tape for all users. A service provider however can write strings on the bulletin board). A functionality $\mathcal{F}_i$ is called public if $\mathcal{F}_i \in \mathcal{P}$. A functionality $\mathcal{F}_i$ is called private if $\mathcal{F}_i \in \mathcal{F} \setminus \mathcal{P}$.

We say a functionality $\mathcal{F}_i \in \mathcal{F}$ is available if there exists an onto mapping ϕ such that $\phi(\mathcal{F}_i) \subseteq \mathcal{I}$. If an available functionality $\mathcal{F}_i \in \mathcal{P}$, we say $\mathcal{F}_i$ is publicly available. If an available functionality $\mathcal{F}_i \in \mathcal{F} \setminus \mathcal{P}$, we say $\mathcal{F}_i$ is privately available.

Definition 1. *Let $\mathcal{F}$ be a set of available functionalities $\{\mathcal{F}_i\}_{i=1}^{\infty}$. Let $C_{\mathcal{F}}$ be a set consisting of all pre-images of $\{\phi^{-1}(\phi(\mathcal{F}_i))\} \subseteq \mathcal{I}$, where $\mathcal{F}_i \in \mathcal{F}$. We call $C_{\mathcal{F}}$ a Cloud. We say $C_{\mathcal{F}}$ is a public Cloud if $C_{\mathcal{F}} = \{\phi^{-1}(\phi(\mathcal{F}_i))\}$, where $\mathcal{F}_i \in \mathcal{P}$. We say $C_{\mathcal{F}}$ is a private Cloud if $C_{\mathcal{F}} = \{\phi^{-1}(\phi(\mathcal{F}_i))\}$, where $\mathcal{F}_i \in \mathcal{F} \setminus \mathcal{P}$.*

Definition 2. *If $C_{\mathcal{F}} = I$, we say the Cloud is complete; We refer to the complementary set $I \setminus C_{\mathcal{F}}$ as the complementary Cloud, denoted by co-$C_{\mathcal{F}}$.*

2.2   A Formalization of Cloud Computing

Throughout the paper, a Cloud $C_{\mathcal{F}}$ refers to a publicly available Cloud. We further assume that the publicly available Cloud $C_{\mathcal{F}}$ is complete, i.e., $C_{\mathcal{F}} = I$.

The Cloud environment. In this section, a new notion which is called Cloud environment $\mathcal{Z}$ is introduced and formalized. We model $\mathcal{Z}$ an environment where all Cloud computing are executed. The environment $\mathcal{Z}$ includes external environment (e.g., a platform, data storage/backup systems and communication channels for applications of the Cloud) and internal environment (e.g., software and hardware in the data-center) of a Cloud. The $\mathcal{Z}$ communicates an probabilistic polynomial time Turing Machine called adversary $\mathcal{A}$ during an execution of a computation freely during the course of computation. The task of Cloud environment Z is to provide inputs to all parties in the Cloud and instruct the adversary $\mathcal{A}$ to communicate with the honest parties and coordinate with corrupted parties in the protocol instances. The Cloud environment Z receives all outputs of parties and will output its internal state eventually.

The monotone adversary structure. It is unknown to the honest players which subset of players is corrupted during the course of Cloud computation. We thus define an adversary structure $\mathcal{A}$, which is simply a family of subsets of players. The adversary structure could comprise all subsets with cardinality less than some threshold value t (i.e., at most t parties can be corrupted by the adversary $\mathcal{A}$). Since in the Cloud computing environment, the adversary's structure can be different in the different Cloud environment, we must require that any adversary structure is monotone.

Definition 3. *Let $\mathcal{A}$ and $\mathcal{B}$ be two adversarial structures. We say $\mathcal{B} \preceq \mathcal{A}$, if the corrupted parties in $\mathcal{B}$ is a subset of $\mathcal{A}$.*

3   Universally Composable Cloud Computing

The universally composable framework defines a probabilistic polynomial time (PPT) environment machine $\mathcal{Z}$. $\mathcal{Z}$ oversees the execution of a protocol π in the real world involving PPT parties and a real world adversary $\mathcal{A}$ and the execution of a protocol in the ideal world involving dummy parties and an ideal world adversary $\mathcal{S}$ (a simulator). In the real world, parties (some of them are corrupted) interact with each other according to a specified protocol π. In the ideal world, dummy parties (some of them are corrupted) interact with an ideal functionality $\mathcal{F}$. The task of $\mathcal{Z}$ is to distinguish between two executions. We refer to [6] for a detailed description of the executions, and definitions of IDEAL$_{\mathcal{F},\mathcal{S},\mathcal{Z}}$ and REAL$_{\pi,\mathcal{A},\mathcal{Z}}$.

Let π be a protocol with an PPT adversary $\mathcal{A}$. Let t be the maximum number of parties $\mathcal{A}$ may non-adaptively corrupt (i.e., the adversary $\mathcal{A}$ may non-adaptively corrupt parties as long as at most t parties are corrupted altogether). Once a party is corrupted, the internal state of a corrupted party becomes available to the adversary.

Definition 4. *Let f be a n-party function and π be a protocol for n-party. We say that π is t-securely evaluates f if for any real world adversary $\mathcal{A}$, there exists an ideal world adversary $\mathcal{S}$ such that for any environment $\mathcal{Z}$, the two random variables IDEAL$_{f,\mathcal{S},\mathcal{Z}}$ and EXEC$_{\pi,\mathcal{A},\mathcal{Z}}$) are computationally indistinguishable.*

Let $\mathcal{A}$ be an adversary that can only corrupt a subset of the players if that subset is in $\mathcal{A}$. Let $A \in \mathcal{A}$, and $B \subseteq A$ (hence $B \in \mathcal{A}$). Let π be a protocol that realizes a functionality $\mathcal{F}$ in the f-hybrid model. Let ρ be a protocol that universally composably realizes the functionality f. By the definition of the UC-security, there exists an ideal world adversary $\mathcal{S}$ such that REAL$_{\rho,\mathcal{A},\mathcal{Z}} \approx$ IDEAL$_{f,\mathcal{S},\mathcal{Z}}$ and thus REAL$_{\rho,\mathcal{B},\mathcal{Z}} \approx$ IDEAL$_{f,\mathcal{S}|_B,\mathcal{Z}}$, where the notion $\mathcal{S}|_B$ means that the simulator is restricted to the adversarial structure $\mathcal{B}$. Without the loss of generality, we simple write $\mathcal{S}|_B$ as $\mathcal{S}$ when the protocol execution is clear in the context). If we assume that π realizes the functionality $\mathcal{F}$ in the f-hybrid model, then there exists an ideal world such that REAL$_{\pi^\rho,\mathcal{B},\mathcal{Z}} \approx$ IDEAL$_{\mathcal{F}^f,\mathcal{S},\mathcal{Z}}$. Roughly speaking, if the first Cloud who invokes the protocol ρ securely computes the functionality f and the second Cloud who invokes a protocol π securely computes the functionality $\mathcal{F}$ in the f-hybrid model, then the combined protocol π^ρ securely computes $\mathcal{F}$. That is, by applying the standard universally composable technique [5] and [6], we are able to show that

Theorem 1. *Let $\mathcal{A}$ and $\mathcal{B}$ be monotone adversary structures such that $\mathcal{B} \subseteq \mathcal{A}$. Let f and g be two n-party functions, and ρ be an n-party protocol that non-adaptively and t-securely evaluates f in the presence of adversary structure A. Let π be an n-party protocol that non-adaptively and t-securely evaluates g in the f-hybrid model in the presence of adversary structure $\mathcal{B}$. Then the composed protocol π^ρ non-adaptively and t-securely evaluates g in the adversary structure $\mathcal{B}$.*

4   Conclusion

We have given various notions of clouds within the multi-party computation framework and have shown a universally composable theorem for monotone adversary structures for public Cloud computing. The result may bridge the security-related gaps between industrial views of clouds and that of theoretical researchers.

References

1. Amazon Elastic Compute Cloud, Amazon ec2 (2008)
2. Amazon Web Services Developer Connection (2008), aws.amazon.com
3. Armbrust, M., Fox, A., Griffith, R., Joseph, A.D., Katz, R.H., Konwinski, A., Lee, G., Patterson, D.A., Rabkin, A., Stoica, I., Zaharia, M.: Above the Clouds: A Berkeley View of Cloud Computing, Technical Report No. UCB/EECS-2009-28
4. Ben-Or, M., Goldwasser, S., Wigderson, A.: Completeness Theorems for Non-Cryptographic Fault-Tolerant Distributed Computation (Extended Abstract). In: STOC 1988, pp. 1–10 (1988)
5. Canetti, R.: Security and composition of multiparty cryptographic protocols. Journal of Cryptology 13(1), 143–202 (2000)
6. Canetti, R.: A new paradigm for cryptographic protocols. In: FOCS 2001, pp. 136–145 (2001)
7. Chaum, D., Crépeau, C., Damgård, I.: Multiparty Unconditionally Secure Protocols (Abstract). In: Pomerance, C. (ed.) CRYPTO 1987. LNCS, vol. 293, p. 462. Springer, Heidelberg (1988)
8. Goldreich, O., Micali, S., Wigderson, A.: Proofs that Yield Nothing But their Validity and a Methodology of Cryptographic Protocol Design (Extended Abstract). In: FOCS 1986, pp. 174–187 (1986)
9. Goldreich, O., Micali, S., Wigderson, A.: How to Play any Mental Game or A Completeness Theorem for Protocols with Honest Majority. In: STOC 1987, pp. 218–229 (1987)
10. Dean, J., Ghemawat, S.: Mapreduce: Simplified data processing on large clusters. Communications of the ACM 51(1), 107–113 (2008)
11. Grossman, R.L.: A Quick introdcution to Clouds, Technical report, University of Illinois at Chicago (2008)
12. Grossman, R.L., Bennett, C., Seidman, J.: Creditstone: A benchmark for clouds that provide on-demand capacity. Technical report, University of Illinois at Chicago (2008)
13. Ghemawat, S., Gobioff, H., Leung, S.-T.: The google file system. In: SOSP 2003: Proceedings of the nineteenth ACM symposium on Operating systems principles, pp. 29–43. ACM, New York (2003)
14. Chang, F., Dean, J., Ghemawat, S., Hsieh, W.C., Wallach, D.A., Burrows, M., Chandra, T., Fikes, A., Gruber, R.E.: Bigtable: A distributed storage system for structured data. In: OSDI 2006: Seventh Symposium on Operating System Design and Implementation (2006)
15. Yao, A.C.-C.: Protocols for Secure Computations (Extended Abstract). In: FOCS 1982, pp. 160–164 (1982)

A Service-Oriented Qos-Assured and Multi-Agent Cloud Computing Architecture

Bu-Qing Cao[1,2,3,*], Bing Li[1,2], and Qi-Ming Xia[1,2]

[1] State Key Laboratory of Software Engineering, Wuhan University, Wuhan, 430072, China
[2] School of Computer, Wuhan University, Wuhan, 430072, China
[3] School of Computer Science and Engineering,
Hunan University of Science and technology, Xiangtan, 411201, China
cao6990050@163.com, bingli@whu.edu.cn

Abstract. The essence of Cloud Computing is to provide services by network. As far as user are concerned, resources in the "Cloud" can be extended indefinitely at any time, acquired at any time, used on-demand, and pay-per-use. Combined with SOA and Multi-Agent technology, this paper propose a new Service-Oriented QOS-Assured cloud computing architecture which include physical device and virtual resource layer, cloud service provision layer, cloud service management and multi-agent layer to support QOS-Assured cloud service provision and request. At the same time, based on the proposed service-oriented cloud computing architecture, realization process of cloud service is simplified described.

Keywords: cloud computing; SOA; Multi-Agent; QOS-Assured; architecture.

1 Introduction

With the significant advances in Information and Communications Technology over the last half century, there is an increasingly perceived vision that computing will be the 5th utility one day (after water, electricity, gas, and telephony) [1].There are many technologies which enable cloud computing are still evolving and progressing, for example, Web2.0 and Service Oriented Computing [2].Now, IT companies are now talking about establishment environments of cloud computing, however, if each company will build its own cloud computing platform, this will result in isolated cloud. Therefore, it is especially important to design architecture for cloud computing. At present, different manufacturers offer different design schemes, which result in readers can't entirely understand cloud computing principles. Combined with SOA and Multi-Agent technology, this paper proposes a new Service-Oriented QOS-Assured and Multi-Agent cloud computing architecture which includes physical device and virtual resource layer, cloud service provision layer, cloud service management and Multi-Agent layer to support QOS-Assured cloud service provision and request.

---

* Corresponding author. Tel.: +86-027-61304188 , fax: +86-027-68754590.

M.G. Jaatun, G. Zhao, and C. Rong (Eds.): CloudCom 2009, LNCS 5931, pp. 644–649, 2009.
© Springer-Verlag Berlin Heidelberg 2009

2 Service-Oriented Qos-Assured and Multi-Agent Cloud Computing Architecture

This section firstly introduces SOA and Multi-agent technology; secondly, cloud service Qos model is established according to the characteristic of cloud service consumer and provider; finally, a Service-Oriented QOS-Assured and Multi-Agent cloud computing architecture is designed to support QOS-Assured cloud service provision and request.

2.1 SOA and Multi-Agent Technology

There are advantages for service management and architect-driven concept in the SOA [3-6].Currently, cloud computing technology has hardly any service management and architect-driven concept. Therefore, many companies choose to wait-and-see attitude rather than rush to adopt it. So, the idea of service management and architect-driven can be applied to cloud computing. By this, cloud computing can be seen an extension which SOA provides resources to "cloud", such as, IaaS, PaaS, SaaS, and its key is to determine which cloud services, information and processes on the cloud is the best candidate, and which cloud services should be abstracted in the existing or emerging SOA.

Software agent is a software entity which runs continuous and independent in a given environment, usually combined other agents with solving problem [7]. Multi-Agent system has been increasingly attracted to researchers in various fields, particularly in the network environment, agent can be used to complete complex task by communicating with many resources and task publishers. Cloud computing refers to both the applications delivered as services over internet and hardware and systems software in the datacenters[8], and it provides a variety of resources, such as network, storage, computing resources to users adopted by IaaS, PaaS, SaaS and other forms of service. These resources are vast, heterogeneous, distributed; it is very important how to provide them to users with high-quality, validity. Described by the above, agent can be used to complete complex task by communicating with many resources and task publishers. So, it can be used in service-oriented cloud computing architecture to support QOS-Assured cloud service provision and request.

2.2 Cloud Service Qos Model

There have many related research work on QOS, but QOS mentioned in many articles mentioned only relate to consumers. Taking into account strong background resource process and service provision capabilities, this paper considers all related QOS attributes of cloud service consumer and cloud service providers. As far as cloud service providers, cloud service Qos provided by the physical device and virtual resources layer mainly focus on data center's performance, reliability, stability; cloud service Qos provided by Iaas likely emphasize on response time, resource utilization, and prices, and so on. As far as cloud service consumers, they are very important, such as, response time, price, availability, reliability, reputation, and they can also be provided by the service provider. Thus, considering Qos of cloud services providers and consumers, the most common attributes of Qos will be illustrated as follows and other attributes can be extended according to different service form.

Definition 1 CloudServiceQOS$_{responsetime}$(S). It represents the interval from the requirement sending of cloud service consumers to cloud service implements competition, which is calculated as follows:

$$CloudServiceQOS_{responsetime}(S)=Time_{transfers}(S)+Time_{run}(S). \tag{1}$$

Among this, Time$_{transfers}$(S) on behalf of the transmission time form requirement sending to results return and it can be gained by cloud service monitor; Time $_{run}$(S) represent cloud service implements time and it also can be obtained by cloud service monitor.

Definition 2 CloudServiceQOS$_{cost}$(S). It represents fees paid when customer use service provided by cloud service provider, that is, pay-per-use, and it can be realized by cloud service meterage.

Definition 3 CloudServiceQOS$_{availability}$(S). It represents that the probability of cloud services can be accessed, which is calculated as follows:

$$CloudServiceQOS_{availability}(S) =A/N. \tag{2}$$

Among this, N express the request times that consumer want to use cloud service S during a certain period of time; A express the accessible times of cloud service S.

Definition 4 CloudServiceQOS$_{reliability}$ (S). It show the capacity that cloud service accurately implements its function and the times of validation and invalidation can be acquired by cloud service monitor, which is calculated as follows:

$$CloudServiceQOS_{reliability} (S)=R/M. \tag{3}$$

Among this,R express the times of called and successful implements of the cloud service S; M on behalf of the total called times of the cloud service S.

Definition 5 CloudServiceQOS$_{reputation}$(S). It expresses the creditability of cloud services. Reputation can be seen as the sum of subjective customer's rating and objective QoS advertising messages credibility (CoWS) (based on the Bayes learning theory),in order to reduce the impact of malicious rating[9], which is calculated as follows:

$$CloudServiceQOSreputation(S)= \alpha \times(\sum_{i=1}^{n} Rating) / n + \beta \times coWS \tag{4}$$

Thus, according to above given definition of cloud services related Qos, an integrated Qos model of cloud service S can be expressed as follows:

$$CloudServiceQOS(S)=W1 |CloudServiceQOS_{responsetime}(S)|+W2$$
$$|CloudServiceQOS_{cost}(S)|+ W3 CloudServiceQOS_{availability}(S)+ W4 CloudSer- \tag{5}$$
$$viceQOS_{reliability} (S) +W5 CloudServiceQOS_{reputation}(S)$$

Here , $W_i \in [0,1]$, $\sum_{i=1}^{5} W_{i=1}$, W_i express the weight of corresponding Qos i and its value can be set according to user preferences, for example, user preferences is lower prices and faster response time in an air ticket booking service, thus, the values of W_1 and W_2 can be set to bigger. |CloudServiceQOSresponsetime (S) | expressed QOS attributes dimensionless or normalized process. Specific dimensionless process method does not belong to the scope of this study. This model sustain the extension of

QOS attributes, that is can add or remove QOS attributes according to specific situation, to support QOS-assured cloud service acquired at any time, used on-demand, pay-per-use and extended indefinitely.

2.3 Service-Oriented QOS-Assured and Multi-Agent Cloud Computing Architecture

Figure1 shows a Service-Oriented QOS-Assured and Multi-Agent cloud computing architecture which includes physical device and virtual resource layer, cloud service provision layer, cloud service management and Multi-Agent layer, to support QOS-Assured cloud service provision and request.

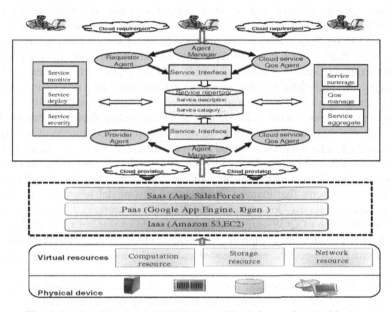

Fig. 1. Service-Oriented and Multi-Agent Cloud Computing Architecture

1) Physical Device and Virtual Resource Layer
Physical resources is all kinds of physical equipment which support upper services of cloud computing, such as a large number of servers in data center, network equipment, storage equipment and so on. Cloud computing is a shared-resource computing method by the form of virtualization. Here, physical resources can be converted into various resources, such as computing resources, storage resources, network resources by virtualization technology, then they can be connected together to form a flexible, unified resources pool in order to dynamically allocated to different applications and service requirement, thereby improve resources utilization rate.

2) Cloud Service Provision Layer
Cloud service provision layer can provide some forms of services by functions composition provided by physical device and virtual resource layer. The forms of service

that cloud computing provides today may be broken down into managed services, SaaS, Web services, utility computing, and PaaS. Figure 1 shows a concentrated services view of cloud computing, including Iaas, Paas, and Saas, which provide IT service capabilities to users.

3) Cloud Service Manager and Multi-Agent Layer

Cloud service manager and multi-agent layer mostly manages a variety of services provided by cloud service provision layer and finds QOS-assured cloud service in service repertory according to user's cloud service requirement. As shown in Figure 1, cloud services management which includes service repertory, service interface, service aggregate, service monitor, service deploy, service meterage, service security, QOS manage. Among them, service repertory similar to UDDI in the SOA, which includes service description, service category, and so on. Service description represents service functional and non-functional information, such as service names, response time, and so on; service category represents service type provided by cloud service provision layer, such as IaaS, Saas, Paas; service interface represents access interface according to services types, for example, Remote Desktop for IaaS, API for PaaS, web services for SaaS; service aggregate represents that new services can be created based on existing services; service monitor represents monitor and alarm according to health status of the services and automatically correct abnormity state of services; service deploy represents automatically deploy and configure specific services examples according to users requirements; service meterage represents cloud services, similar to water, electricity and gas, which are available and pay on-demand by the user; service security represents provide authorization control, trust management, auditing, consistency check for cloud services; QOS manage represents that manage cloud service Qos model which select, calculate and dimensionless process Qos attributes and described in section2.2, at the same time, sustain the extension of QOS attributes, that is can add or remove QOS attributes according to specific situation, to support QOS-assured cloud service acquired at any time, used on-demand, pay-per-use and extended indefinitely, and return the best expected cloud service to user.

Cloud multi-agent management which includes cloud service requestor agent, cloud service QOS agent, cloud service provider agent and agent manager, and it is mainly support QOS-assured cloud service provision and request. Cloud services requester is no longer direct visit cloud service but commit to requestor agent, who mainly collects feedback information of request and submits cloud service request based on QOS. Similarly, Cloud services provider is no longer direct publish services but commit to provider agent, who mainly collects cloud service use information and publishes cloud service. Cloud service QOS agent primarily submits cloud services QOS information. Agent manager primarily manages various managers, such as new, recovery operation.

Thus, the process of cloud service provision can be described: First of all, Cloud service provision layer can provide various cloud service to agent manager and then establish provider agent and cloud service QOS agent. Secondly, service function information, such as service description, service category, which can be standardized by service interface, will be submitted to service repertory by provider agent. At the same time, service QOS information, such as, response time, cost, which can be standardized by service interface, will be submitted to service repertory by cloud service QOS agent. The process of cloud service request is the same to the process of cloud service provision.

4 Conclusion and Future Work

This paper proposes a new Service-Oriented QOS-Assured and Multi-Agent cloud computing architecture to support QOS-Assured cloud service provision and request. There are research challenges in the future for cloud computing that make use of open standards and architecture to allow different clouds for interoperability. Next research work will focus on cloud services interoperability research.

Acknowledgement

This work is supported by National Basic Research Program (973) of China under grant No. 2007CB310801, National High Technology Research and Development Program (863) of China under grant No. 2006AA04Z156, National Natural Science Foundation of China under grant No. 60873083 and 60803025, Research Fund for the Doctoral Program of Higher Education of China under grant No. 20070486065,National Science Foundation of Hubei Province for Distinguished Young Scholars under grant No.2008CDB351 and National Science Foundation of Hubei Province under grant No.2008ABA379.

References

1. Buyya, R., et al.: Cloud Computing and Emerging IT Platforms: Vision, Hype, and Reality for Delivering Computing as the 5th Utility. Future Generation Computer Systems 25(6), 599–616 (2009)
2. Wang, L., von Laszewski, G.: Cloud Computing: a Perspective Study
3. Toward a service-oriented analysis and design methodology for software product lines, http://www.ibm.com/developerworks/webservices/library/ar-soaspl/
4. Vouk, M.A.: Cloud Computing-Issues, Research and Implementations. In: ITI 2008, Cavtat, Croatia (2008)
5. de Leusse, P.: Secure & Rapid composition of infrastructure services in the Cloud. In: The Second International Conference on Sensor Technologies and Applications, Cap Esterel, France (August 2008)
6. van der Burg, S., Dolstra, E.: Software Deployment in a Dynamic Cloud: From Device to Service Orientation in a Hospital Environment. In: ICSE CLOUD 2009, Vancouver, Canada, May 23 (2009)
7. Adshaw, J.M.: An Introduction to Software Agents. In: Bradshaw, J.M. (ed.) Software Agents, pp. 3–46. AAAI Press, Menlo Park (1997)
8. Armbrust, M.: Above the Clouds: A Berkeley View of Cloud Computing, EECS Department, University of California, Berkeley (2009)
9. Li, Z., Su, S., Yang, F.C.: WSrep: A novel reputation model for web services selection. In: Nguyen, N.T., Grzech, A., Howlett, R.J., Jain, L.C. (eds.) KES-AMSTA 2007. LNCS (LNAI), vol. 4496, pp. 199–208. Springer, Heidelberg (2007)

Price-Oriented Trading Optimization for Grid Resource

Hao Li, Guo Tang, Wei Guo, Changyan Sun, and Shaowen Yao

School of Software, Yunnan University, Kunming, China
Lihao707@ynu.edu.cn, tangguo001@gmail.com,
guoweisiwin@126.com, 1200701576@mail.ynu.edu.cn,
yaosw@ynu.edu.cn

Abstract. The resources in the Grid are heterogeneous and geographically distributed. Availability, usage and cost policies vary depending on the particular user, time, priorities and goals. Quality of service (QoS) in grid cannot be guaranteed. This article proposes a computational economy as an effective metaphor for the management of resources and application scheduling. It proposes a QoS-based grid banking model. The model is divided into the application-layer, virtual organization (VO) layer, and the physical resources and facilities layer. At each layer, the consumer agent, service agent, and resource provider agent optimize the multi-dimensionality QoS resources respectively. The optimization is under the framework of the grid banking model and the hierarchical constraints in their respective conditions so that it can maximize the function. The optimization algorithm is price-oriented constant iteration at all levels.

Keywords: Grid banking model,QoS,price,optimization, hierarchical structure.

1 Introduction

In recent years, Globus league brought forward the Open Grid Services Architecture (OGSA) at the OGF(Open Grid Forum) in 2002, and proposed WSRF (Web Services Resource Framework) join IBM in 2004, it makes grid services studies become a hotspot. QoS, which is the primary objective of the Service Grid study, has become the focus in grid. "To provide the extraordinary QoS"[1] is one of the three criteria to determine whether it is the grid or not.

At present, the implementations of the network infrastructure is set up on the basis of "try one's best". Therefore, it cannot guarantee the QoS, especially in grid. It proposed and set up a bank under the grid structure of the model-level QoS based on different objects needs of QoS parameters on the classification at different aspects of QoS description in this paper.

This paper is organized as follows: In Section 2, we describe previous works regarding grid QoS. In section 3, we introduce the architecture of QoS-based grid banking model. In section 4, we analyze optimization solutions in detail under banking model. In section 5, we generate an algorithm. Finally, we conclude the paper in section 6.

M.G. Jaatun, G. Zhao, and C. Rong (Eds.): CloudCom 2009, LNCS 5931, pp. 650–655, 2009.

2 Research of Grid QoS

There are some available methods which can provide QoS on the Internet. For example: DiffServ (differentiated services), which gather the quality of the provision of specific scheduling services on the border of the network. RSVP (Resource Reserve Protocol) ,which reserve part of network resources (i.e. bandwidth), for the transmission of streaming media.GARA[2] (General-purpose Architecture for Reservation and Allocation), which providing advanced and immediate reservation through a unified interface. G-QoSM (Grid QoS Management Architecture),it is an adaptive resource reservation and the QoS management architecture in OGSA grid environment.

Buyya, from an economic point of view, put forward GRACE (Grid Architecture for Computational Economy) [3]. GRACE mainly considerate the deadline and budget constraints, it can control the allocation of resources, supply and demand of resources effectively. More literature [4-6] applied to put the principles of economics in grid resource scheduling and optimization.

3 QoS-Based Grid Banking Model

A grid banking is a grid mechanism after reference the economy grid [3], through simulating the bank's business process. Buyya mentioned QBank and GBank in the GRACE, but it is only used to account. In [7], grid environment can be divided into three roles: Grid Resources Consumer, Grid Bank, and Grid Service Provider.

We make a number of improvements in this paper and refine the function of grid banks. We use the *Grid Dollar* to quantify the parameters of the grid resources, in the meantime, we consider supply and demand of grid resources, using price leverage to allocate resources in the market. Fig 1 shows the Grid Bank model and its interaction.

The resources consumer agent deals with interactive business between resource users and internal part of the grid bank in application layer. The QoS requirements put forward by the consumer agent will be mapped to a particular type of grid QoS by the service agent in VO layer and it will be provided to the appropriate sub-agents. At physical resources and facilities layer, the resources provider agent captures the various QoS attributes to support the various types of QoS from VO layer. When trading occurs, the whole process is organized by the three types of agents under the coordination from the banking model. Resource provider agent acts on behalf of the potential resources' economic interests of the physical resources and facilities layer; the consumer agent acts

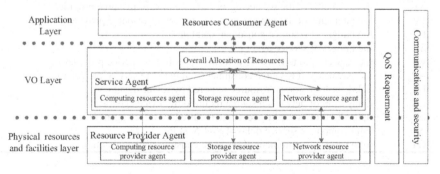

Fig. 1. Grid bank model and its interaction

on behalf of consumers who use the grid to achieve the interests in application layer; the service agent in the VO layer not only acts as a resources buyer from the aspect of resource provider agent, but also acts as a seller from the consumer agent. The three types of agents interact through the operation of the market mechanism. The object of market behavior is to pursuit its own interests in economic field. The supply and demand situation in grid market will be reflected in the price fluctuations.

In market economy, there are multiple service agents in consultation with the consumer agents at the same time. Grid resource scheduler adapt price-oriented algorithm in the model. The main function of the model is to inquiry the appropriate services, which meet the QoS standards, manage local and remote resources, complete the transaction, combine and match resources in a distributed environment.

4   Optimization Solutions

QoS must be distinguished among levels because there are different representations of QoS at different levels [8]. Li Chunlin, who put forward a three-dimensional (cost, time, reliability) QoS formula, it optimized the task agent and resource agent respectively [9-11]. In this paper, the quantitative dimensions have been expanded.

Table 1. The system parameters for the algorithm

Parameter	Description
z_i^l	computing resource prices obtained by service agent i from the computing resource provider agent l
y_i^k	network resource prices obtained by service agent i from the network resource provider agent k
x_i^j	storage resource prices obtained by service agent i get from the storage resource provider agent j
px_i^j	prices of storage resource i provided by storage resource provider agent j
py_i^k	prices of network resource i provided by network resource provider agent k
pz_i^l	prices of processor resource i provided by processor resource provider agent l
S_i	capacity of service agent i
SC_j	capacity of storage resource agent j
NC_k	capacity of network resource agent k
PC_l	capacity of processor resource agent l
T_m	time limits given by the resource consumer agent m to complete its all jobs
SP_i^j	the payments of the service agent i to the storage resource provider j
NP_i^k	the payments of the service agent i to the network resource provider k
PP_i^l	the payments of the service agent i to processor resource provider l
E_m	the budget of resource consumer agent m
SE_i	the budget of service agent i
v_m^i	the service sold to resource consumer agent m by service provider i
AP_m^i	the payments of resource consumer agen m to the service provider i
LS_i	delay limit of storage resource required by sevice agent i
LN_i	delay limit of network resource required by sevice agent i
LP_i	delay limit of proceding resource required by sevice agent i
AD_i	total composite service delay=LS_i+LN_i+LP_i
GT_m^n	total service requirement of resource consumer agen m's nth job.

Express the QoS needs more careful at different levels and interaction between those levels. Table 1 shows the symbol in this paper.

The ultimate goal of optimization is maximize $U_{Grid}(Q_{global})$, at the limit of respective conditions at three levels [11].

$$MaxU_{Grid}(Q_{global}) = \sum (SP_i^j \log x_i^j + NP_i^k \log y_i^k + PP_i^l \log z_i^l) + \sum_m AP_m^i \log v_m^i + \frac{g}{f}$$

$$s.t. \sum_i z_i^l \leq PC_l \ , \sum_i y_i^k \leq NC_k \ , \sum_i x_i^j \leq SC_j \ , \sum_j SD_i^j \leq LS_i \ , \sum_k BD_i^k \leq LN_i \ , \sum_i PD_i^l \leq LP_i \ ,$$

$$\sum_{n=1}^{N} t_m^n \leq T_i \ , \sum_i AP_m^i \leq E_m \quad , \quad \sum_j SP_i^j + \sum_k NP_i^k + \sum_l PP_i^l \leq SE_i$$

Lagrange method is introduced to solve this problem in this paper, according to the ultimate goal to be achieved, Lagrangian function is constructed as follows:

$$L = \sum (SP_i^j \log x_i^j + NP_i^k \log y_i^k + PP_i^l \log z_i^l) + \lambda (SE_i - (\sum_j SP_i^j + \sum_k NP_i^k + \sum_l PP_i^l))$$

$$+ \sum_m AP_m^i \log v_m^i + \beta(E_m - \sum_i AP_m^i) + \gamma(T_i - \sum_{n=1}^{N} t_m^n) + \frac{g}{f} \ . \tag{1}$$

Where λ, β, γ is the Lagrange multipliers, to solve (1) directly is very difficult, and the maximum of the Lagrange problem can be decomposed into three questions at different layer:

$$F_1 = Max \sum (SP_i^j \log x_i^j + NP_i^k \log y_i^k + PP_i^l \log z_i^l) \quad s.t. \sum_i z_i^l \leq PC_l \ , \sum_i y_i^k \leq NC_k \ , \sum_i x_i^j \leq SC_j$$

$$F_2 = Max \left\{ \left(SE_i - \sum_j SP_i^j - \sum_k NP_i^k - \sum_l PP_i^l \right) + \sum_m AP_m^i \log v_m^i + \frac{g}{f} \right\}$$

$$s.t. \sum_j SD_i^j \leq LS_i \ , \sum_k BD_i^k \leq LN_i \ , \sum_i PD_i^l \leq LP_i \ , \sum_m v_m^i \leq S_i \tag{2}$$

$$F_3 = Max \left\{ \left(E_m - \sum_i AP_m^i \right) + \left(T_i - \sum_{n=1}^{N} t_m^n \right) \right\} \quad s.t. \sum_{n=1}^{N} t_m^n \leq T_i \ , \sum_i AP_m^i \leq E_m \ .$$

Physical resources and facilities layer is to resolve F_1 with constraint conditions in (2). we get Lagrangian function [10]:

$$L_{phy}(x_i^j, y_i^k, z_i^l) = \sum (SP_i^j \log x_i^k + NP_i^k \log y_i^k + PP_i^l \log z_i^l) + \lambda \left(SC_j - \sum_i x_i^j \right) + \beta \left(NC_k - \sum_i y_i^k \right) + \gamma \left(PC_l - \sum_i z_i^l \right) \tag{3}$$

$$= \sum (SP_i^j \log x_i^k + NP_i^k \log y_i^k + PP_i^l \log z_i^l - \lambda x_i^j - \beta y_i^k - \gamma z_i^l) + \lambda SC_j + \beta NC_k + \gamma PC_l \ .$$

VO layer must resolve F_2 with constraint conditions in (2). According to service agent acting roles: consumer to the physical layer, provider to application layer, the corresponding Lagrange can break down into the following two functions [10] :

$$L_{VO\_1} = SE_i - \sum_j SP_i^j - \sum_k NP_i^k - \sum_l PP_i^l + \lambda \left(LS_i - \sum_j SD_i^j \right) + \eta \left(LN_i - \sum_k ND_i^k \right) + \beta \left(LP_i - \sum_i PD_i^l \right)$$

$$= SE_i - \sum_j SP_i^j - \sum_k NP_i^k - \sum_l PP_i^l + \lambda \left(LS_i - \sum_j \frac{px_j}{SP_i^j SC_j} \right) + \eta \left(LN_i - \sum_k \frac{py_k}{NP_i^k NC_k} \right) + \beta \left(LP_i - \sum_i \frac{pz_l}{PP_i^l PC_l} \right) ; \tag{4}$$

$$L_{VO\_2} = \sum_m AP_m^i \log v_m^i + \frac{g}{f} + \delta \left(S_i - \sum_m v_m^i \right) \ . \tag{5}$$

Application layer is to resolve F_3 with constrained conditions in (2). Where t_m^n is the time of the grid resource consumer agent m for the nth job, in order to simplify the study, assume $t_m^n = GT_{mn} / v_m^i = (GT_{mn} \bullet ps_i)/(S_i \bullet AP_m^i)$. Combined with its constraints, construct Lagrange function of consumer agent as follows:

$$L_{APP}\left(AP_m^i\right)=\left(E_m-\sum_i AP_m^i\right)+\left(T_m-\sum_{n=1}^{N}\frac{GT_{mn}\bullet ps_i}{S_i\bullet AP_m^i}\right)+\lambda\left(T_m-\sum_{n=1}^{N}t_m^n\right) \qquad (6)$$

5 Algorithm Implementation

This algorithm has been modified and expanded on the basis of literature [10, 11]. It calculated out the price expressed, finally, the feedback is outputted to other relevant agents. Continuous iterative process is repeated until all participants have reached a common solution. The price iteration algorithm described as follows:

5.1 Resource Provider Agent

1. To receive $x_i^{j(n)}$, $x_i^{k(n)}$, $x_i^{l(n)}$) from service agent;
2. To maximize F_1 in (2), according (3), computing

$$x_i^{j*}=\frac{SP_i^j\bullet SC_j}{\sum_{i=1}^{n}SP_i^j} \quad ;y_i^{k*}=\frac{NP_i^k\bullet BC_k}{\sum_{i=1}^{n}NP_i^k} \quad ;z_i^{l*}=\frac{PP_i^l\bullet PC_l}{\sum_{i=1}^{n}PP_i^l}$$

3.Calculate new price of storage resource j [10] : $px_i^{j(n+1)}=\max\{\varepsilon, px_i^{j(n)}+\eta(\sum_i x_i^{j*}-SC_j)\}$

(Note:$\eta>0$, it is a smaller step size of price, n is the number of iterations, ε is a protected price after considering the cost of a variety of revenue. This formula can ensure the largest benefit of the resource provider agent.)
New price of network resource k: $py_i^{k(n+1)}=\max\{\varepsilon, py_i^{k(n)}+\eta(\sum_i y_i^{k*}-NC_k)\}$;

New price of computing resource l: $pz_i^{l(n+1)}=\max\{\varepsilon, pz_i^{l(n)}+\eta(\sum_i z_i^{l*}-PC_l)\}$;

4. Return to the storage resource agent:$px_i^{j(n+1)}$; Return to the network resource agent: $py_i^{k(n+1)}$;Return to the computing resource agent: $pz_i^{l(n+1)}$.

5.2 Service Agent

1. To receive demand v_m^i from consumer agent m;
2. Maximize L_{VO_2} in (5), calculates: $v_m^{i*}=AP_m^i\bullet S_i/\sum_m AP_k^i$
3. Calculate new services prices, return $ps_i^{(n+1)}$ to all consumer agent;
$ps_i^{(n+1)}=\max\{\varepsilon \quad , ps_i^{(n)}+\eta(\sum_m v_m^{i*}-S_i)\}$
;
4. Receive the new price $px_i^{j(n)}$, $px_i^{k(n)}$, $px_i^{l(n)}$; Maximize of L_{VO_1} in (4), calculate

$$SP_i^{j*}=\left(\frac{px_j}{SC_j}\right)^{\frac{1}{2}}\bullet\frac{\sum_j\left(px_j/SC_j\right)^{\frac{1}{2}}}{LS_i} ,SP_i^{j*}=\left(\frac{py_k}{NC_j}\right)^{\frac{1}{2}}\bullet\frac{\sum_k\left(py_k/NC_j\right)^{\frac{1}{2}}}{LN_i} ,PP_i^{l*}=\left(\frac{pz_l}{PC_j}\right)^{\frac{1}{2}}\bullet\frac{\sum_l\left(pz_l/PC_j\right)^{\frac{1}{2}}}{LP_i}$$

5.Calculate: $x_i^{j(n+1)}=SP_i^{j*(n)}/px_i^{j(n)}$; $x_i^{k(n+1)}=NP_i^{k*(n)}/px_i^{k(n)}$; $z_i^{l(n+1)}=PP_i^{l*(n)}/pz_i^{l(n)}$;
6. Return the new price $x_i^{j(n+1)}$, $x_i^{k(n+1)}$, $x_i^{l(n+1)}$ to the resource provider agent.

5.3 Consumer Resources Agent

1. To receive $ps_i^{(n)}$ from service agent i;
2. Maximize F_3 in (2), according (6),calculate [10]

$$AP_m^{i*} = \left(\frac{GT_{mn} \bullet ps_i}{S_i}\right)^{1/2} \bullet \frac{\sum_{n=1}^{N}\left(\frac{GT_{mn} \bullet ps_i}{S_i}\right)^{1/2}}{T_m} ;$$

3. Calculate the demand of services: $v_m^{i(n+1)} = AP_m^{i*(n)} / ps_i^{(n)}$;

Return $v_m^{i(n+1)}$ to the service agent i.

6 Summary

Based on the research of existing grid QoS, by using hierarchical thinking, we put forward the QoS-based grid bank model, and the model is divided into three layers. Three types of agent optimize resource among the layers and the interaction between the various agents may be done through the SLA. Optimization algorithm is based on the principle of economic. Continuous iterative process is repeated until all participants have reached a common solution.

Acknowledgment. This work is supported by the National Natural Science Foundation of China (Grant No.60763008) and the Science and Engineering Foundation of Yunnan University (2008YB014).

References

1. Foster, I.: The Grid: Blueprint for a New Computing Infrastructure (1999)
2. Foster, I., Roy, A., Sander, V.: A Quality of Service Architecture that Combines Resource Reservation and Application Adaptation. In: Proceedings of the Eight International Workshop on Quality of Service, pp. 181–188 (June 2000)
3. Buyya, R.: Economic-based distributed resource management and scheduling for Grid computing, Doctor'S Thesis, Monash University (2002)
4. Subramoniam, K., Maheswaran, M., Toulouse, M.: Towards a micro-economic model for resource allocation in Grid computing systems. In: Proceedings of the 2002 IEEE Canadian Conference on Electrical & Computer Engineering (2002)
5. Stuer, G., Vanmechelen, K., Broeckhove, J.: A commodity market algorithm for pricing substitutable Grid resources. Future Generation Computer Systems 23, 688–701 (2007)
6. Wolski, R., Plank, J.S., Brevik, J., Bryan, T.: Analyzing Market-based Resource Allocation Strategies for the Computational Grid. International Journal of High-performance Computing Applications 15 (Fall 2001)
7. Li, H., Zhong, Y., Lu, J., Zhang, X., Yao, S.: A Banking Based Grid Recourse Allocation Scheduling. In: GPC Workshops (2008)
8. Kenyon, C.: Architecture Requirements for Commercializing Grid Resources. In: Proceeding of the 11th IEEE International Symposium on High Performance Distributed Computing (HPDC) (2002)
9. Chunlin, L., Layuan, L.: A distributed multiple dimensional QoS constrained. Journal of Computer and System Sciences (72), 706–726 (2006)
10. Chunlin, L., Layuan, L.: Cross-layer optimization policy for QoS scheduling in computational grid. Journal of Network and Computer Applications 31, 258–284 (2008)
11. Chunlin, L., Layuan, L.: QoS based resource scheduling by computational economy in computational grid. Information Processing Letters, 98, 116–126 (2006)

A Requirements Recommendation Method Based on Service Description

Da Ning and Rong Peng

State Key Lab. Of Software Engineering, Wuhan University, Wuhan, China
ningdadh@163.com, rongpeng@sklse.org

Abstract. The development of Service oriented architecture (SOA) has brought new opportunities to requirements engineering. How to utilize existing services to guide the requestors to express their requirements accurately and completely becomes a new hotspot. In this paper, a requirements recommendation method based on service description was proposed. It can find web services corresponding to user's initial requirements, establish the association relationship between user's requirements and service functions, and in turn, recommend the associated service's functions to the requestor and assist him to express requirements accurately and completely. The effectiveness of this method is evaluated and demonstrated by a case-study in travel planning system.

Keywords: SOA; service description; service functions; requirements recommendation.

1 Introduction

SOA (Service-Oriented Architecture) has become a popular framework for software design. The independence of services in SOA allows different providers to provide different business functions according to their own specialty. Service requestors can select the services provided by various providers according to their own preferences. SOA doesn't only change the way how software is designed, implemented, deployed and utilized, but also provides a new way to satisfy user's requirements. In SOC (Service-Oriented Computing), using the existing services to satisfy user's real-time requirements has been considered as the first choice [1, 2]. Only when the needed service doesn't exist, a new development will start.

From another point of view, the initial requirements description proposed by users always has some fuzziness or ambiguity. Their target is not really very clear. So it can be adjusted or complemented according to the similar functions which can be supplied by existing services. In this paper, the emphasis is placed on how to assist requestors to express their requirements accurately and practically through utilizing the existing services. It is organized as follows: Session 2 discusses the related work; a framework based on service description for requirement recommendation is given in Session 3; and a requirement recommendation algorithm is presented in Session 4; Session 5 gives an experimental example; Session 6 is the conclusion.

M.G. Jaatun, G. Zhao, and C. Rong (Eds.): CloudCom 2009, LNCS 5931, pp. 656–661, 2009.
© Springer-Verlag Berlin Heidelberg 2009

2 Related Work

In SoC, demand-driven service discovery [3] method has already existed. On the one hand, researchers have tried to improve the existing requirements elicitation approach according to service feature [5], making requirements elicited hold the service specific features such as QoS to facilitate the service matching. On the other hand, they try to enhance the service semantic description capability to fill the gap between the requirements and service description [4, 6].

Andreas, et al, present an alignment method between business requirement and service by using the model comparison techniques [4]. But how to automatically generate the Tropos goal model of requirements and services is the bottleneck. Hausmann, et al, present a model-based service discovery method [6], which utilizes software models and graph transformations to describe the service semantics. It is well known that modeling is a difficult task for both service providers and service requestors. Whatever the automated requirement modeling tool or service semantic modeling tool is hard to practice. Thus, in this paper, we presents a service requirement recommendation method based on the concept of the initial keywords description of user's requirement and service description, establishing the association between them by similarity calculation. And then, guide the user to modify and perfect the requirement expression according to the existing services' functions.

3 Recommending Requirements Framework Based on WSDL

As it is well known, web services often use WSDL/OWL-S to encapsulate the description of service, which is regarded as the information source for requirement recommendation. The recommendation framework is shown in Figure 1.

In the framework, user is regarded as service requestor, using the requirement template of the requirement elicitation platform SklseWiki [7] to present the initial requirement. And then, the keywords of the requirement are extracted to facilitate service matching. Varieties of service registrations, such as Seekda, include a large amount of web service using WSDL to describe its functions. The service semantics

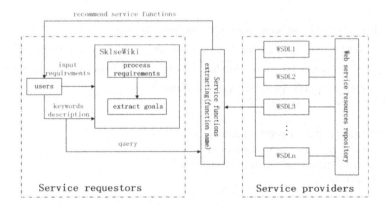

Fig. 1. A requirement recommendation framework based on service description

represented by functional keywords will be analyzed by the service function extractor according to the WSDL description. After the similarity calculation between the keywords, the most suitable services will be found out, and the related recommendations can be given to guide the requestor's expression.

4   Automatic Service Requirements Recommendation

The automatic service requirements recommendation method consists of following three steps.

4.1   The Keywords of Initial Requirement Extracting

The user's requirements are captured by the Sklsewiki platform [7] (see Figure 2). The requirement is described according to various templates. In this method, we mainly concern functional requirements template, which is described as follows:

FuncTemplate= {reqDesc, funcName, roleSet, subFuncSet, keywordSet}

reqDesc: describing the user's original requirements, for instance, "The system should be able to provide the function of travel planning. It should be able to book flights, hotels and cars for vacations."

funcName: the function name extracted from user's requirements, for example, the above requirements can be named as "Provide TripPlan".

roleSet: the roles corresponding to requirements, such as traveler.

subFuncSet: sub functions resolved from the initial requirements, such as "Book Flights", "Book Hotel" and "Book Cars" .

keywordSet: keywords description for the original requirement. This element is a connection hub between the service requestors and service providers. The user may further describe requirements by using the keywords such as TravelPlanning, BookFlights, BookHotel, etc.

4.2   Service Functions Extracting

We only considered the service described by WSDL. It can be regarded as the following five-tuple.

SERVICE = {types, message, portType, binding, service}

In which, portType is responsible for defining the operation executed in service, which is similar to the function, module or class in traditional programming language. The element portType is defined as follows:

```
<portType name="port name">
   ...
   <operation name="operation name_N">
      <input message="operation input">
      <output message="operation output">
   </operation>
   ...
</portType>
```

Through traversing sub-element <operation> of <portType>, extracting each operation name, we will obtain an operational set S = (operation$_1$, operation$_2$, ... , operation$_N$), which is used to express all the functions each service can provide.

4.3 Automatic Service Requirements Recommendation

Requirement recommendation algorithm based on service description aims to query service resource repository according to user's initial requirement. And then, find out his genuine requirement by the matched service.

Assumption: Traversing the services registered in the repository, and building a service function set {Fs}, the Fs$_i$ denotes the i-th service function set.

Algorithm ServAutoMatch({Req}):
1) Establishing user's requirement function set {Fu} according to the keywords description of initial requirement Req;
2) Compared each item of {Fu} with that of {Fs}(see the similarity calculation method in [8]);
   a) if {Fu}={Fs$_i$}, then return entire service to the user as well as record the corresponding relation between the requirement and service, goto 3;
   b) else if {Fu} ⊂ {Fs$_i$}, then record the functions in {Fs$_i$}-{Fu} as a **recommendation set** and the service matched to the requirement;
   c) else if {Fu} ⊃ {Fs$_i$}, then record the service matched to the requirement and call **ServAutoMatch({Fu}-{Fs$_i$})**;
   d) else if {Fu} ∩ {Fs} ≠ ∅, then record the functions in {Fs$_i$}-{Fu} as a **recommendation set** and the service matched to the requirement, call **ServAutoMatch({Fu}-{Fs$_i$})**;
3) Sort the recommendation records by the size of **recommendation set**, and recommend them to user.
4) Stop.

Note: Recording service functions matched aims to provide guidance for later development.

5 The Example and Experimental Results

According to the above method, an example of travel planning is given. The requirement created by the user using the Sklsewiki platform is shown in Figure 2. For the requirement "The system should be able to provide the function of travel planning. It should be able to book flights, hotels and cars for vacations.", the user can use the keywords "TravelPlanning", "BookFlights", "BookHotel", "BookCars" to tag the requirement.

Using the keyword "BookHotel", the service "Booking Engine" in the service resource repository Seekda[1] can be found since the "SearchAccommodation" is one of the operations of the "Booking Engine". On the other hand, the other operations "AddBooking", "GetAllAirports", "GetAllDestinations", "GetResortInfo", and "GetResortList" is recommended to the user who can use these information to complement his original requirement.

---

[1] http://seekda.com/

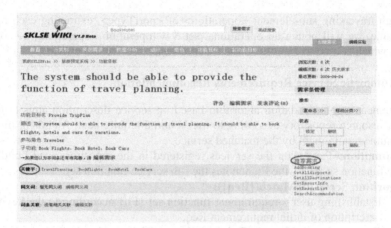

Fig. 2. Sklsewiki platform for requirements elicitation

Fig. 3. The webpage of Seekda, which is used as a service repository in SKLSEWiki

6   Conclusion and Future Work

With the development of SOC, how to utilize the existed services' functions to adjust and improve the user's requirements becomes a new direction of requirement elicitation. The main advantages of the requirements recommendation method are as following:

1) It is based on the similarity calculation algorithm which is mature comparatively.

2) Converting the issue of automatic service requirements recommendation to the matching problem between user's requirements and existing services. Through the matched service, the additional operations of the service are used to adjust and perfect the initial requirement;

3) Converting the matching problem between user's requirements and service to that between original keywords description of user's requirements and service functions. The conversion makes it possible to compute the similarity between them;

4) This method provides a flexible requirement engineering process for future applications based on services. Through utilizing the method we can not only find a suitable service, but also it can advance user to make use of the current existing service meet to the requirements.

The future work is focused on improving the efficiency of algorithms and developing better recommendation strategies.

Acknowledgments. This research project was supported by the National Natural Science Foundation of China under Grant N.o.60703009, the National Basic Research Program of China (973) under Grant No. 2007CB310801, the "Chen Guang" project of Wuhan under Grant No. 200950431189, and the 111 Project of China under grant No. B07037.

References

1. Colombo, M., Di Nitto, E., Di Penta, M., Distante, D., Zuccalà, M.: Speaking a Common Language: A Conceptual Model for Describing Service-Oriented Systems. In: Benatallah, B., Casati, F., Traverso, P. (eds.) ICSOC 2005. LNCS, vol. 3826, pp. 48–60. Springer, Heidelberg (2005)
2. van Eck, P.A.T., Wieringa, R.J.: Requirements Engineering for Service-Oriented Computing: A Position Paper. In: 1st International E-Services Workshop, PA, Pittsburgh, pp. 23–28 (2003)
3. Zachos, K., Maiden, N.A.M., Zhu, X., Jones, S.: Discovering Web Services to Specify More Complete System Requirements. In: 19th International Conference on Advanced Information Systems Engineering, Trondheim, Norway, pp. 142–157 (2007)
4. Andreas, G., Nadine, B., Klaus, P.: Goal-Driven Alignment of Services and Business Requirements. In: 2008 International Workshop on Service-Oriented Computing Consequences for Engineering Requirements, Barcelona, Spain, pp. 1–7 (2008)
5. Xiang, J., Liu, L., Qiao, W., Yang, J.: SREM: A Service Requirements Elicitation Mechanism based on Ontology. In: 31st Annual International Computer Software and Applications Conference, vol. 1, pp. 196–203. IEEE computer society, Beijing (2007)
6. Hausmann, J.H., Heckel, R., Lohmann, M.: Model-Based Discovery of Web Services. In: IEEE International Conference on Web Services, CA, San Diego, pp. 324–331 (2004)
7. http://61.183.121.131:8080/sklsewiki/
8. Zhang, X., Li, Z.-J., Li, M.-J.: An Approach and Implementation to Semantic Web Service Matchmaking. Computer Science 134(15), 99–103 (2007)

Extending YML to Be a Middleware for Scientific Cloud Computing

Ling Shang[1,3], Serge G. Petiton[1], Nahid Emad[2], Xiaolin Yang[1], and Zhijian Wang[3]

[1] Lifl, University of Science and Technology of Lille, France
{ling.shang,serge.petiton}@lifl.fr
[2] PRiSM - Laboratoire d'informatique - UVSQ, Versailles, France
[3] College of Computer and Information Engineering, Hohai University, China

Abstract. Grid computing has gained great success in harnessing computing resources. But its progress of gridfication on scientific computing is slower than anticipation. This paper analyzes these reasons of hard gridfication in detail. While cloud computing as a new paradigm shows its advantages for its many good features such as lost cost, pay by use, easy of use and non trivial Qos. Based on analysis on existing cloud paradigm, a cloud platform architecture based on YML for scientific computing is presented. Emulations testify we are on the right way to extending YML to be middleware for cloud computing. Finally on going improvements on YML and open problem are also presented in this paper.

Keywords: Grid computing, Cloud computing, YML, Scientific computing, Cloud middleware.

1 Introduction

Grid computing has become a mature paradigm aiming at harnessing high performance distributed computing resources (CR) in a simple and standard way. And it widely diffused in many aspects of scientific computing such as biochemical, Physics, Astronomical Sciences, Ocean Sciences, Earth Sciences...Two kinds of Grid platform has been established which are service based grid platform and desktop grid platform. In which service based grid platform, utilized to harness dedicated CR belongs to 'push model'; while desktop grid platform is 'pull model' mainly collecting non-dedicated CR. Scalability is poor to service based grid for non-technology reason and high costs. Desktop grid is famous for its scalability and low costs but high volatility is its key problem. Lots of grid platform has been established based on these two kinds of platforms for scientific computing. Such as service based Grid: TeraGrid, Open Science Grid, LCH Grid, EGEE, Earth System Grid; Desktop Grid: Bonic, Seti@home, Xtremweb, Entropia. Some problems met during the practice of running scientific computing on these platforms and which can be summarized as follows: 1) From the end users' viewpoint: the grid interfaces for users are complete and it is hard for end user to find appropriate interface they need. To utilize the grid platform, users are required to know system details ranging from resource configuration to service availability to hardware configuration. In a word, grid is hard to use for end users.

M.G. Jaatun, G. Zhao, and C. Rong (Eds.): CloudCom 2009, LNCS 5931, pp. 662–667, 2009.

This is the reason why so many scientific computing are still based on clusters and supercomputer. 2) From the Gird itself viewpoint: most schedulers in grid middleware are based on batch scheduler, which can't adapt tasks to appropriate CR. Thus causes lower efficiency of platform. Additionally, almost data transfer/migration model in grid is based on client/server, which leads to a lot of time spent on unnecessary data transfer and ultimately decreases the efficiency of platform. In a word, scheduler and data transfer model in most grid system are two bottlenecks which decrease the efficiency of grid platform.

Cloud computing has been a spotlight since at the end of 2007 and it arouses great concerns for it can provide flexible, on demand, non-trivial quality and easy-to-use service to end users. As well known to us all, Grid computing is presented to make distributed CR as services work collaboratively. And cloud computing is raised to make sure those services can be invoked in low cost, easy-of-use and non-trivial Qos way. Researches on cloud products from famous IT enterprises such as Google, Amazon, IBM and Microsoft have testified our viewpoints. Cloud computing belong to a special problem solving environment (SPSE). In other word, cloud platform is utilized to solve a special kind of problem or achieve a definite goal with a simple interface. For example, the goal of Google's cloud platform is to index valuable information from huge volume of data. These SPSEs are always based on large scale computing platform. It also can provide end user an easy-of-use, pay-by-use interface and on demand, low cost services. Users can invoke these services as they need in a very simple way without knowing about inner structure of cloud platform. Through the analysis above, a definition of cloud computing can be: *cloud computing is a specific problem solving environment based on large scale resources pool (consist of clusters, grid, desktop grid, super computer or hybrid platform); It encapsulates all technological details through virtual technology and can provide end users with on demand provision, non-trivial quality of service and pay by use, easy of use, high level program interface; End users can utilize all these services provided by cloud platform in a very simple way without knowing where these services come from and on what kinds of platform/ system/ infrastructure these services run.* According to this definition, we propose a cloud model based on YML [1][2][3][6] for scientific computing. Finally, our on-going works for extending YML to be a middleware of cloud computing is summarized and an open problem is also presented in this paper.

2 Lesson Learned from Practice on Gridification

The reason of hard gridification can be summarized from the following two aspects:

2.1 Viewpoint from End Users

Grid platform is hard to utilize for end users: Grid expose all the interfaces to users, though a lot of interfaces are useless to a special user. And users need to spend a lot of time to find and learn how to use them. The second reason is that grid platform is a kind of very complex system. End users need to book CR they need and then deploy appropriate environment they need. This is another hard point for non expert users.

Grid middleware is hard for end users to develop application: To successfully utilize middleware, developers are required to know system details ranging from resource configuration to service availability to hardware configuration. When creating Grid applications, proper management of the underlying resources has to be done. Some factors such as resource availability, fault tolerance, load balancing and scheduling have to be taken into account. These requirements significantly increase the burden of responsibility on Grid users.

2.2 Viewpoint from Gird Itself

Scheduler in many grid middleware is a bottleneck: Most schedulers in grid middleware are based batch scheduler. This kind of scheduler doesn't support adaptive scheduling in Grid system. Thus causes the scheduler can't dispatch tasks to appropriate CR. Grid platform belongs to heterogeneous environment in both available and capability of CR. So static and a single level scheduler can't meet the requirement of grid platform.

The method of data transfer is another bottleneck: Most data transfer models are almost based on Serve/Client model. All the data are store in a data server. When a task to be executed, it need get the data needed from data server and send back to data server when the task finishes. If another task's input is the output of the first task, unnecessary data transfer generate.

3 Extending YML to Be a Middleware for Cloud Computing

Researches on products from very famous It enterprises show that cloud computing is a specific problem solving environment based on large scale resources pool (consist of clusters, grid, desktop grid, super computer or hybrid platform); It encapsulates all technological details through virtual technology and can provide end users with on demand provision, non-trivial quality of service and pay by use, easy of use, high level program interface; End users can utilize all these services provided by cloud platform in a very simple way without knowing where these services come from and on what kinds of platform/ system/ infrastructure these services run. Based on that, A cloud model based on YML is presented as follows:

Computing Resources pool: The CR pool of this cloud paradigm consists of two different kinds of CR which are dedicated CR (servers, supercomputer, clusters) and non dedicated CR (personal PCs). Generally speaking, supercomputer, clusters are too expensive to scale up for a research institute or enterprise. At the same time, there are a lot of PCs of which a lot of cycles wasted. So it is appealing (from the view of both economic and feasibility) for users to harness these two kinds of CR. CR pool consisting of a lot of non dedicated PCs, is easy to contribute to low cost, scalability by nature. And these features are key points for cloud computing platform. As to these two different kinds of CR, we can use gird middleware OmniRPC to collect cluster and grid CR. And middleware XtremWeb can manage volunteer CR. Now YML can support to integrate these two different kinds of middleware to harness the CR in the cloud pool.

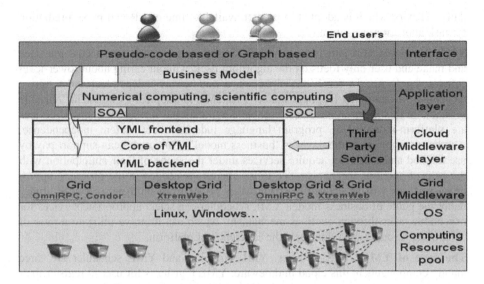

Fig. 1. Architecture of Cloud Platform Based on YML

Operating System: you can use the operating system you would like to use (now only windows and Linux can be supported). And different middleware visions have been put forward to adapt to different operating system.

Application layer: The application of scientific computing or numerical computing is better based on service of architecture (SOA). Service of computing technology is adopted in this layer. And the reason is that it is helpful to invoke the third parts service and the services developed can be reused very easily.

Interface: users can describe their algorithm through an easy of use interface based on YvetteML language which is a XML based description language. It belongs to pseudo code. This interface makes sure the pseudo code is platform independent and middleware independent. See detail in [5]

    Business model is used for describing user's requirement on their expected costs. This is the base for the selection of third part services and CR.

YML backend: YML backend encapsulates different middleware underlying to provide a consistent execution environment to YML services. Concurrently it permits to utilize one or several middleware through providing the specific interface for each middleware. The back-end layer consists in three parts named Monitor, worker coordinator and data manager. Data manager is a component for managing all data exchanges between nodes and data server. This component provides two services to its local or distant worker: distributing appropriate data to workers in advance and retrieving the final results. Worker coordinator maintains a list of active requests and a list of finished requests. The polling of the middleware allows the back-end to move requests from the active queue to the queue of finished requests. It is also in charge of allocating tasks to different virtual resources. Monitor component is used for monitoring the status of computing nodes. The monitoring mechanism is based on users' daily behavior which is adopted to predict available time of CR and make prediction for task allocation/migration [4].

YML frontend: This part is to provide end user with a transparent access interface and make end user only focus on the algorithm itself without caring about lower-level software/hardware. To reach this objective, a middleware-independent and intuitive workflow programming language called YvetteML is adopted. Component 'reusable services' in this layer orchestrates reusable computational services and these services are platform-independent, program language independence, system independence. Another component in this layer is 'business model'. This model can support pay by use method and users can acquire services under the scope of their anticipation with the help of auctions mechanism. To those operations needed in the program, appropriate services will be chosen referring to its prices from third part services library under the guide of business model. YML scheduler can select appropriate services for executable tasks through auctions mechanism, which can improve utilization ratio of computing resources and thus raise the efficiency of platform.

The core of YML: YML register, YML compiler and YML scheduler are three mainly components in this cloud middleware. YML register is for user to register their developed or pay by use services in cloud platform. Once registered, these services can be invoked by YML scheduler automatically. YML compiler is composed of a set of transformation stages which lead to the creation of an application file from XML based program. YML compiler parses the program and an application file consisting of a series of events and operations, is generated. Events are in charge of sequence of operations. Operations are a series of services registered through YML register. An important thing in this paper is to add data flow table into the application file. Through which data dependence between operations can be dealt with. As well known to us all, these data dependence determine the execution way (in parallel/sequence) of those operations. So through data flow table, data persistent and data replication mechanism can be realized in cloud middleware. YML scheduler is a just-in-time scheduler which is in charge of executing the application on the underlying runtime environment defined by the back-end layer. YML scheduler is always executing two main operations sequentially. First, it checks for tasks ready for execution. This is done each time once a new event/fact is introduced and leads to allocate tasks to the back-end. The second operation is the monitoring of the work currently being executed. Once a new worker begins executing, the scheduler of the application regularly checks if the new worker has entered the finished state. The scheduler interacts with the back-end layer through the data manager and backend components. The scheduler takes tasks with an input data set and corresponding operations from application file and executes these tasks on underlying virtual resources until completion or unexpected error. To realize the process presented, some things have to be done. Firstly, a trust model will provide scheduler with availability of a computing node in a future time span. The scheduler allocates tasks to CR according to its trustiness degree. Secondly, YML service will tell YML scheduler the expected time of being executed on a standard virtual machine (VM). The standard VM can be set in advance. For example, the VM is set through a series of parameters like that (Ps, Ms, Ns, Hs), in which Ps stands for processor of VM (2.0 Hz CPU), Ms represents memory of VM (1G Memory), Ns means network bandwidth of VM (1G) and Hs stands for hard space left (10 G). According to reality, you can add/minus the number of parameters. A real machine 'Rm' can be set as (Pr, Mr, Nr, Hr). the capacity (Crm) of 'Rm' can be presented as follows: Crm= a1*Pr/Ps +a2*Mr /Ms+a3*Nr/Ns+a4 *Hr/Hs, in which a1+a2+a3+a4=1. The value of ax can be set according to real case. Based on these two points presented above, scheduler can choose appropriate CR for tasks. Of courses, business model is also important factor for scheduler to take into account. Scheduler will choose better computing resources based on users' expected costs.

4 Conclusion and Open Problem

To make/extend YML suit for cloud computing environments, detail descriptions have been described in section 3. Here I want to make a summary on our on-going work for extending YML to be middleware for cloud computing: 1), Introduce the business model to support pay by use method for cloud platform and it also can be used as a guider cost to bid up in third part service market. At the same time, this model also helps to select appropriate CR for these tasks to be executed in low costs. 2), Data flows are added in the application file. Through adding this flow, data persistence and data replication mechanism can be realized in our cloud platform, which will improve the efficiency of platform greatly. Some emulation experiments have been made to testify our point. 3) Monitor and Trust model is introduced to predict the available status of non dedicated CR. Also a method to evaluate expected execution time based on standard VM is adopted.

Open problem: How to allocate tasks to different CR is key issue. Because two kinds of CR which are dedicated CR and non-dedicated CR are harnessed in the cloud platform based on YML. Making full use of dedicated CR and appropriately utilize the non dedicated CR will generate incredible computing power with lowest cost. Appropriate CR selection during the process of scheduling can improve the efficiency of cloud platform greatly.

References

1. Delannoy, O., Petiton, S.: A Peer to Peer Computing Framework: Design and Performance Evaluation of YML. In: HeteroPar 2004, Ireland. IEEE Computer Society Press, Los Alamitos (2004)
2. Delannoy, O., Emad, N., Petiton, S.G.: Workflow Global Computing with YML. In: The 7th IEEE/ACM International Conference on Grid Computing, pp. 25–32 (2006)
3. Delannoy, O.: YML: A scientific Workflow for High Performance Computing, Ph.D. Thesis, Septembre, Versailles (2008)
4. Shang, L., Wang, Z., Zhou, X., Huang, X., Cheng, Y.: Tm-dg: a trust model based on computer users' daily behavior for desktop grid platform. In: CompFrame 2007, pp. 59–66. ACM, New York (2007)
5. Shang, L., Wang, Z., Petiton, S., Lou, Y., Liu, Z.: Large Scale Computing on Component Based Framework Easily Adaptive to Cluster and Grid Environments. Third Chinagrid Annual Conference Chinagrid 2008. IEEE Computer Society, 70–77 (2008)
6. YML, http://yml.prism.uvsq.fr/

Power-Aware Management in Cloud Data Centers

Milan Milenkovic, Enrique Castro-Leon, and James R. Blakley

Intel Corporation, Hillsboro, Oregon, USA
{milan,enrique.g.castro-leon,jim.r.blakley}@intel.com

Abstract. Power efficiency is a major concern in operating cloud data centers. It affects operational costs and return on investment, with a profound impact on the environment. Current data center operating environments, such as management consoles and cloud control software, tend to optimize for performance and service level agreements and ignore power implications when evaluating workload scheduling choices. We believe that power should be elevated to the first-order consideration in data-center management and that operators should be provided with insights and controls necessary to achieve that purpose.

In this paper we describe several foundational techniques for group-level power management that result in significant power savings in large data centers with run-time load allocation capability, such as clouds and virtualized data centers. We cover VM migration to save power, server pooling or platooning to balance power savings with startup times so as not to impair performance, and discuss power characteristics of servers that affect both the limits and the opportunities for power savings.

Keywords: power management, power-aware scheduling, cloud management, virtualization management, power efficiency, energy-proportional computing.

1 Introduction

Power efficiency is a major concern in operating cloud data centers. It affects operational costs and return on investment, with a profound impact on the environment. Power consumption in a data center is driven by the operation of the information technology (IT) equipment, including servers, networking, and storage, directly and indirectly through coupling with cooling. Current data center operating environments, such as cloud control software stacks and commercial management consoles, tend to optimize for performance and service-level agreements (SLAs) and largely ignore power implications when evaluating workload scheduling choices.

Our objective is to elevate power consumption to a first-class consideration in data center resource allocation and workload scheduling. The hypothesis and our experimental experience is that power-aware placement, management and balancing of workload can reduce power consumption in a data center with negligible impact on performance. Additional savings are possible through power capping policies that manage power-performance tradeoffs in accordance with business objectives. Key power management techniques include consolidation and migration of workloads to keep active machines at optimal operating points, creation of pools of standby

M.G. Jaatun, G. Zhao, and C. Rong (Eds.): CloudCom 2009, LNCS 5931, pp. 668–673, 2009.
© Springer-Verlag Berlin Heidelberg 2009

machines with different wakeup latencies (and proportionally reduced power consumption) to accommodate dynamic up and down capacity scaling in response to load variations, matching workload characteristics to individual machine power-performance profiles, and placement and balancing of workload to minimize thermal variance in the data center and thus reduce cooling inefficiencies.

2 Power Characteristics of Servers

Energy proportional designs have been proposed to improve energy efficiency data centers. Actual energy savings attainable with the current state of the art in server design are somewhat more limited. The power consumption of a server can be represented by the following model:

$$P_{actual} = P_{baseline} + P_{spread}L$$

where P_{actual} is the actual power consumption, $P_{baseline}$ is power consumption at idle, P_{spread} is the power consumption spread between idle and full power, and L is the per unit workload on the server, ranging from 0 to 1.

Loading factors in today's data centers are usually in the 10 to 50 percent range, so the actual power consumption from servers is less than the peak. However, even when loading factors are low, power consumption remains significant due to relatively high power use at idle.

A low $P_{baseline}$ is better. Current technology imposes a limit on how low this number can be. Just a few years ago, idle power use was close to 90% of maximum power, while today it stands closer to 50%.

Literature and our experience indicate that power proportionality can be closely approximated in cloud services via pools of virtualized servers that collectively yield a value of $P_{baseline}$ much lower than the 50 % attainable with a single server through application of integrated power management processes.

At higher load factors another technology is available, Intel® Dynamic Power Node Manager (DPNM) that allows rolling back power consumption by as much as a third of the full load. The reduced power consumption comes at the expense of performance. The loss of performance varies with the type of workload.

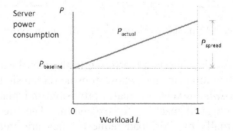

Fig. 1. Power Proportional Computing Model for Servers

3 VM Migration to Save Power

This section describes a specific prototype designed to explore the components, policies, behavior, and power savings made possible in virtualized environments by power-aware rebalancing of the workload.

Group-Enabled Management Systems (GEMS) is a prototype group-enabled management system designed for autonomic management of collections of server nodes. Its variant developed for virtualization with power management, GEMS-VPM, specifically implements rebalancing of workload in collections of virtualized systems in order to save power by (1) proactively consolidating the active workload on a subset of machines that can run it at optimal power-performance settings, and (2) shutting off unused capacity.

Basically, the system consists of a collection of physical servers that are virtualized and effectively create a pool of virtual machines for execution of user workloads in response to incoming requests. This is a common setting for cloud operators that provide Infrastructure as a Service (IaaS) offerings, essentially running customer workloads, packaged and managed as virtual machines, for a fee.

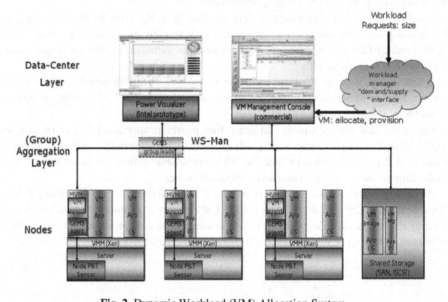

Fig. 2. Dynamic Workload (VM) Allocation System

In a typical usage, work requests are arriving to the workload manager that communicates with virtualization manager (whose console screen shot is shown above the *VM Management Console* server) to create, provision and place virtual machines (VMs) on a suitable physical machine for execution. The life cycle of individual VMs is dictated externally by workload requests; they are created, activated, suspended, or terminated as appropriate.

In this prototype, GEMS adds power and thermal awareness to workload allocation and binding to physical servers. In particular, instead of random allocation of VMs to suitable nodes that is quite common in contemporary cluster and cloud schedulers, GEMS is used for power-aware placement and balancing of workload. In general, power-aware placement implies optimal placement of workload among a collection of eligible physical machines based on power projections of specific workload allocations and selection of an optimal one.

GEMS-VPM prototype implements workload rebalancing to minimize global power consumption. It operates as a policy-driven automation mechanism that proactively seeks opportunities to migrate VMs away from lightly loaded nodes and to save system power by shutting off vacated nodes (servers) left with no active workload.

All nodes contain built-in power and thermal sensors, designated as Node P&T sensor, that are common in contemporary commercial server offerings. GEMS group leader and Power Visualizer, an early prototype of Intel Data-Center Manager (DCM) offering, collaborate to provide real-time individual server and aggregate cluster power readings. These are valuable operator tools that allow added insights such as correlating of workloads with power usage and measuring power savings resulting from policy-based VM migrations described here.

Power-aware policies, running in GEMS leader node, are evaluated in response to significant system events, such as creation and deletion of VMs whose lifecycle is dictated by workload requests that are external to the system. The policy manager activates live VM migration by issuing the necessary APIs to VM management console. Nodes that are shut down to save power during comparatively low overall utilization of the VM execution pool, can be programmatically brought back into operation when needed in response to workload demand fluctuations.

Savings resulting from shutting off of unused nodes are significant due to the fact that contemporary server platforms tend to consume on the order of 50% of their maximum power consumption when idle. As in illustration, consider a pool of 20 physical servers that consume 500W each at full load and 250W at idle. At 100% total aggregate load, the server pool consumes 10,000 W. At 50% aggregate load, the unbalanced pool would consume somewhat in excess of 7500W, depending on load distribution. With VM migration to save power described here, the system could use as little as 5000W while executing the same workload by consolidating it on 10 active servers and shutting off the remaining ones, thus yielding power savings on the order of 30%. Even though in practice operators tend to set a limit below 100% for maximum server utilization, power-aware VM migration results in significant power savings often in double digit percentages.

4   Energy Proportional vs. Power Proportional Computing

Power consumed by a server can vary instantaneously and continuously. The energy consumed by a server can be represented by the integral of its power consumption over that particular interval:

$$E = \int P(t)\, dt$$

A power saving mechanism can also yield energy savings. Let's build a simple model to compare the power consumed by a server without any power saving mechanism vs. a server that does. The server without power management would exhibit a constant

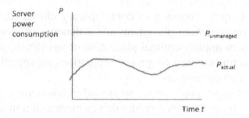

Fig. 3. Measuring Energy Saved

power consumption $P_{unmanaged}$ regardless of the operational state. Let's also track the actual power consumption P_{actual} over time. The energy saved by the power mechanisms in effect would be the area determined by the difference between $P_{unmanaged}$ and P_{actual} over time:

Energy saved is represented by the equation

$$E = \int (P_{unmanaged}(t) - P_{actual}(t))\, dt$$

From this analysis it becomes clear that in order for a power saving mechanism to yield meaningful energy savings, power savings need to be maintained for a long time and the difference between $P_{unmanaged}$ and P_{actual} be as large as possible.

A single mechanism will not yield the desired benefits. For instance, a typical power consumption of a Nehalem generation server is about 300 watts when utilization is close to 100 percent. Applying DPNM power capping can bring the power consumption to about 200 watts. If the server is brought to idle, power consumption will descend to about 150 watts.

Applying a power management mechanism may have a performance impact: DPNM works through voltage and frequency scaling, that is by reducing the voltage applied to the CPU and the frequency at which it works in discrete steps. Doing so impacts performance. The actual penalty is a function workload type.

Another limitation imposed by power management mechanisms is a restricted operational envelope: DPNM works best at high loading factors, while mechanisms like demand based switching (DBS) work best when workloads are light.

One way to maximize the difference $P_{unmanaged}$ and P_{actual} is to reduce $P_{baseline}$ as much as possible. In virtualized cloud environments where server resources are pooled, it is possible to bring down $P_{baseline}$ collectively for the pool by shutting down servers not needed to meet the current load. Doing so allows extending the power dynamic range with workload considerably. A system exhibiting a large dynamic range is said to be workload power *scalable*. Since it takes several minutes to restart a server, it may be necessary to designate an extra pool of servers in a higher energy state to pick up load spikes while dormant servers are restarted.

We describe a scheme whereby a large pool of servers is divided into sub-pools supporting each other for the purposes of meeting a time-varying workload. For this reason we call this scheme *platooning*.

A platooning example is depicted in Figure 4 using ACPI S5 sleep as the dormant state and a sub-pool of power capped servers as the reserve pool. The reserve pool is operational and can be used to run low priority loads. PSMI stands for Power Supply Management Interface, a standard that allows real-time power supply readouts.

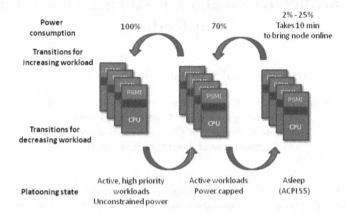

Fig. 4. Platooning: Achieving High P_{spread} and Low $P_{baseline}$ Power Management with Server Pools

It is important to note that this scheme is not viable in a traditional application environment where applications are bound to physical servers. A key factor is to have fungible pools of compute and storage resources.

References

1. Barroso, L.A., Hölzle, U.: The Case for Energy-Proportional Computing. IEEE Computer, 33–37 (December 2007)
2. Nathuji, R., Schwan, K.: VirtualPower: Coordinated Power Management in Virtualized Enterprise Systems. In: ACM Symposium on Operating Systems Principles, SOSP 2007 (2007)
3. Ranganathan, P., Leech, P., Irwin, D., Chase, J.: Ensemble-Level Power Management for Dense Blade Servers. In: International Symposium on Computer Architecture, ISCA 2006 (2006)
4. Moore, J., Chase, J., Ranganathan, P.: Weatherman: Automated, Online, and Predictive Thermal Mapping and Management for Data Centers. In: IEEE International Conference on Autonomic Computing, ICAC 2006 (2006)
5. Nathuji, R., Canturk, I., Gorbatov, E.: Exploiting Platform Heterogeneity for Power Efficient Data Center. In: ICAC 2007 (2007)
6. Castro-Leon, E.: The Web within the Web. IEEE Spectrum 42(2), 42–46 (2004)
7. Castro-Leon, E., He, J., Chang, M., Peiravi, P.: The Business Value of Virtual Service Oriented Grids. Intel Press (2008)
8. DCMIspecification, http://download.intel.com/technology/product/ Data_Center_Manageability_Interface_whitepaper.pdf
9. IPMI specification, http://www.intel.com/design/servers/ipmi/
10. WS-Management specification, http://www.dmtf.org/standards/wsman/

Parallel K-Means Clustering Based on MapReduce

Weizhong Zhao[1,2], Huifang Ma[1,2], and Qing He[1]

[1] The Key Laboratory of Intelligent Information Processing, Institute of Computing
Technology, Chinese Academy of Sciences
[2] Graduate University of Chinese Academy of Sciences
{zhaowz,mahf,heq}@ics.ict.ac.cn

Abstract. Data clustering has been received considerable attention in
many applications, such as data mining, document retrieval, image segmentation and pattern classification. The enlarging volumes of information emerging by the progress of technology, makes clustering of very
large scale of data a challenging task. In order to deal with the problem,
many researchers try to design efficient parallel clustering algorithms.
In this paper, we propose a parallel k-means clustering algorithm based
on MapReduce, which is a simple yet powerful parallel programming
technique. The experimental results demonstrate that the proposed algorithm can scale well and efficiently process large datasets on commodity
hardware.

Keywords: Data mining; Parallel clustering; K-means; Hadoop; MapReduce.

1 Introduction

With the development of information technology, data volumes processed by
many applications will routinely cross the peta-scale threshold, which would
in turn increase the computational requirements. Efficient parallel clustering
algorithms and implementation techniques are the key to meeting the scalability
and performance requirements entailed in such scientific data analyses. So far,
several researchers have proposed some parallel clustering algorithms [1,2,3].
All these parallel clustering algorithms have the following drawbacks: a) They
assume that all objects can reside in main memory at the same time; b) Their
parallel systems have provided restricted programming models and used the
restrictions to parallelize the computation automatically. Both assumptions are
prohibitive for very large datasets with millions of objects. Therefore, dataset
oriented parallel clustering algorithms should be developed.

MapReduce [4,5,6,7] is a programming model and an associated implementation for processing and generating large datasets that is amenable to a broad
variety of real-world tasks. Users specify the computation in terms of a *map* and
a *reduce* function, and the underlying runtime system automatically parallelizes
the computation across large-scale clusters of machines, handles machine failures, and schedules inter-machine communication to make efficient use of the

M.G. Jaatun, G. Zhao, and C. Rong (Eds.): CloudCom 2009, LNCS 5931, pp. 674–679, 2009.
© Springer-Verlag Berlin Heidelberg 2009

network and disks. Google and Hadoop both provide MapReduce runtimes with fault tolerance and dynamic flexibility support [8,9].

In this paper, we adapt k-means algorithm [10] in MapReduce framework which is implemented by Hadoop to make the clustering method applicable to large scale data. By applying proper <key, value> pairs, the proposed algorithm can be parallel executed effectively. We conduct comprehensive experiments to evaluate the proposed algorithm. The results demonstrate that our algorithm can effectively deal with large scale datasets.

The rest of the paper is organized as follows. In Section 2, we present our parallel k-means algorithm based on MapReduce framework. Section 3 shows experimental results and evaluates our parallel algorithm with respect to speedup, scaleup, and sizeup. Finally, we offer our conclusions in Section 4.

2 Parallel K-Means Algorithm Based on MapReduce

In this section we present the main design for Parallel K-Means (PKMeans) based on MapReduce. Firstly, we give a brief overview of the k-means algorithm and analyze the parallel parts and serial parts in the algorithms. Then we explain how the necessary computations can be formalized as map and reduce operations in detail.

2.1 K-Means Algorithm

K-means algorithm is the most well-known and commonly used clustering method. It takes the input parameter, k, and partitions a set of n objects into k clusters so that the resulting intra-cluster similarity is high whereas the inter-cluster similarity is low. Cluster similarity is measured according to the mean value of the objects in the cluster, which can be regarded as the cluster's "center of gravity".

The algorithm proceeds as follows: Firstly, it randomly selects k objects from the whole objects which represent initial cluster centers. Each remaining object is assigned to the cluster to which it is the most similar, based on the distance between the object and the cluster center. The new mean for each cluster is then calculated. This process iterates until the criterion function converges.

In k-means algorithm, the most intensive calculation to occur is the calculation of distances. In each iteration, it would require a total of (nk) distance computations where n is the number of objects and k is the number of clusters being created. It is obviously that the distance computations between one object with the centers is irrelevant to the distance computations between other objects with the corresponding centers. Therefore, distance computations between different objects with centers can be parallel executed. In each iteration, the new centers, which are used in the next iteration, should be updated. Hence the iterative procedures must be executed serially.

2.2 PKMeans Based on MapReduce

As the analysis above, PKMeans algorithm needs one kind of MapReduce job. The map function performs the procedure of assigning each sample to the closest center while the reduce function performs the procedure of updating the new centers. In order to decrease the cost of network communication, a combiner function is developed to deal with partial combination of the intermediate values with the same key within the same map task.

Map-function The input dataset is stored on HDFS[11] as a sequence file of <key, value> pairs, each of which represents a record in the dataset. The key is the offset in bytes of this record to the start point of the data file, and the value is a string of the content of this record. The dataset is split and globally broadcast to all mappers. Consequently, the distance computations are parallel executed. For each map task, PKMeans construct a global variant *centers* which is an array containing the information about centers of the clusters. Given the information, a mapper can compute the closest center point for each sample. The intermediate values are then composed of two parts: the index of the closest center point and the sample information. The pseudocode of map function is shown in Algorithm 1.

Algorithm 1. map (*key, value*)

Input: Global variable *centers*, the offset *key*, the sample *value*
Output: <*key', value'*> pair, where the *key'* is the index of the closest center point and *value'* is a string comprise of sample information

1. Construct the sample *instance* from *value*;
2. $minDis = Double.MAX\_VALUE$;
3. $index = -1$;
4. For i=0 to *centers*.length do
       dis= ComputeDist(*instance*, *centers*[i]);
       If $dis < minDis$ {
            $minDis = dis$;
            $index = i$;
       }
5. End For
6. Take *index* as *key'*;
7. Construct *value'* as a string comprise of the values of different dimensions;
8. output < *key', value'* > pair;
9. End

Note that Step 2 and Step 3 initialize the auxiliary variable *minDis* and *index*; Step 4 computes the closest center point from the sample, in which the function *ComputeDist* (*instance*, *centers*[i]) returns the distance between *instance* and the center point *centers*[i]; Step 8 outputs the intermediate data which is used in the subsequent procedures.

Combine-function. After each map task, we apply a combiner to combine the intermediate data of the same map task. Since the intermediate data is stored in local disk of the host, the procedure can not consume the communication cost. In the combine function, we partially sum the values of the points assigned to the same cluster. In order to calculate the mean value of the objects for each cluster, we should record the number of samples in the same cluster in the same map task. The pseudocode for combine function is shown in Algorithm 2.

Algorithm 2. combine (*key*, *V*)

Input: *key* is the index of the cluster, *V* is the list of the samples assigned to the same cluster
Output: < *key'*, *value'* > pair, where the *key'* is the index of the cluster, *value'* is a string comprised of sum of the samples in the same cluster and the sample number

1. Initialize one array to record the sum of value of each dimensions of the samples contained in the same cluster, i.e. the samples in the list *V*;
2. Initialize a counter *num* as 0 to record the sum of sample number in the same cluster;
3. while(*V*.hasNext()){
       Construct the sample *instance* from *V*.next();
       Add the values of different dimensions of *instance* to the array
       num++;
4. }
5. Take *key* as *key'*;
6. Construct *value'* as a string comprised of the sum values of different dimensions and *num*;
7. output < *key'*, *value'* > pair;
8. End

Reduce-function. The input of the reduce function is the data obtained from the combine function of each host. As described in the combine function, the data includes partial sum of the samples in the same cluster and the sample number. In reduce function, we can sum all the samples and compute the total number of samples assigned to the same cluster. Therefore, we can get the new centers which are used for next iteration. The pseudocode for reduce function is shown in Algorithm 3.

Algorithm 3. reduce (*key*, *V*)

Input: *key* is the index of the cluster, *V* is the list of the partial sums from different host
Output: < *key'*, *value'* > pair, where the *key'* is the index of the cluster, *value'* is a string representing the new center

1. Initialize one array record the sum of value of each dimensions of the samples contained in the same cluster, e.g. the samples in the list *V*;
2. Initialize a counter *NUM* as 0 to record the sum of sample number in the same cluster;
3. while(*V*.hasNext()){
       Construct the sample *instance* from *V*.next();
       Add the values of different dimensions of *instance* to the array
       NUM += *num*;
4. }
5. Divide the entries of the array by *NUM* to get the new center's coordinates;
6. Take *key* as *key'*;
7. Construct *value'* as a string comprise of the *center*'s coordinates;
8. output < *key'*, *value'* > pair;
9. End

---

3 Experimental Results

In this section, we evaluate the performance of our proposed algorithm with respect to speedup, scaleup and sizeup [12]. Performance experiments were run

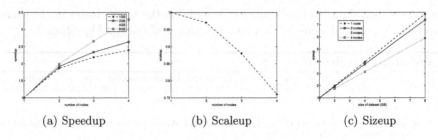

(a) Speedup   (b) Scaleup   (c) Sizeup

Fig. 1. Evaluations results

on a cluster of computers, each of which has two 2.8 GHz cores and 4GB of memory. Hadoop version 0.17.0 and Java 1.5.0_14 are used as the MapReduce system for all experiments.

To measure the speedup, we kept the dataset constant and increase the number of computers in the system. The perfect parallel algorithm demonstrates linear speedup: a system with m times the number of computers yields a speedup of m. However, linear speedup is difficult to achieve because the communication cost increases with the number of clusters becomes large.

We have performed the speedup evaluation on datasets with different sizes and systems. The number of computers varied from 1 to 4. The size of the dataset increases from 1GB to 8GB. Fig.1.(a) shows the speedup for different datasets. As the result shows, PKMeans has a very good speedup performance. Specifically, as the size of the dataset increases, the speedup performs better. Therefore, PKMeans algorithm can treat large datasets efficiently.

Scaleup evaluates the ability of the algorithm to grow both the system and the dataset size. Scaleup is defined as the ability of an m-times larger system to perform an m-times larger job in the same run-time as the original system.

To demonstrate how well the PKMeans algorithm handles larger datasets when more computers are available, we have performed scaleup experiments where we have increased the size of the datasets in direct proportion to the number of computers in the system. The datasets size of 1GB, 2GB, 3GB and 4GB are executed on 1, 2, 3 and 4 computers respectively. Fig.1.(b) shows the performance results of the datasets. Clearly, the PKMeans algorithm scales very well.

Sizeup analysis holds the number of computers in the system constant, and grows the size of the datasets by the factor m. Sizeup measures how much longer it takes on a given system, when the dataset size is m-times larger than the original dataset.

To measure the performance of sizeup, we have fixed the number of computers to 1, 2, 3, and 4 respectively. Fig.1.(c) shows the sizeup results on different computers. The graph shows that PKMeans has a very good sizeup performance.

4   Conclusions

As data clustering has attracted a significant amount of research attention, many clustering algorithms have been proposed in the past decades. However, the enlarging data in applications makes clustering of very large scale of data a challenging task. In this paper, we propose a fast parallel k-means clustering algorithm based on MapReduce, which has been widely embraced by both academia and industry. We use speedup, scaleup and sizeup to evaluate the performances of our proposed algorithm. The results show that the proposed algorithm can process large datasets on commodity hardware effectively.

Acknowledgments. This work is supported by the National Science Foundation of China (No.60675010, 60933004, 60975039), 863 National High-Tech Program (No.2007AA01Z132), National Basic Research Priorities Programme (No.2007CB311004) and National Science and Technology Support Plan (No.200-6BAC08B06).

References

1. Rasmussen, E.M., Willett, P.: Efficiency of Hierarchical Agglomerative Clustering Using the ICL Distributed Array Processor. Journal of Documentation 45(1), 1–24 (1989)
2. Li, X., Fang, Z.: Parallel Clustering Algorithms. Parallel Computing 11, 275–290 (1989)
3. Olson, C.F.: Parallel Algorithms for Hierarchical Clustering. Parallel Computing 21(8), 1313–1325 (1995)
4. Dean, J., Ghemawat, S.: MapReduce: Simplified Data Processing on Large Clusters. In: Proc. of Operating Systems Design and Implementation, San Francisco, CA, pp. 137–150 (2004)
5. Dean, J., Ghemawat, S.: MapReduce: Simplified Data Processing on Large Clusters. Communications of The ACM 51(1), 107–113 (2008)
6. Ranger, C., Raghuraman, R., Penmetsa, A., Bradski, G., Kozyrakis, C.: Evaluating MapReduce for Multi-core and Multiprocessor Systems. In: Proc. of 13th Int. Symposium on High-Performance Computer Architecture (HPCA), Phoenix, AZ (2007)
7. Lammel, R.: Google's MapReduce Programming Model - Revisited. Science of Computer Programming 70, 1–30 (2008)
8. Hadoop: Open source implementation of MapReduce, http://lucene.apache.org/hadoop/
9. Ghemawat, S., Gobioff, H., Leung, S.: The Google File System. In: Symposium on Operating Systems Principles, pp. 29–43 (2003)
10. MacQueen, J.: Some Methods for Classification and Analysis of Multivariate Observations. In: Proc. 5th Berkeley Symp. Math. Statist, Prob., vol. 1, pp. 281–297 (1967)
11. Borthakur, D.: The Hadoop Distributed File System: Architecture and Design (2007)
12. Xu, X., Jager, J., Kriegel, H.P.: A Fast Parallel Clustering Algorithm for Large Spatial Databases. Data Mining and Knowledge Discovery 3, 263–290 (1999)

Storage and Retrieval of Large RDF Graph Using Hadoop and MapReduce

Mohammad Farhan Husain, Pankil Doshi, Latifur Khan,
and Bhavani Thuraisingham

University of Texas at Dallas, Dallas TX 75080, USA

Abstract. Handling huge amount of data scalably is a matter of concern for a long time. Same is true for semantic web data. Current semantic web frameworks lack this ability. In this paper, we describe a framework that we built using Hadoop[1] to store and retrieve large number of RDF[2] triples. We describe our schema to store RDF data in Hadoop Distribute File System. We also present our algorithms to answer a SPARQL[3] query. We make use of Hadoop's MapReduce framework to actually answer the queries. Our results reveal that we can store huge amount of semantic web data in Hadoop clusters built mostly by cheap commodity class hardware and still can answer queries fast enough. We conclude that ours is a scalable framework, able to handle large amount of RDF data efficiently.

1 Introduction

Scalability is a major issue in IT world. Basically what it means is that a system can handle addition of large number of users, data, tasks etc. without affecting its performance significantly. Designing a scalable system is not a trivial task. This also applies to systems handling large data sets. Semantic web data repositories are no exception to that. Storing huge number of RDF triples and the ability to efficiently query them is a challenging problem which is yet to be solved. Trillions of triples requiring peta bytes of disk space is not a distant possibility any more. Researchers are already working on billions of triples[1]. Competitions are being organized to encourage researchers to build efficient repositories[4].

Hadoop is a distributed file system where files can be saved with replication. It provides high fault tolerance and reliability. Moreover, it provides an implementation of MapReduce programming model. MapReduce is a functional programming model which is suitable for processing large amount of data in parallel. In this programming paradigm, MapReduce processes are run on independant chunks of data making parallelization easier. MapReduce is an evolving technology now. The technology has been well received by the community which handles large amount of data. Google uses it for web indexing, data storage, social networking [2]. It is being used to scale up classifiers for mining peta-bytes

---

[1] http://hadoop.apache.org
[2] http://www.w3.org/RDF
[3] http://www.w3.org/TR/rdf-sparql-query
[4] http://challenge.semanticweb.org

M.G. Jaatun, G. Zhao, and C. Rong (Eds.): CloudCom 2009, LNCS 5931, pp. 680–686, 2009.
© Springer-Verlag Berlin Heidelberg 2009

of data [3]. Data mining algorithms are being rewritten in different forms to take the advantage of MapReduce technology [4]. Biological data is being analyzed by this technology[1].

Current semantic web frameworks like Jena[5] do not scale well. These frameworks run on single machine and hence cannot handle huge amount of triples. For example, we could load only 10 million triples in a Jena in-memory model running in a machine having 2 GB of main memory. In this paper, we describe our work with RDF data and Hadoop. We devise a schema to store RDF data in Hadoop. In a preprocessing stage, we process RDF data and put it in text files in the distributed file system according to our schema. We chose Lehigh University Benchmark[5] (LUBM) data generator to generate our data. We have a retrieval mechanism by MapReduce programming. We find that for many queries, one MapReduce job is not enough. We need to have an algorithm to determine how many jobs are needed for a given query. We devise such an algorithm which not only determines the number of jobs but also their sequence and inputs. We run all the LUBM benchmark queries. We run them on different sizes of data sets starting from 100 million triples to 1 billion triples.

The remainder of this paper is organized as follows: in section 2 we discuss the architecture of our system and data storage. We discuss how we answer a SPARQL query in section 3. Finally, we present the results of our experiments in section 4.

2   Proposed Architecture

Our architecture consists of several software components. We make use of Jena Semantic Web Framework in data preprocessing step and Pellet OWL Reasoner[6] in query execution. Our framework consists of two components: data generator-preprocessor and MapReduce framework for query processing.

We have three sub-components for data generation and preprocessing. The LUBM [5] data generator creates data in RDF/XML serialization format. We take this data and convert it to N-Triples serialization format using our N-Triple Converter component. This component uses Jena framework to convert the data. The Predicate Based File Splitter takes the converted data and splits it into predicate files. The predicate based files are then fed into the Object-Type Based File Splitter which split the predicate files to smaller files based of type of objects. These steps are described in section 2.1. The output of the last component are then put into HDFS[7].

Our MapReduce framework has three sub-components in it. It takes SPARQL query from the user passes it to Job Decider and Input Selector. This component decides how many jobs are needed and selects the input files and passes the information to the Job Handler component which submits corresponding jobs to Hadoop. It then relays the query answer from Hadoop to the user. To answer queries that require inferencing, we use Pellet OWL Reasoner.

---

[5] http://jena.sourceforge.net
[6] http://clarkparsia.com/pellet
[7] http://hadoop.apache.org/core/docs/r0.18.3/hdfs_design.html

2.1   File Organization

In HDFS a file takes space replication factor times its size. As RDF is text data, it takes a lot space in HDFS to store a file. To minimize the amount of space, we replace the common prefixes in URIs with some much smaller prefix strings. We keep track of this prefix strings in a separate prefix file. This reduces the space required by the data by a significant amount.

As there is no caching in Hadoop, each SPARQL query needs reading files from HDFS. Reading directly from disk always have a high latency. To reduce the execution time of a SPARQL query, we came up with an organization of files which provides us with the capability to determine the files needed to search in for a SPARQL query. The files usually constitute a fraction of the entire data set and thus making the query execution much faster.

We do not store the data in a single file because in Hadoop file is the smallest unit of input to a MapReduce job. If we have all the data in one file then the whole file will be input to MapReduce jobs for each query. Instead we divide the data in multiple steps. **Predicate Split (PS)**: in the first step, we divide the data according to the predicates. **Predicate Object Split (POS)**: In the next step, we work with the type information of objects. The *rdf_type* file is first divided into as many files as the number of distinct objects the *rdf:type* predicate has. This further reduces the amount of space needed to store the data. For each distinct object values of the predicate *rdf:type* we get a file. We divide other predicate files according to the type of the objects. Not all the objects are URIs, some are literals. The literals remain in the file named by the predicate i.e. no further processing is required for them. The objects move into their respective file named as *predicate_type*. In our work we found 70.42% space gain after PS step and 7.04% more gain for 1000 universities dataset.

3   MapReduce Framework

3.1   The *DetermineJobs* Algorithm

To answer a SPARQL query by MapReduce jobs, we may need more than one job. It is because we cannot handle all the joins in one job because of the way Hadoop runs its map and reduce processes. Those processes have no inter process communication and they work on idependent chunks of data. Hence, processing a piece of data cannot be dependent on the outcome of any other piece of data which is essential to do joins. This is why we might need more than one job to answer a query. Each job except the first one depends on the output of its previous job.

We devised Algorithm 1 which determines the number of jobs needed to answer a SPARQL query. It determines which joins are handled in which job and the sequence of the jobs. For a query Q we build a graph $G = (V, E)$ where V is the set of vertices and E is the set of edges. For each triple pattern in the query Q we build a vertex v which makes up the set V. Hence $|V|$ is equal to the number of triple patterns in Q. We put an edge e between v_i and v_j, where $i \neq j$, if and only if their corresponding triple patterns share at least one variable. We label the edge e with all the variable names that were shared between v_i and v_j. These edges make up the set E. Each edge represents as many joins as the number of variables it has in its label. Hence, total number of joins present in the graph is the total number of variables mentioned in the labels of all edges. An example illustrates it better. We have chosen LUBM [5] query 12 for that purpose. Listing 1.1 shows the query.

Listing 1.1. LUBM Query 12

```
SELECT ?X WHERE {                                               1
?X rdf:type ub:Chair .                                          2
?Y rdf:type ub:Department .                                     3
?X ub:worksFor ?Y .                                             4
?Y ub:subOrganizationOf <http://www.University0.edu> }         5
```

The graph we build at first for the query is shown in figure 1. The nodes are numbered in the order they appear in the query.

Algorithm 1. DETERMINEJOBS(*Query q*)

Require: A Query object returned by RewriteQuery algorithm.
Ensure: The number of jobs and their details needed to answer the query.

```
 1: jobs ← φ; graph ← makeGraphFromQuery(q); joins_left ← calculateJoins(graph)
 2: while joins_left ≠ 0 do
 3:     variables ← getVariables(graph); job ← createNewJob()
 4:     for i ← 1 to |variables| do
 5:         v ← variables[i]; v.nodes ← getMaximumVisitableNodes(v, graph)
 6:         v.joins ← getJoins(v.nodes, graph)
 7:     end for
 8:     sortVariablesByNumberOfJoins(variables)
 9:     for i ← 0 to |variables| do
10:         if |v.joins| ≠ 0 then
11:             job.addVariable(v); jobs_left ← jobs_left − |v.joins|
12:             for j ← i + 1 to |variables| do
13:                 adjustNodesAndJoins(variables[j], v.nodes)
14:             end for
15:             mergeNodes(graph, v.nodes)
16:         end if
17:     end for
18:     jobs ← jobs ∪ job
19: end while
20: return jobs
```

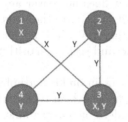   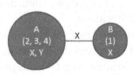

Fig. 1. Graph for Query 12 in Iteration 1   **Fig. 2.** Graph for Query 12 in Iteration 2

Table 1. Iteration 1 Calculations

Variable	Nodes	Joins	‖Joins‖
Y	2, 3, 4	2-3, 3-4, 4-2	3
X	1, 2	1-2	1

Table 2. Iteration 1 - After choosing X

	Variable	Nodes	Joins	‖Joins‖
√	Y	2, 3, 4	2-3, 3-4, 4-2	3
	X	1		0

Table 3. Iteration 2 Calculations

Variable	Nodes	Joins	Total Joins
X	1, 2	1-2	1

In figure 1, each node in the figure has a node number in the first line and variables it has in the following line. Nodes 1 and 3 share the variable X hence there is an edge between them having the label X. Similarly, nodes 2, 3 and 4 have edges between them because they share the variable Y. The graph has total 4 joins.

Algorithm 1 is iterative. It takes a *Query* object as its input, initializes the *jobs* set (line 1), builds the graph shown in figure 1 before entering first iteration (line 2). It also calculates the number of jobs left (line 3). It enters the loop in line 4 if at least one job is left. At the beginning of the loop it retrieves the set of variables (line 5) and creates a new empty job (line 6). Then it iterates over the variable (line 7 and 8), lists the maximum number of nodes it can visit by edges having the variable in its label (lines 9). It also lists the number of joins that exist among those nodes (line 10). For example, for variable Y we can visit nodes 2, 3 and 4. The joins these nodes have are 2-3, 3-4 and 4-2. The information it collects for each variable is shown in table 1.

It then sorts the variables in descending order according to the number of joins they cover (line 12). In this example, the sort output is the same as table 1. Then, in greedy fashion, it iterates over the variables and chooses a variables if the variable covers at least one join (line 13 and 14). In each iteration, after it chooses a variable, it eliminates all the nodes it covers from subsequent variable entries (lines 17 to 19). It then calculates the number of joins still left in the graph (line 16). For example, once the algorithm chooses the variable Y, the nodes and joins for X becomes like table 2.

It also merges the nodes visited by the chosen variable in the graph (line 20). Hence, after choosing Y it will not choose X as it does not cover any join any more. Here the inner loop terminates. The joins it picked are the joins that will be done in a job. The algorithm then checks whether any join is not picked (line 4). If such is the case, then more jobs are needed and so the algorithm goes to the next iteration.

At the beginning of the subsequent iteration it again builds a graph from the graph of the previous iteration but this time the nodes which took part in joins by one variable will be collapsed into a single node. For our example, nodes 2, 3 and 4 took part in joins by Y. So they will collapse and form a single node. For clarity, we name this collapsed node as A and the remaining node 1 of the graph in figure 1 as B. The new graph we get like this is shown in figure 2. The graph has total 1 join. We have listed the nodes which were collapsed in braces.

After building the graph, the algorithm moves on to list the maximum number of nodes, joins and total number of joins each variable covers. This is shown in table 3. The algorithm chooses X and that covers all the joins of the graph. The algorithm determines that no more job is needed and returns the job collection.

4   Results

Due to space limitations we choose to report runtimes of six LUBM queries which we ran in a cluster of 10 nodes with POS schema. Each node had the same configuration: Pentium IV 2.80 GHz processor, 4 GB main memory and 640 GB disk space. The results we found are shown in table 4.

Table 4. Query Runtimes

Universities	Triples (million)	Query1	Query2	Query4	Query9	Query12	Query13
1000	110	66.313	146.86	197.719	304.87	79.749	198.502
2000	220	87.542	216.127	303.185	532.982	95.633	272.521
3000	330	115.171	307.752	451.147	708.857	100.091	344.535
4000	440	129.696	393.781	608.732	892.727	115.104	422.235
5000	550	159.85	463.344	754.829	1129.543	132.043	503.377
6000	660	177.423	543.677	892.383	1359.536	150.83	544.383
7000	770	198.033	612.511	1067.289	1613.622	178.468	640.486
8000	880	215.356	673.0	1174.018	1855.5127	184.434	736.189
9000	990	229.18	727.596	1488.586	2098.913	214.575	821.459
10000	1100	273.085	850.503	1581.963	2508.93	286.612	864.722

Table 4 has query answering times in seconds. The number of triples are rounded down to millions. As expected, as the number of triples increased, the time to answer a query also increased. Query 1 is simple and requires only one join. We can see that it took the least amount of time among all the queries. Query 2 is one of the two queries having most number of triple patterns. We can observe that even though it has three times more triple patterns it does not take thrice the time of query 1 answering time because of our storage schema. Query 4 has one less triple pattern than query 2 but it requires inferencing to bind 1 triple pattern. As we determine inferred relations on the fly, queries requiring inferencing takes longer times in our framework. Query 9 and 12 also require inferencing and query 13 has an inverse property in one of its triple patterns.

We can see that the ratio between the size of two datasets and the ratio between the query answering times for any query are not the same. The increase in time to answer a query is always less than the increase in size of datasets. For example, 10000 universities dataset has ten times triples than 1000 universities but for query 1 time only increases by 4.12 times and for query 9 by 8.23 times.

The later one is the highest increase in time which is still less than the increase in dataset size. Due to space limitations, we do not report query runtimes with PS schema here. We observed that PS schema is much slower than POS schema.

References

1. Newman, A., Hunter, J., Li, Y.F., Bouton, C., Davis, M.: A Scale-Out RDF Molecule Store for Distributed Processing of Biomedical Data Semantic Web for Health Care and Life Sciences. In: Workshop WWW 2008, Beijing, China (2008)
2. Chang, F., Dean, J., et al.: Bigtable: A Distributed Storage System for Structured Data. In: OSDI Seventh Symposium on Operating System Design and Implementation (November 2006)
3. Moretti, C., Steinhaeuser, K., Thain, D., Chawla, N.V.: Scaling Up Classifiers to Cloud Computers. In: IEEE ICDM (2008)
4. Chu, C.-T., Kim, S.K., Lin, Y.-A., Yu, Y., Bradski, G., Ng, A.Y., Olukotun, K.: Map-reduce for machine learning on multicore. In: NIPS 2007 (2007)
5. Guo, Y., Pan, Z., Heflin, J.: LUBM: A Benchmark for OWL Knowledge Base Systems. Journal of Web Semantics 3(2), 158–182 (2005)

Distributed Scheduling Extension on Hadoop

Zeng Dadan, Wang Xieqin, and Jiang Ningkang

Software Engineering Institute, East China Normal University
ddzeng@sei.ecnu.edu.cn

Abstract. Distributed computing splits a large-scale job into multiple tasks and deals with them on clusters. Cluster resource allocation is the key point to restrict the efficiency of distributed computing platform. Hadoop is the current most popular open-source distributed platform. However, the existing scheduling strategies in Hadoop are kind of simple and cannot meet the needs such as sharing the cluster for multi-user, ensuring a concept of guaranteed capacity for each job, as well as providing good performance for interactive jobs. This paper researches the existing scheduling strategies, analyses the inadequacy and adds three new features in Hadoop which can raise the weight of job temporarily, grab cluster resources by higher-priority jobs and support the computing resources share among multi-user. Experiments show they can help in providing better performance for interactive jobs, as well as more fairly share of computing time among users.

Keywords: Hadoop, Distributed Scheduling, MapReduce, Fair Share.

1 Preface

Cluster resource allocation is the key of the efficiency in a distributed computing platform. The quality of the scheduling strategy will directly affect the operational efficiency of the entire cluster. Google's MapReduce framework is a typical representative for distributed computing platform[1,2]. Hadoop is the open source implementation of Apache Software Foundation's MapReduce which is used to deal with the parallel computing on large-scale data sets (TB orders of magnitude)[3]. Hadoop splits calculation into map and reduce in order to distribute the computing tasks to various nodes in clusters and finally complete the parallel computing on large-scale data sets through summarizing the results of each node. Because of its open source and the powerful processing capabilities of distributed computing, Hadoop has been the most widely used platform in the industry. Besides Yahoo, Facebook ,Amazon and other major companies, researchers at Cornell University, Carnegie Mellon University, University of Maryland, and Palo Alto Research Center use Hadoop for such distributed computing as seismic modeling, natural language processing, and Web data mining[5,6,7,8].

This article studies the scheduling model Hadoop used. Then, analyses the limitations of the existing scheduling strategy, the imperfect of it. On the basis of that, three improvements are added to the existing scheduling strategy combined with the specific needs in the distributed environment.

M.G. Jaatun, G. Zhao, and C. Rong (Eds.): CloudCom 2009, LNCS 5931, pp. 687–693, 2009.

2 Scheduling Strategies of Hadoop

Hadoop with the FIFO scheduling strategy is mainly for large batch operations, such as Web search, Log Mining and so on [4]. FIFO scheduling strategy is not able to meet the new demands of multi-user's sharing of cluster while it is hard to deal with the highly-demanded response time in the aspect of the interactive task. In this case, the third-party companies develop some new scheduling strategy according to their business. Take some famous example, Facebook's FairScheduler and Yahoo's Capacity-Scheduler. FairScheduler is based on the principle of fair sharing. Fair sharing aims at the pro-rata sharing of resources among the users.

Similar to FairScheduler, CapacityScheduler is also applicable to multi-user share cluster. In CapacityScheduler, the user could define a series of naming queues while he could configure the number of maps and reduces' computing resources that each queue needs. When there is a job in the queue, CapacityScheduler will provide the queue with the computing resources according to the configuration, meanwhile, it will allocate the surplus computing resources equally. Inside each queue, capacityscheduler simulate Hadoop's FIFO scheduling strategy which is that the scheduler decides the processing sequence according to the job's priority and submit time.

3 Design and Implementation to Improve the Hadoop-Based Scheduling

Hadoop is assumed to be mainly used for large-scale batch processing operations in design, for example Web search, log mining, and so on. Its built-in scheduler Job-QueueTaskScheduler is based on FIFO scheduling thought. However, with more and more data added to HDFS by the Hadoop users, a new demand comes into existence. When multi-users are sharing the cluster resources, the scheduler should provide rapid response capability to the interactive jobs. Since that Hadoop scheduling strategy is hard to deal with multi-users sharing of clusters, in the July of 2008 Apache Software Foundation designs the Hadoop scheduler as a pluggable component. Which enable the organizations or individuals define the distributed computing scheduling strategy according to their own business demands.

But the current scheduling strategy of third-party developers has their limitations too. Take fair scheduling strategy for example, provides each job with some computing resources. The short jobs will not be starved by the high-priority, but the schedule doesn't specifically optimize the performance of the interactive job. On the other hand, fair scheduling strategy does not allow jobs to preempt.

3.1 Temporary Weight Enhancement Mechanism

The scheduling algorithm of FairScheduler tracks and maintains the weight in real time. Through modifying the scheduling algorithm for reading the configuration information and endowing the enhancement of their weight after defining each new run time T (which may be user configured, the default is 10 minutes).The scheduling strategy can significantly reduce more response time of interactive operations. At the same time, the mechanism is dynamically guaranteed to the fairness of all the jobs because each job has access to the temporary weighting enhancement after running the first T time.

Job is an instance of the object, JobInProgress, which means the job enters the processing queue. CurrentWeight means the current weight of the job which is value that takes job's priority, job's size and job's waiting time into consideration. FACTOR is the weight enhancement cause of the algorithm maintained in configuration file. Its default value is set to 3. DURATION is the running time has to be waited in order that the program can be enhanced by the weight. Its default value is set to 600000 (10 * 60 * 1000, 10 minutes) and it is maintained in configuration file too.

3.2 Preempting Mechanism

Users may accidentally submit the long-running jobs. Or they have to process the mass data which may lead to longtime running. In order to meet demands of the fair scheduling strategy to ensure the basic computing resources of the determined queue and the response time of the interactive jobs, the article introduce the preempting mechanism.

The job is able to preempt other jobs' computing resources if a job doesn't get the smallest computing resources ensured by cluster in at least T1 time or the computing resources it gets is less than the certain percentage (for example, 1 / 3) of its Fair Share in T2 time. Of which, T1 will be smaller than T2 so as to first ensure the smallest guaranteed amount of computing resources, and T2 is used to ensure that those queue not important and there is no guarantee amount will not be starved. T1, T2 can be configured by the user.

First, GrabTasksNecessary () need to check the jobs needing to preempt the resources. If such operations exist, GrabTasksNecessary () will sort all the jobs according to computing resources' shortage monitored and maintained by scheduling strategy. And then GrabTasks() will consider preempting the job that has the largest idle resources by sequence.

TasksToGrab () is used to define the jobs need to preempt how many computing resources of the designated type. If the job's waiting time exceed the given minShareTimeout and its resources is less than the minimum quota, the job can preempt the computing resources (the preemptive computing resources is decided by margin of the deserved computing resources and its occupied computing resources); if the job's waiting time exceed the given fairShareTimeout, and its resources are less than the certain amount of the Fair Share (can be configured, the default is 1 / 3), the job can preempt the computing resources until it meet the allocation of he Fair Share value. Meeting the above two situation, the job will preempt the maximum of resources. According to the time out configured by users, the situation generally does not occur unless the user deliberately set the same time out. (Under normal circumstances, minShareTimeout is smaller than fairShareTimeout).

GrabTasks () will preempt the maximum tasks number that doesn't exceed the specified number of specified type (map or reduce) while ensuring that the computing resources of the job being preempt will not less than their minimal guaranteed amount or a certain ratio of Fair Share (1/CONST_RATE, can be configured).The algorithm is preferred to select the active task.

3.3 The Fair Share of Computing Resources among the Resource Pool

FairScheduler will default the jobs as equal entities in the aspects of sharing resources so that it can share the surplus computing resources fairly among the jobs with the minimal of guaranteed computing resources. It results the situation that users who submit two jobs get twice computing resources as the users who submit one. Apparently, this allocation is inadequate because the user can submit multiple jobs intentionally to get more computing resources. This article will take the strategy that each user is allocated a separate computing pool while they are regarded as equal entities to share the surplus computing resources fairly. On the other hand, weight can be added to the computing pool so that several users or organizations who actually need can acquire greater share of the cluster.

4   The Realization and Experiments

The FairScheduler tool developed by Facebook in this text will realize the temporally raising of weight, preemption by higher priority and the resource sharing between users by the java, and will load it on the Hadoop scheduler.

4.1   The Realization

1) Temporarily raising of weight

Define a class named WeightBosster in the FairScheduler, the structure is in Figure 1.

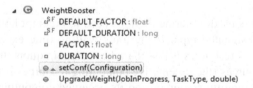

Fig. 1. Class WeightBooster

DEFAULT_FACTOR is assigned to the default factor of the raised weight and the default value is 3.DEAFAULT_DURATION is used to assign when default temporally raised weight happen, and its default value is 10*60*1000(10 minutes); set-Conf(Configuration) maintained FACTOR and DURATION these two vital factor of raising weight algorithm dynamically through the configuration file.

```
public void setConf(Configuration conf) {
    if (conf != null) {
        FACTOR = conf.getFloat("mapred.weightbooster.factor",DEFAULT_FACTOR);
        DURATION = conf.getLong("mapred.weightbooster.duration",DEFAULT_DURATION);
    }
    super.setConf(conf);
}
```

UpgradeWeight(JobInProgress,TaskType,double) is the realization of the raised weight by java.

```
public double UpgradeWeight(JobInProgress job, TaskType taskType,double curWeight) {
    long start = job.getStartTime();
    long now = System.currentTimeMillis();
    if (now - start < DURATION) {
        return curWeight * FACTOR;
    } else {
        return curWeight;
    }
}
```

2) Resource sharing between users

FairScheduler scheduler define the way of resource allocating in the FairScheduler.java. In order to change to our new way, override the method assignTasks(). Meanwhile, the over defining of the computing pool allocation in the PoolManager.java adopts the way of sharing resource. It must provide each user its own computing pool whose default name is its computer name

3) Preemption of higher priority

Define a class named GrabTasks in the FairScheduler.

Fig. 2. Preemption realization

GRAB-INTERVAL is used to define the interval of the preemption algorithm, the default value is 300000(five minutes); grabEnabled determines whether scheduler actives the preemption .LastGrabCehckTime, lastTimeAtMapMiniShare, lastTimeAtReduceMinShare, lastTimeAMapFairShare, LastTimeAtReduceFairShare, each of these define the key attribution value of realizing preemption algorithm. These values combine with the methods isStarvedForMinShare() and isStarvedForFairShare(), which provide the reference of the preempting algorithm. UpdateGrabVariables() is used to maintain the various attributes of class GrabTasks. GrabTasksIfNecessary() calls the methods TasksToGrab() and GrabTasks() to scan the Hadoop task queue and if any task needs preempt resource then the preemption happens.

4) Test environment

We get four simple personal computer(CPU:1.86HZ*1,Memory:2GB*1)that are connected to a switch board to make up a LAN. One of the computerss is preinstall cygwin to simulate linux environment and is regarded as NameNode. The rest three of the computers are preinstalled linux environment and are regarded as SecondNameNode and the other two DataNode. Meanwhile, install Hadoop on these four computers and active the dfs and mapred these two process. The total testing data is about a thousand txt files(The total size is about 1GB).

4.2 Performance Test

1) Raised weight

The raised weight is designed for prompt the response of small tasks. The test involves in two distributed tasks, task A and task B. Task A runs wordcount on 10MB data, and task B runs wordcount on 500MB data. Suppose that the quality of task A is similar to interactive task, and user wants to get the result of task A as soon as possible. What's more, when the task A is submitted, task B has already executed for about three minutes. In this test, task A is spilt into 300 small tasks and task B is split into 25000 tasks. When the raised weight is not used, in the premise of that task B occupies the resource and is running, the performance of A's process is stable which is about 38 per minute. The Figure 3 shows the result.

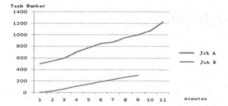   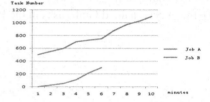

Fig. 3. Result without raised weight   **Fig. 4.** With using weight raised

When using the raised weight, in order to make the result of test more obvious, we set the multiply to five and the time to 3 minutes.The moment that the running time of task A is three minutes, the speed of it rise from 28 per minute in the first three minutes to 83 per minute, while task B's process speed decrease obviously. So 300 tasks take six minutes.

2) Task preemption

Without preemption, it's hard for task A and task B to obtain adequate resource in the condition that task C occupies huge amounts of resource result in that they must wait for the completion of task C and release its resource. In the 10 minutes, they all finish 200 small tasks.

After using the preemption, task A and task B grab the task C's resource in their one minute's running which shows the prompt of process is about 250%. In the ten minutes' running, task A and task B have each processed 500 small tasks.

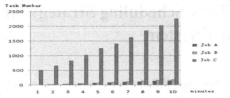
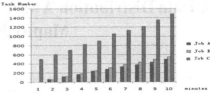

Fig. 5. Without Job-grabbing   **Fig. 6.** Preemption Scheduling

5 Conclusion

Schedule strategy is an important part of a distributed system. This article focuses on the Hadoop's schedule model and its disadvantages to solve the processing interactive task problem, low priority tasks hungry and the sharing resource in Multi-user clusters problem.The experiments show that these improvement can meet the specified need properly to advance the hadoop scheduling.

With the increase of data and the expansion of users, the schedule will certainly meet more and more challenges such as safety in distributed system, refinement of users' pool and hierarchical solution and so on which could be done in the future work.

References

[1] Lammel, R.: Google's mapreduce programming model revisited. Science of Computer Programming 70(1), 1–30 (2008)
[2] Dean, J., Ghemawat, S.: MapReduce: Simplified Data Processing on Large Clusters. Communications of the ACM 51(1), 107–113 (2008)
[3] http://hadoop.apache.org/core/docs/r0.17.2/
mapred_tutorial.html
[4] Zaharia, M., Konwinski, A., Joseph, A.D., Katz, R., Stoica, I.: Improving MapReduce Performance in Heterogeneous Environments. University of California, United States (2004)
[5] Amazon EC2 Instance Types, http://tinyurl.com/3zjlrd
[6] Yahoo! Launches World's Largest Hadoop Production Application,
http://tinyurl.com/2hgzv7
[7] Chu, C.-T., Kim, S.K., Lin, Y.-A., Yu, Y., Bradski, G., Ng, A.Y., Olukotun, K.: Map-reduce for machine learning on multicore. In: Advances in Neural Information Processing Systems, pp. 281–288. MIT Press, Cambridge (2007)
[8] Lin, J.: Brute Force and Indexed Approaches to Pairwise Document Similarity Comparisons with MapReduce. In: Proceedings of the 32nd Annual International ACM SIGIR Conference on Research and Development in Information Retrieval (SIGIR 2009), Boston, Massachusetts (July 2009)

A Data Distribution Aware Task Scheduling Strategy for MapReduce System

Leitao Guo, Hongwei Sun, and Zhiguo Luo

China Mobile Research Institute,
53A, Xibianmennei Ave., Xuanwu District, Beijing 100053, P.R. China
{guoleitao,sunhongwei,luozhiguo}@chinamobile.com

Abstract. MapReduce is a parallel programming system to deal with massive data. It can automatically parallelize MapReduce jobs into multiple tasks, schedule to a cluster built by PCs. This paper describes a data distribution aware MapReduce task scheduling strategy. When worker nodes requests for tasks, it will compute and obtain nodes' priority according to the times for request, the number of tasks which can be executed locally and so on. Meanwhile, it can also calculate tasks' priority according to the numbers of copies executed by the task, latency time of tasks and so on. This strategy is based on node and task's scheduling priority, fully considers data distribution in the system and thus schedules Map tasks to nodes having data in high probability, to reduce network overhead and improve system efficiency.

Keywords: MapReduce, Task Scheduling.

1 Introduction

MapReduce is a new parallel programming system proposed by Google Inc [1, 3], which summarizes the data processing in two steps: map and reduce. Library provided by mapreduce system can automatically handle the parallel processing, fault tolerance, data distribution, load balance and etc. As the system architecture shown in Figure 1, mapreduce system is mainly composed of 3 parts. Client is used to submit the user's mapreduce program to the master node; master node can initialize the program into map and reduce tasks automatically, and schedule them to worker nodes; worker nodes request and execute tasks from master. At the same time, a distributed file system (DFS) built on worker nodes is used to store input/output data for mapreduce jobs [1,2] .

The major feature for the task scheduling strategy in MapReduce system, is to schedule the tasks to the workers which store the data for map task. This location-based scheduling policy can reduce the network overhead and improve system performance when map task can be executed on the workers which have data. Due to the reliability and storage capacity of the different worker nodes, the uneven distribution of the data will be caused. The existing scheduling strategy doesn't fully consider the situation of data distribution, and will result in more network load.

M.G. Jaatun, G. Zhao, and C. Rong (Eds.): CloudCom 2009, LNCS 5931, pp. 694–699, 2009.

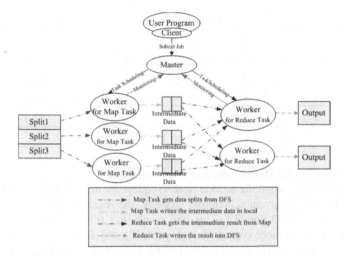

Fig. 1. System Architecture of MapReduce System

2 Problems in the Existing MapReduce Scheduling Methods

Scheduling of MapReduce is divided into 2 phases: initialization and task scheduling.

Initialization process is as following:

1. Master receives submitted tasks, and initializes it as map and reduce tasks;
2. After initialization, put the task into the pending task list;
3. Calculated local task list for each worker node;
4. Waiting for the worker to request tasks.

Task scheduling process is as following:

1. Master receives the task request from worker. It examines whether there are runnable tasks in local task list of worker, if there are, return the first task in local task list; otherwise, continue;
2. From near to far, to inquire the worker' nearby worker neighbors about whether there is runnable task in their local task list, if there is, return the first runnable task; otherwise, continue;
3. traverse local task list to return the first runnable task; if not found, continue;
4. Do following steps such as speculative scheduling [1] and so on.

The existing task scheduling ignored the data distribution situation for map task, such as the number of local task for a worker and the number of data copies for each map task. In the following scenarios, more map task cannot run locally and will cause more network overheads.

Scenario 1, there are different number of local tasks in worker nodes
As shown in Table 1, when the worker nodes request for new task in the order of H4-H1-H2-H3, based on current scheduling strategy, the result is: H4 gets T1, H1 gets T2, H2 gets T3, and H3 gets T4. This will result in 3 times of network data copy. Since there are 2 splits of data on H3, the best scheduling result is scheduling T3 or T4 to H4.

Table 1. Scenario 1

Worker node	Data splits stored in the worker	Local task list
H1	S1	T1
H2	S2	T2
H3	S3 , S4	T3,T4
H4	-	-

Scenario 2, there are different number copies of data.

As shown in Table 2, when the worker nodes request for new task in the order of H4-H1-H2-H3, based on current scheduling strategy, the result is: H4 gets T1, H1 gets T2, H2 gets T3, and H3 gets T4. This will result in 3 times of network data copy. Since T2 and T3 have more copies of data, while T1 and T4 have only one copy, the best scheduling result is: H4 gets T1, H1 gets T4, H2 gets T2 and H3 gets T3.

Table 2. Scenario 2

Worker node	Data splits stored in the worker	Local task list
H1	S1, S2, S3, S4	T1, T2, T3, T4
H2	S2,	T2
H3	S3	T3
H4	-	-

Scenario 3, there are only one copy of data, and the data are uniformly distributed.

As shown in Table 3, when the worker nodes request for new task in the order of H4-H1-H2-H3, based on current scheduling strategy, the result is: H4 gets T1, H1 gets T2, and H2 gets T3. This will result in 3 times of network data copy. Since every task has the same number of copy, the best scheduling result is: refuse the request of H4 and wait for H1, H2 and H3 request for task.

Table 3. Scenario 3

Worker node	Data splits stored in the worker	Local task list
H1	S1	T1
H2	S2	T2
H3	S3	T3
H4	-	-

According to the above analysis, current mapreduce task scheduling strategy doesn't consider the data distribution of tasks, and will result in more network overhead

3 Data Distribution Aware Task Scheduling Strategy

There are 2 main phases in this Strategy: in the initialization phase, statistics number of copies of data processed by each map task. At the same time, statistics the number of localizable tasks for each worker; in the scheduling phase, according to the information above, calculating the scheduling priorities for each task and each works that requesting task, and scheduling the task to works based on this priority.

3.1 Main Modules in Master Node

In addition to the existing data structure that included in the current system, the master node needs to enhance the following modules:

(1) Module for calculating the scheduling priority for each task

The master node needs to calculate the scheduling priority for each map task, which is P_Task, based on the distribution of data to be processed by this map task. A map task with a higher P_Task will have higher priority to be scheduled. P_Task is related to the following parameters:

- *Replica_Num*: number of workers that can execute the map task locally. P_Task is inversely proportional to Replica_Num, map tasks have lower Replic_Num will have higher priority to be scheduled.

- *Worker_TaskList*: length of localizable tasks list for the workers who keep the data to be processed by the map task. The task with bigger Worker_TaskList has higher P_Task.

- *Task_WaitTime*: time period for a task from the initialization to the current moment of time. Task with longer Task_WaitTime has higher scheduling priority.

Therefore, the scheduling priority for each task can be calculated by the following formula:

$$\text{P\_Task} = \alpha F_3(replica\_num) + \beta F_4(worker\_tasklist) + \gamma F_5(task\_waittime) + C$$

While, C represents some impact factor that should be considered, $F_3(replica\_num)$ is a decreasing function, and $F_4(worker\_tasklist)$ and $F_5(task\_waittime)$ are increasing function.

(2) Module for calculating the scheduling priority for each workers which requesting task

This module is responsible for the calculation of the scheduling priority for workers, P_Worker. The master will schedule the task to the workers with higher P_Worker. P_Workers can be calculated by the following parameters:
- *Worker's local task list*: task list kept for each worker. Every task in this list can be processed locally on this worker. If the worker's local task list is not empty, P_Worker can be set as the maximum priority, and master will schedule the task in this list to the worker first.

- *Request_Num*: number of requests since the worker gets a task last time. A bigger Request_Num shows that this worker has low load and can handle more tasks. Worker with a bigger Request_Num has higher P_Worker.
- *History_Info*: the success rate for task processing on the worker. History_Info is proportional to P_Worker.

Therefore, the scheduling priority of a worker can be calculated as the following formula:

$$P\_Wor\,ker = \begin{cases} P\_Wor\,ker\_Max & \theta = 1 \\ \alpha F_1(request\_num) + \beta F_2(history\_\inf o) + C & \theta = 0 \end{cases}$$

In this formula, $P\_Wor\,ker\_Max$ represents the maximum value of P_Worker, C represents some impact factor that should be considered. When the worker's local task list is not empty, $\theta = 1$ otherwise $\theta = 0$. $F_1(request\_num)$ and $F_2(history\_\inf o)$ are increasing function.

(3) Refinement for job initialization process

Regarding to the scheduling priority of task and workers, the job initialization process will be refined as the following:

1. Master node instantiations the map and reduce tasks after receiving the job.
2. Master puts the initialized job into the pending job list.
3. Calculate the Replic_Num for each map task.
4. Calculate the Worker_tasklist for workers who keep the data for this job.
5. Waiting for the worker to request a new task.

(4) The scheduling decision-making module

The scheduling decision-making module determines whether to schedule a task to a worker based the value of P_Worker and P_Task. A simple decision-making system just like: $\alpha * P\_Wor\,ker + \beta * P\_Task > \tau$, τ is a threshold value for decision-making, when the value is bigger that τ, the master schedules the task to this worker.

In the case that worker's scheduling priority is omitted, the scheduling decision-making module can be simplified as the following process:

1. Firstly, master node checks the local task list for the workers, and scheduler the task with the minimum Replic_Num to the worker. If the length of local task list is 0, go to the next step.
2. Scan the workers that near to this worker, and schedule the map task with the minimum Replic_Num from their local task list. If cannot find a proper map task, then continue.
3. Calculate the length of worker_tasklist for workers that can process the tasks locally. Pick the worker with the longest worker_tasklist, and schedule its map task with the minimum Replic_Num. if cannot find a proper map task, then continue.
4. Start to handle the speculative scheduling.

3.2 Main Modules in WorkerNode

In addition to the existing data structures that included in the current system, the worker node needs to have the function to handle the request fault by dynamically adjusting the period of task requesting.

When workers request master for a new task, but master failed to schedule a task to this worker, the worker should wait for a while and request again. To decrease the resource waste when waiting for a new task in workers, worker should shorten the task request period. Once the worker gets a runnable task, the task request period will be reset to the default value.

4 Analysis of Application Effectiveness

Using the proposed schedule algorithm, the results of three scenarios described in Section 2 are as follows,

Scenario 1: The schedule result is : H4 executes T3, H1 executes T1, H2 executes T2, and H3 executes T4.

Scenario 2: The schedule result is : H4 executes T1, H1 executes T4, H2 executes T2, and H3 executes T3.

Scenario 3: Since replica_num of T1 and T2 is 1, and worker_tasklist of every node is 1, so P_Task is high, this results in no task to be processed in H4. The schedule result is : H1 executes T1, H2 executes T2, and H3 executes T3.

5 Conclusions and Future Works

This paper proposed a data distribution aware MapReduce task schedule strategy based on data distribution, which can increase the probability of the localized task implementation. Future works include the optimization of this schedule strategy, such as the management of the used resources by jobs and the schedule algorithm based on the loads of all nodes.

References

1. Dean, J., Ghemawat, S.: MapReduce: Simplified Data Processing on Large Clusters. In: OSDI 2004, 6th Symposiumon Operating Systems Design and Implementation, Sponsored by USENIX, incooperation with ACM SIGOPS, pp. 137–150 (2004)
2. Ghemawat, S., Gobioff, H., Leung, S.-T.: The Google File System. In: Proceedings of the 19th ACM Symposium on Operating Systems Principles, pp. 20–43 (2003)
3. Hadoop opensource project, http://hadoop.apache.org/

Cloud Computing Based Internet Data Center

Jianping Zheng, Yue Sun, and Wenhui Zhou

53A, Xibianmennei Ave, Xuanwu District, Beijing, 100053, China
{zhengjianping,sunyue,zhouwenhui}@chinamobile.com

Abstract. Cloud computing offers a great opportunity for Internet Data Center (IDC) to renovate its infrastructure, systems and services, and cloud computing based IDC is promising and seem as the direction of next generation IDC. This paper explores the applications of cloud computing in IDC with the target of building a public information factory, proposes the framework of cloud computing based in IDC, and probe into how to build cloud services over the cloud platform in the IDC.

Keywords: Internet Data Center, Cloud Computing, Public Information Factory.

1 Introduction

The Internet Data Center (IDC) and its services evolve with the development of Internet and information technology. The first generation IDC only provides the simple and basic services like web hosting, server renting and bandwidth renting. The second generation IDC offers value-added services such security and load balance, and improves its quality of service. However, the 2nd generation IDC faces new challenges. First, the IDC customers demand the gradual increase of IDC resources including computing, storage and bandwidth resources to meet their business growth, while they do not expect service break due to the system upgrade. Second, the IDC consumes mass power and faces the energy saving problem. Cloud computing seems to be the best solution to overcome these challenges. It realizes elastic computing and also improves the efficiency of server utilization to save power. Cloud computing based IDC is promising and is the direction of 3rd generation IDC.

Google, Amazon and Microsoft are running cloud computing based data centers across the globe to provide competitive cloud services. Google App Engine (GAE) [1] is built over Google cloud computing infrastructure including GFS, BigTable and MapReduce, and provides the web service development environment as well as web hosting for the developers. Amazon Web Service (AWS) [2] is Amazon's cloud computing platform that provides companies of all sizes with an infrastructure web services platform in the cloud. Amazon provides EC2, S3, CloudFront, SQS and other cloud services over AWS. The Azure Services Platform [3] is an internet-scale cloud computing and services platform hosted in Microsoft data centers. The Azure Services Platform provides a range of functionality to build applications that span from consumer web to enterprise scenarios and includes a cloud operating system and a set of developer services.

Telecom operators, the main players of IDC services, are also active in introducing cloud computing to IDC to develop new services. For example, recently AT&T launched synaptic hosting service. The telecom operators have advantage network

M.G. Jaatun, G. Zhao, and C. Rong (Eds.): CloudCom 2009, LNCS 5931, pp. 700–704, 2009.

resources and a very large number of customers. With cloud computing, the telecom operator can turn the IDC into a public information factory. Such a public information factory provides the virtual, security, reliable and scalable IT infrastructure. Moreover on top of the IT infrastructure the telecom operator can build open platforms that enable the third party to develop new applications. Finally, the public information factory can provide variety of information services to the consumer, enterprise and government on demand and in a pay-as-you-go manner, just as the way of providing gas or water service.

This paper, from the viewpoint of telecom operators, explores the applications of cloud computing in IDC with the target of building a public information factory, proposes the framework of cloud computing based in IDC, and probe into how to build cloud services over the cloud platform in the IDC.

2   Framework of Cloud Computing Based IDC

Cloud computing offers a great opportunity for Internet Data Center (IDC) to renovate its infrastructure, systems and services, and make the IDC as a public information factory. As a public information factory, the IDC should provide its customers all kinds of IT services on demand. The IT services by the telecom operator are all around. Basically, the infrastructure services including computing, storage and networking services should be provided to the web hosting customers. Second, the telecom services such as voice, SMS, MMS, WAP and location service should be opened as capabilities to the developers to develop new applications. In addition, the IDC needs to provide services to help Internet Software Vendors (ISV) to host their on-line software in the IDC.

To offer the above IT services, the IDC utilizes the cloud computing to construct a cloud platform, on top of which three kinds of cloud services including Infrastructure as a Service (IaaS), Platform as a Service (PaaS) and Software as a Service (SaaS) are provided. Fig. 1 illustrates the framework of cloud computing based IDC. The IT resources including computing, storage and networking resources in the IDC are

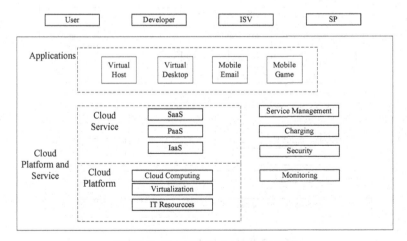

Fig. 1. Framework of cloud based IDC

virtualized and managed by cloud platform. Based on the cloud platform, IaaS, PaaS and SaaS are provided to the customers to develop and deploy applications in the IDC. To guarantee the Service Level Agreement (SLA) with the customers, all the cloud services are well managed with powerful management systems.

With IaaS, PaaS and SaaS, the developers can develop and deploy their applications in the IDC and do not need to take care of constructing the servers for the applications. The IDC offers the developers with elastic computing resources on demand. The consumer can have his computing desktop in IDC and access it anywhere by any device. The enterprise and government can build their virtual data centers in the cloud based IDC, which saves their IT Capex and Opex.

3   Services in Cloud Based IDC

3.1   Infrastructure as a Service

IaaS is the delivery of computing infrastructure as a service. The providers rent computing power and disk space and access them from desktop PCs through a private network or across the Internet. Amazon EC2 and S3 services are typical IaaS. The telecom operator has mass IT resource in its IDC. Traditionally, the operator has limited kind of services and business model in renting the resource. Typically, the customer rent servers or bandwidth for a fixed term e.g. one year. With cloud computing, the operator can be much more flexible in renting resources, and the customer can have scalable resource on demand and pay for utility. The elastic computing service, cloud storage service and content delivery service are the most important infrastructure services in IDC for telecom operators.

Fig. 2 shows the system architecture of IaaS. Built on top of the IT infrastructure, the cloud platform consists of cloud computing system, cloud storage system and Content Delivery Network (CDN) system, which have API open to the cloud services

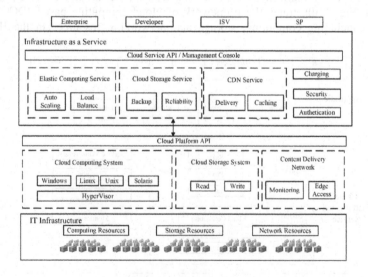

Fig. 2. System Architecture of IaaS

for accessing the IT resource. The cloud services e.g. elastic computing service are provided to the customer by service API or management console.

3.2 Platform as a Service

As pointed out in [4], PaaS can add significant value to enterprise IT by enabling IT to better serve the business, operate at a strategic level with business divisions and rapidly deliver application solutions to business partners. Google App Engine and Microsoft's Azure are the examples of PaaS that benefits the Internet society and enterprise in developing and delivering new applications. To promote the telecom services and solutions, the telecom operator need to construct its own PaaS.

The telecom PaaS is a platform for the customers to develop, deploy, execute and manage their applications. It consists of three main components, i.e. telecom service gateway, runtime environment and development environment, as shown in Fig. 3. The core value of telecom PaaS is that it opens the telecom enablers, such as SMS, MMS and WAP, to the 3rd parties so that they can create innovative applications that combined the Internet and telecom services.

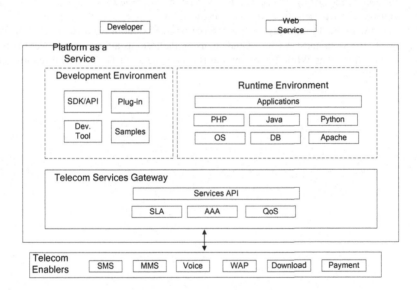

Fig. 3. System Architecture of Telecom PaaS

4 Summary

Cloud computing can provide large scale, low cost, reliable and scalable IT infrastructure for IDC, which offers great opportunities for the IDC to renovate its system and services to make itself more competitive. IaaS, PaaS and SaaS are cloud services that will make the IDC as a public information factory providing all kinds of information services to the customers on demand.

Building cloud based IDC is one of the important strategies for the telecom operators. With cloud based IDC, the telecom operators not only innovate in the IDC services but also reduce the operation cost. Furthermore, it helps the telecom operators to exploit the long tail market of IDC services, and keeps their competitive position in the Internet services.

However, the cloud based IDC faces challenges, among of which availability and security are the most vital. As a public information factory, high availability is the basic requirement of IDC. Even a short outage of cloud service could cause widespread panic. Security concerns arise because both customer data and program are residing in IDC. However, the cloud based IDC faces the problems such as vulnerability in virtualization, denial of services, and information confidentiality. Much work is needed to overcome these challenges to make a cloud based IDC as an operable and trustable information factory.

References

1. Google App Engine, http://code.google.com/appengine/
2. Amazon Web Service, http://aws.amazon.com/
3. Microsoft Azure Platform, http://www.microsoft.com/azure/default.mspx
4. Cheng, D.: PaaS-onomics: A CIO's Guide to using Platform-as-a-Service to Lower Costs of Application Initiatives While Improving the Business Value of IT. Technical report, Long Jump (2008)

Author Index